REVISED AND ENLARGED EDITION

Missouri Government and Politics

Edited by

Richard J. Hardy, Richard R. Dohm,

and David A. Leuthold

University of Missouri Press   Columbia and London

Copyright © 1995 by
The Curators of the University of Missouri
University of Missouri Press, Columbia, Missouri 65201
Printed and bound in the United States of America
5   4   3   2   1   99   98   97   96   95

Library of Congress Cataloging-in-Publication Data

Missouri government and politics / edited by Richard J.
    Hardy, Richard R. Dohm, and David A. Leuthold.–Rev.
    and enl. ed.
        p.   cm.
    Includes bibliographical references (p. –) and index.
    ISBN 0–8262–0990–4
    1. Missouri–Politics and government.   2. Local
government–Missouri.   I. Hardy, Richard J.   II. Dohm,
Richard R.   III. Leuthold, David A.
    JK5416.M57   1995
    320.9778–dc20   95-6552
                                                          CIP

♾ This paper meets the requirements of the
American National Standard for Permanence of Paper
for Printed Library Materials, Z39.48, 1984.

Designer: Kristie Lee
Typesetter: BOOKCOMP
Printer and Binder: Thomson-Shore, Inc.
Typefaces: Minion, Frutiger Bold

To our children,

*Amanda and Thomas Hardy, Greg and Chris Dohm,
and Janet Holt and John Leuthold*

Contents

IV LOCAL GOVERNMENT AND POLITICS IN MISSOURI

Preface

Some parts of Missouri government have changed considerably in the ten years since the first edition of *Missouri Government and Politics* was published. The personnel have changed—every statewide elected official and every member of the Supreme Court has changed; more than half of the members of the legislature were first elected since the previous edition was published. On the other hand, these new officials are dealing with some of the same issues, particularly the issue of distributing the scarce resources of government as effectively and efficiently as possible. This second edition is designed to help Missourians keep abreast of the myriad changes taking place constantly in their government.

The three themes of the earlier edition—complexity, conflict, and conservatism—are reflected in this work as well. Complexity is a continuing factor in state government, and also aptly describes the legal setting for both state and local government. Conflict over values continues to be the most salient element of politics, and virtually every chapter identifies at least one conflict that has had impact. A case study has been included to describe and provide insights into one of the most important conflicts. Lastly, the theme of conservatism is reflected in many ways beyond Missouri's identification as the Show-Me State. Missourians continue to emphasize individualism, minimal government, dispersed political authority, and low levels of taxation and spending. Changes are not adopted without careful consideration of potential impacts. "If it ain't broken don't fix it" appears to be a corollary to the Show-Me posture, again reflecting commitment to conservatism and traditional values.

Five chapters are completely new in this edition, covering topics that were not available in the first edition. An additional seven chapters have been written by new authors, bringing their viewpoints to the book. Each of the remaining chapters has been revised, in some cases substantially rewritten to reflect the changes that have taken place in the last ten years.

The authors are specialists on Missouri government and politics. More than twenty of the authors are teaching or have taught in Missouri colleges and universities. Eight have participated in Missouri political campaigns or have been candidates or officeholders themselves. Three of the authors hold public administration positions in Missouri government. About half the authors have published books or articles elsewhere about Missouri government.

The book is divided into four parts. Part I (chapters 1–5) provides an overview of government and politics in Missouri. In the first chapter, Richard J. Hardy and Michael P. McConachie discuss the role of Missouri in the federal system, delineating the various powers and obligations possessed by the Show-Me State relative to the national government and other states. The second chapter, by Richard R. Dohm, examines the setting of Missouri's political culture, describing how Missouri's history, physical makeup, population characteristics, and economy have helped shape the state's political institutions and public policies. In chapter 3,

Gregory Casey, James Endersby, and James D. King analyze the types of interest groups in Missouri and discuss their influence. Important tactics employed by interest groups include traditional lobbying, electioneering, and public relations. Missouri's political parties are the subject of chapter 4, in which R. E. Burnett and Cordell Smith present the history of political party competition in the state and illustrate the regions of Democratic and Republican strength today. They analyze Missouri's political parties from three viewpoints: voters who participate in parties; the organizational structure of the parties; and the operation of parties within the government. In chapter 5, David A. Leuthold analyzes public opinion in Missouri by looking at the history of votes on public issues—constitutional amendments, initiatives, and referenda. Leuthold examines in detail four issues long important to Missouri—prohibition, gambling, government debt, and tax increases for roads and highways.

The chapters in part II (chapters 6–12) cover the state governmental framework. Chapter 6, by Roy Blunt and Larry Whatley, traces the historical development of the Missouri Constitution and summarizes its major provisions. In chapter 7, James V. Young discusses the types of law under which Missourians live, concentrating on statutory law developed by the legislature, administrative law developed by executive agencies, and common law developed by the judicial branch. The Missouri General Assembly is the subject of chapter 8, in which David Valentine examines the organization, powers, membership, and procedures within Missouri's house and senate. Valentine also analyzes the impact that the term limits amendment will have on the legislature. In chapter 9, David A. Leuthold scrutinizes the ex-

ecutive, legislative, and judicial powers possessed and used by Missouri's governors. Denny E. Pilant discusses the other state constitutional officers—lieutenant governor, secretary of state, treasurer, auditor, and attorney general—in chapter 10. In chapter 11, C. Cartwright Young explores the nature, functions, and structure of public administration in Missouri, focusing on the changed procedures stimulated by publication of the book *Reinventing Government*. Finally, in chapter 12, Richard J. Hardy and Joseph J. Carrier delineate the functions and jurisdiction of Missouri's courts, judges, and juries.

Part III (chapters 13–20) examines Missouri state policies and politics. In chapter 13, Earl Hawkey analyzes the state's executive budget, which he defines as a political tool for setting the legislative agenda. Tax policies are the subject of chapter 14, by Donald Phares. He analyzes the principal taxes used in the state of Missouri, including the individual income tax, the general sales tax, and the property tax. He also discusses debt financing and the implications of the tax limitation amendment to the constitution. In chapter 15, Bryan Forbis and Richard J. Hardy analyze educational policies in Missouri and profile the major political actors (citizens, interest groups, legislators, school boards, and administrators) who influence education policies in the state. They include an analysis of the controversial desegregation issues in St. Louis and Kansas City. Jeanette B. Welch analyzes policy making in higher education in Missouri in chapter 16, focusing particularly on the efforts by the legislature and the Coordinating Board of Higher Education to provide direction for higher education in Missouri. In chapter 17, Gregory Casey and James W. Endersby present a case study of Missouri's efforts to increase funding for education in the early 1990s, focusing on the unsuccessful Proposition B effort in 1991, followed by the Outstanding Schools Act of 1993. In chapter 18, Jerena E. Giffen and Richard L. Koon provide a history of the health, mental health, and welfare programs in Missouri, and analyze the current welfare policies of the state as well as the proposals for change. Robert Dewhirst analyzes state policy in the interrelated fields of economic development, energy, and the environment in chapter 19. In chapter 20, Rickert Althaus underscores the importance that agriculture plays in Missouri's economy and discusses the people and institutions that help shape the state's agricultural policies.

Finally, part IV (chapters 21–26) examines local government and politics in Missouri. Chapter 21, by John Ballard, details the development, classification, organization, personnel, operations, and importance of Missouri's 115 county governments. In chapter 22, Richard R. Dohm explores the fastest-growing but least-known local governments in the U.S.—special districts. Chapter 23, also by Professor Dohm, examines the important elements of land regulation in Missouri, summarizing the development and complexities of comprehensive planning and zoning. Municipal government is the topic of chapter 24. In his analysis, Dohm details the classifications, variations, structures, and operations of the state's incorporated cities and villages. The final two chapters are devoted to government and politics in Missouri's largest metropolitan areas—St. Louis and Kansas City. In chapter 25, E. Terrence Jones describes the economic and demographic setting of St. Louis and St. Louis County, identifies the major political issues facing the area, and analyzes how local government officials deal with these issues. And in chapter 26, G. Ross Stephens profiles the Kansas City

metropolitan area, concentrating on its unique economy and demographics.

We would have liked to have included the text of the Missouri Constitution in our appendix, particularly because many of our authors refer to sections of the constitution. Unfortunately, the constitution has become quite long, long enough to be printed in a book of its own, albeit a thin book. Instructors may obtain free copies of this important document for classroom purposes by writing to the Office of Secretary of State, State Information Building, 600 W. Main Street, Jefferson City, Missouri, 65101. Those wishing a current listing of Missouri's governmental personnel should also request copies of the *Missouri Roster*. We have included a glossary of relevant terms and concepts at the end of the text, as well as a list of suggested readings relevant to Missouri government and politics.

A number of individuals and groups have contributed in important ways to the development of this reader. Obviously, we are greatly indebted to our outstanding contributors, whose experience, research, and analyses made this work possible. We are also indebted to the Department of Political Science, University of Missouri–Columbia, for helpful comments and criticisms by our colleagues, and for support by the department chairmen, David Wood and Birol Yesilada, and the office staff. We give special thanks to Beverly Jarrett, Director of the University of Missouri Press, for her encouragement and support, and to John Brenner for his conscientious and thoughtful editing of the text. We appreciated very much the help of Chris Kelly, who reviewed a chapter for us, and to numerous administrators, public officials, and interest group representatives and lobbyists who provided information and clarification on the complexities of state government. Finally, we express special appreciation to the University of Missouri for its assistance to retired faculty. The early retirement of Professors Dohm and Leuthold allowed them sufficient time to complete this edition, and the University continued to provide them the facilities and support needed for completion of this book.

Richard J. Hardy
Richard R. Dohm
David A. Leuthold

Tables

Figures

PART I

The Context of Missouri Politics

CHAPTER 1

Missouri in the Federal System
by Richard J. Hardy and Michael P. McConachie

> The American system is a federal one; it is, as the Supreme Court has put it, "an indestructible Union, composed of indestructible States." Neither government is judged to be paramount over the other except with respect to a very few well-defined areas. . . . It remains to this day an experimental system, one which probes constantly for pragmatic accommodation where legal principle fails.—Roscoe C. Martin, *The Cities and the Federal System*

Missouri government and politics are difficult to comprehend without a rudimentary understanding of federalism. In this chapter we first define American federalism, giving special attention to the various powers and limitations of both national and state governments. Next, we examine the concept of vertical federalism—the relationship between the national government and the states. The pervasive theme of that section is the increased role and power of the national government in relation to Missouri and the rest of the states. Finally, we analyze the concept of horizontal federalism—the relationship of Missouri to her sister states—delineating both the formal and informal aspects of interstate cooperation and competition.

I. American Federalism

Every nation can be classified according to the formal distribution of power among its governmental units. In general, there are three forms of government—unitary, confederate, and federal. All three exist or have existed in the United States.

Unitary Form. Under a unitary form, one central government wields power over all political subdivisions. These political subdivisions (such as states, provinces, cities, and nations) owe their creation and continued existence to the central government, and they possess only powers granted to them by the central government. Nations with unitary governments include Great Britain, France, and Belgium. It should be noted that Missouri and all other states have unitary forms of government in relationship to their political subdivisions. As will be seen in Part IV of this book, "Local Government and Politics in Missouri," Missouri's local governments are subordinate in varying degrees to the state government. The chief advantage of a unitary system is its relative uniformity; the same policies apply basically to everyone. Conversely, the chief disadvantage is the system's inflexibility; the same policies are applied to all political subdivisions without regard to local differences or special needs.

Confederate Form. A confederate form of government is one in which two or more governments join together to accomplish

3

some common purpose, such as providing for national defense or conducting foreign affairs. Under such an arrangement, each government retains its own independence or sovereignty and confers only limited powers upon the central government. Normally, confederate governments are highly unstable. Consider our nation's first constitution—the Articles of Confederation (1781–1789). Under this confederate system, the national government was completely at the mercy of the thirteen original states; it was unable to regulate interstate commerce, raise revenue by taxation, or enforce its laws effectively. These inherent flaws prompted our founders to create an entirely new federal system in the Constitution of 1787.

Federal Form. The United States has operated under a federal form of government since our Constitution was ratified in 1789. Our federal system is one in which powers are divided by the U.S. Constitution between the national government and the component state governments. These powers typically are classified as delegated, implied, reserved, prohibited, and concurrent.

Delegated powers are those powers expressly granted to the national government in the Constitution. (Thus, they are sometimes referred to as "expressed powers.") For example, Article I grants Congress the power to tax, regulate interstate commerce, prescribe rules of naturalization, regulate bankruptcies, coin money, establish weights and measures, and declare war. Article II grants the president power to appoint and receive ambassadors and to command the army, navy, and militia. And under Article III, the U.S. Supreme Court is given jurisdiction over suits between states and over cases affecting ambassadors.

Implied powers are powers not expressly granted in the Constitution, but which exist because they are "necessary and proper" to carry out delegated powers. According to the "elastic clause" (Article I, Section 8.18), Congress has the power "To make all Laws which shall be necessary and proper for carrying into Execution the foregoing Powers, and all other Powers vested by this Constitution in the Government of the United States." Implied powers were established in the case of *McCulloch v. Maryland* (1819) when the U.S. Supreme Court upheld the national government's right to create the Bank of the United States even though such a power is not expressly stated in the Constitution. The Court reasoned, in part, that this power to create a bank was "implied" from Congress's delegated power to tax and coin money. As we will see, the application of implied powers has given the Constitution a great deal of flexibility and has greatly expanded the role of the national government in relation to the states.

Reserved powers are defined in the Tenth Amendment of the U.S. Constitution: "The powers not delegated to the United States by the Constitution, nor prohibited by it to the States, are reserved to the States respectively, or to the people." Although there is no definitive list of reserved powers, the Supreme Court has broadly defined them as the powers of state governments to limit personal and property rights to protect (1) the public health (for example, to license medical personnel, establish quarantine laws, and inspect food and drugs); (2) the public safety (for example, to regulate building construction, license firearms, and establish motor vehicle laws); (3) the public welfare (for example, to regulate utilities, prohibit discrimination, and provide workmen's compensation); (4) the public morals (for example, to restrict obscene literature, prohibit gambling or prostitution, and regulate sales of tobacco and alcohol); and (5) the public convenience (for example, to provide public parks and public transportation). Furthermore, because the U.S. Constitution makes no reference to education, education too is considered a reserved power; indeed, education remains the single most important function of state governments. Hence, the importance of the reserved powers cannot be overemphasized since they serve as the basis for a vast amount of legislative power in Missouri.

Prohibited powers are powers denied to either the national government, the state governments, or both. Article I, Section 10, of the Constitution, for instance, prohibits the states from (1) impairing the obligation of contracts, (2) coining money, (3) regulating imports or exports, or (4) entering into treaties or confederations. Furthermore, both state and national governments are forbidden to (1) infringe on the freedoms of speech, press, religion, and assembly (First and Fourteenth Amendments); (2) deprive any person of "life, liberty, or property, without due process of law" (Fifth and Fourteenth Amendments); or (3) restrict the right to vote because of race (Fifteenth Amendment) or gender (Nineteenth Amendment).

Concurrent powers, or shared powers, are powers that both the national and state governments may possess. For example, both the United States and Missouri governments have the power to tax, charter corporations, regulate banks, pass legislation, establish highways, and maintain court systems. Missouri may thus exercise any power that is not exclusively conferred on the national government and that does not conflict with national law.

Supremacy of National Laws. From time to time, conflicts arise between Missouri laws and national laws. When this occurs, Article VI, Section 2, of the Constitution (known as the "supremacy clause") provides that the national laws must prevail. More specifically, the article states, "This Constitution, and the Laws of the United States which shall be made in Pursuance thereof; and all Treaties made, or which shall be made, under the Authority of the United States, shall be the supreme Law of the Land." The following cases show how Missouri's laws have sometimes been revoked or preempted by national laws.

The first example concerns a conflict between Missouri statutory law and a U.S. treaty. In 1916, the United States and Canada entered into a treaty in which the two nations agreed to propose legislation to protect migratory birds. Then in 1918 Congress passed legislation forbidding the capturing, selling, or killing of specified migratory fowl. When a U.S. game warden named Holland tried to enforce the national government's regulations, the state of Missouri sued to prevent him on grounds that (1) the regulation of migratory fowl is not specifically granted in the U.S. Constitution (delegated powers) and (2) that such regulation violated Missouri's reserved powers (Tenth Amendment). In the landmark case of *Missouri v. Holland* (1920), however, the Supreme Court ruled against Missouri on grounds that the U.S. treaty represented the "supreme Law of the Land" (Article VI) and that subsequent congressional action was "necessary and proper" (implied powers) to carry out the treaty.

A second illustration concerns a dispute between a state regulation and the U.S. Constitution in the case of *Missouri ex rel Gaines v. Canada* (1938). For many years, Missouri law prohibited Black students from attending the University of Missouri School of Law. Lloyd Gaines was a qualified Black student who applied for law school admissions, but was denied solely on the basis of his race. In denying his admission, university officials offered to pay Gaines's tuition to any law school in the surrounding states that accepted out-of-state Black students. At the time, these states included Iowa, Illinois, Kansas, and Nebraska. Gaines found this offer unacceptable and sued the registrar (Canada), contending his action violated the "equal protection" clause of the Fourteenth Amendment. The Supreme Court agreed and ordered that Gaines be admitted to the law school.

A third example concerns the conflict between state and national constitutions. Note that the *Gaines* decision was limited strictly to the issue of racial segregation in law schools; it did not affect elementary and secondary schools. After the *Gaines* decision, the U.S. Supreme Court gradually began to chip away at racial segregation. Finally, in 1954 the U.S. Supreme Court ruled in *Brown v. Board of Education* that every state must integrate its public elementary and secondary schools "with all deliberate speed." The epoch *Brown* decision had a profound impact on Missouri; it rendered null and void Article IX of the Missouri Constitution of 1945, which called for "separate but equal schools for children of African descent."

However, the issue of racial segregation and federal preemption of state constitutional law did not end there. Take the controversial Kansas City school desegregation case of *Missouri v. Jenkins* (1990). This case began in 1977 when a federal district court ruled that the Kansas City, Missouri, School District (KCMSD) and the State of Missouri had illegally operated segregated schools. As a remedy, the KCMSD proposed, and Federal District Judge Russell G. Clark accepted, a "magnet school" plan. The plan required pouring hundreds of millions of dollars into the inner-city schools with the goal of attracting White, suburban students into predominantly Black neighborhoods. The State of Missouri was to pay 75 percent of the cost, while the KCMSD was to pay 25 percent. However, after he determined that the KCMSD was unable to raise its portion of the bill, Judge Clark ordered an increase in local property tax rates, nearly doubling the rate. The State of Missouri maintained that the judge's actions violated both the Missouri Constitution and the U.S. Constitution's Tenth Amendment. The argument fell on deaf ears. In a five-to-four decision, the Supreme Court upheld the plan with one caveat: In the future, the judge must not set the tax rates, although he retains the authority to order the school board to do so.

Advantages and Disadvantages of Federalism. American federalism merits both praise and criticism. On the one hand, our federal system represents a blend between state and national powers. Given the great diversity among the states (see chapter 2), federalism permits the states to tailor their policies to fit their own particular needs, yet also enables the national government to handle common problems, such as providing for national defense or preventing racial discrimination. On the other hand, our federal system lacks uniformity (states differ over such things as divorce laws, criminal penalties, traffic violations, tax policies, professional licensing, and educational requirements), which results in an uneconomical overlapping of functions (for example, both the nation and the states maintain law enforcement agencies, courts, and highway systems). In Section II, some of these problems and possible solutions in dealing with national-state relations are examined in greater detail.

II. Vertical Federalism

Vertical federalism refers to the relationship between the national and state governments. It is important to examine this relationship because Missouri's government and politics are often greatly affected by national developments. The national government influences the states in a number of important ways, and vice versa. These include the regulation of interstate commerce, the extension of the Bill of Rights, the use of emergency powers, and financial assistance.

Regulation of Interstate Commerce. Interstate commerce is one area in which the national government has greatly increased its power. Recall that Article I, Sections 8.3 and 8.18, of the Constitution grant Congress the power to regulate interstate commerce (delegated power) as well as the power to pass laws that it deems "necessary and proper" to implement this provision (implied power). The Constitution, however, does not spell out precisely what is meant by interstate commerce (or, more precisely, "commerce among the several states.") For instance, does the term refer to the shipment of goods, services, people, or airwaves? Certainly the founders did not have airplanes, telephones, or fax machines in mind when they wrote this provision.

However, the Supreme Court has gradually enlarged the meaning of interstate commerce to enable our nation to deal with ever-changing social and economic problems. In 1824 the Supreme Court in *Gibbons v. Ogden* first defined interstate commerce as not only the transportation of goods, but the movement of services and people as well. Subsequently, interstate commerce has been expanded to include labor relations, agriculture, insurance companies, and civil rights.

Note that each judicial redefinition of interstate commerce both sanctioned and enlarged congressional authority over areas once thought to be controlled only by the states. Important legislation that the courts considered to be within the commerce clause included the Sherman Antitrust Act of 1890 (which prohibits monopolies and restraint of trade), the Wagner Act of 1935 (which protects labor unions and ensures the right to collective bargaining), the Fair Labor Standards Act of 1938 (which established minimum wages and maximum hours, and restricts child labor), the Civil Rights Act of 1964 (which bans discrimination in public accommodations, empowers the federal government to bring suit to desegregate public schools, and forbids discrimination in public and private employment), and the Highway Beautification Act of 1965 (which regulates outdoor advertising along major highways).

Extension of the Bill of Rights. A second way in which the national government has expanded its authority over the states is through the extension of the Bill of Rights. Because many early opponents of the U.S. Constitution feared oppression by a strong central government, the Bill of Rights (or first ten amendments) was added to the U.S. Constitution by 1791 to protect citizens *from the national government.* Thus, such guarantees as freedom of speech, right to counsel, and protection from illegal searches and seizures were thought to apply only to the national government—not to the states. Moreover, this interpretation was upheld by the Supreme Court in *Barron v. Baltimore* (1833).

But as time passed, it became apparent that our founders' fears were misplaced. Most discrimination and infringement upon civil rights came not from the national government, but from the states. This was no better illustrated than in the case of *Dred Scott v. Sanford* (1857). Dred Scott was a slave who lived in Missouri, then a slave state under the conditions of the Missouri Compromise in 1820 (the document that brought Missouri into the Union as a slave state and Maine as a free state). After living in Missouri, Scott was taken by his owner to live in the free state of Illinois, but he later returned to Missouri. Upon his return, Scott filed a lawsuit claiming freedom by virtue of having lived on free soil. Unfortunately, the U.S. Supreme Court held that Dred Scott had no standing to sue because he was not a citizen, and that Blacks (whether free or slave) could never be U.S. citizens. This controversial decision helped fuel the fires that led to the Civil War and engendered myriad forms of racial discrimination.

Following the Civil War, Congress proposed, and the states ratified, the Fourteenth Amendment in 1868. This amendment makes clear that "All persons *born* or naturalized in the United States . . . are citizens of the United States." Note the reference to "born," which renders the *Dred Scott* decision null and void. The Fourteenth Amendment also establishes that "*No State* shall make or enforce any law which shall abridge the privileges or immunities of citizens of the United States; *nor shall any State deprive any person of life, liberty, or property, without due process of law; nor deny . . . the equal protection of the laws*" (emphasis added). The purpose of the Fourteenth Amendment was to confer full rights of citizenship to former slaves.

Unfortunately, it took many years for the Fourteenth Amendment to have its intended impact because subsequent Supreme Court decisions severely restricted its scope. In *Gitlow v. New York* (1925), however, the Court ruled that the Fourteenth Amendment's "due process" clause incorporates the First Amendment's free speech provision. That is, the due process clause "absorbed" that portion of the First Amendment and extended individual protection against state as well as federal

governmental infringement. Since *Gitlow*, the Supreme Court has "selectively incorporated" those sections of the Bill of Rights that are considered essential "to the scheme of ordered liberty"—but only on a case-by-case basis.

Today only three amendments have been totally incorporated to protect citizens from both federal and state violations. These include the First (freedom of speech, press, religion, and assembly), Fourth (protection from unreasonable searches and seizures), and Sixth (rights to counsel and speedy, public trial). Amendments that have been partially incorporated are the Fifth (freedom from self-incrimination and double jeopardy, and protection of due process—but not the right to a grand jury trial) and Eighth (protection from cruel and unusual punishment—but not protection from excessive bail or fines). Finally, those amendments that have yet to be incorporated are the Second (right to keep and bear arms), Third (protection against quartering soldiers), Seventh (right to trial by jury in suits at common law), Ninth (fundamental rights retained by the people), and Tenth (reserved powers).

Although total incorporation is highly unlikely, those amendments that have been incorporated, either in full or in part, have greatly expanded the federal government's role in the area of civil liberties and in relation to the states. Additionally, as will be seen in chapter 6, nearly all of these guarantees are also found in the Missouri Constitution of 1945.

Emergency Powers. A third area in which the national government has expanded its authority is through the use of emergency powers. Article IV, Section 4, of the Constitution guarantees that the national government shall protect each state against "invasion" and "domestic violence."

And Article II, Section 3, provides that the president "shall take care that the laws be faithfully executed." During wartime, insurrection, civil commotion, or natural disasters, these constitutional provisions have been interpreted broadly. Several examples illustrate this point.

In 1894 President Grover Cleveland ordered troops to Chicago to quell the Pullman railway workers' strike despite the objections of Governor John P. Altgeld of Illinois. When Arkansas Governor Orval Faubus ordered the National Guard to stop Black students from attending Little Rock Central High School in 1957 following court-ordered desegregation, President Dwight Eisenhower then "nationalized" the troops and ordered them to enroll and protect the Black students. Emergency measures include the national government's imposition of daylight savings time and the fifty-five miles per hour speed limit at the height of the OPEC oil embargo in 1974. More recently, President Bill Clinton offered to send federal troops to Missouri and other midwestern states affected by the unprecedented flooding along the Mississippi and Missouri Rivers in 1993.

Financial Powers. Perhaps the most pervasive aspect of vertical federalism in recent decades is the national government's financial power. The national government has exerted financial leverage over the states in at least three major ways—through grants-in-aid, threats of withholding federal funds, and tax credits.

Grants-in-aid. Grants-in-aid are considered by many to be the most important source of federal influence over state policy. A grant-in-aid is a form of money payment from the national government to state or local governments for specified programs under whatever conditions the national government wishes to impose.

Grants-in-aid work on a matching basis. For example, it may be a two-thirds to one-third agreement, meaning that the national government agrees to provide two-thirds of the funding if Missouri agrees to provide the remaining third. There are numerous types of grants, but most may be classified as either categorical or block grants.

Categorical grants are distributed for a specific purpose (such as highway construction, lowering juvenile delinquency rates, or agricultural extension programs), and place many restrictions on the recipient state or local government. Categorical grants grew in popularity in the 1960s as part of the federal government's Great Society. Proponents of categorical grants argue that they enable the federal government to set national priorities and minimum uniform standards, to give aid directly to cities, and to help redistribute funds from affluent states to poorer states. Opponents maintain that such grants are poorly coordinated, stimulate extravagant expenditures by luring states into spending funds they would not normally spend, and undermine state independence both because too many strings are attached and because money goes directly to the cities.

Because of these criticisms, block grants have become especially popular in recent years. Block grants channel federal monies through the states, rather than going directly to local governments, and permit state officials to allocate funds for general purposes such as "community development" or "law enforcement." Advocates of block grants included the Reagan and Bush administrations in the 1980s and early 1990s as well as most state governors and legislators. Critics of block grants include big-city mayors and minority groups who feel their needs are being ignored.

Withholding Funds. Because Missouri and other states lean heavily on the national government for funding of state programs, the national government has been able to achieve significant degrees of uniformity by either withholding or threatening to withhold federal funds. Important examples of standards established in this way include the Hill-Burton Act of 1946 (which prohibits discrimination in state hospitals receiving federal construction funds), the Elementary and Secondary Act of 1965 (which prohibits racial discrimination in public schools), Title IX of the 1972 Education Amendments Act (which prohibits sex discrimination in athletics), and the Civil Rights Act of 1991 (which bans discrimination in state institutions of higher education).

Tax Credits. Tax credits have been used by the national government to equalize tax burdens that would otherwise vary widely among the states, or to encourage states to adopt or alter particular public policies. Perhaps the best example is the Social Security Act of 1935. To encourage state development of unemployment compensation programs, the Social Security Act of 1935 levied a tax on all employers in the United States, but permitted them to deduct on their federal income tax up to 90 percent of what they paid into state unemployment taxes. Before 1935 few states had state unemployment programs; after 1935, Missouri and all other states developed such programs in response to this tax credit.

Revenue Sharing. To help end excessive federal guidelines and revitalize state and local power, revenue sharing was established under the State and Local Fiscal Assistance Act of 1972. Revenue that was collected by the national government was redistributed automatically and directly to state and local governments on the basis of population, income, and local tax effort. Under this plan, state and local governments had virtually complete discretion in spending these funds. There were some restrictions (for example, discrimination was prohibited, while public hearings and uniform reporting were required), but these paled in comparison to those of block grants. Whether good or bad, revenue sharing was short-lived; it was terminated in 1986 due to the growing federal deficit. Put simply, there were no longer enough revenues to share.

Federal Funding for Missouri. Missouri has indeed become quite dependent on federal funding in recent years. In the 1993–1994 fiscal year Missouri received $3.46 billion, about three-tenths of its total revenues, from the national government. Two-thirds of these funds were for three programs: Medicaid, highways, and elementary and secondary education, with Medicaid alone accounting for more than 40 percent of the funds received from the federal government. The growth in health care costs, and thus in Medicaid payments, has fueled an increase in federal government payments to Missouri.[1]

State Influence on the National Government. It would be wrong to assume that the states are completely dominated by the national government. On the contrary, the national government often must rely on the states. The national government, for instance, depends on the states to send representatives to Congress, establish voting machinery for national elections, choose members of the Electoral College, ratify amendments to the U.S. Constitution, and implement numerous federal policies.

Congressional Representation. The national government depends on the states to elect representatives to the U.S. Senate and House of Representatives. According to Article I, Section 2, the Senate, or "upper

---

1. Interview with Mark Reading, Division of Budget and Planning, November 7, 1994.

house," is composed of two senators from each state (giving a total of one hundred), thus giving each state equal representation. By contrast, the House of Representatives, or "lower house," is composed of 435 members apportioned by the states on the basis of population. (See Table 1–1.)

To ensure that congressional districts are roughly equivalent in population, the U.S. Constitution requires states to reapportion their House seats following each decennial census. In 1972 Missouri sent ten representatives (or about one representative for every 467,000 people) to the U.S. House of Representatives. However, in 1982 Missouri *lost* one seat in the House, even though the Show-Me State's population actually increased by 4.8 percent between the 1970 and 1980 censuses. That was because Missouri's population growth was quite modest relative to that of other states. During the 1970s the U.S. population grew by 11 percent; the greatest percentage increases were registered by the "Sun Belt" states, notably Florida (41.1), Arizona (52.9), and Nevada (63.8).

The loss of a U.S. representative was a bitter pill for Missouri to swallow. Initially, Missouri's attorney general at the time, John Ashcroft, threatened to challenge the census data in federal court. Then the Missouri General Assembly, which was supposed to redraw the state's congressional districts, could not settle on a reapportionment plan. The central issue was whether a Democrat or a Republican would lose a seat in Congress. The Democratically controlled General Assembly wanted to retain three Democratic districts in St. Louis at the expense of a Republican district; conversely, Republicans and many outstate interests in the state legislature wanted to eliminate one of the St. Louis districts—particularly the seat of Black congressman William Clay—on the grounds that St. Louis had lost population relative to the rest of the state. The issue was finally laid to rest when the Missouri Supreme Court drew a plan that eliminated the former Eighth District congressional seat held by Republican Wendell Bailey.

The 1990 census revealed continued changes in the U.S. population. From 1980 to 1990, the population grew from about 226 million to nearly 250 million Americans. This growth was far from even as the South and West continued to register the fastest gains, while the Midwest and Northeast grew slowly. The states with the greatest percentage growth were Nevada (+50.1 percent), Alaska (+36.9), Arizona (+34.8), Florida (+32.7), and California (+25.7). Four states actually lost population: West Virginia (–8.0 percent), Iowa (–4.7), Wyoming (–3.4), and North Dakota (–2.1). Missouri's population grew a modest 4.1 percent to about 5.1 million.

This population shift has likewise had a significant impact on congressional representation, as nineteen House seats were reapportioned beginning in January 1993. As Table 1–1 reveals, the states gaining the most seats were California (+7), Florida (+4), and Texas (+3), while the states losing the most seats were New York (–3), Illinois (–2), Ohio (–2), Michigan (–2), and Pennsylvania (–2). Fortunately, Missouri managed to retain its nine seats in Congress. The General Assembly made minor changes in congressional district boundaries, resulting in the districts shown in Figure 1–1.

Election Machinery. Under Article I, Section 4, of the U.S. Constitution, the state governments are called upon to furnish election machinery for national elections. This gives the state authority (subject to certain federal laws) to regulate voter registration, select ballots, supervise voting, prevent voter fraud, count votes, and publish election returns. In Missouri,

Table 1-1. Effects of the 1990 Reapportionment on Congressional Representation

State	Population	No. of House Seats	Change in Seats 1980–1990	State	Population	No. of House Seats	Change in Seats 1980–1990
Alabama	4,040,587	7		Montana	799,065	1	−1
Alaska	550,043	1		Nebraska	1,578,385	3	
Arizona	3,665,228	6	+1	Nevada	1,201,833	2	
Arkansas	2,350,725	4		New Hampshire	1,109,252	2	
California	29,760,021	52	+7	New Jersey	7,730,188	13	−1
Colorado	3,294,394	6		New Mexico	1,515,069	3	
Connecticut	3,287,116	6		New York	17,990,455	31	−3
Delaware	666,168	1		North Carolina	6,628,637	12	+1
District of Columbia	606,900	0		North Dakota	638,800	1	
				Ohio	10,847,115	19	−2
Florida	12,937,926	23	+4	Oklahoma	3,145,585	6	
Georgia	6,478,216	11	+1	Oregon	2,842,321	5	
Hawaii	1,108,229	2		Pennsylvania	11,881,643	21	−2
Idaho	1,006,749	2		Rhode Island	1,003,464	2	
Illinois	11,430,602	20	−2	South Carolina	3,486,703	6	
Indiana	5,544,159	10		South Dakota	696,004	1	
Iowa	2,776,755	5	−1	Tennessee	4,877,185	9	
Kansas	2,477,574	4	−1	Texas	16,986,510	30	+3
Kentucky	3,685,296	6	−1	Utah	1,722,850	3	
Louisiana	4,219,973	7	−1	Vermont	562,758	1	
Maine	1,227,928	2		Virginia	6,187,358	11	+1
Maryland	4,781,468	8		Washington	4,866,692	9	+1
Massachusetts	6,016,425	10	−1	West Virginia	1,793,477	3	−1
Michigan	9,295,297	16	−2	Wisconsin	4,891,769	9	
Minnesota	4,375,099	8		Wyoming	453,588	1	
Mississippi	2,573,216	5		Total	248,709,873	435	
Missouri	5,117,073	9					

Source: *The Universal Almanac*, John C. Wright, General Editor (New York: Andrews and McMeel, 1993), pp. 276–77.

the secretary of state, county clerks, and boards of election commissioners are responsible for supervising elections.

Electoral College. The national government also relies on the states to choose electors to the electoral college. In the United States, the people do not vote directly for president and vice president; rather, voters select slates of candidates or electors, who in turn vote for the nation's highest officials. According to Article II, Section 1, as amended (Twelfth and Twenty-Third amendments), each state gets electoral college votes equal to the total number of senators and representatives it has in Congress (hence, Missouri has eleven). The District of Columbia also has three votes, which are granted in the Twenty-Third Amend-

Figure 1-1 Missouri's Congressional Districts after the 1990 Census

Source: *Missouri Roster 1993–1994.* Office of Secretary of State.

ment. States may select electors by a variety of partisan methods, including conventions, primaries, or committees. To become president and vice-president, the winning ticket must receive a majority (270) of the total electoral college vote (538). If no ticket receives a majority of the electoral votes, then the election is decided in the House of Representatives, where each state gets one vote to decide from among the three tickets that received the most votes.

Ratification of U.S. Constitutional Amendments. The U.S. Constitution can-

not be amended without the approval of the states. According to Article V, amendments may be *proposed* in two ways: by a two-thirds vote of both houses of Congress, or by a constitutional convention called by Congress at the request of two-thirds (today thirty-four) of the state legislatures. To date, only the first method has been used. Article V also provides for two methods for *ratifying* proposed amendments: by a vote of three-fourths (today thirty-eight) of the state legislatures, or by conventions in three-fourths of the states. Only the

Twenty-First Amendment (repeal of prohibition) was submitted to state conventions.

History suggests that it is extremely difficult to amend the U.S. Constitution. Although more than ten thousand proposals have been introduced in Congress, only twenty-seven have been adopted by the states. The Twenty-Seventh Amendment, which delays the implementation of any future congressional pay raises until after the next congressional election, was ratified by the states in 1992. Ironically, this amendment was introduced by James Madison in 1789—long before Missouri was even a state!

Implementation of Federal Policies. Aside from these constitutional provisions, the national government relies heavily on state officials to carry out many of its policies. Important national legislation implemented by the states includes Medicaid, Food Stamps, Aid to Families with Dependent Children (see chapter 18), the Elementary and Secondary Education Act (see chapter 15), and Title IX of the Education Amendments Act, to name but a few.

With all of these ways by which the states affect the federal government—sending representatives to Congress, establishing voting machinery for national elections, choosing members of the electoral college, ratifying amendments to the U.S. Constitution, and carrying out numerous federal policies—it is obvious that Missouri and her sister states have played and will continue to play a vital role in our federal system.

III. Horizontal Federalism

Horizontal federalism refers to both the formal and the informal relationships between state governments. Formally, the U.S. Constitution requires the states to grant full faith and credit to one another's public acts, records, and judicial proceedings; to return persons who are fleeing from justice in another state; to extend to one another's citizens the privileges and immunities of their own citizens; to consult with Congress before entering into interstate agreements; and to use the federal courts in settling legal disputes. Informally, states have developed a number of methods for settling interstate conflicts, such as interstate compacts, adoption of uniform laws, and participation in the Council on State Governments. A more detailed description of each of these formal and informal aspects of horizontal federalism follows.

Formal Horizontal Relations

Full Faith and Credit. A recurring problem during the Articles of Confederation (1781–1789) was the movement of Americans from one state to another to avoid debts and court judgments. Because the national government was weak and each state was considered sovereign, a person could easily renege on a contractual obligation or ignore one state's judicial decree by simply moving to another state. To remedy this problem, the "Full Faith and Credit" clause was incorporated into the Constitution.

More specifically, Article IV, Section 1, of the Constitution provides that "Full Faith and Credit shall be given in each State to the public Acts, Records, and judicial Proceedings of every other State." In lay terms, this means that such documents as wills, deeds, mortgages, vital statistics, hearings, official records, birth certificates, contracts, and civil proceedings of one state must be recognized as legal by another state.

Consider some examples of full faith and credit. Say that Mr. Smith sues Mr. Brown over a contract in Missouri's thirteenth

Judicial Circuit Court and is awarded one thousand dollars. Soon thereafter, Mr. Brown moves to Iowa and refuses to pay. According to the Constitution, Iowa must grant full faith and credit to the Missouri judgment, even if such a decision could not have been possible in Iowa. Or let's say that Ms. Jones, a Missouri resident, injures Mr. White, a Florida resident, while she is vacationing in Florida. Following some rather complicated legal maneuvers, Mr. White could then file a civil suit in Florida and, should he win, force Missouri to uphold the Florida judgment, regardless of whether Ms. Jones appears in court.

In general, full faith and credit works reasonably well, but several problems continue to plague its application. One problem is that Congress has failed to establish adequate legislation to ensure smooth compliance. As Robert Karsch points out, "Persons desiring to evade their obligations are often able to delay or thwart completely the operation of the clause by questioning either the jurisdiction of the court or some phase of the proceedings."[2]

Another problem is that full faith and credit does not apply to criminal decisions. What may be a crime in Missouri need not be recognized as a crime in another state. If, for instance, John Doe flees to Arkansas to avoid a drunk-driving conviction in Missouri, Arkansas is not compelled to enforce Missouri's sanction. However, the Constitution does establish an extradition mechanism to handle such cases—a point that will be elaborated later.

A final complaint about the full faith and credit clause concerns the recognition of marriage and divorce laws. Over the years some states—particularly New York, Massachusetts, and North Carolina—have successfully challenged the legality of "quickie" divorces secured in other states. The Supreme Court, though, has stipulated that where both husband and wife participate in the divorce proceeding and are given ample opportunity to contest one state's jurisdiction, the divorce must be accorded full faith and credit in every other state.[3]

Interstate Rendition. The gap created by the failure of the full faith and credit provision to extend to criminal sanctions is largely closed by the Constitution's provision for interstate rendition or extradition. According to Article IV, Section 2, "A Person charged in any State with Treason, Felony, or other Crime, who shall flee from Justice, and be found in another State, shall on demand of the executive Authority of the State from which he fled, be delivered up, to be removed to the State having Jurisdiction of the Crime." Furthermore, the Sixth Amendment stipulates that a person charged with a crime can only be tried and prosecuted in "the State and district wherein the crime shall have been committed."

Anticipating frequent jurisdictional conflicts, Congress in 1793 established certain procedures to implement interstate rendition. Additionally, since 1936 all states, including Missouri, have adopted the Uniform Criminal Extradition Act, which delineates specific procedures for handling interstate fugitives. The process works like this: the accused must first be formally charged with a crime, either through an information or indictment (see chapter 12), in the state where the alleged offense was committed. Police officers in the state where the charge was filed then request the police in the asylum state (the state to which the fugitive has fled) to detain the fugitive until the necessary paperwork is

2. Robert F. Karsch, *The Government of Missouri*, 14th ed. (Columbia: Lucas Brothers, 1978), 231.

3. *Sherrer v. Sherrer*, 334 U.S. 343 (1948).

completed. The governor of the requesting state must then submit a certified copy of the indictment along with a formal request for rendition to the governor of the asylum state. The governor of the asylum state then checks the document regarding the accused, and may ask his attorney general for advice. If extradition is granted, the requesting state sends officers to the asylum state to return the fugitive. All expenses incurred in the process (such as transportation and food) are borne by the requesting state. Once the accused is returned to the requesting state, he or she is accorded due process of law. Missouri both honors and requests two or three hundred extraditions annually.

As with the case of full faith and credit, interstate rendition proceedings have not always run smoothly. Historically, the most controversial issue has been whether extradition is mandatory; that is, does the governor in the asylum state have the right to refuse extradition to the requesting state? In *Kentucky v. Dennison* (1861) the Supreme Court held that governors were not compelled to grant another state's request for extradition. The case arose when the State of Kentucky (then a slave state) sued to compel Governor William Dennison of Ohio (a free state) to surrender a fugitive named Willis Lago. Lago was a free Black who was accused of smuggling slaves into Ohio in violation of Kentucky law. In upholding Dennison's actions, the Supreme Court ruled that extradition was a moral, but not a legally enforceable, duty.

Following *Kentucky v. Dennison*, governors typically would refuse to cooperate in cases where the alleged offense was not punishable in the asylum state, where the accused had "turned over a new leaf," or where public opinion opposed extradition. Until a few years ago, Missouri would deny,

and in turn be denied, about a half-dozen extradition requests annually.[4]

One of the most amusing cases concerning extradition involved the theft of a chimpanzee named "Mr. Moke" from the St. Louis Zoo. After the thief had fled with Mr. Moke to Florida, the state of Missouri requested that Florida officials extradite the two as soon as possible. However, the governor of Florida, "discovering that the 'chimpnapper' had originally trained Mr. Moke, had sold him to the zoo, had missed him badly, had tried unsuccessfully to buy him back, and had left $1,000 in Mr. Moke's cage as part payment for him, showed no eagerness to return the wanted man."[5]

The *Dennison* decision remained the rule on extradition for nearly 126 years. However, in 1987 the U.S. Supreme Court took a 180-degree turn and reversed itself in *Puerto Rico v. Branstad*. The *Branstad* case involved a man who fled to Iowa after being charged with manslaughter in Puerto Rico. When the Governor of Puerto Rico sought extradition, Iowa Governor Terry Branstad refused the request on grounds that the accused could not get a fair trial. On appeal, the Supreme Court unanimously held that extradition requests must be honored. Writing for the Court, Justice Thurgood Marshall (ironically, a descendant of slaves) held that *Dennison* was "the product of another time" and "that the commands of the extradition clause are mandatory and afford no discretion to the executive officers or courts of the asylum state."[6]

---

4. Karsch, *Government of Missouri*, 232.

5. Thomas H. Eliot, *Governing America*, 2d ed. (New York: Dodd, Mead and Co., 1964), 759.

6. Kenyon Bunch and Richard J. Hardy, "Continuity or Change in Interstate Extradition? An Analysis of *Puerto Rico v. Branstad*," *Publius: The Journal of Federalism* 21:1 (1991), 1.

The extradition process can also involve numerous legal challenges and bureaucratic red tape. Basically, a criminal suspect can either waive extradition and return to the requesting state or test the validity of extradition proceedings by requesting a writ of habeas corpus, a procedure that occasionally results in release. Moreover, many officials argue that the extradition process has become too cumbersome and time-consuming. According to one report, "Action must occur by at least nine agencies from the asylum and demanding states before the wanted person is available for the first step in the criminal justice process in the demanding state."[7]

A final problem of interstate rendition procedures concerns the posting of bail or bonds. A suspect facing a stiff prison sentence in another state can often fight extradition and gain freedom by posting bail.[8] Some experts feel that bond in the asylum state is often set too low. Two cases illustrate this point. In 1980, the governor of Missouri requested the state of Kansas to extradite Homer Lewellen Jr. for the 1977 attempted murder of a Cole County sheriff. Lewellen petitioned the Leavenworth (Kansas) County District Court for a writ of habeas corpus, was freed on a ten thousand dollar bond, and then traveled to Joplin, Missouri, where he robbed a jewelry store at gunpoint. Needless to say, Lewellen did not make his court appearance in Kansas. Another incident involved country-western singer Johnny Paycheck. Following a free concert at the Missouri State Penitentiary in 1981, Paycheck was arrested by Missouri authorities on a warrant issued by the state of Wyoming charging the performer with sexually assaulting a twelve-year-old girl in Casper. Paycheck posted a ten thousand dollar bond, was released, and returned immediately to his home in Florida.

Of course, not every interstate flight to avoid prosecution necessitates extradition proceedings. One exception is "hot pursuit" or "fresh pursuit." Since 1951 Missouri has permitted police officers from bordering states to track down and arrest fugitives inside the state provided that the pursuit and arrest are conducted without "unreasonable delay" and that the state involved accords the same privilege to Missouri's law enforcement officials.[9] In addition, it is now a federal offense to flee to avoid prosecution of a state crime or to transport stolen vehicles, kidnapped persons, or illegally killed animals across state lines.

Privileges and Immunities. Because the founders feared that states would attempt to favor their own citizens over citizens from other states, they included the so-called Comity Clause (meaning courtesy or civility) into the Constitution. Article IV, Section 2, provides that "The Citizens of each State shall be entitled to all Privileges and Immunities of Citizens in the several States." As is so often the case, the Constitution does not specify the meaning of the term *privileges and immunities*. Once again we must rely on the Supreme Court to interject some general guidelines concerning the application of this clause. The

7. Laurie Baker, "Extradition Policies Complicate Law Enforcement," *Jefferson City News Tribune*, April 6, 1980. A writ of habeas corpus is a formal order directed to law enforcement personnel to bring the prisoner to court and to state the time and cause of arrest. If the cause is insufficient, the accused must be released. This writ is important because it guards against arbitrary punishment by guaranteeing judicial intervention and review.

8. The chief purpose of a bond at any state of a criminal proceeding is to assure that the defendant will appear in court. Bond is set by the court after considering such things as the defendant's prior record, mitigating circumstances, employment, residency, etc.

9. Karsch, *Government of Missouri*, 232.

Supreme Court has ruled that *privileges and immunities* means that U.S. citizens have the right to (1) travel through any state, (2) take up residence in any state, (3) buy and sell property in any state, (4) attend another state's public schools, (5) use another state's judicial system, and (6) secure the equal protection of the law.

There are some notable exceptions to the privileges and immunities clause. One exception concerns "beneficial services"— the resources and institutions that a state has property rights in and may reasonably reserve for its own residents. Thus, Missouri may charge out-of-state residents higher tuition to attend its tax-supported universities or increased fees for hunting and fishing licenses. A second exemption concerns political rights. Missouri may require new residents to dwell in the state for a specified period before they are permitted to vote or run for public office. A third exception concerns business and professional activities. The courts have held that Missouri does not have to recognize corporation charters or professional licenses (for example, licenses to practice law or teaching certificates) granted in another state.

Interstate Compacts. Interstate compacts are formal agreements between two or more states relating to such diverse matters as flood control, regional planning, forest fire protection, educational facilities, health services, traffic enforcement, disaster assistance, transportation, waste disposal, and public utility regulation. Article I, Section 10.3, of the U.S. Constitution makes it clear that "No State shall, without the Consent of Congress . . . enter into any Agreement or Compact with another State." Not surprisingly, the Constitution fails to specify when or how congressional consent should be registered. In any event, no case has arisen in which an interstate compact has

been held unconstitutional by the Supreme Court.

Throughout its history, the state of Missouri has entered into more than thirty interstate compacts. Some of the more noteworthy include the Interstate Crime Compact, the Adoption Assistance Compact, the Missouri-Kansas Boundary Compact, the Nonresident Violator Compact, the Tennessee-Missouri Bridge Compact, the Interstate Compact of Education, the St. Louis Bi-State Development Compact, the Southern Interstate Nuclear Compact, and the Interstate Compact on Juveniles.

Suits between States. From time to time, states have locked horns over matters that could only be resolved through litigation. Article III, Section 2, of the Constitution stipulates that the U.S. Supreme Court has exclusive original jurisdiction (as opposed to appellate jurisdiction) over suits between states. This means that only the nation's highest court has the power to hear and decide such cases.

The most notable interstate lawsuits involving Missouri have concerned water rights and boundary disputes. In 1906, for example, Missouri sued Illinois when a drainage canal from the Chicago sanitary district emptied raw sewage into a tributary of the Mississippi River, polluting one of Missouri's water sources. Another example is the early border skirmish between Missouri and Iowa. In 1816 the original survey of the two territories declared Missouri's northeastern boundary "to run east and west of the rapids in the Mississippi River which were near the mouth of the Des Moines River." Missouri, however, erroneously believed its northeastern boundary "to run east and west along a line from the rapids of the Des Moines River." Because the original markers had washed away, Missouri resurveyed the land in 1837 using the Des Moines River as its guide. When

Missouri declared the new boundary to be approximately thirteen miles north of where it was supposed to be, Iowa protested vehemently. This dispute lasted until 1850, when the Supreme Court declared that the confluence of the Des Moines and Mississippi rivers was to be the northeastern tip of Missouri.[10]

Informal Horizontal Relations

Uniform Laws. In addition to the formal/legal aspects of horizontal federalism, there are a number of informal methods of interstate cooperation. The oldest cooperative effort is the National Conference of Commissioners on Uniform State Laws, organized in 1892 by the American Bar Association. The purpose of this organization is to draft and recommend "model" laws to the various state legislatures. The major successes have been in commercial transactions; all states have adopted model laws on warehouse receipts, stock transfers, and negotiable instruments. Of the more than 170 model laws drafted by the commission, Missouri has adopted or modified 21. It must be stressed, though, that model laws are no panacea for reducing legal inequities. Even where such laws are adopted, they may be subsequently amended by state legislatures or interpreted differently by the state courts.[11]

Council on State Governments. Another organization aimed at improving interstate relations is the Council on State Governments. Established in 1925, the council serves as a clearinghouse for interstate research, information, and cooperation. It publishes *State Government* (a monthly journal) and *The Book of the States* (an annual reference book on state government), and serves as the secretariat for such interstate cooperative groups as the American Legislators Association, the National Association of State Budget Officers, the National Association of Attorneys General, and the National Legislative Conference. Like all other states, Missouri supports the council's various activities.

Reciprocity. Perhaps the simplest form of interstate cooperation is reciprocity, meaning "We'll respect your state laws if you'll respect ours." Thus, Missouri and Kansas allow each other's residents, under limited conditions, to enroll as state residents in their university systems. Missouri also honors temporarily all out-of-state driver's licenses with the knowledge that other states will honor ours. Despite these areas of cooperation, though, reciprocity in many instances has given way to retaliation.

Interstate Conflict. One area of interstate bickering concerns the imposition of quarantines for health purposes. In the early 1980s Missouri was at odds with Florida and Texas over the shipment of diseased cattle. After the discovery of high incidences of brucellosis, a contagious cattle disease that causes abortions and weak calves, Missouri imposed tougher inspection procedures on all livestock coming from these states. Florida officials were especially upset because they felt that Missouri's laws were highly unnecessary and discriminatory.[12] Similar feuds have occurred between California and Hawaii over the shipment of med-fly-infested fruit.

A second area of interstate rivalry centers around the competition for energy.

10. Margaret L. Posten, *This is the Place—Iowa,* 2d ed. (Ames: Iowa State University Press, 1967), 199–202.

11. David L. Martin, "Uniform State Laws and Interstate Compacts," *Capitol, Courthouse, and City Hall,* 6th ed. (Boston: Houghton, Mifflin, 1981), 70–72.

12. David A. Wiesler, "As States Fight over Water, Energy and Jobs," *U.S. News and World Report,* August 23, 1982, 49–50.

After the OPEC oil embargo of 1973–1974, many energy-rich states—particularly in the West—began to watch out for their own interests by levying severance taxes on the extraction of their natural resources. For example, Montana placed a 30 percent tax on coal, and Texas levied a 7.5 percent tax on natural gas. In Louisiana, severance taxes are the state's largest single source of revenue. This proliferation of severance taxes has brought an outcry from those in energy-poor states, who feel that such taxes merely allow energy-rich states to shift their tax burdens to nonresidents. In the future, look for nonseverance states to retaliate.

A third area of interstate conflict concerns water diversion. For example, in the early 1980s Missouri was at loggerheads with South Dakota over the proposed diversion of water from the Missouri River to Wyoming. South Dakota's governor at the time, William Janklow, wanted to sell 16.3 billion gallons of Missouri River water per year to private corporations that would send Wyoming coal to power plants in Oklahoma and Louisiana. Missouri officials threatened to take this matter to court on grounds that such a project would have harmful effects on navigation, hydroelectricity production, and the environment. The controversy ended when the proposed project was scrapped.

A final area concerns interstate competition for business and industry. Recent economic difficulties, coupled with significant federal government cutbacks, have forced many states, including Missouri, to move more aggressively to attract new business. A few years back, Michigan, for instance, learned that business development scouts from Indiana were trying to persuade Michigan companies to relocate in the Hoosier State. The ongoing economic war between South Dakota and Minnesota also illustrates this point. In the past decade, South Dakota eliminated its corporate and personal property taxes and reduced its unemployment insurance and workmen's compensation rates as an incentive for new businesses.

These are just a few of the interstate problems that currently exist. As natural resources become scarce, the economy tightens, and states perceive they are being discriminated against, interstate bickering will no doubt increase.

IV. Conclusion

The purpose of this introductory chapter has been to explain briefly the concept of American federalism, and to reveal how Missouri relates both formally and informally to the national government as well as to other states. It should now be obvious that Missouri's role in the federal system is not static, but instead is highly complex, dynamic, and subject to change. To understand Missouri government and politics—past, present, and future—one must not only understand the nature of American federalism but also keep abreast of the many legal, social, economic, and cultural changes that significantly affect Missouri in the federal system.

CHAPTER 2

Political Culture of Missouri
by Richard R. Dohm

> Nor is it possible to devote oneself to Culture and declare that one is "not interested" in politics.
> —Thomas Mann

Culture is an inclusive concept that refers to the generalized attitudes, values, and orientations that distinguish one group of people from another. Political culture refers to those aspects of culture that are concerned with politically relevant objects, such as attitudes toward laws, institutions, and leaders. The purpose of this chapter is to examine the political culture of Missouri. The chapter begins with a survey of the state's physical makeup, economy, population, migrational patterns, and history. Next, a cultural typology is offered, and Missouri's political characteristics are discussed within that context. Finally, the effects of Missouri's political culture are analyzed with reference to specific policies and institutions.

I. The Setting

Any discussion of Missouri's political culture must be framed in a setting of the state's physical makeup, economy, population, population characteristics, and history.

Physical Makeup

Missouri is located near the center of the United States, with the Mississippi River serving as its eastern boundary. Although the state is landlocked, it does have approximately one thousand miles of navigable rivers, including the Missouri and the Mississippi. The topography varies from gently rolling hills in the northern and west-central areas to the Ozark Mountains (more accurately described as highlands) in the south and southwest. The Bootheel in the southeastern corner is flat Mississippi River delta land that has been noted since 1922 for its cotton production. However, soybeans have surpassed cotton in dollar volume. The rest of the southern third of the state is rugged because of the Ozark highlands, and is famed for its fishing, hunting, and numerous caves and springs.

Economy

The economy of Missouri is varied, with the top industries including agriculture, manufacturing, aerospace, and tourism, although not necessarily in that order. Mineral production is also important, with lead and crushed stone (as well as Portland cement) accounting for $924.6 million in sales in 1992.[1]

---

1. *The World Almanac and Book of Facts—1994* (New York: Newspaper Enterprises Association), 644.

Manufacturing. The state has a large transportation-equipment manufacturing industry, which is led by McDonnell-Douglas Company. Missouri also ranks high in number of defense contracts (almost every county has some), which leaves the economy vulnerable to the ending of the Cold War. The state's industries produce such items as space capsules, rocket engines, and aircraft, as well as automobiles and electrical equipment (Emerson Electric). Food processing is also important and includes meat packing, grain milling (Ralston-Purina), beer brewing (Anheuser-Busch), and other beverage processing. Production of chemicals is another important industry, in which Monsanto Company plays a leading role. Kansas City–based Hallmark, which produces greeting cards, is another major world company.

Agriculture. Agriculture is an important income producer in Missouri. Farm marketing totaled $4.4 billion in 1992, with more than half coming from livestock. The state is a major producer of cattle and cows, hogs, and turkeys. Other important products include soybeans, corn and clover crops, winter wheat, tobacco, apples, peaches, alfalfa, popcorn, and cotton. The state ranks sixth in the nation in rice production, and it also has a growing wine industry that ranks seventh in number of wineries and eighth in production.

Although agriculture is very important to the state's economy, farm income varies widely among geographic areas. For example, the southern third of the state, excluding the Bootheel, is lower in per capita farm income than other areas, primarily because of the hilly terrain. Excellent farmland elsewhere, however, contributes to higher farm income.

Tourism. Tourism, now claimed by its leaders to be the state's second-largest industry, generated an estimated $8.6 billion in 1993, according to the Missouri Division of Tourism. The state offers a wide range of vacation facilities, with many resorts at the larger lakes, which include Lake of the Ozarks, Taneycomo, Bull Shoals, and Table Rock. Lake of the Ozarks has two world-class resorts and is continuing to experience considerable growth. The city of Branson (in Taney County, which borders Arkansas) has several new multimillion-dollar country-western theaters, and is rivaling Nashville as country-western capital of the nation.

The Army Corps of Engineers has constructed two new lakes, the Harry S. Truman and Mark Twain reservoirs, which should further increase tourism's impact on the economy. In addition, there are forty-seven state parks and numerous caves and springs, many of which are privately owned.

Minerals. Missouri is rich in minerals, including large deposits of lead. With lead now banned from gasoline and paint for health reasons, however, demand has decreased and the industry has declined. The state is also a leader in barite and lime mining, and has coal (although with high sulfur content, which means it does not burn as cleanly), iron ore, copper, and zinc. Missouri manufactures cement and asphalt and mines clay for the production of fire brick.

Personal Income. Missouri has usually ranked near the middle among the fifty states on personal income per capita. Missouri ranked twenty-second in 1965, twenty-ninth in 1980, twenty-third in 1987, and twenty-seventh in 1993. Personal income per capita in Missouri in 1993 was $19,463, slightly below the national figure of $20,817.[2]

2. *Statistical Abstract of the United States 1994* (Washington, D.C.: Bureau of the Census, 1994), 457.

Population

Missouri's population is expanding, but at a rate below the national average. According to the 1990 Census, the population was 5,117,073, which maintained Missouri's position as the nation's fifteenth most populous state.[3] Although the state's population has increased every decade since 1880, it has been outpaced by the nation's population growth throughout the twentieth century.

In general, the national patterns of migration have held for Missouri since World War II. Suburban and exurban areas continue to increase in population, although some older suburban cities have declined, as have the central cities of St. Louis and Kansas City. Outstate Missouri has seen increases in the lake counties, but most of the agricultural counties lost population. Thirty-five northern Missouri counties lost population through the 1980s and early 1990s, reflecting the economic depression in agriculture.

Two important factors related to population should be emphasized: the state has exported many of its youth during the last several decades, with the highest outmigration rates found among those from twenty to thirty years old;[4] and the state ranked tenth in the percentage of residents sixty-five years of age and older as of 1990.

Social System

The social system of Missouri is highly diversified, due in part to Missouri's earlier role as the "gateway to the West" and to the instate migration of many different ethnic groups. Early migrations included German immigrants and their descendants who, among other things, developed the large brewing industry in St. Louis. Those who settled in the southwest and the Ozark Mountains came primarily from the hill country of Kentucky and Tennessee, and they opposed slavery (which helps explain why this region is largely Republican today).

In addition, there was a substantial slave population in 1860, with 114,931 blacks, almost 10 percent of the total population of 1,182,012.[5] Indeed, in seven counties slaves accounted for more than 35 percent of the population (including 59 percent in Howard County). These concentrations occurred in counties bordering the Missouri and Mississippi Rivers, probably because the rich flood plains and the availability of river transport made plantation-style farming feasible.

The existence of slavery influenced the social systems in these counties and aggravated the schism that resulted in the Civil War. Indeed, some of the effects still linger. One section extending from the center of the state to the Mississippi River in the northeast is still known as "Little Dixie," and these counties have voted Democratic since the Civil War with few exceptions, although recently they have supported some Republican candidates for state office.

Civil War. The schism between slaveholders and nonslaveholders was reflected in some peculiar events of the Civil War. Missouri's government at the start of the war included a majority of Southern sympathizers. However, after a series of military and political events, federal troops from St. Louis (primarily German-Americans who were sympathetic to the Union) occupied the state capital. The legally elected government passed an act declaring Missouri's

3. Office of Social and Economic Data Analysis, University of Missouri–Columbia, *The State of the State: Missouri's Changing Economy and People*, 7.

4. Office of Social and Economic Data Analysis, *Trendletter* (Columbia: University Extension, May–June 1991), 1.

5. Duane Meyer, *The Heritage of Missouri: A History* (Hazelwood, Mo.: State Publishing Co., 1970), 316.

secession from the Union, but was deposed by the federal troops. The deposed government did not meet during most of the war, although it sent representatives to the Southern Confederacy legislature. In its absence, members of a former state convention were reconvened in Jefferson City and became the provisional government (surprisingly, none of these earlier-elected members of the convention were Southern sympathizers). With these developments, the state was kept within the Union, even though there were numerous military skirmishes between the opposing armies. Together with the schism of the Civil War, the great diversity in economy, personal income, population, and social systems has affected the state's political culture, which in turn has affected Missouri's institutions and politics.

II. Political Culture and Comparative Studies of State Government

Political culture is a concept that has been developed to help explain how political systems differ among countries and even among states. An excellent work that has examined state political institutions is Daniel Elazar's *American Federalism: A View from the States.* Elazar argues convincingly that the United States is still a federal system, despite the concentration of power in Washington, D.C.:

> [I]t becomes very likely, if not inevitable, that each state will possess its own particular characteristics simply by virtue of its settled existence over generations. In turn, its bundle of individual characteristics is what transforms each state into a civil society, possessing a political system that is in some measure autonomous. And despite the apparently great and continuing pressures for

centralization, this autonomy is no mean thing.[6]

Thus, Elazar is convinced that even though the states have lost power to Washington, they possess a political system developed sufficiently to continue operation should some catastrophe befall the nation's capital. In addition, the states have civil societies that differ from each other.

The Concept of Political Culture

The concept of political culture, then, "is rooted in the historical experience of particular groups of people," which in turn affects the ways individuals and groups view government. It influences what people expect from government, what types of individuals seek elective office and government employment, and the "actual way in which the art of government is practiced by citizens, politicians, and public officials in the light of their perceptions."[7] Furthermore, the cultural components within a state will make themselves felt in three additional ways: (1) in the kind of civic behavior dictated by conscience and internalized ethical standards, (2) in the character of law-abidingness displayed by citizens and officials, and (3) in the positive actions of government.

Elazar argues that the United States as a whole shares a general political culture based on two contrasting conceptions of the political order: (1) that of a marketplace in which "the primary public relationships are products of bargaining among individuals and groups acting out of self-interest" (often termed *pluralism*), and (2) that of a commonwealth or community where "citizens cooperate in an effort to create and maintain the best government

6. Daniel Elazar, *American Federalism: A View from the States,* 2d ed. (New York: Thomas Y. Crowell Co.), 1972.
7. Ibid., 5, 85.

in order to implement certain shared moral principles."[8] These two conceptions have profoundly influenced attitudes and politics, sometimes conflicting with and sometimes complementing each other.

This broad general political culture is a synthesis of three basic political subcultures: individualistic, moralistic (better termed community or commonwealth), and traditionalistic. These subcultures are the result of various immigrations of Europeans and reflect differing views of society. New England was settled mostly by Puritans and their descendants, who were concerned with "an earthly vision of the holy commonwealth."[9] The middle Atlantic states were settled mostly by the Germans and English, who were concerned primarily with individual opportunity, making even religion an individual matter. The southern Atlantic states also were settled by people motivated by individual opportunity, but they founded a plantation-based, rather than commercial, economy.

From the Eastern seaboard, various individuals and groups struck out westward for new opportunities, taking their views of government, society, and religion with them. Pennsylvania and Missouri were key states in this westward migration, and consequently, the development of their governmental institutions was influenced by many diverse groups that chose to settle rather than move on. Some of those influences persist today.

Three Political Subcultures

The three political subcultures—individualistic, moralistic, and traditionalistic—and their mix are what provide a state with its unique bundle of political characteristics. Elazar has identified the major characteristics of the political subcultures in this way:

1. The *individualistic* political subculture emphasizes minimal government and minimal governmental interference in the economy (examples include Indiana, Illinois, and Pennsylvania).

2. The *moralistic* political subculture strongly emphasizes cooperation in improving the community or commonwealth (Massachusetts, Wisconsin, Oregon, Utah, Minnesota).

3. The *traditionalistic* subculture emphasizes a strong commitment to the existing social and political order and is primarily associated with the precommercial area of the South (Alabama, Mississippi, South Carolina).

In analyzing the various cultures of the states, Elazar breaks down this typology into a mix of eight components. In general, the moralistic (community–commonwealth) subcultures are found in the northern states, although the Rocky Mountains diverted this culture to the Southwest. The individualistic subculture is found throughout the middle states, while the South is traditionalistic (see Figure 2-1). Missouri, Elazar notes, is one of only two states having a mixed individualistic–traditionalistic political subculture. This means that while the individualistic is dominant, there are also strong traditionalistic elements.[10]

III. Missouri's Political Characteristics

Missouri has been nicknamed the Show-Me State, which suggests skepticism regarding change, whether it be change in institutions or change in the old way

8. Ibid., 90.
9. Ibid., 90, 91.

10. Ibid., 108.

Figure 2-1 Dominant Political Cultures, by State

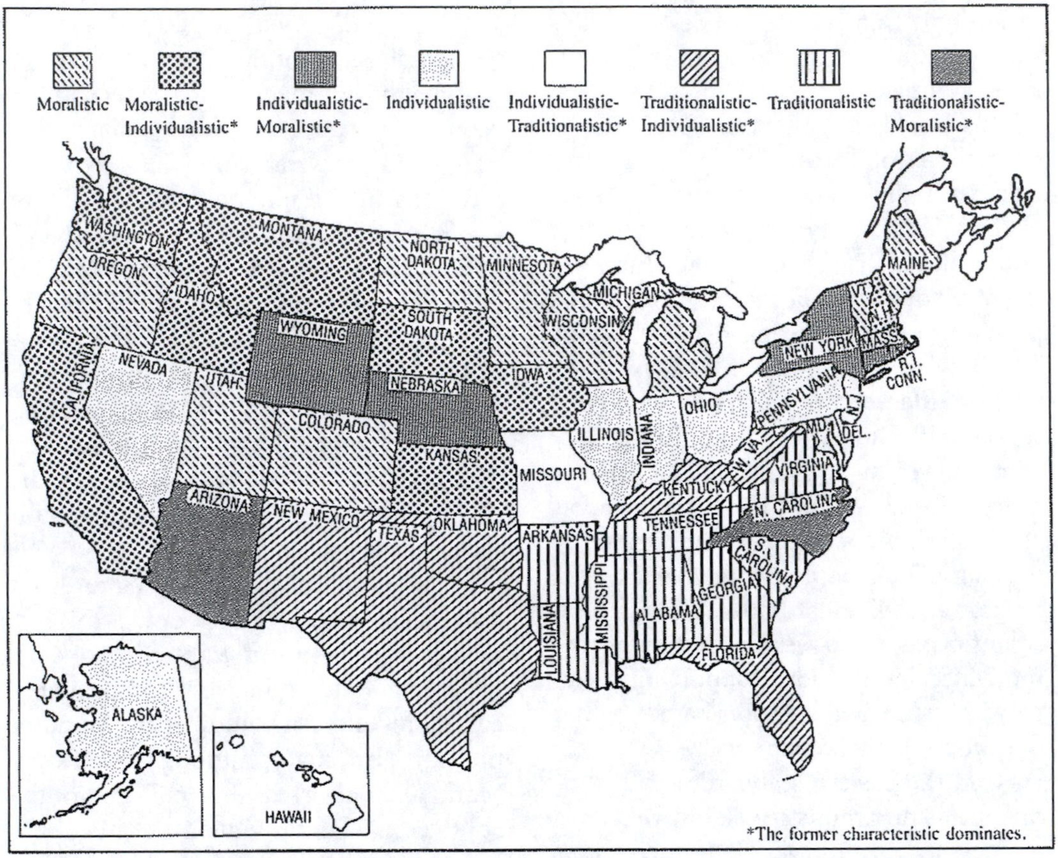

Source: *American Federalism: A View from the States*, Daniel J. Elazar. Copyright © 1984 by Harper and Row. Reprinted by permission of Harper Collins Publishers, Inc.

of doing things. For example, the state is one of fifteen that did not ratify the equal rights amendment—nine of the fifteen were part of the old South (see Table 2–1). Missouri's state government is more conservative than most other states, at least with respect to taxation, expenditures, and innovative programs that cost money. It is noted for its low tax effort and low expenditures, and in 1991 it ranked forty-ninth in state and local tax revenue per one hundred dollars of personal income.[11]

On the other hand, Missouri was one of twenty states that adopted TELS (tax and expenditure limitations) between 1976 and 1986. The Hancock Amendment, put on the ballot in 1980 by initiative petition, was Missouri's answer to California's Proposition 13, passed in 1978. Even though the state had rigid restrictions on governmental indebtedness and a long history of commitment to low taxes, then-businessman Mel Hancock of Springfield (he later became a Republican congressman) circulated petitions calling for additional restrictions on state and local taxation. Through his Taxpayers Survival Association efforts and, more importantly, the efforts of the Missouri Farm Bureau, the issue was placed

11. *State Legislatures*, 5.

Table 2-1. Political Culture and Ratification of the U.S. Equal Rights Ammendment
Predominant State Political Culture*

	M	MI	IM	I	IT	TI	T	TM
Not Ratified	Utah		Ill.	Nev.	Mo.	Ala. Ark. Fla. Ga. La. Okla.	Miss. S.C. Va.	Ariz. N.C.
Ratified and Rescinded		Idaho	Neb.				Tenn.	
Ratified	Colo. Maine Mich. Minn. N.D. Ore. Vt. Wisc.	Cal. Iowa Kan. Mont. N.H. S.D. Wash.	Conn. Mass. N.Y. Ohio R.I. Wyo.	Alaska Ind. N.J. Pa.	Del. Hawaii Md.	Ky. N.M. Tex. W. Va.		

*M = moralistic; I = individualistic; T = traditionalistic. When two characteristics are given, the preceding culture is the dominant one.

Source: John Kincaid, ed., *Political Culture, Public Policy and the American States* (Philadelphia: Institute for the Study of Human Issues, 1982), p. 20.

on the ballot on November 4, 1980. It was approved by a substantial margin, 1,002,935 to 807,187. In only 20 of Missouri's 115 counties did a majority vote against the proposal. A proposed constitutional amendment further limiting state government revenues, initiated again by Hancock and his supporters, was soundly defeated in 1994.

Although Missouri has long been noted for its conservatism, partly due to its many schisms including cultural aspects of North and South, that conservatism has been modified by the same recent developments that have influenced the rest of the nation. National television has had a homogenizing effect, as have fast-food outlets, chain stores, and economic development in general. However, several

historians suggest that the South is not disappearing as a distinct region but is continuing to maintain a commitment to the military, support for prayer in public schools, strong religious affiliation, anti-unionism, and a concern for race somewhat different from that in the North.

These southern characteristics have been part of Missouri as well, although the state has supported unions for the private sector while resisting them for public employees. While Republican Governor John Ashcroft was in office (1985–1993), considerable efforts were made to oppose abortion. The Missouri legislature passed several laws designed to restrict abortions in the state, embroiling the state in various court cases. On the other hand, Missouri has supported recent gambling initiatives, at least in the case of riverboat gambling and horse racing. This has occurred despite the opposition of Southern Baptists.

The Individualistic Political Culture

The major characteristics of an individualistic political culture can be examined by looking at the way that type of culture views six elements: (1) society and the role of government, (2) the role of political parties, (3) party regularity and discipline, (4) the level of governmental activity, (5) political professionalism, and (6) the commitment to professionalism in government employment.

Society and the Role of Government. Individuals in an individualistic political culture see the society of the United States as a democratic marketplace. That is, the economic marketplace is viewed as an end in itself, and government should only mediate between special interest groups. It should not concern itself with questions of "good society" but rather should play only a minimal role as an umpire between competing interest groups. This conception of society and the role of government closely resembles the ideas of Thomas Jefferson, who believed that government should "restrain men from injuring one another, and should leave them otherwise free to regulate their own pursuits of industry and improvement, and shall not take from the mouth of labor the bread it has earned." Jefferson thought that public power threatened liberty and favored dispersing it: "It is not by the consolidation or concentration of powers, but by their distribution, that good government is effected."[12] Jefferson also believed that government which

is closest to the people and which governs least is best.

Andrew Jackson also left a legacy of ideas affecting state and local government. Like Jefferson, he believed in keeping government from becoming powerful and tyrannical. This was to be accomplished by having frequent elections (short terms of office) and electing as many public officials as practicable. This led to a "long ballot," so-called because of the many offices to be filled. Also, he believed in eliminating property restrictions on voting, at least for free, white males.

Several indicators reflect Jeffersonian-Jacksonian values in Missouri. The large number of local governments is an excellent example of the preference for small, personal governments. According to the U.S. Bureau of the Census, in 1992 Missouri ranked eleventh among the states in local units per one hundred thousand population. Other indicators are (1) twenty-three counties have the rural-township form of government—these counties have lost some functions (property tax assessment, for example) but gained optional planning and zoning authority in 1989; (2) commitment to decentralization in county government, with the election of as many as twenty-five officials per county; (3) preference of most cities for the traditional mayor–council form of government, with its elected administrative officials; (4) deep suspicion of many municipal populations toward the council–manager form of government (the city administrator form has been developed as an alternative—see the section in this chapter on the commitment to professionalism in government employment); and (5) commitment to direct democracy and the desire to vote on many local and state issues (the use of the initiative and referendum has been common in both state and local elections,

12. Jefferson is quoted in Charles M. Wiltse, *The Jefferson Tradition in American Democracy* (New York: Hiss and Wang, 1963), 87, and in Leonard D. White, *Introduction to the Study of Public Administration* (New York: Macmillan, 1955), 16.

with voters casting ballots on a variety of issues).

Two additional indicators reflect conservative positions on property rights and governmental finance. Only about 25 percent of the counties have adopted planning *and* zoning, reflecting the strong resistance to governmental controls over use of property. This opposition is most associated with rural counties, but it is not confined to them. Jefferson County, located next to St. Louis County on the south and long impacted by urbanization, opposed planning and zoning for many decades before finally voting for adoption. Then it voted it out before finally readopting it for good. (The recent authorization of township planning and zoning is consistent with minimalizing the use of such powers, but such small scale is heresy to professional planners.)

Lastly, general obligation bond issues and above-limit school levies require extraordinary majorities (more than 50 percent plus one) for approval, reflecting a conservative fear that a minority of voters might raise taxes or put the community in debt. With turnouts in local elections often being 30 percent or less, a simple majority might represent as little as 15 percent of eligible voters. A two-thirds or four-sevenths majority requirement certainly reduces this possibility, even though it gives greater weight to votes against the issue (a "no" vote in a two-thirds election is equal to two "yes" votes).

The Role of Political Parties. With respect to the role of the political party in the individualistic political culture, Elazar notes that "such a political culture encourages the maintenance of a party system that is competitive, but not overly so, in the pursuit of office."[13] Supporting the contention that individualistic political cultures en-

courage semicompetitive party systems is the existence of many one-party counties, at least in courthouse elective offices.

Although party influence has certainly declined in recent decades and voting patterns reflect less straight-ticket voting, there is a striking persistence of party loyalty in county offices. About one-third of all counties elect Democrats in at least 90 percent of all elections for county offices, a pattern that existed from 1966 to 1974 and persisted in the 1980s. The proportion of counties that elected Republicans as county officials at least 90 percent of the time declined slightly, from about one-fifth of all counties in 1966–1974 to one-seventh in the 1980s.[14]

Although voters have learned to split their tickets and are now electing more Republicans to state and national offices, there is still considerable party loyalty operating in contests for county offices. Election outcomes for seats in the General Assembly also continue to reflect traditional party patterns.

Party Regularity and Discipline. As Elazar notes, "party regularity is indispensable in the individualistic political culture because it is the means for coordinating individual enterprise in the political arena and is the one way of preventing individualism in politics from running wild." Such a system demands party regularity or discipline because the all-important goal is to achieve office and patronage. "Party regulars" are considered essential to achieve this end. In addition, an individual can achieve success in such a system not by dealing with issues or concerns about good

---

13. Elazar, *American Federalism*, 95.

14. The 1966–1974 data are from Robert F. Karsch, *The Government of Missouri*, 13th ed. (Columbia: Lucas Brothers, 1976), 46. The 1979–1988 data were compiled by Cordell Smith and R. E. Burnett for chapter 4 of this textbook.

government, "but by maintaining his place in the system of mutual obligations."[15]

Several factors have undermined patronage and party discipline, including reorganization of the executive branch of state government in the early 1970s, the elimination of party identification from employment forms, and several United States Supreme Court decisions (including *Elrod v. Burns* in 1976) that have removed partisanship as a factor in firing state government employees. These efforts have been successful nationally, but recent Missouri governors have had some success in maintaining partisanship.

The tools for gubernatorial use of patronage include appointment of division and department heads, the nomination process for the nonpartisan court appointments, and appointments to other boards and commissions. For example, in his two terms as governor Ashcroft appointed all members of the seven-member Missouri Supreme Court and the nine-member University of Missouri Board of Curators. Complaints surfaced regarding the politicization of such bodies, but such practices are not new or limited to governors of one party. State license fee offices are another patronage opportunity, and although one governor attempted to remove them from patronage, most are still operated by political appointees.

Party discipline is also maintained in the house of representatives. The Democrats, the majority party, control committee assignments and other perks. Party-line votes are not uncommon, and the operation is quite different from that of the senate, in which nonpartisanship has continued for decades. The different ground rules in the senate allow Republicans to play an important role and at times even dominate the legislative process in that body, despite being in the minority.

Elazar's contention that an individual can achieve success "by maintaining his place in the system of mutual obligations" is supported by the existence of an "old boy" network in Jefferson City and the state. By dint of being in the right friendship circles or knowing the right people, men and women have gained employment and had long careers, despite not being of the party in power, or having to be processed through a classification system.

In summary, party regularity and discipline has certainly weakened in Missouri as it has nationally. However, there is still sufficient patronage in state government to assure some party discipline, and governors will undoubtedly use it for such purposes.

The Level of Governmental Activity. Since the role of government in the individualistic political culture is minimal, government generally is not expected to initiate new programs until the demands by legislators or the public are overwhelming. In a study of innovation and adaptation of innovative programs by state governments, Jack L. Walker of the University of Michigan ranked Missouri thirty-ninth among the forty-eight contiguous states in "innovation." After identifying eighty-eight innovative programs developed by various state governments and tracing their adoption rate by other states, Walker found that Missouri ranked low, supporting the "show-me" pattern. As Elazar states, "In general, government action is to be restricted to those areas, primarily in the economic realm, which encourage private initiative and widespread access to the marketplace."[16]

---

15. Elazar, *American Federalism*, 95.

16. Jack L. Walker, "The Diffusion of Innovations among the American States," *American Political Science Review* 63:3 (September 1969), 883. Elazar, *American Federalism*, 94.

Political Professionalism. The individualistic political culture holds politics to be just another means by which individuals may improve themselves socially and economically. There also is a strong tendency among the public to believe that politics is a dirty business best left to professional politicians—that is, people who have dedicated their lives to a career in politics and political parties. The opposite of this belief is found in moralistic (community/commonwealth) political cultures, where the entire citizenry is expected to participate in politics and amateurs often are encouraged to run for elective office. Naturally, in moralistic cultures party regularity is minimal and not particularly encouraged. Elazar further notes that in individualistic political cultures, "since a fair amount of corruption is expected in the normal course of things, there is relatively little popular excitement when any is found unless it is of an extraordinary character."[17]

The Commitment to Professionalism in Government Employment. Citizens in individualistic political cultures are somewhat ambivalent about the place of bureaucracy in the political order. An appointed bureaucracy based on objective and competitive examinations for employment and promotion is considered efficient, but it flies in the face of the favor or patronage system. To quote Elazar:

> In the end, bureaucratic organization is introduced within the framework of the favor system; large segments of the bureaucracy may be insulated from it through the merit system but the entire organization is pulled into the political environment at crucial points through political appointments at the upper echelons and, very frequently, the bending of the merit system to meet political demands.[18]

The best indicator of this view is the status of the merit system, or rather merit systems, in state government. The central merit system that cuts across organizational lines in state government departments presently covers less than one-half of all state employees, although there are several additional single-department merit systems (including those in the departments of Conservation and Highways, the State Highway Patrol, and the university and college systems). There is a program to extend the central merit system to cover the departments of Revenue and Agriculture, but it will not take effect until 1996 and will still provide flexibility in employment hiring practices.

The sixteen hundred patronage employees of the Department of Revenue have constituted a political football for many years. Former governor Warren E. Hearnes acted to put them under the merit system, but only after Christopher Bond, a Republican, was elected to succeed him. Bond attempted to do the same but was thwarted by the General Assembly. Teasdale also tried the same by executive order but with the same results. Thus, sufficient employees still remain under the patronage system to undercut the concept of professionalism in state government.

The same ambivalence toward professionalism in government can be seen at the local level in Missouri. For example, only thirty-six of the more than nine hundred municipalities have adopted the council–manager plan, which is available to all cities of the third class and others with the requisite population. (Some of the twenty-nine home rule cities also have a variation of the council–manager plan.) The plan is the

---

17. Elazar, *American Federalism*, 95.

18. Ibid., 99.

most professional of local forms, centralizing authority under the city manager and requiring at-large elections.[19] The thirty-six manager cities are a rather small number when compared with other states of somewhat equal populations, but this figure must be modified by the large number of cities (114 in 1991) having the city administrator form of government. The city administrator form retains the traditional mayor-council structure, but adds the position of city administrator. This change can be accomplished by ordinance rather than a vote of the people. The community retains a mayor and ward elections while gaining some centralization under the administrator. In these communities, elected officials realized the need for full-time management but also recognized the unpopularity of the manager plan (which when first adopted must be retained for six years). The resulting compromise illustrates the attachment to traditional governmental structures while modifying them to meet present needs.

Despite some recent change, two generalizations can be suggested: (1) anti-professionalism can still be a force in Missouri politics, and (2) Missourians prefer to adjust their existing local governmental structures rather than adopt new forms of government.

The Traditional Political Culture

Society and the Role of Government. Citizens in a traditionalistic political culture hold an elitist conception of the community or commonwealth. This means they are committed to preserving a privileged position for traditional "elites" or established old families. In this political culture, hierarchy is accepted as the natural order, and those at the top of the social structure are expected to play a dominant role in government. People support the existing order and generally oppose change, and good government is considered to be government provided by the leadership or traditional elites.

This type of political culture is most associated with the South before industrialization, particularly before the Civil War. Although these attitudes are somewhat difficult to document, there is some evidence of their existence in outstate Missouri, especially in counties that once had large slave populations and that are now without substantial growth centers. A common indicator is the importance of family, rather than profession or work, to an individual's identity within the county. For example, in many counties candidates for elective office emphasize that they are natives of the county because "nativeness" is still considered important in winning elections. Elazar explains:

> The traditionalistic political culture accepts government as an actor with a positive role in the community, but it tries to limit that role to securing the continued maintenance of the existing social order. To do so, it functions to confine real political power to a relatively small and self-perpetuating group drawn from an established elite who often inherit their "right" to govern through family ties or social position.[20]

The Role of Political Parties. Political parties in traditionalistic cultures are considered useful but of secondary importance. They are useful in recruiting candidates, but only those candidates considered acceptable by the leadership. In addition,

19. In 1985, an amendment to chapter 78 authorized an alternative to the council–manager plan. The alternative (78.700) requires five wards and a council of seven members, one each from the five wards and two at large.

20. Elazar, *American Federalism*, 99.

the political elites regard political parties with some suspicion because those parties encourage a degree of openness that may conflict with the hierarchical social order.

Political competition in a traditionalistic culture usually involves factional alignments rather than conflicts between two parties; that tendency is a logical extension of the personal politics characteristic of the system. "Hence political systems within the cultures tend to have loose one-party systems if they have political parties at all."[21] Indeed, party ties are highly personal and are based upon family and social ties.

The Level of Governmental Activity. Government may foster worthy projects, but only with respect to the existing social order. If there is a threat to the prominent elites, then government may initiate programs to perpetuate elitist rule. In states with predominantly traditionalistic cultures, government is usually highly centralized but does not initiate innovative programs.

The Commitment to Professionalism in Government Employment. The elitist approach to government means, in most instances, that those who have no legitimate claim to political careers should not participate—government leaders should only include those who are part of the social elite. This conception is held by both social leaders and the population at large, resulting in a paternalistic approach to governing.

Since traditionalistic cultures are generally antibureaucratic, they display a minimal commitment to professionalism. A merit or civil service system "by its very nature interferes with the fine web of informal interpersonal relationships that lie at the root of the political system."[22] Where

bureaucracy is introduced, it is introduced in a limited way and is firmly controlled by the established power holders.

It should be noted, though, that the traditionalistic political culture is breaking down in many instances, and has not prevented some innovative state and local programs. The rapid industrialization of the South has obviously modified traditional political patterns, and Virginia has gained a reputation for being innovative in state and local relations.

With the exception of Louisiana and Virginia, the states of the South fell near or below the median in the Walker study of governmental innovation among the forty-eight contiguous states. Louisiana ranked nineteenth and Virginia twenty-first.[23] The other southern states are ranked in this order: North Carolina, twenty-fourth; Alabama, thirtieth; Florida, thirty-first; Arkansas, thirty-second; Tennessee, thirty-fourth; Georgia, thirty-seventh; Texas, forty-fourth; South Carolina, forty-fifth; and Mississippi, forty-eighth. Thus, although most states with strong traditionalistic cultures ranked below the median on the Walker scale, they certainly did not all group at the bottom. As a final note, traditionalistic cultures place a very high value on "community," similar to the emphasis found in moralistic cultures.

IV. Effects of Political Culture on Missouri

In political party strength, Missouri's traditional Democratic dominance has eroded in the last twenty-five years. Although Democrats still dominated at the local level, in the General Assembly, and in the congressional delegation in the late 1980s and early 1990s, Republicans won about

21. Ibid.
22. Ibid., 102.

23. Walker, "Diffusion of Innovations," 883.

half of the contests for statewide executive office, and both U.S. Senate seats.

In presidential contests since 1932, Missouri has a split-ticket record and a history of supporting the winner in most cases. Democratic candidates fared better at first, but more recently the state supported Republicans Ronald Reagan and George Bush. The 1976 contest between Gerald Ford and Jimmy Carter was very close, but the state went for Carter, the Democrat, by a very slim margin. The Reagan/Bush tickets won by large margins in 1980 and 1984, and Bush and Dan Quayle won in 1988, but by a much smaller margin (1,084,953 to 1,001,619). In 1992, however, the state reverted back to its traditional Democratic voting pattern and supported Bill Clinton and Al Gore over Bush/Quayle by a margin of 1,053,873 to 811,159 (the Perot/Stockdale ticket gained 518,741 votes). Only 32 of 115 counties gave the majority of their votes to Bush/Quayle. (At this same election Democrats were elected to five of the six state offices, completely reversing the previous situation, in which Republicans held five of the six offices.)

At the state and local levels, the Democratic dominance is more pronounced. The General Assembly has been dominated by Democrats since 1900, particularly in the senate, where Democrats have been the majority party for all but eight years. Republicans have had better success in the house, where they were the majority for twenty-two years, but this occurred before 1955. At the county level, as noted, there are more single-party Democratic counties than Republican, at least in terms of elected county officials.

Despite the weakening of the parties in Missouri and the nation and the resulting increase in ticket splitting, Missouri remains a modified two-party state. This means that there is some competition between the parties, particularly for state offices, where Republican pressures and successes have been increasing. In many counties, for example the eight counties in Little Dixie,[24] voters retain their party loyalty (Democratic) for county elective offices.

Elazar's findings support the characterization of Missouri as conservative and bring some additional factors to light:

> Five states, all located along the middle of the country between North and South and all ranking low in internal cohesiveness, are united primarily by their concern with maintenance of the established political patterns which give them power against various pressures, usually external. Since there is little that unites the public in these states, the problems of the powerholders remain the most significant ones. They include the maintenance of low tax rates against the rising needs for governmental services, the maintenance of patronage systems in the face of pressures for civil service reform, and the maintenance of entrenched political organizations and alignments against disturbing elements that are generated from outside the state boundaries.[25]

Thus, although Missouri does not have a great deal of internal unity or cohesiveness, there is some agreement that the state's political patterns should be preserved, particularly against outside pressures—usually generated by the federal government.

In contrast, in some other states the preservation of cultural patterns is most significant for internal unity. For example, prior to 1965 the southern states were unified on the preservation of their way

24. Audrain, Boone, Callaway, Howard, Monroe, Pike, Ralls, and Randolph counties, as identified by Milton D. Rafferty in *Historical Atlas of Missouri* (Norman: University of Oklahoma Press, 1982), 33.

25. 25.

of life, which excluded a role for blacks. The same concern with cultural patterns is found in Minnesota, Oregon, and Utah (states with moralistic political cultures), and these states continue to have a high degree of internal unity. In Minnesota, for example, opinion polls show a consensus that "the state is more 'honest,' more 'community-minded,' more 'stable,' more 'homey,' and more concerned with the individual immediate neighbors." The same polls found "that all this is due to the state's more isolated position; and that it is worth preserving."

Elazar also attempts to analyze the relationship of localities or political subdivisions to their respective state governments. In so doing, he identifies variables that affect such relationships: political culture, sectionalism, rural-urban and metropolitan-nonmetropolitan cleavages, and localism. If a state has many variables or a few very active ones, it appears there is an increase in state and local conflict. In addition, Elazar notes, "there is some evidence that these states with more significant variables do less governmentally to help their civil communities than their sisters." Pennsylvania and Missouri, it should be noted, are the only two states that have the full complement of seven variables.

Missouri ranks rather low in terms of the help states give their political subdivisions. As illustrated in Table 2-2, the state ranked forty-seventh in 1990 in per capita state aid to local governments (excluding education and welfare expenditures). Of the seven upper Midwest states (Iowa, Kansas, Minnesota, Missouri, Nebraska, North Dakota, and South Dakota), Missouri ranked last. Both South Dakota and Missouri provide less than one-half of the national per capita average for financial help to local governments.

State aid, then, has not been substan-

Table 2-2. State Aid Per Capita to Local Governments in Plains States, 1990

		Rank Nationally
Minnesota	$350.65	(5)
Nebraska	258.62	(10)
Iowa	209.98	(13)
North Dakota	185.92	(20)
Kansas	107.71	(34)
South Dakota	82.18	(42)
Missouri	71.39	(47)
U.S. Average	$177.64	

Source: U.S. Census Bureau, as reported in *Governing*, article by Jonathan Walters, "Set Us Free," January 1992, page 42.

tial except for school districts. The usual answer to local financial needs is to authorize new optional local taxes, such as the local-option sales taxes for cities and counties, which must be approved by voters.

An important consideration for any state aid, however, relates to the tax effort being made by a given state. If there is a considerable tax effort, it is likely that the state will at least consider greater support of local government. If not, there is not much to share, regardless of the willingness of state government to do so. In Missouri the state tax effort is in keeping with the state's essentially conservative political culture, despite greater tax effort over the last decade or so. In 1977–1978 the state ranked fiftieth in per capita general revenue, but jumped to forty-fifth in 1992. The jump reflects adoption of several sales tax increases, including an additional one cent for schools, one-tenth cent for parks and soil conservation, and an increase in the tax on gasoline.

Missouri's general revenue was $988.13 per capita in 1992. States that ranked lower included Texas, Mississippi, Tennessee, South Dakota, and New Hampshire. The national average for 1992 was $1,288.14. With Missouri $300.01 below the average, the state lost (or taxpayers saved) about $1.5 billion in 1992 alone by falling below the average for that year.

V. Conclusions

Several points can be made regarding Missouri's economy, population, and political culture, and the effects of the political culture on existing political institutions and public policy.

• Missouri ranks near the median of all states in wealth and economic development, with manufacturing, tourism, and agriculture being the major income producers.

• Missouri's population has increased steadily since 1880, but its rate of growth from 1960 to 1990 was below the national average. The population includes a disproportionate number of older adults, with the state ranked tenth in 1990 (down from sixth in 1987) in percentage of those older than 65. The population is also dispersing. The counties with the largest percentages of population increases are in southwest Missouri and in the outer suburban areas of the St. Louis metropolitan area.

• Missouri's ranking in personal income has fluctuated over the last three decades, but remained close to the median. In 1959 the state ranked eighteenth. It dropped to twenty-ninth in 1980, then rose slightly to twenty-seventh in 1993. There may be several reasons for this fluctuation, but changes in agriculture may be the most prominent one.

• Missouri has a highly diverse social system with many religious and ethnic groups represented.

• Politically, Missouri is a modified two-party state, although a Republican resurgence is evident. The state is interested in maintaining its political patterns against federal pressures (such as federal court orders that make the state pay for desegregation costs in St. Louis and Kansas City). The state government can be characterized as conservative, and it maintains its characteristically low tax effort.

• With respect to political culture, Missouri is primarily individualistic, but with strong traditionalistic elements in outstate areas and some suburbs. This reflects just one of the many cleavages or schisms in the state, but it helps account for the state's slow adoption of innovative programs. The many cleavages both reduce the level of demand for innovative government programs and effectively hinder the passage of such programs.

• From their attitudes toward the role of government and the political process, Missourians as a whole appear to (1) emphasize individualism and individual opportunity—often at the expense of community; (2) want a minimal role for government; (3) favor dispersing political and government authority because of a suspicion of large-scale government and a preference for personalized government; and (4) have a minimal commitment to a highly competitive two-party system, at least at the county level.

• The effects of Missouri's political culture on existing institutions and public policy include (1) a large number of local governmental units of all types; (2) a preference for direct democracy with many votes on special issues; (3) a commitment to extraordinary voting majorities, such as two-thirds and four-sevenths on local general-obligation bond issues and two-thirds for school levies over a certain level; (4) a large number of traditional local governments with many independently elected officials; (5) the development of the city–administrator form of government as a compromise between traditional, decentralized structures and the need for full-time management; (6) a tremendously complex and restrictive legal system for local government; (7) a low revenue effort by state government; (8) a lack of significant state revenue sharing with counties and municipalities; and (9) a small percentage of counties that have adopted zoning by a vote of the people.

CHAPTER 3

Interest Groups in Missouri

by James W. Endersby, Gregory Casey, and James D. King

> In no other country in the world has the principle of association been more successfully used
> or applied to a greater multitude of objects than in America.—Alexis de Tocqueville

Interest groups are organizations formed to influence public officials and public policies in the direction of group members' shared attitudes and objectives. Group members possess common goals; they think along similar lines and generally want to accomplish the same things. Rather than acting separately as individuals, group members pool resources, such as time, money, management, and skills, and follow a coordinated plan of action. Through unity, group members expect to increase the likelihood of favorably influencing government policy, and to do so at a much lower cost.

Political parties also seek to influence public policy, but parties are composed of a diverse constituency of groups and individuals with broad and often conflicting goals. The chief functions of political parties are to win elections and to control the government. The primary function of an interest group, however, is limited to pressuring for certain policies relevant to the economic and ideological concerns of the members of the organization. In recent years, political partisanship among the electorate and among public officials has been in decline. Interest groups, which have been increasingly active in politics, are taking over many of the traditional functions of political parties.

Public awareness of the role of interest groups in the political process also has grown in recent years. The news media have highlighted connections between certain interest groups and specific government policies. Among the better-known group-policy linkages are the National Rifle Association and gun control legislation, the American Medical Association and health care policy, farm organizations and agricultural price supports, the American Association of Retired Persons and benefits for senior citizens, and pro-choice and pro-life organizations and policy on abortion. But most media attention has focused on interest group activity on the national political scene. Less widely recognized is the extent of interest group involvement at the state and local levels of government.

The purpose of this chapter is to explore the role of interest groups in Missouri state government. First, we offer a general classification of interest groups in the contemporary setting. Second, we look back at the history of interest group influence in the Show-Me State and discuss the relative strengths of interest groups in Missouri as compared to those in other states. Finally, we examine the most common strategies used by interest groups to affect public policy.

I. Types of Interest Groups

Interest groups' primary political function is to influence public policy, but political goals are often a secondary issue when interest groups are created. Frequently, associations are formed to rally citizens and organizations around some common economic or social interest, and political purposes are later, natural outgrowths of their unity. Interest groups can be classified in a variety of ways. One simple way is to categorize organizations by their constituency and fundamental purpose. Interest groups can then be placed into three general categories—economic, public interest, and governmental.

Economic Interest Groups. This category includes organizations representing common economic interests and is by far the largest and most influential sector. Economic organizations encompass interests of both business and labor as well as interests of competing businesses. The rubric of economic groups includes individual businesses (often corporations), trade associations (organizations of companies operating in a given industrial sector), agricultural organizations (individuals and businesses engaged in similar farming interests), professional associations (which represent individuals employed in a common occupation), and labor organizations (for union workers).

Economic interests, particularly business interests, have consistently dominated group politics. For example, in one nationwide study, legislators were asked to identify the most powerful groups in their states. More than 75 percent of the legislators responding specified business

interests. Similarly, another study, of the legislative process in four states, found that business interests were most influential. In a listing compiled in 1982 of prominent interest groups in each of the fifty states, 70 percent of the groups listed were business related. These three studies also discovered that organized labor plays an important role in state politics.[1]

Public Interest Groups. This second category comprises the greatest variation among groups. Public interest groups form to advance broader political and social issues, including questions of morality. Mutual economic concerns seldom unite members of public interest groups. Occasionally, public interest groups are established to counterbalance the influence of economic interests; more often, citizens' groups develop as mass membership organizations with a theme. These groups seek to protect the common interests of members (such as women, students, or gun owners). Some public interest groups promote a political agenda that seeks societal benefits rather than political action to provide direct benefits to members of the group.

Public interest groups may be concerned with broad policy areas such as civil rights, environmental protection, advancement of the arts, governmental reform, consumer protection, morality, or ideology. The scope of a particular group, however, may be broad, encompassing one or more policy areas, or narrow, focusing on only one or two issues, such as abortion, prayer in

1. Wayne L. Francis, "A Profile of Legislator Perceptions of Interest Group Behavior Relating to Legislative Issues in the States," *Western Political Quarterly* 14 (December 1971): 703–5; John C. Wahlke, Heinz Eulau, William Buchanan, and Leroy C. Ferguson, *The Legislative System* (New York: John Wiley, 1962), 314–15; Sarah McCally Morehouse, *State Politics, Parties and Policy* (New York: Holt Rinehart and Winston, 1982), 108–12.

school, or capital punishment. "Economic interests" and "public interests" are not mutually exclusive. On the contrary, many groups serving a public interest seek favorable economic policies, while economic groups often give attention to political and social issues. For instance, civil rights groups seek political, social, and economic equality for ethnic minorities, and the AFL-CIO works for civil rights as well as for the economic benefit of its members. Most economic interests argue that benefits for their group also provide economic stimulus, tax revenue, and employment extending beyond personal business. Despite these natural overlaps, however, most groups can be classified according to their clientele and goals.

Governmental Interest Groups. The final category is quite different from the first two. Economic and public interest groups are private organizations with a membership of individual citizens or private-sector firms. Governmental groups are public organizations representing state agencies, individual local governments, or associations of governments. These groups generally represent cities, counties, and special districts before the state legislature, usually seeking state aid, tax advantages, or other localized interests. Although public officials who are part of governmental interest groups may have much influence over policy decisions of a legislature or agency, scholars seldom consider these individuals as representatives of interest groups.[2] Missouri statutes, however, do require unelected bureaucrats to register as lobbyists if they seek to influence policy decisions of other public officials in the legislative or executive branches.

The Missouri state code contains an interesting and unusually expansive definition of a lobbyist: it includes all individuals who attempt to influence legislative or executive policy, except for elected legislators and state officials.[3] The number of registered governmental lobbyists, then, is larger in Missouri than in many other states. Unelected members of the executive branch who appear before the legislature, discuss legislation with a member of the General Assembly, or influence policy with members of other executive branch departments must register as lobbyists. Statements filed with the Missouri Ethics Commission do indicate whether a lobbyist is a state employee. This registration requirement includes presidents and curators of state universities, members of the governor's staff, members of state regulatory boards, and many others. Nevertheless, the number of state officials registering as lobbyists declined from almost five hundred in 1982 to about one hundred a decade later.

II. Interest Group Influence in Missouri

While complete enumeration of Missouri's interest groups is impossible, Tables 3–1 and 3–2 provide an indication of the variety of groups and interests represented. Missouri law requires state lobbyists to register and to identify the organizations that they represent. Table 3–1 classifies these registered interest groups by type.[4]

2. Representatives of *foreign* governments, however, are traditionally defined as lobbyists on either the federal or state levels (despite the absence of a nongovernmental organization).

3. Section 105.470 RSMo 1992. Changes in the 1992 reform legislation expanded the exceptions from the requirement to register to include not only members of the General Assembly and elected state officers but also those individuals who are responding to a request for or are obtaining public information. This additional exemption may clarify the statutes, but its effect on the number of registered individuals seems limited.

4. Sometimes the classification of an organization into one of these categories may seem arbitrary. The Missouri National Education Association, for example, might be

The vast majority (more than three out of four) of registered groups in early 1993 were concerned with economic interests. Registered lobbyists represent business interests in particular; 62 percent of all organizations were individual businesses or trade associations. Given the large number of state government agencies that must register under Missouri law, the ratio of economic interests is underestimated in the table. Economic groups, for instance, outnumber public interest groups almost eight to one. Overall, the number of interest groups represented in Jefferson City doubled from 1982 to 1993. Excluding state agencies, only 400 interest groups were represented by lobbyists in 1982, but the number rose to 783 in 1993. Only the number of labor organizations (and state government officials as noted above) has declined, and, despite the importance of agriculture to the state economy, farm interests still maintain few lobbyists. Trade and professional associations, public interests, and, especially, individual businesses have many more lobbyists than they had in 1982.

A sample of Missouri interest groups is offered in Table 3–2, with organizations arranged alphabetically within each category. Since these organizations include only those lobbying during the 1993 session of the General Assembly, many groups active only in other political arenas are ex-

cluded. Nevertheless, the listing does give an indication of the diverse interests active within state politics. Several organizations in a complete listing of all interest groups might be counted more than once. Similar interests may have several representative organizations; these include a parent company and its subsidiaries, a state trade or professional association and regional chapters, or a union and its local. Some lobbyists are careful to register all corporate subsidiaries, but most are not. Individuals and businesses may also be represented by more than one association.

The discussion of types of interest groups thus far has not focused on any particular policy area but instead has classified groups on the basis of membership. Yet the policy area(s) in which the group operates can also be an important characteristic. One policy area prominent at the state and local area that warrants special mention is education, which is the single most expensive and costly service provided by state and local governments. Because of education's dominant position, educational interests often have been treated as a specific category in classifications of interest groups. In the four-state study, for example, educational interests ranked second in group prominence among legislators. In the nationwide survey, 16 percent of the respondents named educational interests (school boards, teachers unions, and state universities) as among the most powerful groups; this made education the category with the second highest response rate, behind business and slightly ahead of labor interests. A recent ranking of the most influential interests among all fifty states placed teachers associations at the top of the state interest group hierarchy, followed by general business organizations, associations of bankers, manufacturers, and labor organizations.

considered a union or a professional association; the Missouri Sheriffs Association might be a professional association or a governmental interest group. This classification, like categories for groups on the national level, may provide a better picture of which interests have political influence since it depends on the characteristics of the clientele represented by the organizations. Regardless of the classification scheme, however, group strategies for political influence are notably similar. See Kay Lehman Schlozman and John T. Tierney, *Organized Interests and American Democracy* (New York: Harper & Row, 1986).

Table 3-1. Classification of Interest Groups in Missouri, 1993

Type of Group	Number	Percent
Economic Interest Groups	693	75.4%
Individual Businesses	392	42.7
Trade Associations	177	19.3
Agricultural Organizations	8	0.9
Professional Associations	91	9.9
Labor Organizations	25	2.7
Public Interest Groups	90	9.8
Governmental Interests	136	14.8
Total	919	100.0%

Source: Senate Lobbyist Registration Reports, Missouri Ethics Commission

This national trend is also found in Missouri. Educational politics at midcentury were dominated by a single interest group, the Missouri State Teachers Association. Operating within that era's weak interest group system, the MSTA maintained a united front for a limited educational agenda.[5]

Although educational interests in Missouri have retained their influence on state policy making, they are now fragmented into many groups. Educational groups across all categories of Table 3–1 make up about 5 percent of registered organizations, but may still have a disproportionate impact on education policy decisions. Other industrial sectors are represented by an even larger number of organizations when considered across the clientele categories. Approximately 8 percent of registered groups in Missouri represent the insurance industry, and about 11 percent are for health-related businesses and occupations. The relatively large number of organizations in these areas may stem from recent legislative efforts regarding malpractice, insurance, and health reform. Other industrial sectors that appear to have disproportionate representation in Missouri are communications, transportation, banking, and utilities. Law enforcement and other public employee groups are also well represented. Few public interest groups opposed to business interests, however, lobby in Jefferson City.

The power of interest groups in Missouri politics has changed greatly in the past few decades. In the middle part of this century, Missouri politics was dominated by

5. Wahlke et al., *The Legislative System,* 314–15. Francis, "Profile of Legislator Perceptions," 703–5. Clive S. Thomas and Ronald J. Hrebenar, "Nationalization of Interest Groups and Lobbying in the States," in Allan J. Cigler and Burdett A. Loomis, *Interest Group Politics,* 3d ed. (Washington: CQ Press, 1991), 68, based on data from Thomas and Hrebenar, "Interest Groups in the States," in Virginia Gray, Herbert Jacob, and Robert B. Albritton, *Politics in the American States,* 5th ed. (Glenview: Scott, Foresman, 1990), 123–58. Nicholas A. Masters, Robert H. Salisbury, and Thomas H. Eliot, *State Politics and the Public Schools: An Exploratory Analysis* (New York: Alfred A. Knopf, 1964). When asked in a 1966 survey to designate the most powerful interest groups, about half of all Missouri legislators mentioned the Missouri State Teachers Association, and about 40 percent mentioned "education," "school lobby," or other education groups. See David Leuthold, *The Missouri Legislature: A Preliminary Profile* (Columbia: Research Center of the School of Business and Public Administration, University of Missouri, 1967).

Table 3-2. Examples of Registered Interest Groups, 1993

Economic Interest Groups	Agricultural Organizations
Individual Businesses	MO Corn Growers Association
Anheuser-Busch Co., Inc.	MO Dairy Products Association
Bristol-Myers Squibb	MO Farm Bureau Federation
Burlington Northern Railroad	MO Poultry Federation
Chrysler Corp.	Professional Associations
Commerce Bancshares	MO Association of Realtors
Great American Life Insurance Co.	MO Association of Trial Lawyers
GTE (General Telephone)	MO Bar Association
Kansas City Power & Light	MO Sheriffs Association
Leggett & Platt Inc.	MO Society of CPAs
McDonnell Douglas Corp.	MO State Medical Association
Mercantile Bancorporation, Inc.	MO State Teachers Association
Monsanto	MO Veterinary Medical Association
RJR Nabisco Inc.	Labor Organizations
St. Louis Baseball Cardinals	Intl. Brotherhood of Electrical Workers
St. Mary's Health Center	MO AFL-CIO
Southwestern Bell Telephone	MO Highway Employees Association
State Farm Insurance	MO National Education Association
Truman Medical Center Corp.	United Auto Workers
Union Carbide Corp.	**Public Interest Groups**
Union Electric	ActUp
Western Resources, Inc.	American Civil Liberties Union
Trade Associations	Associated Students of the Univ. of MO
Home Builders Assn. of MO	Common Cause in MO
Mining Industry Council of MO	Conservative Foundation of MO
MO Assn. of Mutual Insurance Cos.	League of Women Voters of MO
MO Chamber of Commerce	MO American Cancer Society
MO Hospital Association	MO Catholic Conference
MO League of Savings Institutions	National Rifle Association
MO Oil Council	YMCA
MO Restaurant Association	**Governmental Interest Groups**
MO Travel Council	Cities of Columbia, Kansas City, O'Fallon,
MO Wine & Spirits Association	Springfield, St. Louis, St. Peters, etc.
Tobacco Institute	MO Association of Counties
	MO Lottery
	MO Municipal League
	MO School Boards Association

Source: Senate Lobbyist Registration Reports, Missouri Ethics Commission

an establishment elite. In a modified one-party state, controlling state policy only required manipulating the Democratic party primary. A historic alliance linked state Democratic party officials and the Central Missouri Trust Company of Jefferson City, which received state funds in noninterest-bearing accounts. This alliance influenced candidate selection and nominations for state offices in the low-turnout party primary. The establishment elite, however, began to break apart after the death in 1961 of Richard Nacy, former state treasurer, Democratic state chair, and Central Bank officer. Nacy was the broker who maintained the Bank's influence and kept the diverse courthouse crowds in the Democratic party together. In 1964, maverick Warren Hearnes successfully challenged the party leaders' choice for the Democratic gubernatorial nomination, proving the elite had lost its grip. Other candidates for statewide office soon followed the precedent of challenging party leadership; this change coincided with the rise of the Missouri Republican party. The Central Missouri Trust Company also eventually lost influence in the political process, in part because of the Democratic party leadership's inability to control the nomination process. Policy reforms caused public funds to be placed in federal government obligations and in banks throughout the state. These reforms reduced the incentive for banking interests to dominate state politics.[6]

Since the mid–1960s, Show-Me State politics has evolved into a more pluralistic system with a number of interest groups competing for influence in state government. When the Democratic party was strong, interest groups were relatively weak.[7] As political party control of state

government lessened, interest groups began to grow in number and influence. The election of Republican Kit Bond as governor in 1972 corresponded with rapid growth in the number of lobbyists and interest groups. A cooperative working environment between public officials and a few lobbyists (such as the relationship between the Central Bank Trust Company and executive officials, or that between the MSTA and the legislature) within a few policy areas evolved into a more competitive environment characterized by a fragmentation of interests, a larger number of lobbies, and a greater variety of access points to state government.

Relative Strength of Missouri Interest Groups. The strength of the interest group system varies greatly from state to state. In some states, interest groups are powerful forces that virtually control state government; in other states, interest groups are quite weak, playing only minor roles while the political parties dominate the scene. Recent analyses of all fifty states list Missouri among states with "moderate" interest group strength. One analysis also developed a list of interest groups considered "powerful" in the state. Of six influential interest groups identified, only one, the Missouri Farmers Association, has lost its political base, and its position has been replaced by another organization, the Missouri Farm Bureau Federation. A roster of powerful interests in Missouri today might include unions, teachers, brewers, health care groups, lawyers, gambling in-

6. Gregory Casey and James D. King, "Missouri: From Establishment Elite to Classical Pluralism," in Ronald J. Hrebenar and Clive S. Thomas, eds., *Interest Group Politics in the Midwestern States* (Ames: Iowa State University Press, 1993), 165–91. John Fenton, *Politics in the Border States* (New Orleans: Hauser Press, 1957).

7. Although research in this area is not conclusive, past indicators suggested that interest groups in Missouri were once relatively weak. A 1950 American Political Science Association study of state legislative systems, the first complete categorization of interest group strength, classified Missouri's interest group system as "weak." In the mid–1960s Missouri scored low on an index computed to measure interest group conflict for each

state. Belle Zeller, ed., *American State Legislatures* (New York: Thomas Y. Crowell, 1954), 190–91; L. Harmon Ziegler and Hendrik van Dalen, "Interest Groups in State Politics," in Herbert Jacob and Kenneth N. Vines, eds., *Politics in the American States*, 3d ed., (Boston: Little, Brown, 1976), 95; Wayne L. Francis, *Legislative Issues in the Fifty States* (Chicago: Rand McNally, 1967), 28–29, 44–45.

terests, bankers, and groups with positions on abortion.[8]

Missouri Ethics Commission. The proliferation of interest groups in Missouri, combined with the growth of political distrust, has led to new attempts to regulate their influence. Reform legislation signed by Governor John Ashcroft at the end of the 1992 session created a new Missouri Ethics Commission to coordinate reporting requirements of groups.[9] Individuals who attempt to influence executive or legislative policy decisions and those who represent an interest group must register. These lobbyists also must file expenditure reports relating to lobbying activities.

III. Strategies and Tactics of Interest Groups

Interest group activity is often equated with lobbying, but actually a variety of strategies and techniques may be available to accomplish goals. The incidence of organizational lobbying of the General Assembly has unquestionably increased in recent years. But many groups also appear to be using other points of access as well. Lobbying occurs not only within the legislature but also within executive agencies. Interest groups may also use alternative strategies including participation in elections, influencing public opinion, filing lawsuits, and resorting to other political activities.

Traditional Lobbying. Lobbying is un-doubtedly the most common form of interest group influence on the political process. Lobbying involves communication with legislators, legislative staff members, and administrative officials to influence decision making. A lobbyist has the responsibility of promoting the group's interests and persuading government officials to act in a manner consistent with the well-being or desires of the group's members. To be effective, interest group representatives must have access to important decision makers, and they must have valuable information to provide.

As the number of lobbyists in the halls of state governments has increased, their style of influence has changed as well. Increased competition among interest groups has caused lobbyists to become more professional and to more closely resemble their counterparts in the nation's capital.[10] Some public interest groups such as the League of Women Voters and the Associated Students of the University of Missouri use volunteer lobbyists as well as paid lobbyists. Large corporations and associations are more likely to have an in-house lobbyist or a legislative liaison. In addition, interests represented by paid, professional lobbyists have become more common. Most lobbyists serve only one organization, but contract lobbyists may represent a large number of client organizations. John Britton became the first contract lobbyist in Missouri, with Anheuser-Busch as his principal client. He later expanded his business into the largest lobbying firm in Jefferson City. Registration does not obligate the lobbyist to report the capacity in which he or she serves. But records do indicate that, in 1993, 73 (7.5 percent) of the 973 registered lobbyists served more than three organizations, a

8. Morehouse, *State Politics,* 110; Ronald J. Hrebenar, "The Changing Nature of Interest Group Activity in the Midwestern States," in Hrebenar and Thomas, *Interest Group Politics,* 351; Clive S. Thomas and Ronald J. Hrebenar, in Virginia Gray and Herbert Jacob, *Politics in the American States,* 6th ed. (forthcoming).

9. RSMo 1992, sections 105.470 and 105.955 and chapter 130. Before 1993, lobbyists filed registration and expenditure reports with the clerk of the house of representatives and the secretary of the senate. Political action and other election committees filed reports with the secretary of state.

10. Thomas and Hrebenar, "Nationalization of Interest Groups," 63–80.

reasonable indicator of contract lobbying. Twenty-three lobbyists represented ten or more organizations.

Lobbyists communicate with legislators and other public officials in a variety of ways. When a committee within the General Assembly considers legislation connected with a group's interest, the lobbyist for that group usually testifies concerning the impact the bill will have on the group's members and suggests why the legislature should or should not approve that measure. For instance, in early 1993 Britton, representing Anheuser-Busch, testified against Speaker Bob Griffin's health care plan, which would have been financed with various sin taxes. Although Missouri was then tied with Wisconsin for the lowest tax on a gallon of beer (set at six cents), and although the tax hadn't been increased for twenty-two years, Britton argued that sales of beer would drop, citing studies showing a 0.5 percent drop in sales for every 1 percent price increase in beer. Britton claimed that "this tax will be the highest tax increase imposed on an individual industry in the state." He was also testifying as the representative of the Tobacco Institute. Also in 1993, Steve Weber, a lobbyist for AT&T, testified against a proposed tax on long distance telephone calls (proceeds were to be earmarked primarily to fund new mental health and prison facilities). He argued that absence of the tax was good for the economic climate, since it could be used as a selling point to persuade telemarketing firms and other heavy long distance users to locate in Missouri, whereas adopting the tax would cause business departures. Weber also argued that the tax would fall disproportionately on the poor, citing figures suggesting that poor telephone users spend about 12 percent of their income on telephone charges, while wealthy telephone users spend only about 1 percent of

their income on such charges. Weber also suggested that the proposal would be less damaging to business if volume users were exempted.[11]

Formal testimony is one method of reaching legislators and bureaucrats. Informal, personal contracts may be a more direct means of persuading public officials to adopt political positions on issues. Visits to senators' and representatives' offices are common, as are dinner invitations, where the conversation turns to pending legislation and the lobbyist picks up the tab. In the words of one Missouri state senator, "One of the hardest things to get used to when I first came here was not buying my own dinner."[12] Lobbyists representing economic interests are more likely to have entertainment budgets to establish and maintain contacts with public officials. As shown in Table 3–3, in the 1986 session, lobbyists for economic organizations spent nearly three-fifths of their budget for entertainment. Lobbyists for other interests are less likely to use this tactic, yet between one-third and two-fifths of their funds went for entertainment.

Despite public perceptions of lobbyists as fat cats who buy influence with money, the most highly treasured commodity available to the lobbyist is *information*. A good lobbyist must be persuasive and knowledgeable on all of the topics of concern to the interest group. An unprepared or uninformed lobbyist will rarely achieve success. State legislators operate under severe time constraints and generally find lobbyists useful in the information gathering process. The diversity of interest group representatives can assist

11. "Griffin Pushes His Proposal for Health Care," *Columbia Tribune,* February 16, 1993. Rudi Keller, "Kelly Wants Phone Tax to Counter New Debt," *Columbia Tribune,* February 10, 1993.

12. Virginia Young, "Lobbyists Everywhere, but Harry Picks Up the Tab," *Missouri Times,* March 23, 1981.

Table 3-3. Lobbyist Registration and Expenditures in Missouri, 1986

Lobbyists	Economic Organizations	Social Organizations	Local Governments	State Agencies
Number	323	46	41	534
Number with	74	7	1	33
Multiple Clients	(25%)	(15%)	(2%)	(6%)
Number Incurring	183	20	18	22
Expenditures	(57%)	(43%)	(44%)	(4%)
Total Expenditures	$708,017.22	$22,787.07	$31,507.71	$40,814.57
Mean of Those with Expenditures	$3,868.95	$1,289.35	$1,750.42	$1,855.21
Total Expenditures by Function				
Entertainment	57%	40%	38%	36%
Travel	15	18	24	37
Printing	12	24	4	18
Honoraria	2	0	3	3
Other (unspecified)	14	19	31	5

Source: Clerk of the Missouri House of Representatives; Gregory Casey and James D. King, "Missouri: From Establishment Elite to Classic Pluralism," in Ronald J. Hrebenar and Clive S. Thomas, eds., *Interest Group Politics in the Midwestern States*, (Ames: Iowa State University Press, 1993), p. 179.

lawmakers in obtaining a broader understanding of political issues without conducting extensive personal research. Perhaps one Missouri legislator spoke for his colleagues as well as himself when he noted, "I use lobbyists as much as they use me." To generate and maintain support for group goals, a good lobbyist will develop a close personal relationship with important contacts in government. The key component in the relationship between lobbyists and that contact is a high degree of credibility. Information provided should be honest and pertinent, or else the lobbyist will no longer be useful as a source. But accurate, relevant information alone is not enough to influence state policy. Lobbyists must also have *access* to those individuals who have power to make governmental policy.[13]

Several points of access are available to lobbyists hoping to gain more favorable outcomes from the legislative process. Among the most important contacts in the Missouri General Assembly are the party leadership offices in each chamber of the legislature. The Speaker of the House in particular wields the greatest amount of power by controlling the legislative agenda, committee assignments of members of both parties, chairpersons, and so forth. Party leadership in the senate is more diffuse, but concentrating on key leaders may still be the most efficient way of influencing the legislative process. Contact with party leadership can be important for advancing favorable legislation and for blocking unfavorable legislation.

Other important points of access are also available. The committee system is also important to the decision-making process.

13. Young, "Lobbyists Everywhere." For two good descriptions of effective lobbying practices, see Jeffrey M. Berry, *The Interest Group Society,* 2d ed. (Glenview: Scott Foresman, 1989), and Alan Rosenthal, *The Third*

House: Lobbyists and Lobbying in the States (Washington: CQ Press, 1993).

Chairs and members of key legislative committees also have disproportional influence on the language and success of proposals within their policy areas and thus are important targets for lobbyists seeking contacts. Legislative staffers are also productive contacts for lobbyists, useful in gaining access to legislators and as sources for important information.

A final point of access should not be ignored. Officials in the executive branch are also important players in the governmental process. Effective lobbying in the executive branch may encourage the governor to sign or veto a bill (or item veto a portion of an appropriations bill, or to threaten/promise to sign/veto legislation with particular provisions, thus providing a compelling strategic setting in which the lobby can maneuver). Executive officials also have leeway in interpreting or enforcing the law, and they may expand on the law with administrative regulations. One new feature of the 1992 reform legislation was to specifically include an individual contacting the executive branch within the statutory definition of a lobbyist. Any individual attempting to influence an action of an executive official is now also required to register and report expenditures.

Electoral Activities. Public officials who are favorably disposed toward an interest group's positions are a tremendous advantage for any lobby. A lobby's chances of gaining a lawmaker's support on a particular piece of legislation are obviously greater when the group and the legislator agree on the issue from the start. In addition, given the extensive reliance on colleagues as voting cues within state legislatures, one supporter of the group's position may translate into several votes in the final tally. To gain such an advantage, interest groups use their financial and human resources to aid in the election of certain candidates with views favorable to the group's positions.

One of the more highly publicized and controversial activities of interest groups in recent years involves their participation in the electoral process. Amendments to the Federal Election Campaign Act in the 1970s established legal standards for the multicandidate committee, more commonly known as the political action committee or PAC. PACs are committees created by groups, including business, labor, associational, and ideological organizations, to collect contributions and to distribute or spend the money for the purpose of influencing election campaigns. Levels of campaign receipts, expenditures, and contributions are somewhat higher in presidential election years than in off-year elections. But both the number of political action committees and the amount of their contributions are large and growing. Table 3–4 demonstrates this trend.

Interest groups and PACs make contributions to office seekers who might help the group achieve its goals. Supporting candidates whose political philosophies closely reflect the group's is one tactic, but it pays no dividend if the candidate loses the election. Therefore, some interest groups, particularly economic groups, may contribute to any candidate with a reasonable chance of winning and to obvious winners of noncompetitive races. Resourceful groups may hedge their bets by contributing to opponents in the same race! For interest groups, winning an election is in itself unimportant; public policies determined by the winner are important. Lobbyists can do more with a lukewarm supporter winning office than with an ardent supporter who loses.

PAC contributions have become an important source of revenue for many candidates, particularly incumbents, in campaigning for legislative and statewide executive office. Interest groups, however,

Table 3-4. PAC Financial Activity, 1979–1993

Year	Number of PACs	Total Receipts	Total Expenditures	Total Contributions
1979	93	$1,050,327.57	$ 197,977.18	$ 378,810.03
1980	163	2,615,887.36	261,036.28	1,351,590.07
1981	133	1,822,869.75	222,780.73	417,464.26
1982	164	2,826,092.64	368,942.93	1,436,216.48
1983	137	2,168,513.05	193,264.92	670,805.12
1984	209	4,218,403.73	524,340.42	2,343,714.88
1985	162	2,611,746.43	221,211.72	606,631.36
1986	184	4,316,423.30	460,007.22	1,893,909.01
1987	175	4,040,067.42	384,432.96	1,028,235.65
1988	200	5,557,315.79	579,550.73	2,734,052.87
1989	182	4,738,153.49	473,955.80	1,064,190.75
1990	206	6,786,428.89	1,034,807.40	3,008,547.63
1991	204	5,525,965.08	526,239.35	2,122,883.58
1992	198	7,481,309.80	981,005.90	4,827,820.96
1993	180	5,198,026.11	640,381.93	1,340,860.62

Source: Marion N. Sinnett, Administrative Secretary, *1993 Missouri Annual Campaign Finance Report* (Jefferson City: Missouri Ethics Commission, 1994), 96.

are not solely preoccupied with candidate elections. Missouri elections frequently feature ballot questions in addition to candidate races. The initiative petition is a direct democracy device allowed to set state policy, and interest groups usually are involved in attempts to place questions on the ballot and take sides if the initiative petitions are successful. A 1990 ballot proposition to establish a Natural Streams Commission led to $810,612 in reported expenditures by supporters and opponents. Reported spending on failed initiative petitions in the same year reached $252,022 on an ethics proposition removed from the ballot by a court decision and $128,000 on an initiative that would have eliminated restrictions on abortion.[14] Pro-gambling interests raised nearly $11 million for the amendment allowing slot machines on riverboats. The debate on ballot questions frequently centers on the interests of certain groups in the state.

The political action committees with the highest level of financial activity generally represent economic interest groups. Table 3–5 shows the thirty-five political action committees with the largest amounts of contributions and expenditures during 1992. Virtually all of the PACs have connected organizations that are businesses, unions, and trade or professional associations. In some instances, financial activity may be higher than that shown when spending from local branches of organizations is totaled. The six regional chapters of the Missouri Farm Bureau collected more than $111,000 in total contributions. Two locals of the Teamsters Union (Kansas City and St. Louis) spent almost $71,000. Issue or ideological groups, often single-issue

14. *1990 Missouri Annual Campaign Finance Report* (Jefferson City: Secretary of State, May 1990), 272–75.

Table 3-5. Financial Activity of Leading PACs, 1992

Committee Name (Connected Organization)	Total Financial Activity
Missouri NARAL PAC (National Abortion Rights Action League)	$224,071.55
Missouri Right to Life PAC	196,199.91
Central Bancompany PAC (Central Bank, Jefferson City)	153,891.33
MERC PAC (Mercantile Bancorporation, St. Louis)	152,718.75
Southwestern Bell Missouri Employee PAC	145,761.79
Missouri Medical PAC (Missouri State Medical Association)	124,665.93
Missouri National Education Association PAC (MNEA)	122,673.44
Missouri Association of Trial Attorneys PAC	117,889.53
Missouri Health Care Association PAC	117,248.24
Electrical Workers Voluntary Political Education and Legislative Fund (International Brotherhood of Electrical Workers Local 1, St. Louis)	92,409.60
Missouri State UAW PAC (United Auto Workers)	89,092.50
Realtors PAC (Missouri Association of Realtors)	87,925.64
Pipefitters Fund (Pipefitters Local #562, St. Louis)	86,841.33
Home Building Industry PAC (Home Builders Association of Greater St. Louis)	83,917.11
Missouri Bankers Association State PAC	71,993.64
Hallmark PAC (Hallmark Cards)	70,268.01
Missouri State Chiropractors Association PAC	69,765.98
CWA District #6 Political Education Committee (Communication Workers of America)	66,316.32
Political Action Committee of Emerson (Emerson Electric Co.)	63,180.34
Enterprise Leasing Co. PAC	62,000.00
Missouri Progress Committee (Missouri Chamber of Commerce)	61,232.50
Civic Progress Action Committee, St. Louis	59,694.89
AGC MO PAC (Associated General Contractors of Missouri)	58,601.07
Missouri Cable PAC (Missouri Cable TV Association)	56,661.28
Health PAC (Missouri Hospital Association)	55,585.77
Heavy Constructors PAC (Heavy Constructors Association)	54,700.00
North County (St. Louis) Labor Legislative Club	51,730.06
Blue Cross–Blue Shield of Missouri State Government Affairs Committee	51,572.00
MODENT PAC (Missouri Dental Association)	50,900.00
Missouri State Council of Fire Fighters PAC	50,032.38
Association of Missouri Electric Cooperatives PAC	49,311.20
Kansas City Life Insurance Co. Employees PAC Fund	46,030.54
General American Life Insurance Co. Associates PAC	45,925.00
Pipefitters Local Union #533 Volunteer Political Fund (Kansas City)	45,467.78
Labor's Voluntary Political and Education Club Independent (Teamsters Joint Council No. 13, St. Louis)	44,969.85

Source: Marion Sinnett, *1992 Missouri Annual Campaign Finance Report* (Jefferson City: Missouri Ethics Commission, 1994), pp. 174–87

groups, also create PACs. A single-issue group evaluates candidates solely on the basis of their support or opposition to the particular policy of interest to the group. Pro-choice and pro-life groups led the list in 1992, demonstrating the salience of the abortion issue for voters in the election. Although this particular social issue has been hotly debated in state politics, most political action committees form around traditional economic interests and most campaign finance activity stems from these lower-profile groups.

In Missouri statutes, political action committees representing ongoing interest groups are included in a larger category of "continuing committees." Continuing committees include other groups such as partisan groups not directly affiliated with the political party apparatus and ideological groups unaffiliated with a parent organization, party, or candidate(s). Continuing committees include neither candidate committees nor political parties. Official state reports often do not list some continuing committees as PACs, although they obviously should be counted as such. Neither total financial activity of political action nor continuing committees accurately describes the full range of campaign contributions by interest groups.[15]

Formation of a political action committee is not a necessity for most business interests. Missouri election law permits direct contributions from corporation and union treasuries; indeed, many businesses make direct contributions and campaign expenditures without resorting to the creation of PACs. For many years, Missouri was somewhat unusual among states because it had no limits on the size of contributions by organizations. This changed in 1994 when stringent limits on contributions to campaigns were imposed by new legislation and by an initiative proposal approved by voters. These new limits do not, however, apply to independent campaigns that organizations and corporations may conduct for or against a candidate.

Interest groups, both directly and indirectly through political action committees, make more than one-fourth of all contributions for Missouri state executive and legislative elections. They also have a large, though variable, effect on campaign finance for ballot propositions. The relative influence of interest groups in Missouri elections, however, is somewhat difficult to determine. Per capita spending on legislative elections in Missouri appears somewhat lower than expenditures in other states; campaign spending for gubernatorial elections, however, appears somewhat higher.[16] Table 3–6 outlines how economic PACs and other interest groups compare to other sources of campaign finance in Missouri elections in 1990 and 1992. The single largest source of contributions for candidates remains individual donations. Yet political action committees, businesses, and unions are an important source of campaign finances for candidates in an era of costly campaigns.

---

15. For example, two of the three continuing committees with large combined expenditure and contribution totals, Citizens for Missouri Courts ($368,242) and Missourians for Choice ($595,280), are not listed with connected organizations, although they probably should be so defined as PACs. A number of organizations reporting as continuing committees are merely Democratic and Republican clubs. Other committees clearly representing organizations such as the Greater St. Louis Labor Council, the Missouri Chamber of Commerce, and the Missouri State Council of Carpenters should clearly be labeled PACs in the 1992 reports, but were not. For comparison among states, see Herbert E. Alexander, *Financing Politics: Money, Elections, & Political Reform,* 4th ed. (Washington: CQ Press, 1992), 127–28.

16. Frank J. Sorauf, *Money in American Elections* (Glenview: Scott, Foresman, 1988), 264, 271.

The postelection effect of contributions remains subject to debate. In general, however, interest group campaign contributions do not actually buy votes or support. Instead, interest groups use contributions as a means to obtain access to an incumbent legislator or executive official. A good lobbyist needs access to decision makers, and electoral participation increases the likelihood of getting an elected official's attention on important issues. Rather than meeting their overall objectives through the electoral process, interest groups use electoral support to prepare and supplement their lobbying efforts.

Campaign contributions and expenditures, however, are not the only methods of electoral participation. Economic interest groups probably seek to influence the political process through campaign finance; other organizations with large membership may influence elections decisively by providing votes. Unions and professional associations have a large number of potential voters with similar economic interests. In their communities, these organizations enjoy prestige, which can be transformed into influence. The Missouri State Teachers Association makes no contributions, but through its members' community standing it enjoys access to most legislators (especially in outstate areas). Certain public interest organizations serving large constituencies such as the American Association for Retired Persons, the National Rifle Association, and the abortion issue groups have mass membership with similar, intense ideological beliefs. Interest groups can use their human resources in a variety of ways. Simple get-out-the-vote campaigns may encourage candidates to concentrate on issues important to the interest group. Some groups provide information on candidate and party platforms or incumbents' voting records to mem-

bers; others may specifically endorse some candidates, hoping members will vote for those endorsed.

Other available electoral strategies usually are less successful. Interest groups may become actively involved in the recruitment of candidates. The Central Missouri Trust Company certainly serves as one example of an interest group that has successfully followed this tactic. In 1986 and 1988, the American Agriculture Movement (AAM) also adopted the strategy of recruiting candidates for congressional seats.[17] For example, Wayne Cryts unsuccessfully challenged incumbent Congressman Bill Emerson in the 8th District. Failed attempts to win public office, however, can have dire consequences for interest groups attempting to influence public policy. Officeholders may be less likely to respond to traditional methods of lobbying if interest groups are actively engaged in electoral politics against them. Nevertheless, a positive demonstration of popular support can always assist interest group lobbying.

Public Relations. Supporting an unpopular cause or organization can be hazardous to a legislator's political health. Therefore, it is not surprising that when a lobbyist approaches a lawmaker to ask for support on a matter before the General Assembly, the task is much easier if the interest group the lobbyist represents has significant popular support. In order to improve their lobbying efforts, interest groups often engage in public relations campaigns, also known as grassroots lobbying, to enhance their image. Through public relations, a group hopes to remove any negative stigma it may have acquired. Sometimes a public relations campaign can even produce

17. See Allan J. Cigler, "Organizational Maintenance and Political Activity on the 'Cheap': The American Agriculture Movement," in Cigler and Loomis, *Interest Group Politics.*

Table 3-6. Total Group Contributions in Missouri by Source, 1990 and 1992

Groups Making Contributions	1990 Candidates Amount	%	1990 Ballot Measures Amount	%
Corporations, Businesses, and Associations	$803,604.43	8.4	$218,307.94	26.1
Corporate, Trade, and Association PACs	1,516,396.86	15.9	39,380.00	4.7
Labor Organizations	71,009.00	0.7	.00	0.0
Labor PACs	270,757.11	2.8	2,000.00	0.2
Other Continuing Committees	348,566.23	3.7	35,042.98	4.2
Subtotal, Group Contributions	$3,010,333.63	31.6	$294,730.92	35.3
Total, All Contributions	$9,514,116.21	100.0	$836,036.74	100.0

Groups Making Contributions	1992 Candidates Amount	%	1992 Ballot Measures Amount	%
Corporations, Businesses, and Associations	$5,257,935.52	16.1	$1,914,250.32	88.0
Corporate, Trade, and Association PACs	2,551,391.45	7.8	12,000.00	0.5
Labor Organizations	260,767.36	0.8	.00	0.0
Labor PACs	889,779.12	2.7	.00	0.0
Other Continuing Committees	426,959.13	1.3	10,082.50	0.5
Subtotal, Group contributions	$9,386,832.58	28.7	$1,963,332.82	89.0
Total, All contributions	$32,696,793.50	100.0	$2,205,989.59	100.0

Data for candidate elections includes primary and general elections and, for 1990, special elections.
Sources: Roy D. Blunt, *1990 Missouri Annual Campaign Finance Report* (Jefferson City: Secretary of State), p. 344; Marion Sinnett, *1992 Missouri Annual Campaign Finance Report* (Jefferson City: Missouri Ethics Commission), pp. 168–70, 199.

a groundswell of public support for the group's positions, making it more likely that the legislator will heed the lobbyist's calls.

The public relations tactic is a major strategy of many large, national interest groups. Membership groups often need attention to attract and maintain membership; corporations and trade associations sometimes need to explain or defend their practices to the general public. Print advertisements for energy companies are placed in newspapers and magazines to tout efforts by the companies to enhance environmental preservation. Bumper stickers are distributed to members of citizens' groups

for publicity and to assure members that they are part of an important organization. Utility companies, often state and local regulated monopolies, advertise on television, not to increase consumption but to describe their rising operating costs, promote safety and conservation, and express concern for the general well-being of the average citizen. All are instances of an interest group advertising itself and using public relations to build a positive public image for the group.

Some large membership organizations, like the National Rifle Association and the abortion issue groups, can also use public relations techniques effectively to mobilize public support. When lobbyists need to bolster support within the legislature, a grassroots campaign urging members to send cards and letters to their elected representatives may assist in their efforts. A demonstration of widespread support may influence legislators who are looking ahead to the next election to support the causes of a group with a large number of members. These strategies, however, are usually more effective on the national level. Far fewer citizens have even rudimentary knowledge of the political process at state and local levels of government. One way to bolster support, then, is to educate the public on issues of concern to the interest group.[18]

Litigation. Interest groups that fail to achieve goals through traditional legislative and executive lobbying and through influencing voters and public opinion may appeal to yet another access point, the courts. Litigation is often used as the tactic of last resort, when other access points have failed. For example, initiative petitions to place issues on the ballot (such as the 1990 ethics initiative, the Right-to-Work bill, the Hancock Amendment to limit taxes and government spending, and a bill permitting larger trucks on state highways) are frequently challenged in court. Groups have tried to invalidate the petitions by claiming improper or misleading collection of signatures. Religious organizations that oppose legalized gambling, such as the Missouri Baptist Convention, have also filed lawsuits. In general, appeals to the state judiciary have not been successful for interest groups because their occasional successes at the trial court level usually are overturned on

appeal. The Missouri judiciary is generally committed to judicial restraint and is therefore unreceptive to efforts at policy reform.

Litigation in two policy areas, however, has been successful for organizations appealing to the federal courts. Pro-choice groups seeking to overturn state statutes restricting access to abortion and civil rights groups seeking to impose court-ordered desegregation plans on school districts in the St. Louis and Kansas City areas have found some success. Lawsuits challenging the constitutionality of Missouri's 1974 and 1988 statutes restricting abortions were appealed to the U.S. Supreme Court.[19] In the 1989 case of *Webster v. Reproductive Health Services,* seventy-eight amicus curiae briefs were filed, a record number. Occasionally, interest groups such as the American Civil Liberties Union may provide legal advice or assistance without actually participating in a case as one of the litigants. In general, activity in the judicial branch is pursued by interest groups only when other avenues are no longer available.

Other Forms of Interest Group Activity. Expense budgets for lobbying and for political action committee and other campaign contributions are legal activities that can be used to influence the decisions of politicians. Too often citizens associate legal interest group activity with illegal extortion and bribery. In spite of occasional publicized cases of influence peddling, most interest group representatives and public officials perform their duties in a legal, honest, and open manner. Some famous historical incidents involving bribery show what can happen to Missouri officials who violate the law. In 1977 Richard Rabbitt, former Speaker of the House, was convicted in federal court on fifteen counts of extortion and

---

18. A related tactic is to use membership to educate public officials. A group such as the Missouri State Teachers Association, which has a membership that maintains personal contacts with officials, may be able to use its members' acquaintances to affect policy decisions.

19. *Planned Parenthood of Central Missouri, Inc., v. John Danforth et al.,* 428 U.S. 52 (1976); *Webster v. Reproductive Health Services,* 492 U.S. 490 (1989).

mail fraud involving payoffs and kickbacks. One count involved a twenty thousand dollar payment for not killing a bill that the Greater St. Louis Automobile Dealers Association wanted passed; another involved kickbacks on state contracts awarded to an architectural firm.[20] Other classic cases of bribery in Missouri politics go back further. For instance, Kansas City political boss Tom Pendergast was convicted in 1939 of failure to pay federal income tax on his illegal payoffs from insurance companies; this bribery involved not legislators but administrative officials. Most interest groups, however, would not see bribery as a viable alternative to traditional lobbying.

Interest groups, however, may resort to alternative tactics if more traditional methods prove unsuccessful. Protests and demonstrations are occasionally organized by interest groups to attract media attention and public support for their cause. While protest is normally associated with issues such as civil rights and opposition to nuclear power, more mainstream groups may also use demonstrations to successfully attract attention. For instance, when budget cuts were proposed for funding of mental health programs in 1980–1981, rallies staged by mental health workers, parents of handicapped children, and public school teachers generated public sympathy. Opponents of mental health cuts succeeded, partly through more traditional lobbying efforts and partly because of the attention and support the demonstrations generated.

The issue most often responsible for organized protests in recent years has been abortion. Both pro-life and pro-choice groups have held numerous demonstrations to attract and maintain media attention for their positions. Most effective strategies, however, require working within the state's political system. Even major reforms can occur through constant exertion of political pressure.

IV. Conclusion

Interest groups have many strategies available to influence state policy making. Traditional lobbying remains the most effective overall means to influence public policy. But the choice of a particular strategy of political action depends on the group's environment, including the particular issue involved, the constituency represented by the group, and the resources available to the organization. For an example of how these factors shape a lobbying campaign, see chapter 17, "Funding for Education in the 1990s," which presents an illustrative case study of contemporary interest group activity.

Unlike the elitist structure of the state's recent past, Missouri politics today is characterized by pluralism and competition among a variety of interests. In a democratic society, all citizens, regardless of the popularity of their causes, have a right to articulate their views and to petition the government. Yet not all interest groups have the same amount of resources available to them, and not all interests in society are represented by a lobbying organization. The challenge of republican government is to represent this diversity of interests and, through deliberation and compromise, to choose wisely among many public policy alternatives.

20. Roy Malone, "Rabbitt's Fraud, Extortion in Case Goes to Jury," *St. Louis Post-Dispatch*, July 28, 1977; Roy Malone, "Rabbitt Convicted of Extortion, Mail Fraud," *St. Louis Post-Dispatch*, July 29, 1977; Terry Ganey and Roy Malone, "Rabbitt Case Sparks Debate on Need for Reform," *St. Louis Post-Dispatch*, July 31, 1977.

CHAPTER 4

Missourians and the Political Parties

by R. E. Burnett and Cordell E. Smith

> I am deeply sensible of the fact that the majority of you are not of my political party. To that extent we do differ, and we shall probably be on the hustings, in the next campaign, giving and receiving the same time-honored and lusty blows to which we have all grown accustomed.— Republican Governor Arthur M. Hyde, to the Fifty-Second General Assembly, January 3, 1923

Governor Hyde's remarks, to a legislature dominated by his partisan opponents, suggest a key theme useful in understanding political parties in Missouri and elsewhere: the contest to gain control over government and to make government work upon achieving that control. Political parties operate in an environment in which citizens may pledge their loyalty to either of two large parties, to an array of small third parties, or even to no party at all. In the latter case, voters may decide to support only specific candidates or to support nonparty entities like political action committees.

After the voters have acted and the candidates they elect move into government positions, political parties become a means of organizing the government itself. The structure of Missouri's government, with its three branches, fosters a further division of political parties into separate power bases that reflect both the separation of governmental powers and the different norms and traditions within each branch.

Analyzing Missouri's political parties thus becomes a complicated—maybe even intimidating—task. Fortunately, the discipline of political science has devoted significant effort to the job. University of Minnesota scholar Frank J. Sorauf in particular has created an especially helpful framework; Sorauf suggests studying political parties in three different arenas: within the electorate, within the party organization itself, and within the government.[1] Although Sorauf's work examines parties across the nation, his structure applies within Missouri as well. First, however, a review of historical developments will help in analyzing the parties, by pouring a foundation on which Sorauf's superstructure can be constructed.

I. History of Political Parties in Missouri

Contests within and between Missouri's Early Parties. When President James Monroe declared Missouri a part of the Union on August 10, 1821, the United States was enjoying the so-called Era of Good Feelings, in which party conflict largely did not exist. The Federalist party, formed in

1. Frank J. Sorauf and Paul Allen Beck, *Party Politics in America*, 6th ed. (Glenview, Ill.: Scott, Foresman/Little, Brown, 1984), 8–12. Sorauf and Beck build upon a similar analytical approach used by V. O. Key Jr., *Politics, Parties, and Pressure Groups*, 5th ed. (New York: Thomas Crowell, 1964).

the previous century to advocate passage of the U.S. Constitution, had died out, leaving only the Democratic-Republican party. The Democratic-Republicans, organized by Thomas Jefferson to oppose the Federalists, appealed to the agrarian commonfolk of the nation and found Missouri a hospitable place.

A particularly fractious presidential election in 1824, however, ended the Era of Good Feelings. The 1824 presidential race featured four candidates: John Quincy Adams, Henry Clay, William H. Crawford, and Andrew Jackson. Missouri voted for Clay, but because no candidate won a majority in the electoral college, the presidential race was thrown into the House of Representatives. When Clay endorsed Adams, and Missouri's Representative John Scott followed Clay's recommendation, Adams was elected—barely.[2]

The 1824 election created a schism in the state's political life that disrupted Democratic-Republican unity. Representative Scott and U.S. Senator David Barton sided with the faction backing Henry Clay and John Quincy Adams, while Missouri's other U.S. Senator, Thomas Hart Benton, supported Andrew Jackson. During the 1830s, the Adams-Clay faction bolted from the Democratic-Republican party and ultimately became known as the Whig party, while the Jacksonians, who succeeded in electing their man president in 1828, became known simply as the Democratic party. As an agrarian frontier state, Missouri consistently supported the Democratic party, voting for every Democratic presidential candidate before the Civil War.

Moreover, every pre–Civil War governor was a Democrat.[3]

In the years leading to the Civil War, however, the contentious issue of slavery altered Missouri's partisan landscape. The divisive point in Missouri, a slave state, was not whether slavery should be abolished but whether Congress should limit slavery's introduction into the territories. Within the Democratic party, one faction sought to block the spread of slavery; Benton aligned himself with this faction, but he did not follow when much of the group bolted from the Democrats to organize the Free Soil party behind former Democratic President Martin Van Buren. The other Democratic group, represented in Missouri by U.S. Senator David Rice Atchison, supported a popular sovereignty approach to slavery, in which voters in a territory would decide the issue for themselves. This group prevailed in the Democratic party, and under its control the Missouri legislature adopted resolutions ordering Benton to support popular sovereignty.[4]

The Democratic leadership and the Free Soilers managed to reunite in 1852, in support of Franklin Pierce for president and Sterling Price for Missouri governor, both of whom won. The Free Soil issue—blocking slavery's spread into the territories—was taken up by the infant Republican party, which replaced the disintegrating Whig party as the Democrats' main opponent. In 1856 the Republicans nominated Benton's son-in-law John C. Fremont for president; Benton nevertheless remained in the Democratic party, whose gubernatorial and presidential candidates both won.[5]

Civil War Rift and Realignment. The division over slavery continued to widen during the 1850s, ultimately fracturing the

2. William E. Parrish, Charles T. Jones Jr., and Lawrence O. Christensen, *Missouri: The Heart of the Nation,* 2d ed. (Arlington Heights, Ill.: Harlan Davidson, Inc., 1992), 83–84. This work is an especially valuable survey history of Missouri.

3. Parrish et al., 84–87.
4. Ibid., 125–27.
5. Ibid., 128–29, 136–38.

nation as South Carolina seceded from the Union in December 1860 and ten other southern states followed in the first few months of 1861. Missouri itself split just as the Union did, with Missourians divided in their loyalties to either North or South; the state government itself reflected this breach.

When war began at Fort Sumter, in South Carolina, on April 12, 1861, Democrat Claiborne Fox Jackson held the governorship of Missouri. A Southern sympathizer, Jackson called for a special convention to decide whether Missouri should also secede. Astonishingly, not a single pro-secession delegate was selected for the convention. Eventually, the convention declared itself the provisional government of Missouri and replaced Jackson with the pro-Union Hamilton R. Gamble.[6]

After the war Missouri entered the Reconstruction era under the control of the Radical Union party, a group organized in 1863 by several delegates from the special convention who felt that Gamble was moving too slowly in abolishing slavery in Missouri. The Radical Unionists controlled the governorship in 1865; more important, they dominated the convention that drafted the Missouri Constitution of 1865.[7]

This constitution, known as "Drake's Constitution" after delegate Charles Drake, a major player in the convention, attempted to remove from public life any person who had acted in behalf of the secessionist cause. To participate in public life, including voting or holding office, a person had to take the "test oath" to swear that he had never acted disloyally either to the Union or to Missouri as a state in that Union. This essentially eliminated the opposition to the Radical Unionists, at least until January 1867 when the U.S. Supreme Court found the test oath unconstitutional.[8]

In 1872 the Democrats finally regained control of the governorship and the legislature. Missouri also voted Democratic in the presidential race, although Republican Ulysses S. Grant won the national election. Entrenched hostility during the Civil War and Reconstruction hardened party loyalties, and Democrats remained the principal governing party of Missouri until well into the twentieth century.

Republican Interludes, Third Party Ferment, and Current Trends. The Democrats, however, did not achieve exclusive control of Missouri elections. In 1904, for example, Missouri shocked the political pundits of that era by voting for Republican Theodore Roosevelt for president. This marked the beginning of a new era in which Missouri reflected the national patterns, almost always voting for the winning presidential candidate. The first few years of the twentieth century were Republican years, and in Missouri, Republicans won the General Assembly and in 1908 the governorship. Democrats returned to power in 1912.

During this early period of the twentieth century, Missouri adopted a significant electoral change that greatly affected the way the state's parties conducted their business. The caucus system, in which the official candidates of each party are designated in meetings of the party faithful, was replaced by the direct primary, in which a party's candidates compete in a preliminary election to receive the official sanction of the voters of the party. The party's slate of nominees would then campaign against the nominees of other parties in a general election. This change increased the number of people who could participate in the

6. Ibid., 166–67, 171.
7. Ibid., 183–84, 189–90.

8. Ibid., 190–93.

nomination process, since it was generally less burdensome to cast a primary election ballot than to attend the long and often boring caucus meetings.

In addition to changing the workings of Missouri's political parties themselves, the adoption of the direct primary demonstrated a key feature of the party system as a whole: the ability of the two major parties to remain dominant by expropriating the ideas and platforms of the smaller third parties. While the bill enacting the primary election system passed a Democrat-controlled legislature with the approval of a Democratic governor, the idea itself actually arose from the Progressive party.

The Progressives, a reform-minded third party, sought to open the political process through not only the primary but also the popular election of U.S. senators and through direct, popular enactment of legislation by the initiative. Both of these Progressive goals succeeded; direct election of senators was adopted through the Seventeenth Amendment in 1913, and the initiative process was adopted in Missouri in 1908. However, these reforms took effect without the Progressives actually taking control of state government. Instead, the Democrats simply expropriated the ideas and made them their own.[9]

Other third parties in Missouri history include the People's party (or Populist party), a largely rural movement advocating monetary policies favorable to farmers and government regulation of railroads; the Prohibition party, primarily concerned with outlawing alcoholic beverages;

and the Socialist party, organized to obtain "the collective ownership of the means of production and distribution."

Third party activities and occasional Republican victories undoubtedly made Missouri political life more interesting, but Missouri generally remained Democratic in inclination.[10] Beginning in 1968, though, when Republican John Danforth won election as Missouri's attorney general, Republicans proved increasingly competitive in statewide elections, although Democrats continued to control the General Assembly. In 1988, Republicans won all statewide offices except lieutenant governor; four years later, Democrats recaptured all these posts, in part by focusing on allegations of ethical violations by Republican gubernatorial candidate William Webster.

II. The Party in the Electorate

This survey discussion of political parties in Missouri history, however, relies on a questionable assumption. Do the election results for president and governor reflect the partisan preferences of the voters in that election? Using statewide races to make comments about the state's overall partisanship presents a problem of aggregation, hiding regional or local variations in partisanship behind overly broad generalizations; a statement that "Missouri is a Democratic state because a Democrat lives in the governor's mansion" obscures regional differences in the urban centers, along the Missouri River, or in the Bible Belt of the southwest portions of the state.

9. Parrish et al., 236, 247–49; Sorauf and Beck, 56. Parrish, Jones, and Christensen list other reasons that third parties did not become principal parties; Sorauf argues that the major parties take up third party issues mainly after the issues have garnered popular support, but the public's support may result from sources other than third party agitation.

10. Another Republican interlude began in 1920 with the election of Governor Hyde, quoted at the opening of this chapter. Hyde initially had a Republican legislature as well, but the Democrats recaptured the General Assembly in 1922. Republicans won control of one or both houses in seven of the next fifteen elections, through the 1952 election.

Intuitively, it seems obvious that partisanship must be viewed closer to the level of the individual voters. Interpreting election results at the county level, then, could reveal the partisan loyalties of different regions of the state. Further, using the results of countywide races instead of statewide races could eliminate nonparty influences, such as PACs, which focus mainly on higher-level races in the state's executive and legislative branches.

Figure 4–1 attempts to highlight regional partisanship through such countywide races. The number of elected county offices held by each party was counted for the five biennial periods from 1979 through 1988, and a percentage of offices held by Republicans was calculated. A 0 rating therefore indicates the most Strongly Democratic counties, since no officeholders during the period were Republicans. Likewise a 100 rating indicates the most Strongly Republican counties. Other counties fell somewhere between these extremes.

The map that results from these data does in fact provide some insights into regional variations in party preference. Democratic areas include: (1) the urban centers in Jackson County (Kansas City) and St. Louis; (2) the Little Dixie counties along the Missouri River that were major slaveholding areas in pre–Civil War days; and (3) the Bootheel region, settled by migrants from southern states. Republican areas include: (1) the southwest Missouri Bible Belt around Greene County (Springfield), and (2) certain agricultural counties near the Iowa border, such as Harrison, Mercer, and Putnam.

Still, even this analysis does not escape the problems inherent in using elections as a measure of partisanship. The problem of aggregation is still there—regions within a county may differ in partisanship from the county as a whole. For example, Saline County, classified as strongly Democratic, includes three Republican precincts and four precincts that lean Republican.

The Party and the Individual Voter. All measures of partisanship in the electorate in which the individual is not the unit of measurement will involve some error due to aggregation. Individual humans vote; precincts, counties, and states do not. Although secret balloting blocks access to election data about individual voter behavior, data gathered through survey research can provide some insight into what Sorauf calls "the political party as an electorate."[11]

A classic early study of voter behavior and of voter attitudes toward political parties is based on responses surveys conducted during the 1952 and 1956 election campaigns.[12] This study found that voters generally fit within four broad categories:

1. Some voters grounded their attitudes toward the political parties, and toward politics in general, in ideological terms. That is, these citizens referred to some kind of issue (sometimes very vaguely) in assessing the parties. The study estimated this group made up about 15 percent of voters.

2. A second set of voters saw the parties as favoring or opposing different groups in society, such as big business, the working class, or farmers. These voters seemed to have little if any understanding of the specific issues that might affect these groups, instead merely branding the parties as friendly or unfriendly to their favorite groups. These voters accounted for about 45 percent of the electorate.

3. Other voters appraised the political parties in still vaguer terms, crediting or

11. Sorauf, 155.

12. Angus Campbell et al., *The American Voter*, Midway Reprint ed. (New York: John Wiley and Sons, 1960; reprint, Chicago: University of Chicago Press, 1980), 227–49. Page numbers given below are references to the reprint edition.

Figure 4-1 Party Strength by County, 1979–1988

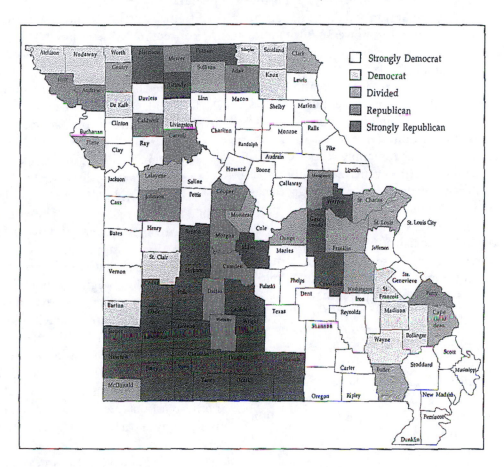

blaming the party in power (usually meaning the president's party) with the perceived state of affairs in general—whether the economy was good, the nation was at peace, or like concerns. This group of voters made up about 23 percent of the electorate.

4. Finally, the last group of voters seemed to have little rationale for their attitudes toward the parties and the parties' candidates. Some members of this group identified with the parties, and some aligned themselves with specific candidates instead, but none of them could explain why, even in vague terms. These voters accounted for the remainder of the electorate, about 18 percent of the total.

Identification with Political Parties. The last group of voters in particular illustrates how even the most uninformed voters still have acquired some attitudes toward the parties. Indeed, even the "higher" types of analysis in the first three groups may disguise the true process at work in shaping the voters' attitudes. If a voter claims to be Democratic because he or she is ideologically liberal, could the truth be instead that the liberal ideology is caused by an earlier commitment to the Democratic party? Might a Republican claim that "times are good" whenever Republicans are in power, rather than objectively appraising the nation's condition and then deciding to endorse the party in power? Which came first, the voter's party identification or the voter's rationale?

Arguably, the party identification came first, through a process termed political socialization. As children grow to adulthood, they acquire early political attitudes from sources such as family, school, church, peers, and political events that they observe. Children usually pick up a party identification from their family first; if they grow up in a relatively homogeneous society, the other socializing agents may simply reinforce that identification. In a more heterogeneous environment, the child's early party identification may be challenged (by peers, for example), although the family's influence often remains the most significant.[13]

This socialization process helps account for the remarkable stability of party identification over time. Socializing agents such as the family help pass party identification along from generation to generation; in addition, a major political event such as the Civil War doubtless proved a powerful socializer, inculcating party identifications that reflected the divisions in regional loyalties.

As durable as it is, though, party identification remains largely nominal and does not translate into active party participation. Indeed, to claim membership in one of Missouri's political parties, a voter does not have to pay dues or serve on an elected party committee. He or she does not even have to declare a party affiliation to register to vote; "voter branding," in which the election authorities maintain a record of a voter's party identification as part of

the voter's registration, is not practiced in Missouri.

Party membership is, therefore, an elusive concept in Missouri. Only on one occasion does a voter have to formally declare a party affiliation: at a primary election. Since the primary election determines which candidates become the nominees of their party, making the primary essentially a party function, the voter must declare a party preference in order to vote; the voter will then receive the primary ballot of the declared party and will vote to nominate candidates for that party. The primary election becomes the one event that defines the party support in the electorate.

However, the absence of voter branding leaves the election judges no choice but to accept the voter's party declaration. As a result, even highly visible activists in one party may vote, legally, in the primary of an opposing party. But since a voter receives only one party's ballot in the primary election, a person crosses over to vote in another party at the cost of forgoing the opportunity to participate in his or her own party's primary.

Registering and Voting in Missouri. An unregistered citizen may register to vote up to twenty-eight days before the election at a registration site, often in the county courthouse. Citizens may also register by mail, submitting an application to the local election authority. If a person has registered by mail, he or she must vote in person, rather than absentee, at the first election. Missouri citizens may also register when they apply for driver's licenses or for services at major public service agencies.

Registered voters who have moved since the last election but not filed their new address can vote at a place determined by the election authority, often the county courthouse. Voters who will be absent on election

13. Ibid., 146–67.

day can vote absentee by requesting a ballot from the election authority.

In Missouri the primary election is held in August, the general election is held in November, and municipal elections are held in April. Special elections may be called in February, March, June, and October.

III. The Party as an Organization

While Missouri's political parties seem unorganized and casual when examined in the electorate, the parties take on a lot more structure in Sorauf's second tier of analysis: the party as an organization. As organizations with great influence on the process of electing public officials, the parties are closely regulated by Missouri's election laws.

Chapter 115 of the *Revised Statutes of Missouri* sets out the criteria by which new political parties become established and the process by which they shall organize. In general, political parties are formed and organized into committees that reflect the political subdivisions and districts of the state: counties, state and federal legislative districts, judicial circuits, and the state as a whole.

To form a new political party, its founders must file petitions stating the name of the new party, the candidates to run under its name, and two noncandidates who will serve as the new party's chairman and treasurer. To obtain ballot space in a county or district, the party's petition must be signed by enough registered voters to equal 2 percent of the votes cast in the last election for the offices the new party's candidates are seeking. Different thresholds apply if the new party is seeking to run statewide.

Whether the new party becomes an established political party entitled to bal-

lot space in future elections is determined by the voters. If one of the new party's statewide candidates receives more than 2 percent of the votes cast in that race, the party becomes established statewide. Otherwise, the new party becomes established only in any county or district in which the party's candidate for office in that county or district receives more than 2 percent of the vote.[14]

Once a party becomes established under this definition, it organizes itself into a series of committees as specified by state law. In a newly established party, the candidates have the power to appoint the members of these committees; these appointees serve as the party organization until the next primary election, at which time the newly established party's committeemen and committeewomen are elected by the voters, as they are in already established parties.

The primary election day, of course, is the key to selecting the party as an organization, for it is in the primary that voters declare a party affiliation in order to receive a ballot. When primary voters cast their ballots, then, they determine not only the candidates for governor or senator but also the party committeeman and committeewoman. In general, a committeeman and a committeewoman are elected from each township or ward within each county of the state. These committee members serve two-

---

14. In 1992, the Libertarian party became established statewide under these rules. The most successful Libertarian was Janet Lewis, who received 6 percent of the votes cast for state treasurer. *Official Manual, State of Missouri, 1993–1994* (Jefferson City: Secretary of State, 1993), 534. In contrast, the Green party became established in the Ninth Congressional District, where it received 4 percent of the vote, and in state House District 45, where it received 10.5 percent of the vote. The Natural Law party became established in the Fifth Congressional District with 2 percent of the vote. *Official Manual 1993–1994*, 705, 707, 713.

year terms, until the next primary, except in St. Louis city and county, where they are selected in gubernatorial primary years and serve four-year terms.

On the third Tuesday in August, after the primary, the committeemen and committeewomen assemble in each county seat across the state and organize themselves into the county party committees. The county committee elects a chairman and vice chairman, one a man and the other a woman, as well as a secretary and treasurer, also one man and one woman. Unlike the chairman and vice chairman, the secretary and treasurer need not be members of the county committee as such.

The county committees serve as the basic foundation of the party as an organization. The party also organizes into legislative district committees, whose members are the elected committeemen and committeewomen within each of Missouri's 163 districts for the state house of representatives. In the same manner as the county committees, the legislative district committees elect a chairman, vice chairman, secretary, and treasurer.

The chairmen and vice chairmen of the several county and legislative district committees in turn become members of the congressional, state senatorial, and judicial circuit party committees. These committees also elect a slate of officers. The senatorial district committees, in addition to electing officers, select two registered voters within their senatorial districts to serve on the state party committee. Each senatorial district sends one man and one woman to the state level.

The state committee is organized in Jefferson City on the second Saturday in September through the election of a slate of officers. According to state law, the state committee consults with party candidates to prepare a platform, and it may call conventions to elect delegates to national committees and national conventions and to select the party's presidential electors, who cast the formal votes for president in the electoral college if the party's candidate wins the state.

The state committee therefore carries out the functions that require the party to speak as one voice at the state level. The state committee hires a professional staff and maintains a year-round office, usually in Jefferson City.[15] Similarly, the local committees act for their party in functions specific to their particular districts. For example, if a special election occurs in a state senatorial district to fill a vacant senate seat, the senatorial party committees nominate the candidates to represent their parties in the election. At the county level, the county committee often recommends candidates to the governor for appointment to fill vacated county offices, and also supplies the county election authority with names of persons eligible to serve as that party's election judges in the county's precincts.

The parties of Missouri thus reflect the decentralization common to U.S. and Missouri politics. Instead of a centralized party committee that acts for a monolithic party, each party has special committees that act independently. Moreover, the party has a bottom-up structure instead of a top-down one; the state party committee is ultimately selected by the local committees. Perhaps instead of Sorauf's analysis of "the party as an organization," it would be better to speak—as Sorauf himself implies—of "the party as a series of organizations."

Reality Check: The Party as Disorganization. Even that characterization might be misleading, however. State law may create, on paper, an impressive per-party network

---

15. The Libertarian Party lists an address in Springfield. Secretary of State, *Official Manual 1993–1994*, 850.

of 115 county committees, 163 legislative district committees, 34 senatorial committees, and so on, but the law cannot force those committees to be vigorous or even active. A quick examination of the *Official Manual of the State of Missouri* reveals countless vacancies for committeeman and committeewoman; primary election ballots often have blank spaces instead of candidate names for these positions. Moreover, those who actually hold these positions often do so only nominally, rarely attending county committee meetings or working for party candidates.

For a measure of party committee vitality, one need only consult the reports these committees file to disclose their finances. The Missouri Campaign Finance Disclosure Law (Chapter 130 RSMo.) requires that committees involved in election campaigns file reports to disclose their receipts and outlays to appropriate election authorities, usually the Missouri Ethics Commission and the relevant county clerk. According to state regulations, a party committee must file these reports if it receives more than $1,000 in aggregate contributions, makes more than $1,000 in aggregate expenditures, or receives more than $250 from any one contributor in any reporting period. Most party committees do not reach these reporting thresholds.

In the 1992 election, for example, only 45 Democratic and only 52 Republican county committees filed disclosure reports. None of the 326 Democratic and Republican state legislative district committees filed. These data speak convincingly about the reality of party committee vitality.[16]

Nevertheless, the party committees are thoroughly interwoven into the fabric of Missouri elections. Whether the party committees succeed in advancing the party's flag in electoral battles is a question the election laws do not worry much about; such a question is of more concern to the party's own activists and identifiers within the electorate. As semipublic organizations, though, the party committees have public functions under Missouri election laws, and the laws assume they will carry out these functions when the need arises.

IV. The Party in Government

The most essential public function of the parties is to supply candidates to fill the positions in the government itself. Without people to staff its agencies and write its laws, government would stop functioning. The parties, as machines devoted to the election of candidates, are by far the leading recruiters for government positions, the occasional independent candidate or nonpartisan election notwithstanding.

The party in government, then, becomes the third tier of Sorauf's analysis. In Missouri, the party in government to some degree takes in all three branches of the state government, as well as the administrative bureaucracy. Like the party organization, the party in government on closer inspection splits into several elements, mirroring the separated institutions of the government itself.

The most visible representatives of the party in government undoubtedly are the elected officials of the executive branch: the governor, lieutenant governor, sec-

---

16. Even these data probably overstate party committee strength. Many committees file "Annual Supplemental" reports to close their books for the calendar year, even when not required to file under the $1,000/$250 threshold. Of the ninety-seven county committees filing, fifteen filed Annual Supplementals. (However, this does not mean that all fifteen fell below the $1,000/$250 threshold.) Data are from the Missouri Ethics Commission, *1992 Missouri Annual Campaign Finance Report* (Jefferson City: Missouri Ethics Commission, 1993), 188–91.

retary of state, state treasurer, attorney general, and state auditor. Because these officers run for election independently, any number of them may come from different parties—even the governor and lieutenant governor, who do not run as a team like the federal president and vice president.

Of the executive branch offices, the governor's office clearly offers the most reward to a political party. The governor appoints the heads of some executive departments as well as the members of many commissions. In addition, article IV, section 4, of the state constitution charges the governor with filling vacancies in public offices by appointment; this can provide a means for the governor to reward local supporters as well as to establish a foothold in a county that otherwise might be hostile to the governor's party.

The governor's power to fill vacancies by appointment does not extend to vacancies in the General Assembly, of course, since the legislature is a separate branch of state government with its own powers, traditions, and party structure. The house of representatives and the senate organize along party lines, with the majority party members selecting the leaders in each chamber: the Speaker of the house and the senate president pro tempore.

Like their federal counterparts, the Missouri senate and house of representatives divide their workload by organizing into committees, typically based on particular subject areas such as agriculture, higher education, and transportation. These committees also can provide the parties with power to encourage party loyalty among the legislators, since appointment to desirable committees may depend on one's party loyalty.[17]

Explicit partisanship, as in the executive and legislative branches, all but disappears when the focus turns to the judicial branch. Outside of the St. Louis and Kansas City areas, most judicial circuits still select their judges through partisan election. Once elected, though, the judges have little motive to push a partisan agenda. While risking removal from office, an overtly partisan judge would have little to gain, as appointment to higher positions in the judiciary is covered by the nonpartisan court plan discussed in chapter 12. Some observers contend that partisanship still operates within the judiciary,[18] but explicit partisanship—especially in one's judicial proceedings—is definitely disapproved.

Likewise, partisan political activity has a limited role in the bureaucracy, particularly in state agencies whose personnel are covered by the merit system. Such agencies rely on competitive examinations and on review of applicant résumés to determine the qualifications of job applicants; support of the governor's political party is not an acceptable criterion for hiring an employee. Even agencies not legally covered by the merit system, such as the Missouri Highways and Transportation Department (MHTD), often have internal personnel systems that prohibit partisan activity by employees.

Still, the parties do have a presence in the bureaucracy, if only to keep each other in check. Not all department directors are appointed directly by the governor; in some departments, a bipartisan commission selects the agency chief. The MHTD, for instance, is headed by a chief engineer,

---

17. See chapter 8 for a description of the process of appointing in each chamber. The Speaker of the House

is particularly powerful, appointing both majority and minority party members in the house.

18. Kenyon D. Bunch and Gregory Casey, "Political Controversy on Missouri's Supreme Court: The Case of Merit vs. Politics," *State and Local Government Review* 22 (Winter 1990): 5–16.

selected by the bipartisan State Highways and Transportation Commission. The governor appoints the commissioners, with senate consent, but the state constitution expressly limits each party to no more than half of the commission seats. Moreover, the commissioners serve six-year terms, so that no governor appoints the entire commission unless that governor serves two successive terms. For the bureaucracy, then, the presence of both major parties serves as a means to control partisanship, not to extend it.

The party in government thus fragments along the lines separating the powers of government institutions. Whether it is the legislature organizing its agenda according to partisan control or an administrative commission using built-in bipartisanship to enhance the bureaucracy's political independence, Missouri state government expressly recognizes a role for the parties in conducting its business.

Other Committees: Supporting and Competing Influence. Not surprisingly, though, state law allows or authorizes other kinds of committees that diversify the options available to those who wish to participate in politics. Some of these committees function as party auxiliaries—they provide a broader membership base for the party and often carry a partisan label, but exist outside of the formal party committees that constitute the party as organization. Others draw contributions and volunteer help away from the parties, contributing to a weakening of party loyalties.

The party auxiliary groups include the College Republicans and the Young Democrats, the Missouri Federated Republican Women and the Jefferson Women's Democratic Clubs, and the Pachyderms and Muleskinners civic groups. These membership groups provide a larger base of supporters for their parties than the party committees themselves could; instead of getting elected as a committeeman or committeewoman, a person need only pay dues to the auxiliary group to join.

Accordingly, the party auxiliaries provide the party committees with essential support: new volunteers to carry out party activities, new funds to pay campaign costs, new avenues to reach particular constituencies (youth, women, business leaders, etc.). For the member, the auxiliaries can provide socialization that enhances cohesion among party supporters, reinforces the member's identification with the party, and possibly contributes an element of fun to party activities.

Less supportive of party activities are the candidate committees. These committees serve one purpose: election of a specific candidate to public office. They seek to enhance partisanship among their supporters only if that will increase the candidate's chances of being elected. Often they downplay partisanship to attract independents and voters from both major parties into a coalition behind the candidate. Campaign finance reports in the 1988 primary and general elections emphasize the relative importance of candidate committees. Committees for candidates in statewide races spent $21,766,122 in the primary and general elections of 1988; together, the Republican and Democratic state committees spent only $1,533,578—about one-fourteenth of that spent by the candidate committees. These data suggest that contributors are less concerned with advancing a partisan cause than with promoting a specific candidate. They also demonstrate that candidates have developed independent sources of contributions that free them from slavish devotion to their parties.

Nevertheless, party committees and candidate committees do have overlapping interests, in that victory for the party's candidates translates into victory for the party itself. This is not as true, however, for another type of committee, the political action committee (PAC). Many though not all PACs are associated with a trade association, business, labor union, or (less frequently) an ideological group. The parent organization, termed a "connected organization" under state law, uses its resources to raise funds for the PAC from the organization's members. The PAC, in turn, contributes its funds to candidates.

PACs, then, pursue the specific interests of their connected organizations, as they see it. It is in a PAC's interest to interact directly with the candidates, thereby evading the buffer that political parties otherwise would provide. By appearing to act more reliably on behalf of the members of the connected organization, the PAC offers its contributors a competitive reason to support the PAC instead of a more independent-minded party.

For candidates, PACs become an alternate source of revenues that help them act independently of their parties. In 1992, political action committees contributed $3,441,171 to statewide and legislative candidates, nearly four times the $890,086 contributed to those candidates by political party committees.[19] Financially, candidates stand to benefit substantially by soliciting from PACs rather than from their own parties.

The objectives and interests of PACs therefore conflict almost directly with those of the parties. The growth of candidate-driven campaign organizations further

weakens the political parties. One would expect to find, then, that Missouri elections would reflect this weakening of party loyalties.

The inclination of voters to split their tickets, by voting for candidates of different parties for different races rather than simply for all candidates of the same party, supports the proposition that the voters' allegiance to political parties has weakened. Consider, for example, the outcome of the 1988 general election for governor, in which Republican John Ashcroft defeated Democrat Betty Hearnes. While Missouri's counties have a variety of partisan leanings, as reflected in Figure 4–1, 112 of the 115 counties (including the independent city of St. Louis as a "county") voted for Ashcroft. The measure used in Figure 4–1 had placed 48 counties in the Strongly Democratic category, but 45 of these counties voted for the Republican governor. All of the 13 counties rated as Democratic voted for Ashcroft, as did all the counties in all the other categories.

In the 1992 gubernatorial election between Democrat Mel Carnahan and Republican Bill Webster, ticket-splitting was still present but was less pronounced. Eighty-nine of the 115 counties voted for Mel Carnahan, who won with 58.7 percent of the votes cast. Of the 25 counties rated as Strongly Republican in Figure 4–1, 8 voted for Carnahan; 11 of the 14 Republican counties voted for him.

Clearly, the attachment Missourians have felt for their parties has diminished, at least to the point of permitting them to wander away from their favorite party when a candidate of the other party attracts them.

V. The State of the State's Parties

Political parties in Missouri, then, find themselves facing new challenges as the new

---

19. Missouri Ethics Commission, *1992 Missouri Annual Campaign Finance Report*, 199. Candidates do receive, however, many contributions that are party-related, such as $462,672 in 1992 from the committees of other candidates. In addition, millions of dollars are given to candidates by individuals, corporations, and labor unions that are known as regular party supporters to whom party candidates can turn for help.

century approaches. Voters feel less need to adhere to their party's candidates when casting their ballots; the competing influences from candidate-oriented campaigns and from interest group political action committees dilute the electorate's commitment to a party, although the parties' membership auxiliaries provide an opportunity for the parties to reach out to broader slices of the electorate than the party committees themselves could reach. The party in the electorate, as Sorauf has labeled it, is fragmented and evasive of the parties' appeals.

Sorauf's other analytical tiers demonstrate fragmentation as well. The party as an organization seems more like a series of organizations, each free to pursue an agenda independently of the state party committee. Likewise, in the government, the parties divide along the lines separating the powers of the different branches of state government. An observer of political parties, hoping for a simple monolith irresistibly pulling party loyalists in a uniform direction, finds instead a complicated array of different elements. Accordingly, an understanding of and appreciation for this complexity must accompany any serious effort to appraise Missouri's political parties.

CHAPTER 5

Public Opinion and Issue Votes in Missouri
by David A. Leuthold

> There must be public opinion back of the laws or the laws themselves will be of no avail.—Theodore Roosevelt

Public opinion in Missouri is usually much like that in the nation as a whole, because Missouri is both northern and southern, eastern and western, urban and rural. In presidential elections since 1932, the vote in Missouri has correlated closely with the national vote, more closely than in every state but one. Occasionally, surveys include the same question at the same time in Missouri and in the rest of the United States; usually the response patterns are the same. As a result, one rule of thumb in estimating public opinion in Missouri is to assume that it is similar to data shown in national surveys, which are more readily and frequently available.

The votes of Missourians on public issues are another useful measure of public opinion. Missouri voters have been asked to vote on more than 385 statewide issues in the past 160 years. The rate has accelerated to about five statewide issues per year in the last two decades. Missourians have considered each of these issues and made decisions on them.

As measures of public opinion, issue votes have some advantages over public opinion surveys. The number of voters is much larger than the number of respondents in a sample survey, and most of the voters have given more thought and

consideration to the topic than have survey respondents. Often this is because the issues are concrete and the results will determine public policy, whereas public opinion survey results create policy only indirectly. On the other hand, public opinion surveys, if available, have other advantages. They can include questions on many topics that may never make it to a ballot. They can, by sampling the total population, include the opinions of nonvoters as well as those of voters. In addition, surveys can give more accurate and complete data on why voters act as they do, as well as on the thought processes of issue supporters and opponents.

The history of issue voting in Missouri is examined in this chapter, with focus given especially to some recurring issues that have reflected changes in public opinion over time—two moral issues, prohibition and gambling; and two financial issues, government debt and tax increases for roads and highways. This last issue will lead to consideration of patterns of "yes" and "no" voting on tax issues. Finally, this chapter includes an analysis of the impact of other factors that affect voting results and thus structure public opinion, such as the number of issues on the ballot and the sponsorship of an issue.

I. History of Issue Voting

Constitutions and Constitutional Amendments. In America, issue voting can be traced back to the 1640s, when New England town meetings allowed freemen to make the laws. In 1778, Massachusetts submitted a constitution to the public for approval. Although two or three other states adopted a similar pattern, Missouri leaders did not submit their 1820 constitution to the people. The first statewide issue vote in Missouri was a call in 1835 for a constitutional convention; it was rejected by the voters. A similar call was approved in 1844, but two years later voters rejected the constitution proposed by that convention.[1] In 1865 another convention submitted another constitution, which was adopted by Missouri voters. This constitution provided that constitutional amendments passed by the legislature must receive voter approval to be effective, triggering many more state issue elections. The first such amendment, an 1868 proposal calling for Negro suffrage, was defeated. The next constitution, in 1875, included a similar provision requiring a public vote on amendments proposed by the legislature, and 47 of 117 amendments proposed by the legislature were adopted. The 1945 constitution contained a similar provision; in the first fifty years legislators referred 125 proposals to voters, who approved 65 percent of them.

Tax Levy Issues. Many other issues also have been sent to voters in local communities or counties. Using an 1839 law, voters in local school districts levied taxes upon themselves for school buildings and raised nearly two hundred thousand dollars for schools by 1859. The 1849 legislative session allowed St. Louis voters to decide if they wanted to levy a local school tax, and the voters promptly agreed to do so, by a five-to-one margin. Many local communities voted to issue bonds to finance railroads. In 1865, a statewide vote was held on a similar topic; two railroads had received state aid and were supposed to repay the state from their revenues. The issue, presented on the ballot as the question, "Shall the railroads pay their bonds?" was adopted, giving an early indication of how ballot titles could influence voters. Even so, one of the railroads asked for and received a court order saying that it did not have to pay the money.[2]

Initiative and Referendum. Missouri adopted the initiative and referendum in 1908, becoming the sixth state to do so. Four years earlier, Missourians had voted against an initiative and referendum (a negative vote against the initiative and referendum has happened only four times in U.S. history). The initiative allows groups of voters to submit their own proposed law or constitutional amendment to the people. To get a proposal on the ballot, supporters must secure almost 80,000 valid signatures on an initiative petition for a proposed law and more than 125,000 valid signatures for a proposed constitutional amendment. The referendum allows groups to use the same procedure to bring to a popular vote a decision on whether to rescind or retain a law passed by the legislature.

Missouri's 1904 vote against the initiative and referendum, as well as the narrow approval of the proposal in 1908, revealed divisions within the state that reflected regional divisions within the nation. At the turn of the century, western states were adopting the initiative and referendum, but

---

1. Priscilla Bradford, "The Missouri Constitutional Controversy of 1845," *Missouri Historical Review* 32 (October 1937), 37, 38, 51.

2. Eugene Fair, *Public Administration in Missouri* (Kirksville, Mo.: State Teachers College, 1923), 40–41; Frederick N. Judson, *A Treatise upon the Law and Practice of Taxation in Missouri* (Columbia: E. W. Stephens, 1900), 53.

southern states (which had large black populations) and eastern states (which had large immigrant populations) were reluctant to take their chances with a procedure that offered such direct democracy. Missouri was in the middle, and Missourians echoed both the inclination of the West and the reluctance of the South and the East. The passage of the initiative and referendum in Missouri was a tribute to the hard work of Missouri reformers, who overcame not only the state's internal regional differences but also the powerful liquor interests in Missouri (including the world's largest brewery in St. Louis), which, scared of the possibility of prohibition, often fought direct democracy proposals. Since 1908, Missouri voters have cast ballots on an average of more than seven initiative proposals and three initiated referenda in each decade.

The number of issues on which Missourians have been asked to vote—constitutional amendments, initiatives, referenda, calls for constitutional conventions, and constitutions, amendments, and ordinances proposed by those conventions—has increased over the years, as is indicated in Table 5–1. One high point was reached in the 1910s and 1920s. This peak reflected the initial interest in the initiative as well as the efforts of a 1922 constitutional convention, which submitted twenty-one amendments to the constitution. A second high point began in the 1970s and continues today with more than five statewide issues per year being referred to voters.

II. Missouri Attitudes toward Issues over Time

The variation from decade to decade in the percentage of issues approved by the voters, as indicated in Table 5-1, can be classified into three different time periods:

1835–1875: 83 percent of issues passed

1876–1941: 35 percent passed
1942–1988: 64 percent passed

Why is there such variation over time? Economic conditions provide one explanation. Voters apparently are more willing to approve proposals when times are good. During the 1930s, the era of the Great Depression, only 37 percent of the issues on the ballot passed. Similarly, voters defeated all six proposals offered in 1894 and 1896, during the depression following the financial panic of 1893. In contrast, the period from 1942 through 1988 was one of fairly continuous prosperity, and most ballot issues were approved. In 1990 the nation entered another recession, and poll results indicated a substantial and continuing drop in consumer confidence while election results for two years reflected a decline in willingness to approve public issues (only 43 percent of the public issues were approved).

Another explanation could be found in the level of confidence citizens have in their government. One indicator of a loss of confidence in the 1880s and 1890s was the rise of the Populist and Progressive movements, which were in part protests against the political machines of the major parties and which included proposals for reforming government procedures. This was also an era of low rates of approval for public issues. Similarly, in the 1990s citizen confidence is lower than in some earlier eras, a trend indicated by increasing public support for third parties and for antigovernment measures such as term limits and tax limitations, as well as by declining public support for officeholders, which includes a declining percentage in votes for retention of Missouri judges.

Public opinion data on trust in government since the 1950s follow roughly similar patterns. Confidence in government, as measured in public opinion sur-

Table 5-1. Issue Voting in Missouri by Decade

Time period	Number of votes	Percent passed	Time period	Number of votes	Percent passed
1830s	1	0	1920s	74	47
1840s	2	50	1930s	28	37
1850s	0	—	1940s	20	45
1860s	4	75	1950s	14	69
1870s	12	92	1960s	24	58
1880s	4	25	1970s	45	72
1890s	8	25	1980s	44	61
1900s	30	63	1990–1994	29	52
1910s	48	5	Total	387	49

The "percent passed" figures exclude referenda submitted by the people, in which the initiators are hoping that the act will get less than 50 percent and thus not go into effect.

veys, was high in the 1950s, then gradually declined for twenty years. After a slight upturn in the early 1980s came another decline, which became fairly rapid in the early 1990s. Approval of public issues was high from the 1950s through the 1970s (although there was a dip in the 1960s), then began to decline in the 1980s and especially in the 1990s.

An examination of particular issues that were presented to voters time and again can help provide understanding of patterns over time. The prohibition movement gained strength in the latter half of the nineteenth century and secured majority votes in the 1920s; since then voters have been less and less supportive. Gambling was widely practiced in the first half of the nineteenth century, then fell out of public favor until it was finally revived in the 1970s. Support for highway and bridge taxes has been consistently limited, with the only successes coming in two elections in the 1920s and one in 1987. On the other hand, Missouri voters have regularly supported proposals for statewide bond issues. In addition, they have often supported, though more cau-

tiously, proposals allowing local government debt expansion.

III. Prohibition

During the nineteenth century, prohibitionists, often outstate activists, attempted to convince the legislature to follow the example of Maine, which enacted statewide prohibition in 1851. The legislature did not do so. Moving in the opposite direction, St. Louis city voters in 1858 voted to permit the sale of beer and wine on Sunday. By 1880, however, the General Assembly, dominated by legislators from the then populous rural areas, began to pass restrictions on the sale or use of liquor, considering at least one such bill in every session up to 1916. In 1887 the legislature passed a local option law, and within nineteen months, 83 of the 114 counties in Missouri voted in local-option referenda, with 61 voting dry. Another 35 voted dry in succeeding years. In 1913, the wets gained a temporary victory and the General Assembly passed a law eliminating the local option opportunity for cities with populations greater than twenty-five hundred. That law was challenged by

Table 5-2. Selected Public Issue Votes in Missouri, 1934–1994

Types
C—Constitutional amendment placed on ballot by
    legislature
IC—Initiated constitutional amendment
IS—Initiated statute

RP—Referendum initiated by the people
RL—Referendum referred by the legislature
O—Other, usually a proposal to call a constitutional
    convention

Date	Yes vote	No vote	Percent yes	Type of issue	Subject
5-15-34	288,195	166,607	64	C	$10 million building bond issue
11-3-36	879,213	351,962	71	IC	Created Conservation Commission for fish and game
11-5-40	535,642	445,194	55	IC	Nonpartisan system for appointment and election of judges of certain courts
11-3-42	366,018	265,294	58	O	Shall there be a convention to revise the constitution?
11-7-44	364,794	401,900	48	IC	Proposal for unicameral legislature of 50–75 members
2-27-45	312,032	185,658	63	O	Adoption of the 1945 constitution
11-2-48	462,323	694,960	40	C	Proposed 1.5 cent increase in motor vehicle fuel tax
4-4-50	179,094	528,201	25	RP	Proposal for 2 cent increase in motor fuel tax
10-4-55	230,851	95,717	71	RL	Cigarette tax to be used for schools
1-24-56	114,570	46,609	71	C	$75 million building bond issue
11-6-62	295,972	519,499	36	O	Shall there be a convention to revise the constitution?
8-17-65	204,987	75,968	73	C	Allowed governors a second term
4-7-70	364,546	468,597	44	RP	Income tax referendum, special election
8-4-70	174,989	423,942	29	C	Proposal to construct and operate toll roads
10-5-71	406,055	130,565	76	C	$150 million bonds for water pollution control
11-5-74	751,078	219,584	77	IS	Campaign financing and election law, later nullified by Missouri Supreme Court
8-3-76	598,897	442,103	58	C	Repealed segregated schools provision of Missouri Constitution
8-3-76	463,198	684,818	40	IC	Proposal for public aid to children in private schools
11-2-76	901,535	873,421	51	IC	1/8 cent sales tax for Conservation Commission
11-2-76	742,627	970,560	43	IC	Proposal to eliminate sales tax on groceries and prescription drugs
11-2-76	1,132,664	663,486	63	IS	Prohibited charging customers for construction costs of electrical power plants until the plant was completed
8-19-78	112,425	803,936	12	IC	Proposed 3 cent increase in motor vehicle fuel tax
11-7-78	631,829	948,387	40	IC	Right-to-work proposal to prohibit contracts requiring union membership for employment

Continued

Table 5-2. *Public Issue Votes (continued)*

Date	Yes vote	No vote	Percent yes	Type of issue	Subject
11-6-79	437,345	187,463	70	C	$200 million water pollution bonds
11-4-80	1,338,272	533,458	71	C	Allowed bingo
11-4-80	1,002,935	807,187	55	IC	Hancock Amendment. Limited state tax revenue
11-4-80	772,597	1,201,821	39	IS	Proposal to prohibit operation of nuclear plants prior to development of permanent waste storage sites
4-6-82	405,471	463,585	47	RP	Proposal to allow larger trucks on Missouri highways
*6-8-82	226,232	217,320	51	C	$600 million bonds for state buildings
11-2-82	406,446	927,056	31	O	Shall there be a convention to revise the constitution?
*11-2-82	492,293	905,289	35	RL	Proposal for 4 cent per gallon motor fuel tax
*11-2-82	757,756	667,190	53	IS	Proposition C, a 1 cent sales tax for education, half to be used to reduce property tax
*8-7-84	425,148	423,449	50	C	1/10th cent sales tax for state parks and soil and water conservation
11-6-84	1,369,910	590,648	70	C	Authorized state lottery
11-6-84	1,157,664	771,437	60	IC	Allowed pari-mutuel wagering on horse races
11-6-84	650,895	1,317,444	33	IS	Proposal to prohibit electricity charges for cost overruns and unneeded plants
*5-7-87	459,760	359,215	56	RL	4 cent per gallon gasoline tax increase, increased fees for large trucks
*11-8-88	1,235,023	600,751	67	C	$275 million bonds for water pollution
*11-8-88	1,263,644	576,790	69	C	Extended 1/10th cent sales tax for soil and water conservation and state parks
*11-8-88	550,974	1,372,102	29	IC	Proposal for a state health care system
11-6-90	320,958	969,082	25	IS	Proposal for state management of Missouri streams
11-5-91	304,049	623,660	33	RL	Proposition B. Proposal for tax increase for education
11-3-92	1,610,311	535,562	75	IC	Term limits—8 years for Missouri Senate or House
11-3-92	1,397,750	839,568	63	RL	Riverboat gambling on Mississippi, Missouri rivers
4-5-94	527,011	528,278	49.9	C	Allowing games of chance on riverboat casinos
8-2-94	416,787	409,912	50	C	$250 million building bond issue
11-8-94	943,752	807,707	54	IC	Slot machines on riverboats
11-8-94	558,642	1,195,483	32	IC	Hancock II. Proposal to limit state revenues
11-8-94	1,186,113	418,630	74	IS	Campaign contribution limitations

* Votes included in the compilation of pro-tax and anti-tax voting patterns in Missouri counties.

referendum, and the public vote restored local option.

Across the nation liquor interests had opposed the initiative and referendum, fearing that the device would be used to institute prohibition. Not surprisingly, it was used almost immediately for that purpose in Missouri. In 1910, two years after the initiative and referendum were adopted, liquor opponents put on the ballot an initiative proposal prohibiting the manufacture and sale of intoxicating liquors. The prohibition proposal was defeated by a two-to-one margin. For five more elections, prohibition and liquor interests fought at the polling booths, with each side winning some battles. Prohibitionists won 64 percent of the vote in 1914, 41 percent in 1916, 43 percent in 1918, 53 percent in 1920, and 66 percent in 1926.

Support for prohibition declined, however, and when Congress passed the Twenty-First Amendment repealing prohibition, Missourians gave 76 percent of their votes to those who favored repeal in the 1933 election of delegates to the convention to ratify the amendment. Missouri law still allowed local option; gradually Missouri cities dropped local prohibition, with larger cities dropping it more quickly.

Support for prohibition was found especially in rural areas. Opposition to prohibition, as measured by the 1920 vote, was strongest in St. Louis and nearby counties, especially counties with heavy concentrations of German ethnic groups. The anti-German feeling associated with World War I helped increase the prohibition vote.[3]

The long-term pattern seems to have been one of widespread acceptance of alcohol in much of the nineteenth cen-

tury, then gradually increasing strength of prohibition, especially in the rural areas. In 1920, Missouri prohibitionists won a clear majority, mirroring the movement's success nationally. But the experiences of the prohibition era—bootlegging, crime, and hazardous liquor—reversed public opinion, and Missourians voted heavily for repeal in 1933, once again mirroring the national pattern. Since then, Missourians in smaller and smaller cities and towns have been voting to allow liquor by the drink.

IV. Gambling

In the early nineteenth century lotteries were used by many states, then eliminated by all but Missouri and two other states. The "Missouri State Lottery," a private lottery despite its name, developed from an 1833 authorization of a lottery to raise fifteen thousand dollars to build a one-mile railroad from New Franklin to the Missouri River. The lottery continued for forty years, even though the proposed railroad was changed to a macadam or plank road, portions of that road collapsed into the river, and the town of New Franklin was abandoned (temporarily). The lottery owner continued to do a large nationwide business for many years despite an 1835 Missouri antilottery law, an 1839 repeal of the authorization for the New Franklin lottery, an 1842 antilottery law, and an antilottery provision in the 1865 constitution. The Missouri State Lottery was finally ended as the result of internal problems of misrepresentation and corruption, a St. Louis newspaper crusade against it, and an antilottery vote after a bitter battle at the 1875 constitutional convention.

Interest in gambling seems to revive once every one to three generations. The Great Depression brought numerous proposals

3. James H. Timberlake, *Prohibition and the Progressive Movement, 1900–1920* (Cambridge: Harvard University Press, 1966), 165, 179.

for state lotteries, although nationally the major changes of the 1930s were the legalization of gambling in Nevada and of pari-mutuel betting along the eastern seaboard and in parts of the Midwest.

The adoption of a state lottery by New Hampshire in 1964 revived interest in gambling in the United States. Subsequently, lotteries were adopted in all the New England and Middle Atlantic states, some midwestern states, and a few western states. Not until 1986 did a southern state—Florida—adopt a lottery. This pattern reflects the national pattern found in a Gallup Poll of 1951, that support for legalization of gambling was much stronger in the New England and Middle Atlantic states than in the rest of the nation, and much weaker in the South. Gallup also reported that support for legalization of gambling was much higher among urban residents than among rural residents.

The acceptance of legalized gambling in recent years has been accompanied by reduced opposition from churches. Just as churches had profited from lotteries in colonial America, so also have some churches profited in recent years from raffles and bingo games, a pattern that changed parishioner attitudes. The Roman Catholic church has had no strict teaching against gambling, and often has used bingo or raffles for fund-raising. Thus it is not surprising that states in which Catholics are relatively numerous—New Hampshire, Massachusetts, and New York—are the states that led the way to legalized gambling. The denominations most strongly opposed to gambling have been the Southern Baptists, United Methodists, and Assemblies of God—churches heavily represented in the South, which has been slow to accept legalized gambling. These patterns were reflected in a 1976 study that reported the percentage of people who gambled was somewhat higher among Catholics and Jews than among Protestants.

These nationwide patterns have been reflected in the votes on gambling issues in Missouri. The percent voting yes on the first thirteen gambling votes in Missouri this century were:

46 percent, October 1971 (legalization of horse racing)

73 percent, November 1978 (authorization of sweepstakes in which players did not have to pay to play, such as the Reader's Digest Sweepstakes)

72 percent, November 1980 (legalization of bingo)

70 percent, November 1984 (legalization of state lottery)

60 percent, November 1984 (legalization of horse race betting)

58 percent, August 1986 (liberalization of horse race betting procedures)

57 percent, November 1986 (authorization of horse race betting by individual counties)

57 percent, August 1988 (removal of some restrictions on the lottery and reduction of proportion of income to be given to the state)

47 percent, August 1990 (liberalization of bingo procedures)

49.9 percent, August 1992 (allow off-track betting parlors)

62 percent, November 1992 (allow riverboat gambling on Mississippi and Missouri Rivers)

49.9 percent, April 1994 (allow games of chance on riverboat casinos)

54 percent, November 1994 (repeat of April 1994 issue)

One surprising pattern is the high level of support in the initial votes for sweepstakes, bingo, and lottery—more than 70 percent on each issue. Only about one-ninth of all public issue votes in Missouri have received

70 percent or greater support. By 1988, however, support for the lottery had fallen to 57 percent, and by 1990 support for bingo had fallen to 47 percent. Similarly, support for horse racing fell from 60 percent in 1984 to less than 50 percent in 1992. The exception to this decline in the 1990s was the November 1992 riverboat gambling measure. The reason for that exception may well have been the $1.9 million campaign conducted for the measure, a campaign large enough to change public attitudes. Continued decline in public support for casino gambling was indicated by the decline below 50 percent in April 1994 despite a $1.3 million campaign and the rise to only 54 percent in November 1994 despite a $9 million campaign.

As with the national patterns, the greatest support on gambling issues came from metropolitan areas—St. Louis, Kansas City, St. Joseph (Buchanan County), and Columbia (Boone County). In contrast to rural counties, urban counties tend to have higher proportions of young people, people with higher incomes, and people with more years of education, all groups that are more likely to support gambling. Greene County (Springfield) did not provide comparable support but was nevertheless somewhat more in favor than were the rural counties surrounding it.

Another pattern repeated from national data is fairly strong support from counties with relatively larger percentages of Roman Catholics, such as St. Louis, Franklin, Jefferson, Ste. Genevieve, and Perry. Opposition was consistently strong in many of the counties with larger percentages of Southern Baptists and Methodists, such as many of the Ozark counties and a few north central counties.

V. Government Debt

The national debt is a frequent topic in political speeches. No one openly argues for a large national debt, but the political advantages of increasing the debt are so great that it more than doubled during the terms of Ronald Reagan, even though Reagan before his election had frequently flailed the big spenders who ran up the earlier debt. State governors and legislators argue that the federal government should balance its budget just like state governments do each year. In fact, however, state and local governments incur some debt, although they often must secure approval of voters. (Even so, the amounts of state debt are much lower than federal debt; debt service constitutes only 2 percent of Missouri's state budget, whereas it constitutes more than 20 percent of the federal budget.)

Missouri voters have approved increases in the state debt thirteen of the fifteen times they have been asked to do so. Five of the approvals were for constructing new buildings, three were for financing water pollution and sewage treatment facilities, three were for bonuses for World War I veterans, and four were for highway construction. The two disapprovals were for two initiated highway bond issues in 1914 when the need for highways was not as widely acknowledged as it is today.[4]

Approvals of state debt increases have been one-sided, with water pollution bonds receiving on average 71 percent of the vote; building bonds, 62 percent; and veterans bonus bonds, 60 percent. In contrast, the average on highway bond issues has been 36 percent. For all fifteen issues, the average yes vote has been 55 percent.

In comparison with issues to approve increases in state debt, voters have been somewhat less willing to give local governments the authority to incur debt, although they still have approved fifteen of the thirty

4. Not included in this compilation are two losing toll road proposals that would have allowed the state to issue bonds to be paid by the toll receipts. In each case, voters focused on the toll roads rather than the bonds.

proposed constitutional amendments that would have eased or lifted restrictions on local debt. The average yes vote on the thirty issues was 47 percent.

Missouri's history of statewide votes on debt (including measures for both state government and local government debt) can be divided into four periods:

I. *Nineteenth century.* No statewide votes were taken, although the legislature could incur debt. An 1868 law allowed local governments to loan their credit, if two-thirds of the voters approved. Millions of dollars were raised in this way to help build railroads, and some of the railroad debt was not repaid. The 1875 Constitutional Convention delegates responded by drafting stiff prohibitions against incurring debt.

II. *From 1900 to 1930,* twenty-four issues, an average of 1.5 issues in each general election, were presented to Missouri voters, with 58 percent being approved.

III. *From 1931 to 1960,* the Great Depression and World War II years and their aftermath, only four issues, an average of only 0.3 issues in each general election, were presented to voters, although all four of these issues passed.[5]

IV. *Since 1961,* the pattern has been much like the predepression pattern: an average of about 1.1 debt-lifting proposals per general election have been presented to Missouri voters, with 61 percent being adopted.

This pattern correlates fairly closely to economic conditions, with more proposals of debt issues, and more approvals of them, occurring in prosperous times. One

exception is that the "depression era" cycle lasted from 1931 to 1968, whereas the Great Depression ended in about 1940. State leaders who governed in the 1940s and 1950s offered few proposals to raise debt, doing so only in 1952, 1956, and 1960. The voters approved each of these proposals.

VI. Tax Increases for Roads and Highways

In the past 110 years Missourians have voted twenty-eight times on proposals to fund roads and highways. Only ten of those proposals passed. Another seven proposals were resoundingly defeated, with 70 percent or more of the voters voting against them. While Missourians have been willing to increase taxes for many purposes, this willingness has not extended to roads and highways.

The first statewide votes on taxes for roads would have allowed counties to levy a property tax for road construction. Such proposals were defeated in 1884, 1886, and 1894, but one was finally passed in 1900 after being amended to give taxing power to townships in counties that had township organization and to exclude the large cities of St. Louis, Kansas City, and St. Joseph.

Sales of newly invented automobiles stimulated interest in improved roads, but Missourians still voted against each of the five proposals offered between 1908 and 1918. Public attitudes shifted sharply in 1920, however, and Missourians approved a $60 million bond issue for the construction of roads and highways, as well as a tax measure to pay for other roads. The public also approved the use of motor vehicle license fees for highway construction and maintenance. In 1924 a successful initiative imposed a two cents per gallon tax on gasoline, which worked so well that by 1928, motor vehicle and motor fuel taxes accounted for more than 44 percent of

---

5. A 1938 omnibus measure that included a bonding proposal among its many provisions was not included in these calculations because the measure was initiated to provide advertising revenue to newspapers rather than to change public policy. The state is required to buy advertising space to print the full text of each proposal in many newspapers.

the state's total tax revenues. To secure good roads more quickly, voters authorized another $75 million bond issue in 1928, agreeing to repay the bonds from the motor fuel tax proceeds as well as the vehicle and driver's license fees. This was the last such approval of a highway improvement measure for fifty years.

In 1937 the legislature increased the motor fuel tax to three cents per gallon, fulfilling Democratic campaign promises. Opponents, especially the Automobile Club, the oil industry, and automobile dealers, circulated petitions for a referendum on the new law, and Missouri voters overwhelmingly rejected the gas tax increase in 1938. In the same election, voters were faced with a three cents per gallon proposal initiated by employees of the Missouri Highway Department, perhaps as a counter to the referendum. The Missouri Farmers Association and the petroleum industry opposed the initiative, and it was narrowly defeated. Another proposal for a three cent motor fuel tax was put on the ballot in 1940 by the Missouri Farmers Association, but received only 40 percent of the vote.

The legislature proposed a 1.5 cent gas tax increase for county and municipal roads in 1948, but voters rejected the proposal. In 1949 the legislature increased the gasoline tax to four cents per gallon, but the oil interests, the Automobile Club of Missouri, and the Missouri Bus and Truck Association circulated a referendum asking for a public vote on the issue. Although the governor and the Missouri Farmers Association campaigned heavily for the tax increase, it was defeated by a wide margin. In 1948 and 1950 voters split on rural-urban lines, with rural voters, especially those in northern counties, providing strong support for the rural-dominated legislature's proposal. In contrast, only 30 percent of St. Louis and St. Louis County voters supported the issue

in 1948 and only 7 percent supported it in 1950.

Nevertheless, as part of a state modernization program, the legislature increased the gasoline tax to three cents per gallon in 1952, a smaller increase than that proposed in the 1948 and 1950 measures. The legislature increased the rate to five cents per gallon in 1969 and to seven cents per gallon in 1972; opponents did not use the referendum procedure to kill either tax increase. In 1978, an initiative proposal to increase the tax to ten cents per gallon was overwhelmingly defeated, with 88 percent of the voters opposing it. Nevertheless, the legislature referred a four cents per gallon increase to voters in 1982; this proposal was also defeated, but it did receive more than one-third of the vote. Only two counties, Cole and Boone in central Missouri, gave the proposal a majority vote.

In 1987, the legislature combined a four cents per gallon tax increase with increased fees for larger trucks and limits on administrative costs, referring the entire package to voters, who approved it with 56 percent of the vote. In that campaign, supporters had more than $1 million to spend and opponents did not organize. Specific improvement projects, including major river bridges, were promised if the tax passed. Voters in the areas of St. Louis, Kansas City, and Columbia provided the strongest support. On the other hand, every county in southwest Missouri, and many counties in southeast and south central Missouri, opposed the tax increase.

In 1992 the legislature voted, and the governor signed, a six cent increase in the motor fuel tax to be phased in over a four-year period. The public officials stoutly resisted efforts to send the issue to voters for their approval. Given the history of limited support by Missouri voters for gas tax increases and the recession mood of 1992, the proposal might well have lost if it had gone to the voters.

The general pattern on road and highway taxes has been a continuing reluctance by Missouri voters to provide financing. Only on those occasions when the proponents were well organized and extremely active have Missourians approved additional funding for roads and highways. One essential aspect of organization has been to develop proposals that would secure support across the state, in both metropolitan and rural areas.

VII. Pro-Tax and Anti-Tax Voting in Missouri Counties

According to political folklore, some counties in the state are certain to vote against almost any tax issue on the ballot, while other counties will support almost any tax, almost any time. For example, some metropolitan political leaders have argued for a larger share of certain bond issue or tax proceeds, noting that the issues would not have passed except for the solid votes in their counties.

In the 1980s, eight tax or bond issue proposals were presented to Missouri voters. Six of these issues passed and two failed, reflecting a continuing statewide trend in which two-thirds of the thirteen tax or bond issues offered since 1955 have passed. (Such frequent voter approval raises interesting questions about why Missouri has low rates on so many taxes.) The votes on these eight measures have been averaged to compare voting patterns in Missouri counties.[6]

The counties that most often vote "yes" are led by Boone (Columbia), which has

6. David Leuthold, "Pro-Tax and Anti-Tax Voting in Missouri Counties," *Governmental Affairs Newsletter* 24 (March 1990), 1–7. The eight issues are identified with an asterisk in Table 5–2.

had an average vote of 63 percent yes, well above second-place St. Louis city, which has averaged 58 percent yes. Counties that have voted yes least frequently (or no most frequently) include Shannon, with an average yes vote of 32 percent, and Texas, with an average of 33 percent. Figure 5–1 indicates the percentage of yes voters in each county.

Patterns of "Yes" and "No" Voting. A clear metropolitan versus rural pattern appears, in that St. Louis, St. Louis County, St. Charles County, and Jackson County are four of the six areas to vote yes the most often. Other urban and suburban counties have voted yes less often, but even so, almost every county that is part of a metropolitan area is in the top half of the listing.

A second immediately apparent pattern is regional: many counties in southern Missouri, especially southwest Missouri, tend to vote no. Among the forty counties that have voted no most frequently, thirty-nine are in a southwest Missouri block extending from Bollinger, Wayne, and Butler counties on the east to Osage County on the north and the Kansas border on the west. The only southwestern counties not in this group are Greene (Springfield), Jasper (Joplin), Taney (Branson and Bull Shoals Lake), and Phelps (Rolla)—urban, lake, and college counties. The only nonsouthern county in the top forty is Schuyler, a small rural county on the Iowa border.

A third pattern relates to income and education. National voting behavior studies have found that voters with more income and more years of education are more likely to support tax increase proposals than are voters with less income and fewer years of education. Part of the explanation commonly given is that higher-income people feel the pinch of increased taxes less severely because their disposable incomes are still quite high, even after the tax increase. Given this pattern, we should expect that counties

Figure 5-1. Pro-Tax and Anti-Tax Voting in Missouri Counties, 1980–1988

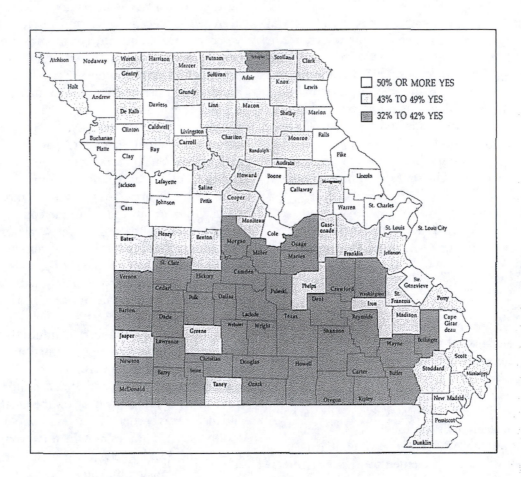

with higher average levels of income and education would be more likely to vote yes.

One statistical measure of the relationship between tax voting and income or education is the correlation coefficient, which can range from 0.0, no relationship, to 1.0 (or –1.0), perfect relationship. The correlation of 1985 per capita county income with the average percent voting yes on the eight statewide tax and bond issues was .60; the correlation of the percentage of county adults who had graduated from high school with the average percent voting yes was .50. Both of these relationships are strong, indicating that counties with high levels

of income or education were much more likely to vote yes on tax and bond issues than were counties with lower levels of income and education.

A fourth pattern is partisanship. Most southwestern Missouri counties are noted for their solid Republican votes, and the Seventh Congressional District almost always has been represented by Republicans in Congress. In comparing the average yes vote with the Democratic vote, the correlation coefficient was .35, using the average percentage for the six elections for governor and treasurer in the 1980s. This means that the more likely a county was to vote yes, the more likely it was to vote for Democratic candidates. Conversely, counties that voted no were more likely to vote for Republican candidates. The relationship, however, is not as strong as the relationship of yes voting with income or education.

VIII. Number of Issues on the Ballot

The fate of any issue on the ballot may well be determined by how many other issues are on the ballot. If many issues are on the ballot, it is less likely that any particular issue will pass. In the past fifty years, more than 60 percent of the statewide issues on the ballot have been approved by voters. · The November 1982 election was an exception. With thirteen issues on the ballot, only three passed. Three of the issues were submitted again in later elections when fewer issues were on the ballot, and each passed on the second effort.

Other elections that indicated a similar pattern were those of 1910, 1912, 1914, 1918, 1920, 1922, 1924, and 1938, each of which had nine or more proposals on the ballot. Only 22 percent of the proposals on election ballots in those years passed (excluding the referenda initiated by the people). Most of the successes came in 1920 and in the February 1924 election in which voters adopted one-third of the amendments proposed by a constitutional convention. One reason for the low approval rate was that long ballots were more likely to include a controversial issue. Encouraged by the campaigns, many voters voted against all issues in an effort to be sure to kill the controversial one. From 1910 to 1920, most elections included one or more controversial proposals on prohibition, women suffrage, or the single tax system. Another explanation may be a tendency on the part of voters to stick with the status quo if they are faced with numerous issues and insufficient time to study them.

Another factor affecting voter approval of issues is who sponsors them. Proposals referred to voters by the legislature are much more likely to be successful than are proposals referred to voters by their fellow voters through the initiative. Since 1835, voters have approved 54 percent of the constitutional amendments referred to them by the legislature, but only 28 percent of the constitutional amendments referred to them by initiative. Similarly, voters have approved five of the six laws referred to them by the legislature, but only 31 percent of the laws referred to them by initiative.

In examining only those constitutional amendments referred to the people by the legislature and offered at elections in which the total number of issues was less than nine, the percentages that passed were:

1868–1874: 89 percent (9 issues)
1878–1896: 23 percent (13 issues)
1900–1921: 70 percent (33 issues)
1928–1948: 40 percent (20 issues)
1950–1962: 58 percent (22 issues)
1965–1988: 81 percent (67 issues)
1990–1994: 53 percent (15 issues)

To a large extent, this pattern reflects changes in economic conditions. The 1878 to 1896 period included the aftermath of the depression of 1873 and the depression of 1893. The pattern in these depression periods suggests that voters react more slowly than do the economic indicators, continuing to approve measures even as the nation enters the depression, then continuing to disapprove ballot issues even as the nation emerges from the depression.

IX. Conclusions

Economic Cycles. Although the data raise as many questions as answers, they do help us to understand more about the public opinion of Missourians. Except for two "cautious" cycles, one associated with the 1873 and 1893 depressions, and one associated with the Great Depression, Missourians have regularly approved about two of every three constitutional amendments and referenda referred to them by the legislature. The cautious cycles are explained in large part by the financial uncertainty associated with depressions and recessions. This pattern is similar to the year-in and year-out pattern in which lower-income voters are less willing than higher-income voters to support tax increases. In times of economic uncertainty, voters are less willing to experiment with change.

Technical Factors. Just as the results of opinion surveys are affected by the way in which the questions are worded and other technical factors, so also are public issue vote outcomes affected by technical factors, such as the number of issues on the ballot and the sponsorship of the issue. Voters are less likely to approve an issue if it is presented at the same time as numerous other issues. In addition, they are much more likely to approve proposals from the legislature than from their fellow voters.

Just as farmers have learned how to get much better crop yields than they did at the turn of the twentieth century, so also have political leaders learned how to improve the prospects for receiving majority support from Missouri voters. Political leaders have worked hard to gain legislative sponsorship of proposals to increase their chances of passage. Similarly, the governor has distributed proposals over special, primary, and general elections rather than bunching them all in the general election. In addition, sponsors have learned campaign techniques, such as stimulating turnout among people likely to be most supportive of their proposal.

Even so, voter support is not automatic. Since 1979, voters have rejected one of every three proposals referred to them by the legislature in elections with small numbers of issues on the ballot. The elections in the 1990s have reflected lower rates of approval of issues, as well as less support for incumbent officeholders running for reelection. Only time will tell whether 1990 was the introduction to another cautious cycle.

PART II

State Governmental Framework

CHAPTER 6

The Constitution of Missouri
by Roy Blunt and Larry Whatley

> Laws and institutions must go hand in hand with the progress of the human mind. . . . As new discoveries are made, new truths disclosed, . . . institutions must advance also, and keep pace with the times. . . . Each generation . . . has [the] right to choose for itself the form of government it believes the most promotive of its own happiness. A solemn opportunity of doing this every nineteen or twenty years should be provided by the constitution.—Thomas Jefferson

Constitutions are designed to create a framework for government. That framework is at least as important in what it does to define and limit government as it is in what it does to legitimate and empower government. The purpose of this chapter is to trace the development and summarize the basic features of the current state constitution, the Missouri Constitution of 1945.

I. The Development of Missouri's Constitution

Americans were fortunate in 1987 to be able to celebrate the bicentennial of the U.S. Constitution. The Constitution has served not only as a most enduring framework for government but also as a prototype for the many state constitutions written after it. Many of the concepts that frame government in the fifty states were initiated in the federal constitution drafted during a hot Philadelphia summer. Among the most important was the notion of limited government. The logic of "checks and balances"—an idea we accept so easily today—was a unique governmental structure in 1787.

Former Chief Justice Warren Burger, who left the U.S. Supreme Court to dedicate himself to the bicentennial of constitutional government, observed that in earlier times "the value of the horse depended on the harness you could keep on it." His point is clear: a constitution harnesses the forces of government. Although it is a document with tremendous potential to grant power, the U.S. Constitution defines government and by that definition actually limits the powers of government.

The Constitution continues to stand as a model of resilience. In the words of nineteenth-century British Prime Minister William Ewart Gladstone, "the American Constitution is the most wonderful work ever struck off at a given time by the brain and purpose of man." It is remarkable in its endurance, almost unchanged in form for two centuries. The first ten amendments, the Bill of Rights, were put in place immediately. The next two amendments were added in the first clarifying years of the

Constitution and only fifteen other changes have occurred since 1804. Of the 160 constitutions at work in the world today, nearly half are less than ten years old and only fourteen predate World War II.

Another new element of government, reinforced with the Tenth Amendment, was the idea of leaving much of the power of government with the states. This new concept of federalism has worked well in the United States. It was based on the idea that the states also had to have a framework of government, and that creating that framework was part of achieving statehood. The current Missouri Constitution is the state's fourth, with two other constitutions presented by constitutional conventions and defeated by voters.

No state constitution is more associated with controversy than Missouri's first one, which, when it was submitted to the U.S. Congress in 1820, marked the beginning of four decades of constitutional controversy regarding slavery. Thomas Jefferson said that the impact of Missouri's application for statehood was "like a fire bell in the night."

In spite of the controversy it caused, the 1820 constitution plowed no new ground but rather was built on the revolutionary model of great trust in the legislative body. The legislature not only was given substantial authority over the government, but also held the sole authority to change the state constitution. Like the states before it, Missouri initiated a two-house legislature. Even the state treasurer was chosen by the legislature.

The governor and lieutenant governor were elected by the people. The remaining state officials were chosen by the governor, as was the case in most of the New England states at the time. Judges were appointed to serve "during good behavior."

After a constitutional convention in 1845, a new constitution was offered to Missourians, but they rejected it. The system was, however, ready for change, and the 1820 constitution was amended often. These changes were often Jacksonian in their extension of democracy. Judges and statewide officials, formerly appointed, began to be elected by popular vote, and the previously broad powers of the legislature became more limited.

A new constitution was produced in 1865, immediately after the Civil War. The 1865 constitution is often called the Drake Constitution after its principal drafter, Charles Drake. This Reconstruction-era constitution was quickly replaced by the constitution of 1875, which served as the basis for Missouri state government for seventy years.

The 1875 constitution was longer than its predecessors and eventually was lengthened further by sixty amendments. The constitution itself included two innovations that still affect government in Missouri today. The first was the constitutional recognition of education as a high priority for state funds and the new requirement that 25 percent of general revenue go to elementary and secondary education. The 1875 constitution also gave each city with more than one hundred thousand inhabitants the power to design its own "home rule charter." No other state had this charter provision in its constitution, but many have since added it.

One innovation, added by amendment in 1908, was the initiative and referendum. Only half of the states have given the electorate the power to initiate laws and constitutional changes or to refer current laws to a popular vote. This innovation was part of the Populist-Progressive movement that marked the transition from the nineteenth to the twentieth century. States had not extended this right to their citizens before

Table 6-1. State Adoptions of Initiative and Referendum, 1898–1977

Year	State
1898	South Dakota
1900	Utah
1902	Oregon
1904	Nevada (referendum only)
1906	Montana
1907	Oklahoma
1908	Maine, Missouri
1910	Arkansas, Colorado
1911	Arizona, California, New Mexico (referendum only)
1912	Idaho, Nebraska, Nevada (initiative only), Ohio, Washington
1913	Michigan
1914	North Dakota
1915	Kentucky (referendum only), Maryland (referendum only)
1918	Massachusetts
1959	Alaska
1968	Florida (constitutional initiative only), Wyoming
1970	Illinois (constitutional initiative only)
1977	District of Columbia

Source: Thomas E. Cronin, *Direct Democracy: The Politics of Initiative, Referendum, and Recall* (Cambridge: Harvard University Press, 1989), 51.

that time, and only a few states have added it since.

Missourians have used the initiative and referendum process to create the conservation commission, limit the legislative ability to increase taxes, extend a parks and soil conservation tax, and limit terms of members of the Missouri General Assembly. Other areas where the state's citizens have used this tool have included the passage of Missouri's first campaign and personal financial disclosure law in 1974 (which was later found to be too onerous by the Supreme Court) and a 1981 reversal of a legislatively enacted law easing the regulations for tractor-trailer trucks on Missouri's roads and highways.[1]

Many see the initiative and referendum as the ultimate oversight that citizens can ap-

ply to their government, while others think it lacks the important benefit of legislative debate and discussion. The initiative is not an easily accomplished process and has not been used when the legislature dealt with issues. The referendum, an equally difficult process, has been used much less frequently.

Another significant addition to Missouri's constitution process was made in 1920, when voters approved an initiated proposal requiring that Missourians vote once every twenty years on whether a constitutional convention should be called to propose a new constitution. The first use of this new provision, in 1921, did not result in the proposal of a new constitution, but it did lead to twenty-one proposed amendments. All but six of these amendments were rejected by voters. While Missouri voters rejected fifteen of the amendments

1. See also the discussion of the initiative and referenda in chapter 5.

proposed by the 1921 constitutional convention, the 1875 constitution still had become weighted down with changes. By 1943, the voters had approved 60 of the 173 amendments proposed to them.

Missourians were given their second opportunity to call a constitutional convention by majority vote in 1942, and once again said they would like to see what a convention could produce. At the April election in 1943, eighty-three delegates were elected. Deliberations began in Jefferson City in September 1943, and on September 29, 1944, the part-time deliberations of the drafters produced a final document.

At a special election in February 1945, one-fifth of the eligible voters went to the polls and adopted a new constitution by a vote of 312,032 to 185,658. The constitution they adopted has been confirmed by many more Missouri voters, who passed up the opportunity to call another convention in 1962 and in 1982.

II. The Provisions

The twelve articles of the 1945 constitution begin with a preamble expressing gratitude to and reverence for the "Supreme Ruler of the Universe." Like most state constitutions written since the addition of the Bill of Rights to the U.S. Constitution, a bill of rights is the first item following the preamble.

Article I. Even though many of the nationally confirmed rights apply to the states, the states still retain their own versions of these traditional provisions and may design them to suit their own circumstances and conditions. Missouri has expanded the guaranteed rights in a number of areas, such as the addition of the victim's rights provision in 1992. The most important element of this amendment is the guarantee of a constitutional right for victims to participate in the legal process. Victims now have the right to appear at sentencing hearings and to have a voice at parole hearings, and they have other specific rights during proceedings involving crimes in which they were a victim.

In addition to the traditional rights of freedom of religion, speech, and assembly, and freedom from unreasonable search and seizure, ex post facto laws, and bills of attainder, the Missouri bill of rights also provides for free elections and the right of employees to collective bargaining. Article I of the bill of rights also indicates that "all political power is vested in and derived from the people," is founded on their will, and is instituted "solely for the good of the whole."

Article II. Article II consists of only one paragraph. It succinctly proclaims that the three branches of government are to be distinct and that no person in one branch may exercise any power that belongs to another department of government, unless permitted by the state constitution. This reaffirms our belief in "checks and balances" and ensures that governmental power is not concentrated in the hands of a few.

Article III. The third article is significant and lengthy, longer than the entire U.S. Constitution. It creates the legislature, the first branch of state government, and mandates the title of "The General Assembly of the State of Missouri." This legislative body follows the traditional bicameral pattern and consists of a senate and a house of representatives. The Missouri Senate consists of 34 members. The Missouri House of Representatives has 163 members, making it the fourth largest in the United States. Interestingly, the largest house of representatives is in one of the smallest states, New Hampshire, where 400 legislators meet for a short time and receive little pay. Conversely, the large states of California and Illinois have only 80 and 118 members respectively in their houses of representatives.

Prior to the U.S. Supreme Court ruling in *Baker v. Carr,* the case that led to the one person, one vote decisions after 1962, each Missouri county elected one member to the house of representatives and only the remaining forty-eight seats were allocated on the basis of population.[2] After *Baker v. Carr,* each of the districts in both the house and the senate were to be as nearly equal in population as possible, with some small deviation acceptable. Every ten years the inequities created by population shifts are the focus of redistricting efforts that follow each national census. Redistricting commissions are chosen by the governor from names submitted by the two major political parties. If the commissions fail to act, the judiciary is given the final responsibility for redistricting.

While the U.S. Constitution in brief and straightforward fashion creates a national legislative body and grants enormous power to it (but with some limitations on congressional prerogatives), the Missouri Constitution grants modest powers to the state legislature or General Assembly. In addition, it includes laborious detail and provides significant limitations on legislative power. Some of the major provisions of Article III include qualifications for legislators; the legislative process that is to be observed as the two houses create law and policy for the state; limitations on state debt; and permission to sell bonds for financing state buildings, paying for water pollution control, and covering a few other expenditures. The rules for the operation of the initiative and referendum processes are also included.

2. In 1921, twenty-seven seats were allocated on the basis of population. The number gradually increased to forty-eight in 1963.

Several amendments were added to Article III in the years after 1982. Some of the more significant changes include changes in session length and granting the state legislature power to approve a state lottery with proceeds going to public education, as well as legislative authority for bingo, pari-mutuel wagering, and riverboat gambling. Term limits for legislators were also added and were arguably the most fundamental of these changes. Legislators elected after 1992 may serve a maximum of eight years in each house, or a total of sixteen years.

Article IV. Article IV creates the executive branch of Missouri government. "Supreme executive power" is vested in the governor, who is also given the authority to appoint many public officials in the state including the "cabinet." Provision is also made for filling emergency or unanticipated vacancies in most executive offices, including the office of governor.

The line of succession for the office of governor is lieutenant governor, president pro tempore of the senate, speaker of the house, secretary of state, state auditor, state treasurer, and attorney general. In a case of gubernatorial disability, a "disability board" composed of the state's top executive officials may notify the legislature that a governor is unable to discharge the powers and duties of the office, in which case the lieutenant governor or the next person in the order of succession who is able to perform becomes the acting governor. If the originally elected governor subsequently seeks to resume the office, he or she may do so unless denied by the disability board. In case of disagreement between the board and the governor, a majority of all the members of the Missouri Supreme Court must vote that the governor is unable to serve; otherwise the originally elected governor assumes the powers and duties of the office.

The disability board has not been needed in Missouri since its adoption in 1968.

In addition to delineating the major executive departments of Missouri government, Article IV also specifies the modes of selection as (1) direct election of the governor, lieutenant governor, auditor, secretary of state, state treasurer, and attorney general by the people, (2) appointment of some departmental executives by the governor with the approval of the senate, and (3) other arrangements such as selection of some departmental executives by a board. For most of the departments, broad goals and objectives are stated and specific powers may be listed, then the legislature is empowered to enact laws relative to the department and its mission. In regard to the Missouri Department of Agriculture, for example, "The general assembly shall provide the department of agriculture with funds for adequate administration of its functions; and shall enact such laws and shall provide such other appropriations as may be required to protect, foster, and develop the agricultural resources of the state."

The governor and lieutenant governor are elected separately. In the four elections from 1976 through 1988, Missourians elected a governor and lieutenant governor of different political parties. In 1992 voters decided to give the lieutenant governor additional duties significantly beyond the minor responsibilities assigned to that officer since 1821. The other four officials elected statewide also find the authority to carry out their responsibilities in Article IV. The auditor is elected at a different general election from the other state officials, in an effort to ensure more independence. Only the governor and treasurer are limited in their terms of office, each being limited to two terms.

Article V. The fifth article is given an overview in Section 1, which states, "The judicial power of the state shall be vested in a supreme court, a court of appeals consisting of districts as prescribed by law, and circuit courts." In addition, each county has at least one resident associate circuit judge. Each circuit also has "such municipal judges as provided by law."

The terms of office are also established in Article V. Supreme court and court of appeals judges serve for twelve years. Circuit court judges serve for six years, and associate circuit judges serve for four years. Salaries are determined by the state legislature and may not be diminished during a judge's term of office.

The power of the Missouri Supreme Court includes exclusive *appellate* jurisdiction involving the validity of a treaty or statute of the United States, or of a Missouri statute or provision of the Missouri Constitution, or of cases involving the construction of Missouri revenue laws, title to state office, or the death penalty. The court of appeals has appellate jurisdiction in all other cases. The circuit courts have *original* jurisdiction over all cases, both civil and criminal. Associate circuit judges have jurisdiction over all cases formerly handled by magistrate and probate judges as well as other cases that may be provided by law. Magistrate courts had previously decided minor civil and criminal cases. Municipal judges in each circuit hear and determine violations of municipal ordinances.

The Missouri Supreme Court is composed of seven judges. One member is elected by the others to serve as chief justice. The supreme court has general superintending control over all lower courts and may establish rules relating to practice, procedure, and pleading for all courts.

With the exception of municipal judges, selection of judges in Missouri follows two basic plans. In most Missouri counties associate and circuit judges are elected by direct popular vote after being nominated by party balloting during the primary election. The judges in the other state courts, including the supreme court, court of appeals, and circuit and associate circuit judges in St. Louis City and Jackson County, are chosen by a nonpartisan selection plan that is mandated in Article V. Voters in Platte, Clay, and St. Louis counties have also adopted the use of the nonpartisan technique to select their judges. This nonpartisan court plan was labeled the "Missouri Plan" after a 1940 citizen initiative added it to the 1875 constitution, and it has been adopted by a number of other states as a "good government" alternative.[3]

Article VI. Article VI contains basic information and rules for the creation of city and county governments in Missouri. All of Missouri's counties were established by 1861, long before the 1945 constitution. The constitution preserved the existing county structure, although voters in the counties can consolidate or make other changes if they choose to do so. County courts, now county commissions, consisting of three members called commissioners, are to be elected to conduct county business as prescribed by the law of the state. Counties with more than eighty-five thousand inhabitants are allowed to adopt a home rule charter, drafted and approved locally by voters. Home rule charters have been adopted in St. Louis, Jackson, and St. Charles counties. The city of St. Louis is also constitutionally mandated to be a county. This "landlocking" of the city has limited its growth in size and tax base, whereas other Missouri cities can change and cross county lines. Both counties and cities are to be classified or placed in categories, so that a law passed by the state legislature or a power granted by that body would apply to all counties or cities in a particular class. A maximum of four classes of counties is allowed, with the same number permitted for cities. While not explained in the constitution, one of the reasons for classification is to free (or restrict) the legislature from local legislation, that is, from establishing particular laws for particular cities or counties. Also, some uniformity in the organization and powers of cities and counties results from this scheme. Despite this provision in the constitution, the legislature passed many laws that applied to only a single county. A 1994 Missouri Supreme Court decision raised doubts about the constitutionality of such laws, and the legislature proposed a constitutional amendment to retroactively make those laws constitutional.

The remaining provision of Article VI allows cities with more than five thousand inhabitants to adopt home rule charters for city government, although these governments may be limited in power by the constitution or by state law. Several other limitations are placed on cities and counties. They are not allowed to own stock in or lend credit to corporations except as allowed in the constitution. There are also limitations on the amount of indebtedness that political subdivisions may incur.

Articles VII through XII. The remaining articles are significant but relatively brief. Article VII allows for impeachment for several types of wrongdoing. Also, any public employee who is guilty of nepotism, defined in this case as hiring a relative within the fourth degree (a first cousin or closer), will be forced to forfeit his or her office.

Article VIII specifies the date of general elections as being "on the Tuesday next following the first Monday in November

---

3. See chapter 12 for a description of the operation of the Missouri plan for selection of judges.

Table 6-2. Procedures for Proposal and Ratification
of Missouri Constitutional Amendments

Proposal	*Ratification*
By the *General Assembly* at any time, if a majority of each house agree. This is by joint resolution.	By a simple majority of the votes cast in a popular election (either the next general election in November, or an earlier one specially called by the Governor).
By *popular initiative.* Initiative petitions stating the proposed amendment must be signed by at least 8% of the legal voters (the number who voted for Governor at the last election) in each of at least 2/3 of the state's nine congressional districts. These petitions must be filed with the Secretary of State at least 4 months before the election. Such an amendment proposal may contain only one amended or revised article.	Same as above.
By a *constitutional convention.* The question of calling a convention is to be voted upon by the people every 20 years (next time 2002), or at any other general or special election if the General Assembly so orders. Election of delegates takes place from 3 to 6 months after the vote which calls the convention. The convention meets within 6 months after election of delegates.	By the people from 2 to 6 months after adjournment of the convention. The convention itself decides on all terms and arrangements for submitting the new amendments (or new constitution) to the people.

Source: Robert F. Karsch, *The Government of Missouri*, 7.

of each even year." Provisions relating to qualifications for voting and absentee voting are also included.

Article IX guarantees a free elementary and secondary education to students under the age of twenty-one. A state board of education is created along with the position of commissioner of education. A state university and free public libraries are also mandated.

Article X grants taxing power to the General Assembly, which then may authorize counties, cities, and other political subdivisions to levy taxes. Some limitations are placed on local tax rates, and the Hancock Amendment provides that state taxes are

not to rise faster than the personal income of Missourians.

Article XI stipulates that corporations are to be established under general laws, not by special laws that would relate to only one corporation.

Article XII provides the procedures for proposing and ratifying changes in the constitution. Robert Karsch, in his work explaining the process, has summarized the processes in Table 6–2.

III. Conclusion

Missouri's history is reflected in the constitutions that have served as its framework for government. The first constitution was part of the painful debate that led to statehood in 1820. The changes forged by the Civil War required a new document in 1865, and the dramatic political changes in the state following the war produced another constitution just ten years later. That framework gave way to the current constitution approved by Missouri voters at the end of World War II.

Missourians have seen their last two constitutions as flexible documents that the "owners" of state government could change in significant ways. Items as fundamental as the limits on taxation by state officials and the procedures to ensure effective represen-

tation in the General Assembly have been hotly debated as voters decided on such constitutional amendments as the Hancock Amendment and term limits. Missouri voters make governmental decisions every two years as they deal with proposed amendments.

The addition of more than forty amendments by the fiftieth anniversary of the 1945 constitution may mean that Missourians will have a more detailed discussion of the constitution in 2002, the year when the next vote on whether to call a constitutional convention will occur.

CHAPTER 7

Types of Law in Missouri
by James V. Young

Law is the highest reason, implanted in nature, which commands what ought to be done and forbids the opposite.—Cicero

For many centuries, philosophers have inquired about the nature of, and the need for, law. Whereas Cicero, as well as Plato, Aristotle, and others before them, focused primarily on law as a unified whole, more recent writers such as Bentham and Austin emphasize the need for classification in their legal system. Today, a Missourian who is attempting to write a valid will or put together a legal defense against a charge of careless and imprudent driving has an even greater need to understand the various parts of our state's legal system.

By its very nature, the law divides people and things into categories, and then attributes certain legal rights and responsibilities to each category. Landlord-tenant, debtor-creditor, citizen-alien—all are categories of people, and the law has assigned certain legal characteristics to each category.

Growth of the law and efforts to organize it into a logical system have led to the subdivision of law into various *types*. One of the most common typologies is in part based on the *source* of the law: statutory law stems from documents called *statutes* that are enacted by the legislature, constitutional law at least originally emanates from an instrument called a constitution, common law and equity flow from the courts, adminis-

trative law comes from the administrative or executive branch of government, and popular law comes from the people.

This chapter will focus on most of these types of law and other types that are an important part of Missouri's legal system. This focus on a particular state's legal system is appropriate, in part because of the decentralized nature and development of American law, as will be explained in the section on common law. This decentralization is manifest in the fact that our states, more than the national government, are involved in legal education and in the control of the legal profession. In fact, most legal rules in the United States are matters of state rather than federal law.

The purpose of this chapter is to identify, describe, and illustrate the major types of law applicable to Missouri citizens: statutory, administrative, constitutional, and common. In addition, this chapter will discuss some other classifications of law that have been useful for citizens: civil law and criminal law, private law and public law, and natural law and positive law.

I. Statutory Law

The first response to a question about the law often will be to pull out a copy of Missouri's statutory laws—the binding rules of conduct that have been passed by the Missouri legislature. Each year the legislature passes 150 or more new laws, adding some rules and deleting others that are no longer appropriate. Every other year, statutes passed by the General Assembly are arranged alphabetically by subject matter in the *Laws of Missouri.* These "session laws" are prepared by the secretary of state's office, which also makes them available to the public.

All applicable Missouri statutes, regardless of date of enactment, are included in a multivolume set called *Revised Statutes of Missouri,* often abbreviated to RSMo. When the legislature passes a law, it often specifies the particular chapter in RSMo into which the laws will fit. Every ten years, in years ending in "9," the Joint Committee on Legislative Research of the General Assembly publishes a new edition of the *Revised Statutes of Missouri.* Biennial supplements update this reference source. In addition, *Vernon's Annotated Missouri Statutes,* a privately published set of volumes, contains the laws set forth in the *Revised Statutes* plus extensive annotations and historical materials.

II. Administrative Law

In the traditional sense, administrative law is the body of law involving the powers of agencies in the executive branch of government, the procedures that they must follow, and the relations between citizens and such agencies. In this sense, for example, administrative law prescribes the methods of initiating actions before an administrative agency, the rights that one has before an agency, the amount of evidence necessary for the agency to make a decision, and the scope of judicial review of the agency's decisions.[1]

When the General Assembly passes a law setting up a new program, it either establishes an agency in the executive branch to enforce the law or adds such a responsibility to an already existing agency. In addition, the legislature may delegate some of its *law-making* power to such an agency, empowering it to make rules and regulations that have the effect of filling in the details of the broadly worded statute that the agency is to enforce.

Such administrative rule making enables the agency to cope with day-to-day challenges and changes that otherwise would require amendment of the basic statute, an inflexible approach. The rules have the same legal force and effect as does the statute. A citizen affected by the rule must abide by it or pay a penalty such as a fine. The rules and regulations promulgated by the agency become part of administrative law.

Public universities offer one example of administrative rule making. The General Assembly created most of the public institutions of higher learning in the state. These administrative institutions, along with their boards of regents, have been given the quasilegislative authority to make rules and regulations applicable to student life on campus. The rules are then enforced by campus security personnel. Most of the rules with which students must comply while on campus are probably of this nature rather than of the statutory variety.

Some agencies are also given the power to settle disputes in which citizens or clientele groups affected by the agencies are parties. The results of such administrative adjudication also become part of the body of administrative law. Rulings by the Missouri Public Service Commission as to the reasonableness of rates charged by private

---

1. For a discussion of the scope of administrative law, see Kenneth F. Warren, *Administrative Law in the American Political System* (St. Paul: West Publishing Company, 1982), pp. 6–16.

utility companies are an example of this type of administrative law.

In emergency situations, the governor of a state may issue an executive order that has the effect of creating law as far as the general public is concerned. When Governor Joseph Teasdale decreed that trucks heavier and longer than those allowed by the General Assembly could travel on Missouri's highways on a temporary basis, he was adding to administrative law.

Administrative laws now outnumber statutory laws. In Missouri, a person who wants to learn the administrative law on a subject will usually consult the *Code of State Regulations*, which includes all Missouri regulations currently in force. In addition, proposed new regulations or changes in existing regulations are published in the *Missouri Register*, which is issued twice each month.

III. Constitutional Law

In Missouri, constitutional law is supreme, superior to any conflicting form of positive law. The basis of constitutional law is the Missouri Constitution of 1945, including its amendments. In addition, all Missouri citizens have rights guaranteed in the U.S. Constitution (see chapter 1). Most constitutional law is derived from judicial interpretations of state and federal constitutions and their amendments in cases brought before the courts. Much constitutional law stems from the exercise of judicial review, the power of a court to declare unenforceable laws that the court considers to be in conflict with the constitution.[2]

Judicial review and the formation of most constitutional law occur in situations in which a type of law (such as common, statutory, or administrative) is alleged to be in conflict with the supreme law—the constitution—and a court is called on to determine whether a conflict exists. An example of this predominant form of judicial review occurred in 1994 when the Missouri Supreme Court voided parts of a 1993 statute authorizing riverboat gambling. The Missouri Constitution makes it unlawful for the General Assembly to authorize lotteries or "gift enterprises." In *Harris v. Missouri Gaming Commission*, the Missouri Supreme Court ruled that keno, numbers tickets, pull tabs, jar tickets, push cards, punchboards, and traditional slot machines constituted lotteries forbidden by the state constitution. Thus, the authorization of these games on riverboats by the 1993 act was unconstitutional.[3]

The court reasoned that games are not lotteries if they have an element of skill that increases the possibility of "winning" and enables one participant to be a better player than others. The court upheld the General Assembly's authorization of the games of poker and twenty-one, on the grounds that these games possessed the necessary element of skill. The games disapproved by the court were regarded as having no such element of skill.[4]

2. See Henry J. Abraham, *The Judicial Process: An Introductory Analysis of the Courts of the United States, England, and France,* 6th ed. (New York and Oxford: Oxford University Press, 1993), p. 271.

3. Missouri Constitution, Article III, section 39(9). The prohibition was amended in 1978 to allow Missourians who won prizes in the Reader's Digest Sweepstakes or similar contests to accept their prizes; in 1980 to allow bingo to be conducted by religious, charitable, or similar organizations; and in 1984 to allow the Missouri state lottery and pari-mutuel betting on horse racing. For more detail on the ruling that slot machines on riverboats were unconstitutional, see *Harris v. Missouri Gaming Commission,* 869 S.W.2d 58 (1994).

4. The 1993 act had also authorized some other forms of gambling, including baccarat, craps, roulette wheel, klondike table, faro layout, and video games of chance. The Missouri Supreme Court ordered the circuit court to consider evidence and determine whether these games constituted lotteries or games of chance.

IV. Common Law and Equity

As the previous example illustrates, much of the meaning of the law comes from the interpretations of judges, based in part on their understanding of the constitution, the laws passed by the legislature, or the rules made by an administrative agency. In fact, much of the original development of the law came from the decisions of judges, and this body of decisions has come down to us as common law. For some lay people, the term *common law* was first heard with regard to a "common law marriage"—a situation in which a couple was not formally married, but had lived together for some time. If one spouse died without a will, the other might sue to win control of the estate. The law usually provided that the estate should go to the nearest living relative. Over time, judges decided that some couples had lived together for enough years that the arrangement could be considered a marriage and that the surviving spouse had the same rights as if the couple had been formally married. It should be noted that by statute in Missouri, common law marriages are regarded as null and void, although such marriages entered into before 1921 are considered valid.[5]

Common law is the judge-made body of laws that originated in custom in medieval England,[6] and which developed largely by means of the rule of *stare decisis* (that is, that judges should base their rulings on the legal principles of similar judicial decisions made in the past). When judges decide such cases, they do not have the benefit of a document such as a constitution or statute to which they can look for the applicable legal rule. Instead, the applicable legal rule is derived from the judicial process itself.

In deciding an issue at common law, the court will look to the past for similar cases. Having discovered such a case, the court declares the legal principle (or *ratio decidendi*) that was the basis of that ruling, then by the process of deductive reasoning applies the principle to the slightly different factual situation of the current case. Thus, the process is said to involve discovery, declaration, and deduction.

Common law is often called "unwritten," because it is not found in a single document or collection of volumes that can conveniently fit on a bookshelf. Perhaps with modern computer databases the common law will become as accessible as statutory law. But traditionally, common law has been considered to exist in thousands of appellate court opinions accumulated through the ages in the Anglo-American legal system.

Common law is found in appellate court opinions because it is mainly judges with jurisdiction or power to decide cases on appeal from lower or trial courts who write formal, written opinions. Courts with such appellate (rather than primarily original) jurisdiction usually have more

---

Soon thereafter, the legislature referred to voters a constitutional amendment to allow games of chance on riverboats, but this was narrowly defeated in April 1994. Subsequently, proponents of riverboat gambling circulated petitions for another constitutional amendment to allow games of chance on riverboats, and this was adopted by public vote in November 1994.

5. RSMo, 1986, Sec. 451.040(5). See also Jack Cochran, *Missouri Practice*, vol. 21, *Family Law* (St. Paul, Minn.: West Publishing Company, 1990), 391. Cochran notes that Missouri courts have recognized the validity of common law marriages that are contracted elsewhere, but not when the parties were (1) residents of Missouri before, at the time of, or after the alleged marriage, or (2) only brief residents of the state in which the marriage was allegedly contracted.

6. To traditional jurists such as Blackstone, the notion that judges made law was anathema. They contended that judges *discovered* the law. In their view, the legal rule could be found, for example, in local custom, in precedents (prior judicial decisions), or in nature (or the nature of things). In regard to the latter, see the quotation from Cicero at the beginning of this chapter, and the section on natural law later in this chapter.

manpower—several judges per bench—and decide fewer cases. Thus, they can explain their decisions in written form, following an informal outline that includes the facts, issues, holdings, and reasoning of the cases. These opinions eventually are published and find their way to bookshelves in law libraries. (Trial courts or courts of original jurisdiction decide so many cases that they normally do not have time to write opinions accompanying their decisions.)

While common law principles are written down in the form of countless appellate court opinions, they are not conveniently marked as "principles" per se, and mastering them requires experience and training. Certain helpful jurists, such as Sir Edward Coke, Sir William Blackstone, Chancellor James Kent, and Justice Joseph Story, wrote commentaries on the common law in which they set forth what they considered to be its most important principles. These were convenient sources for students such as Abraham Lincoln, who taught himself the law. But these commentaries were not the law itself—just esteemed judges' opinions as to its essence.

The common law was transported by the British to their far-flung colonies, and the legal system spread throughout the world. When the American colonies became independent states, each one, being sovereign, could decide whether to retain the common law, and if so, to what extent. Although the new states' decisions varied, for the most part they retained the system. Each state then further developed the common law on its own, with its own hierarchy of courts, at the same time referring to the precedents from other states and nations. The common law (with some modifications) became the basis of the law of each state.

In the American colonies and independent states, the common law composed by far the largest part of the law that was available. It retained this status until the early twentieth century, when it was surpassed in quantity by statutory law. Before the nineteenth century, legislatures had been relatively weak, and even after that, they met infrequently and for short periods. They would pass a few laws, but their output would not be extensive.

The common law held the capacity for change, because (1) previous similar rulings were not always found by lawyers and judges; (2) past cases needed to be similar to be regarded as binding, and similarity was a matter of judgment; (3) no two cases were ever exactly alike; and (4) *stare decisis* was not an absolute rule. In the latter regard, for example, the Missouri Supreme Court is not bound by rulings of the Illinois Supreme Court or the Queen's Bench in England.

Despite this capacity for change, the common law could not keep pace with the drastic wrenching of the political, social, and economic systems set in motion by the Industrial Revolution. Political interest groups and parties began to clamor for rapid and wholesale change, and legislatures, responding to pressures from an expanding number of voters (as the population increased and voting barriers began to fall), passed statutes changing or in some cases restating the common law rules. Accordingly, statutes were passed providing remedies that the common law did not grant.

One of the most famous common law principles was the doctrine of sovereign immunity. Originating in the questionable assumption that "the King can do no wrong," the principle prohibited suits against the sovereign government without its consent. In Missouri, the rule, with considerable modification and amplification, survived until recently, when the Missouri Supreme Court abolished it. Prior to 1977, Missouri courts' treatment of the principle had resulted in protection of the state, counties, and most other political subdivisions such as school, road, and drainage districts from liability in lawsuits. Cities enjoyed immunity from citizen lawsuits if the suits involved the governmental function of the city, but not if they involved a proprietary function, such as providing water or electricity.

Missouri courts not only had fashioned these specific rules in regard to sovereign immunity but also had determined, by a series of cases, which functions were governmental (such as regulating street traffic, managing schools and hospitals, and operating police and fire departments) and which were proprietary (such as managing waterworks or utility plants, and maintaining streets, sidewalks, parks, and swimming pools). Even in the case of governmental activities, a municipality could be liable if its activities constituted a nuisance.

In *Jones v. State Highway Commission* (1977) the Missouri Supreme Court ruled by a four-to-three vote that the doctrine of sovereign immunity was abrogated, or no longer valid.[7] The *Jones* case involved a suit for money damages against the state's highway commission for injuries suffered by a woman who lost control of her car after it left the road on a curve and dropped onto a lower shoulder of uneven surface. She alleged that the commission was negligent in its maintenance of the road and in its failure to warn motorists of the road's condition. The supreme court sent the case back to the trial (circuit) court, which had relied on the sovereign immunity doctrine because it was the accepted common law up to that point. A jury of the circuit court subsequently ruled in favor of the state highway commission.

The arguments made by the supreme court indicated that the justices were trying to explain their decision so that others would accept this change in the common law. For example, the supreme court noted that the Missouri courts had eroded the doctrine of sovereign immunity as it applied to municipalities, and it reasoned that if courts could modify the principle, then they could also cancel it completely. The court also noted that twenty-nine states and the District of Columbia had abrogated by judicial decision either completely or partially the doctrine of sovereign immunity from tort liability (torts are private or civil wrongs or injuries). The court also said that the ruling did not apply to the exercise of governmental functions by governmental bodies.

One of the bases on which the Missouri Supreme Court decided against this common law doctrine was its conflict with statutory law. A Missouri statute provided that the state's highway commission "may sue and be sued in its official name." Although previous decisions of the Missouri Supreme Court had held that this language did not mean the agency could be sued for wrongs that it had committed, the court in *Jones* applied what is known as the "plain meaning rule" of statutory interpretation and ruled in effect that the statute meant what it said. The court thereby provided a statutory basis for its decision. Shortly thereafter, however, the legislature, responding to fears of local officials that eliminating the immunity doctrine would cause a deluge of lawsuits, passed a law partially reestablishing sovereign immunity.[8]

7. 557 S.W.2d 225 (1977). Since 1957, opinions of the Supreme Court of Missouri have been found in the *South Western Reporter, Second Series,* published by the West Publishing Company of St. Paul, Minnesota.

8. *Revised Statutes of Missouri* 1969, Sec. 226.100. For law partially reestablishing sovereign immunity, see, for example, *Revised Statutes of Missouri,* 1978, Sec. 537.600.

The fact that the statute displaced the conflicting common law rule illustrates that statutory law is more powerful than common law. The types of law that exist are not all entitled to the same status or respect. Constitutional law is at the apex of the hierarchy among types of positive law; statutory law ranks in the next highest echelon. The courts, of course, can interpret statutory law and can determine what it means (subject to subsequent amendment by the legislature to correct an erroneous judicial interpretation). But barring a finding that the statute conflicts with the constitution, the courts cannot reject the statutory rule or begin developing common law on the subject as if the statute had not been passed.

Equity is a body of law that was developed to overcome rigidities in the common law. In earlier days, courts were governed primarily by the common law rules. (In those days, legislatures passed few laws of any kind, and even fewer laws correcting judicial decisions that were no longer equitable.) In certain circumstances, indiscriminate application of a common law rule would be unfair, and justice required that an exception be granted to the rule.

Originally, those aggrieved by such circumstances would petition the king for a remedy, which he could grant as a matter of grace. Overwhelmed by such petitions, the king of England delegated these matters to his legal officer, the Lord Chancellor. With the ever-increasing workload, the legal officer's staff gradually expanded into an entire court system known as the Chancery.

In the United States, equity and common law actions have always been handled by the same courts in the federal judiciary, but the states have followed various patterns. In equitable actions, a jury usually is not employed. The cardinal rule of equity is that it will not provide a remedy unless the remedy "at law" is inadequate.

A typical remedy used in equity law is an injunction, a court order that prohibits someone from performing a certain act, or requires someone to do something. The penalty for noncompliance is the penalty for contempt of court. One reaction to Governor Teasdale's 1979 executive order allowing longer and heavier trucks on the highways was an attempt by railroads, which competed with trucks, to obtain an injunction barring implementation of the order. At common law, the railroads would have had to wait until the order was carried out and then sue for money damages.

V. Other Legal Classifications: Civil and Criminal Law

All law can be classified as either civil or criminal. When called to serve on a jury, citizens may be assigned to civil or criminal cases, all in the same court. Civil law consists of rules enforced by government that ordinarily involve relations between private persons or groups. Thus, the categories of torts, contracts, property, family law, and decedents' estates are civil law subjects. Civil law also includes situations in which the state is not the prosecutor, but is suing or being sued.

In civil law situations, the plaintiff is claiming to have been damaged by the defendant's action and thus is suing for money damages. The damage, perpetrated against the plaintiff and not the community, is not regarded as sufficiently serious to be considered a crime against the state. The plaintiff probably has asked the defendant for compensation for the damage, and the defendant has refused to provide compensation, or at least enough to satisfy the plaintiff. The plaintiff subsequently has initiated the action by filing an original action or complaint in court. The costs are borne by one or both parties, usually by the loser, in accordance with state law and the judge's decision.

Criminal law consists of binding legal rules that define offenses against the public or state and that prescribe punishment by fine, imprisonment, or both for those convicted of such offenses in actions prosecuted by the government. Such offenses are considered sufficiently serious to justify action against the alleged wrongdoer by the government, which bears the expense of the action. Criminal law is divided into felonies (major crimes) and misdemeanors (minor crimes). Most criminal law is state law rather than federal law. Missouri's criminal law is typical of that in most states.

Missouri defines a crime as a statutorily prescribed offense for which a sentence of death or imprisonment is authorized. In Missouri, a crime is a felony if it is so designated or if a person convicted of it may be sentenced to death or imprisonment for more than one year. If a fine is imposed for a felony conviction, normally the penalty exceeds one thousand dollars. A crime is a misdemeanor in Missouri if it is so designated or if a person convicted of it may be sentenced to imprisonment for one year or less. If a fine is imposed for a misdemeanor conviction, the penalty normally does not exceed one thousand dollars. Missouri has four classes of felonies and three classes of misdemeanors.

In Missouri, an offense is an infraction if it is so designated or if no sentence other than a fine, fine and forfeiture, or other civil penalty is authorized upon conviction. Thus, there is no authorized imprisonment, and an infraction is not a crime. Ordinarily, the penalty for an infraction does not exceed two hundred dollars. Most traffic offenses fall under this category, but some serious traffic offenses can be regarded as misdemeanors,[9] and very serious ones can be regarded as a felony.

VI. Private and Public Law

13 The classification between private and public law is also useful. Private law generally involves binding rules applicable to relations between nongovernmental individuals or groups. Law courses such as torts, contracts, property, family law, trusts and estates, commercial law, corporations, and corporate finance are typical private law subjects.

Public law consists of binding rules that regulate relations between government and private persons, and relations between governmental branches or units. Since the late nineteenth century, when the study of political science became a separate academic discipline (by breaking away from political economy and history), public law has been recognized as one of the major subdivisions of political science.[10] This feature of the discipline helped make political science a popular "pre-law" major, a status that it has maintained to this day.

Public law has been popular with political science professors as well as with undergraduates. During the early years of the profession, the chairman of the department often taught the public law courses. Typical public law courses in a political science curriculum include, for example, "The American Constitution" and "The Constitution and Civil Rights."

VII. Natural Law and Positive Law

An ancient and long-established classification of law is based on whether the rules of human conduct are made by human beings. Natural law is composed of universal, eternal, and basic rules of justice that are

9. See Title 19 of *RSMo*, Cum. Sup. 1993, especially Sec. 302.340, for example.

10. For an informative account of the development of the discipline, see Albert Somit and Joseph Tanenhaus, *The Development of Political Science: From Burgess to Behavioralism* (Boston: Allyn and Bacon, 1967). See also Oscar Ibele, *Political Science: An Introduction* (Scranton, Pa.: Chandler Publishing Company, 1971), pp. 7–17.

ascertainable either by (1) human reason or logic, or (2) divine revelation. Many people accept the Ten Commandments as a divine revelation embodying fundamental principles of human conduct that differentiate right from wrong. Adherents regard these tenets as superior to conflicting law made by human beings and institutions. Collectively, they represent Truth. Natural law just exists; it is not made by humans but is discovered by them, or revealed to them.

Social contract theorists such as Hobbes, Locke, and Rousseau, in explaining the reasons for the establishment of government, wrote of a pregovernmental state of nature in which natural law was applicable. In the late seventeenth century, Locke explained that humans left the state of nature and entered into society by giving up some of their natural rights that existed in natural law. People retained their inalienable rights to life, liberty, and property, and the main job of the government that was established by the social contract was to protect these rights, especially property.

These Lockean concepts, with slight modification, were carried over into the Declaration of Independence by Thomas Jefferson: "We hold these truths to be self-evident, that all men are created equal, that they are endowed by their creator with certain unalienable rights, that among these are life, liberty and the pursuit of happiness—that to secure these rights, governments are instituted among men." These concepts were also carried into the contract clause and other provisions of the U.S. Constitution—as well as the due process clauses of its amendments—and became part of the American constitutional heritage. Obviously, natural law has affected Missouri jurisprudence in such areas as criminal law, property law, and rules of civil and criminal procedure.

In contrast to natural law, which according to its adherents simply exists and is not made by humans, positive law *is* made by humans and their institutions. Positive law includes all of the other types of law discussed in this chapter, although natural law helped shape legal rules in those areas.

VIII. Conclusions

Although frequent references are made to "the law," law is of various types or forms. Many types of law that are made, enforced, and interpreted in Missouri can be differentiated on the basis of their source. According to the separation-of-powers principle, legislatures make the law, but in the opinion of many writers, the executive agencies make administrative laws, and courts make common law. An important dichotomy concerns law that just simply exists and has no apparent human source, and law that emanates from human beings or governmental institutions.

Any particular law or legal rule may fall under several categories of law. For example, a negligence case would be classified under the law of torts, which is part of private law, civil law, and positive law.

Types of law are not all accorded the same respect. Among the types of positive law, constitutional law ranks at the top of the hierarchy, followed by statutory law and then common law.

There are many differences of opinion as to the definition, the scope, and even the existence of certain types of law; typologies will differ. Some analysts view administrative law, for example, in a much narrower sense than do others, while still others do not recognize it as a separate type of law at all.

CHAPTER 8

The Missouri General Assembly
by David Valentine

[The state legislator] is always confronted with more demands than he can satisfy; he is always in danger of displeasing someone and is never sure of just what it will take to please them; . . . he is always depending on someone else's judgment for his equanimity and his security.
—Edward A. Shils

Each year in early January, the legislators of the Missouri General Assembly meet in one of the finest state capitols in the nation.[1] The Missouri State Capitol, built between 1913 and 1919, sits majestically on a bluff above the Missouri River. The interior of the capitol abounds with murals, paintings, and statues depicting the history and settlement of Missouri. It is a lavish setting in a state without lavish resources, and it attracts thousands of students and tourists each year. It is also where both the executive and legislative leaders conduct their business. The third floor is the legislative floor, which contains the senate chamber, the house chamber, and the offices of the legislative leadership.

The Missouri General Assembly consists of 34 senate seats, one of the smallest senates in the nation; and 163 house seats, one of the nation's largest houses of representatives (see Figures 8–1 and 8–2). General elections for seats in the house are held every two years. Senators are elected for four-year terms: those from odd-numbered senatorial districts run in presidential election years and those from even-numbered districts run in nonpresidential election years. The general elections are held in November of every even year, and the new members are installed the following January.

Space for the legislature in the capitol is divided between the house and senate, and thus senators receive convenient and ample office space. The house leaders and the more senior members receive offices of moderate size, but new members share rather crowded quarters. Each senator represents about 150,000 people while each house member represents about 31,000 people. A senator must be at least thirty years old, whereas a house member must be at least twenty-four. Senators and representatives receive a salary of eighteen thousand dollars per year plus a yearly adjustment; in fiscal year 1995 this resulted in a total salary of $24,313. Legislative leaders receive slightly more. In addition, all legislators receive $35 per day for each day of session attended as well as mileage for one round trip per week between their homes and the capitol.

The Missouri legislature is in session every year, from January through mid-May.

1. An earlier version of this chapter was coauthored with Wayne L. Francis.

Figure 8-1. Missouri's Representative Districts

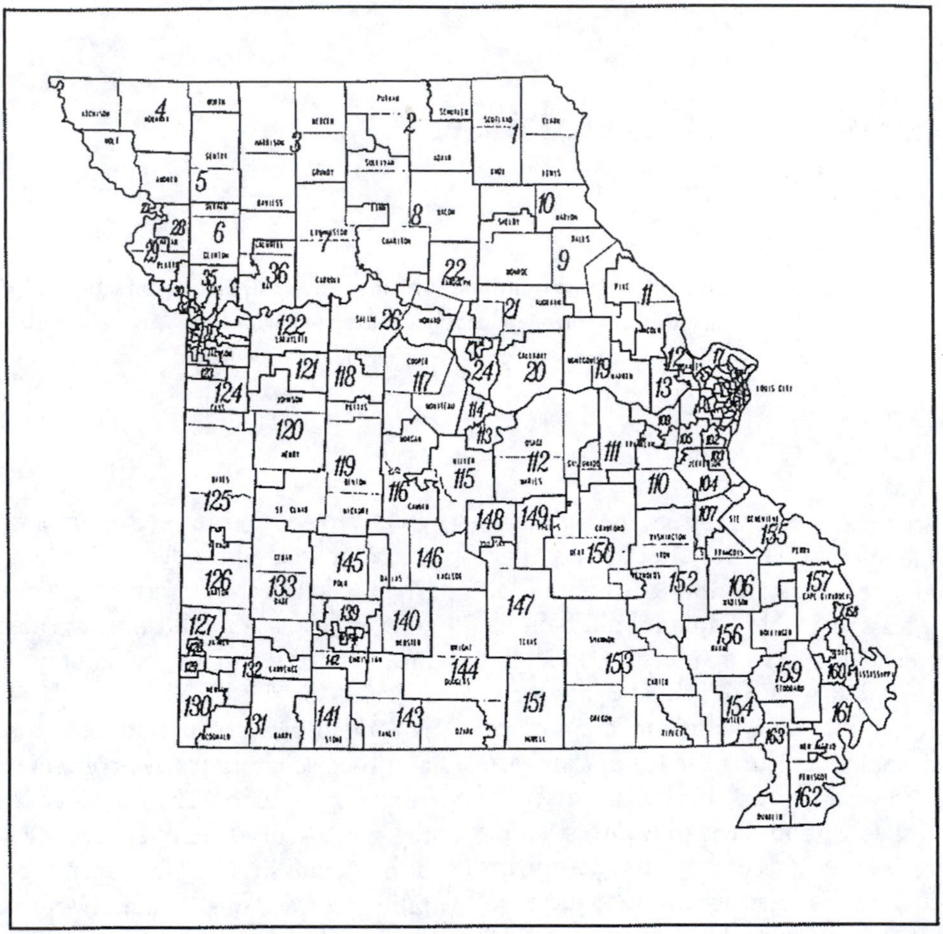

Source: *Missouri Roster 1993–1994*, Office of Secretary of State

The members normally are in Jefferson City four days a week, Monday through Thursday, and typically the chamber proceedings begin shortly after noon on Monday.

Legislators may also be called into session to address items of special importance to the state. Special sessions are usually called by the governor and are limited to sixty calendar days. In a special session, legislators can only consider items specifically mentioned in the governor's call. In 1989, the governor called a special session to raise revenue to pay for tax refunds for retirees of the federal government required by federal and state supreme court decisions.[2] In 1993 Governor Mel Carnahan called a special session to appropriate moneys for flood recovery efforts following major flooding on the Missouri and Mississippi rivers. In 1994 Carnahan called a special session to consider impeachment of Secretary of State Judi Moriarty. Since 1988 the General Assembly has had the authority to call itself into special session if the session is

2. *Hackman v. Director, Department of Revenue*, 771 S.W.2d 77 (Mo 1989).

Figure 8-2. Missouri's Senatorial Districts

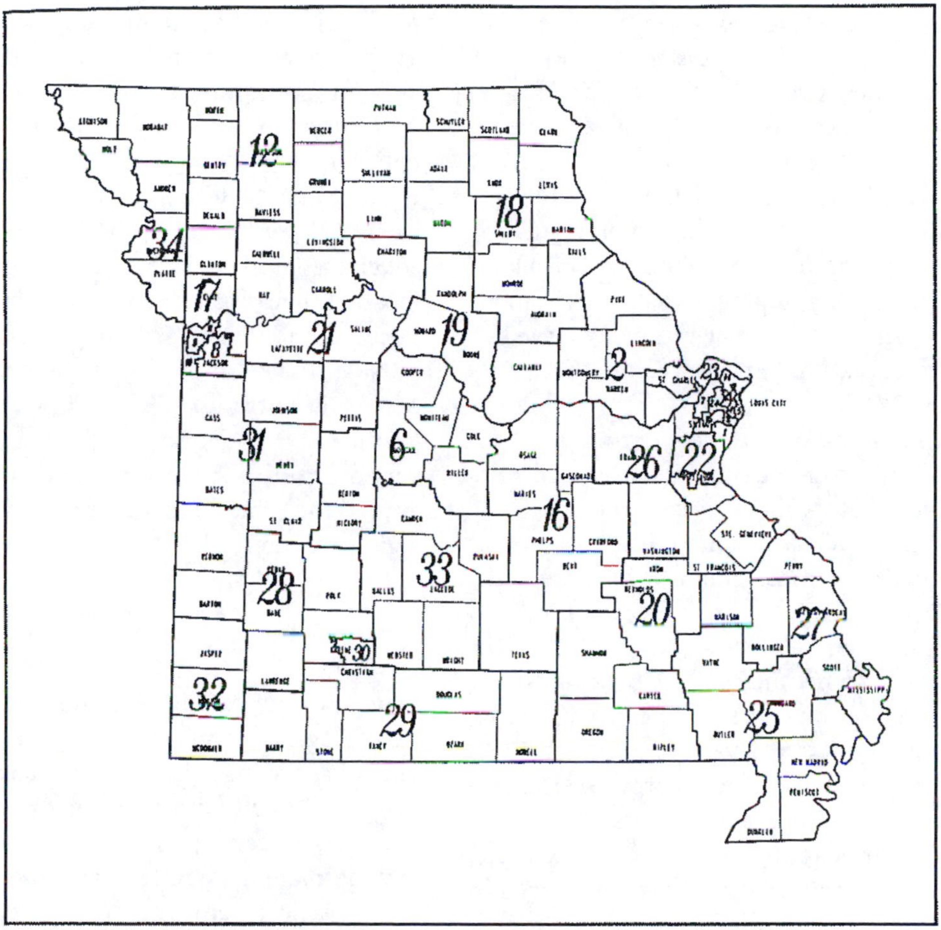

Source: *Missouri Roster 1993–1994*, Office of Secretary of State

supported by three-fourths of the members of both chambers, but it has yet to use this authority.

I. Legislators and Legislative Roles

Legislators have backgrounds that in some ways are representative of and in other ways are distinct from the districts that send them to the General Assembly. Most legislators, nearly 80 percent of those in office in 1991, were born in Missouri, and almost all of them have been longtime residents of the communities from which

they were elected. The typical legislator is a college-educated white male who is in his late forties or early fifties. The number of women in the legislature has increased in recent years, but women still constitute only about 20 percent of the house and only about 10 percent of the senate.[3]

For most of its history, the Missouri General Assembly was predominantly composed of men drawn from farming, small

3. The changing role of women in the legislature is described by Virginia Young, "The Woman's Touch," *St. Louis Post-Dispatch*, March 30, 1993.

town "main street" business, and legal backgrounds. In earlier times, fewer demands were made of legislators. The dominant views of the district were stable, constituents required few services, single-issue interest groups were rare, and the responsibilities of lawmaking were relatively light. The typical legislative act, for example, was a one- or two-page affair regulating business, agriculture, or the powers of local governments, matters that the farmers, businessmen, and lawyers who served in the legislature experienced in their daily lives.

But none of these conditions hold today and, consequently, the lives and roles of legislators have become increasingly complex. Constituent opinion is not as stable and, more important, there often are sharp differences of opinion within the district. Conflicting demands from the public, sometimes fueled by single-issue interest groups, create uncertainty about public opinion and force legislators to spend more time and energy ascertaining the views of their constituents.

Major economic interests, for example, are able to mount intensive campaigns in support of their objectives. In 1994, for example, Southwestern Bell launched a campaign, complete with television ads and hundreds of letters written to legislators, in support of legislation that would free the company from regulation by the Missouri Public Service Commission. Likewise, during the final days of the 1994 session, one senator, whose district happened to contain a major insurance company, received more than one hundred phone calls in a single day, all in opposition to proposed health care legislation.

Similarly, the issues that the legislator as lawmaker must consider have become more difficult. In recent legislative sessions, for example, the General Assembly

has grappled with issues like the funding of public education, health care, and air quality; issues that are not merely beyond the everyday experiences of legislators but also are so complex that they are fully understood by only a few people in the entire state.

The Missouri General Assembly is considered a part-time legislature, and Missouri legislators are generally proud of the fact that theirs is a citizen legislature, composed of individuals who have "real" jobs outside of government. But the demands of constituency and of lawmaking are such that many conscientious legislators have a very difficult time meeting these demands and, at the same time, those of their non-legislative careers.[4]

II. Electoral Competition

Much has been made of the "incumbency advantage" in both state and national legislative bodies. Incumbents are viewed as having inherent advantages that make it difficult for a challenger to mount a successful campaign. These advantages include name recognition and the ability to intercede in government on behalf of constituents.

Measures of the incumbency advantage do not take into account legislators who voluntarily retire, some of whom may have chosen to retire rather than face a bruising campaign and possible defeat. Nonetheless, incumbents contest about two-thirds of the 180 legislative seats up for election every two years and only a handful are defeated. Between 1980 and 1994, for example, only four incumbent senators were

---

4. For an interesting description of the complexity of the legislative roles and the legislative process in Kansas during the 1989 legislative session, see Burdett A. Loomis, *Time, Politics and Policies* (Lawrence: University of Kansas Press, 1994).

Table 8-1. Percentages of Legislative Districts
Uncontested, Primary and General Elections, 1986–1994

	Percent Uncontested in Primary					Percent Uncontested in General				
	1986	1988	1990	1992	1994	1986	1988	1990	1992	1994
House										
Uncontested by Republicans	90	83	85	86	88	37	37	39	28	22
Uncontested by Democrats	76	71	82	67	72	13	18	17	13	16
Senate										
Uncontested by Republicans	88	94	76	89	65	29	35	12	29	12
Uncontested by Democrats	71	94	76	42	48	12	12	18	18	6

Source: *Official Manual, State of Missouri*, for the years indicated.

defeated, and each contest involved extenuating circumstances that made the incumbent vulnerable.

A large part of the incumbency advantage in Missouri arises from the lack of competition, both within and between the parties, as shown in Table 8–1. From 1986 to 1994 the Democrats had primary competition in only 27 percent of the seats up for election while the Republican candidates faced competition from within their party in only 14 percent of the elections. Intraparty competition is uncommon for candidates of both parties, but Democrats are more likely to face competition from within their own party than are Republicans, possibly because serving in the legislature as a member of the majority party is more attractive than serving as a member of the minority party.

Interparty competition is also relatively low. In recent years, about half of the seats in the house had only one candidate in the general election. For the period shown in Table 8–1, 33 percent of the house seats went uncontested by Republicans and 15 percent were uncontested by Democrats. There has been greater interparty competition in the senate, but fully 35 percent of the seats were uncontested by one party.

The lack of competition does not reflect the power of incumbency, but rather the weakness of party organizations at the local level. Candidates for election in the house in 1992 who did not have general election opposition had the same average tenure (7.6 years) as that of state representatives as a whole.

III. Incumbency Competition and Campaign Costs

Almost every observer of the American political scene laments the high cost of campaigns, and with good reason. The cost of campaigns continues to rise at every level of government. As costs increase, fund-raising becomes an essential component of the candidate's efforts and interest group contributions become more critical to success. The increase in expensive legislative campaigns is indicated by the increase in the number of candidates for the house of representatives who spent more than fifteen thousand dollars in the general election, an increase from eight in 1986 to thirty-two in 1992. Among candidates for the senate, the number who spent more than seventy-five thousand dollars in the primary and general election combined increased from five in 1986 to

Table 8-2. **Competition and General Election Campaign Costs, Missouri Senate, 1992**

Competitiveness	# of Districts	Average Expenditure Per Candidate	Expenditure Range
Incumbent without opponent	5	$ 6,634	$ 908 – $ 14,162
Incumbent with opponent	9	$18,769	$ 1,000* – $ 57,460
Open district/two candidates	3	$77,994	$33,452 – $139,345

*Four challengers spent less than $1,000 in the general election.
Source: *1992 Missouri Annual Campaign Finance Report*, Missouri Ethics Commission.

eleven in 1992.[5] More and more often, legislative candidates feel that they must raise and spend large sums of money to be elected.

Not surprisingly, competition for office is a major factor influencing the magnitude of campaign costs. Consider the 1992 general election costs for the senate shown in Table 8–2. Most people, other than perhaps incumbents, believe that electoral competition is a healthy and necessary component of a democratic society. Yet perversely, competitiveness can increase the candidate's dependency on generous contributions and especially on interest group contributors. Competition between two candidates when neither is an incumbent can be both intense and costly, as is shown in Table 8–2.[6]

On balance, an incumbent legislator has opportunities to raise campaign funds that are not available, or as available, to an opponent. The incumbent has established a voting record of support for and opposition to various legislative proposals, which affected citizens and interest groups can use to determine whether he or she should receive a campaign contribution. The in-cumbent has a working relationship with representatives of and lobbyists for these groups. The incumbent, then, is likely to be a known quantity, while the challenger's positions are less well known and his or her voting behavior is unpredictable.

Since the mid–1970s, Missouri has struggled with the complex problems of campaign finance and campaign reporting. In 1974 a revision of Missouri's campaign laws was submitted to the voters by initiative petition. Although it was approved by 78 percent of the voters, the Missouri Supreme Court subsequently declared the initiative unconstitutional on a number of grounds in a decision that was consistent with the Buckley decision of the U.S. Supreme Court.[7]

In 1994 the General Assembly adopted a major revision of the Campaign Finance Laws. The new law prohibited legislative candidates from accepting contributions during the legislative session and limited the contributions that an individual could make to a candidate. The law established "voluntary" expenditure limits and imposed significant penalties for noncompliance with the "voluntary" limits. The sponsors hoped to limit campaign costs without violating Missouri and U.S. Supreme Court decisions that held that

5. Data are from *Missouri Annual Campaign Finance Report,* for 1986, published by the Secretary of State, and for 1992, published by the Missouri Ethics Commission.

6. See also Gary Moncrief and W. David Patton, "Upping the Campaign Ante as Parties Compete to Control State Legislatures," *State and Local Government Review* 25 (Winter 1993), 39–44.

7. *Labor's Educational and Political Club-Independent v. John C. Danforth et al,* 501 S.W.2d 339; *Buckley v. Valeo,* 424 U.S. 1 (1974).

campaign spending is a form of free speech that can only rarely be limited.

Later that same year the Association of Community Organizations for Reform Now (ACORN), a citizens' group, proposed by initiative a lower limit on the size of contributions to candidates, and Missouri voters adopted their proposal, known as Proposition A, by an overwhelming 74 percent. This proposal limited contributions from any single source to one hundred dollars per term for members of the house and two hundred dollars per term for members of the senate, and required the return of excess funds after each election. The contribution limits in Proposition A were immediately challenged in federal court and the court temporarily stayed enforcement of the contributions limits. Earlier, identical limits adopted in Minnesota had been ruled unconstitutional by the U.S. Eighth District Court of Appeals.

None of the limits in either law apply to independent expenditures—expenditures made by individuals, organizations, or corporations that are not under the control of the candidate. Court decisions have cautioned that limits on such expenditures would be restrictions on the freedom of speech of those individuals or groups. Independent expenditures have been used increasingly in congressional election campaigns, which have been more tightly regulated than state campaigns; for example, the National Rifle Association purchased advertisements against Missouri Congressman Tom Coleman in 1992. The net effect of these two Missouri reform efforts may be to change the way money flows in campaigns without reducing the overall cost of campaigns; to make it more difficult to identify the supporters (and opponents) of any particular candidate; and to diffuse control over campaigns, especially media campaigns, by reducing

the candidate's accountability for the tone and content of the campaign.

IV. The Leadership

Observers of state legislatures typically find that legislatures have become more decentralized over the last three decades. At one time, legislative power was centralized in the hands of the governor, legislative leaders, and policy committees, themselves composed of legislative leaders. Today, leadership is much more diffuse. The Missouri legislature is moderately centralized, although there are significant differences in the centralization of each chamber.[8]

Formal and Informal Leadership

The formal leadership of the Missouri Senate includes the lieutenant governor, who is the president of the senate, and the leader of the majority party, who is the president pro tem of the senate. The lieutenant governor is elected separately in a statewide contest and as a consequence may or may not be of the same party as the senate majority. In Missouri, the Democrats have held until recent years a two-to-one advantage in each legislative chamber, yet, for example, a Republican lieutenant governor, William C. Phelps, served as president of the senate from 1973 to 1981 in the face of a substantial Democratic majority in the senate.

In some states, the lieutenant governor has important legislative responsibilities, including assigning bills to committee and arbitrating contested points of order during floor debate. The authority of the president of the senate—that is, of the lieutenant governor—was defined narrowly by the

8. Alan Rosenthal, *Legislative Life* (New York: Harper and Row, 1981); Alan Rosenthal, "A Vanishing Breed," *State Legislatures*, November/December 1989, 30–34; Wayne L. Francis and James W. Riddlesperger, "State Legislative Committee Systems: Structure, Procedural Efficiency and Party Control," *Legislative Studies Quarterly* (November 1982), 453–71.

Missouri Supreme Court in 1973 following a protracted battle between two successive lieutenant governors and the senate. In 1969 the Democratically controlled senate adopted rules removing some of the powers formerly exercised by the lieutenant governor and vested those powers in the president pro tem, leaving the lieutenant governor, Democrat William Morris, with significantly less authority than his predecessor, Tom Eagleton, had held. The battle was renewed in 1973 when Phelps became lieutenant governor and instituted a lawsuit to regain the authority of the office. The Missouri Supreme Court ruled that the president of the senate (the lieutenant governor) did not have the power to assign bills or rule on points of order if the membership voted to place those powers elsewhere, as it had.[9]

The president of the senate, however, does have the right to preside and to vote in case of a tie. The senate, protecting its powers, assiduously avoided tie votes while the lieutenant governor was presiding until 1993, when Democratic Lieutenant Governor Roger Wilson, a former senator, cast two tie-breaking votes.

The second formal leader of the senate is the president pro tem, who is elected by the senate membership. He is the leader of the legislative majority party, and most of the authority of the senate is vested in him.

In the Missouri House of Representatives, the membership elects two principal offices: the speaker, who not only presides but also makes all chair and committee appointments, and his chief stand-in, the speaker pro tem, who is generally a close ally of the speaker.

In each chamber, each party caucus selects a floor leader. The floor leaders are

9. *State ex. inf. Danforth v. Cason,* 507 S.W.2d 405 (1974).

not a part of the formal leadership, since their positions are not established by law, but they exercise important responsibilities nonetheless. The floor leader of the majority party becomes responsible for the day-to-day management of debate in the chamber. He sets bills for debate and determines the time and length of each day's session. The floor leader's skill in "moving the calendar," getting legislation through the chamber, is critical for making a session a success. Senator J. B. Banks of St. Louis has been the majority leader of the senate since 1989 and is the first black to hold that position. The minority floor leader is the spokesman and legislative strategist for his party within the chamber.

Leadership Contests

Battles for the chamber leadership positions can be intense, bitter, and protracted. Legislators campaign for leadership positions using the chairmanship of committees, appointment to choice committees, and campaign contributions to cement their coalition.

The most recent conflict in the senate occurred in 1980–1981 when two-term pro tem Norman Merrell (D, Lewis County) was challenged by Phil Snowden (D, Platte County). Snowden won the support of the Democratic caucus, but when the senate voted on the nomination in early January, a coalition of disgruntled Democrats and Republicans voted for Merrell, thereby electing him to his third term as pro tem.

Conflicts in the house are no less intense. Speaker Bob Griffin has the distinction of serving longer than any other speaker in Missouri history, since 1981. But immediately after Griffin's 1989 reelection, majority floor leader Tony Ribaudo made known his candidacy for the 1991 speakership; their long-running battle, won by Griffin, affected the tone and performance of the house during the 1989 and 1990 sessions.

On the first day of the 1995 session, dissident house Democrats joined with Republicans to challenge Griffin's claim to the speakership. At the end of a tumultuous day, the vote was tied 81–81; the next day Speaker Griffin eked out an 82–80 victory. Later the Democratic caucus ejected one of its freshman members for suggesting that the speaker resign. This acrimonious start set the tone for both the 1995 and 1996 legislative sessions.

Leaders in Missouri and elsewhere now tend to retain their positions longer than did their predecessors. Until the 1980s there was an informal norm that leaders retained their positions for no more than four years. Griffin has been reelected to his post every two years since his first election in 1981. Two of the last three presidents pro tem of the senate, Norman Merrell (1977–1983) and John Scott (1983–1989), were elected as pro tem three times, and the third, James Mathewson (1989–), was elected four times.

Leadership contests produce winners and losers, especially among the vocal supporters of each candidate. The losers can expect to receive undesirable committee assignments, are unlikely to be appointed to chair a committee, and are likely to have their bills bottled up in committee. The trend has been for particularly visible losers to voluntarily retire from the legislature within a short time.

Leadership Powers

Power wielded by the legislative leaders is derived from three major sources. The first is found in the characteristics of the leaders themselves: their aggressiveness, capabilities, willingness to bargain and ability in bargaining, and capacity to maintain their balance in a complex and ambiguous environment.

The second source of power is the formal rules of each legislative chamber. For example, these rules give the leaders the power to select committee chairmen, to make appointments to committees, and, although full chamber approval is required, to increase or decrease the number of committees. A committee chairmanship is important to majority party members, and there are always a number of influential committees to which all members seek to be assigned.

Appointment to influential committees and selection as a committee chairman are critically important in enhancing the visibility, influence, and impact of a legislator. Appointment to a "backwater" committee can effectively exclude a legislator from significant policy debates, reduce his or her visibility to almost zero, and dampen zest for the job.

Legislative leaders are aware of the value of committee and chair appointments and try to enhance their power by granting or withholding these appointments. Members who supported an opponent for a leadership post may be "rewarded" by an appointment to an insignificant committee chairmanship, by having a committee chairmanship withheld, or by appointments to committees in which they have no interest. Committee chairmen can be removed, although few are, and most ensure that their actions will not jeopardize their position. A rare exception was Senator Jack Gannon, a Democrat from Jefferson County, who supported Republican John Ashcroft for governor in 1984. President pro tem John Scott refused to reappoint Gannon as chairman of the Senate Banking Committee when the legislature reconvened in 1985. Gannon voluntarily retired when his term expired.

A third source of power is derived from knowledge of and ability to use the informal norms of the institution. Each chamber has its own set, with those of the senate being much more important in structuring behavior of the leadership. A successful leader of the senate must adapt his personal style to exploit the informal norms. For example, the press frequently describes that chamber as "clubby." Consequently, a confrontational senator is unlikely to become a leader in the senate, and a successful leader will not be confrontational. The leader must meld together a series of unique coalitions over the course of a session. Each coalition may contain an unlikely combination of senators representing the diverse elements of the state.

Leadership and Partisanship in the House

In the Missouri General Assembly, chamber leadership has been the exclusive prerogative of the Democratic party since 1954. The Democrats held substantial majorities for most of the intervening years, and Democratic leaders in the house especially did not need to be overly concerned about the Republican opposition. The speaker appointed all members, including Republicans, to committees. If he chose to do so, he could neutralize Republican influence by appointing the most capable Republicans to the least significant committees.

The strategy of the house Republicans in the late 1970s was largely one of cooperation. Individual Republicans were able to exert considerable influence over legislation, but a Republican party position on any given piece of legislation was unlikely. This strategy, with its focus on governing, provided Republican house members with experience in policy development and in negotiating that would have been critical if the party ever became the majority. Similarly, cooperation enhanced the job satisfaction of Republican legislators, making it more likely that the party would retain experienced and capable representatives.

Conversely, house Republican strategy through most of the 1980s and the early 1990s focused on establishing campaign positions rather than governing. Republican representatives largely gave up the opportunity for influence on specific pieces of legislation in favor of expressing a clear party position for electoral purposes. This approach assumed that the party had little internal power and sought to exert influence outside of the house—on the governor, powerful interest groups, and the public. In using this strategy, house Republicans largely forwent the governing experience that would have been gained by more extensive participation in the legislative process, but were able to establish themselves as an electoral alternative to the Democrats. The electoral strategy was effective in increasing the number of Republicans elected. Republicans gradually increased their strength in the house from fifty-one (31 percent) in 1981 to seventy-six (46 percent) in 1995. Although they failed to win a majority on November 8, 1994, an election in which Republicans were winning majorities in Congress and in many other states, house Republicans entered the 1995 session prepared to take their place as equals in the legislative process after decades on the periphery. They engineered the almost successful challenge to the speaker and effectively undermined his authority. They used constitutional provisions to remove bills from committee, where they were being held, and place them on the house perfection calendar. They challenged the rules used by the house to govern its proceedings, arguing that the rules centralize power in the hands of the speaker and committee chairmen, to the detriment of less favorably situated members, including members of the minority party. Due to conflicts over the rules, the house operated under temporary rules, rules from the previous session, for well over two months.

Leadership and Partisanship in the Senate

The situation is quite different in the senate, even though Democratic numeric dominance there has been equal to that of the house. But as in the house, Republican membership has been increasing. In 1995 Republicans held fifteen of the thirty-four seats, more than at any time since the 1950s.

The president pro tem's authority is not as expansive as that of his house counterpart. The senate's rules, informality, and friendship patterns tend to diffuse authority. As a result, senate leaders are most successful when they couple their authority with the ability to bargain with the various factions in the senate. Consequently, members of the minority party in the senate are in a very good position compared to their house counterparts. In the senate, the minority party leader selects minority members of committees.

V. Committee Structure

In most states, the number of committees tends to increase with time, until at some point the legislature decides that reorganization is necessary. In Missouri, the president pro tem and the speaker determine committee structure in their respective chambers, and thus the numbers and kinds of committees have fluctuated over the years according to their interests.

In 1974 a citizens' advisory committee issued a series of recommendations for improving legislative organization. It suggested, for example, that the number of committees should be reduced to nineteen in the house and fifteen in the senate. At that time there were forty-four in the house and twenty-five in the senate. The number of committees has never been reduced to the number recommended, and in 1993 there were forty-two in the house and twenty-one in the senate. Only three of the remaining ninety-seven state legislative bodies have more committees than those of Missouri.[10]

Most observers agree that there are too many legislative committees in Missouri. Other states manage to function with far fewer committees, and there is little doubt that Missouri could also operate effectively with fewer committees. Many states manage with fewer committees by using subcommittees. Would a subcommittee system be possible for Missouri? Recall that one way the majority leaders satisfy a member is to offer a chairmanship as a plum. Fewer chairs mean fewer plums. A subcommittee chair is not as desirable—unless perhaps subcommittees are given substantial autonomy. Further, in most systems the subcommittee chairs are appointed by the committee chair, which in turn tends to decentralize the decision making. The party leaders thus lose some ability to exchange favors for support, and they lose considerable ability to direct legislative actions on major policies.

Different committees in the various states are important for different reasons. The education committees are important in Missouri because so much of the state budget goes to education. In fiscal year 1995, almost half of state general revenue of $5.2 billion was allocated to elementary and

---

10. *Book of the States 1992–1993* (Lexington, Ky.: Council of State Governments, 1992), 191. Missouri's committees are listed in each edition of the *Official Manual, State of Missouri*.

secondary education, desegregation, and higher education. The judiciary committees are important because they deal with the structure and responsibilities of the state judicial system as well as the salaries of judges. Some committees are intermittently important when they touch on a hot issue, such as reapportionment, pollution control, energy shortages, or crime control. Finally, the so-called money committees are important because they determine levels of support for government services and the extent to which various groups may pay for such support. The money committees usually are considered the core of the committee system. In Missouri these committees are the appropriations and ways and means committees in each chamber, the budget committee in the house, and the state budget control committee in the senate.

The Budget Committees

In recent years, leaders in both the house and the senate have developed new strategies to enhance their control over the flow of legislation through their respective chambers. Any bill with a fiscal note of more than one hundred thousand dollars annually is sent to the budget committee before final action is taken by the chamber on the bill. A fiscal note is an estimate of the probable financial impact of legislation prepared by the Oversight Division of the Joint Committee on Legislative Research. Legislative leaders typically have chaired these committees or have appointed a very close ally as chair. The committees have been used as a major leadership bargaining chip to advance legislative priorities. For example, certain bills may be held "hostage" until the other chamber acts upon a legislative priority of the leadership.

The Money Committees—Taxation and Appropriation

The house and senate committees on ways and means determine both the level of state taxes and the groups that will bear the brunt of the taxes. Likewise, the appropriations committees in both the house and the senate set the amount of state funding for all state agencies and programs, and thus affect the distribution of benefits.

Most tax proposals considered by these committees in a typical year, however, are quite modest. In fact, very few major tax proposals have been considered in recent years. Major tax increases were considered in 1983, 1988, and 1989, but were not passed by the General Assembly. In 1991 the General Assembly submitted, by referendum, a major tax increase to fund both elementary and secondary education and higher education, but the referendum was soundly defeated by the voters. In 1992 the General Assembly enacted a six cents per gallon tax increase for highways, and in 1993 the General Assembly enacted a tax increase of approximately $300 million for elementary and secondary education.

The appropriations committees are the second major type of money committee. They are the most visible legislative committees because they review Missouri's more than $12 billion budget. Budget preparation is begun by state agencies soon after the fiscal year starts in July. Each department's budget is submitted to the governor, who revises budget requests according to his priorities and revenue estimates and then submits the entire budget to the appropriations committees. These committees rarely make major changes in the governor's budget request. In most years, the final budget passed by the General Assembly is less than 1 percent larger than the governor's request. (For a detailed description of the budget process, see chapter 13.)

Nonetheless, the marginal changes made by the appropriations committees can be extremely important to those affected. A change in the Medicaid reimbursement rate for prescription drugs, for example, will directly affect the state's pharmacists. Or the small amount of dollars added to the capital improvements budget for a new building at a state university might benefit not only the faculty and the students, but the local economy as well.

VI. Legislative Committees

In Missouri, as in most states, the chair of a committee is in a very powerful position. First, he or she has the ability to set the agenda—to decide which bills will be considered and in what order. In recent years, leaders in both chambers have attempted to limit congestion of the legislative calendars by restricting the number of bills that a committee can report to the floor. This has greatly strengthened the power of the committee chair because the chair decides which of the bills voted out of committee will be reported to the floor and the order in which they will be reported.

Tremendous demands are made on committees of the Missouri General Assembly. A member of the house can expect to sit on four committees that will consider 90 to 100 bills each year, while a member of the senate can expect to serve on five or more committees that will consider 140 to 150 bills. Under these circumstances, committee activity is almost frenetic. Virtually all bills introduced will receive a hearing, but for most, even if they are voted out of committee, the committee hearing is the beginning and end of their legislative careers.

Since only a small number of bills can be considered on the floor, there is pressure to report bills out of committee as quickly as possible. Because of the shortened legislative week and the numerous committees, overlapping committee hearings are impossible to avoid. Senate members are particularly hard-pressed because they are fewer in number, serve on an average of six committees, and thus must cope with more meetings and more legislation. Average attendance is about 75 percent in house committee meetings and 67 percent in the senate.[11] Out of necessity, much of the legislation never gets serious consideration.

VII. The Processing of Legislation

To understand what takes place in the Missouri General Assembly, it is necessary to understand the relationships between the leadership offices, the regular committee meetings, and the action on the floor. Although important policy decisions are made in all three arenas, different types of decisions are made in each. Leadership offices are likely to decide which issues will be the chamber's priority—and pushed forward ahead of others. Committees make more of the substantive policy decisions concerning the content of legislation, and the committee chairman determines the priority of the legislation. Major policy divisions among legislators are evident in floor debate.

Most bills are initially proposed by a state agency or a regulated interest group such as bankers, insurance companies, or generators of hazardous waste. A legislator's involvement in the drafting of bills varies significantly by individual legislator and by issue. Sometimes a bill will be drafted on a legislator's initiative. Sometimes legislators

11. Francis and Riddlesperger, "State Legislative Committee Systems."

may participate with other interested parties in almost every aspect of the development and final drafting of a bill, but at other times they may be asked to sponsor legislation only after the drafting is complete. In many cases, legislation is devised by interested groups in meetings held throughout the interim.

Once a legislator agrees to sponsor a bill, the group or agency that proposed it or is affected by it is expected to locate other legislators who will act as cosponsors and to conduct a lobbying campaign sufficient to generate support for the bill in committee, on the chamber floor, and in the other chamber. Each bill m' st overcome a series of obstacles to become law (see Figure 8–3). In recent years, 10 to 15 percent of all bills introduced have been approved by both houses of the legislature.

After a bill is introduced, it is assigned to committee by the president pro tem of the senate or the speaker of the house. If the bill's sponsor is an ally of the leadership, the bill will probably be assigned to the committee the sponsor desires. Otherwise, the bill may be assigned to a committee less disposed to vote it out of committee and onto the floor of the chamber.

It is the sponsor's responsibility to request a hearing on his or her bill. Hearings on most bills are pro forma; little information is presented or requested. This is due in part to the large number of bills, many of which are repeats from previous years. Unlike many states, Missouri does not carry over bills from the first to the second session of the General Assembly. With carryover, a bill retains in the second session the position gained in the first. But in Missouri, each bill must begin the process anew each session. The resulting pressure upon committees contributes to inadequate committee scrutiny of many bills.

Figure 8-3. The Legislative Process in Missouri

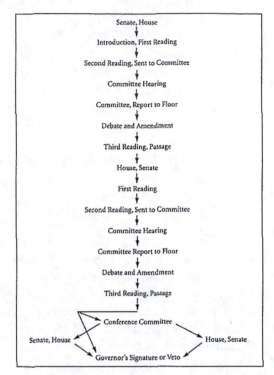

Source: *Missouri's Voter's Handbook,* League of Women Voters of Missouri.

Lobbyists can also influence the degree of scrutiny a bill will receive in committee. An effective lobbyist will discuss pending legislation with legislators well before the hearing and frequently before the beginning of the legislative session. These informal discussions can enable the advocates of legislation to resolve many of the questions that a legislator might otherwise ask during a hearing.

A bill's sponsor cannot relax even after the bill has been voted out of committee, since leaders have limited the number of bills that a single committee may report to the floor at any one time. In the past, committee chairmen were allowed to report in as many bills as were approved by their committees. The inevitable result was a mad scramble to hear and report bills to the floor early in the session—those reported out of committee after just two weeks of hearings would probably be too far down on the calendar to be considered by the full chamber, and all too often, inconsequential and noncontroversial legislation was reported out early while more important and more controversial legislation languished in committee for want of agreement. In the early 1980s, legislative leaders in both houses began to restrict the number of bills that committee chairs could report to the full chamber. This procedure enhances the power of chamber leadership and committee chairmen to determine legislative priorities.

When a bill is reported to the floor, it is placed on the Perfection Calendar, which is a list of bills awaiting floor debate and possible amendment. Normally, bills are taken up in order of their placement on the calendar. But under some circumstances, both chambers can take bills from the Perfection Calendar out of order. As an alternative, the sponsor may take the bill off the Perfection Calendar and place it on the Informal Perfection Calendar, to be taken up later. The rules of the house give its leaders much greater freedom to call bills up out of sequence than do those of the senate.

After floor debate and decisions on amendments, a motion is made to declare the bill "perfected." If that motion passes, the bill is reprinted and then goes to the calendar for a third reading and final vote. A bill "third read" or passed by one chamber must gain the approval of the second chamber in a similar manner. If a bill is approved by the second chamber without changes, it is automatically signed by the leaders of both chambers and sent to the governor. If changes were made in the bill by the second chamber that are not acceptable to the first, five conferees are appointed from each chamber to work out the differences.

Relatively few bills make it this far (see Table 8–3). In 1994, only 15 percent of the bills introduced were sent to the governor.

This summary of the process by which bills become law glosses over the central role of strategy in maneuvering a bill around legislative roadblocks. For each bill introduced, the sponsoring legislator must make a series of decisions, usually based on intuition and inadequate information. For example, is compromise with interest group X necessary? What must be traded among other legislators for support for the bill? And who is interested in trading? Legislators skillful enough to get their bill through their own chamber will face the same questions in the second chamber, where the rules and personalities may seem even more ambiguous.

VIII. Sources of Legislative Information

State governors are given abundant resources for obtaining information related to policy making. Governors not only have a sizable personal staff but also can rely on the reporting function of many administrative agencies. In recent years, state legislatures have attempted to increase their leverage, in part by improving their access to information relevant to state policies. Legislators are limited by the time demands of their position, however, to sources that are readily available. These sources include other legislators, lobbyists, constituents, and staff. In search of information, legislators will draw upon one or more of these sources, depending on personal preference and the nature of the issue.

Legislators often develop special relationships with other legislators who represent similar constituencies or who have compatible political philosophies or personal styles. Within such groups, vote

Table 8-3. Action on Legislation, Missouri General Assembly, 1994

	Senate		House	
	N	Percent	N	Percent
Introduced	409	100	838	100
Sent to second chamber	130	38	168	20
Truly agreed to*	95	23	88	11

*Sent to the Governor

trading is frequent. Exchanging information about the legislation is a by-product of vote trading.

Lobbyists are the most important external source of information. Lobbyists entertain legislators and contribute to their campaigns in order to ensure access to those legislators. Lobbyists rarely are able to provide specific information about the impact of proposed legislation. Rather, their major function is to convey the opinions of a group or business to the legislature. Legislators use this information to map the "political geography" of the issue. In truth, political intelligence such as this is frequently seen as more valuable than a detailed description of the effects of proposed legislation.

Legislators vary greatly in their attitude toward following the opinion of their constituents, but constituency opinion is most meaningful to legislators on emotional social issues and on economic issues that affect the major industries or activities of the district. On those issues, the dominant views of the district will be forcefully presented and quite evident to the lawmaker.

Finally, legislators normally rely heavily on both their staff and outside experts in dealing with complex legislation that has statewide implications. With these issues, other sources are unlikely to command the information necessary to guide legislative decisions. In addition, differences of opinion on these issues usually do not follow standing partisan, economic, or ideological divisions.

Legislators who are active, either on behalf of or in opposition to a particular bill, must also have internal information about opportunities and obstacles that present themselves as the legislative process unfolds. Lobbyists frequently provide that information. Lobbyists follow only a small number of the roughly fifteen hundred bills introduced each year and, unlike all of the other participants in the process, a lobbyist will be present at every stage in either chamber where formal action is taken on a bill. Lobbyists are also likely to be in continuing informal contact with both internal and external proponents and opponents of a particular bill. Consequently, lobbyists are in a unique position to provide invaluable strategic information that the legislator can use to further his or her legislative agenda.

IX. Legislative Relationships with Executive Agencies

The state agencies and the legislature frequently seem to be opponents. Legislators are part-time public employees who see themselves as private citizens. Most are independent business persons or lawyers who may neither understand nor trust complex bureaucratic organizations. Agency heads, furthermore, are likely to exaggerate the importance of their individual units or functions, whereas legislators are more likely to respond to a broad variety of needs or demands. These differences in perspective provide a basis for tension and potential for conflict.

The legislature has three major mechanisms, other than the law itself, that it may use to influence agency policy. The first is the budget. An agency that raises the ire of the legislature risks having its budget cut by the appropriations committee. Some of these cuts are purely symbolic, and such cuts are usually restored before the appropriations bill is finally passed. The use of this tactic, however, sends an agency a message that is almost always effective.

Second, many legislatures also use legislative oversight as a tool to evaluate and change agency policy. Legislative oversight is a periodic and systemic review of an agency's mandate and the efficiency with which it carries out its mandate. Developed in the early 1970s, legislative oversight is now used in 80 percent of the states. Oversight is accomplished through formal legislative audits, reviews of administrative regulations, and in many states with the aid of "sunset" legislation, which terminates an agency at given intervals unless it is reestablished by the legislature prior to the specified date. The Missouri General Assembly experimented with sunsets in the 1970s but has not regularly used them since. Legislative review of agency performance has not been conducted systematically in Missouri.

Finally, the General Assembly retains the authority to review specific rules and regulations issued by state agencies. When agency rule making burgeoned in the early 1970s, the legislature in 1976 and 1982 proposed and sent to the voters constitutional amendments that would have given the General Assembly clear and explicit authority to overturn proposed rules. These amendments were defeated, but the legislature has continued to exercise its legislative veto, even though in doing so it is operating on murky constitutional grounds. Two lawsuits were initiated in 1992, both at the behest of Governor Ashcroft, which challenged the rule review procedure used by the General Assembly. One of these was resolved without addressing the authority of the legislature, and the other was left pending. Perhaps as a result of these suits, the General Assembly revised its review procedures for administrative rules in 1993.

Only a very small number of the roughly two thousand rules promulgated each year are actually reviewed and only an infinitesimal number of these are suspended, but legislators cling to rule review because it gives them a means of intervening directly with agencies on behalf of their constituents or interest groups.

X. Legislative Tenure and Public Policy

In 1990 an initiative drive was organized to propose a constitutional amendment to limit the length of time that legislators can hold office to eight years in each chamber of the legislature. Missouri voters approved the limits by a majority of 75 percent in 1992. Advocates typically argue that term limits will reduce "careerism," inject new blood into the legislature, and increase competition by retiring incumbents before they would otherwise leave office. But many observers see a less public-spirited motive: "Conservative Republicans have recently promoted term limits as a way to break the Democratic hegemony over Congress and most state legislatures. The 1988 Republican party platform embraced the idea." Term limits were endorsed by the 1992 Republican party platform as well.[12]

Whatever their motivation, advocates of term limits have tapped into a powerful strain in American politics. The proposal has been successful almost everywhere it has been presented to the voters. Yet while voters have strongly supported term limits, they have simultaneously returned incumbents to office. Only time will tell whether term limits will increase Republican electoral success, but it is obvious that term limits will have far-reaching consequences for legislatures as lawmaking institutions, regardless of their partisan composition.

The term limit movement asks voters to accept the notion that a legislator in his first year is more capable, more dedicated, more honest, and makes a larger contribution to the citizens of Missouri than a ninth-year legislator. Voters may have accepted the premise, but its validity is not supported by other than anecdotal evidence. The average tenure in office is barely more than eight years in the senate and is actually less than eight years in the house. Turnover for the Missouri General Assembly from 1979 to 1989 was 72 percent.[13]

There is ample evidence that term limits will inhibit the ability of the General Assembly to resolve the complex issues that confront it. The substance of legislative activity—the drafting, evaluating, modifying, and passing of legislation—requires knowledge and a variety of skills that few new legislators bring to their position. The required knowledge for effective lawmaking includes information about the subject matter, an awareness of the positions of the groups affected by a particular piece of legislation, an understanding of the informal norms governing what legislators may and may not do while advancing their legislation, and knowledge of the rules of parliamentary procedure. A very small number of legislators are able to make a valuable contribution within their first year in office, but most require two to three years to become effective lawmakers.

Effective lawmaking requires experience, and effective leadership requires more experience. Generally, skillful members will step into positions of significant responsibility by their sixth year of service, but it is common for the more important positions to be filled by legislators with more than eight years' experience. That was the pattern in 1979 when house leaders averaged 10-year tenures and senate leaders averaged 8-year tenures, as well as in 1989, when house leaders averaged 11.8 years in office and senate leaders averaged 9.3 years. The chairs of the most powerful house committees averaged 10.7 and 11 years in office in 1979 and 1989 respectively. The comparable figures for chairs of the most important

12. Many of the individuals active in the initiative drive were associated with the ultimately unsuccessful 1990 petition drive to limit the powers of the General Assembly. According to reports filed with the secretary of state, the group spent more than $250,000 in the 1990 drive and more than $284,000 in the 1992 effort. There was little organized opposition to the term limits initiative, as evidenced by the fact that the group opposing term limits spent less than $12,000 in their effort, 4 percent of the amount spent by supporters of term limits.

For more on term limitations, see Richard Hardy, "Term Limitations for Legislators—Point/Counterpoint," *Governmental Affairs Newsletter* 25 (April 1991), 2–8, and Gerald Benjamin and Michael Malbin, eds., *Limiting Legislative Terms* (Washington, D.C.: CQ press, 1992); the quotation is from Andrew C. Miller, "Tough Partisan Fight Is Looming over Term Limitations," *Kansas City Star*, November 11, 1990.

13. John Ballard, "Term Limitations for Legislators—Point/Counterpoint," *Governmental Affairs Newsletter*

25 (April 1991), 2–8; Jack Stapleton Jr., "Unintended Consequences," *Daily Dunklin Democrat*, August 13, 1991, and "The Dangers of Experience," *Daily Dunklin Democrat*, September 24, 1991; *Book of the States, 1992–1993*, 127.

senate committees were 10 years and 9.8 years.[14]

The fact that current leaders typically have more than eight years of experience does not prove that such experience is required, but when the length of apprenticeship is factored into the equation, it is obvious that term limits will remove legislators from the General Assembly just as they become capable of making an important contribution to the legislature and the state. At the same time, term limits will bring new blood into legislative leadership positions, but whether these new leaders would have the breadth of experience and the depth of knowledge required for successful performance is another matter.[15]

Term limits will have serious consequences for the legislature as an institution. The removal of longer-tenured members deprives the remaining members of institutional memory, a critical element in the successful performance of any complex organization. Similarly, the removal of those with the substantive knowledge of the law and the issues will weaken the General Assembly as a policy-making institution. But if the legislature is weakened, other forces involved in policy development, especially interest groups and their lobbyists and state agencies, will be strengthened.[16]

XI. Conclusion

More than twenty years ago, the Citizens Conference on State Legislatures published a study of the capacity of all fifty state legislatures. The group studied each state's weaknesses, ranked the states, and made recommendations for each one. The impetus for the study was the widely held view that state legislatures were operating under laws, rules, and norms more suitable for the nineteenth than the twentieth century, but the conference members believed that legislatures could and "should become genuinely creative institutions capable of anticipating public needs and originating public policy."[17]

Each state legislature was rated on how functional, informed, independent, and representative it was. The Missouri General Assembly had an overall ranking of thirty-sixth—that is, thirty-five state legislatures were found to perform better overall than the Missouri General Assembly. Missouri's rankings on the four measures varied widely. The legislature was ranked fifth in representativeness, the degree to which it mirrored the social and ethnic composition of the state and the extent to which the procedures of the legislature allowed members to assist their constituents. But the legislature ranked forty-ninth in independence, the ability of the legislature to act as a policy-making body, independent of interest groups, state agencies, and the governor.

The Missouri General Assembly adopted a number of the recommendations from the conference in the decade after the study, *The Sometime Governments,* was published, but in the absence of another study, no one can say for certain how much the legislature's performance has improved. One can say for certain, however, that the en-

14. Data from *Official Manual, State of Missouri,* for the years indicated. House leaders included the speaker, speaker pro tem, majority floor leader, and minority floor leader. Senate leaders included the president pro tem and the floor leaders. Committees included education, judiciary, ways and means, and appropriations.

15. See Terry Ganey, "How Fast Can Legislators Learn?" *St. Louis Post-Dispatch,* November 5, 1992.

16. The enhanced position of California's veteran lobbyists with term limits is explored by Charles Price, "Advocacy in the Age of Term Limits: Lobbying after Proposition 140," *California Journal* (October 1993), 31–34.

17. Citizens Conference on State Legislatures, *The Sometimes Governments: A Critical Study of the 50 American Legislatures* (New York: Bantam Books, 1971); the quotation is from page 4.

vironment that confronts the legislature, including the number and sophistication of lobbyists, the scope of state agencies and state programs, and the issues that require resolution, is vastly more complex than it was in 1971. Even if the General Assembly had adopted all of the recommendations, and even if every one had its expected effect on legislative performance, the General Assembly would still be hard-pressed to meet the demands made of it in the 1990s.

Legislators may recognize the increasing complexity and difficulty of their roles, but the public does not, creating an inevitable tension between public expectations and legislative performance. The general public must learn almost all of what it knows about the legislature from the press, but on most issues, coverage of the legislature is insufficient to provide readers with enough information about the issues or the legislative process to enable them to draw any reasonable conclusions about either.

Legislative institutions are alternately castigated for inefficiency and pummeled for the real and imagined sins of their members, yet candidates still launch legislative careers and experienced legislators continue to seek reelection. Why? Legislatures may have fallen into disrepute, but legislators are granted a status in their own communities that few would otherwise earn. In addition, most legislators draw inspiration from people who were helped by their personal efforts, such as students assisted by the state's "bright flight" scholarship program, families coping with the terror of Alzheimer's disease, or a constituent in need of services provided by the state. Finally, whether they win or lose, legislators participate in the drama of politics, and that participation enhances their sense of involvement and their satisfaction with their service. For all of its drawbacks, legislative service provides psychological and emotional rewards in a measure unequaled by most other occupations, and these rewards help legislators to sustain their interest and commitment.

CHAPTER 9

The Governor of Missouri
by David A. Leuthold

> True leadership, which inspires the willing confidence of men, cannot be crystallized into constitutional grants of power. Each governor must win it anew.—Leslie Lipson

The governor is the chief executive of state government and the official leader of the state of Missouri. The governor is the state's political leader and is one of the state's most skillful politicians, as indicated by election to the top office in the state. Missouri's governors have substantial legal power, at least as much as the average governor across the United States.[1] Even so, numerous restraints—fiscal, legal, and political—can be imposed on governors. Therefore, many Missouri governors have maintained their political popularity, an important source of their political power, by heeding the restraints and exercising their powers cautiously.

I. Characteristics of Missouri Governors

The governor shall be at least thirty years old and shall have been a citizen of the United States for at least fifteen years and a resident of this state at least ten years next before election. —Missouri Constitution, Article IV, Section 3

Presumably, every Missouri child has some chance of becoming governor. But in fact, all governors elected have been white males; most have been in their forties or fifties (Christopher "Kit" Bond was the youngest, first elected at age thirty-three). The last eight governors have all been attorneys. The requirement that a governor be a resident for at least ten years before election dissuaded some potential candidates until 1972, when Bond filed for nomination despite having been out of the state for an extended period of time. The Missouri Supreme Court ruled, however, that he had intended to return to Missouri, and thus had maintained his residency and was eligible to be governor.[2]

Political Careers. All governors elected in the last fifty years have held some other elective public office prior to becoming governor, serving on average about twelve years in other offices. The most frequent pattern in recent years has been election to one or more of the other statewide offices—lieutenant governor, secretary of

---

1. Thad L. Beyle, "Governors," in Virginia Gray, Herbert Jacob, and Robert B. Albritton, eds., *Politics in the American States: A Comparative Analysis*, 5th ed. (Glenview, Ill.: Scott, Foresman, 1990), 228.

2. *State ex rel. King v. Walsh* 484 S.W. 2d 641 (Mo. 1972). In 1954 Bond had transferred from public school in Mexico, Missouri, to Deerfield Academy in Massachusetts. After two years there he spent four years at Princeton University, New Jersey, three years at the University of Virginia law school, one year as a law clerk to a federal judge, and three years practicing law with Covington and Burling, a Washington, D.C., law firm.

Table 9-1. Recent Governors of Missouri

Governor	Years Elected	Party	Occupation	Previous Offices	Later Office
Phil M. Donnelly	1944, 1952	Democrat	Attorney	Prosecuting attorney, Legislator	
Forrest Smith	1948	Democrat	Public office	State Auditor	
James T. Blair, Jr.	1956	Democrat	Attorney	Legislator, Mayor, Lieutenant Governor	
John M. Dalton	1960	Democrat	Attorney	Attorney General	
Warren E. Hearnes	1964, 1968	Democrat	Attorney	Legislator, Secretary of State	Appointed judge
Christopher S. Bond	1972, 1980	Republican	Attorney	State Auditor	U.S. Senate
Joseph P. Teasdale	1976	Democrat	Attorney	Prosecuting attorney	
John Ashcroft	1984, 1988	Republican	Attorney	Auditor, Attorney General	U.S. Senate
Mel Carnahan	1992	Democrat	Attorney	Legislator, Treasurer, Lieutenant Governor	

state, treasurer, auditor or attorney general (Table 9–1). This pattern has been so strong that 60 percent of the people elected to other statewide offices from 1968 through 1988 subsequently ran for governor. (Another 15 percent ran for other statewide offices.) These statewide offices have become important because of the decline in political organizations that at one time could provide a substantial vote for a favored candidate for governor. In their absence, candidates need a highly recognizable name and numerous personal contacts across the state to have any chance of winning the governorship. These attributes can be purchased by wealthy people; those without personal wealth secure these attributes gradually, by running for and serving in minor statewide offices.

Campaigns for the governorship are increasingly expensive. The amounts spent by the winning candidates (in 1992 dollars) were $3.1 million in 1980, $4 million in 1984, $4.1 million in 1988, and $4.7 million in 1992. At the same time, losing candidates were spending sometimes more, sometimes less. This record indicates that a gubernatorial candidate needs to be able to raise at least $3 million or more, and probably $5 million to be competitive. Such fund raising usually requires that the candidate spend thirty or more hours per week asking for money, and that he or she have sufficient recognition and reputation to attract individual contributions of five thousand dollars or more.[3]

3. A campaign finance law passed by the 1994 General Assembly provided for voluntary expenditure limits for future gubernatorial candidates of $1.5 million in the primary election campaign and $1.5 million in the general election campaign. The same law limited contributions to one thousand dollars per candidate per election. A 1994 initiative, approved by Missouri voters, limited contributions further, to three hundred dollars for gubernatorial candidates.

For most incumbents, the governorship has been the peak of their careers and the last office they have held. Among the eight governors who have been elected and completed their terms in the last fifty years, only two, Bond and John Ashcroft, have been elected to another office (U.S. senator). The difficulties in building a political career through the governor's office are indicated by the fact that two (Bond in 1976 and Joseph Teasdale in 1980) of the last four governors failed to win reelection and a third (Warren Hearnes) lost races for the U.S. senate and for state auditor.

Missouri's governors have rarely received national recognition for their accomplishments. Only two Missouri governors have gone on to hold federal cabinet posts (Arthur Hyde, governor from 1921 to 1925, who served as Secretary of Agriculture under President Herbert Hoover in the late 1920s, and David Francis, governor from 1889 to 1893, who served as Secretary of the Interior during Grover Cleveland's last year in the White House in 1896). No Missouri governor has ever been a serious candidate for president. In contrast, there have been several presidential candidates among Missouri's U.S. congressmen and senators, including "Silver Dick" Bland in 1896, "Champ" Clark in 1916, James Reed in 1928 and 1932, Harry Truman in 1948, Stuart Symington in 1960, and Richard Gephardt in 1988.

II. Executive Powers

The supreme executive power shall be vested in a governor. The governor shall take care that the laws are distributed and faithfully executed, and shall be a conservator of the peace throughout the state. — Article IV, Sections 1 and 2

Article IV, sections 1 and 2, of the Missouri Constitution potentially give the governor great latitude and authority. That authority is enhanced by the public's expectation that the governor will provide leadership on a wide range of matters. This "supreme executive power" is, however, limited by numerous formal and informal restrictions.

The governor's executive authority applies to local governments as well as the state government. Local governments are created by the state and are subject to detailed state laws.[4] Therefore the governor's power to recommend and veto legislation gives the governor influence over the laws affecting local governments. In addition, the governor appoints boards of police commissioners in St. Louis and Kansas City, as well as election officials in the metropolitan areas. The state took control of the St. Louis police department in 1861 as a means of cleaning up problems of mismanagement and corruption. The state exercised control of Kansas City police from 1861 to 1932, and has since retained control from 1939 to the present. State control of St. Joseph police existed from 1909 until 1965. In addition, the governor appoints replacements for vacancies in county governments. In most such cases, however, the chief executive follows the recommendation of the party's county central committee or of his or her local supporters.

Directing State Agencies

Supreme executive power allows the governor to exercise control over many state agencies. The governor's power is enhanced by virtue of the 1974 reorganization of state government, which limited the number of state departments to fourteen (now increased to sixteen). Earlier, agencies had been so numerous that it was difficult for the governor to influence many of them.

---

4. See chapter 21 on county government in Missouri, chapter 22 on special districts, and chapter 24 on municipal government.

The governor's ability to direct state agencies is restricted, however, by the detailed laws and regulations that govern state agency action, by requirements imposed on the governor and the state by the federal government and the courts, by budget limitations that often provide funding for only the same actions as the previous year, and by the limited number of employees that the governor can remove if they fail to carry out his directives. As a result, governors who wish to exercise executive power will probably use their political skills of persuading, cajoling, and threatening more than their administrative skills of directing, decreeing, and requiring. Two areas of concern—preserving the peace, and developing the economy—illustrate the governor's powers and limitations.

Preserving the Peace and Enforcing the Law

The governor shall be the commander in chief of the militia, except when it is called into the service of the United States, and may call out the militia to execute the laws, suppress actual and prevent threatened insurrection, and repel invasion. —Article IV, Section 6

Seemingly, the power of the governor as commander in chief of the militia is substantial. In actuality, however, the militia is the National Guard, whose expenses are appropriated by the federal government. Having provided the funding, the federal government exercises strong control over the Guard, as was indicated by a 1990 Supreme Court decision in which the court ruled that governors could not restrict the federal government from sending National Guard units to Central America for training.[5] Some governors (but not

Missouri's) had tried to prohibit such training, maintaining that this was simply a way in which the Reagan administration could build up the American military presence in Central America without congressional supervision, and that Honduras was not a safe place to train because of guerilla activity. The governors lost.

Missouri governors have used the National Guard for important tasks and emergencies, calling out the guard once or twice a year through much of the twentieth century. In recent years call-ups have been less frequent, in part because better training has meant that local emergency management specialists were able to handle many crises. The largest call-up ever was in 1993, when five thousand men and women from the Army and Air National Guard, about half the state's National Guard force, helped fight the Missouri River and Mississippi River floods.

The governor also has general authority over civil defense matters, a power that has additional significance because Missouri has a nuclear power plant in the center of the state. For many years, the state was a potential enemy target because of the presence of intercontinental missiles in and around Whiteman Air Force Base.

A related power is the governor's authority in case of disaster relief. Although the governor might call out the National Guard in an emergency (at state rather than federal expense), the more common approach is to inspect the troubled areas and to request federal aid. The most frequent disasters in Missouri are floods on the Missouri and Mississippi rivers, and tornadoes. In 1980 Teasdale skillfully exploited a summer heat wave, traveling to Washington, D.C., to secure promises of federal aid that helped his efforts to defeat challenger James Spainhower for the Democratic nomination for governor.

5. *Perpich et al. v. Department of Defense et al.* (1990) 406 U.S. 334.

In the past, the governor had direct control over the Missouri State Highway Patrol. This allowed Hearnes to send a busload of highway patrol officers to the University of Missouri–Columbia campus when he feared that anti-Vietnam student protests might turn violent. (They did not, and the patrol officers returned to their normal duty stations.) In 1974 state government reorganization put the highway patrol under the director of the Department of Public Safety, who is appointed by the governor. Governors occasionally still ask the highway patrol's Criminal Investigation Bureau to conduct investigations of alleged criminal activities.

Similarly, the governor had direct control over liquor licenses and thus over liquor law enforcement until 1974, when the Division of Liquor Control was transferred from the governor to the Department of Public Safety. The supervisor of the division is still appointed by the governor on recommendation of the director of the Department of Public Safety.

Economic Development. Although Missouri governors have no specific constitutional powers in economic development other than the power to appoint the director of the Department of Economic Development, community and economic development has been a political issue on which Missouri governors have worked hard for the past thirty years or more.[6] Their activities have included public pronouncements, development trips to other countries, opening trade offices in Germany, Japan, Korea, and Mexico, and entertaining visiting delegations.

6. In 1962 Governor Dalton headed a delegation of Missouri businessmen to both coasts in an effort to attract new industry. He urged New York industrialists to build in Missouri because it was a low tax state, a frequently repeated argument that seems not to have been effective, given Missouri's lower than average growth rate. *St. Louis Post-Dispatch,* December 10, 1962.

Governors frequently have lobbied to convince firms to locate new factories in Missouri. Soon after his inauguration in 1985, Ashcroft spearheaded a substantial effort to convince General Motors to build its new Saturn plant in Missouri. This included persuading the legislature to pass mandatory seat belt legislation, which General Motors wanted. In the end General Motors selected neighboring Tennessee. Other automobile plants that Missouri courted eventually were built in Ohio and Kentucky (and in 1987 Missouri lost to Ohio its long-held position as the nation's second largest assembler of automobiles). One success was the establishment of a Briggs & Stratton small engine plant in Rolla, achieved with substantial effort from Governor Mel Carnahan. One California business owner reported that he had received a personal phone call from Carnahan, with promises of various forms of assistance if he would move to Missouri. The proffered assistance included complimentary tickets to St. Louis Symphony concerts.

A second pattern has been to encourage the expansion of business already in Missouri. In 1989 the state agreed to pay for the training of new workers to help Ford Motor Company expand its Claycomo production plant in the Kansas City area. About one thousand workers were trained at a state cost of approximately $1.6 million; the plant later received recognition as Ford's most productive auto plant in North America. Similarly, Carnahan signed a bill allowing a $7 million tax waiver for TWA to help ensure the continued economic success of the beleaguered airline company, and undoubtedly to help convince the company to select Missouri as its national headquarters. (The effort was successful; in 1993 TWA announced a shift of national headquarters from New York to St. Louis.)

A third procedure has been to stimulate economic activity in Missouri through state government expenditures. In 1982, when the country was beset by a substantial recession, Bond pushed through the legislature and spearheaded a popular vote in support of a proposal to borrow $600 million to construct new buildings in the state. In 1992, in the midst of another recession, Ashcroft pushed through the legislature a substantial increase in the state gasoline tax to secure more federal funds to stimulate more road building in the state.

Appointment of State Employees

The governor shall fill all vacancies in public offices unless otherwise provided by law, and his appointees shall serve until their successors are duly elected or appointed and qualified. —Article IV, Section 4

The heads of all the executive departments shall be appointed by the governor, by and with the advice and consent of the senate. —Article IV, Section 17

The head of each department may select and remove all appointees in the department except as otherwise provided in this constitution, or by law. All employees in the state eleemosynary and penal institutions, and other state employees as provided by law, shall be selected on the basis of merit, ascertained as nearly as practicable by competitive examinations. —Article IV, Section 19

The sections of the state constitution quoted above seem to both give to and take away from the governor extensive appointive powers. In actual practice the governor makes numerous appointments, always keeping an eye on both the formal and informal limitations and restrictions on his powers. How many appointments? One chief executive's assistant estimated that a governor made approximately two hundred "political plum" appointments, which would be less than one-half of one percent of all state employees. Another governor's assistant still learning the job suspected there might be as many as two thousand appointments to process, counting members of numerous state boards and commissions, replacements for vacancies for county offices, and members of advisory commissions.

This responsibility saddles the governor and his staff with an enormous task of receiving and reviewing applications, searching for candidates when well-qualified ones do not apply, receiving and responding to telephone calls from supporters of particular candidates, interviewing leading candidates for the more important positions, and persuading people to leave their present positions and work for state government. Given the extensive amount of time required, most governors have at least one staff person, often two or three, working full time on appointments. The governor is likely to meet personally only with the leading candidates for the most important positions. In many cases, the governor will have had no contact with the appointee, and will be relying on the recommendation of a trusted friend or associate. The magnitude of the task was indicated by the report that Ashcroft's 1984 transition team received about forty-five hundred résumés and interviewed two thousand to three thousand people.[7]

Political Office Appointments. The most prestigious appointment opportunities are vacancies for short terms to the United States Senate or for a statewide elected office. There are not many such openings, on average less than one per gubernatorial term. Governor James Blair (1957–1961)

7. Dean L. Yarwood and Richard J. Hardy, "The Norm of Standing Aside: Gubernatorial Transition in Missouri in 1984," in Thad Beyle, ed., *Gubernatorial Transitions: The 1983 and 1984 Elections* (Durham: Duke University Press, 1988), 92.

appointed a U.S. senator and a Missouri secretary of state. Bond appointed an auditor in each of his two terms, and Teasdale also appointed an auditor. Presumably as party leader, the governor would try to appoint a person who would be able to win subsequent election to the office, thus holding it for the governor's party. Among these five recent appointees, however, two failed even to file for the nomination and one lost the general election.

Agency Heads and Administration Leaders. The governor appoints some of the decision makers of state government, including the heads of ten of the sixteen major agencies. Commissions, often dominated by a predecessor's appointees, appoint the other six department heads—conservation, elementary and secondary education, higher education, highways and transportation, labor and industrial relations, and mental health.

The governor has an often difficult task of convincing potential appointees to give up their present positions and accept a new appointment, frequently at a substantial pay cut. Many new appointees must move from their present homes to Jefferson City, transferring children into new schools and reducing contact with family and old friends. No wonder most governors encounter some refusals, especially when they search for candidates of outstanding quality. Similarly, it should be no surprise that governors will appoint people who are already in Jefferson City; about half of Ashcroft's cabinet appointees, and a much higher proportion of lower-level appointees, were holdovers from the administration of his fellow-Republican predecessor.[8]

The governor's power to appoint even the ten directors is restricted, both by formal requirements of securing state senate approval and by the informal expectations of the chief executive's supporters or other politically important groups. In 1993 the Black Caucus of the legislature complained that Carnahan had not appointed enough Blacks to reflect the importance of Black support in his nomination and general election contests. Black senators threatened to disapprove of the one Black department director that Carnahan had appointed, as well as one other appointee who lived in the district of a Black senator. Carnahan successfully convinced the minority legislators to support his nominees, pointing out that he had in fact offered additional cabinet posts to Blacks who had declined.

Other senators attempted to influence another Carnahan appointee. In an effort to protect the Highway Patrol superintendent, the senators told the prospective director of the Department of Public Safety that they might not confirm him if he didn't agree *not* to fire the superintendent. Carnahan responded by saying that he would *immediately* fire the superintendent if the senate did not confirm the governor's choice without any such guarantee. Subsequently the senate confirmed the nominee without a promise to retain the superintendent, who later announced his retirement.

In 1979 Teasdale reappointed consumer advocate Alberta Slavin to the Public Service Commission. The senate did not confirm Slavin, but Teasdale refused to make another appointment, which meant that Slavin could serve until her successor had been selected and approved. This tactic meant, however, that if Democrat Teasdale left the state, Republican Lieutenant Governor Bill Phelps could appoint a replacement, thereby ending Slavin's service. Teasdale stayed in Missouri (except for one time when he took Phelps with him),

---

8. Yarwood and Hardy, "The Norm of Standing Aside," 93.

and Slavin served until the inauguration of Bond, who defeated Teasdale for reelection.

Commissions. The governor appoints members of most commissions in state government, including the Missouri Public Service Commission, the Conservation Commission, the State Tax Commission, the State Highways and Transportation Commission, the Labor and Industrial Relations Commission, the Mental Health Commission, the Missouri Ethics Commission, the State Lottery Commission, and the Horse Racing Commission. The governor appoints the governing boards for each of the higher education institutions in the state. Many of these appointments must receive senate approval, which may restrict the governor.

On their own initiative, governors frequently construct special commissions to advise them. In 1991 Ashcroft received a report issued by "Jobs for Missouri's Future," a commission he had appointed to develop a strategy to strengthen the state's economy by improving the skills of its work force. Carnahan, Ashcroft's successor, appointed a Business Council in 1993 to draft a comprehensive economic development plan for the state.

Patronage. In years gone by, governors could have a major impact on employment in state government. Many departments were operated on a patronage basis, so a new governor might replace many of the employees in a state agency. Civil service reform in state government was stimulated in the 1930s when the federal government required that state agencies which relied in part on federal funds must adopt merit programs. Further indications of this movement in Missouri were the adoption of initiative constitutional amendments for the Conservation Commission in 1936 and the metropolitan and appellate judiciary in 1940, each involving merit appointments.

The movement finally culminated in a provision of the 1945 constitution that authorized a merit system to cover some agencies. Today the Missouri Merit System covers thirty thousand employees in part or all of nine departments. Another twenty thousand employees serve under uniform compensation guidelines or guidelines for labor management relations. The six thousand faculty and many more staff people in the state's colleges and universities fall under merit systems administered by individual institutions.

As a result, few patronage opportunities are available to governors today. The only departments that are regarded as "patronage" departments are Revenue and Agriculture. Even in those departments, turnover is limited. The Department of Revenue has voluntarily adopted many provisions of the Missouri Merit System, but is not officially covered by that program. One area of the department still subject to some patronage expectations is the network of 164 motor vehicle and driver's license fee offices. Governors occasionally will replace the licensee in such an office with a "more deserving" person.

Limits on Appointments. While the authority to appoint people can be an important source of power, the governor's power is limited in many ways. Large numbers of state employees are in agencies under one or another merit system. Similarly, employees for each of the other five statewide elected officials are appointed by that official rather than by the governor.

Even in the cases in which the governor does make an appointment, he or she may be severely restricted. In the case of merit plan judges or the redistricting and ethics commissions, the governor is restricted to appointing persons appearing on short lists developed by commissions or groups. Most major appointments require approval by the state senate, with senate rules allowing the senator in whose district a nominee resides to singlehandedly reject an appointment. Informal rules established and enforced by the senate preclude a governor from making "midnight appointments," appointments at the end of the governor's term. In 1984 outgoing governor Bond made no appointments after September 30.[9]

Statutes may also restrict selections. The statute creating the Office of Administration at first required that the commissioner of administration have a master's degree "in public administration," as well as other provisions. The first nominee, Robert James, had a master's degree in business administration but not public administration. Senators contended that he failed to meet the statutory requirements and James withdrew his name after two years of debate.[10]

Other standards or restrictions may be provided informally; Ashcroft was criticized by the National Women's Political Caucus because his cabinet ranked third lowest in the nation in the number of women members (one reason being that Missouri could not count some agencies headed by women because they were divisions, or subcabinet posts, in Missouri but cabinet posts in some other states). Most governors come under some pressure to appoint the friends or supporters of other public officials. In addition, the governor's choice may be restricted by an inability to persuade some people to accept a government post.

Removal of Appointees

All appointive officers may be removed by the governor. —Article IV, Section 17

The governor's removal power was first established by law in 1933, designed for two purposes: to enhance the power of the governor, and to allow a Democratic governor to remove appointees selected by his Republican predecessor. Governor Guy Brasfield Park (1933–1937), however, used the law cautiously, allowing many Republican officeholders to continue in office.[11] Most subsequent governors have been cautious in exercising power of removal. Teasdale used the power more than most governors, firing, among others, three of his own cabinet appointees.

The seemingly sweeping powers given in the constitution are in fact greatly restricted. For example, Bond was unsuccessful in his 1974 effort to remove the head of the State Labor and Industrial Relations Commission. Bond claimed that reorganization had ended the old Industrial Commission of Missouri, leaving him free to appoint a director for the newly reorganized State Labor and Industrial Relations Commission. The Missouri Supreme Court disagreed and the incumbent director remained in office. Teasdale asked four members of the Public Service Commission to resign to allow him to appoint a commission that would be less willing to grant utility rate increases. All four refused. However, within six months Teasdale was able to appoint a majority to the commission when the term of one commissioner ended and one of the remaining three resigned. An analysis two years later indicated that the new appointees had allowed rate hikes at about the same rate as previous commissions.[12]

9. Ibid., 83.
10. Ibid., 88.

11. Stanley Botner, "The Office of Governor of the State of Missouri" (Ph.D. diss., University of Missouri–Columbia, 1963), 201–3.
12. "Teasdale Public Service Commission: Little Change in Rate Hikes," *St. Louis Post-Dispatch*, June 14, 1979.

Such powers as governors had to remove employees were restricted by *Elrod v. Burns,* a 1976 decision in which the U.S. Supreme Court held that the First Amendment prevents the political firing of county and local workers who are below the policy-making level. While the court seemed to waver some in 1980 and 1983 cases, a 1990 decision, by a five-to-four vote, clearly prohibited the state of Illinois from basing decisions about promotion, transfer, recall after layoff, and hiring of low-level public employees on their party affiliation and support.[13]

III. Legislative Powers

Fiscal Legislation

Budget

The governor shall . . . submit to the general assembly a budget for the ensuing appropriation period, containing the estimated available revenues of the state and a complete and itemized plan of proposed expenditures of the state and all its agencies, together with his recommendations of any laws necessary to provide revenues sufficient to meet the expenditures.—Article IV, Section 24

The budgetary authority of the governor is particularly strong. The governor's budget usually emerges fairly intact from the legislative session.[14] On the other hand, both the governor and the legislature are severely restrained by outside constraints, including:

• limited state revenues
• mandates accompanying federal funds (which make up more than one-fourth of total state expenditures)

• restrictions on earmarked taxes and funds (which make up more than one-fourth of total state expenditures)
• orders and potential orders from federal and state courts, such as the desegregation programs, prison improvement programs, and the state foundation formula
• previous governmental decisions, especially those requiring the repayment of money borrowed by the state, and the requirement that elementary and secondary education receive at least 25 percent of all general revenue funds
• widespread acceptance of most governmental programs (especially education and human services, which make up more than two-thirds of the state general revenue operating budget)
• the power of significant interest groups, which can protect "their" agency's appropriations from severe slashes.

Given the number of restraints on the state budget, a governor who wants to make significant changes probably will have to engineer a tax increase, substantial reallocation, or spending cuts. Such actions, especially the tax increase, can be politically risky. During his second term, Hearnes pushed through the Missouri legislature a bill to increase income taxes and make them more progressive. One of the senators with an eye on the governorship, Earl Blackwell, circulated petitions for a referendum, easily got enough signatures, and won the referendum election, stopping the governor's tax increase. Hearnes had been very popular during his first term but lost popularity during his second, one reason being his effort to raise taxes. Subsequent governors were very cautious about raising taxes.

Significant tax increases in the 1980s and 1990s recommended by a governor

13. *Rutan v. Republican Party of Illinois* (1990) 497 U.S. 62. The earlier court decisions were *Elrod v. Burns* (1976) 427 U.S. 347; *Branti v. Finkel* (1980) 445 U.S. 507; and *Connick v. Meyers* (1983) 461 U.S. 138.
14. See chapter 13 and its extensive description of the budget.

and adopted by the legislature included temporary corporate income tax and sales tax increases passed as an emergency in 1989, and a gasoline tax increase passed by the legislature in 1992. Both of these tax increases came during the administration of Ashcroft, who demonstrated substantial political skill in getting the taxes increased without raising strong public opposition or having public irritation focused upon him. In 1993 Carnahan recommended and secured legislative approval for increases in the personal and corporate income tax and cigarette tax, and a new tobacco products tax for use in financing a circuit court–ordered revision of the foundation program for elementary and secondary schools. Opponents reacted by securing signatures to put a more stringent tax limitation proposal on the ballot, a proposal defeated by voters in November 1994.

The Item Veto

The governor may object to one or more items or portions of items of appropriation of money in any bill presented to him, while approving other portions of the bill. . . . The governor shall not reduce any appropriation for free public schools, for the payment of principal and interest on the public debt.—Article IV, Section 26

The item veto can be a formidable weapon, especially for governors who want to reduce expenditures for a program or for state government in general. Legislatures rarely, if ever, override an item veto. The provision protecting the public schools has only limited authority. In 1953 Governor Phil Donnelly vetoed a $9 million item for the public schools, saying a complete veto was not a "reduction," and was upheld by the Missouri Supreme Court. However, the governor cannot use the item veto to disapprove of nonappropriation portions of the bill. In 1973 Bond used the item veto

to strike language designating the purpose of the appropriation, but not the appropriation itself. For example, he deleted the words "West Side" on the description of renovation of the capitol building because renovation needs were not limited to the west side. The supreme court ruled that he could not veto the purpose of the item without vetoing the item itself.[15]

Withholding Funds

The governor may control the rate at which any appropriation is expended during the period of the appropriation by allotment or other means, and may reduce the expenditures of the state or any of its agencies below their appropriations whenever the actual revenues are less than the revenue estimates upon which the appropriations were based.—Article IV, Section 27

A related power of the governor is that of withholding funds from state agencies, if revenues appear to be falling short. This power applies only to general revenue funds and not to earmarked funds, such as those supporting the Conservation Commission or the Department of Highways and Transportation. Standard procedure is for the governor to withhold 3 percent of each agency's general operating revenue at the start of the fiscal year, then release that amount at the beginning of the fourth quarter, if revenues are sufficient. Because withholding is more painful later in the fiscal year than earlier, given the difficulty in planning, governors normally would prefer to withhold as early as possible.

In 1991 school desegregation costs in Kansas City were unexpectedly high, and Ashcroft was forced to withhold funds. He

---

15. *State ex rel. Cason v. Bond* (1973) 495 S.W. 2d 385. See also the description of the case in James M. Vaughan, "Constitutional Law—The Governor's Item Veto Power," *Missouri Law Review* 39 (1974):105–10.

chose to withhold in part from the public schools, prompting a lawsuit by the Missouri National Education Association, which charged that the withholding violated the constitutional prohibition against reducing funds for the public schools. The court upheld Ashcroft's action, reasoning that the desegregation payments were part of the state expenditures for public schools, so that a transfer, in effect, from other public schools to the Kansas City schools was not a reduction below the amount originally appropriated for public schools.

Recommending Legislation

The governor shall . . . give to the general assembly information as to the state of the government, and shall recommend to its consideration such measures as he shall deem necessary and expedient.— Article IV, Section 9

The procedures that governors have used to secure legislation include:[16]

1. The State of the State message, given by each governor at the start of each session of the General Assembly. Governors also make major policy recommendations when they present their proposed budgets to the legislature. Governors Blair and Teasdale went a step further by testifying before legislative committees. Teasdale commented, "Most of these guys just want you to hold their hand, do them a little favor like come into their district and give a speech at a fund raiser or something."[17]

2. Closely following the legislative session, usually by having staff people attend legislative sessions and report on legislative actions and debates. Ashcroft relied heavily on these first two procedures. In 1991 "right to die" legislation finally passed after long negotiations among Ashcroft's staff, the Missouri Bar, the Missouri Catholic Conference, and the Missouri Right to Life organization produced an agreement that the governor and legislators would accept.

3. Personal lobbying of legislators. In 1993 Carnahan stood in the side lobbies and spoke individually with legislators, urging them to support a revision of the school foundation formula. In 1939 Governor Lloyd Crow Stark held personal conferences with many legislators in his successful effort to gain state control over the police department of Kansas City, whose city government was dominated by Tom Pendergast.[18] In 1961 Governor John Dalton contacted many legislators and mobilized interest groups across the state in his successful effort to secure adoption of income tax withholding. Later the governor said, "These fellows understand a club better than a nudge."

4. Patronage or "log rolling." Little documentation exists about the use of log rolling to pass legislation. Both parties to a supposed agreement usually deny its existence. In fact, such agreements may be unspoken and perhaps multifaceted. An example was the 1992 appointment of Democratic State Senator Edwin L. Dirck to a short term on the Industrial and Labor Relations Commission. Speculation prior to the appointment focused on the senator's support for Republican Ashcroft's proposal to reorga-

16. Not all governors want legislation. In his 1925 inaugural address, Governor Sam A. Baker said, "There can be such a thing as too much legislation. Sometimes it is desirable to give the people a rest and a chance to work out their own problems." State Historical Society of Missouri, *Messages and Proclamations of the Governors of the State of Missouri* (Columbia: State Historical Society of Missouri, 1922), vol. XII, 269. Quoted in Botner, "The Office of Governor," 73.

17. Dana L. Spitzer, "Governor: Proud of Job Done," *St. Louis Post-Dispatch,* October 7, 1979.

18. Botner, "The Office of Governor," 252–64, 290,

nize state agencies providing children's services. Speculation later focused on the increase in the senator's retirement benefits by the boost to the much higher commission salary, and the opportunity for the governor's party to win another senate seat, which it did.

5. Appeals to voters. In 1939 Stark made numerous radio addresses and orchestrated an extensive media and grassroots campaign to convince legislators to support his proposal for a state takeover of the Kansas City Police Department.[19] A governor may also become involved in political contests. Since the governors can raise funds more effectively than anybody else in the state, it is not surprising that they have quietly helped candidates, particularly in special elections.

Democratic governors, who usually are more liberal and more supportive of governmental activity, are more likely to be heavily involved in legislative lobbying than are Republican governors who are more conservative and less supportive of government action. Other factors probably affect legislative lobbying patterns. Two of the three most recent Democratic governors had served previously in the legislature, while neither Republican governors Bond nor Ashcroft had done so. In addition, each of the Democrats had a party majority in the legislature while neither of the Republicans had a partisan majority in either house in any year. No matter what styles they use, governors have some success; Bond reported in 1981 that 39 percent of his legislative recommendations had passed, and Ashcroft said in 1985 that more than 85 percent of the bills he supported had become law.

The Veto

The governor could say no quite effectively. One of his strongest powers—the veto power . . . was a power to prevent action. . . . The governor was better equipped to stop action than to initiate it.—Richard Kirkendall, *A History of Missouri, 1919 to 1953*, vol. V (Columbia: University of Missouri Press, 1986), 344

Nationwide, year in and year out, about 5 percent of the bills passed by legislatures are vetoed, a pattern also found in Missouri. Not surprisingly, the number of vetoes is slightly higher when the governor and legislature are of opposite parties than when they are of the same party. About one in twenty-five vetoes nationwide are overridden.[20] In Missouri, however, the governor's veto is rarely overridden. One governor's veto was overridden in 1820 (a legislative pay allowance bill), seven were overridden in 1833 (all on divorce bills), and one was overridden in 1839 (a bill to establish a criminal court in St. Louis County), the last to be overridden for 135 years! In 1976 the legislature overrode a veto by Bond of a nursing regulation bill and in 1980 the legislature overrode Teasdale's veto of the authorization of the Truman Office building, a large state office building in Jefferson City.[21]

In the past, much of the reason for the strength of the governor's veto was the legislature's pattern of postponing passage of most bills until the last two or three weeks of the session. For decades, this meant that the governor did not have to sign or veto the bill until the legislature had gone home and

19. Ibid., 259–62.

20. Beyle, "Governors," 225.
21. For a more complete description of the legislature's override of Bond's veto, see Robert F. Karsch, *The Government of Missouri*, 13th ed. (Columbia: Lucas Brothers Publishers, 1976), 135. For a more complete description of the Truman building situation, see chapter 13.

could no longer consider the veto. A constitutional amendment adopted in 1970 and later amended allows a September session of the legislature that considers bills vetoed by the governor. Even so, in the twenty-two years in which vetoes have been considered, only two were overridden. During sixteen of those twenty-two years, the legislature was controlled by Democrats while the governor was Republican.

Indicative of the power of the governor's veto and the restraints on that power was the battle over a "state minimum wage." In 1989 and again in 1990, the legislature passed bills providing a state minimum wage, which Ashcroft vetoed. Subsequently, legislative sponsors began actively considering use of a referendum, which bypasses the governor and sends a bill directly to the people for a public vote. In addition, they negotiated with the governor about his objections to the state minimum wage bill. In the end, the legislature passed and the governor signed a bill that extended most aspects of the federal minimum wage to employees of amusement parks and large hotels and restaurants.

A similar battle was waged over Sunday liquor sales. In 1991 the legislature passed such a bill, which Ashcroft vetoed, ostensibly because of a provision that would have allowed an increased amount of liquor in candy, which in turn would be available to children. In 1992 the legislature passed another Sunday liquor sales bill, the governor vetoed it, and the veto was upheld. In 1993 when the legislature passed a Sunday liquor sales bill for the third time, it was signed by Carnahan, the newly elected governor.

Other Legislative Powers

Calling Special Sessions. The power to call special sessions was more significant in the 1950s and 1960s than it has been

since. Prior to 1952 governors called special sessions once every five years, on average. A limit on the length of special sessions adopted in 1952 led to numerous special sessions, in which governors had the authority to designate the agenda. The adoption in 1970 of a constitutional amendment providing for annual sessions reduced the need for special sessions. Subsequently, special sessions have been held only for unusual reasons, such as in 1981 when Bond called one in hopes that the legislature would agree on a congressional redistricting proposal more acceptable to him than the redistricting proposal he expected if the issue went to a federal court. A special session was called in 1989 by Ashcroft to pass a temporary increase in corporate income taxes in an attempt to make up the revenue lost when a court interpretation of a state law exempted public employee retirement pensions from personal income tax. In 1994 Carnahan called a special session to consider impeachment of Secretary of State Judi Moriarty.

IV. Judicial Powers

Judicial Appointments

The governor fills all vacancies on the Missouri Supreme Court and the three courts of appeals, and all circuit court vacancies in the St. Louis and Kansas City metropolitan areas. The governor's power over these appointments is restricted by the constitutional provision that the governor shall choose from among three nominees submitted by a judicial nominating commission. Even so, governors often are able to influence the nominating commissions sufficiently so that the governor's preferred candidate is included among the three nominees.[22] The number of vacancies

22. Richard A. Watson and Rondal G. Downing, *The Politics of the Bench and the Bar: Judicial Selection under*

available may vary enormously: Hearnes appointed two supreme court judges during each of his two terms, Bond appointed one in his first term and three in his second, and Teasdale appointed three in his single term. Ashcroft appointed all seven supreme court judges, two in his first term and five in his second, all young enough so that if they serve until the normal retirement age of seventy years, his successors will have few appointments and an Ashcroft majority could remain on the court until 2018!

In addition, the governor fills vacancies for nonmetropolitan circuit courts when an incumbent dies or resigns during a term. About one-fifth of the circuit court judges originally were appointed to a circuit court position by a governor.

Pardons, Extraditions, and Investigations

The governor shall have power to grant reprieves, commutations and pardons, after conviction, for all offenses except treason and cases of impeachment, upon such conditions and with such restrictions and limitations as he may deem proper.—Article IV, Section 7

The power to pardon is not a major power, nor one frequently used by governors. Most of the usage appears to be for humanitarian cases, for people who have paid the penalty for their crime and led exemplary lives since. In 1980 Teasdale stirred substantial comment by pardoning thirteen people convicted of drunken driving—four times as many pardons for drunken driving as had been granted by his two predecessors combined. On the other hand, despite substantial public pressure, Teasdale had earlier refused to pardon a

Southwest Missouri State University student who had been sentenced to seven years in prison for a five dollar sale of marijuana.

Governors may also commute sentences, reducing them to a less severe punishment. In 1992 when Ashcroft wanted to resolve questions about the mental competency of a man who had been imprisoned for murder and then had killed a guard in prison, he delayed the man's scheduled execution. Several months later, Carnahan, upon becoming governor, commuted the man's death sentence to life in prison without parole, citing his very limited mental capacity.[23] In this case as in all other pardons, commutations, and reprieves, the governor received an investigation and perhaps recommendations from the Missouri Board of Probation and Parole.

The governor also is the state's agent for extraditions, the process of sending criminal suspects from the state where they have been caught to the state where the crime was committed. Missouri's governor requests the extradition of Missouri suspects from other states and approves the extradition requests from other states. A recent U.S. Supreme Court decision seems to require that all extradition requests be granted, so that this task is largely a ministerial function performed by the governor's legal counsel.[24]

V. Political Powers

As with the president, the power and influence of the governor depends in part upon a chief executive's political popularity. Public and party approval increases a governor's ability to persuade legislators to pass his or her program or to secure acceptance from administrators of directives or

---

the *Missouri Nonpartisan Court Plan* (New York: John Wiley & Sons, Inc., 1969), especially chapter 5.

23. Virginia Young, "Carnahan Commutes Killer's Death Sentence," *St. Louis Post-Dispatch*, June 3, 1993.
24. See the discussion of extradition in chapter 1.

suggestions. An officeholder who is popular has good prospects for continuing in one office or another for some time, a prospect that attracts supporters and cautions opponents.

Leader of State Politics. By virtue of the office, the governor has many opportunities to influence and direct state politics. The governor receives numerous requests for speeches and personal appearances, many of which are likely to receive television or newspaper coverage. When the governor sponsors a conference, such as Bond's 1976 Conference on Education, people from all over the state step forward to participate. When the governor telephones Missourians, those calls are returned (or at least most of them are). The governor is usually a good fund raiser, good enough so that the chief executive's position on issues can be well presented in a campaign. Both Ashcroft and Hearnes held major fund raisers each year on their birthdays.

Leader of the Party. The governor usually receives overwhelming recognition and acceptance as the leader of a state political party. Governors can probably pick the state party chairman if they wish; certainly Teasdale picked the Democratic party chairs when he was governor. If so desired, the governor can lead party delegations to national party conventions, as Hearnes did in 1968 and 1972. This can be a mixed blessing if a governor gets embroiled in an intraparty dispute. In 1980 Teasdale stayed out of the national delegate selection process because he was concerned about the challenge to his own governorship from within the party.

The governor also appoints some commissions closely tied to partisan politics, including the redistricting commissions for each house of the Missouri legislature (once every ten years) and the Board of Election commissioners in Clay, Jackson, and St. Louis counties, as well as in Kansas City and the city of St. Louis. By virtue of the authority to pick the members of redistricting commissions, the governor can have some influence over the districts of state legislators. Such infighting is rarely discussed publicly so that it is difficult to know how involved various governors have been. In 1971 Hearnes was apparently fairly influential; in 1991 Ashcroft apparently deferred to Republican members of the senate in the development of senatorial districts.

Another indication of restrictions on the governor was revealed by the first appointments to the potentially explosive Ethics Commission. When the commission was first authorized in early 1992, Democratic party committees refused to submit nominations to Ashcroft, in hopes that a Democrat would be elected governor that November. Republican party committees submitted nominations and Ashcroft appointed three Republicans, but the Democratic-controlled senate did not act on these nominations. Once Democrat Mel Carnahan was elected governor, the Democratic committees quickly submitted nominees. This time Republican committees submitted nominees only in certain districts, hoping to restrict the governor's choice to particular Republicans.

The governor may also play a role in the party at the national level. Hearnes helped lead support for the presidential candidacy of Senator Henry "Scoop" Jackson of Washington in 1972. Ashcroft served as co-chairman of the Republican National Convention platform committee in 1992, and was an unsuccessful candidate for the national party chairmanship in 1993.

Of course, the party leadership may be a mixed blessing when the opposite party controls an office or a branch of government. Legislators who see governors as not only heads of competing branches of government but also heads of competing parties have double incentive for opposing or undermining their programs.

An example of the impact of the governor's political power is the influence over the use of the initiative and referendum, an area in which the governor has no special legal powers. Nevertheless, as the state political leader, the governor can exercise considerable influence. Teasdale was an early signer and vocal supporter of a tax limit amendment petition, finally enacted in 1980 as the Hancock Amendment. Ashcroft was reported to have raised the quarter of a million dollars used by opponents to kill a health care initiative in 1988. In 1990 Ashcroft pushed hard for a "Yes on ethics" proposal by contributing $135,000 from his own campaign treasury to the campaign, using license fee office personnel to help collect signatures, and personally soliciting signatures himself. In the end, the proposal was deleted from the ballot by the Missouri Supreme Court, a majority of whose members had been appointed by Ashcroft, for having more than one subject. In 1991 Ashcroft allowed his chief of staff to devote part-time efforts to help manage the campaign for Proposition B, a referendum that would have provided additional funding for education.

VI. Conclusion

The Missouri governorship has sufficient power and prestige that it attracts many of the state's brightest and most capable people. The Missouri political culture, however, has not expected or wanted governors to move boldly in new directions. Furthermore, competition from other states and rising political expectations may force the governor (and all of state government) to run harder and harder to stay in place. In 1992 Mel Carnahan won the governorship with a campaign focused on providing additional funding to stimulate "world class" elementary and secondary schools. Almost immediately, however, he was faced with a court decision requiring additional funding and more equitable state funding for public schools. Setting aside his program for "world class" schools, the governor proposed and pushed through the legislature a tax increase to meet the court requirements. Therefore, while Missouri would not have "world class" schools, at least state funding for public education would be distributed more equitably, and the state's contribution would be a little higher than it had been.[25] Such was the contribution a governor could make.

25. See chapter 17 for a discussion of the 1993 effort to revise the school foundation formula.

CHAPTER 10

Missouri's Other State Constitutional Officers
by Denny E. Pilant

Those [delegates to the constitutional convention who were opposed to having numerous statewide elected offices] were principally the older delegates, those who nurtured no future political ambitions, and the academic group. Such offices as attorney general, secretary of state, [and] treasurer . . . were eyed covetously by the younger and politically ambitious delegates.—Martin Faust, *Constitution Making in Missouri: The Convention of 1943–1944*

In Missouri, as in a number of other states, the governor is not the sole executive officer elected statewide. The Missouri Constitution of 1945 calls for five elected executive officials in addition to the governor: lieutenant governor, secretary of state, auditor, treasurer, and attorney general. All of these executives carry out predominantly ministerial and nondiscretionary tasks. They are responsible for some of the most essential work of state government. But they are not policy makers. They are a part of the state executive branch, but the governor has little or no administrative control over their offices. In terms of public administration, this results in a divided government and divided responsibility, which many students of state government deplore.

These officials may belong to a different political party than the governor, and they all have their own campaign organizations. These statewide executive officeholders can employ virtually whomever they please and pay them whatever they determine is appropriate, within the constraints of the funds granted by the legislature.

There is no formal merit system. All of these offices are considered to be stepping-stones to the governorship, with the offices of attorney general, lieutenant governor, and secretary of state being particularly good platforms for aspiring to higher office.

The most dramatic political change in the statewide offices over the past quarter-century has been the end of the Democrats' long predominance. Beginning in 1968 with the election of Republican John Danforth as attorney general, the Republicans have gradually assumed more control of the statewide offices. After the 1988 elections they held all of the statewide offices except the lieutenant governor's office. In the 1992 election the Democrats regained control of all except the auditor's office; the statewide executive offices can now be classified as two-party competitive. The functions and politics of these offices make up an important part of the political history of Missouri.

I. Lieutenant Governor

Since the governor is the most powerful executive official in the state, one might assume that the lieutenant governor would be the second most important executive elected statewide. But this is far from true. Like the vice president of the United States, who has little to do so long as the president remains healthy, the lieutenant governor has very few jobs to perform as long as the governor remains in office.

The lack of constitutional duties to perform has led to the same kinds of quips about the lieutenant governor that circulate about the vice president. Former U.S. Senator Thomas F. Eagleton once occupied the post of lieutenant governor and was quoted as saying that "the biggest event of [the] day there was watching the Missouri River flow by [the] office window."[1]

The qualifications for lieutenant governor are relatively modest and relate to age, residence, and citizenship. One must be at least thirty years old, a U.S. citizen, and a resident of the state for at least ten years—the same qualifications as for governor. As is usually the case in offices of this type, there is no formal education requirement. Not even a high school diploma is required to be eligible to serve as lieutenant governor.

The lieutenant governor serves a four-year term and may be returned to office for as many terms as he or she manages to be reelected. If the office becomes vacant for any reason, it remains vacant until the next scheduled election.

Constitutional Duties. The lieutenant governor is in the direct line of succession to the governorship should the governor become ill, die, or resign. In the past the lieutenant governor became the acting governor whenever the governor was absent from the state, but a 1991 Missouri Supreme Court decision has largely eliminated this duty.[2]

In addition to his or her role as direct successor in case the governor becomes incapacitated, the lieutenant governor is supposed to preside over the state senate as ex officio president, and he or she may break tie votes. But even this job is not exclusive, since most of the presiding duties must be shared with the president pro tem of the senate.

Extra-Constitutional Duties. Nearly all recent lieutenant governors have taken on extra duties not mentioned in the law or the state constitution. Harriet Woods, for example, established Statewide Volunteers for Efficiency (SAVE). Through this program she encouraged state workers and other citizens to telephone anonymously to report perceived inefficiency on the part of state agencies.

Governors also can assign extra tasks to the lieutenant governor. When Warren Hearnes was governor (1965–1973), he appointed Lieutenant Governor William Morris chairman of the State Goals Commission. The announced purpose of the commission was to give citizens an opportunity to declare their opinions about state policy. But the position also gave Morris the opportunity to travel throughout the state holding "nonpolitical" hearings for the commission. It is probably fair to say, however, that most governors have not been enthusiastic about handing over additional duties to the lieutenant governor.

William C. Phelps, elected to the office in 1972 and 1976, was one of the first to emphasize the lieutenant governor's role as a citizen ombudsman. The lieutenant governor's office continues to refer citizen

---

1. Terry Ganey, "Rothman Plans Enhancement of Lieutenant Governor's Post," *St. Louis Post-Dispatch*, January 4, 1981.

2. During such times when he is acting governor, the lieutenant governor receives the governor's salary.

questions and concerns to appropriate state agencies.

In the 1992 general election, voters approved Proposition C, which assigned additional duties to the lieutenant governor. These duties included memberships on six additional boards and commissions. The proposition also made the lieutenant governor an "advocate for the elderly," and an adviser for early childhood education and the Parents as Teachers program.

The Politics of the Office. Surprisingly, many of the most heated political controversies in recent times concerning the lieutenant governor have centered on the proper way to interpret the meager constitutional duties of the office. Early in his first term as lieutenant governor, Phelps, a Republican, became embroiled in a dispute with William J. Cason, president pro tem of the senate and a Democrat. The controversy was over Phelps's power to preside over the state senate. Cason did not want Phelps to be presiding when important matters came before the senate. The dispute eventually was settled by the Missouri Supreme Court, which ruled that the lieutenant governor did not have the authority to assign bills or make rulings on points of order if senators had elected to vest those duties elsewhere.

Another political controversy has arisen over the lieutenant governor's power to act as governor whenever the sitting governor leaves the state. In March 1979 Lieutenant Governor Phelps signed a bill while Governor Joseph Teasdale, a Democrat, was out of the state at a national governor's conference. Subsequently, Teasdale refused to leave the state in order to keep state government out of the hands of Phelps. Teasdale was quoted as saying that he was "virtually a prisoner of Missouri" because Phelps "is ready to take over the governorship every time I leave." Phelps's response was that Teasdale should be worried! Teasdale was

quoted as saying that Phelps "might do anything—sign bills, veto bills, or make appointments."[3]

The relationship between governor and lieutenant governor can, however, be cordial, even when they are members of opposing political parties. Lieutenant Governor Rothman stood in for Governor Christopher Bond for a total of eighty-seven days in 1981 alone, while Bond was out of state—often on trade missions.

As lieutenant governor, Carnahan contended that he became acting governor whenever Governor John Ashcroft was absent from the state. Ashcroft maintained that he retained his power even if he was absent from the geographical boundaries of Missouri. In an action that some political observers claimed was prearranged, Ashcroft faxed from Japan some documents to Secretary of State Roy Blunt and asked that his facsimile signature be authenticated. Blunt refused to authenticate the signature from out of state, leading to a ruling by the Missouri Supreme Court in *State ex rel. Ashcroft v. Blunt.*[4]

The supreme court distinguished "physical absence" from the state from "effective absence." Modern technology makes it possible, the court ruled, for governors to fax or telephone instructions back to the state when necessary. Only if a governor is effectively prevented from exercising the duties of the office, regardless of whether he or she is out of the state or not, does the lieutenant governor assume the powers, duties, and emoluments of governor.

To clarify the issue, Carnahan, after being elected governor, and Roger Wilson, Car-

3. "Prisoner in State Teasdale Says," *St. Louis Post-Dispatch,* February 26, 1980. Kevin Horrigan, "Phelps: Teasdale Should Be Worried," *St. Louis Post-Dispatch,* March 7, 1980. "Rift with Phelps May Keep Teasdale from Convention," *St. Louis Post-Dispatch,* May 20, 1980.

4. 813 S.W. 2d 849 (Mo banc, 1991).

nahan's successor as lieutenant governor, signed an agreement in January 1993, just before Carnahan left the state to attend the presidential inauguration in Washington, D.C. According to the agreement, Wilson may occasionally substitute for the governor, but he will not be able to make appointments, veto bills, grant pardons, or call out the Missouri National Guard while Carnahan is out of the state.

Campaigning for Lieutenant Governor. Because the constitutional duties of the office have been so limited, candidates for lieutenant governor generally have campaigned on public policy issues that have absolutely nothing to do with the office, or are at best very remotely related to the office.

Until the early 1970s, candidates for lieutenant governor tended to be lawyers who drew their salary (which was not large), showed up during the legislative sessions that met every other year, and continued their private law practices. This tradition ended when Phelps ran for the office in 1972. He campaigned under the slogan "Full-Time" Phelps and promised that, if elected, he would not practice law but instead would be a full-time lieutenant governor. Phelps kept his promise and restricted himself to the duties of the office for two terms of four years each. His annual salary during several of those years was only sixteen thousand dollars. Phelps later said that he nearly starved to death while he was lieutenant governor. Nevertheless, the office of lieutenant governor was for him, as for his predecessors and successors, a "bully pulpit" from which to run for the governorship or the U.S. Senate.

In spite of the obvious campaign advantages in running for governor from the security of the lieutenant governor's office, the record shows that very few lieutenant governors go on to become governor. Only six of Missouri's former lieutenant governors have won election to the governor's office—out of the forty-two who have served.

II. Secretary of State

The office of secretary of state has become very visible in recent years because of its role in elections and because of the exposure derived from publishing the state manual (Blue Book). Its duties are largely ministerial. Historically, the post has had a "clerical" reputation, and the secretary of state often has been referred to as the state's chief clerk.

The secretary of state deals with the real nuts and bolts of state government. His or her work is essential for the day-to-day operation of state government. The office has not been a particularly glamorous or prestigious post in the past. But this old image has changed dramatically, and today the office is viewed as an excellent stepping-stone to the governorship.

The state constitution lists no required qualifications to be secretary of state. The secretary of state has a four-year term and can be reelected indefinitely to the position. He or she is in the line of succession to the governorship.

Constitutional and Legal Duties. Once elected, the new secretary of state takes the oath of office and enters a bond of ten thousand dollars. About two hundred people work for the secretary of state. One employee is designated to serve as deputy secretary of state, with all the power of the secretary of state. The deputy must also have lived in Missouri for at least two years before being appointed. The deputy also has the duties of registration of lands, issuance of patents, and authentication of title to saline or swamp lands. According to law, aggrieved persons must be paid one hundred to five hundred dollars if the deputy neglects or refuses to perform his or her duties.

The secretary of state must report to the governor and the General Assembly annually or whenever requested. An additional duty is that of opening new legislative sessions—a ceremonial role carried out each year.

The secretary of state provides four major services to the state:

1. *Election services.* The secretary of state is the state's chief election official and handles all of the basic election chores, including administering all statewide elections on both candidates and issues. He or she aids county clerks, publishes the Missouri Election Laws, and establishes the rules overseeing electronic voting tabulation systems. The secretary of state also conducts voter education programs and processes initiative and referendum petitions. New political parties trying to get on the ballot must demonstrate to the secretary of state that statutory requirements have been met.

As custodian of the official state seal, the secretary of state carries out a number of commission activities. Examples are affixing the great seal to and attesting to the validity of all commissions of officials elected at the state and local levels, gubernatorial appointments, filing processes, extraditions, commutations, prison sentences, and restorations of citizenship. The same service is performed for all acts signed by the governor.

About twenty thousand notaries public a year are processed and commissioned by the secretary of state. All bonds and oaths of office by state officials are also stored by the secretary of state's office.

The election services division of the secretary of state's office keeps a registry of trademarks and service marks. Twice as much revenue as is needed to run the division is generated annually.

The secretary of state formerly was responsible for campaign reports, including campaign financial statements, for all candidates and organizations required by law to file such reports. This is no longer the case. Today campaign finance reports are the responsibility of the state Ethics Commission.

Sometimes the secretary of state has been embroiled in political controversy over whether or not initiative or referendum petitions have been properly filed. On September 18, 1985, a new law went into effect that made it easier for signers of petitions for statewide referendums to know what they are signing and how it will appear on the ballot. Ballot titles now must be drafted at the beginning instead of the end of the petition process. Moreover, both the secretary of state and the attorney general are required to approve the petition form to be used in advance of the circulation of the petition. The purpose of the law is to reduce, if not eliminate, the rejection of petitions for technical reasons. Candidates for state office file for office with the secretary of state. Many candidates believe that voters do not read all the names on the ballot, and that those names listed first have an advantage of as much as 10 percent of the vote. Since filing was done on a "first come first served" basis, the lineup of candidates often began in front of the secretary of state's office weeks in advance of the filing day so they could get their names on the coveted first line of the ballot. During his tenure as secretary of state, Blunt attempted to end this Missouri tradition by establishing a lottery to determine the filing order. Candidates who showed up at 8 A.M. on the filing day (the second Tuesday in January) were to be given numbers. The candidate with the lowest number was listed first on the ballot; the next lowest, second; and so forth. This procedure, however, was overturned in *Wealton v. Blunt* (1986) as unauthorized by law.[5]

2. *Business services.* The office of secretary of state has a corporate division that provides for the incorporation of new businesses (about sixteen thousand a year) and the annual registration report required of all corporations. As of January 1988 the secretary of state began collecting franchise taxes. This duty was transferred from the Department of Revenue and coupled with the annual corporate registration report so clients could take care of all their business in one office.

A securities division works to protect the public from securities fraud by applying the Missouri Uniform Securities Act, also called the "Blue Sky Law." Proposed securities offerings are screened to see that they meet the intent of the law regarding fairness and other concerns. If brokers do not comply with the law, the secretary of state can order them to stop doing business in the state. In serious cases, violators can be turned over to the attorney general for prosecution. The secretary of state also conducts investor education programs to protect the consumer.

The secretary of state administers the provisions of the Missouri Uniform Commercial Code. Established in 1965, this part of the secretary of state's office keeps data on approximately 750,000 commercial loans, including the debtors' and lenders' names and addresses and the nature of the collateral provided for the loans.

3. *Administrative services.* This division of the secretary of state's office is responsible for producing and preserving a huge volume of publications and records. Administrative rules are published in the *Code of State Regulations* after having been previously published in the *Missouri Register* for public comment prior to becoming effective.

The secretary of state is responsible for publishing numerous items, including the *Official Manual* (Blue Book), *Constitution, State of Missouri, Laws of Missouri, House and Senate Journals, Securities Laws, Corporation Laws, Uniform Commercial Code Handbook, Election Laws, General Assembly Roster,* the results of primary and general elections, various bulletins and newsletters, and *Missouri Roster,* the listing of members of the General Assembly and state, district, and county officers. This large number of publications illustrates why rural newspaper publishers traditionally felt they had special expertise qualifying them for the office of secretary of state.

4. *Library services.* In 1993 the Missouri State Library was added to the secretary of state's office. The library serves the information needs of state government and coordinates some statewide library development programs.

Politics and Reform Proposals. Three patterns can be discerned in the politics of the office. The first and most traditional pattern involved small-town publishers who ran for the office and typically held it for about three terms, then retired from state office. The potential of the office as a springboard for higher office was not generally appreciated. But the publication of the state Blue Book plus the secretary of state's role in elections provides considerable public visibility.

A second pattern was initiated by Warren Hearnes. A lawyer–legislator rather than a publisher, Hearnes succeeded in moving from the secretary of state's office to the governor's office, demonstrating the potential of the office for further political

5. 725 S.W. 2d (Mo. Ap. 1986).

success. James Kirkpatrick, the successor to Hearnes, reflected the more traditional approach to the office with the exception that he served a full five terms instead of the usual three. His successor, Blunt, returned to the Hearnes pattern and ran for governor in 1992—although unsuccessfully. Judi Moriarty, Blunt's successor, may reflect yet a third pattern in the careers of secretaries of state. Like Blunt, Moriarty was a county clerk before running for the office. Both emphasized the fact that county clerks were responsible for conducting elections in Missouri counties and hence were particularly well prepared for the duties of secretary of state, which include election services. Perhaps in the future the career pattern for this office will be county clerk—secretary of state—governor. In other states, secretaries of state also have moved on to become governor, Jerry Brown of California being one example.

In campaigns for the office itself, the lack of policy issues related to the position forces candidates to turn to issues that really have little to do with the duties of the office. In the 1984 campaign the main issues turned on the appropriateness of the educational backgrounds of the candidates and the best color for the state manual. Kirkpatrick, during his unprecedented five terms as secretary of state, changed the color of the state manual to green to celebrate his Irish heritage (and to red, white, and blue during the bicentennial). Some felt it should be returned to its traditional blue color. This is clearly the stuff of which great campaigns are made! (Blunt did reestablish blue as the color for the four manuals published during his term in office, but Moriarty changed the color to mauve.)

The numerous duties of the position and the large number of employees in the office require the secretary of state to have substantial management skills. In 1994 two employees in Moriarty's office, a husband and wife team, resigned and publicly charged favoritism and mismanagement in the office. Moriarty responded that the husband had lost out in a power struggle within the office. The charges forced Moriarty to appoint an administrative review team, which recommended some changes in the management of the office but also commended some procedures. In addition, the county prosecutor brought charges, and Moriarty was found guilty of falsely certifying that her son had filed to run for the state legislature. (The son had paid his filing fee and completed a filing form, but the absence of his signature on the form in the office meant that he could not be legally certified as a candidate.) Governor Carnahan called a special session of the legislature, and the house impeached Moriarty, necessitating a trial before the Missouri Supreme Court. Moriarty was tried, found guilty, and removed from office.

III. Auditor

The office of auditor is not the most glamorous post in state government, but it is one of the most important. The auditor is elected in "off-year" elections on the theory that he or she is more likely to perform an independent check on other statewide elected officials if elected separately from them. The off-year election does insulate the office from the issues that are attached to the races for president and for governor and other statewide elected officials. The drawback is that the duties of the office and the activities of its officeholder are not well known to the voter. When the U.S. Senate race comes up in an auditor's election year, the office is even more overshadowed. It is difficult to capture the public's imagination with debates between candidates for the office over preferred accounting practices.

The auditor must have the same qualifications as the governor, that is, he or she must be at least thirty years old, a citizen of the United States for fifteen years, and a Missouri resident for ten years before the election. (In a court challenge in 1978, James F. Antonio established that the ten years of required Missouri residency do not have to be continuous.)[6] Since 1974 every successful candidate for auditor has emphasized his or her credentials as a certified public accountant and the need for such credentials, a point that has been sufficiently well made to preclude most non-CPAs from candidacy. The term of office is four years with no limit on the number of terms one can serve.

Constitutional and Legal Duties. The auditor is responsible for auditing the books of all the units of state government, including establishing appropriate systems of accounting, conducting postaudits of state agencies, annually auditing the treasury, and making all other inquiries required by the legislature. Reports must be submitted to the governor and the General Assembly annually.

Under Missouri law, the legislature and governor appropriate the budget for all state agencies, and the law and the constitution mandate that the money be spent only for the purposes appropriated. Offices must stay within their budgets. The auditor makes sure that this has been done. He or she reports to elective officers the findings on their appointees and reports in writing the findings on county offices and institutions to the county commissioners or prosecuting attorney. The auditor is also required to furnish budget forms and other help and advice, if so requested, to political subdivisions.

The office of the state auditor not only oversees the books of all the state agencies, boards, commissions, and special programs but also conducts special audits of local governmental entities if enough registered voters request such an audit. The local governmental unit must bear the cost of the audit.

The auditor has no power to force changes in the management of any governmental unit, but he or she does have the capability of focusing the glare of publicity on inefficient agencies. This usually brings about some, if not all, of the changes recommended by the office. If laws are violated by an agency, the auditor may report it to the proper authorities.

The state auditor may calculate whether Missouri taxpayers are owed income tax refunds under the tax and spending limitations (Hancock Amendment) approved by voters in 1980. The auditor's calculations are not final, since other agencies such as the state's Office of Administration can challenge the auditor's estimates.

Along with the governor, the auditor must approve the banks that receive state funds before they are allocated by the state treasurer. By law, the auditor officially certifies and notifies Missouri counties as to whether they are classified as first, second, third, and fourth class counties. The determination is made on the basis of assessed valuation of property in the county.

In the early years of the office, officeholders viewed their primary responsibility as conducting *financial compliance* audits on units of state government. In recent years the auditor's office has expanded its operation to include the investigation of the actual processes of government. This type of operation is often referred to as *performance auditing*, in which in addition to seeing if appropriated money was properly spent, the management of agencies is examined for possible improvement as well.

6. *Antonio v. Kirkpatrick*, 579 F. 2d, 1147 (1978).

Politics of the Office. Traditionally, the state auditor's post was a position almost unnoticed by the general public. Officeholders were elected with little fanfare and served out their terms with almost no publicity. All this changed in 1970, when Republican Christopher Bond defeated the incumbent, Democrat Haskell Holman, by relying on new "high tech" campaign techniques that included radio and television advertising.

Bond proceeded to modernize the office and is credited by some observers for moving it "from a non-controversial, seldom-heard-from agency to a very dear piece of political property." The *St. Louis Post-Dispatch* cited two reasons the auditor's office moved from a bush league position to the major leagues in state politics. One, Bond used the office as a springboard to the governor's office, becoming the first Republican in thirty-two years to capture the governorship. The other reason was that the public was becoming more interested in the auditor's office due to increased public cynicism toward government resulting from the Watergate scandals surrounding President Richard Nixon's administration. This led the public to favor a more independent occupant in the auditor's office.[7]

Upon being elected governor, Bond appointed John Ashcroft to fill out his term as auditor. In 1974 Ashcroft was defeated in his reelection bid by George W. Lehr. Lehr and Ashcroft campaigned hard, spending a sum of more than four hundred thousand dollars. The campaign was significant in that Lehr convinced the voting public that one needed to be a CPA in order to be a qualified auditor.

After a series of resignations and turnovers in the auditor's office, Governor Bond, serving a delayed second term, appointed Margaret Kelly to fill out an unexpired term. Kelly won reelection on her own in 1986, 1990, and 1994, bringing some continuity to an office that had seen considerable turnover since 1970. At the time of her appointment, Kelly was the state's seventh auditor in fifteen years as well as the first woman to hold statewide office in Missouri.

In 1992 Kelly was defeated in a bid for the lieutenant governorship. Her defeat, along with Ashcroft's defeat in 1974, points out what are possibly inherent difficulties in using the auditor's office as a political stepping-stone. It may turn out to be the case that Bond and Forrest Smith (a Democrat who served as auditor for four terms and then was elected governor in 1948) are exceptions to the usual career patterns of auditors. The traditional pattern would tend to indicate that the office holds limited possibilities for getting elected to higher political office.

Reform Proposals. Several former auditors, including Democrat Lehr and Republican Antonio, have called for making the auditor's office an appointed position, with professional credentials (such as a CPA certificate) required to hold the position. In about thirty states the auditor is appointed; the other twenty states elect their auditor.[8] One might argue that if appointed, the auditor should not be directly under the control of the governor because as a watchdog over billions of dollars in state funds, the office should be completely independent of the executive branch. The legislature could employ the auditor, who could run the office in much the same way the

7. Richard K. Weil Jr., "Lehr, Ashcroft Look beyond Auditor's Job," *St. Louis Post-Dispatch*, October 6, 1974.

8. *The Book of the States*, 1988–1989 ed., vol. 27 (Lexington, Ky.: Council of State Governments), Table 2.9, 51–52.

comptroller general runs the General Accounting Office for Congress. But if independence and professionalism are both highly valued, perhaps the simplest change would be to constitutionally require that the state auditor be a CPA or the equivalent. This would provide the state with a professionally qualified auditor who would also be free from the direct control of the other branches of government.

IV. Treasurer

The state treasurer's office is primarily a banking operation through which most of the state's annual budget of more than $13 billion is handled. State expenditures are determined on a yearly basis by the governor, the governor's budget office, and the legislature. The Division of Accounting in the Office of Administration sends to the treasurer the bills that need to be paid on a day-to-day basis. The state constitution specifies that no money shall be withdrawn from the state treasury unless a warrant is presented to the state treasurer. The treasurer signs the warrants and converts them into a check or draft on a banking institution that is a designated depository of state funds. The treasurer is the custodian of state funds. He selects, with the approval of the governor and the auditor, the banks in which to invest state funds not needed for current operating expenses. There are about forty employees in the treasurer's office.

There are no specific qualifications listed in the state constitution for treasurer. In Missouri's first constitution in 1820, the treasurer was elected by the legislature, but the office is now elective. Once elected, treasurers are limited to two terms in office.

Constitutional and Legal Duties. Within sixty days of assuming office, the treasurer must be bonded for five hundred thousand dollars or forfeit the office.[9] The governor must check the solvency of the bond every six months. A curious statutory provision provides that the treasurer forfeits five thousand dollars if he or she doesn't take the oath of office.

The treasurer has the authority to appoint one assistant treasurer along with other clerical employees and to set their salaries. He or she may administer oaths and use the seal of the office. The treasurer is required to keep duplicate receipts for all sums of money paid into the treasury and to turn the copy over to the commissioner of administration.

As state treasurer, he or she must make a monthly report to the governor on disbursements and receipts. The treasurer also reports to the commissioner of administration monthly. The treasurer has access to the books of other state officers so far as they concern the treasurer's duties, and the treasurer provides blank forms for clerks of courts and county officers.

Beginning in February 1986 the legislature authorized the MO-BUCKS subsidized loan program, which allocated $150 million for farm loans and $50 million for small-business loans. The program authorized the state treasurer to make deposits in banks, savings and loans, and credit unions that agree to provide low-interest farm and business loans. The state does not guarantee the loans, but it puts one-year deposits at the participating banking institutions at three percentage points below the one-year Treasury Bill rate.

Robert Holden, a Democrat elected in 1992, said that to prevent favoritism, he would change the MO-BUCKS program so the treasurer would not know who was applying for loans. He also said that he wanted to expand the MO-BUCKS program to

9. The state pays the premium for the bond.

give loans for retraining workers who are laid off. Holden labeled his program the "linked-deposit program."

Holden's predecessor, Wendell Bailey, set up a panel of private and public experts to forecast state revenue, believing that "appropriations for major state services have been affected by disagreement over how much money the state will have to spend in approaching fiscal years."[10] The goal was to try to end arguments among the governor, the house, and the senate over how much money the state will bring in and therefore how much can be appropriated for state revenues.

The treasurer's office is closely regulated by law, but the treasurer still has great discretion in choosing where to invest state funds. The treasurer has the power, with the approval of the governor and state auditor, to select banking institutions in which to place idle state funds (those not needed for current expenses) that may then earn interest for the state.

Extra-Constitutional Duties. The state treasurer can also use the office to advance certain policy objectives. James Spainhower, for example, announced during his tenure as treasurer that his office would review the lending practices of banks that received state treasury deposits. If any of those banks were found guilty of "redlining," a banking practice in which mortgage loans are systematically denied in certain parts of the city, then their status as state depositories would be reviewed. Both Bailey and Mel Carnahan were opposed to the state putting its money in South African investments so long as the South African government practiced apartheid.

Several state treasurers, including Spainhower and Bailey, have encouraged the deposit of state money in minority owned or minority linked banks so they can lend money to other minority businesses.

Politics of the Office. The election of 1972 was the first campaign in recent times in which the race for state treasurer took on its own identity separate from the regular party state ticket. Both candidates campaigned on their own personal platforms and emphasized issues separate from their party's ticket. Before 1972, treasury candidates generally associated themselves closely with the party ticket. Since Democrats usually were in the majority, the Democratic candidate usually won by riding on the coattails of the party. But between 1969 and 1972 the Democratic officeholder in the treasurer's office was accused of the misuse of idle state funds, cozy arrangements with favorite bankers, and even alleged payoffs. For many years state treasurers kept some state money in noninterest-bearing accounts in banks that had helped them get elected. This was free money for the banks, who used it to make more loans. For nearly half a century there was a close relationship between the state treasurer's office and Central Trust Bank of Jefferson City. For years the state treasurer belonged to the same political party as the governor, and Central Trust was allowed to control much of the state's idle money. Between 1965 and 1972, the average daily cash balance—idle uninvested state funds—exceeded $23 million. It has been estimated that as much as $6.5 million could have been made by favored banks in years with high interest rates.

Democrat Spainhower ran as a "Mr. Clean" candidate and was elected in 1972. Spainhower changed the tradition of leaving millions of state funds in noninterest-bearing accounts. By the end of his first term, Spainhower had developed a comprehensive formula for depositing idle state

---

10. Fred W. Lindecke, "State Treasurer's Campaign Stirs Limited Interest," *St. Louis Post-Dispatch*, October 20, 1984.

money and began investing more than 98 percent of available state funds. This earned the state additional income estimated by Spainhower to total about $75 million over nearly four years.

Campaigns for state treasurer in recent years have revolved around management, money, and experience. Virtually all candidates have agreed that the state's money should be invested to earn the highest possible interest rates. The conflict has tended to occur over campaign money "invested" by bankers in various candidates. This had led to charges of conflict of interest and cozy relationships between the treasurer and specific banks in the state. But the need for campaign funds (bankers or their PACs typically contribute from 40 to 50 percent of the winning candidate's money) has made candidates very reluctant to give up this source of money.

After the 1980 campaign, in which the usual charges were traded about favoritism on the part of the treasurer's office toward certain banks, Treasurer Mel Carnahan changed the office's banking and investment practices. While Central Trust Bank of Jefferson City continued to process state checks and handle other essential recordkeeping chores, other major banks around the state such as Boatmen's Bank of St. Louis, United Missouri Bank of Kansas City, and Mercantile Bank of St. Louis were also given some of the state's business. To prevent future charges of favoritism in selecting banks to deposit state funds, Carnahan set up a committee to determine which banks would be chosen using a revolving list and a special formula.

The winner of the 1984 election was Bailey, a Republican. One of his first acts was to transfer more than $500 million in state funds from New York banking institutions to Missouri banks. This action was intended to benefit businesses within the state by establishing larger loan services for patrons and businesses.

The August following his election, Bailey switched the state's bank account from Central Trust Bank of Jefferson City to United Missouri Bank in the capital. The change was supposed to save the state money and also make an acceptable profit for United Missouri Bancshares, which won the competitive bid for the state's business.

The most important consequence of the change in banks was probably political rather than financial. Central Trust traditionally has been a supporter of Democrats for state office. Moving to another bank made the Republicans potentially more competitive with the Democrats in raising campaign funds for the office.[11] Democrat Robert Holden accepted support from the Central Bank in his successful 1992 campaign for state treasurer, but said he would use bids to award state banking business.

In 1994 Treasurer Holden's policy was to deposit in each Missouri bank sufficient funds to cover the amount that the bank had loaned under MO-BUCKS or similar economic development programs, and also to deposit in any Missouri bank any amount requested by the bank, so long as the bank put up equivalent collateral and paid interest at the current Treasury bill rate. Requests from banks covered only about 20 percent of available funds, and the remaining 80 percent were invested in U.S. Government Obligations, earning additional interest for the state. The state's checking account was maintained at

---

11. Switching banks is not as easy as it might seem. In 1981 when Mel Carnahan began the first competitive bidding for the state's banking business, only Central Trust bid on all the services. Most banks were willing to bid for only part of the state's business. Wendell Bailey also found only two banks, United Missouri and Central Trust, interested in making complete bids for the state's accounts.

Central Trust Bank, but the state deposited in its major account only an amount equal to the checks that had cleared that day, thus retaining for the state the opportunity to invest for a few days the funds for checks that had been written but not yet cashed.

Reform Proposals. As in the case of the other elected state executives, it has been suggested that the treasurer's office be made appointive rather than elective.

Certainly, if treasurers were appointed there would be no need for campaign contributions from banks and any possible conflict of interest would be eliminated. A possible drawback would be the removal of a very sensitive area from intensive public scrutiny. Critics of election, however, point to the fact that there is little intensive public scrutiny with the present system of statewide election.

V. Attorney General

The attorney general is the chief legal officer for the state and represents the state in both federal and state courts. He or she represents the state in cases in which the state is a party and represents Missourians as a group, but does not represent citizens in private legal disputes. As the state's chief legal representative and because of the office's visibility to the public, the attorney general is one of the most powerful persons in state government. But paradoxically, the office is only mentioned in the state constitution in listing the order of succession to the governorship, as one of the state executive offices, and in those sections discussing elections. The state office originated in 1806 when Missouri was not yet a state but was part of the Louisiana Territory. The first state constitution mandated an appointed attorney general, but the post was made elective in the 1865 constitution and thereafter. The functions of the office are considered to be

traditional and hence are not defined by the constitution.[12]

There are no formal requirements as to age, citizenship, residency, membership in the state bar, or whether one must be a voter or licensed attorney to be eligible for the office. In 1984 a St. Louis man announced that he was filing for the post even though he was not a licensed attorney. Secretary of State Kirkpatrick, on the advice of Attorney General Ashcroft, informed the candidate that state laws give the attorney general courtroom duties and "[b]eing a lawyer is the '*sine qua non*' [essential condition] of the attorney general's duties."[13]

Legal Duties. The attorney general must devote his or her full time to the office and is not permitted to engage in the private practice of law. The attorney general is elected to a four-year term and may be reelected indefinitely. There are nearly 250 employees in the office—which has long been criticized for having too many inexperienced young attorneys due to the relatively low salaries available. This has led most of Missouri's recent attorneys general to lobby the legislature for increased funding in order to hire more and better lawyers.

The office may institute *quo warranto* proceedings against any person unlawfully holding office and can oust any public official for misfeasance, nonfeasance, or malfeasance in office. This is a relatively rare proceeding, yet it was instituted by the attorney general's office in 1985 against a Jefferson County assessor who was accused by county executives of sabotaging the reassessment process and thereby jeopardizing the county's tax base.[14] In 1994

---

12. The duties of the attorney general are found in RSMo., 1986, Chapter 27.

13. Fred W. Lindecke, "Gibson Disqualified in Attorney General Race," *St. Louis Post-Dispatch*, April 6, 1984.

14. Mary E. Chollet, "Suit Seeks Ouster of Assessor," *St. Louis Post-Dispatch*, March 15, 1985.

Attorney General Jay Nixon threatened ouster proceedings against Secretary of State Judi Moriarty if she did not resign or was not impeached.

The attorney general is required by law to issue legal opinions to all statewide executive officials, members of the General Assembly, local prosecutors, and the heads of the various state departments on the interpretation of statutes relating to their legal duties. The attorney general does not give opinions on the constitutionality of bills or ordinances. His or her opinions do not have the force of law, and the Missouri Supreme Court has ruled that the attorney general's opinions have no more weight than the opinion of any good attorney. Nevertheless, the opinion of the attorney general is constantly solicited, and recent occupants of the office have attempted to decrease the amount of time required to produce opinions requested by legislators.[15]

The duties of the attorney general's office are carried out in six divisions.

Litigation Division. All major or complex litigation is sent here for consideration. Such major cases as *Webster v. Reproductive Health Services* and *Cruzan v. Harmon* are worked on in this part of the attorney general's office. This is the division that pursued the Kansas City and St. Louis school desegregation cases.

The attorney general defends state law when challenged on federal constitutional grounds. During much of his tenure as attorney general from 1977 to 1985, Ashcroft was preoccupied with defending the state against a school desegregation plan mandated for St. Louis by the federal courts. Federal court decisions found the state a "primary constitutional wrong-doer" and

held it responsible for paying for most of the costs associated with the St. Louis desegregation plan. This still allowed Ashcroft (and later Bill Webster) to dispute legally which costs were related to desegregation and which ones were not. The attorney general's office contended that the St. Louis School District was using desegregation as a guise to force the state to pay for the rebuilding of the city's school system. Ashcroft charged the desegregation plan with being "a monumental drain on the state treasury."[16] Webster followed Ashcroft's confrontational lead and was forced to deal with court-ordered desegregation of the Kansas City School District as well.

Missouri attorneys general from John Danforth (1969–1977) through Ashcroft (1977–1985) and Webster (1985–1993) have taken very conservative positions in regard to the abortion issue, which blossomed after the U.S. Supreme Court's *Roe v. Wade* decision that legalized abortion in 1973. Webster successfully argued a Missouri-based abortion case before the Supreme Court, winning a decision in *Webster v. Reproductive Health Services* that modified in some respects the *Roe v. Wade* decision and returned more discretion on the abortion issue to the state legislatures.

Another case that drew national attention concerned Nancy Cruzan, who was left in a permanent coma after an automobile accident. Her parents petitioned to remove her from intravenous nutrition, but the Missouri Supreme Court upheld the interest of the state in maintaining life.[17] Her case was appealed on her behalf by her parents to the U.S. Supreme Court, where Webster argued Missouri's position against

15. *Gershmann Investment Corp. v. Danforth*, 517 S.W. 2d 33 (Mo en banc, 1974). Fred W. Lindecke, "Watching the Websters," *St. Louis Post-Dispatch*, September 2, 1985.

16. Joan Little, "To Head Off Cuts in Services Bond Says, Ashcroft Pledges Fight," *St. Louis Post-Dispatch*, October 21, 1983.

17. *Cruzan v. Harmon*, 760 S.W. 2d, 408 (Mo en banc 1988).

a "right to die." The "right to life" movement has been very strong in Missouri, and the legislature even enacted a law effective January 1, 1988, declaring that life begins at conception.

Jay Nixon, a Democrat elected attorney general in 1992, declared that the state of Missouri had no business being involved in right-to-die disputes. One of his first acts in office was to end the state's fight to prevent an accident victim's father from moving his daughter from the state so her feeding tubes could be removed.

Criminal Division. This is one of the most traditional activities of the office. The attorney general is required to defend state convictions in every felony criminal case appealed to a court of appeals or the Missouri Supreme Court. He or she is authorized to assist local prosecuting attorneys in difficult trials and also has the authority to initiate local prosecutions for specific crimes that have been committed. The attorney general represents all state agencies related to law enforcement in state and federal civil litigation.

One of the attorney general's concerns in recent years has been the control of paramilitary-type activities. Webster called for tougher laws that would make it illegal for paramilitary organizations to assemble in the state for purposes of training individuals in violent techniques.

Environmental Protection Division. The attorney general's office enforces laws on environmental protection, mental health, and human services. It provides legal services to state agencies that are concerned with these issues. The attorney general works to speed cleanup of hazardous waste sites and to make polluters clean up or reimburse the state for cleanup costs. According to Webster, environmental litigation is the "single most rapidly growing area of litigation in the attorney general's office."

Consumer Protection Division. One of the more glamorous responsibilities of the attorney general's office is the protection of a free and open marketplace for the Missouri public. The attorney general enforces the Consumer Protection Act and the state's antitrust laws prohibiting monopolies and restraint of trade. He or she also prosecutes securities fraud for the secretary of state. The attorney general has established offices in St. Louis, Kansas City, and Springfield to expedite handling consumer complaints. The attorney general also is involved in consumer protection in areas involving "deception, fraud, misrepresentation or the concealment of material facts in the sale or advertisement of goods or services."[18]

The attorney general's office has sued a number of auto dealers over odometer tampering. All of the suits have typically demanded restitution to the victims and a one thousand dollar civil penalty for each violation.

Governmental Affairs Division. At the request of any state agency, the attorney general's office must assign an assistant attorney general to assist them in performing the duties required by law. The office will conduct litigation for administrative agencies, issue official advice, interpret statutes or regulations, prepare and review legal documents, and review administrative rules and regulations for legality.

The attorney general is charged with enforcing the state liquor laws and represents the public in proceedings affecting "the administration of charitable trusts" and the Workers Compensation Second Injury Fund.[19]

18. Secretary of State, *Official Manual: State of Missouri,* 1991–1992, 57.
19. Ibid., 58.

Labor Division. The attorney general's office represents the state in claims involving the Second Injury Fund, the claims of victims of crime, workmen's compensation claims if state employees are involved, and prevailing wage disputes. The attorney general also provides legal assistance to the Missouri Department of Labor and Industrial Relations and those who report to it.

Politics of the Office. The enormous publicity surrounding some of the cases argued by the attorney general makes this office a natural platform from which to run for higher office. Indeed, in this respect the office rivals that of governor or U.S. senator in terms of its potential influence on future public policy in the state.

Thomas Eagleton was attorney general from 1961 to 1965, then was elected lieutenant governor, and from that post went on to be elected U.S. senator in 1968, where he served three terms. Several of the assistants hired in the office by Eagleton later moved up to very influential positions in government service.

Danforth won the office in 1968. Under him, the office also became a fertile training ground for future political leaders. Those who trained under Danforth included Bond, later governor and then U.S. senator; Ashcroft, governor and then U.S. senator; Al Sikes, chairman of the Federal Communications Commission; and Clarence Thomas, who took a seat on the U.S. Supreme Court after a lengthy and controversial confirmation fight.

Campaigns for the office have grown more lively in recent years. Since the late 1960s, candidates for the post have tended to see the attorney general as a spokesman for a better system of law enforcement and administration of justice instead of just as a routine pleader of the state's position in civil and criminal matters. Most of the recent attorneys general have presented annually their own "legislative package" of laws that they think the legislature should pass to protect Missourians against crime.

In 1992 Webster, then attorney general, lost a hotly contested gubernatorial contest with Mel Carnahan. Webster, unable to get legislative appropriations to pay for in-house lawyers to defend the Second Injury Fund, appointed lawyers who represented the fund on a contract basis. (The Second Injury Fund makes payments to workers with job-related injuries that are intensified because of previous medical problems.) A series of articles in the *St. Louis Post-Dispatch* charged that many lawyers appointed by Webster to defend the fund contributed campaign funds to him. Also, according to the St. Louis newspaper, lawyers who contributed to Webster tended to get larger settlements from the Second Injury Fund.

Webster was charged with political favoritism and wrongdoing by his primary election opponents, but still won his party's nomination. In the general election the negative publicity surrounding the Second Injury Fund was a major factor in Webster's loss to Carnahan. After the election, Webster pleaded guilty to two charges, including conspiring to defraud the state by using the Second Injury Fund to raise campaign money. Jay Nixon, the newly elected attorney general, said that he would only use staff attorneys to defend the Second Injury Fund and was supported with appropriations for that purpose from the General Assembly.

VI. Conclusion

The five statewide executive offices examined in this chapter are administrative posts that do not make policy. Strong arguments can be made to make the treasurer and secretary of state appointed by and directly responsible to the governor. The lieutenant governor's office serves primarily to provide the occupant with a dependable salary while he spends his time campaigning for higher office. The duties of this office could be transferred to the secretary of state and president pro tem of the senate, especially now that the lieutenant governor does not act as governor when the governor is out of the state. The auditor's office should be retained as an elective post with the constitution being amended to reflect the growing custom of only electing CPAs to that post. The attorney general could also be an appointee of the governor, just as at the federal level, where he is an appointee of the president. Since the governor is legally responsible for the faithful execution of the laws and is the conservator of the peace, it makes sense to have the attorney general, the state's lawyer, directly responsible to him.

This would leave only two elected state executives. Such an administrative model would increase the concentration of executive authority and responsibility in the governor's office. It would also make the Missouri governor much more clearly accountable for the policies of the executive branch of state government. This administrative model appeals to many students of public administration. It would undoubtedly be less attractive to many Missouri voters who are accustomed to voting for statewide administrative officials and consider it a right to be able to do so.

CHAPTER 11

Public Administration: Structure, Process, and Reinvention

by C. Cartwright Young

> Today's environment demands institutions that . . . deliver high-quality goods and services, squeezing ever more bang out of every buck. It demands institutions that are responsive to their customers, offering choices of nonstandardized services; that lead by persuasion and incentives rather than commands; that give their employees a sense of meaning and control, even ownership.—David Osborne and Ted Gaebler

To appreciate public administration, one must analyze it in the context of modern government. The breadth of services now expected by society makes the work of public agencies more significant and more challenging. Financial constraints on governments have caused increased scrutiny of the efficiency and effectiveness of government agencies and bureaucrats. The ongoing pressures for growth exacerbate the problems public agencies face. Not only do elected leaders and government agencies initiate ideas for additional government programs but also constituents, interest groups, and citizens place increased demands on governments. Furthermore, these demands are frequently for programs that are extremely difficult to provide. Health care, welfare, and economic development demands are not easily met. Nevertheless, existing government programs, even those that are costly and produce mediocre results, develop strong support among constituencies, making them extremely difficult to eliminate.[1]

1. James Q. Wilson, "The Rise of the Bureaucratic State," *The Public Interest* 41 (Fall 1975): 77–103.

As new needs emerge, the typical response is to add programs. Constituency support blocks reduction or elimination of existing programs, and thus political pressure leads to expansion of government rather than to substituting new programs for less needed services. Ultimately, the public bears some of the responsibility for this tendency toward government growth because citizens are quick to demand new government services, even though they are often reluctant to pay for them. This expansion of government activity has inevitably increased the number and role of public administrators and makes their work even more important to study.

Woodrow Wilson wrote in 1887, "Administration lies outside the proper sphere of *politics*. Administrative questions are not political questions." It was Wilson's view that elected public officials should make policy and that administrators should only serve to carry out policy. Wilson argued, "It is the object of administrative study to discover, first, what government can properly and successfully do, and, secondly, how it can do these proper things with the utmost possible efficiency and at the least cost either of money or of energy."[2] Thus Wilson's focus was a legal, structural, and managerial one in which administrators were to implement the policies passed by elected officials efficiently and effectively.

Much of the public administration literature of the last fifty years is in direct conflict with Wilson's policy–administration dichotomy. Over the last half-century, scholars have taken a much more political approach in analyzing public administration. The political approach focuses on the political, entrepreneurial role that public administrators must play if they hope to be effective. In his classic article "Power and Administration," Norton Long asserted, "The lifeblood of administration is power. Its attainment, maintenance, increase, dissipation, and loss are subjects the practitioner and student can ill afford to neglect." Consequently, an administrator cannot rely on formal grants of authority from the legislature in carrying out the activities of the agency. The administrator instead must play the role of entrepreneur to cultivate political support: "It is clear that the American system of politics does not generate enough power at any focal point of leadership to provide the conditions for an even partially successful divorce of politics from administration."[3]

Public administrators rely on formal grants of authority such as regulatory and rule-making authority, but they also rely on less formal forms of authority, such as the power to determine policy through discretionary interpretation of legislative phrases (often so vague as to demand interpretation). One scholar notes, "Even when an administrator's discretion is constrained by many rules, procedures, and checks, . . . public administration has become a center for the development of policy choices for American society as a whole."[4] As a repository of expertise, commitment, and interest, the public administrator is a useful partner in the legislative process of drafting and passing bills. Similarly, public administrators need the financial resources and legal authority the legislature has to offer. This symbiotic relationship develops into an even stronger political base when administrators are joined by supportive interest groups.

Recognizing the importance of the political realm of public administration does not lessen the need to understand its legal/structural realm. In many cases the structures of the national and state governments and the public agencies influence administrative politics and processes. Thus, the first section of this chapter explains the formal structure of Missouri's executive branch and explores how these formal elements influence the public administrator's resources of power as well as the agency's political environment. The second section of this chapter focuses on the political nature of public administration processes. This section investigates the symbiotic executive–legislative relationship, the political budget process, and the territorial nature of the jurisdictional claims of agencies.

The third section examines a relatively new orientation to public administration promoted in David Osborne and Ted Gaebler's recent book *Reinventing Government*.[5] The book's insights into increasing the effectiveness of government

2. Woodrow Wilson, "The Study of Administration," *Political Science Quarterly* 56 (December 1941): 494, 481. (Originally published in 1887.)

3. Norton Long, "Power and Administration," *Public Administration Review* 9 (Autumn 1949): 257–58.

4. David H. Rosenbloom, *Public Administration: Understanding Management, Politics, and Law in the Public Sector*, 3d ed. (New York: McGraw Hill, 1993), 52.

5. David Osborne and Ted Gaebler, *Reinventing Government: How the Entrepreneurial Spirit is Transform-*

have caught the attention of the Clinton and the Carnahan administrations. Osborne and Gaebler's approach to public administration assumes both the need for formally structured accountability and the reality and advantages of empowering employees in executive organizations. In this way, reinventing government strategies and assumptions provides an opportunity to synthesize the primary schools of thought within public administration literature—legal/structural, managerial, and political.

I. The Structure of Public Administration in Missouri

Since public administration resides primarily in the executive branch of government, a good place to begin a structural review of Missouri public administration is with a review of Missouri's executive branch organization chart (see Figure 11–1). Missouri's current administrative structure reflects the Administrative Reorganization Act of 1974, with a few adjustments. The Department of Highways and Transportation is a merger of two once separate agencies. In 1984 the Department of Consumer Affairs, Regulation, and Licensing was renamed the Department of Economic Development. The Department of Corrections and the Department of Health, which were previously part of the Department of Social Services, became autonomous departments in 1981 and 1985, respectively. The Department of Insurance (formerly part of the Department of Economic Development) was established in 1990.

Note in Figure 11–1 that in addition to the sixteen departments whose department heads, boards, or commissioners are gubernatorial appointments, there are four other important executive department heads and a lieutenant governor who are elected directly by the people every four years and who are therefore able to be independent of the governor. This structure may exacerbate coordination problems, particularly because Missouri voters have, since 1968, elected at least one statewide official of the major political party opposite that of the governor. Thus, electing statewide officials contributes to the fragmentation of power, complicating the task of achieving efficiency and coordination.

The ability of the governor to coordinate departments and agencies is also limited by the many administrative organizations run by commissions or boards rather than by officials appointed by the governor. In 1993 five of the state's fifteen departments were headed by a commission or board with authority to appoint chief executive officers.[6] These commissions are composed of a specified number of members who serve staggered terms and who in some instances must represent certain sectors of society.

Commissions can help shield administrative departments from political forces. For example, the Department of Conservation was specifically designed to be as free as possible from political interference. The department is headed by a bipartisan commission of four members appointed by the governor for staggered six-year terms.

---

6. Conservation, Department of Elementary and Secondary Education, Department of Higher Education, Department of Highway and Transportation, and Department of Mental Health. The Department of Labor and Industrial Relations also has a three-member board, but the board and the governor share the power to appoint the director. The board nominates and the governor appoints with the advice and consent of the senate. The Department of Health also has a board appointed by the governor that serves in an advisory capacity to the department director. See "Guide to Missouri State Government," 1993 Directory, a pamphlet produced by the Missouri Commission on Intergovernmental Cooperation, Jefferson City.

---

ing the Public Sector (Reading, Mass.: Addison-Wesley, 1992).

Figure 11-1. Missouri State Government Executive Branch

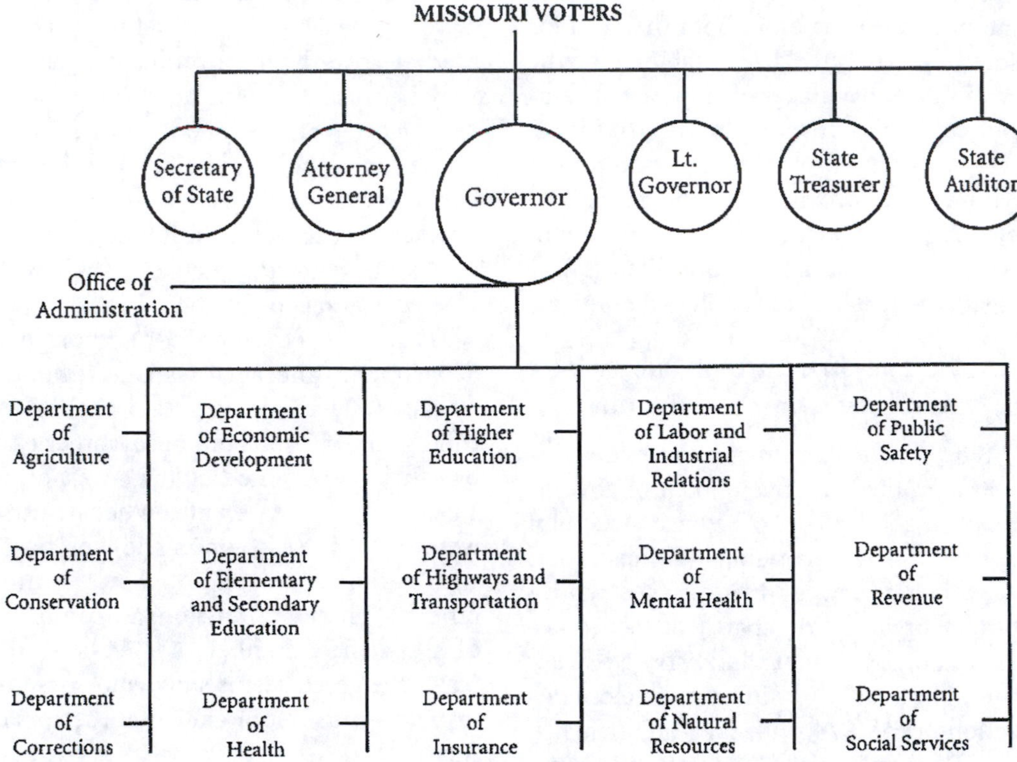

Accordingly, the governor cannot upon election select his own four people to head the commission. He can only appoint a new member when a current member's term is completed, and at any time half the commissioners must be from a political party other than the governor's.[7] The Conservation Department is even more independent from the governor and legislature since it receives revenue from an earmarked one-eighth-cent sales tax and does not depend on appropriations from the general revenues controlled by the legislature and governor.

7. There are procedures for early removal in the case of misconduct in office.

It is obvious that department structures and sizes are extremely varied. Some also have more direction from Washington, D.C., than do others. For example, since the Department of Natural Resources administers many programs under guidelines set by the Environmental Protection Agency, it is directly influenced by national as well as state policy. Federal funding can also mean more federal influence over policy. In the 1993 fiscal year, five state agencies—Highways and Transportation, Health, Social Services, Labor and Industrial Relations, and Economic Development—received more than half of their funds from federal sources (see Table 11–1).

Table 11-1. 1993 Federal Funds
as a Percent of Total Missouri
Department Revenues

Highways and Transportation	79
Health	72
Social Services	62
Labor and Industrial Relations	61
Economic Development	58
Conservation	32
Natural Resources	23
Public Safety	19
Mental Health	14
Elementary and Secondary Education	14
Administration	5
Insurance	3
Agriculture	3
Higher Education	2
Corrections	1
Revenue	0.1

Personnel practices among Missouri's departments also vary. Six departments, the departments of Administration, Corrections, Health, Mental Health, Natural Resources, and Social Services, and specific divisions and agencies in the departments of Economic Development, Labor and Industrial Relations, and Public Safety, are under the Missouri Merit System. The Division of Personnel located within the Office of Administration administers the merit system, which covers approximately thirty thousand employees. The merit system includes standardized job descriptions and pay levels, competitive examinations for employment, and objective and consistent personnel policies and appeals from disciplinary actions. The Division of Personnel classifies all positions, develops and maintains the pay plan, recruits and examines applicants, audits payroll and personnel transactions, and administers rules governing appeals, layoffs, and other matters. Other departments have their own personnel systems that typically provide for systematic practices similar to the merit system. However, the Department of Economic Development and the Department of Revenue still maintain some vestiges of a patronage system for some of their employees. Furthermore, a number of policy-making positions within each department are exempt from the merit system.

One study of Missouri state government workers compared employment equity in the Social Services Department, a merit department, with that of the Department of Revenue, a "patronage" department. While 78 percent of the staff of both departments were women in 1987, the average earnings for women in the Social Services Department were 86 percent of the average earnings for men, while the average earnings for women in the Department of Revenue were only 70 percent of the men's average. Even more discouraging, average earnings for women in the Department of Revenue in 1951 had been 80 percent of men's average earnings, and thus the department's pay equity over time has actually dropped by ten percentage points. Pay equity in the Department of Social Services improved by four percentage points over the same period.[8] One other implication is the difficulty of achieving change by imposition of legal rules; equal pay for equal work had not been achieved even in government agencies after twenty-five years of the Equal Pay Act.

The last structural feature addressed here is the General Assembly's Joint Committee on Administrative Rules. Five members of the senate and five members of the house fill this joint committee. Created to allow the legislature to intervene if an agency promulgates rules that exceed its statutory authority, the committee provides a potential constraint on agencies.

8. Helen V. Cartwright, "Equality in the Workplace: Myth or Reality," Ph.D. diss., University of Missouri, December 1993, chapter 5.

The Committee on Administrative Rules reviews a small number of rules and rarely suspends them. Politics obviously influences the degree to which this procedure is used. Nevertheless, it is one more structure of Missouri state government, this time within the legislative branch, that may affect public administration.

II. The Political Process of Public Administration

Missouri public administrators must often become involved in the political process to carry out the duties of their position. Department directors are expected to be the primary spokespersons for policy in their departmental areas of expertise. In addition, this expertise and intense interest in the policy area often causes the executive departments to work alongside the legislature and the agency's attentive publics and interest groups. Consequently, this section of the chapter examines the power of public administrators and their influence on legislation and public policy.

Executive–Legislative Relations

The astute public administrator knows that it is political suicide to isolate oneself from the governor or the state legislature. Modern administrators are directly involved in the identification, formulation, and implementation of public policies. Thus, department officials try to maintain good relations with the governor, his advisers, and the legislature (especially with legislators who are members of committees that directly affect their own department). After identifying a problem area, public administrators who wish to establish or expand a program in their agency are wise to cultivate political support for their proposal. Convincing powerful legislators on the pertinent committees and also the governor of the need for such expansion is essential to improve chances for approval. The shrewd agency leader will also strive to gain vocal support from key interest or clientele groups and influential individuals. Thus, public administrators cannot simply respond to legislative or gubernatorial directives, but instead must become entrepreneurs—selling their agencies and ideas, initiating legislative action, testifying at legislative hearings, and maintaining the pressure necessary to push legislation through the General Assembly's maze of personalities, jurisdictions, and institutional procedures and rules.

In an interview study of seventy members of the General Assembly, legislators acknowledged the reliance they have on others for issue information.[9] When asked, "To what extent do you rely on the relevant state agencies for information on bills?" 55 percent answered "extensively," 26 percent answered "some," 11 percent reported "not often," and 5 percent reported "almost never." Asked to what extent they relied on lobbyists for information on bills, 39 percent responded "extensively," 40 percent "some," 18 percent "not often," and 3 percent "almost never." Legislators, recognizing the agencies' closer proximity to information, depend heavily on agency officials for information. In comments, it was easily discerned that many legislators lament this dependence on others for information. Often the legislator would mention that both state agencies and lobbyists can be expected to package information to benefit their interests. One senator suggested that information from agencies was more reliable because the legislature has more leverage over agencies, while other legisla-

9. Seventy legislators who had a bill reach the perfection calendar prior to the first week of March in 1989 and 1990 were interviewed by the author using a structured interview. The average interview lasted thirty minutes.

tors felt that lobbyists were more likely to give an unbiased view because they tended to have longer careers than agency legislative liaisons and needed to maintain their legitimacy.

A final example of the political nature of the executive-legislative relationship is that rules require bills and joint resolutions to include a fiscal note. A fiscal note predicts the fiscal impact of each proposal, and all bills accompanied by a fiscal note of one hundred thousand dollars or more must be heard by the Budget Committee in addition to a substantive committee. Legislators have to rely on state agencies to predict the monetary costs of legislative proposals. Because high-cost bills are more difficult to pass, conflict may occur over the projected fiscal costs of legislation. Legislators frequently accuse departments of playing politics by granting relatively lower fiscal notes to bills the department favors than to bills that the department opposes.

After legislation is passed, public administrators continue to make important political decisions through their discretionary powers. Rarely can the legislature, which is pressed for time and lacks expertise in most technical areas, write legislation that is all-inclusive and specific. The legislature typically passes bills with a mixture of specific duties and constraints as well as more vague broad directives. Hence, it is up to administrators to develop procedures and rules under the legislature's specified and delegated rule-making authority and to apply them to individuals, businesses, and corporations. This discretionary power of agencies diverges from and even clashes with the policy-administration dichotomy advocated by Woodrow Wilson.

A legislator who gains the support of the relevant departments and organized interest groups has a much better chance of passing legislation. Research on the Mis-souri legislature indicates that when three or more proponents testify on behalf of a bill, chances for passage improve significantly. In a 1991 study, agencies testified at 46 percent of the hearings and made up 12 percent of the total testifiers. As might be expected, while the presence of agencies in the legislative process is significant, it is substantially less than the presence of interest groups, whose representatives testified at 74 percent of the hearings and constituted 52 percent of all testifiers. The emphasis on executive agency–interest group coalitions is supported by the fact that neither agencies nor interest group support alone was a statistically significant factor in passing legislation. However, a coalition of an executive agency and at least one interest group testifying on behalf of a bill increased chances of passage at a statistically significant level.[10]

Testifying at legislative hearings is only one way in which agencies influence public policy. Using the media is an additional source of influence. In a content analysis of a random sample of 1990 issues of the *St. Louis Post-Dispatch*, interest group representatives and other interested parties received 24 percent of the attributed remarks.[11] Legislators made 18 percent of the attributed remarks, and agency spokespersons (including university representatives) made 24 percent. Local government officials were not included in this category and made an additional 8 percent of attributed remarks. Assuming the newspaper is an unobtrusive measure of relative

10. C. Cartwright Young and Martin Romitti, "Executive-Legislative-Interest Group Relations: The Formulation and Adoption of Public Policy," paper presented at the Southwestern Political Science Association Meeting, San Antonio, Texas, March 1991, 7–8.

11. Missouri state politics articles for one week of each month in 1990 were analyzed for the source of all attributed remarks. The week from each month was randomly selected.

power, interest groups and state agencies seem to possess great potential influence on public policy. The content analysis results also suggest relative parity in the degree of influence held by the agencies and the interest groups. The balance of agencies and interest groups in the press is similar to the significant presence of both interest group lobbyists and agency legislative liaisons in the capitol. When you see the crowds in the corridors outside legislative chambers and offices, there is little that distinguishes agency from interest group lobbying. It is important to remember, though, that in the end the legislature and the governor have the higher authority; enacting law is their decision.

Budget Politics

Budget processes also cause public administrators to interact with the governor and the General Assembly. State departments attempt to persuade the executive and legislative branches that their budget requests should be funded. The total operating budget of Missouri state government rose from approximately $4 billion in the 1983 fiscal year to approximately $10 billion in the 1993 fiscal year. How agencies fared in terms of budget allocations over the ten-year period is certainly one reflection of an agency's power. In the context of the budget, every agency is in conflict with every other agency. Each agency seeks to maintain and enhance its percentage of the state revenue pie. Since this can only be accomplished by reducing the share received by other agencies, competition among agencies is inevitable.

In addition to state agency influences on the budget, federal mandates for programs such as Medicaid and environmental protection have also directly affected Missouri's budget decisions. Figure 11–2

identifies the revenue of each state department as a percent of total state revenues for 1983 and 1993. If one analyzes the patterns of change in executive department budgets from 1983 to 1993 (relative to each department's percentage of the total state budget), the Departments of Social Services, Revenue, Economic Development, Natural Resources, and Corrections are the winners and the Departments of Higher Education, Elementary and Secondary Education, Highways and Transportation, Mental Health, and Public Safety are the losers. However, in the 1995 fiscal year Elementary and Secondary Education and Highways and Transportation began to receive significantly increased revenues as a result of tax increases.

The data reported in Table 11–2 on Missouri's per capita expenditure rankings demonstrate that Missouri should be classified as a low-tax state. The Missouri political culture and the Hancock Amendment have combined to maintain Missouri's low ranking in direct general per capita expenditures. According to statistics from the U.S. Bureau of the Census, among the fifty states and the District of Columbia, Missouri ranked fifty-first in the 1988 fiscal year; in the 1979 fiscal year Missouri ranked forty-ninth. Between 1979 and 1988, Missouri improved its rank within spending subcategories from fifty-first to forty-third in education spending, but the state fell from twenty-eighth to forty-first in health spending.

Jurisdictional Conflict

As government takes on more and more functions, services, and activities, the potential for interagency jurisdictional conflicts increases. For example, recent conflicts occurred between the Department of Natural Resources and the Highways and

**Figure 11-2. Expenditures of Missouri Executive Departments
as a Percent of Total State Expenditures**

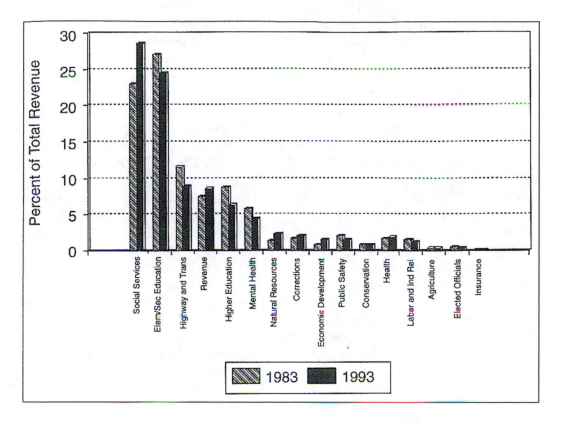

Table 11-2. Missouri Rankings in Per Capita Expenditures, 1979 and 1988

Fiscal Year	Total	Education	Highways	Public Welfare	Health and Hospitals
1979	49	51	31	42	28
1988	51	43	34	41	41

*Includes the 50 states and the District of Columbia

Source: Tax Foundation Incorporated, Facts and Figures on Government Finance, 21st ed., 1981. Computed from Department of Commerce, Bureau of the Census data.

Transportation Department. In one case, the Highways and Transportation Department was cited by the Department of Natural Resources for violating regulations by failing to test the waste residue created by sandblasting lead-based primer from a bridge. In another case, the Highways and Transportation Department opposed rules for ground disturbance permits proposed by the Department of Natural Resources. Similarly, when Senator Jay Nixon and Representative Jim Talent proposed legislation to create a Missouri Bureau of Investigation that would be assigned some duties held or desired by the Missouri Highway Patrol, the Highway Patrol responded by filling a legislative hearing room with more than 125 people, many of them in uniform. Attorney General William Webster, after endorsing the legislation a week earlier, testified against the idea. "Senator Nixon said the bill 'had turned into a lightning rod, where more people were concerned about turf wars than the war on crime.' "[12]

Politics is a quintessential characteristic of public administration, and executive-legislative relations are ongoing. In many respects the separation of governmental power between the executive and the legislative branches requires that public administrators become entrepreneurs on behalf of their agency. Developing support among interest groups is a requisite strategy for enhancing an agency's power. Budget politics are also continual and intense since budget decisions are made annually, fiscal resources are usually quite limited, and budgets typically involve situations in which one agency's gain is another agency's loss. Conflict, however, does not exist only in the budget arena. Vague legislation, overlapping grants of rule-making authority, and the multitude of executive units provide the basis for jurisdictional disputes among agencies and even among subdivisions within an agency.

III. The Reinvention of Missouri Public Administration

By examining a recent approach to increasing the effectiveness of public agencies and the functions they serve, it is possible to merge the structural focus of section one with the political process focus of section two. For decades, public administrators and citizen reformers have been searching for methods that would make government more effective, efficient, and productive. At the national level, the Brownlow Commission of 1937 is a well-known example. The Brownlow Commission proposed to reform public administration by focusing on the structure and legal rules. The commission wrote that to improve the effectiveness of government, one must engineer efficiency into "the structure of government just as it is built into a piece of machinery."[13]

Structural reorganization efforts in Missouri, consistent with the rationale of the Brownlow Commission, have received periodic attention. The 1945 state constitution established some administrative reorganization, the General Assembly adopted the Merit System Law in 1946, and reorganization commissions were created in 1953, 1963, and 1969. However, as the discussion in section two of this chapter pointed out, efforts to control the bureaucracy through structural and legal changes generally overlook the political reality that administrative power is derived from expertise, discretion, and executive–legislative–interest group relations. The latest reform movement, "reinventing government," requires a move away from legislative control based on structure and rules. In essence, the legislature is asked to identify desired outcomes and the agency is asked to use its entrepreneurial skills to achieve those outcomes.

It is unusual for public officials to be as influenced by a single book as seems to

12. Joe Holleman, "Sandblasting Halted on 2 Bridges," *St. Louis Post-Dispatch*, August 15, 1990; Virginia Young, "Troopers Rip Plan for Agency," *St. Louis Post-Dispatch*, January 28, 1992; Young, "Lobbying by Troopers Cited in Bill's Defeat," *St. Louis Post-Dispatch*, January 28, 1992.

13. President's Committee on Administrative Management, *Report of the Committee* (Washington, D.C.: Government Printing Office, 1937), introduction.

be occurring with Osborne and Gaebler's *Reinventing Government.* The book outlines a series of successful case studies for entrepreneurial governance, and recommends a set of principles around which entrepreneurial organizations are built. Among the book's important principles are:

1. Government should steer, not row.
2. Government should arrange for the necessary services to be provided but should not be compelled to deliver them directly.
3. Communities should be empowered to solve their own problems.
4. Authority should be decentralized.
5. Decisions should be made by those who are closest to the customer, improving the quality of the decisions and the morale of employees.
6. When designing responses to citizen demands, government agencies should encourage competition rather than monopolies.
7. Government organizations should be driven by missions, not rules.
8. Government should be results-oriented. The quality of desired results should be the basis for judging the quality of government programs.

The ideas in *Reinventing Government* caught the attention of both the Clinton and the Carnahan administrations. In Missouri, Governor Carnahan and his staff were intrigued by the ideas for a changed orientation to government processes and roles. In the summer of 1993, Missouri public administrators were encouraged to attend a state-sponsored, daylong workshop with Ted Gaebler. The conference also included a panel of department heads and legislators and a panel focused on the Department of Mental Health's strategic plan to implement the principles described

above. The DMH Reinventing Government Steering Committee (consisting of the Department of Mental Health's key central office managers, the director of the state's Office of Administration, and members of the governor's staff) established thirteen special task groups, which included DMH customers and parents, advocates, providers, and DMH field managers and staff. These groups developed specific proposals around two themes:

Creating a mission-driven organization: Removing bureaucratic barriers, eliminating unnecessary personnel and policy regulations, and developing strategies that reinforce an organizational culture driven by customer outcomes.
Implementing targeted initiatives: Conducting local demonstration projects, consistent with DMH vision and values, which will demonstrate the efficacy of specific Reinventing Government principles.[14]

Proposed initiatives include developing specific, measurable outcomes goals and a continuing database, privatizing state-operated community mental health centers in the St. Louis area, and initiating employment opportunities for DMH clients by providing incentives to private- and public-sector industries.

A primary motivation for developing measurable outcomes is the belief that agency needs and effectiveness should be based on evidence from multiple measurements. This focuses attention on the success of agency efforts and lessens the emphasis of earlier reform movements on structure and rules.

Currently, the relative merit of various government programs is being judged intuitively; rarely is there a set of predeter-

14. Missouri Department of Mental Health, "Reinventing Government in Missouri's Department of Mental Health: An Interim Report," June 15, 1993, 1.

mined, measurable objectives. Appropriations rarely reward evidence of agency progress toward desired results; it is much more common for appropriations to reward agencies that have successfully built political power.

Furthermore, even if efforts are made to convert public thinking to outcomes or results, it is crucial to use proper measures of quality. For example, over the past two decades leaders in higher education have attempted to alter the criteria for judging quality. Traditionally, quality in higher education has been measured in terms of resources and reputation. These two measures are highly correlated and fall into the trap of measuring inputs to an organization rather than outputs. Thus quality by these input measures tells one little about the quality of student learning or faculty research at a university. Yet many parties interested in securing more resources for higher education in the state continue to rely on Missouri's low per capita spending as the primary rationale that universities need more money. Over the past fifteen years Missouri has tended to rank among the lowest states in the country on this indicator. In 1990 Missouri ranked forty-sixth in per capita appropriations for higher education. In actuality, one must ask whether low cost should necessarily be seen as a negative. The ideal condition for any state ought to be high levels of student learning (as well as high levels of other key objectives relative to a university's mission, for example research for a research university) at a relatively low cost.[15]

Another measurement, appropriation per pupil, is less often used but is certainly a better measure of resource allocation. On this measure, Missouri tends to be at or near the median of all states. In 1988, Missouri ranked twenty-fifth in per pupil spending on higher education.[16] The vast difference in these two measures should sensitize one to the difficulty of identifying valid and reliable measures. Reinventing government principles would encourage deemphasizing spending level measures and focusing instead on more direct measures of student learning. To focus on results, the legislature needs to develop multiple measures for desired outcomes. The best programs should be those that produce the highest levels of student learning, not those that receive the most money. Thus, while per capita spending figures are appropriate measures for analysis of state revenues, they are not very appropriate measures of university effectiveness.

In the early 1990s the Coordinating Board for Higher Education (CBHE) developed a plan for identifying more precise missions for public universities in the state based on program focus and admission standards. A plan for collecting data from each of the universities and colleges based on multiple outcomes also was established as a part of this long-range plan. Americans value higher education and believe that most people should be able to pursue a college degree at a reasonable cost. Thus the state system not only has to provide for a broad range of quality programs but also has to provide education that is appro-

---

15. For a discussion of how educational quality has been measured, see Alexander Astin, "Why Not Try New Ways of Measuring Quality?" *Educational Record* (Spring 1971), 10–15; for statistics on per capita spending for education, see "Grapevine," Center for Higher Education, Department of Educational Administration and Foundations (Illinois State University, Normal, Ill.,

December 1989), 2270, as reprinted in "Background Information," Missouri Business and Education Partnership Commission, July 31, 1990.

16. NCHEMS (National Center for Higher Education Management Systems), "Background Information," Missouri Business and Education Partnership Commission, July 31, 1990.

priate for students of a very wide range of aptitudes and levels of achievement.

The realization that the state cannot afford to have public institutions providing programs that unnecessarily duplicate those on other campuses, along with the governor's and CBHE's leadership toward an outcomes focus, may lead to a more effective, efficient, and diversified state system of higher education. The *Critical Choices* long-range plan adopted by the CBHE in 1993–1994 identifies efforts the state should undertake to encourage universities to improve the quality of student learning. The national reliance on funding formulas based on head counts seems particularly counterproductive to an emphasis on quality. Missouri abandoned this funding strategy years ago. The Coordinating Board has recommended that a small amount of additional money be appropriated to universities and colleges by the General Assembly based on results (as determined by assessment of student learning performance and by graduating students in areas of critical needs). Carnahan has recommended appropriations based on performance results, and in the 1995 fiscal year the funding appropriated for each institution did include some funds allocated on the basis of an outcomes formula.

Switching the state's focus from inputs to intended results is necessary for implementing the "reinventing government" principles, but such a switch appears unlikely when one considers the requirements of implementation, since those requirements include a legislative commitment to a results orientation, particularly a legislative willingness to allow agencies discretion in determining how to reach the designated goals. The authors of *Reinventing Government* give little attention to the difficulty of changing public officials' focus from ap-

propriations, audits, and procedural rules to the specification and monitoring of results. Legislators perceive processes to reinvent government as a threat to their control over government bureaucracies and programs. Merely identifying desired outcomes and leaving it up to agencies to use their resources and procedural discretion to reach them makes many legislators anxious.[17]

The traditional managerial approach emphasized control of executive agencies by elected officials. The political approach emphasizes realistic acceptance of the need for agency discretion. More recently, this approach has been supported by management literature that has advocated increased concern for human motivation in the workplace. An agency employee who is given responsibility for achieving agency objectives is more likely to make quality contributions than the employee who is held responsible for meticulous adherence to rules. The public sector will undoubtedly receive continuing reinforcement for empowering employees, for developing mission-driven organizations, and for making decisions based on outcomes if these strategies are perceived to be successful in private organizations.

IV. Conclusion

Returning to the challenge presented in the introduction of this chapter, what does the citizen need to know about public administration to understand modern government? First, public administration is affected by its political context. Public administrators must successfully navigate the agency's relationship with the legislature, the governor, other agencies, and interest

17. Statements of several members of the Missouri General Assembly, Legislator Panel, Missouri Reinventing Government Conference, July 1990.

groups. The legislative relationship is particularly important given that it defines the nature of government programs and many of the structures and procedures of executive agencies. The legislature and the governor also determine revenues available to agencies through their authority over annual appropriations. Perhaps the most difficult political challenge for public administrators and elected officials alike is to meet public expectations for programs and services that exceed the resources citizens are willing to provide for the programs.

Secondly, public administrators must identify ways to mobilize agency personnel to effectively provide the services expected of the agency. To some, this means developing elaborate hierarchical structures, procedures, and rules. To others, this means getting agreement on the overarching objectives of the organization and systematically measuring which agency approaches best accomplish them. In the end, each of the political and managerial strategies are important. Truly successful public administrators in Missouri will need to be able to synthesize these varied perspectives and approaches as they seek to provide quality programs with relatively few resources.

CHAPTER 12

Missouri Courts, Judges, and Juries

by Richard J. Hardy and Joseph J. Carrier

> We are under a constitution, but the constitution is what the judges say it is, and the judiciary is the safeguard of our liberty and of our property under the constitution.—Charles Evans Hughes, chief justice and presidential candidate

Whenever humans interact, there will be periodic conflicts. Conflicts might include disputes between business partners over shares of company profits, arguments between former spouses over child custody, fights between neighbors over barking dogs and the placement of fences, consumer complaints about product liability, disagreements between tenants and landlords over rent payments, or crimes committed against persons or their property. The list of potential conflicts is seemingly limitless. Indeed, in 1993 there were more than 802,000 civil and criminal disputes filed in Missouri alone![1]

The purpose of this chapter is to examine the various courts, judges, and juries that resolve such legal conflicts in Missouri. We begin with an examination of Missouri's court system from the lowest levels to the highest. The jurisdiction, structure, and operation of Missouri's circuit courts, court of appeals, and supreme court will each be discussed. Special consideration will be given to the functions and problems of the jury system in the state. The discussion will then turn to the qualifications, selection, and tenure of judges in Missouri. It will be emphasized that judges, like the executive and legislative members of state government, act within a political context.

I. The Missouri Court System

Development of the System

The judicial branch of government is established in Article V of the Missouri Constitution of 1945. While Article V makes it clear that the Missouri Supreme Court is the ultimate authority on state law, the state court system was for many years highly decentralized. Until recently, the state court system consisted of a hodgepodge of rural and urban courts (such as the probate, magistrate, municipal, common pleas, and police courts) that nearly defied classification. As the former administrator of the state courts, James Robinson, hyperbolically stated, "there were as many kinds of courts as there were judges."[2]

In general, there were three criticisms leveled against the court system in Missouri prior to 1979. First, many municipal

1. *Missouri Judicial Report,* Fiscal Year 1993, Office of State Court Administrator, Jefferson City, Missouri, 1993, 7.

2. Judy Gibbs, "Court Reform: Slow but Sweeping," *Columbia Daily Tribune,* October 8, 1978.

and magistrate judges lacked sufficient legal training. Although many judges were lawyers by profession, many others possessed little or no legal training. Second, state financing of judicial personnel was grossly inadequate. Because local governments bore almost the entire cost of operating the courts, some judges were paid nothing, some were paid on a per-case basis, and still others were paid a salary. In 1978, for example, the towns of Ashland and Rocheport relied solely on volunteers for their municipal court judges; Centralia and Cedar City paid their municipal judges $2.50 and $4 per case, respectively; while other trial judges were paid salaries ranging from $20 per month in Hallsville to $40 per hour in Holts Summit. Finally, there was little coordination among Missouri's lower courts. Some judges were overworked, others were underworked, and each had pretty much a free hand within his or her own courtroom, with little or no supervision from above. Hence, similar cases could be treated differently by judges at the same level.[3]

Recognizing the urgent need for court reform, the Missouri Bar Association began lobbying for a unified court system in the early 1970s. The General Assembly finally drafted a proposed constitutional amendment to replace the old judicial article. This referendum was submitted to the voters in August 1976 and was approved statewide by only 32,985 votes. Once the amendment was approved, the General Assembly then developed a more specific bill to implement court reform. The bill that was

eventually passed and signed into law by Governor Joseph Teasdale in 1978 was 230 pages long—at that time, the longest single bill ever passed in Missouri. This new law, known as the Court Reform and Revision Act, took effect on January 2, 1979, and created three notable changes in Missouri's court system.

First, the revised judicial article upgraded standards for judges. The new law requires all municipal judges in cities with populations of more than seventy-five hundred to be lawyers, and requires all non-lawyer municipal judges to attend state-provided training programs. This change was welcomed by nearly everyone except nonlawyer judges in large municipalities, who felt that the Missouri Bar Association had exerted too much influence in state politics. As Fulton's former municipal judge, Russell Shafer (a full-time employee of Sears who lost his part-time judgeship as a result of this new requirement), put it, "a bunch of lawyers passed a law to keep a bunch of lawyers."[4]

Second, the revised judicial article significantly revamped court financing throughout the state. Beginning in 1981, the state assumed responsibility for paying the salaries of all circuit clerks, circuit judges, and associate circuit judges. This change enabled the state to provide comparable pay for comparable work, uniform personnel policies, uniform fringe benefits, and similar staffing for similar courts. In addition, the state prohibited judges from being paid on a per-case or fee basis. Critics believed that the fee system had encouraged local magistrates to drum up business by entering into agreements with local police—resulting in such things as speed traps designed to fleece out-of-town drivers.

Finally, and perhaps most significantly,

---

3. Justices of the peace were eliminated by the Missouri Constitution of 1945. After 1945, justices of the peace became magistrate judges. Magistrate judges are now associate circuit judges.

Judy Gibbs, "Municipal Judges: Reorganization May Leave Them without Jobs," *Columbia Daily Tribune*, October 8, 1978.

4. Ibid.

the new plan established a unified court system to foster accountability, creating a three-tiered judicial system (shown in Figure 12-1). At the lowest level are the circuit courts, which absorbed all the courts of limited jurisdiction—municipal, probate, juvenile, magistrate, common pleas, and so on. Each circuit court is headed by a presiding judge, who is responsible for managing and coordinating every court within the circuit. The presiding judge can reassign judges and cases throughout the circuit to relieve administrative backlogs. At the next level is the court of appeals, with three divisions that may review decisions made by the trial courts. At the apex is the state supreme court, which remains the final authority on Missouri law. Each of these three levels will be discussed in turn.

Circuit Courts

The circuit courts, commonly known as trial courts, are courts of original jurisdiction; in other words, nearly all civil and criminal cases originate in the circuit courts. As indicated in Figure 12-2, Missouri is currently divided into forty-five contiguous judicial circuits, with each circuit encompassing from one to five counties. These courts include municipal, probate, juvenile, associate, and circuit divisions. Each division hears and determines different classes of cases within its jurisdiction.

Municipal Division. The municipal division handles city ordinance violations, such as housing code or traffic violations. Kansas City and St. Louis are required by statute to provide municipal courts to hear ordinance violation cases. Twelve other large municipalities have the option of maintaining municipal courts or having their cases turned over to the associate circuit. The advantage of abolishing municipal courts is that this releases the local governments from the burden of financing such courts. Most municipalities, however, have opted to maintain their municipal courts on the grounds that they want to preserve some semblance of local control, even though those courts are now under the purview of the circuit courts. Missouri currently has 336 municipal judges who hear roughly 390,000 cases—mainly traffic violations—annually.[5] It should be noted that municipal courts do not have jury trials. If such a trial is requested, the case must go to the appropriate circuit judge for reassignment to an associate circuit or circuit court.

Probate Division. The probate division deals with incompetency proceedings and the administration of deceased persons' wills and estates. In the 1993 fiscal year Missouri's probate division handled more than thirteen thousand cases.[6]

Juvenile Division. The juvenile division has jurisdiction over cases dealing with persons under the age of seventeen. In counties with populations of less than seventy thousand, juvenile cases may be handled by associate circuit courts. The juvenile division is designed to provide treatment and rehabilitation—not punishment—for children needing care, education, protection, and guidance. Cases heard before this division involve: (1) adoptions and parental rights; (2) children who are habitually truant from school or are runaways; (3) children who have criminal propensities; and (4) children who are sexually, emotionally, or physically abused. Approximately twenty-three thousand juvenile cases are heard in Missouri annually.[7]

---

5. *Missouri Judicial Report, Fiscal Year 1993,* 7.

6. Ibid.

7. Missouri Press-Bar Commission, *News Reporter's Handbook on Law and Courts* (Jefferson City, 1991), 75–78. *Missouri Judicial Report,* Fiscal Year 1993, 7.

Figure 12-1. Missouri Court System

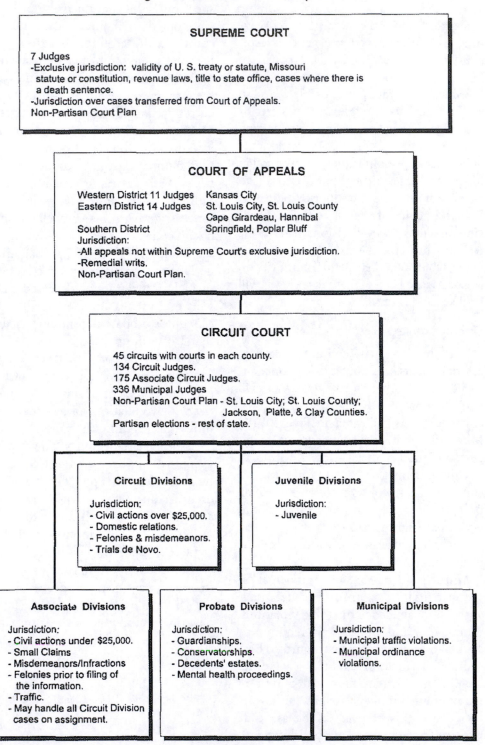

SUPREME COURT

7 Judges
-Exclusive jurisdiction: validity of U. S. treaty or statute, Missouri
   statute or constitution, revenue laws, title to state office, cases where there is
   a death sentence.
-Jurisdiction over cases transferred from Court of Appeals.
Non-Partisan Court Plan

COURT OF APPEALS

Western District 11 Judges   Kansas City
Eastern District 14 Judges   St. Louis City, St. Louis County
                             Cape Girardeau, Hannibal
Southern District   Springfield, Poplar Bluff
Jurisdiction:
-All appeals not within Supreme Court's exclusive jurisdiction.
-Remedial writs.
Non-Partisan Court Plan.

CIRCUIT COURT

45 circuits with courts in each county.
134 Circuit Judges.
175 Associate Circuit Judges.
336 Municipal Judges
Non-Partisan Court Plan - St. Louis City; St. Louis County;
                          Jackson, Platte, & Clay Counties.
Partisan elections - rest of state.

Circuit Divisions

Jurisdiction:
- Civil actions over $25,000.
- Domestic relations.
- Felonies & misdemeanors.
- Trials de Novo.

Juvenile Divisions

Jurisdiction:
- Juvenile

Associate Divisions

Jurisdiction:
- Civil actions under $25,000.
- Small Claims
- Misdemeanors/Infractions
- Felonies prior to filing of
  the information.
- Traffic.
- May handle all Circuit Division
  cases on assignment.

Probate Divisions

Jurisdiction:
- Guardianships.
- Conservatorships.
- Decedents' estates.
- Mental health proceedings.

Municipal Divisions

Jursidiction:
- Municipal traffic violations.
- Municipal ordinance
  violations.

Source: *Missouri Judicial Report, Fiscal Year 1992,* Office of State Courts Administrator.

**Figure 12-2. Missouri's Forty-Five Judicial Circuits
and Three Courts of Appeal**

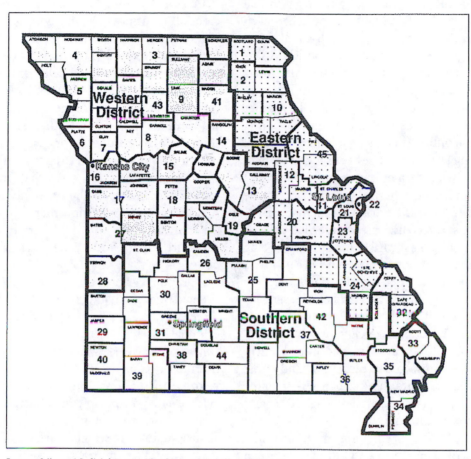

Source: *Missouri Judicial Report, Fiscal Year 1992*, Office of State Courts Administrator.

Associate Division. The associate division handles violations of municipal ordinances (for municipalities not having separate municipal courts), criminal cases, and civil cases involving sums of less than twenty-five thousand dollars. Civil law is concerned with resolving disputes between private citizens such as rent and possession suits, dissolutions of marriage, legal separation proceedings, attachment and mechanics' liens, actions against railroads for killing animals, nuisance cases, and automobile negligence suits. Each year the associate circuit division hears about one hundred thousand cases—municipal, criminal, and civil. Additionally, many civil cases may be classified as "small claims" cases.

Missouri's small-claims courts were established under the 1976 reform to hear civil cases involving sums of less than five hundred dollars. Due to inflation, that threshold figure was raised to fifteen hundred dollars. These courts offer several interrelated advantages over regular trial courts. One advantage is that they offer a relatively easy and inexpensive way for injured parties to bring cases to court.

Typically, filing fees are less than twenty-five dollars, depending on the amount of the claim involved. Additionally, a nominal sheriff's fee is usually charged for each defendant summoned, and a small fee is charged should the case be appealed. A second advantage is that small-claims courts can resolve highly emotional conflicts that would not normally be heard in regular courts, such as the case of the boy suing his neighbor to collect ten dollars in baby-sitting fees, or the case of the young woman suing her former fiancé to recover the cost of collect phone calls he had made to her. A third advantage is that small-claims courts dispense with formal rules of procedure. Parties have the option of being represented by attorneys, but since no juries are used, the judge usually makes the final decision on the spot. Cases can be reheard if appealed to the circuit court, but this option is seldom exercised. About twenty-two thousand cases are filed in Missouri's small-claims courts each year, and most of them fall into three categories—tenant-landlord claims, vehicle damage suits, and unpaid accounts.[8]

The associate division may also dispose of criminal cases. Criminal cases can be classified as either misdemeanors or felonies. Although there is no ironclad distinction between these terms, as a general rule misdemeanors are infractions punishable by fines or by jail sentences of less than one year, while felonies are offenses punishable by incarceration for more than one year. Most misdemeanors are tried before an associate circuit judge after the prosecuting attorney files an "information" verifying the criminal complaint. In the 1993 fiscal year approximately twenty-six thousand felony and eighty-eight thousand misdemeanor cases were filed in circuit courts.[9]

Circuit Division. The circuit division decides all cases not specifically assigned to one of the other divisions. These include: (1) all felony cases; (2) civil cases exceeding twenty-five thousand dollars; (3) equity cases, such as injunctions and domestic relations; (4) probate matters in counties with populations of more than sixty-five thousand; (5) misdemeanor cases that are initiated in this division; (6) extraordinary remedy cases; and (7) cases that are reassigned from one of the other divisions. It is at the circuit division that jury trials are most frequently initiated. Jury trials in Missouri are of two varieties—grand and petit.[10]

A grand jury is a special panel of citizens ordered by a circuit judge to decide whether there is sufficient evidence to prosecute in criminal cases. In Missouri, grand juries consist of twelve persons who usually serve from three to six months. Because the sole purpose of the grand jury is to discover evidence rather than to convict, strict rules of procedure are not followed. Although all proceedings are secret, hearsay evidence (secondhand testimony) is admissible, and potential defendants are not allowed to be present when testimony is offered concerning them, unless permitted by the prosecuting attorney. If the grand jury believes there

---

8. Rhonda Stansberry, "Do-It-Yourself Justice," *Columbia Daily Tribune*, July 9, 1981.

9. *Missouri Judicial Report*, Fiscal Year 1993, 8.

10. "Extraordinary remedies" are those involving unusual procedures and include *Writ of Prohibition* (an order from a higher court to a lower court or agency preventing a public official from acting outside of his or her jurisdiction); *Writ of Mandamus* (an order compelling a public official to perform a ministerial duty); *Quo Warranto* (an order to prevent an official from exercising authority in an unlawful manner); and *Writ of Habeas Corpus* (a proceeding to test the legality of one's confinement). See *News Reporter's Handbook*, 1991, chap. 6.

Technically, in addition to grand and petit jury trials, Missouri also has a six-person coroner's jury that can be called to investigate suspicious deaths.

is probable cause to call for a jury trial, it returns a "true bill," or indictment, to the court. A vote of nine jurors is sufficient to render an indictment.

Although the Fifth Amendment of the U.S. Constitution provides that no person shall be held accountable for a crime unless on an indictment by a grand jury, this guarantee has never extended to the states. Therefore, each state has the option of using either the grand jury or some other method to charge a person formally with violating state law. In Missouri, grand juries are used continuously in metropolitan circuits but are used only sporadically throughout the rest of the state.

In lieu of a grand jury trial, most persons are charged with a crime through information gathered at a preliminary hearing conducted before a judge. A question frequently raised concerning these preliminary methods is: Why use a grand jury instead of a preliminary hearing? The answer involves costs and practicality. A grand jury is extremely expensive and cumbersome to gather, but once impaneled it can dispense with a backlog of cases quickly because it does not have to wait for the availability of a busy judge. The use of grand juries to eliminate case backlogs may be on the wane, however, since court reform has enabled circuit judges to reassign caseloads and thus have more time free for preliminary hearings. Nevertheless, the grand jury will probably remain an important tool for investigating violations of state law relating to public officials and elections.

Once a person is formally charged with a crime—either by an indictment or by information—he or she is bound over for a jury trial. In Missouri a trial, or petit, jury consists of twelve persons whose function is to evaluate the evidence and determine guilt or innocence in criminal cases, or judgment for the plaintiff or defendant in

civil cases. In criminal cases, verdicts must be unanimous in order to convict; in civil cases, at least nine jurors must concur.

Numerous criticisms have been leveled against Missouri's jury system. One major criticism concerns jurors' qualifications and exemptions. Theoretically, every citizen should have an equal chance to draw jury duty. In practice, this is not the case. Missouri law requires every juror to be a citizen of the state, a resident of the county or of a city not within a county for which the jury may be impaneled, and at least twenty-one years of age. Missouri law automatically disqualifies (1) convicted felons (unless their civil rights have been restored); (2) persons convicted of misdemeanors involving moral turpitude; (3) persons unable to read, write, speak, and understand the English language; (4) persons on active military duty; (5) licensed attorneys; (6) judges of courts of record; (7) persons with mental or physical infirmities who are judged by the court to be incapable of performing jury duty; and (8) persons who have served on a grand jury within the previous ten years (this applies to grand jury duty only).

In addition to these automatic exemptions, Missouri law permits the following persons to be excused from jury duty: (1) any person older than sixty-five; (2) clergy; (3) any person licensed and engaged in the practice of medicine, osteopathy, chiropractic, or dentistry; (4) professors or teachers; (5) any person who has served on a state or federal petit jury within the previous year; (6) any government employee; and (7) any person whose employment would be jeopardized by the jury duty.

Interestingly, until 1979 Missouri law allowed any woman to request exemption prior to being sworn in. However, in *Duren v. Missouri*, the U.S. Supreme Court declared that the state's exemption for women was unconstitutional.[11] In its ruling, the court overturned a first-degree murder conviction of a Kansas City man for the shooting death of a woman. The court ruled that the male-dominated jury that convicted him did not represent a fair cross section of the state's population as required by the U.S. Constitution.

One attempted modification concerned the minimum age requirement for jurors. In 1974 the Missouri attorney general ruled that since eighteen-year-olds can vote (based on the Twenty-Sixth Amendment), they should also be allowed to serve as jurors.[12] Later the Missouri Supreme Court disagreed, upholding the constitutionality of the twenty-one-year-old minimum age qualification. A bill to reduce the minimum age for jurors to eighteen died in the 1993 legislative session.

To ensure better representation, Missouri law provides that prospective jurors be selected from a "master jury list," compiled by the county board of jury commissions. In compiling the master list, officials "shall consult one or more public records." Until recently, nearly all potential jurors were drawn exclusively from voter registration lists. However, many county officials now draw from driver's license records as a way of expanding the pool. Whatever the source, Missouri law stipulates that the master jury list shall contain the number of names equal to 5 percent of the jurisdiction's population, and in no event shall the master list fall below four hundred names.

Once the master list is compiled, the names of prospective jurors are drawn at random. Those selected are usually notified by mail and asked to complete a questionnaire. The questionnaire is used to determine eligibility and availability of prospective jurors. Typically, prospective jurors are asked to select the time period in which it would be most suitable for each of them to serve, or to give reasons why they cannot serve. Those who qualify based on the questionnaire are next summoned to appear before the court for either grand jury or petit jury cases. However, just because one is summoned does not mean that one will serve. Further sifting and winnowing of potential jurors continues in the courtroom.

In grand jury cases, jurors may be selected by a circuit judge, a board of jury commissioners, or even the sheriff. Consider the case of Boone County. In the past, most of Boone County's grand jurors were first loosely selected by the board of jury commissioners from the list of registered voters. Then the presiding judge made the final selection from a random pool of prospective jurors summoned to the courthouse. However, in February 1983 a Boone County grand jury was handpicked by Sheriff Charlie Foster under the authority of state statute. When asked how he selected the seven women and eight men who composed his jury and alternates, Foster replied, "I would ask a person to recommend some real outstanding person they knew in the neighborhood. . . . I pretty well know all of them or know of them."[13]

In petit jury cases, jurors are chosen through voir dire proceedings. Voir dire ("to speak the truth") is the preliminary questioning of prospective jurors by the court and attorneys to determine their qualifications to sit on a jury in a particular case. Jurors may be excused either "for cause" (prejudice or bias) or by "peremptory challenge" (at the discretion of the

11. *Duren v. Missouri,* 439 U.S. 357 (1979).

12. Irving R. Kaufman, "Harbingers of Jury Reform," *American Bar Association Journal,* July 1972, 698.

13. Jeff Truesdell, "Sheriff Is Handpicking 15 Residents for Grand Jury," *Columbia Daily Tribune,* February 8, 1983.

attorneys). There is no limit to the number of people who can be disqualified "for cause," and the attorneys may each use an equal number of peremptory strikes (usually six) without citing justification.

Studies reveal that neither method of selection results in a jury that is a true cross section of the general public. First, nonvoters are systematically excluded from the jury selection process; this is why some counties now use driver's licenses for jury selection. Second, attorneys on each side will try to exclude jurors who are likely to favor the other side. Although state and federal laws prohibit the systematic exclusion of any class of citizen, every attempt is made by attorneys to impanel jurors who may be sympathetic to their clients. For example, it has been shown that in criminal cases Black and Catholic jurors are more likely than White or Protestant jurors to decide in favor of the defendant. Likewise, evidence suggests that jurors of Slavic descent are more likely to find for the defendant in criminal cases than are jurors of German or British descent.[14]

Another criticism of Missouri's jury system is its low pay. As compensation, jurors get fifteen dollars per day and travel expenses determined by the local circuit court. Few jurors feel that this constitutes sufficient remuneration for what may amount to long hours of work. People who work for hourly wages are obviously discouraged from serving.

Most cases that come to trial are terminated following decisions in circuit court. However, the losing attorney may contest the decision by filing a notice of appeal with the clerk of the trial court. That no-tice is then transmitted to the appropriate appellate court along with all records pertaining to the case, such as pleadings, testimony, arguments, instruction, judgment, and motions. The attorneys for both sides then file written briefs presenting their legal arguments to the proper appellate court.

Court of Appeals

The Missouri Court of Appeals reviews decisions rendered in trial courts and certain administrative agencies, except in cases in which the state supreme court has exclusive appellate jurisdiction. As seen in Figure 12–1, the court of appeals is divided into three districts—eastern, western, and southern. The eastern district court meets in St. Louis and periodically in Clayton, Hannibal, and Cape Girardeau; the western district court meets in Kansas City and periodically in other county seats in the district; the southern district court meets in Springfield and periodically in Poplar Bluff. To enable the court of appeals to hear more cases, each district is divided into smaller groups consisting of at least three judges. The orders, judgments, and decrees of a majority of the judges in any division within a district have the force and effect of those of the full court. In 1993 the Missouri Court of Appeals handled 3,786 new appeals.[15]

In jury-tried cases, the court of appeals reviews both the facts and the law to verify that the evidence corroborates the jury's verdict and that no reversible legal error has been committed by the trial court. In non-jury cases, the court of appeals must uphold the trial court's judgment unless it finds that (1) there is no substantial evidence to support it; (2) it is against the weight of evidence; (3) it erroneously declares the law; or (4) it erroneously applies the law.

---

14. See, for example, Deborah Shapley, "Jury Selection: Social Scientists Gamble in an Already Loaded Game," *Science*, September 20, 1974, 1033–34; and Harry Kalven Jr. and Hans Zeisel, *The American Jury* (Boston: Little, Brown and Co., 1966).

15. *Missouri Judicial Report*, Fiscal Year 1993, 4.

Decisions of the court of appeals are final unless they are transferred to the state supreme court. A case may be transferred if (1) a majority of the judges of the appeals court feel that it involves a question of paramount importance; (2) a dissenting member of the appeals court believes that the decision is contrary to previous decisions rendered by an appellate court; or (3) the state supreme court orders it transferred.

Missouri Supreme Court

The state supreme court is the highest court in Missouri. It has general appellate jurisdiction (cases may be appealed to it) over decisions made by the trial courts, certain administrative agencies, or the court of appeals. The supreme court also has exclusive appellate jurisdiction (cases may be appealed only to it) in cases involving (1) validity of U.S. treaties or statutes; (2) validity of Missouri statutes or the Missouri Constitution; (3) construction of Missouri's revenue laws; (4) title to a state office; and (5) the punishment of death. Finally, the high court has original jurisdiction (cases only it can try) in cases involving impeachment (other than of the governor or members of the supreme court), election contests, and the issuance of certain writs.

The supreme court consists of seven members who are appointed for twelve-year terms under the nonpartisan court plan (this plan is discussed later in the chapter). The seven judges in turn select one of their members to be chief justice. The chief justice presides over the court and handles administrative details. The court's practice is to rotate the position of chief justice every two years.

The supreme court hears oral arguments three times per year—in January, May, and September. Today, the entire court sits en banc (all seven justices together). In the past, the court sat in two divisions to facilitate decision making, with Division I consisting of four justices, and Division II comprising three justices. Each division was headed by a presiding judge and could hear and dispose of cases independently of the other division. In the 1993 fiscal year a near-record 1,015 cases were filed with the supreme court.[16]

II. Missouri Judges

Qualifications, Compensations, and Tenure

Missouri has a variety of judges. State judges may be categorized as either municipal, associate circuit, circuit, appellate, or supreme court judges. For each category of judge, Missouri law establishes different qualifications, compensations, and tenures.

Municipal Judges. Municipal judges are chosen in a manner prescribed by municipal ordinances or charters. In some cities, municipal judges are selected by the city's governing body or mayor; in other cities, they are elected by popular vote. The Kansas City charter provides that all municipal judges be selected by a nonpartisan court plan. Terms and salaries of municipal judges are also decided by municipalities. Terms may not be less than two years, and compensation ranges from nothing to more than forty thousand dollars per year in Kansas City. To qualify as a municipal judge, a person must be a Missouri resident between the ages of twenty-one and seventy. If a municipality has a population of more than seventy-five hundred, its judge must be an attorney. In municipalities of less than seventy-five hundred, all nonlawyer judges are required to complete

16. Ibid., 10.

a course of instruction prescribed by the supreme court. Finally, each municipality determines its own judge's compensation.

Associate Circuit Judges. Associate circuit judges are elected for four-year terms in most counties of the state. The number of associate circuit judges per county varies according to the county's population, but state law mandates that there be at least one resident associate circuit judge per county. In 1993 there were 175 associate circuit judges in the state. An associate circuit judge must be at least twenty-five years old, a qualified Missouri voter, a resident of the county in which he or she presides, and a licensed attorney. Salary for an associate circuit judge in 1994 was $73,134.

Circuit Judges. Circuit judges, like associate circuit judges, are popularly elected in most counties. Circuit judges, however, serve six-year terms. The Missouri Constitution requires that there be at least one circuit judge in each of Missouri's forty-five judicial circuits. In 1993 there were a total of 134 circuit judges in the state. Each circuit is headed by a presiding judge who has general administrative authority over case loads and judicial personnel. To qualify as a circuit court judge, one must be at least thirty years old, a U.S. citizen for ten years, a qualified Missouri voter for three years, a resident of the circuit for one year, and an attorney licensed to practice law in Missouri. In 1994 the salary for a circuit court judge was $82,967.

Appellate Judges. All appellate and supreme court judges are selected for twelve-year terms under the nonpartisan court plans discussed below. There are seven supreme court judges, and the number of appellate judges per district is determined by statute. Currently, the western district has eleven judges, the eastern district has fourteen, and the southern district has seven. To qualify for either the appellate courts or the supreme court, judges must be citizens of the United States for at least fifteen years, registered voters for at least nine years preceding selection, licensed attorneys in Missouri, and at least thirty years of age. Salaries in 1994 ranged from $89,558 for appellate court judges to $95,897 for supreme court judges and $98,397 for the chief justice.

Judicial Selection

There are three methods by which judges are selected in Missouri—appointment, election, or a mixed method commonly referred to as the "Missouri plan." Each of the three methods offers certain advantages and disadvantages.

Appointment. During the first three decades of Missouri's statehood, judges of the chancery, circuit, and supreme courts were appointed by the governor with the advice and consent of the state senate. However, this method generated a great deal of controversy. Supporters of the appointive system argued that the governor and senate were in the best position to select the most qualified judges. Opponents of the system argued that judges are more apt to be chosen for their political loyalty than for their legal expertise. Moreover, it was believed that judges should be directly accountable to the people. After a great deal of debate, the state constitution was amended in 1849 to provide for the popular election of judges, and this system continues in effect for most of Missouri's trial courts. The only judges who are regularly appointed now are some municipal judges who are selected by their city's governing body or mayor. About one-fourth of the circuit and associate circuit court judges serving in districts where judges are elected were originally appointed to their office by the governor when a resignation or death created a vacancy.

Elections. Most of the judges in Missouri's municipal, associate circuit, and circuit courts are thus popularly elected on partisan ballots. In partisan elections, each judicial candidate must first win the August primary of his or her own party— Democrat, Republican, or Independent. Party nominees then face each other in the November general election to determine the winner.

The election of judges still raises doubts about the quality of the judges. Although elections are intended to give democratic control over the courts, it appears that few voters are prepared to accept this responsibility. Studies reveal that most persons are unaware of those who are seeking judicial office, let alone their qualifications.[17] Many judges seeking reelection are unopposed, and those who are opposed are seldom defeated. In Missouri in 1992, 42 percent of the twelve judges seeking reelection were opposed, and 8 percent were defeated. This suggests that many elected judges enjoy a degree of independence from popular control.

Missouri Plan. Recognizing that selection of judges by either appointment or election was not totally satisfactory, in 1940 the voters adopted a hybrid court plan, popularly known as the Missouri plan because it was first adopted in Missouri. The plan, which has been used as a national model for selection of judges, represents an innovative attempt to combine the best of both the appointive and the elective systems of judicial selection. Under the plan, prospective appellate court judges are first screened by a seven-member, nonpartisan

commission. These nonsalaried commissioners include the chief justice of the state supreme court, who serves as chair; three lawyers, one from each district of the court of appeals, who are elected by the bar of their districts; and three lay members, one from each district of the court of appeals, who are appointed by the governor. Except for the chairperson, all commissioners serve six-year, staggered terms and are ineligible to succeed themselves.

After careful screening, the commission gives the governor the names of three candidates from which to choose. The governor's choice must then be approved by a majority of voters at the first general election held after the newly appointed judge has served in office for twelve months. The judge's name is placed on a separate judicial ballot, without political party designation, and the people are asked to vote yes or no on the question, "Shall Judge __ of the __ Court be retained in office?" If the voters say no, the governor must select a new commission-recommended judge, and the process of public approval is repeated. If the voters say yes, the judge is entitled to a full term in office. At the end of each judge's term, this same question is once again submitted to the voters to determine if the judge should serve another term.

The Missouri Constitution stipulates that not only all appellate court judges but also all associate and circuit court judges in the city of St. Louis and in Jackson County must be selected under this nonpartisan court plan. The constitution also permits this nonpartisan court plan to be adopted in any trial court jurisdiction if 10 percent of the voters in each county in the circuit sign petitions requesting a vote on the plan and if a majority of the voters then approve it. The commissions that nominate trial-court judges are composed of five members— the presiding judge of the appellate court

17. Charles A. Johnson, Roger C. Schaefer, and R. Neal McKnight, "The Salience of Judicial Candidates and Elections," *Social Science Quarterly* 59 (September 1978): 371–78.

district, who acts as chair; two lawyers elected by the bar; and two lay members appointed by the governor. Currently, associate and circuit-court judges in St. Louis, Platte, and Clay counties are selected by this method, and municipal judges in the Kansas City Municipal Division are elected by modified nonpartisan methods.

It is not certain that the Missouri plan has produced its intended effects. Studies of its impact reveal two important findings. First, the use of this hybrid plan does not necessarily result in the selection of higher-caliber judges. Separate studies comparing the judges selected under different systems—election, appointment, and the Missouri plan—indicate that there are few differences in the judges' social backgrounds, educational qualifications, or experience. Second, the Missouri plan does not remove politics from judicial selection. Rather, it tends to shift the responsibility of judicial selection from the electorate to the lawyers on the nominating commission and to the governor. As Richard A. Watson and Rondal G. Downing point out, governors still "use their appointment power to reward friends or past political supporters."[18]

Another advantage envisioned for the Missouri plan was that it relieved judges from problems of political campaigns. In Missouri prior to 1940, and in some other states today, candidates for judicial posts, especially on the state supreme court, must raise large sums of money and conduct extensive campaigns. The use of the merit system appointments and the retention elections was designed to free judges from such expensive, enervating campaigns. For many years in Missouri the percentage of votes cast in favor of retaining judges was quite high, often more than 70 percent yes. The percentages declined, however, in the 1970s and 1980s, and dropped precipitously in 1990. As a result, judges up for retention in Missouri in 1992 began making "educational" tours of the state, telling groups of voters about the judicial selection process. Supporters of the Missouri plan collected more than four hundred thousand dollars and ran radio and newspaper ads urging retention of judges on the ballot. The campaign was successful in that the percentage voting yes increased, but it also raised concerns that Missouri plan judges were beginning once again to be involved in political campaigns.

Retirement and Removal

Based on a constitutional amendment adopted by the voters in 1970, the General Assembly created the Commission on Retirement, Removal, and Discipline of Judges, which is responsible for investigating all requests for retirement based on disability and all complaints of alleged misconduct or incompetency. The commission is composed of six persons who serve six-year terms each. Included are two lawyers appointed by the bar, two nonlawyers appointed by the governor, and two judges—one circuit court judge and one appeals court judge selected by their respective colleagues.

Retirement. According to the 1976 constitutional amendments, all judges other than municipal judges must retire by age seventy. It is, of course, possible for a judge

18. For comparative studies of judicial selection systems, see Richard A. Watson and Rondal G. Downing, *The Politics of the Bench and the Bar: Judicial Selection under the Missouri Nonpartisan Court Plan* (New York: John Wiley and Sons, 1969); and Larry Berg et al., "The Consequences of Judicial Reform," *Western Political Quarterly* 29 (June 1975): 263–80. For an analysis of the politics of judicial selection in the Missouri plan, see Kenyon D. Bunch and Gregory Casey, "Political Controversy on Missouri's Supreme Court: The Case of Merit vs. Politics," *State Government Review* (Winter, 1990): 5–16. Watson and Downing, 45.

to retire at any time, but retirement benefits are contingent upon age and length of service. State law stipulates that any state court judge who has served for a total of twelve years and has reached the age of sixty-five may retire and receive benefits equal to 50 percent of his or her salary on the highest court on which he or she served. Even after a judge retires, he or she may still be called into active duty by the supreme court (with the consent of the retired judge) to serve on a temporary basis. In addition to retirement benefits, the 1970 judicial revision provides for payments to surviving spouses, unemancipated minor children, or the judge's estate in the event of a judge's death.

Removal and Discipline. Any Missouri judge may be removed from office for misconduct or incompetency. According to the state constitution, judges of the supreme court, court of appeals, or circuit courts may be impeached for "crimes, misconduct, habitual drunkenness, willful neglect of duty, corruption in office, incompetency, or any offense involving moral turpitude or oppression in office." Impeachment proceedings are initiated by the house of representatives, which serves as prosecutor. Once charges are brought, a trial is conducted by the supreme court. Should the person being impeached be a member of the supreme court, a special commission composed of seven jurists chosen by the senate must hear the case. In order for there to be a conviction, five of the seven justices or commissioners must concur. Once removed from office, the convicted judge may then be subject to criminal prosecution in a regular trial court. Thus far only six judges—all of them from the circuit court—have been impeached, with four of the impeachments being in the nineteenth century. Two of the judges resigned before trial, two were removed, one was acquitted, and charges against one judge were dropped.

Although impeachment is recognized as a valuable method for removing unfit judges, the process is extremely cumbersome and vulnerable to political manipulation. It is for these reasons, in part, that the General Assembly created the Commission on Retirement, Removal, and Discipline of Judges. All complaints concerning judicial misconduct or incompetency must first go to the commission, which then conducts an informal investigation. If at least four commissioners believe there is probable cause to find the accused guilty or incompetent, a formal investigation is called. If after a formal hearing at least four commissioners still believe the accused should be disciplined, a report containing all relevant information and recommendations for discipline is made to the supreme court. The supreme court is then responsible for making a final decision.

The commission has received several hundred complaints concerning judicial misconduct, but only about a dozen have been recommended to the supreme court for discipline. Several of the most notorious cases in recent years included the 1976 removal of St. Louis County Circuit Judge Paul Conning for failure to carry out his duties adequately, the 1980 conviction of Jackson County Circuit Court Judge William J. Marsh for driving while intoxicated, and the removal of Scott County Judge Lloyd Briggs for partisan political activities.[19]

III. Conclusion

This chapter should provide at least a rudimentary understanding of the myriad courts, judges, and juries in the state of Missouri. It should now be obvious that the state has made remarkable strides in

19. Meriemil Rodriguez, "Judges' Emotions Put to Test When Defendant Is a Peer," *Kansas City Star*, February 11, 1980 39.

recent years toward improving its methods for resolving conflicts. Significant reforms include compulsory legal training for judicial personnel, elimination of the fee system, creation of a unified court system, and improved methods for dealing with judicial misconduct and incompetence. Despite these important changes, Missouri's judicial system is far from being completely neutral. Jurors typically do not reflect a cross section of their community, and judges are frequently selected on political grounds. If it is true, however, that "politics arises out of conflict," then Missouri's courts, judges, and juries are, and will remain, political institutions.

PART III

Policies and Policy Making in Missouri

CHAPTER 13

Politics of the Budgetary Process
by Earl W. Hawkey

> Most public organizations are driven not by their missions, but by their rules and their budgets. They have a rule for everything that could conceivably go wrong and a line item for every subcategory of spending in every unit of every department. The glue that holds public bureaucracies together, in other words, is like epoxy: it comes in two separate tubes. One holds rules, the other line items. Mix them together and you get cement.—David Osborne and Ted Gaebler, *Reinventing Government: How the Entrepreneurial Spirit Is Transforming the Public Sector*

According to the Missouri Constitution and state law, no money may be spent by any state department unless it has been properly appropriated and budgeted. Consequently, everyone in the executive branch from the department managers to the governor is involved in preparing the annual budget request. The requests themselves range from well-conceived guides for the coming year's activities to wish lists produced solely to fulfill the letter of the law.

The Division of Budget and Planning, which is part of the Office of Administration, coordinates the budget process and analyzes all funding requests for the governor and his staff. By state statute, the division is also charged with setting guidelines for departments to follow in preparing their funding requests. For example, the division has determined that the state departments must begin preparing their fiscal year (FY) budgets by August of each year and complete their requests by October 1.[1] (See Figure 13-1 for the calendar and steps in the formulation of the Missouri budget).

I. Budget Guidelines and Terminology

Since the early 1970s Missouri has used a line-item budget; that is, each department details in its budget request the funding requested for each item of personal service and for each item of expense and equipment. Personal service items include such things as salaries, wages, and staff benefits. Expense and equipment items are broken down into several subclasses, such as travel and vehicles, fuel and utilities, and office and communications equipment (telephones, file cabinets, desks, chairs, and computers). The use of these subclasses provides budget analysts and the General Assembly with detailed information about how the personal service and expense and equipment money will be spent. In addition, each budget request is accompanied by an explanation of the problems faced by the department, a listing of the goals

---

1. *Revised Statutes of Missouri,* 1986, Sec. 33.220.

Figure 13-1. The Budget Process in Missouri

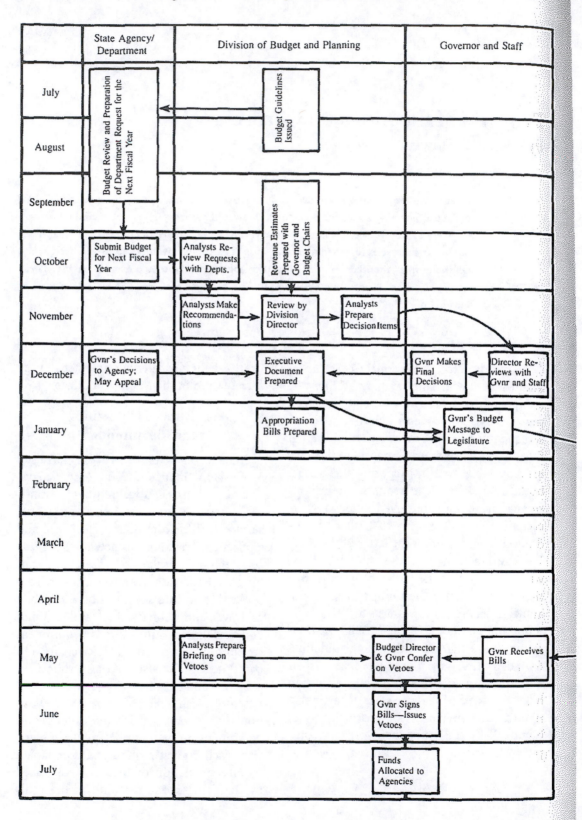

House Appropriations Committee	House Budget Committee	House of Representatives	House-Senate Conference	Senate	Senate Appropriations Committee
	Bills Referred to Substantive Comm.	Gvnr's Budget to Appropriations Comm.			
Hearings & Subcom. Recommendations	Substantive Comm. Decisions Amended	Budget Comm. Recommendations Amended		House Bill Referred to Senate App. Comm.	Senate Comm. Hearings, Formulates Amendments
		Accepts Senate Changes or Conference	Confer to Resolve Differences	Senate Substitute Passed by Senate	
		Compromise Passed by House		Compromise Passed by Senate	
				Bills Sent to Gvnr for Signature	

and objectives for the coming years, and performance measures that illustrate the present workload of the department and explain what will be accomplished with any additional funds.

Other guidelines proposed by the Division of Budget and Planning pertain to inflationary increases for the continued operation of state government. The division notifies departments of the percentage increase that will be allowed each year for items such as fuel, food, and communications. The division also establishes guidelines for cost-of-living and merit salary increases to be calculated for state employees. Cost-of-living adjustments are increases of a set percentage that are added to the salaries and wages of each full-time employee within a department to keep up with inflation. Merit increases are intended to award employees whose job performances have been outstanding. The amount of money given a specific division for merit increases is a percentage of the total salaries of all the employees within that division (in many years the percentage is zero, because of shortages of state revenue). Each of these guidelines is approved by the governor prior to budget preparation.

Since 1980, the Statewide Accounting System for Missouri (SAM) has been used in preparing departmental budgets. Data on actual expenditures for previous fiscal years are fed into the SAM from accounting records. Before SAM, budget analysts had to rely on the departments to give them accurate expenditure information. SAM makes budget presentation easier for the analysts in other ways as well. The governor's recommendations can be bulk-loaded into the system at night, and a corrected budget will be completed by morning. This saves the analyst from having to calculate each change in the budget by hand and

allows more time to evaluate individual budget requests. SAM also helps the departments assemble a more accurate budget because it does all the addition and automatically calculates cost-of-living and merit increases.

Three years of financial history are presented in each budget request. Prior-year expenditures indicate how a department actually spent its money from July 1 through June 30 of the previous fiscal year. Expenditures for FY 1994 (July 1, 1992, through June 30, 1993), for example, will show up as prior-year expenditures in the FY 1996 request. Current-year expenditures show how the department plans to spend the funds allocated to it for the current fiscal year. In the FY 1996 request, these would be the projected expenditures for FY 1995. Budget-year expenditures are the department's request for funding in the upcoming fiscal year. Because the FY 1996 budget will start July 1, 1995, and end June 30, 1996, preparation of the budget must begin during the summer and fall of 1994. This presents obvious problems of timing for many departments since they must begin preparing their budget request for the next fiscal year before they are sure what their funding will be for the current one. They are budgeting for a period that will not begin for at least another ten months and will stretch twenty-two months into the future. In times of uncertainty or change, this can be a difficult task.

Each division within a department is a budgeting organization and prepares a group of decision items (for example, requests for funds). There are two main types of decision items: core requests and expansions. A *core* decision item is a request for funds to continue operating a division at the existing level of service. This means only doing the same amount of work as in the current year. An *expansion* decision item is a request for funds to do more than is being done in the current year. For example, if 350 tax auditors are employed by the Department of Revenue and the department wishes to maintain that staff, funds are requested in a core decision item. If the department wants to hire an additional 50 auditors, the funds to do so would be requested as a separate expansion decision item.

Decision items (both core and expansion) are summarized at both the divisional and department levels through the SAM system. After all of the decision items have been entered into the system, departments must assign a priority ranking to each one. Core items usually receive the highest rankings, and expansion items of less importance are given the lowest priorities. Those items with the lowest rankings usually receive less consideration and attention by both the department and the Division of Budget and Planning.

II. Department and Division Interactions

Whenever a set of guidelines such as the one prepared by the Division of Budget and Planning is sent to the sixteen different departments, it inevitably is interpreted sixteen different ways. Analysts within Budget and Planning must continually explain the format of the budget, the information to be included in each request for new funds, and why the governor recommended the cost-of-living and merit allowances contained in the guidelines. This type of interaction serves important purposes: it gives the analysts some idea of what the department will request in the coming year, and it gives the department some indication of how Budget and Planning might react to certain types of requests for additional money. This helps both the department officials and the budget analysts in the division choose their strategies for the coming budget cycle.

Once the department's budget request is completed and forwarded to the Division of Budget and Planning, analysts begin reviewing the request for content, mathematical accuracy, and compliance with the published guidelines. By the time the analysts receive the budget requests, chances are they already have a good idea of what the department will ask for in the way of expansion items and which items the department is most interested in receiving. It is important for the analyst to know this because items are sometimes included within a request strictly for negotiating purposes or to pacify certain groups within or outside the department.

After reviewing the budget and listing every discrepancy or question they have concerning the document, the analysts meet with staff of the various departments to determine the importance of various decision items. Information acquired from these meetings provides analysts with data they can use to brief the budget director on departmental requests. As a result of such review meetings, decision items with a high priority for the department and of interest to the governor and his staff receive additional review. Analysts gather more information on these decision items and prepare special analyses, including such things as a cost/benefit analysis, a review of the benefits and disadvantages of funding the item, alternatives to the existing process or program, and a review of who might favor or oppose the decision item.

Analysts must gather these data from department officials who may be reluctant to give out additional information on their internal operations. Agencies are often fearful of providing a division analyst with too much information because a knowledge-able analyst might see a particular decision item as unnecessary. On the other hand, if an analyst knows too little about a decision item, he or she will be unable to effectively present the department's position in planning meetings. The amount of cooperation an individual analyst receives from a department depends largely on the department's assessment of what the analyst is seeking to do with the information requested. Regardless, the analyst must prepare briefing papers for presentation to the budget director, the governor's staff, and the governor. The analyst must also be able to discuss each of the department's other expansion items, the operations of the department, the personalities involved, and what may have happened to the previous year's budget requests.

III. Decision Making within the Division

Analysts go into budget meetings as both advocates and adversaries of the departments. On decision items they support, analysts must convince the budget director of the merits of the request. On items they oppose, analysts must present an equally credible argument. The director must view each analyst's argument from his strategic political position. If one item is funded, another program cannot be funded because of limited fiscal resources. The director must consider whether an item is required to address a vital need, or if it can be ignored for now. The director also must be aware of the possible reactions to the proposed item by the legislature, interest groups, and (most important) the governor and his staff. This requires a great deal of political sensitivity. Finally, the director must attempt to coordinate recommended decision items into a total spending plan that can be easily defended before the legislature.

It would be ideal if each request for additional funds could be evaluated strictly on its own merits, based on a complete and rational analysis of its advantages and disadvantages. But the reality of the situation is that decision items are compared against other requests from within the same department as well as against those requested by other departments. Prior to any decision making within the division, economists prepare estimates of how much revenue will be generated by the state during the next fiscal year and how much will be available to fund new decision items. In recent years these revenue projections have been jointly agreed to by the governor and the chairs of the house and senate budget committees. This has eliminated one source of friction between the governor and the legislature during the budgetary process since everyone agrees on the size of the revenue "pie." Instead, both sides can focus on the policy implications of the budget.

Once the preliminary meetings between analysts and the budget director are complete, budget items are presented to the governor's senior staff. The same process of being both an advocate and an adversary takes place once again, only this time the budget director has the key role and may often take a position opposing that of the governor's staff. When these discussions are complete, decisions are made on many of the items that were undecided in the first round. Those items that are still up in the air or that are extremely political in nature are usually presented to the governor for a final decision.

Once the final decision is made concerning which items will be requested and which will be denied, analysts must notify their departments. During the last few days of December, departments are besieged with questions concerning the success or failure of funding requests. On particularly sensitive items, analysts often must tell department officials that they know the answer but cannot give it out yet. Such notifications are often handled directly by the governor and his staff rather than by the division. When agencies are finally given formal notification of the governor's decision, they are often given an opportunity to appeal the decision directly to the governor. Such appeals usually concern the denial of an expansion item that the department feels is particularly important. Budget analysts must then defend the governor's decision, and in most cases the decisions reached by the budget office and the governor stand.

The final task for the budget analyst is to help prepare the executive budget document. This hefty book explains the recommendations made by the governor for each division within the departments of state government. Any new decision items, core reductions, or program transfers are explained. Analysts also must prepare the appropriation bills to be introduced in the General Assembly by the chair of the House Budget Committee.

IV. The Governor's Budget Message

The governor's budget message, delivered before a joint session of the General Assembly each January, marks the beginning of the legislative phase of the budgetary process. Although the governor's budget is supposed to be a secret prior to his message, in reality budgetary decisions are usually "leaked" piecemeal to the press in the weeks before the speech or cleared with legislative leaders and department directors long before they are publicly announced. However, the budget message reveals the details of the budget to both government personnel and the representatives of special interest groups. Analysts within the division are given strict orders as to when and how copies of the governor's speech, as well as copies of the executive budget itself, can be distributed.

Despite these public relations efforts, the governor's speech is important for the public attention it draws to the chief executive and for its articulation of his program. The air of mystery and the massiveness of the executive budget lend a sense of hard work, judicious deliberation, and expertise to the governor's recommendations. The budget message is the primary forum in which the governor can explain in full the reasoning for decisions (even if it is self-serving). The address sets the tone and the agenda for the current legislative session, since the governor puts forth both the administration's legislative program and the executive budget. If the two mesh and have no major contradictions, both stand a better chance before the legislature. For example, in 1981 Governor Christopher Bond faced one of the state's worst fiscal crises in many years. With dwindling state resources, he was able to make few new budgetary expenditures. In a tough speech before the legislature, Bond called attention to the state's money problems and emphasized the absolute restraint necessary for the new fiscal year. To emphasize the need for restraint he also proposed a relatively austere legislative program consisting of items that required little in the way of new budget outlays. In this way Bond sought to bolster his image as a "can-do" person by focusing legislative attention on what he could do (back certain types of legislation) rather than what he could not do (spend money on new government programs).

At other times the opposite could well be true. For example, when he was governor, Joseph Teasdale was alleged to have used most of the state's $240 million surplus in a single fiscal year without launching any bold new legislative initiatives. In fact, some opponents of the governor suspected him of trying to win votes for his 1980 reelection by increasing the funding desired by powerful groups and special interests. At the same time, his opponents argued that the governor's other legislative priorities were nothing more than warmed-over proposals that the legislature had already rejected. In this and similar ways, governors can mix both legislative proposals (nonmonetary) and budgetary proposals (monetary) to give themselves the greatest political benefit.

V. The House of Representatives

By tradition, all appropriation bills in the Missouri General Assembly receive their first hearing in the house of representatives. The governor's proposals are put into bill form and introduced in the house by the budget committee chair as a courtesy to the governor. Each department in state government has a separate appropriation bill, and there are also separate bills for capital expenditures (repair and maintenance as well as new construction), emergency appropriations, and reappropriations (for expenditures such as capital projects that may extend across more than one fiscal year).

In the week immediately following the governor's speech, little public work is done in the house committees on these newly introduced appropriations. This delay serves several purposes. First, it allows the members of the General Assembly time to gauge their constituents' reactions to the governor's recommendations. They are able to analyze how this spending plan will affect their individual districts. Second, the delay allows time for the house staff to become familiar with the policy and budgetary de-

cisions embodied in the governor's recommendations so that they can brief committee members on the details of the decision items and the reasoning behind them. They also need to study which interest groups support or oppose portions of the governor's plan so that they can properly brief the committee.

Appropriations committee staffers have an onerous task. One problem they face is the need to familiarize themselves in just two or three weeks with the results of months of work by the division and the governor's staff. In addition, whereas the governor, through the Division of Budget and Planning, has at least one analyst (and in some cases more than one analyst) to oversee the budget and policy activities of each department, each committee staffer must cover three or more departments. Unless the staffers are intellectual giants with an inexhaustible supply of energy, it is virtually impossible for them to know very much about their budget areas. Finally, aggressive staffers often find themselves at odds with certain members of the committee strongly committed to helping their districts. It is bad form, and not very rewarding, for staffers to make an enemy on the committee.

Once introduced into the lower chamber, the appropriation bills are immediately referred to the house appropriations committees. Until 1980, there was one large appropriations committee in the house. However, beginning in 1981 the appropriations committee was split into five theoretically equal committees, each covering the budget of two or three departments. The Appropriations–Education and Public Safety Committee deals with the Departments of Higher Education, Elementary and Secondary Education, and Public Safety as well as the judiciary and the public defender program. A second committee, named Appropriations–Social Services and Corrections, deals with the massive Department of Social Services and the Department of Corrections. A third, the Appropriations–Health and Mental Health Committee, deals with the Department of Health and the much larger Department of Mental Health. The rest of state government is divided between the two remaining appropriation committees—Natural and Economic Resources, and General Administration and Transportation.

Interestingly, the leadership has carefully avoided calling these groups "subcommittees," even though all of their recommendations must pass through the House Budget Committee, whose members consist of the chair, vice-chair, and ranking minority member of each of the five appropriations, or "substantive," committees plus ten to twenty legislators from within and outside of the appropriations committees. This "super committee" has the power to accept, reject, or modify the recommendations of the appropriations committees. The Budget Committee also deals with capital improvements, emergency and supplemental appropriations, and reappropriations. In addition, the Budget Committee exercises a budget control function, approving or disapproving all bills proposing to authorize more than one hundred thousand dollars in expenditures.

There is sometimes friction between the appropriations committees and the budget committee. Members of the appropriations committees sometimes offer high budget recommendations, knowing that the budget committee will reject or reduce them. In some years the budget committee has assigned dollar limits to the appropriations committees in an attempt to curb their tendency to make unrealistic budget recommendations. This tactic has been at least partially successful, but there will always be a lack of incentives for aggressive budget cutting in these committees.

This two-tiered house committee structure has been with us for a number of years, with mixed results. The size of the committees—more than one hundred members in total—allowed many more people to be part of the decision-making process. The increased number of people can mean, however, that the average member has even less influence and that the leadership can dominate the process. The leadership must, however, be strong, and this has not always been the case. The chairman of one appropriations committee was so weak that in a period of a few days his committee voted three different budgetary allocations for the same agency. Committee members simply could not make up their minds, and neither could the chairman. As a result, the committee soon became a source of amusement around the capitol.[2]

Similarly, the record has been mixed in the development of the expertise needed in budgeting. Some junior legislators used the opportunity to develop knowledge about particular agencies, and thus to acquire the power associated with expertise. But expansion also brought into the process individuals who remained inexperienced and mostly uninterested in fiscal matters. Those involved must have a firm grasp of the policy implications of their recommendations and an understanding of the purpose and workings of the departments they are to oversee.

Once the original appropriations bills have been amended by the budget committee, they are again brought to the house floor. Here bills are debated and voted on by the entire chamber. Between three and five amendments for each bill are offered from

2. Randy McConnell, "Griffin Plan Posts Wins—and a Big Loss," *Columbia Daily Tribune*, March 15, 1981.

the floor by minority committee members who lost something they wanted in committee deliberations. However, such challenges rarely succeed. Usually the bills—at least in this first round—are passed on to the senate exactly as they come out of the budget committee. Any problems that crop up at this stage will be taken care of on the senate side or in the conference committee.

VI. The Senate

The budgetary process on the senate side of the legislature is far different from that in the house. First, the Senate Appropriations Committee is a relatively long-tenured and compact group. While the Senate Appropriations Committee has begun to use subcommittees in recent years, all subcommittee members come from the full committee. Rather than being a decentralizing influence as in the house, the senate subcommittees are primarily vehicles through which budget requests can be more carefully scrutinized and members can develop expertise in certain policy areas. In this sense they operate more like their congressional counterparts in Washington, D.C.

A final important way in which the senate committee differs from its house counterpart is in its relative lack of partisan debate over budget recommendations. This does not imply that there are no disagreements in the committee. It only means that most of the conflicts are ideological or geographical rather than partisan in nature. Most Senate Appropriations Committee members see their primary role as passing upon the recommendations of the house appropriations committees and adjusting them in response to appeals by constituents or important interest groups.

If anything, senators tend to take a more parochial attitude toward the budgetary process than do house members by attempting to shift additional funds toward state institutions or agencies located within their districts. Conversely, they also attempt to restrict funding for agencies or institutions that they (or powerful constituents) dislike. While the same thing occurs in the house, it is at least disguised or hidden somewhat from view. In the senate such attempts are often open and blatant.[3]

Nevertheless, the Senate Appropriations Committee is constrained somewhat by previous budgetary actions. First, by the time the senate receives the appropriation bills for consideration, the basic range of funding will have been set by the governor's recommendation and the house recommendation. By tradition, the senate committee attempts to set its recommendations somewhere between these two levels of support. This not only makes the senators' decision making easier (often they just split the difference) but also allows them room for compromise in the conference committee. If both the house and senate agree on an appropriation amount, then that item is not considered in conference; only those items on which they differ go before a conference.

Despite these differences between the senate and house appropriations committees, their staffs are very similar and are plagued by the same problems. Senate staffers often are spread too thin to develop viable policy options. Instead, they tend to make recommendations from options developed by the governor's staff, department personnel, or the house appropriations committees.

Once the senate committee has completed its work, the amended bills must go to the senate floor for passage by the

3. See Virginia Young, "Highway Patrol Head Hopes Legislative Troubles are Over," *Columbia Daily Tribune,* March 2, 1981.

entire chamber. Usually there are a few minor amendments offered at this time. If a serious threat to the committee's recommendations looms, the appropriations chair (who manages the bills on the floor) will temporarily halt debate and place the bill on the informal calendar so that it can be taken up again at a later time. By doing so the chair has time to get a better idea of the amendment's strength on the floor. If at all possible, the chair will attempt to defeat the amendment or at least blunt its purposes. However, if this is not possible without expending a great deal of political capital, the chair usually will not bother since any serious problems can be worked out in the conference between house and senate.

VII. The Conference Committee

The final stage of the budgetary process in the legislature is the conference between house and senate. The conference committee is always made up of five members from the house appropriations committees and five from the senate committee. Because of the house's peculiar committee structure, it has both permanent and temporary conference representatives. The membership of the house delegation always includes the House Budget Committee chair and often includes the vice-chair, but otherwise the membership depends upon the subject matter under discussion. When discussing funding for education, the committee may include the chair, vice-chair, and ranking minority member of the Appropriations–Education and Public Safety Committee. When discussing another department, it may include the chair, vice-chair, and ranking minority member of the appropriations committee in charge of that department. On the other hand, the senate's conference representatives are permanent. This puts the senators in a distinctly better strategic position, since it is easier for them to trade off decision items. Their continuous membership also allows them to keep track of previous compromises and maximize their bargaining position.

As noted previously, only those items in which the house and senate versions of the bill *differ* are supposed to be eligible for conference bargaining. However, conferees have been known to change budget figures that were the *same* on those rare occasions when both sides agreed it was necessary and had permission from their respective chambers. This is rare since the senate committee usually tries to reach a different funding level for important items. In this way, they can guarantee themselves plenty of political capital and maneuvering room in bargaining with the house conferees.

The conference itself usually starts slowly as each side states its initial bargaining position and tries to find out what items the other side really wants. Normally, items on which the two sides cannot agree after a short discussion are temporarily set aside. In this way, most of the minor differences are ironed out in the first round. This process not only indicates to both sides the items they feel strongly about but also enables them to establish a working relationship with a series of small compromises. Only then do the two sides move to larger and more controversial items that require hard bargaining. By this time, they are working efficiently and know fairly well how far and on what types of items the other side is willing to compromise.

One overriding factor at this stage in the budget process is time. The conference usually does not take place until the final weeks of the legislative session. Since the budget is one of the most important items in any legislative session, a compromise must be hammered out and ratified by both the house and the senate in a relatively short period. This is what makes the conference so important to the final passage of the state budget and is why veteran observers consider the real decision-making process to be contained in the conference committee. In many cases the final conference bill (called the report) is not completed until the last ten days of the session.

To avoid end-of-the-session logjams, the legislature has adopted rules requiring adoption of the budget one week before the end of the session. At that time, there is enormous pressure on the members of both chambers to approve what comes out of the conference. If one chamber feels that it has been taken advantage of by the other, the vote for final passage of the conference recommendations may be very close, but it is usually favorable. Members of the conference often argue that they made the best deal they could with the other chamber. It is when this is patently untrue and there is sufficient time for another conference that the committee's recommendations will be rejected. The conference committee report is considered first in the chamber in which the bill originated; in the case of appropriations bills, this is almost always the house. Only after the report passes in the house chamber does the senate begin to consider the compromise budget recommendations.

An unseen but not unfelt presence in each chamber and at conference is the governor. Just as the chief executive sets the agenda at the beginning of the legislative stage of the budgetary process, he also makes the final disposition of the budget. Because Missouri's governor possesses a line-item veto, conferees are hesitant to make any significant increases above the governor's recommendation. Legislators can, however, make significant decreases with impunity because the governor cannot veto items that are not in the bill. More often, legislators will negotiate agreements with the governor that he will veto or not veto particular items, perhaps in return for inclusion or exclusion of other items.

VIII. Veto Decisions

When the conference bills have been ratified by both chambers, the governor and the Division of Budget and Planning again become the central players in the budgetary process. After receiving final versions of the appropriation bills, analysts within the division once again begin a review process to determine which, if any, items should be vetoed. There are usually only two reasons to veto funds for a particular program: (1) the amount appropriated exceeds the amount needed to accomplish the goal, or (2) the program is politically unacceptable to the governor. This has been especially true in recent years when both the legislature and the governor have agreed on the total revenue available for the upcoming fiscal year.

By the time the legislative session has ended, most analysts have prepared a list of differences between the governor's original recommendation and the amount that actually has been appropriated for each department by the General Assembly. Special attention is given to those items that exceed the governor's recommendation by a large dollar amount. In cases where the General Assembly has appropriated less than the governor's original recommendation, a veto is not considered (unless the cuts made in the program are so severe that the final amount will do little or no good). During the course of the legislative session, analysts within the division become aware of those items that are politically undesirable to the governor. These are also marked for possible veto.

Once again the division's analysts must prepare special briefing papers on items to be considered by the governor for veto. They must compare the differences in the service that would be provided by each level of funding and explain the programmatic consequences of a veto. For example, in FY 1982 the General Assembly made reductions in the governor's recommendations for certain programs to allow the funding of cost-of-living adjustments for all state employees. However, an analysis by the Division of Budget and Planning indicated that the state had a serious cash-flow problem and that the modest pay adjustments could not be supported. Hence, all cost-of-living increases were vetoed by the governor.

A recommendation to veto funds for political reasons is considerably more difficult for the analysts within the division to handle. For example, in FY 1979 Governor Teasdale decided to veto $44 million appropriated from the state's General Revenue Fund to build the Truman State Office Building. The Division of Budget and Planning was forced to defend the veto, even though the state had a $240 million surplus in its General Revenue Fund and most of the analysts within the division supported the construction of the building. This decision was especially hard to reconcile because most insiders knew that the vetoed funds were to be used to bolster a large election-year budget for FY 1981. The veto was finally defended on the basis that the state would be better off borrowing the money to construct the building and that the construction was "extravagant" and "an insult to the hard working taxpayers of the state." The veto was later overridden by the General Assembly.[4]

When all the items that are worthy of a possible gubernatorial veto have been identified, a series of reviews again takes place to determine which items will actually be presented to the governor. The budget director and the governor's senior staff assume the role of advocates for funding, while analysts must present the case for vetoing an item. The final decision is left up to the governor, who must weigh the political consequences of any action.

Vetoes in appropriation bills differ from those of regular legislation, which must be signed or vetoed in their entirety, because any portion of an appropriation can be vetoed by the governor. This is known as a line-item veto, and it is used by the governor to maintain the state's fiscal solvency. In FY 1982, the governor vetoed a portion of each appropriation for personal service so that he could eliminate cost-of-living allowances that the state could not afford. Employees' base salaries remained in the appropriation, but the increase was eliminated.

The primary limitation a governor has in exercising this veto power is that it is a negative power only. The governor can only reduce appropriations, not increase them. This limits what can be done in a situation where the legislature refused to appropriate funds or pass the taxes needed to fund the budget. Such a situation occurred in 1989 when the state became liable for tax refunds of such magnitude that massive cuts in state services were threatened unless additional taxes passed the legislature. In this case Governor Ashcroft used his power to call the General Assembly into special session and threatened to withhold large sums from the FY 1990 budget unless taxes were increased to meet the state's obligation. Recognizing the need to act, the

4. News release from the office of Governor Joseph P. Teasdale, November 29, 1979; *Revised Statutes of Missouri*, 1986, Sec. 33.290. For a fuller explication of the budgetary process in Missouri and especially the role of the Division of Budget and Planning, see Michael D.

Connelly, "Budgetary and Policy Analysis in Missouri" (Ph.D. diss., University of Missouri–Columbia, 1981).

legislature quickly passed the temporary tax increases proposed by the governor. By skillfully using a negative power to force a positive action by the legislature, Ashcroft gave a textbook example of how a governor can dominate the budgetary agenda for the state.

When the appropriation bills are finally approved by the governor, the Division of Budget and Planning and the Division of Accounting (which is also within the Office of Administration) must begin allotting these funds to each department. The departments must first prepare spending plans for the upcoming fiscal year showing how much they plan to expend each quarter. This information is then entered into the state's accounting system, and the actual expenditures of each department are monitored by the Division of Accounting to ensure that the departments do not overspend their appropriations.

During the allotment process, the governor identifies an amount from each appropriation that is to be withheld as an emergency reserve. This so-called Governor's Reserve is typically 3 percent of the total appropriation for each department. It is used to pay for unexpected emergencies and can also be used by the governor to ensure that expenditures do not exceed revenues. During the state's fiscal crisis in FY 1982, the governor increased his withholding from 3 to 10 percent to ensure that the state would have enough cash on hand to pay its bills. This reduced expenditures sufficiently to balance the state's budget as required by the constitution. In most years the governor releases the Governor's Reserve during the fourth quarter of the fiscal year, when he is confident that state revenues will be sufficient to cover appropriations.

IX. Conclusion

It is clear that in Missouri, at least, the governor's role is key to the entire budgetary process because the chief executive sets the legislative agenda. With the line-item veto, a governor has substantial power to reduce appropriations after the legislature has done its work. And, as we have seen in some years, when revenues do not meet expectations it is the governor who decides which appropriations are to be cut, and by how much, to bring expenditures in line with revenues.

This is not to say that legislators, department officials, and outside interest groups are irrelevant to the budgetary process. It does mean that these groups must be constantly aware of the governor as the key player in the process. They must also realize that they can diverge only so far from the governor's initial recommendations before unilateral actions designed to eliminate the divergence will be taken. Unless the governor indicates support for a new proposal (or at least benign neglect), that proposal is not likely to succeed. For this reason, the budgetary process at the state level in Missouri is clearly an executive-dominated one.

CHAPTER 14

State and Local Revenue and Expenditure Policies
by Donald Phares

Tax reform means "Don't tax you, don't tax me, tax that fellow behind the tree." —Senator Russell B. Long

Taxes are what we pay for a civilized society. —Oliver Wendell Holmes, Jr.

"Missouri—The Forty-Something State"; this was the title of a six-part series that ran in the *St. Louis Post-Dispatch*, November 25–30, 1990. The series examined the revenue and expenditure policies of the state and raised a litany of questions about the implications for Missouri residents and businesses. While the focus was more explicitly on the state, it set the tone for an examination of all governments in Missouri.

In the fiscally troubled 1990s, we perhaps pay too little attention to what government does to support our day-to-day activities. Government provides us with essential public services and, of course, raises the revenue necessary to finance these operations. Although our economy is market-based, fully one-third of our national output (gross national product) flows through the coffers of federal, state, and local governments.

While objections can be made to the scope, content, and level of public sector operations, the public sector is essential to our individual and social well-being, and it also supports private business and commerce. In a society and economy as complex and interdependent as ours, government must play an important role in correcting for the failures of private actions. Examples of this role include fighting pollution, illegal activity, or the detrimental use of land; providing services such as education or health care that otherwise would not be adequately supplied; or establishing a framework of laws and regulations within which our market-based economy can function.

Government, at various levels, is an agent that acts collectively on behalf of society to deal with those problems and issues that individuals or groups cause directly, tend to ignore, or cannot deal with effectively. Government can accomplish these objectives through taxing provisions, programmatic spending, or creating laws or regulations.

Several essential services provided by Missouri governments stand out: basic educational opportunities for children and higher education and retraining for adults; public safety; roads and bridges, sewer and water systems, and other infrastructure; and health and welfare services to citizens of all ages. Such services clearly contribute to our individual and collective well-being and to the functioning of our society and economic system. Without government involvement these services would not be provided at all, or they would be provided inadequately by the private market, at prices affordable only to a few. Thus they become the responsibility of group or collective action, that which we call government. Depending upon one's political perspective, they might be labeled government as a necessary evil or government as an agent to improve our individual/societal status.

In terms of government services, what does it mean for Missouri to be a "forty-something state"? Table 14–1 summarizes how this label came about. Of the fifty states, Missouri ranks near the bottom in many categories of revenue raising and spending. Missouri ranks forty-ninth, for example, in the level of taxes imposed on its citizens. Using economic jargon, these rankings reflect *fiscal effort*, or how able and willing we are to tap into the resources at our disposal.

Relatively low spending levels, however, must be viewed in concert with the flip side of the budget issue, the potential to raise resources. Low support for public programs could result from a low resource base, or inadequate *fiscal capacity*. Fiscal capacity is determined largely by the level of citizen income that can be taxed; the amount of natural resources, such as oil, that can be taxed when extracted; and the value of taxable property in the state. Missouri has few taxable natural resources, but as Table 14–1 shows, Missouri ranks twenty-fourth in per capita income. The combination of these factors puts Missouri slightly below average, thirty-first among the fifty states, in state and local tax capacity.

Thus, while Missouri is not a rich state, the data clearly indicate that it certainly is not poor; yet it spends as though it were poor. Missouri has an adequate fiscal

Table 14-1. Missouri's Rankings among the Fifty States

Item	Ranking
Demographic/Economic Factors:	
Population	15
Per Capita Income	24
State Gross Domestic Product	15
Fiscal Factors:	
Tax Burden on Personal Income	49
Per Capita State & Local Taxes	39
State/Local Tax "Capacity" [1]	31
State/Local Tax "Effort" [2]	43
Expenditures:	
State/Local Expenditures Per Capita:	
Total	49
Education	42
Higher Education	45

[1] Capacity refers to resource availability.
[2] Effort reflects utilization of available resources.

Source: *States in Profile; The State Policy Reference Book 1991* (McConnellsburg, PA: Brizius & Foster, 1991), various tables.

capacity to support public programs but has chosen not to use it. Spending on public services and the resulting tax burden on residents have served to invoke the forty-something-state label.

The remainder of this chapter examines how Missouri's state and local governments spend their funds on public programs and how revenues are raised to accomplish this. This will help to put the forty-something-state label in perspective, and to suggest appropriate areas for policy deliberation.

I. Missouri Revenue and Spending Patterns

Missouri state and local governments combined spend more than $18 billion

Table 14-2. Missouri State and Local Expenditures, by Function, 1970 and 1991

	Local	State	
Expenditure Category	*1991*	*1970*	*1991*
Total Expenditures (millions of dollars)	$9,047	$1,505	$9,254
Percentage of Total by Major Spending Category:			
Education	46.1%	17.0%	12.7%
Social Services	7.5	24.6	27.3
Transportation	7.5	19.2	8.0
Public Safety	8.8	1.8	3.3
Environment & Housing	7.4	3.1	2.9
Administration	4.2	2.9	3.0
Interest on Debt	3.4	0.3	3.9
Insurance Trusts [1]	—	5.5	8.4
Intergovernmental [2]	—	23.4	28.9
Miscellaneous & Other	15.1	2.3	1.6

[1] Expenditures for retirement, unemployment compensation, workmen's compensation, and disability.

[2] Primarily funds paid to local governments such as for local education.

Source: Derived from data in *State Government Finances* (Washington, D.C.: Bureau of the Census), various years and tables; and *Government Finances* (Washington, D.C.: Bureau of the Census), various years and tables.

annually. This is divided roughly equally between the state of Missouri and its 3,367 local jurisdictions—114 counties, 933 municipalities, 324 townships, 553 school districts, and 1,443 special districts. At the local level, in 1991 school districts spent the largest portion (43 percent of local-level spending), with municipalities following a close second (36 percent), then counties (13 percent), and special districts (8 percent); townships spend a smaller amount.

Spending by program for the state of Missouri in 1970 and 1991 and for local governments in 1991 is shown in Table 14-2. For Missouri's localities, the spending on elementary and secondary education (also called K–12 education)—46 percent—is clearly dominant. It should be noted that the state of Missouri provides substantial support for K–12 education through in-

tergovernmental revenues, primarily the school foundation formula, but the spending takes place locally. Public safety is a distant second to education at 8.8 percent, while social services, transportation, and environment and housing each account for about 7.5 percent of spending. The "miscellaneous and other" category is high (15 percent), but more than two-thirds of this is accounted for by local utility facilities, including water, gas, electric, and transit.

For the state government, the pattern is quite different. The two largest items are intergovernmental expenditures at almost 29 percent and social services at 27 percent. The bulk of the intergovernmental expenditures are for various funds provided to Missouri localities, primarily to support school districts. Education comes next at 12.7 percent, with almost all of this going to support higher education. Transportation follows at 8 percent, with virtually all of these funds going to the state highway system.

Since 1970, there have been some distinct changes in state spending patterns. The most dramatic change has been in transportation expenditures, which fell from 19 percent in 1970 to 8 percent in 1991. Intergovernmental expenditures have increased by 5.5 percentage points and social services by 2.7 points relative to the total. State support for higher education, on the other hand, has dropped by 4.3 percentage points over this time period. The other two categories with relatively large changes are interest on debt, which increased from 0.3 percent to almost 4 percent, and insurance trust funds, which rose from 5.5 percent to more than 8 percent.

Table 14–3 shows the major sources of revenue for the state of Missouri in 1970 and 1991 and for its local governments in 1991. For local units, the largest source is intergovernmental revenue from the state, primarily to support elementary and secondary education. A close second is the property tax at 22.6 percent, with current charges next at 14 percent. While "miscellaneous and other" is large in total, it is a composite of a number of relatively small items. It is interesting to note that revenue from the federal government accounts for only 4 percent of all local revenue.

At the state level, the pattern is distinctly different. Intergovernmental revenue from the federal government is the largest source at 22 percent; this is followed by the individual income and general sales taxes, which are each more than 18 percent of total state revenues. The corporate income tax is very modest at slightly more than 2 percent. Insurance trust funds, which are primarily for retirement and unemployment purposes,

account for more than 13 percent of all revenues.

Comparisons of 1991 with 1970 reveal several distinct changes in how Missouri derives its revenues. Funds from the federal government have fallen from 27.5 percent of total revenues in 1970 to 22.3 percent in 1991. The most marked change is the shift in the individual income and general sales taxes. In 1970 individual income accounted for 8.8 percent of revenues and general sales for 23 percent. In 1991 they each produced more than 18 percent of state revenues. Selective sales taxes have decreased in relative importance from 13.4 percent to 6.4 percent.

Local governments provide many services that on a daily basis are closer to us as citizens, such as elementary and secondary education, police and fire protection, local transportation facilities, parks and recreation, and sewer and water treatment. State government supports some of these activities such as K–12 education, but it also funds broader-scale programs such as infrastructure projects, higher education, and social services. There is a distinction between local programs and those provided by the state; this is reflected by the data in Table 14–2.

On the spending side of the budget, changes are a function of several factors, including the pressures of urbanization and a larger population; changing demographics; the lessening financial involvement of the federal government in state and local programs; growth in entitlements; and greater earmarking of funds for specific purposes such as education, highways, or conservation.

On the revenue side of the budget, there are similar changes due to a shift in the resource base of the federal, state, and local

Table 14-3. Missouri State and Local Revenues, by Source, 1970 and 1991

	Local	State	
Revenue Category	1991	1970	1991
Total Revenues (millions of dollars)	$8,552	$1,480	$10,002
Percentage of Total by Major Revenue Category:			
Intergovernmental:			
federal	4.0%	27.5%	22.3%
state	24.6	—	—
Property	22.6	**	**
General Sales & Gross Receipts	7.9	23.3	18.6
Selective Sales [1]	3.6	13.4	6.4
Individual Income	2.5	8.8	18.3
Corporation Income	—	1.4	2.2
Current Charges	14.1	6.4	7.4
Insurance Trusts	—	9.1	13.4
Miscellaneous & Other	20.7	10.1	11.4

[1] Primarily taxes on motor fuel, alcoholic beverages, tobacco products, and insurance for the state; and taxes on public utilities for local.

**Rounds to zero.

Source: Derived from data in *State Government Finances* (Washington, D.C.: Bureau of the Census), various years and tables; and *Government Finances* (Washington, D.C.: Bureau of the Census), various years and tables.

sectors; economic factors; voter/taxpayer perception and approval of various revenue sources; entitlement programs and revenue earmarking; and legislative decisions about both how to raise additional funds and how much to raise.

II. An Analysis of Revenue Sources

Guidelines for Revenue Policy

To help understand how state and local governments finance their operations, it is useful to have some criteria to use as a reference. While many could be specified and none are absolute, the following are generally agreed upon as being relevant.

Equity or Fairness. This addresses the issue of who pays for government and how the burden is apportioned. One principle would be to allocate costs in accordance with benefits received, but this is often impossible to accomplish since any linkage may be obscure or nonexistent. A second principle for equity would be to allocate program costs in accordance with taxpayers' ability to pay, usually defined by their income. A tax (or tax system) is progressive when those with higher incomes are taxed a higher percentage of their income; on the other hand, a regressive tax would levy a higher percentage on those with lower incomes. A proportional tax would burden all income levels the same.

The greatest potential for progressivity is offered by a broad-based income tax with graduated marginal rates (that is, each additional thousand dollars of income, for example, is taxed at a higher rate than the previous thousand dollars.) General sales and selective sales taxes tend to be regressive, the latter more so. Examination of the property tax nationwide and in individual states (including Missouri) and local units has found this tax also to be very regressive. Allowances for exemptions, deductions, and credits do have the potential to alter this regressivity or progressivity, but the general pattern holds true.

Revenue Responsiveness. This is a measure of the extent to which revenue from a tax keeps pace with inflation or growth. Revenue sources that are designed to have automatic increases will eliminate the need for legislative or citizen approval to secure new funds. Automatic revenue growth helps government keep up with inflationary pressures and provides for programmatic enhancement.

The greatest degree of responsiveness is derived from broad-based tax levies such as those on income or consumption; their yield expands with growth in the economy. Narrow-based taxes tend not to respond well automatically. This has proved true for taxes on alcohol, tobacco, and motor fuels, which all have a constant or declining consumption base. When yield for these items has increased, it usually has been due to increased tax rates.

Revenue Adequacy. Certain types of public revenues have a much greater capacity to yield funds. The scope of the tax base depends on the items subject to taxation and the geographical area over which the tax applies. A primary concern is whether to pay for government with a few broad-based revenue sources or to rely on the "nickel and dime approach" of creating many revenue sources, each of which yields a relatively small amount. Adequacy is most pronounced with taxes on income and general consumption due to the scope of their coverage.

Economic Efficiency. The imposition of any tax will alter economic decisions made by individuals or businesses. A tax on workers will shift the balance in favor of greater use of capital; a tax on the consumption of an item will tend to shift spending in favor of other items. A similar phenomenon pertains to the geographic area covered by a tax. Taxes for state or local governments vary; either they may not impose the tax at all or the rates may differ. This can lead to changes in economic decisions by individuals and businesses.

Tax policy makers need to take into account the effect of existing taxes or proposed changes on work and income patterns, consumption patterns, and decisions about location. The more inclusive a tax is in terms of its base and geographical coverage, the more difficult it is for businesses and individuals to try to avoid it and the less incentive they have to do so.

Each of the previous four guidelines for revenue policy has an impact on Missouri and its localities. Localities within the state compete with each other and with those in other states. Each locality must consider its need for revenue, the effect that a given tax will have upon equity, the extent to which the tax will provide the finances needed for an appropriate length of time, and the extent to which imposition of the tax will encourage or discourage economic activity. The state also faces the problem of competing with other states in the national marketplace and with foreign nations in global markets.

The Individual Income Tax

The tax on individual income is a major revenue source for Missouri and for most other states. At present, forty-one states have a broad-based income tax (two others tax only interest and dividends), although they vary considerably in their specific structure and provisions. Missouri's tax was first enacted in 1917 at a rate of 0.5 percent. Graduated tax brackets and marginal rates were put in place in 1931. At present, marginal rates begin at 1.5 percent for the first one thousand dollars of income and then increase by 0.5 percent over nine brackets in thousand-dollar increments up to 6 percent on income greater than nine thousand dollars. The rate structure appears to be progressive in that tax rates rise with income. Until Senate Bill 380 was enacted in 1993, the tax had not been modified since 1973.

Although there is an appearance of substantial progressivity, several factors alter the relationship between the nominal or legally specified tax rate and the economically more meaningful effective tax rate, defined as taxes paid as a percentage of income. The effective tax rate more accurately reflects the true burden on taxpayers' ability to pay. Since the top Missouri rate is 6 percent on taxable income greater than nine thousand dollars, and since most taxpayers' income exceeds this, the tax rates and the allowances for exemptions, deductions, and credits make this tax less progressive than the nominal rates would indicate.

Also, as is true at the federal level and for other states, not all income is taxed. There are a plethora of Missouri adjustments, deductions, exemptions, and credits that serve to reduce taxable income, often far below gross income. No one in any state actually pays the specified marginal rate on their income due to the impact of these provisions.

While states vary widely in the nature and magnitude of alterations to determine taxable income and the extent of itemization, two provisions in Missouri's tax law do stand out. First, all income taxes paid to the federal government were fully deductible for many years. Only nine other states allow any deduction for federal tax payments. In 1993 Missouri capped this deduction at five thousand dollars per person or ten thousand dollars per return.

Since the higher your income, the more your federal tax bill will be, the deduction of federal income taxes means that those with higher incomes receive greater reductions in their Missouri taxes. This clearly favors high-income taxpayers and reduces the progressivity in Missouri's income tax. Thus, the recent cap will increase the progressivity of Missouri's individual income tax.

A second provision of Missouri tax law allows for the full deduction of all social security taxes if you itemize on your state return. Only two other states allow this. Given the rapid growth in these taxes, this deduction can reduce tax liability by as much as five hundred dollars for a two-income family and will grow as federal social security laws change.

A not-so-obvious impact of various exemptions and deductions on Missouri's fiscal status is that for every dollar exempted or deducted, the state suffers a revenue loss. The tax base shrinks and, therefore, so does yield from the individual income tax. The cost is far from inconsequential, as is shown in Table 14-4. In fact, the cost in reduced state tax yield exceeds actual collections; this means that revenue from this tax might more than double if all exclusions and deductions were eliminated.

A tax on income is also allowed in Missouri for two local governments: Kansas City and the city of St. Louis. Each city presently derives about $100 million per year from its local "earnings" tax, making the tax a major source of revenue. Unlike most municipal governments nationwide, which instead rely heavily on the property

Table 14-4. Cost of Tax Deductions and Exemptions in Revenue Yield to State of Missouri

Item	Cost in revenue yield
Personal income tax exclusions and deductions:	
Federal income tax deduction*	$ 353 million
Social security tax deduction	110 million
Standard deduction	342 million
Total exclusions	1,053 million
Total deductions	1,629 million
Sales and use tax exemptions:	
Motor fuel	$ 173 million
Services	428 million
Tax exempt institutions	224 million
Total exempt sales:	1,237 million
Personal	699 million
Business	538 million
Corporate income tax deductions	
Accelerated depreciation provisions	$ 191 million
Federal income tax deduction	100 million
Total exclusions, deductions, and credits	472 million

*Now limited due to senate bill 380 enacted in 1993
Source: B&PA Research Center, *Tax Expenditure Report* (Columbia: College of Business & Public Administration, University of Missouri–Columbia, January 1994). Data are for the latest year available, usually 1994.

tax, Kansas City and St. Louis have been able to use the earnings tax because of enabling legislation enacted by the state in 1948.

The present local earnings tax is a flat 1 percent on salaries, wages, commissions, and other earned compensation for all residents of these two cities plus all non-residents who "do business within" the cities. Missouri is one of thirteen states that permit local jurisdictions to tax income (defined in varying ways by state). Some states have even broadened this taxing authority beyond cities to include counties, school districts, and other localities. By far the most extensive use of this authority is in Pennsylvania, where more than twenty-eight hundred local units use such a tax.

The General Sales Tax

A second major source of state revenues is the general sales tax. Despite its name, the general sales tax is not "generally" applied. Hawaii is the only state with a sales tax deserving the label "general." In fact, while a true general sales tax would equate closely to a tax on all consumption, much that is consumed is exempt under Missouri's present system. Actually, taxation applies predominantly to the sale of tangible items and only very selectively to services. In Missouri, unlike in many other states, little action has been taken to expand the base for broader coverage of service-related transactions.

Missouri's general sales tax was first enacted on a temporary basis in 1934 at a rate of 0.5 percent. The tax was modified in coverage and made permanent at 2 percent in 1943. The rate was not increased again until 1963, when it rose to 3 percent. Other than during a nine-month period in 1989–1990, when the tax was increased temporarily to fund the cost of a federal court decision, the state general revenue rate has remained at 3 percent.

In addition to the state general revenue component, other levies have been collected for earmarked purposes. In 1976 a 0.125 percent levy was added for fisheries and wildlife programs; another 0.1 percent was added in 1984 for conservation and parks. In a 1982 statewide election, voters approved another 1 percent by adopting the so-called Proposition C. Half of the proceeds from this levy are earmarked for local education, and the other half are for property tax rollback. Thus, the present overall state sales tax rate stands at 4.225 percent, of which only 3 percent goes into state general revenue.

Two significant issues arise with respect to the general sales tax. The first is its regressive nature: it places a relatively greater burden on lower-income taxpayers. Scores of studies examining the equity of the general sales tax support this overall conclusion and suggest how its regressivity might be softened.

One option to improve the equity of the general sales tax is to exempt food from the tax base, since food expenses account for a much larger percentage of low-income budgets than of high-income budgets. Missouri is one of 20 states, out of 46 with a general sales tax, that does not exempt food; a 1976 initiative to exempt food was defeated by voters. From a fiscally practical point of view, there is reason not to exempt food: an estimated $400 million loss in revenue would be the result. Part of the loss would be to general revenue from the

3 percent rate, and part would be from the 1.225 percent earmarked state portion. Any local jurisdictions that piggyback their own rate (which can exceed 1 percent) onto the state rate would also experience a loss in revenue.

Exempting food from the general sales tax would improve equity, but it would also cost the state and its localities hundreds of millions of dollars. This loss would have to be offset either by increasing other revenues or by drastically cutting state and local programs. Given Missouri's forty-something-state status, the last option would be difficult.

Missouri's general sales tax is also affected by changes in consumer habits, particularly the pattern of relatively less consumption of taxable items and more consumption of mostly nontaxable services. This clear shift in consumer spending means that one of Missouri's largest revenue sources suffers from the increased spending on nontaxable service items, a list that at present includes cable television, medical care, motor fuel, and vehicle maintenance. In addition, research shows that taxing certain services such as recreation and travel could improve equity, since those with higher incomes tend to spend proportionately more on these services.

The local general sales tax is also widely used in Missouri. In fact, Missouri has been one of the states most responsive to allowing local jurisdictions to use this tax. Missouri ranks second only to Texas in the number of localities (780) taking advantage of state enabling legislation for a local general sales tax. As a result, local sales taxes have become a major, if not the dominant, revenue source for many local governments. Local sales taxes began in 1969 for municipalities and in 1979 for counties; they have now expanded to local transit districts as well. They are most often imposed for general revenue purposes or to fund transportation facilities or infrastructure.

As with the individual income tax, the exemption of items from the general sales tax base imposes a loss in revenues for the state government and for many local governments. Table 14–4 provides estimates of revenue loss for certain items. It reflects only the 3 percent state general revenue rate; the losses from all other levies, state (1.225 percent) and local (1 percent or more), would need to be added. The yield loss is substantial; actual collections could be as much as 40 percent higher if these items were taxed.

The Corporate Income Tax

Missouri's corporate income tax was introduced in 1917, the same year as the individual income tax, at a flat rate of 0.5 percent. It was redefined in 1973, along with the tax on individual income, to create greater conformity with federal tax laws. In 1993 the rate changed to 6.25 percent, with a 50 percent cap on federal tax deductibility, due to legislation (Senate Bill 380) resulting from a Missouri state circuit court decision on the adequacy and equity of local school financing.

While not a trivial source of revenue (it amounts to about $280 million per year), this tax is smaller in order of magnitude than either the general sales tax or the individual income tax. Given its structure it is not likely to grow significantly in importance, even with the scheduled changes, for two reasons. First, many of its provisions are tied into federal tax law that erodes Missouri's yield; the federal government is not likely to change these laws. Second, corporations that operate in other states as well as in Missouri can avoid some of the Missouri tax burden because they can choose the less costly of two ways to determine what proportion of their income

was earned in Missouri, and thus subject to Missouri taxes. A corporation can choose to calculate its tax liability based on the proportion of total sales that were in Missouri, or it can select the so-called 3-factor formula, which weights equally the proportions of the corporation's payroll, property, and sales that are in Missouri. Needless to say, corporations select the option that will minimize their tax liability. For example, a firm located in Missouri with a large proportion of out-of-state sales would choose the 100 percent sales apportionment, thus reducing its Missouri liability below what it would be with the 3-factor formula.

As with the general sales and individual income taxes, specific provisions that exclude or exempt items from the tax base cause a loss in yield for Missouri. Table 14–4 provides some estimates. The revenue loss of these provisions is greater than actual collection.

Selective Sales Taxes

While there are several types of selective sales taxes that affect the Missouri fiscal scene, four dominate. Three are fully or predominantly state levies; one is almost exclusively locally imposed. The predominantly state taxes are on alcoholic beverages (100 percent state), tobacco products (80 percent state), and motor fuels (more than 99 percent state); the public utilities tax is more than 99 percent local. It should be noted that the local public utilities tax, usually called a gross receipts tax, has assumed a major fiscal role in the budgets of some county and municipal governments in Missouri, exceeding the property or general sales tax in many instances.

Three reasons are proposed for imposing selective sales taxes. First, these taxes serve as a charge for benefits received from public services. This reason holds strongest with the motor fuels tax as it relates to road and bridge usage. The tax is earmarked for building and repairing roads and bridges, and is also used to assist localities. The taxes on tobacco and alcohol, however, cannot be construed as charges for public services. These taxes are addressed by the second reason proposed: that as "sin" taxes, they curtail consumption of harmful substances. There is reason to doubt this rationale, especially given the low rates of taxation in Missouri. The third reason, now much more appropriate than in the past, is that selective sales taxes provide new sources of funding for public programs.

The gross receipts tax (that is, the tax on public utilities) has become a cash cow for some Missouri local jurisdictions and certainly cannot be justified as either a sin tax or payment for services provided. The federal government, the Missouri state government, and some local jurisdictions in Missouri have turned to these taxes for needed funds in fiscally tight times. At the local level, the gross receipts tax can be a significant source of funds, accounting for 25 percent or more of the revenue for some Missouri cities. All state-imposed selective sales taxes combined, however, are a modest 6.4 percent of the state government's overall revenue.

The Property Tax

The property tax is an ad valorem ("according to the value of") tax on the value of property as assessed by a taxing authority, usually a county. In principle this tax could be applied to all types of property—real estate, personal, and intangible. But in Missouri and most other states, its coverage has been increasingly confined to real estate and limited personal property; in the latter case this includes mostly items that are readily identifiable through licensing or registration such as cars, boats, or planes. The main reason for limiting the tax base is the administrative nightmare involved in locating, identifying, and placing a value on intangible property and many types of personal property.

The process of assessment entails assigning a value to property against which a tax levy can be applied; in Missouri, the tax levy is expressed as a dollar amount per one hundred dollars of assessed value. An assessment is necessary because unlike most other taxes, the property tax cannot be measured by a market-based activity such as sales or income generation. Assessors must determine the value of property using whatever base of information is available to them. This leads to a degree of arbitrariness and variation and instances where properties with an equal value may be assessed differently.

Since the assessment process is so time-consuming and cumbersome, lags in adjusting property to an appropriate value can also occur. In declining real estate areas, houses may be overassessed; in growing areas, they may be underassessed. This led the state government to mandate a total reassessment of all property in the state since in many places such a reassessment had not been done for decades. Taking several years and costing tens of millions of dollars, the reassessment was implemented in 1985. Now held regularly on a two-year cycle, it has helped to correct some of the unfairness in property assessment. As part of the reform, property is now classified into three assessment rates based on market value: residential is 19 percent, farm is 12 percent, and business is 32 percent. Personal property remains at the old rate of 33.3 percent. Thus a residence valued at one hundred thousand dollars would be assessed at nineteen thousand dollars and the owner would pay a tax levy of perhaps one thousand dollars per year. In contrast, a business building in the same district also valued at one hundred thousand dollars would be assessed at thirty-two thousand dollars and the owner would pay a tax of $1,684.

In the past, the property tax has played a fiscal role for all governments. Over time the federal and state governments turned to other revenue sources, primarily income and sales, and left the property tax for local governments. However, even at the local level, this tax has diminished in importance. In 1950 it represented 89 percent of all local taxes nationwide; at present it accounts for less than 75 percent. In Missouri, this trend is even more pronounced—property taxes account for only 60 percent of local tax revenues. This drop is due in large part to legislation that has allowed local governments to use general sales and gross receipts taxes, and to the earnings tax in Kansas City and St. Louis.

The pattern of property tax usage by localities in Missouri varies by government type and by purpose. All of the local tax revenue for school and special districts and townships is derived from property tax revenues. For counties, property tax revenues are 40 percent of this total; for municipalities, 17 percent. The importance of the property tax for school and special districts is common across the nation. For counties and municipalities, the figures reflect greater reliance on sales-based, rather than property-based, taxation, as allowed by state legislation. By function, the property tax in Missouri is used to support a vast array of local public programs. This includes activities by eighteen different types of taxing authorities ranging from ambulance services to zoos.

Property taxation raises several issues. First, it is a regressive tax, since it falls much more heavily on low-income taxpayers. The inequity of the tax is further exacerbated by the fact that the tax is a relatively large percentage of income as well, providing as much money for Missouri local governments as the personal income tax does for the state government. A highly regressive tax with a very low tax rate is far less of a burden than one with a high rate. One consolation is that the situation could be worse—property taxes in Missouri are lower than in many other states.

There are also issues concerning the lack of responsiveness of the property tax. It does not tend to grow automatically, which explains why Missouri voters see so many ballot issues for an increase in the property tax rate. Revenue adequacy is also of major concern. Missouri localities therefore have been forced to turn to other revenue sources whenever possible.

Since school districts vary so widely in their taxable property base, the revenues derived for support of K–12 education differ substantially. For example, in 1992–1993 the assessed property value for each eligible pupil in Clayton, in St. Louis County, was almost ten times the assessed property value for each eligible pupil in Republic, in southwestern Missouri. Even with equalization provided by the state foundation program, Clayton spent more than nine thousand dollars per pupil that year, while Republic spent less than twenty-four hundred dollars per pupil.

Following a national trend, a recent Missouri Circuit Court decision in Cole County declared that the existing system for funding local education "does not pass constitutional muster" under state equal-protection provisions. In essence, the quality and quantity of local education in Missouri is a function of the happenstance of local property wealth within a district. The circuit court ruled that the state of Missouri must deal with the unequal support for local education, as the judge noted in the opinion, "ranging from the 'golden' to the 'god-awful.'" The judge also ruled that the existing state foundation formula for elementary and secondary education is "irrational" and that the present level of state support "does not maintain" an adequate system of education. This decision led to legislation passed in 1993 (Senate Bill 380) for more than $300 million in additional state support for local education. The legislation also raised the minimum property tax levy required, thus increasing the amount per pupil raised in the lowest taxing districts and reducing the disparity among districts noted earlier.[1]

While the property tax remains a fiscal mainstay for many local governments in Missouri, there are major concerns about its equity, revenue adequacy, and growth responsiveness, not to mention legal challenges about its constitutionality in funding local education. Given Missouri's more than twenty-six hundred local property taxing authorities levying almost five thousand rates for eighteen types of activities, the issue is unlikely to go away. This will put even more pressure on Missouri and its localities to cope with the problems related to local property taxation.

Miscellaneous and Other Revenues

Of the many other revenue sources for Missouri, gambling is the one that has received the most attention recently. Enabling legislation was passed in 1980 allowing bingo and in 1984 for a state lottery and pari-mutuel betting on horse races. Pari-mutuel betting, while authorized, has not come about, probably because provisions in the law do not allow for an adequate profit and there is competition from nearby

Kansas and Illinois. Lottery proceeds have grown and currently net about $100 million annually for the state; bingo generates about $7 million.

Riverboat gambling was authorized by a statewide referendum in 1992 that enabled localities to vote for it. Later the Missouri Supreme Court ruled that although games of chance, most significantly slot machines, were prohibited by the constitution, games of skill (poker and blackjack, for example) could be played on riverboats. An attempt to amend the constitution to allow slot machines on riverboats was narrowly defeated in April 1994. Nevertheless, some boats opened their doors in May, providing poker, blackjack, craps, and video poker. Gambling proponents submitted another initiative proposal to allow slot machines and games of chance on riverboats, and this proposal received statewide voter approval in November 1994. The law specifies that 18 percent of net receipts (after payment of winnings) shall go to the state and 2 percent shall go to the locality. In addition, the locality gets one-half of a two-dollar admission fee. Estimated income for the state will be about $80 million per year.

As a result of another statewide vote in 1992, all state proceeds from gaming activities now are earmarked for education. Most local receipts can be used at the discretion of the locality.

Other major state and local revenues in the "Miscellaneous" category are miscellaneous general revenue (primarily interest earnings), and a large number of license taxes on individual and business activities. License taxes are enacted as a condition to engage in some business or nonbusiness purposes such as owning or operating motor vehicles, amusements (such as exhibitions), professional licenses, and hunting and fishing.

---

1. See chapter 17 for a detailed description of the passage of this legislation.

Current Charges

Current charges represent amounts received from the public either for some specific service rendered or for the sale of services and commodities by the state or by a local government. As shown in Table 14–3, these charges provide modest revenues for the state (7.4 percent of total revenue) but are much more important for localities (14.1 percent of total revenue).

There has been a marked trend, especially at the local level, to impose charges for services where there is an identifiable recipient of the benefits. While in the past many services were paid for out of taxes, tight fiscal times have made charges much more attractive and, many would argue, more palatable to citizens. In effect, you pay a "price" for what you get, much like in the marketplace. Trash collection fees represent an excellent example; most localities now charge specifically for this service rather than financing it through general tax proceeds. It should be noted that user charges are a clear trend not just in Missouri, but nationwide.

Intergovernmental Revenues

The American federal system is characterized by a complex system of intergovernmental revenue flows. The federal government grants funds to states and localities, and the states provide funds to their local jurisdictions. Within some states (not Missouri) there are also revenue flows from larger local units such as counties to smaller units such as municipalities. In dollar terms, the largest amount goes from states to their local units. Nationally, this state distribution to localities is dominated by education (64 percent) with public welfare (12 percent) and general support (10 percent) a distant second and third.

Federal grants are second in dollar volume and are dominated by public welfare (43 percent), then education (16.4 percent) and highways (11.8 percent). The share of federal grants in state–local fiscal affairs peaked in 1978 at 26.5 percent of all state–local outlays, accounting for 3.6 percent of gross national product. The trend since 1978 has been continually downward, as measured both by share of state-local outlays and as a percentage of gross national product. Given the federal budget situation, this trend is likely to be maintained and will put added pressure on states to take up the slack.

In the governor's proposed budget for the 1995 fiscal year, $3.1 billion out of Missouri's spending of $12.4 billion will come from federal sources. Almost $2.3 billion of this goes to health and social services, while another $417 million are for elementary and secondary education. In comparison, at the local level the role of federal funds is quite limited at only 4 percent of all revenues.

The major intergovernmental outlay for the state of Missouri is to local school districts (more than 83 percent) for the support of K–12 education. The remainder is distributed to counties and municipalities for a variety of purposes.

Intergovernmental revenues are a major source of funding—for the state of Missouri from the federal government and for Missouri localities from the state of Missouri. This overall pattern is likely to continue, but with two shifts. The federal role in regard to states and local units is likely to diminish due to national budget issues. This will force states to increase their role. This has already begun to happen, as it did when the state of Missouri increased the motor fuel tax from seven cents to eleven cents per gallon in 1987 and from eleven cents to seventeen cents in 1992–1996 for added support for highways and bridges. Like other states, Missouri will be hit by diminished federal funds; expanding federal mandates, rules, and regulations; and judicially imposed reforms such as for local school funding.

III. Debt Financing

In addition to the revenue sources already discussed, Missouri and its local governments can also obtain funds from the issuance of debt. Unlike the federal government, however, the state's debt proceeds cannot be used to cover operating expenses of the types outlined in Table 14–2, except on a short-term or emergency basis. Missouri and its localities use debt funds for capital projects such as buildings, roads and bridges, sewer and water systems, or other public facilities with a usable life of several years. Funds are borrowed in the present for public purposes, and the cost is spread into the future and paid off with revenues in future years. As shown in Table 14–2, interest payments on debt now account for 3.4 percent of local expenditures and almost 4 percent for the state of Missouri.

By far the greatest volume of outstanding governmental debt is federal, and the national debt has been expanding, not only as a percentage of the total but also relative to gross national output. Nationally, about 78 percent of all governmental debt is accounted for by the federal government; 14 percent is with state governments, and 8 percent is with local jurisdictions.

Missouri and its localities currently have more than $11 billion in outstanding debt, of which $5.8 billion is state and $5.4 billion is local. *Full faith and credit debt,* which has the resources of the issuing jurisdiction as collateral, is about 30 percent of the total. Nonguaranteed debt accounts for 70 percent and is paid off through revenues derived from a specific activity or use such as school loans, mortgages, and industrial development.

Debt is an important instrument for Missouri's finances, but not for covering day-to-day operating outlays. It is used to fund a variety of long-term public projects, promote economic development, or support revenue-producing capital facilities. The only exception to this is short-term borrowing using *tax anticipation notes.* These are paid off with the proceeds from incoming revenues within a fiscal year. They are used to smooth out the time discrepancy between when revenues come in and spending is incurred, since revenues often lag behind spending by many months.

IV. Limitations on Missouri State and Local Revenues

Missouri has no limitation on spending at either the state or local level other than the requirement of an annually balanced budget. However, in 1980 Missouri voters passed by a clear margin a constitutional provision that set out limitations on the revenues that the state and its local governments can raise. This provision emerged from the "taxpayer revolt" of the 1970s and resulted in the so-called Hancock Amendment. Since this amendment set limitations on revenues, it constrained expenditures as well, because the state and its localities must have balanced budgets.

At the state level, revenue is limited to 5.64 percent of total personal income in Missouri for the prior calendar year. This percentage is based on the relation between 1979 state personal income and state revenues in Fiscal Year 1981, when the amendment was first passed. State revenues in excess of this percentage of state personal income for any given year must be refunded to taxpayers in proportion to their payment of state individual income taxes. This refund provision has been questioned under the equal protection provisions of both the Missouri and the U.S. constitutions. In essence the argument is, why not refund to all payers of state taxes, not just the payers of income taxes? Thus far the state has not exceeded the spending limit, so no refund of excess receipts has been paid to any taxpayers. As a result, no aggrieved taxpayer has had a basis for bringing a court suit.

The 1980 Hancock revenue limit can be exceeded when taxpayers statewide approve by a majority vote the enactment of a new revenue source such as was done for the lottery, the sales tax for conservation, or Proposition C for local education. By decision of the Missouri Supreme Court, revenues from any voter-approved tax increase do not count in determining the Hancock limitation on state revenues. In 1994 Congressman Mel Hancock spearheaded an initiative petition drive to ask voters to amend the constitution to further restrict state revenues by placing voter-approved tax measures under the 5.64 percent limit. Although Missouri voters rejected this new tax limit proposal, the Hancock amendment remained in effect.

For local governments the Hancock limits are, in many respects, even more constraining. Increases in rates for local revenues must receive the explicit approval of the voters. For several years, many local governments interpreted this requirement to include voter approval of increases in such trivial matters as charges for dog licenses or fees for recreational activities. As a result, voters in some areas were confronted with a staggering array of provisions for increases in fees, charges, and permits. This generated confusion and annoyance for the voters, and fiscal gridlock for local officials trying to keep up with rising program costs, federal mandates, and citizen demands for more and better services. A 1991 Missouri Supreme Court ruling established rules for defining fees, which allowed local governments to increase some fees without the necessity of asking for voter approval.

One provision of the Hancock amendment has been very well received at the local level. No longer can the state of Missouri impose additional costs or mandate new programs for localities unless it provides funding. Prior to the Hancock Amendment, the state could impose new costs and mandate local programs without providing any compensation.

V. Issues for Missouri Budgetary Policy

This chapter has outlined Missouri's state and local revenue and spending policies. While it may set the parameters of what is, it invites numerous questions as to what will be. Many challenges face the state of Missouri and its local governments, such as:

• What is the appropriate response to accommodate the need for certain public services essential for a changing national and global economy? This would include, but not be limited to, capital improvements needed for business and economic activity and investment in education at all levels for our citizens, which is often referred to as investment in human capital.

• How does Missouri cope with the retrenchment and/or abandonment of many state and local programs by the federal government? Given the status of the federal deficit, things may well get worse, with states and localities picking up an even greater share of the cost for programs that were previously supported by federal funds.

• What, if anything, does Missouri do about low-level support for public services, that is, the forty-something-state syndrome?

• How can the state reform its revenue structure to be more equitable, provide adequate resources for public services, and build in automatic growth in revenues without the constant need for legislative and/or voter approval?

• Can the fiscal constraints of the Hancock revenue limitation on Missouri and its local governments be made compatible with budgetary claims imposed by federal spending retrenchment, new and expanded federal mandates, the rising costs of public services, and the need for certain types of programmatic enhancement?

This list is not intended to provide answers or to exhaust all of the issues. Rather, its purpose is to highlight those that are likely to remain relevant for the state of Missouri and its local governments in the foreseeable future.

References

In addition to specific table citations, data and information for this chapter were derived from the following sources:

Census of Governments: 1987 (Washington, D.C.: Bureau of the Census, various volumes and tables).

Committee for Educational Equality, et al. v. State of Missouri, et al. and *Lee's Summit School District R-VIII, et al., v. State of Missouri, et al.*, Memorandum Opinion and Judgment, Circuit Court of Cole County, January 20, 1993.

The Missouri Budget: Fiscal Year 1995 (Executive Budget) (Jefferson City: 1994, various tables).

Review of 1993 Property Tax Rates (Jefferson City: State Auditor, Report No. 94-16, 3/11/94).

Significant Features of Fiscal Federalism, vols. 1 and 2 (Washington, D.C.: U.S. Advisory Commission on Intergovernmental Relations, various years and tables).

St. Louis Post-Dispatch, November 25–30, 1990.

State Government Tax Collections, State Government Finances, and Government Finances (Washington, D.C.: Bureau of the Census, various years and tables).

The author acknowledges the support of the President's office of the University of Missouri for the Missouri State Revenue Study Project, and the support of the Public Policy Research Centers at the University of Missouri–St. Louis.

CHAPTER 15

Elementary and Secondary Education in Missouri
by Bryan Forbis and Richard J. Hardy

Religion, morality, and knowledge being necessary to good government and the happiness of mankind, schools and the means for education shall be forever encouraged. —Northwest Ordinance of 1787

Since statehood, education has been considered by many to be the single most important function of Missouri government. Because early settlers considered education an essential cornerstone of democracy, they stressed that education in the new state should be compulsory, free, and devoid of politics. Today, elementary and secondary education is still compulsory, but education at all levels is neither truly free nor devoid of politics. Educational concerns are among the hottest economic and political issues in this state.

The purpose of this chapter is to provide an overview of elementary and secondary education in Missouri. We provide a framework of the politics of education to help in understanding "who gets what, when, and how." This framework consists of four basic components—inputs, government, outputs, and feedback. Each of these interrelated components is discussed with special reference to educational policy making in Missouri. Within this framework, we examine the various people who make and implement Missouri's education policies, paying special attention to the role of citizens, interest groups, state legislators, the governor,

the federal government, and professional administrators.[1]

I. Inputs

Inputs are the demands and supports that go into the political system. Demands could include citizens' requests for school prayers, teachers' ultimatums for increased salaries, or a lawsuit over discrimination in school athletics. Supports might include a political culture that places a high value on education, votes for local school board members, or cigarette taxes earmarked for education. Although it is impossible to list every input, it is instructive to examine some of the major educational inputs in Missouri.

Citizens

Any discussion of education must start with citizens, the people of Missouri who have the ultimate responsibility for establishing and maintaining public schools. Theoretically, citizens exercise control over

1. For more on constructing political frameworks, see Harold Lasswell and Abraham Kaplan, *Power and Society* (New Haven: Yale University Press, 1950), and David Easton, "An Approach to the Analysis of Political Systems," *World Politics*, April 1957.

public schools by electing government officials (school board members, state legislators, and governors), approving various school referenda (taxing and spending policies), and participating in local school activities.

In practice, however, citizens do not always participate to the fullest extent possible: some are apathetic, others lack the time, and some simply opt to withdraw from the system—home schoolers, for example. Many Missourians do not even vote in school board elections or on school bond referenda. Typically, less than 25 percent of the eligible electorate turns out for school board elections, and perhaps even fewer voters know the names of the candidates or the issues involved. As Walter Lippmann wrote, voters have "been saddled with an impossible task. [They] cannot find time to do what is expected of [them] in the theory of democracy."[2]

A second reason suggested for decreased citizen participation is a sense of separation from the community school. This phenomenon first started with school consolidation. Under the auspices of the state's School District Reorganization Act of 1947, many of Missouri's school districts merged into larger administrative units. In 1942 there were 8,632 school districts in Missouri; by 1993 there were only 538. In general, school district consolidation was supported by those concerned with increased educational expenses, declining rural enrollments, and district inequities. Opponents, however, felt that consolidation destroyed the concept of neighborhood schools—they believed that children should attend schools near their homes under the control of their parents.

The sense of separation generated through consolidation in the 1960s and 1970s was continued by the ultimate outcomes of desegregation lawsuits in the 1980s. Parents who had moved to a certain neighborhood so that their children could attend the local schools now saw their children bused, by court order, across town to reconstituted magnet schools.

A third reason some feel that citizen control over education has been undermined is that education has become increasingly specialized and complex. Citizens, and even popularly elected school board members, are often unable to cope with the myriad problems facing education today, such as textbook selection, special-education requirements, contract negotiations, computer technology, and complicated funding formulas. Thus, citizens and school board members have, out of necessity, deferred to the "professionals"—superintendents, other administrators, and teachers—who control day-to-day operations of the public schools.

Citizen empowerment issues have taken center stage. Nearly every education reform proposal offered in the past five years has included some sort of school choice—or voucher—program. School choice is based on a simple theme: taking power to direct children away from the professionals and giving parents the freedom to send their children elsewhere. According to a Carnegie Foundation for the Advancement of Teaching study, "The decade-long struggle to reform education seems suddenly to hang on a single word: choice."[3] Proponents argue that choice would address drop-out rates, motivate both parents and students, rescue poor children trapped in inferior institutions, and reestablish a sense of belonging. Critics maintain that choice

2. Walter Lippmann, *The Phantom Public* (New York: Harcourt, Brace, 1925).

3. Kathleen Sylvester, "School Choice and Reality," *Governing* (June 1993): 37.

takes the best students away from public schools, increases transportation costs, weakens school systems, and would perhaps allow the expenditure of tax dollars on private or parochial schools.

Taking empowerment to its furthest extent, some parents are now choosing to "home school" their children. In the Kansas City area, for example, it is estimated that eight hundred to one thousand families educate their children at home. Most cite religious reasons for doing so. Home schooling often is undertaken at personal sacrifice— working two jobs, working no job, or additional expense for books and materials.

Resources

A quality educational system is expensive. A great deal of money is required to pay 53,000 teachers, librarians, and administrators; reimburse 41,800 support staff; provide 11,700 school buses; purchase books; serve 105.2 million meals; maintain buildings; and operate programs for 840,000 students (these figures are from the 1991–1992 school year). In Missouri, that money comes from three major sources—federal, state, and local revenues.

Federal Revenues. Although the federal government arguably is increasing its influence over state educational policies, it is decreasing its overall share of educational funding in Missouri. In 1970 federal revenues equaled about 8 percent of the total revenues for education in the state; in 1992–1993 they had dropped to 5 percent. That 5 percent still equaled some $178 million. (See Figure 15–1.)

In general, federal monies are collected through income taxes and redistributed to the states through various grants-in-aid. Once received by Missouri and defined as state dollars, these funds are distributed to local school districts through a web of complex formulas that weigh enrollment, need, poverty, and other factors.

State Revenues. The state government assumes significant responsibility for financing public schools. Revenues provided by the state, including aid for desegregation and Proposition C (an additional one-cent sales tax to decrease property tax and increase education funding), equaled 55.6 percent of elementary and secondary education funding in the 1992–1993 school year. This represents an increase of 8 percentage points in the state's relative contribution over a ten-year period.

Major sources of state educational funding include general revenues, sales taxes, the cigarette tax, the free textbook fund, and lottery earnings. The funds generated are collected and distributed as follows:

(1) The Missouri Constitution mandates that at least 25 percent of general revenues be earmarked for public schools. Historically, the legislature has allocated more than this target amount. The General Revenue Fund is an amalgam of many sources, but primarily derives from sales and income taxes. By far the largest single program funded through general revenue is the foundation program, which is the primary conduit for state aid to education. In 1993, this program underwent major revision— and an expansion—with the Outstanding Schools Act. For the 1996 fiscal year, the governor recommended appropriation of $1.63 billion for the public schools through the foundation formula.

In the 1980s a major debit to the General Revenue Fund became state aid for court-ordered desegregation. These payments come "off the top" each year at budget time, and represent 6 percent of the total education pie. Some $2.5 billion was spent on desegregation expenses between 1986 and 1995. In the 1994–1995 school year, $359 million—or 6.7 percent of the state's

**Figure 15-1. Sources of Funds for Missouri Elementary
and Secondary Education, 1992–1993**

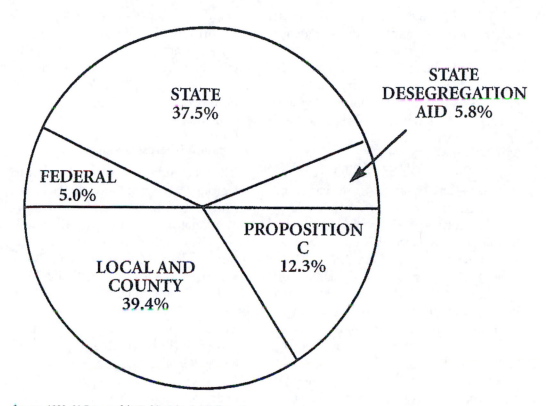

Source: *1992–93 Report of the Public Schools of Missouri*

general revenue budget—went to support the St. Louis and Kansas City desegregation plans.

(2) The State Trust Fund is a dedicated funding source for education. All sources of cash outside the General Revenue Fund are deposited to the account. The State Trust Fund is supplied by three distinct sources.

In 1982, Missouri voters approved Proposition C. Fifty percent of Proposition C revenues are used to reduce, or "roll back," local property taxes. The rest are used for teacher salaries and incidentals like school operating costs. The initial estimates were that Proposition C would generate about $306 million yearly for education; in the 1993–1994 school year, Proposition C generated $450 million for Missouri schools.[4]

All revenue realized from the state cigarette tax is also set aside for education. In 1982 and again in 1993, the General Assembly increased this tax so that it is now 17 cents per pack. In total, the tax brings in more than $100 million per year, part of which is distributed under the foundation program and part of which is distributed on a per-pupil basis.

Last, the free textbook fund comes from a tax that Missouri places on all out-of-state

---

4. As of 1993, state law still requires a property tax rollback, but local districts can now ask voters to forego the rollback benefits to effectively raise the local levy.

insurance companies doing business in the state. This fund provides about $61 million per year.

(3) In 1992, the Missouri General Assembly sponsored a constitutional amendment earmarking the state's lottery earnings for education. This action came in response to public concern that the lottery had been "advertised" by some advocates during the 1984 campaign for its approval as a way to fund educational programs. The amendment approved by the voters in August 1992 mandated that all gambling revenues—lottery, bingo, horse racing, and riverboat gambling—be spent on education. The lottery produces about $100 million per year, and bingo produces about $7 million per year for the state. When riverboat gambling is fully operational, receipts are expected to be about $80 million per year, as estimated in the governor's budget.

Local Revenues. Local educational revenues are drawn from two major sources: county and school district revenues. County revenues include railroad and utility taxes, interest on township permanent funds, fines, forfeitures, and county interests. School district revenues are drawn primarily from the local property tax.

In 1993, the Missouri legislature required that a minimum operating tax levy of $2.75 must be set if a school district is to receive additional aid under the revised foundation program.[5] Most districts have established levies higher than the minimum. Taxes are levied on the basis of 19 percent of the assessed value for residential property, 12 percent for agricultural property, and 32 percent for commercial property. As a result, a home valued at $100,000 would be taxed at the 19 percent rate. Multiplying $19,000 by the minimum levy of $2.75 would generate a property tax bill of $522.50.

The local property tax was, for many years, the principal source of support for Missouri's public schools. Over the years, especially since 1970, the property tax has diminished as a source of local school revenue. In general, reliance on this tax has diminished as criticism of property taxes has increased.[6]

Education Interest Groups

The demands and supports of interest groups are important inputs to government. In Missouri, dozens of formal educational interest groups seek to influence policy makers, including such diverse groups as the Missouri School Boards Association, the National Catholic Education Association, the Missouri Association of School Administrators, the American Association of University Women, the St. Louis School Board, the Home School Legal Defense Association, and Parent-Teacher Associations. Joining these are a variety of ad hoc groups that can spring up around a particular issue or cause, like Missourians for Quality Education and Missourians Against Proposition B, which took opposite sides on the 1991 education tax proposal.

Over the years, the most powerful—or at least the most organized and vocal—educational interest groups have been the teachers' associations and unions. Since the mid-1980s, however, the emergence of organizations representing "management"—school boards and school administrators—have given the traditional groups a run for their money. Regardless of their political base, these groups greatly complicate the diverse world of educational policy making in Missouri.

5. In essence, the Missouri legislature presented local school districts with only two options: raise the levy, or lose certification and state support.

6. In 1994 Michigan voters endorsed a proposal that moved educational funding to a sales and income tax base, ending all reliance on property taxes.

Teacher Associations. Most of Missouri's teachers belong to a teachers' union or association. There are three major teachers' organizations in Missouri: the Missouri State Teachers Association (MSTA); the Missouri National Education Association (MNEA); and the Missouri Federation of Teachers and School-Related Personnel (MFT). Many reasons have been offered for the growth of these unions. Some suggest it is tied to the significant influx of teachers from working-class backgrounds. Others suggest that unionization efforts rest with teachers who were trained during the political, social, and economic upheaval of the 1960s and 1970s. Still others think that working conditions are a factor: even casual observers agree that the job is getting tougher, particularly because of the danger of violence in the schools.[7]

But the primary impetus behind the activism of Missouri teachers, most would agree, has been economic. Missouri's teachers consistently lag behind the national average in salaries. The national average in 1993–1994 was $35,958; Missouri's average reimbursement of $30,311 ranked thirty-sixth.

The Missouri State Teachers Association is the oldest and most moderate teachers' organization in the state. Traditionally, the MSTA has had an outstate, or rural, emphasis, working through local school boards to accomplish its goals. Besides its grassroots efforts, the main tool of the MSTA is its legislative lobby. However, the MSTA does not formally endorse or fund candidates, choosing to let local MSTA leaders work with candidates at home. As the state's largest teachers' association, with

more than thirty-two thousand members (including retired teachers, administrators, and students), the MSTA has taken great care to avoid actions that might cause a split between its teachers and the administrators who are also members. As one early study put it, the MSTA practices "tactics of moderation on behalf of limited objectives."[8]

In response to the other teachers' organizations, however, the MSTA has become more activist. In 1982, for example, the MSTA was able to generate sixty thousand dollars for Proposition C, the successful passage of which is generally considered the organization's greatest accomplishment. It also raised about twenty thousand dollars for Proposition B ten years later, but in that campaign most funds were raised through a special coalition.

Despite its increased activism, MSTA does not support strikes or binding arbitration, believing that teachers are unique public employees and should not slow the wheels of education to accomplish their goals. "It takes two types of people to pass a bill in the legislature, liberal and conservative. We can get to the conservative ones," says Kent King, MSTA's executive director.[9] To reach the rest of the legislature, one should look to the MSTA's closest competitor, the MNEA.

The Missouri National Education Association was formed in 1973. While the NEA is the largest union in the United States and a prominent teachers' organization, claiming 2.1 million of the nation's 3 million teachers, the state chapter is the second largest teachers' organization in Missouri, with twenty-five thousand members. The MNEA hastens to point out, however, that

7. In 1990 the city of St. Louis began using metal detectors in eight high schools to supplement the security guards already hired to monitor for weapons and gang activity. See "St. Louis Schools Armed with Metal Detectors Now," *Kansas City Star*, May 17, 1990.

8. Nicholas Masters, Robert Salisbury, and Thomas Eliot, *State Politics and the Public Schools: An Exploratory Analysis* (New York: Alfred A. Knopf, 1965), 26.

9. "12,000 Teachers to Tackle Politics," *St. Louis Post-Dispatch*, November 1, 1989.

the bulk of its membership is teachers, and that it probably has more active teacher members than MSTA. The MNEA is most powerful in the suburban areas of St. Louis, St. Charles, Jackson, and Clay counties; it also has made inroads in southwest Missouri.

The MNEA has a full-time lobbyist (as does MSTA) who worked hard on Proposition B and the Outstanding Schools Act. The MNEA generally regards the MSTA as a "company union," because its membership includes school administrators. In contrast to the MSTA, the MNEA supports binding arbitration over the right to strike, and publicly endorses and funds candidates.

In the 1992 elections, the MNEA's political action committee distributed nearly $122,000 in "Education Defense Funds" to statewide legislative candidates. In all, the MNEA endorsed 127 different house and senate hopefuls, but targeted its financial help to those more in need. All monies raised for political contributions came from voluntary donations; member dues were not used.

The Missouri Federation of Teachers is the most "militant" teachers' organization in the state. An affiliate of the AFL-CIO formed nationally in 1916, the MFT is a union of teachers and educational employees. Currently the MFT has about five thousand members, half of whom are located in Kansas City and St. Louis.

Like the MNEA, the MFT endorses and supports statewide candidates. Because the MFT is a smaller association, however, its financial impact is limited. It does not have a full-time presence in the state capitol. In addition, its local political activity is limited to endorsing candidates who are screened by local labor councils, and any work on their behalf is done by local volunteers. In contrast to both the MNEA and the MSTA, the MFT favors collective bargaining and the right to strike.

Teacher strikes were a tool used extensively by the MFT in the 1970s and early 1980s, but they have been of little impact in the last decade. Kansas City saw strikes of forty-two days in 1974 and fifty-four days in 1977; St. Louis had strikes of twenty-eight days in 1973 and fifty-six days in 1979. The last strike of note was in September 1983, when twenty-seven hundred St. Louis teachers struck after the St. Louis Board of Education refused a demand for a 17.5 percent pay raise and a reduction of class sizes. Because Missouri law prohibits strikes by public employees, a U.S. district judge ordered them back to work. When they refused, the school board began hiring replacements. After four days and about sixty new hires, the strike ended.

An MFT spokesperson attributes the decline of strikes to several factors. First, local school boards have realized the advantages of working with teachers to accomplish mutual goals collectively. Second, desegregation dollars flowing into Kansas City and St. Louis have improved the working conditions markedly. Third, the willingness of policy makers to support Propositions B and C demonstrates their interest in teachers.

Management Associations. In the late 1980s, management associations emerged to rival the influence and political power of teacher unions. The diverse membership of the teacher groups had sometimes limited their effectiveness. As a result, during the past ten years the Missouri School Boards Association (MSBA), the Missouri Association of School Administrators, the Missouri Association of Elementary School Principals, and the Secondary School Principals Association rapidly grew in power and prestige. Their local membership is well focused, organized, and trained. The administrators and elementary principals fund political action committees. The Missouri School Boards Association has a lobbyist and hosts local training sessions for its members. Some believe that a strong school boards organization can help prevent co-optation by the education professionals, and even counter their influence.

II. Government

Within the framework we have been using, the primary function of government is to convert inputs (demands and supports) into outputs (policies, laws, and regulations). In Missouri, there are numerous federal, state, and local governmental groups and individuals who convert or "authoritatively allocate" educational "values" (for example, money, titles, and certification).

Federal Government

Although education has been traditionally viewed as the responsibility of state and local governments, the role of the federal government is still significant. In 1953 Congress established the Department of Health, Education, and Welfare (HEW), in part to help administer federal educational grants-in-aid. The role of the federal government increased dramatically during the mid–1960s because many—including Lyndon Johnson, perhaps the greatest education president—believed that education was the key to our "great society." Federal aid doubled as a proportion of the nation's total education budget, and numerous categorical grants-in-aid were established to help centralize educational policy making.

In 1980 President Jimmy Carter and Congress reorganized HEW and created the new cabinet-level Department of Education, consolidating approximately 152 education-related programs to further centralize educational policy making. Seeking to reverse direction in the 1980s, the Reagan administration was relatively successful in reducing federal funding for educational programs and in consolidating categorical grants into block grants to give the states more discretion. In the 1990s, however, Congress reasserted itself and began to link funding to state compliance with federal program initiatives. The Reagan administration was unsuccessful in its effort to eliminate the department, which in fiscal year 1995 had a $31.2 billion annual budget and 4,700 employees.

Setting the National Agenda. Until recently, the role of the federal government toward education has been limited mainly to ensuring civil rights, disbursing grants, and administering funds for disadvantaged youth.[10] In 1983 the White House released the now famous report "A Nation at Risk," which proclaimed that "a rising tide of mediocrity that threatens our very future as a nation and as a people" was undermining the nation's educational foundation. In response the states instituted various reforms, but a later review reflected the general feeling that those reforms constituted only a "modest success."[11] In 1989 the federal government took a bold step toward setting the national education agenda; President George Bush convened the nation's governors in a historic meeting. A set of targets for schools was developed from this "Education Summit." Adopted by Congress in 1994, the six national education goals, to be realized by the year 2000, were: all children will start school ready to learn; the high school graduation rate will increase to

10. Sandra Waddock, "The Spider's Web: Influences on School Performance," *Business Horizons* 36:5, 41–42.

11. The study by the Center for Policy Research in Education was reported in "Education: Nation's Schools Still at Risk," *Jefferson City News Tribune*, April 25, 1993.

at least 90 percent; students will leave grades four, eight, and twelve having competency in English, math, science, history, and geography; U.S. students will be first in the world in science and mathematics; every adult will have the skills to compete in the global economy; and every school in America will be free of drugs and violence. Added were two new goals encouraging parents' involvement in education and professional development for teachers. The bill included $647 million for school reform, and passed only after a lengthy filibuster intended to force school prayer.

State Government

The primary responsibility for public education in the United States rests with the individual states. In Missouri, the General Assembly, the governor, and the Department of Elementary and Secondary Education are all of importance in public education decisions.

General Assembly. Aside from the voters, the most important educational decision makers in Missouri are the 197 state legislators. Under Article IX of the Missouri Constitution of 1945, the General Assembly has the authority to establish and maintain public schools (Section 1a); direct the appointment of state board members (Section 2a); and allocate educational funding throughout the state (Section 3).

Today many legislators have educational backgrounds, either as teachers, administrators, or school board members. Teachers are among the fastest-growing segments of American legislatures, in part because their verbal and persuasive skills can translate well to politics. It also can be argued that they do not have businesses to run, and the legislative salary is about the same as a teacher's salary.[12] In 1993, for example,

three of every ten Missouri house members had such backgrounds.

Two important education committees in the General Assembly are the Senate Education Committee and the House Elementary and Secondary Education Committee. All education bills other than funding measures go before these committees. The issues heard there include such diverse topics as teacher qualifications, length of the school year, desegregation, and collective bargaining.

Funds for education are authorized by the Senate Appropriations Committee and the House Appropriations–Education and Public Safety Committee. These two committees have helped total state and federal education expenditures to increase by more than 120 percent between 1980 and 1992. This role, however, was more or less predetermined for the committees. First, many appropriations are formula driven or derive from earmarked funds, leaving the legislators limited discretion as to their budget decisions. Second, governors have made their fiscal support to schools very public and thus have left the committees little choice but to adopt their executive budgets.

The Governor. Even though the General Assembly has overall responsibility for establishing and funding public education in Missouri, it is the governor and his administration who enforce the policies. Hence, the governor is the single most powerful state decision maker concerning education. For many years the governor's role in educational policy making was essentially confined to appointing educational board members and submitting executive budgets. As educational demands accelerated in the 1960s and 1970s, governors began to assume an increasingly visible role in educational policy making. Governors from Teasdale and Bond to Ashcroft and Carnahan each illustrate this increased activism in education.

12. Alan Ehrenhalt, *The United States of Ambition: Politicians, Power, and the Pursuit of Office* (New York: Times Books, 1992), 20.

A notable success for Governor Bond was the Parents as Teachers (PAT) program. Funded by the General Assembly as Bond was leaving office in 1985, PAT is a parent-educator program that provides support for families with children from birth to age five. Through periodic home visits by a trained facilitator, it is designed to help parents serve as early teachers for their children, and to show them how to screen for "at risk" children. PAT is required in all Missouri school districts, and served more than 124,000 families in 1993–1994. While PAT has come under occasional attack from the religious right as governmental intrusion, studies of the program have indicated favorable results. U.S. Senator Bond successfully expanded PAT to a national scale in 1994.

Ashcroft served on the Education Commission of the States and generated an annual report on Missouri's progress toward the national education goals he helped write in 1989. Ashcroft lobbied hard for school choice, longer school years, Parents as Teachers, and early intervention programs. In his first year as governor the General Assembly passed the Excellence in Education Act.

Carnahan's leadership moved the Outstanding Schools Act through the General Assembly in 1993, restructuring the foundation formula and increasing state funding for the foundation program by 20 percent.

Executive Branch. The state educational bureaucracy oversees local school operations and ensures compliance with state directives. The Omnibus Reorganization Act of 1974 vests this responsibility in the Department of Elementary and Secondary Education (DESE). The department is guided by the State Board of Education, which consists of eight lay members appointed by the governor with the advice and consent of the senate. The emphasis on "lay members"

reflects the traditional democratic theme of placing control in the hands of the "people." For continuity, board members serve eight-year, staggered terms. To ensure political and geographical fairness, members must be evenly split between the two major parties, and no more than one member can be appointed from a congressional district.

The Board has general policy-making authority, but local school districts are designed to be independent. As a result, the Board's role is one of leadership and assistance. The Board's duties include: (1) appointing the Commissioner of Education and setting departmental policies; (2) establishing regulations relating to schools; (3) apportioning federal school funds; (4) accrediting local schools; (5) testing and certifying teachers; (6) collecting and disseminating educational information; and (7) defining academic performance standards. The Board has no authority over private, parochial, or home schools.

Because the board is composed of educational "amateurs," some observers believe it possesses neither the time nor the technical expertise to run today's schools. For all of these functions, the board turns to the appointed commissioner of education and the Department of Elementary and Secondary Education. Prior to 1945, the state superintendent had been popularly elected. Today, the commissioner of education is appointed by the board. To date, Missouri has had only three commissioners: Hubert Wheeler, who served from 1947 to 1970; Arthur Mallory, who followed Wheeler and resigned in 1987; and the current commissioner, Robert Bartman.

The powers of the commissioner are far-reaching. First, he heads a state department of twenty-one hundred personnel that supervises nearly every aspect of elementary and secondary education in the state. Second, the commissioner marshals his resources to lobby the state legislature, governor, and media on behalf of his department. Finally, the commissioner and his department advise on the distribution of state revenues and federal grant monies to local school districts. Thus, the commissioner is perhaps the most powerful nonelected educational policy maker in the state. In addition, the 1993 Outstanding Schools Act gave DESE significant new authority for setting academic performance standards, developing curriculum for local school districts, and creating a statewide assessment system.

Local Government

Missouri's elementary and secondary schools are governed at the local level by popularly elected school boards that represent the various school districts. In most small school districts, the school board can be the community's largest employer and thus in charge of the largest local business.

Although this chapter has discussed state (and federal) officials who establish the legal parameters under which schools must operate, school boards still serve important grassroots policy-making functions. Local school boards are, for example, empowered to hire and fire school personnel, levy taxes, borrow money, let contracts, maintain buildings, establish curricula, operate kindergartens, purchase textbooks, choose between middle schools and junior high schools, and decide disciplinary actions. In comparison to other states, Missouri allows local school officials a relatively high degree of autonomy.[13]

Missouri currently has 538 school districts: 87 elementary-only districts and 451 high school districts. Each represents a geographic area designated for the purpose

13. Frederick M. Wirt, "State Policy, Culture and State Decentralization," in *The Politics of Education,* edited by Jay D. Scribner (Chicago: University of Chicago Press, 1977), 164–87.

of providing free public education for all persons living therein "not to exceed 21 years." Enrollment varies considerably. For the 1992–1993 school year, 170 (about 31 percent) of Missouri's school districts enrolled 1,000 or more students, while 47 districts (9 percent) had fewer than 100.

Each school board has seven members, and these members serve three-year terms. Two exceptions are the Kansas City School District, which elects nine members, and the St. Louis City District, which elects twelve members for six-year terms. School board members must be at least twenty-four years old, citizens, and resident taxpayers of their districts for at least one year preceding their election (three years in St. Louis).

III. Outputs

Outputs refer to policies or decisions reached by government. Educational outputs include such items as state laws requiring school attendance, regulations concerning school buses, court rulings on racial segregation, or local tax levies. For simplicity, this chapter concentrates on three significant educational outputs: major federal legislation, recent court decisions, and the distribution of state educational aid.

Federal Legislation

The federal government, having only a secondary role and little money to offer, tries to use what clout it can to move education in particular directions. Federal government programs include: (1) the Smith Hughes Act of 1917, to foster vocational training; (2) the national school lunch and milk programs to help feed students, especially those with low incomes; (3) the National Defense Education Act of 1958, enacted soon after the Soviet Union launched the first space satellite, to improve instruction in foreign languages, mathematics, and science; (4) the Elementary and Secondary Education Act (ESEA) of 1965, the nation's largest federal aid to education program, to help low-income and educationally deprived students; (5) the Carl Perkins Vocational Educational Act of 1984, to provide academic and vocational training for disadvantaged and disabled students; and (6) the Omnibus Trade and Competitiveness Act of 1988, which links economic and academic success and hopes to improve the country's relative trade posture by improving math and science training, foreign languages, technology transfer programs, and adult vocational training.

The federal government also has used education policy to effect social change. Most notable was the prohibition of discrimination. The Civil Rights Act of 1964 authorized the withholding of federal funds from schools that practiced discrimination, and Title IX of the Educational Amendments Act of 1972 prohibits sex discrimination in virtually all phases of education, including admissions, recruitment, financial aid, housing, athletics, and faculty and staff hiring and promotion. Public interest in education has pushed presidents and Congress to take on leadership roles comparable to the roles of their state counterparts.

Judicial Decisions

The federal courts have had profound effects on state and local education policies, especially in the area of civil rights. Article IX of the Missouri Constitution of 1945 originally called for "separate but equal schools for children of African descent." With the landmark case of *Brown v. Board of Education* (1954), the U.S. Supreme Court ruled that de jure (by law) racial desegre-

gation in the nation's public schools was in violation of the "equal protection" guarantee of the Fourteenth Amendment, and ordered that segregation be eliminated in each state—including Missouri—"with all deliberate speed."[14]

The Brown case was just the beginning of federal court activity in the area of civil rights, specifically desegregation. In Missouri, the rulings of federal judges have led to two of the most controversial, and expensive, governmental programs in the state's history. Today, the Kansas City and St. Louis desegregation plans are vying to be the most costly programs per pupil in the forty years since the Brown case. This section looks at both court orders to highlight the similarities and differences between the responses of the two cities, which share the goal of integration but have traveled markedly different paths in their efforts to attain it.

St. Louis's Busing Plan. In 1972, a north St. Louis family filed a federal lawsuit charging that the St. Louis School Board had violated black children's rights by allowing the quality of inner-city schools to deteriorate relative to the predominantly white suburban schools.[15] Soon the National Association for the Advancement of Colored People (NAACP), the U.S. Department of Justice, and the State Board of Education joined in the lawsuit. When the case was finally heard in 1977, Federal District Judge James Meredith ruled against the family. However, three years later a federal court of appeals reversed Meredith's decision and ordered a desegregation plan for St. Louis schools.

In 1981, Judge William Hungate replaced Meredith and gave St. Louis school officials

14. *Brown v. Board of Education*, 347 U.S. 483 (1954).
15. *Liddell et al. v. State of Missouri et al.*, 731 F.2d 1294 (8th Circuit).

the choice either to implement the deseg-regation plan voluntarily or to face federal intervention. The 450-page agreement reached in 1983 created both an "Intra-City" plan and an "Inter-District" plan, the latter settled out of court when suburban districts agreed to participate. Because the judge found the state liable for the segregated condition of the public schools, Missouri was ordered to pay one-half of all costs for implementing the Intra-City plan and making capital improvement, and all expenses related to voluntary Inter-District transfers (busing) and magnet schools.

The plans called for the voluntary exchange of city and county students, expanding libraries, rejuvenating buildings, reducing teacher-student ratios, and recruiting more black faculty and staff. At the core of the agreement was a provision to transport enough students so that twenty-three predominantly white suburban school districts could accept transferred city or county black students until they reached a goal of 25 percent black enrollment. Districts with predominantly white staffs were expected to recruit so that the faculty would be at least 15.8 percent black and administrative staffs at least 13.4 percent black within five years. The operation was to be monitored by a Voluntary Inter-District Coordinating Committee.

Since the arrangements were ordered by the court, all expenses related to St. Louis education—teacher salaries, building improvements, and busing and taxi charges—had to be approved by the judge. The plans also could be amended by the court as appropriate. In 1988, for example, Judge Stephen Limbaugh, who had taken over after Hungate, ordered that the number of spaces in magnet schools be expanded from nine thousand to fourteen thousand.

As of 1994, about 13,500 black students were taking the bus to St. Louis County

schools. The city had twenty-five magnet schools, and about 1,100 white students attended their classes. The average spending on students at magnet schools is 30 percent higher than the spending on students at nonmagnet schools. Approximately $1.3 billion in state funds have helped finance the St. Louis plans since their inception.

Kansas City's Magnets. In 1977 a federal lawsuit accused Missouri, Kansas, and eighteen suburban Kansas City school districts of discriminating against black students. The state of Kansas was dropped from the suit in 1978, and the suburban districts were dismissed six years later. In September 1984, U.S. District Judge Russell Clark found the Kansas City School District and the state of Missouri liable for operating segregated schools.

In 1985, Clark ordered a plan to improve student achievement, including capital improvements, magnet schools, summer school, and smaller classes. A year later, this plan was implemented, with a $500 million price tag for school renovations and construction. By 1992, he expected all the district's middle schools and about half of its elementary schools to be converted to magnets, totaling about fifty-five facilities. Judge Clark has acknowledged, "I got the case because of a segregated district. I did not get it because the quality of education was inferior."[16]

The Kansas City plan differs from its cross-state partner in several ways. In St. Louis, thousands of students are bused to county schools; Kansas City takes voluntary transfers. Only one suburban district had agreed to participate by 1992, and it took just ten students. (Without a viable suburban component, it is argued, the Kansas City plan will be doomed

---

16. Taken from an interview with Judge Clark in the *Kansas City Star*, May 8, 1994.

by demographics—there are not enough white students in the mix.) In Kansas City, the state not only has to pay 75 percent of all program costs and 50 percent of capital improvement costs but also must pick up any portion of the expenses the local district cannot afford to pay. This caveat has cost the state an additional $100 million over its court-ordered share. The most striking difference, however, is in fundamental philosophies: the St. Louis plan mainly sends black students to the suburbs; the Kansas City program tries to attract white students to the city with magnet schools.

Perhaps the best known—and most criticized—of the differences is the funding mechanism ordered by Judge Clark to underwrite the Kansas City plan. In 1987, Judge Clark found that the district had insufficient funds to pay its share of the cost, and he ordered the local tax levy to be nearly doubled. While the Supreme Court had given local judges sweeping powers to begin desegregation in the wake of the original Brown ruling, no one had pushed the limits of judicial authority to that of raising taxes, which was a responsibility constitutionally vested in the legislature or the people. After thousands of district residents had paid property taxes in "protest," an appeal was filed to the Supreme Court. The state argued, "In two-hundred years, no federal court ever assumed the power to mandate a hike in tax levies."[17] Arthur Benson, the school district attorney, argued that the federal courts had broad powers to enforce its rulings, and that the state had no workable plan to live up to its constitutional responsibility.

In 1990, the Supreme Court unanimously decided that Clark had exceeded his powers in ordering a property tax increase on his own, but they upheld—by a five-to-four decision—his ability to override any impediments that would restrict the school board from imposing the taxes. Writing for the majority, Justice White said that "a local government may be ordered to levy taxes where there is reason based in the Constitution." For the dissent, Justice Kennedy wrote that "taxation imposed by the unelected, life-tenured federal judiciary disregards fundamental precepts for the democratic control of public institutions."[18] The protested property taxes were refunded, but the school board immediately imposed the same property tax as the judge had previously ordered.

After all of the construction, busing, and more than $2 billion in costs, sweeping civil rights programs like the Missouri plans are under renewed attack. A 1993 Harvard study found that American schools are more racially segregated than at any time in the nation's history.[19] Some Black parents are decrying the loss of neighborhood schools for magnets that spend more time and money trying to recruit white students than trying to teach black students. Test scores in the magnet schools have not improved markedly, and the relative percentage of black students has remained unchanged in city schools. Neighborhood schools, it is believed, could save $43 million annually in Kansas City by cutting transportation and magnet expenses.

In 1985, for example, 73.6 percent of the students in the Kansas City school district were minorities; in 1992 minority students constituted 74.8 percent of the district's students. (Proponents of desegregation efforts, however, believe that given the con-

17. "Limits to a Judicial Remedy?" *Kansas City Star,* October 15, 1989.

18. "Excerpts from Court's Majority Ruling," *Kansas City Star,* April 19, 1990.

19. "Busing Issue Comes Down to Money," *St. Louis Post-Dispatch,* September 28, 1993.

tinuation of urban white flight, the percentage of black students in city schools would be even higher had it not been for the court's efforts, and that test scores of students in the lower grades are showing some improvement.) Everyone is tiring of the financial burden, and rural schools want more of their tax dollars to stay at home. Fiscal Year 1995 general revenue expenditures for desegregation total more than all the spending on the prison system, the courts, and the Highway Patrol combined.

Recent events may signal the changing sentiments of the public and the civil rights community. Mayor Freeman Bosley, St. Louis's first black mayor, called for an end to the busing program within weeks of his fall 1993 election. He wants more emphasis on educational equity and a sense of local belonging. One ally, State Representative Bill Clay Jr., offered that the desegregation plan "had good intentions, but it was a social experiment that failed."[20] NAACP leaders, however, vowed to continue the program. Ten months later, Judge Gunn required the St. Louis School Board to improve student performance—the first such action in the eleven-year history of the plan. And in Kansas City, all four incumbent school board members were voted out of office in the April 1994 elections. Analysts maintain the voters were expressing their displeasure with the local desegregation efforts.

In 1995 the courts indicated some willingness to relax their stance. In Kansas City, Judge Clark approved a six-month moratorium on court action to allow negotiations to end the lawsuit. The judge also reduced the state's payment for the upcoming school year by $22.5 million. In St. Louis,

20. "The Year In Review," *Report of the Public Schools,* State Board of Education, 1986.

Judge Gunn took under consideration proposals for ending court supervision.

State Education Output

The best index of state educational outputs is state funding for elementary and secondary education. State aid to education involves redistributive policies through which government intends to "equalize" educational expenditures to ensure all children equal opportunity for a quality education. As will be seen, the way a government determines "equality" and redistributes funding is not only highly complex but also emotionally charged and extremely political.

This chapter has already examined the source of state funds and how those funds are allocated. What follows is a look at three major state reform programs, and how each changed education in Missouri.

Excellence in Education Act. Although it is not expressly a funding proposal, the Excellence in Education Act passed in 1985 marked the start of Missouri's education revolution. Key components of the Excellence in Education Act included:

1. A four-year program of increasing minimum teacher salaries to eighteen thousand dollars, giving a raise to some three thousand individuals across the state. This segment was designed to help small districts be more competitive, but later studies by the Department of Elementary and Secondary Education found the minimum salary did not help small districts retain teachers.

2. In what is probably the most criticized aspect of the act, teachers, counselors, and librarians were provided a "career ladder." Salary supplements of up to five thousand dollars were made available to those who had five years of tenure in public schools, met certain performance criteria, and car-

ried out specific duties designed by the district. In the 1994–1995 school year, 270 districts and more than twelve thousand teachers participated in this program.

3. New tests were mandated, designed to assess children in mathematics, science, reading, and social studies. Known as the Missouri Mastery and Achievement Tests (MMAT), they existed for each class level from grade two to grade ten, and were given in at least two nonconsecutive elementary and two nonconsecutive secondary grades each year. The MMAT tests will be phased out during the 1996–1997 school year and a performance measure or process-type test, required by the Outstanding Schools Act of 1993, will be used in their place.

4. The Incentives for School Excellence Program offered grants to teachers, schools, or school districts to encourage innovative programs that would meet specific needs at the local level. Award amounts ranged up to five thousand dollars for an individual teacher and up to fifty thousand dollars for a district; most required a local funding match of between 10 and 30 percent. Individual grants have proved the most popular, rising in number each year. The other categories have shown a decline.

Economic Survival Act of 1991: Proposition B. On the last day of the 1991 legislative session, senate bill 353, calling a state vote on a tax increase for education, was approved. Proposition B, as the issue came to be known, was the result of intense negotiations between Republican Governor Ashcroft and the Democratic legislative leaders, Senate President Pro Tem James Mathewson and House Speaker Bob Griffin. This unique partnership continued through the summer and fall, as Proposition B headed to a November vote of the people.

In the end, voters rejected Proposition B by a two-to-one margin. Uncertainty about the economy; doubts about the measure itself, especially the elementary education component; and growing cynicism about politics in general doomed the project.

Outstanding Schools Act of 1993, and the Foundation Formula. Before examining the Outstanding Schools Act of 1993,[21] a look at the history of the foundation program is in order. Missouri first appropriated money for education on a "flat grant" basis. That is, the state allocated an equal sum for each pupil. Flat-grant allocations did not alleviate the inequalities among school districts because funds were allocated regardless of a district's relative wealth. In addition, flat grants provided no extra help to students with extra needs, such as poor children or disabled children.

The state eventually abandoned flat grants in favor of the foundation program. The foundation fund was designed to consider both local and state revenues and set an amount sufficient for a foundation for education throughout the state.

The foundation formula had two basic components. First the minimum guarantee provided a set amount per eligible pupil based on the projected costs of running the school program. Second, a "guaranteed tax base add-on" was created to provide equal yield for equal effort, taking into account the level of local wealth.

Discussion of the formula dominated the 1980s, and it could not escape the political realities of the legislative process. It became a complex and contradictory formula; most troubling, a formula that was designed to equalize education funding was creating wide disparities between districts. Some districts were providing as much as $9,800 per pupil, while other districts were providing as little as $2,400. Several unsuc-

---

21. For a full discussion of Proposition B and the Outstanding Schools Act, see chapter 17.

cessful attempts at reform were tried in the early 1990s, including Proposition B. Both the legislature and the state board of education had considered changing the formula, but the political constraints of the haves (generally urban districts) versus the have-nots, and the lack of available funds scuttled every proposal.

In 1990 two school districts filed suit in Cole County Circuit Court. They claimed that the formula's reliance on prior year enrollment figures penalized school districts that gained students and helped those districts that lost students. The districts sought to abolish this constraint clause. While the debate began as a "rural versus urban" issue, it soon expanded to encompass the formula as a whole—and all the formula's detractors saw this lawsuit as the long-awaited vehicle for revision. "There are going to be winners and losers in this," said the Lee's Summit superintendent, whose district filed the suit. "And districts know which they are."[22]

In January 1993 Judge Byron Kinder ruled that Missouri's system for funding public education did not "pass constitutional muster." The system was found to be unconstitutional for several reasons: every child has the right to equal opportunity for a good education, and the formula did not afford that chance; the state legislature is responsible for seeing that this opportunity is provided; money makes a difference in the quality of education; and the existing funding system did not give schools enough money to do the job.

The legislature responded by passing, on the last day of the 1993 session, the Outstanding Schools Act. Included in the final 105-page package were:

• A $310 million "Outstanding Schools Trust Fund," financed by raising per-

sonal income tax through capping state-allowed federal tax deductions, and increasing the corporate income tax from 5 percent to 6.25 percent

• Permanent state budget cuts of $50 million, and an anticipated $50 million in riverboat gambling and lower desegregation costs

• Requirements for a school district to adopt a minimum levy of $2.75 per $100 assessed valuation to keep state aid

• Reduction in class sizes for kindergarten through third grade

• Creation of statewide academic achievement standards and a new test to measure them

• More training for teachers

• Full funding of the Parents as Teachers program

• Improvement of vocational training

• Training for local school board members and establishment of a Commission on Performance to advise the State Board of Education

• Establishment of a School Building Revolving Fund for loans for capital improvements

• Plans for an "A+ Schools Program" with grants to develop innovative and challenging school study tracks.

The debate over senate bill 380 will continue. Some educators argue that statewide education standards create a one-size-fits-all mentality. Others say the "outcomes-based" testing system is too subjective, and that it implies that education professionals "know best." There are concerns that the act takes control from the local districts. Last, State Auditor Margaret Kelly maintains the funding enhancements violate Hancock Amendment restrictions (assuming the money from gambling revenues and desegregation savings, called "mystery

---

22. "Challenge on Funding Could Hurt Rural Schools," *Kansas City Star*, June 22, 1990.

money" by Representative Chris Kelly, materializes at all).

IV. Feedback

In this chapter we presented an overview of educational policy making in Missouri. It should be readily apparent that this policy-making process is not static, but dynamic. Rarely, if ever, does government "solve" educational problems or conflicts once and for all. Just as soon as government establishes a policy—a judicial ruling, gubernatorial directive or legislative mandate—there will almost inevitably be some kind of reaction, or "feedback." For example, the loser of a judicial decision may appeal to a higher court, an educational interest group may throw its money and support to the governor's opponent, or parents of schoolchildren might organize a protest against property tax increases. These new demands and supports thus start the political process in motion again. In conclusion, educational policy making in Missouri is constantly changing, very complicated, and highly political.

CHAPTER 16

State Policy Making in Higher Education
by Jeanette B. Welch

> Governance is both a structure and a process. It is a structure legitimatizing power groups and power relationships. It is a process for making basic decisions about purpose, procedure and performance.—John Millett

To the general public, as well as to students, faculty, and alumni, it is almost unbelievable that colleges and universities are engaged in state politics. There is something about the image of the ivy covered tower that seems to contradict the very idea. Yet institutions of higher education, public and private, do not have any other option. Legislators, governors, and administrators routinely make policies that may enhance the institutions or threaten their very existence.

To protect and promote their interests, institutions of higher education must be politically active. However, the type of politics in which they engage—administrative politics at the very highest level of government—is neither visible to the general public nor very well understood by those outside the inner circle.

This chapter explains how public policy in higher education is made in Missouri. Those engaged in state policy making in higher education are divided into two major groups.[1] The core, consisting of the Coordinating Board for Higher Education, its staff, and the institutions of public higher education, are engaged in academically related policy making. On the periphery of the policy community, the governor and the General Assembly set broad policy in higher education and determine the share of the state's resources that will be allocated.

This chapter also describes the roles and political resources of the major participants, and provides case studies of the three major functions of the coordinating board to explain how decisions are made within the policy-making core. A case study of Governor John Ashcroft's reforms, including Proposition B, is included to show the influence of the governor and the General Assembly on higher education policy. Finally, the chapter concludes with an evaluation of coordination as a form of policy making.

I. The Policy Core and Its Political Resources

The Missouri state system of higher education (Table 16-1) includes the University of Missouri with campuses in Columbia,

---

1. This grouping is based on a model created by David M. Welborn and Anthony E. Brown in *Regulatory Policy and Processes: The Public Service Commission in*

Tennessee, Kentucky and Georgia (Knoxville: Bureau of Public Administration, University of Tennessee, 1980).

Rolla, Kansas City, and St. Louis; four regional universities, Central, Northwest, Southeast, and Southwest; one liberal arts university, Northeast; and four state colleges, Harris-Stowe, Lincoln University, Missouri Southern, and Missouri Western. There are twelve community college districts that are jointly supported by the state and citizens of the special junior college districts.

The University of Missouri

The dominant influence in Missouri public higher education is the University of Missouri, with its main campus located in Columbia, a technological campus in Rolla, and urban campuses in St. Louis and Kansas City. Although it has no peer in the public sector, two prestigious, nationally known private institutions in St. Louis, Washington University and St. Louis University, enjoy considerable status and are rivals for philanthropic gifts and research grants.

Among the University of Missouri's many political assets, the nationally recognized extension division is a major source of power and influence. The constitutional status of the university is another political resource. Many legislators still perceive the university as being a constitutional entity, although this status has been heavily qualified by court decisions, attorney general opinions, and legislative actions. Still another source of political power is a vast alumni association whose membership includes many of the state's most prominent citizens, as well as state legislators and other elected officials.

The university's ability to establish its priorities and protect them from outside political influence, however, is undermined by competition between campuses and schools within the system. Each branch of the university, and even each school, has its own loyal supporters and alumni, as well as legislators, who are more loyal to it than to an abstract entity known as the University of Missouri. Administrators of the various schools and campuses frequently take advantage of the situation to promote their own interests in the General Assembly.

Regional Universities and Senior Colleges

Four regional universities, one liberal arts college, and four senior colleges make up the middle level of the state's system of higher education. The FTE (full time equivalent) enrollment of these institutions in the fall of 1993 was 53,835, compared with 38,035 enrolled in the University of Missouri system.[2] The greatest political resource of this group is the concern of local communities for their economic and cultural advancement. These institutions serve a number of regional or local constituencies rather than a single statewide constituency, and their alumni are less numerous, less organized as a political force, and less influential than the alumni of the University of Missouri. The presidents of these schools serve as chief lobbyists, frequently enlisting the support of the Chamber of Commerce, local and regional legislators, influential citizens, prominent alumni, and influential members of their governing boards.

Among this group of institutions, which compete for students and state funds, location and visibility are important political assets. The location of an institution in or near a metropolitan area enhances visibility and enrollments as well as powerful business constituencies, and the larger legislative delegation provides more political

2. *Annual Report to the Governor and General Assembly,* 1994 (Jefferson City: CBHE, January 1994), Table 10.1.

Table 16-1. Missouri's Colleges and Universities

Institution	Location	Year Founded	FTE Enrollment*	Number of Degrees, FY 1992**	Highest Degree Offered
Public Colleges and Universities					
1862 Land Grant University					
University of Missouri–Columbia	Columbia	1839	18,408	5,490	Doctorate
University of Missouri–Kansas City	Kansas City	1929	6,560	2,213	Doctorate
University of Missouri–Rolla	Rolla	1870	4,655	1,054	Doctorate
University of Missouri–St. Louis	St. Louis	1963	8,412	2,219	Doctorate
Subtotal, University of Missouri			38,035	10,976	
1890 Land Grant University					
Lincoln University	Jefferson City	1866	2,547	418	Masters
Statewide Liberal Arts					
Northeast Missouri State University	Kirksville	1867	6,003	1,178	Masters
Regional Universities					
Central Missouri State University	Warrensburg	1871	9,177	2,109	Masters
Northwest Missouri State University	Maryville	1905	5,045	1,056	Masters
Southeast Missouri State University	Cape Girardeau	1873	6,673	1,359	Masters
Southwest Missouri State University	Springfield	1905	15,219#	2,870	Masters
Four-Year Colleges					
Harris-Stowe State College	St. Louis	1857	1,026	68	Bachelor
Missouri Southern State College	Joplin	1965	4,210	727	Bachelor
Missouri Western State College	St. Joseph	1915	3,935	574	Bachelor
Subtotal, public universities and colleges, other than Univ of MO			53,835	10,359	
Two-Year Colleges					
Crowder College	Neosho	1964	1,095	619	Associate
East Central College	Union	1968	1,953	357	Associate
Heart of the Ozarks Technical CC	Springfield	1990	1,638	54	Associate
Jefferson College	Hillsboro	1963	2,726	754	Associate
Metropolitan Community Colleges	Kansas City	1915			
Longview Community College			4,781	738	Associate
Maple Woods CC			2,680	432	Associate
Penn Valley CC			2,903	645	Associate
Mineral Area College	Flat River	1922	1,826	448	Associate
Moberly Area Junior College	Moberly	1927	1,267	249	Associate
North Central College	Trenton	1925	712	163	Associate
St. Charles County CC	St. Charles	1986	2,392	204	Associate
St. Louis Community Colleges	St. Louis city and county	1962			
SLCC at Florissant Valley			4,589	833	Associate
SLCC at Forest Park			3,535	610	Associate
SLCC at Meramec			7,153	983	Associate
State Fair Community College	Sedalia	1966	1,597	344	Associate
Three Rivers Community College	Poplar Bluff	1966	1,710	237	Associate
Subtotal, public community colleges			42,557	7,670	
Subtotal, public institutions			134,427	29,005	

Continued

Table 16-1. Missouri's Colleges and Universities (Continued)

Institution	Location	Year Founded	FTE Enrollment*	Number of Degrees, FY 1992**	Highest Degree Offered
Independent Institutions					
Independent Universities					
Saint Louis University	St. Louis	1818	8,653	2,757	Doctorate
Washington University	St. Louis	1853	9,677	3,139	Doctorate
Webster University	St. Louis	1915	4,814	3,216	Doctorate
Subtotal, independent universities			23,144	9,112	
Independent Four-Year Colleges					
Avila College	Kansas City	1916	934	228	Master
Central Methodist University	Fayette	1844	912	169	Bachelor
College of the Ozarks	Point Lookout	1906	1,476	166	Bachelor
Columbia College	Columbia	1851	3,852	1,347	Bachelor
Culver-Stockton College	Canton	1853	1,065	206	Bachelor
Drury College	Springfield	1873	2,247	539	Bachelor
Evangel College	Springfield	1955	1,362##	350	Bachelor
Fontbonne College	St. Louis	1917	1,355	296	Master
Hannibal Lagrange	Hannibal	1858	631	170	Bachelor
Lindenwood	St. Charles	1827	2,730	521	Masters
Maryville	St. Louis	1872	2,279	668	Masters
Missouri Baptist College	St. Louis	1968	990	124	Bachelor
Missouri Valley College	Marshall	1889	1,149	113	Bachelor
Park College	Parkville	1875	2,678##	N/A	Master
Rockhurst College	Kansas City	1910	1,807	534	Master
Southwest Baptist University	Bolivar	1878	2,235	441	Master
Stephens College	Columbia	1833	824	223	Bachelor
Westminster College	Fulton	1853	681	121	Bachelor
William Jewell College	Liberty	1849	1,469	382	Bachelor
William Woods College	Fulton	1890	799	125	Bachelor
Subtotal, independent four-year colleges			31,475	6,723	
Independent Two-Year Colleges					
Cottey College	Nevada	1884	392	123	Associate
Kemper Military School and College	Boonville	1844	211	52	Associate
Wentworth Military Academy	Lexington	1880	187	23	Associate
Subtotal, independent two-year colleges			790	198	
Subtotal, all independent institutions			55,409	16,033	
Total, all Missouri institutions			189,836	45,038	

Sources: Missouri Coordinating Board for Higher Education, Jefferson City. *The World Almanac and Book of Facts, 1994* (Mahwah, NJ: World Almanac, 1993)

Notes:
*Full-time equivalent (FTE) enrollment, Fall 1993
**Numbers of degrees include certificates. In the case of public two-year colleges about one-third of the degrees awarded are certificates.
#Includes 664 FTE enrollment on the West Plains campus.
##Fall 1992 FTE enrollment

clout. An institution located in a rural area with a declining population and a smaller legislative delegation to provide protection is at a major disadvantage. One former nonurban regional university, Northeast, found a solution to these problems by becoming the state's only public liberal arts college. Having received favorable national publicity, it now turns away hundreds of applicants each year.

Having a speaker of the house or a senate president pro tem from its hometown or district can be of great help to a regional university, as can having a local official who is a member of the House Budget Committee. However, the most highly prized resource is a patron on the Senate Appropriations Committee. This committee is more influential than the house committee, and it has very little turnover.[3] The patron-client relationship traditionally has played an important role in the legislative politics of higher education in Missouri. It is not based on an exchange of favors; rather, a legislator's ties to an institution derive from his regionalism and parochialism and the prestige and income flowing from the location of a college in his or her district. The patrons are strong supporters of higher education and frequently unite behind the board's operating budget recommendation, which is invariably higher than that of the governor. When state funds are available, this has resulted in a higher level of state support for the institutions.

Although they are highly competitive, the regional universities and senior colleges have formed a loose alliance, and with the assistance of their patrons they have managed to maintain a rough balance of power with the University of Missouri. The committee norm of "treating 'em all alike"

works to the advantage of the less powerful. The institutions have also escaped domination by the state university because, as one of their presidents commented, the university has had its hands too full to give them much trouble.

Independent Colleges and Universities

There are some twenty-six widely diverse independent colleges and universities in the state, ranging from small Bible colleges in the Ozarks to the two nationally known universities in St. Louis. During the fall of 1993, the private institutions enrolled more than fifty-five thousand FTE students.[4] The state's independent colleges formed a lobbying association in the early 1960s to enhance their political power. Known as the Independent Colleges and Universities of Missouri (ICUM), the association has sought various forms of state aid, with little success due to the strict limitations imposed by the state constitution, low state revenues, and the opposition of the public institutions.

The ICUM recently achieved a major breakthrough when the coordinating board recommended, and the legislature adopted, a proposal that the state contract with the private institutions for academic programs not offered by a public institution. Of greater importance, students who attend these colleges are eligible for grants under the Missouri student grant program. In 1993 they received almost 80 percent of the funds appropriated for this program.[5]

---

3. For a comparison of the two committees, see chapter 13.

4. CBHE Annual Report, 10.

5. The Missouri Supreme Court ruled that participation by the church-affiliated institutions in the Missouri Student Grant program does not violate the Missouri Constitution (*Americans United v. Rogers*, 538 S.W. 2d 711, 1976). The distribution of state student grant funds in 1993 was as follows:

All state colleges and universities $1,201,822
State community colleges $98,936

State statutes require that the coordinating board include the independent institutions in planning. When approving new degree proposals by the public institutions, the board takes into consideration whether the degree is being offered by another college, public or private. As a requirement for receiving student aid funds, the private institutions are expected to submit new degree proposals for review by the coordinating board. Any recommendations that it may make, however, are not binding on the independent colleges and universities.

Although their political support is not as great as that of the public institutions, the independent colleges and universities do enjoy widespread support scattered throughout the state. Many of the state's private institutions are church-affiliated and receive support from legislative members of their denominations. The policy makers are also receptive to the idea that support for private education saves public dollars by drawing away students who otherwise would be attending public universities. In St. Louis, Washington University and St. Louis University enjoy the support of that city's elite as well as that of the St. Louis delegation, which includes several of their graduates.

Two-Year Colleges

Missouri does not have a comprehensive state community college system. The state currently has twelve community college districts containing sixteen separate colleges, with 60 percent of the enrollment in the six colleges located in Kansas City and St. Louis. Not surprisingly, the greatest support for these colleges comes from the St. Louis and Kansas City legislators. The presidents and other staff members press their case in the General Assembly. The Coordinating Board for Higher Education has been responsive to the goals of this group, that is, to increase state support for operating expenses and capital improvement. The board has required the regional universities to phase out their two-year degree programs, reasoning that this is an expensive form of duplication. It has established guidelines and policies to facilitate articulation between the two-year colleges and the senior institutions. (Articulation involves the rules providing for the transfer of students from one college to another, trying to ensure that students receive appropriate credit for the courses taken in the first college and that they are prepared for the more advanced courses in the second college.)

Coordinating Board for Higher Education

Prior to the 1960s, there had been little state control of higher education. Colleges and universities were elitist, held in high regard by both the legislators and the general public, and there was little demand for accountability. The burgeoning enrollments of the 1960s, however, brought with them empire building and abuses of power by the institutions as well as greatly increased demands for state funding.

As envisioned by its early supporters, coordination would correct the abuses of power, ensure accountability, and at the same time leave the institutions free to develop academically without political interference. Recognizing that they lacked the

---

Independent colleges and universities $8,577,240
Independent two-year colleges $1,560
Professional, technical schools $892,256
Total $10,892,564
Source: CBHE Annual Report 1993, 38.
Student grants are awarded on the basis of costs and family income. A student who is attending a public college where costs are less would not qualify even if his or her family income were the same as that of someone attending a higher-cost college. When the student grant program is fully funded, it is estimated that an additional twenty-five thousand students who now attend the public institutions will be eligible.

necessary expertise, legislators in 1963 created an advisory body, the Commission on Higher Education, consisting of institutional administrators and lay persons. The commission, however, was unable to control the competitive institutions, and finally several abuses of power led the General Assembly to create the coordinating board during the reorganization of state government in 1974.[6]

The new coordinating board was authorized by a constitutional amendment to place it on an equal footing with the University of Missouri Board of Curators. The nine board members, one from each congressional district, are appointed by the governor and confirmed by the senate. The members serve six-year terms, and no more than five members can be from the same political party. To protect the autonomy of the board, state statutes authorize the members to select their own chairman and appoint the Commissioner of Higher Education, who serves as the chief executive officer.

The board's authority falls into three major categories: (1) planning, which includes setting statewide goals and priorities; (2) preparing a consolidated budget request; and (3) reviewing existing and new degree programs, including the approval of new campuses. The board is authorized to establish statewide guidelines on admission, articulation, and residency requirements. In addition, it can gather information and make recommendations to the governor and the General Assembly. The Department of Higher Education, which serves as the administrative arm of the board, is responsible for administering federal and state student aid funds and disbursing any federal funds for postsecondary education received by the state.

The higher education institutions emerged relatively unscathed from the 1974 reorganization. They retained their local governing boards with vast grants of statutory authority, the lump sum appropriation, the right of legislative appeal, and other powers. Their greatest loss of power came from being placed under the jurisdiction of the coordinating board and the Department of Higher Education.

Department of Higher Education

The Coordinating Board for Higher Education makes substantive policy; its staff is responsible for administration and making recommendations to the board. The key member of the staff is the executive director, who also serves as the Commissioner of Higher Education. He or she represents and speaks for the board in its relationship with all persons in and out of the system and acts as secretary to the board, staff director, and chief initiator of policy recommendations.

As the initiator of recommendations, the commissioner wields more power and influence on policy than any other person in the system. The board usually will make no decisions without the commissioner's opinion, and will rarely override one of his or her recommendations. Once the board has made a decision, the commissioner enforces it, interpreting the board's intent and scope, and supplementing policy with the necessary administrative directions.[7]

Traditionally, board members have not played a political role; thus it falls to the commissioner to serve as the major lobbyist

6. For a more detailed account, see Jeanette B. Welch, "The Missouri Coordinating Board: The Politics and Process of State Policy-making in Higher Education" (Ph.D. diss., University of Missouri–Columbia, 1982), 37–40.

7. I am indebted to Lyman Glenny for an understanding of the importance of this position. See *Autonomy of Public Colleges* (New York: McGraw Hill Book Co., 1959), 66–68.

for higher education and to sell the board's recommendations to the governor and legislature. To maintain support, the commissioner must work continuously with the elected officials, providing information and advice, doing favors, and responding to various requests. The political power of the agency rests in no small measure on the commissioner's political skills.

II. The Policy Community Periphery and Its Powers

The powers of the governor and the General Assembly are indicated by the fact that they have developed the statutes establishing most state institutions of higher education, as well as the statutes authorizing voters of local districts to establish community colleges. In addition, the governor and the General Assembly determine each year the share of the state's resources that will be allocated to higher education, and the distribution of those resources among institutions.

While legislators have delegated power to set routine academic policy to the institutional governing boards and to the coordinating board, individual legislators do intervene from time to time in response to constituent complaints. For example, one legislator introduced a bill requiring four-year colleges to accept all credits that students transferred from community colleges. This proposal, reflecting the legislator's view that the coordinating board was not moving sufficiently rapidly in resolving such articulation problems, did not pass but did stimulate faster resolution of differing viewpoints held by various institutions.

Governor

As chief of the executive branch, the governor holds the key to state-level politics of higher education. The governor's powers to propose new legislation and appoint institutional and coordinating board members, added to his budgetary authority, offer many opportunities for shaping state policy. A long tradition of noninterference in the affairs of higher education and the lack of political gains to be made by intervention have caused governors in the past to leave routine decision making to the board and the institutions. Traditionally, the chief impact governors have made on education policy has come through allocating resources and establishing new campuses.

Departing from tradition, Republican Governor John Ashcroft (1985–1993), a former professor of business law at Southwest Missouri State University and chairman of a National Governors Association task force on higher education, assumed a more active role. Ashcroft appointed conservatives to all state boards, including the Coordinating Board for Higher Education, and undertook to restructure and reform the state's system of higher education. In another departure from tradition, Ashcroft is thought to have influenced the selection of the commissioner, Charles J. McClain, formerly president of Northeast Missouri State University.

General Assembly

Its lawmaking functions, as well as the power to appropriate state funds, give the legislature a key role in determining the state's broad policy in education. In the state legislative system, the standing committees on higher education play a minor role in formulating state policy because of the power delegated to the board and the autonomy of the institutions. Because policy and priorities are embedded in the annual appropriations bills, members of the two appropriations committees, particularly the Senate Appropriations Committee, play a more substantial policy role.

Although the governor's line item veto power enables him to control the size of the overall budget, he is unable to prevent the appropriations committees from transferring funds from one program to another within an agency's budget, nor can he restore any cuts they choose to make. A major task of the coordinating agency staff is to protect its budget recommendations from committee interference. The formula budget form makes it more difficult to rearrange items in the operating budget. Most important, if the institutions support the board's budget recommendations, the committees are less likely to make major changes.

III. Policy Making within the Core

Planning

The policy-making role of the Coordinating Board for Higher Education is embodied within its authority to plan. Planning, the gathering and analysis of data and the setting of appropriate goals, is continuous and informs decision making in program and budget review as well as in other areas.

Long-range planning—the formulation of a master plan and the setting of statewide goals—occurs less frequently. Missouri has had only three master plans. The most recent, Master Plan III, was adopted in 1979. The purpose of a master plan is to provide a comprehensive and systematic statement of overall goals by which the various activities of the institutions can be kept in harmony. Its guidelines discourage ad hoc decision making by the legislature, the institutions, and the board. Its clear statement of policy reduces uncertainty and contributes to stability within the system. Because of resistance to change and the lack of resources to effect significant changes, the master plan is necessarily incremental.

Implementation depends on actions by the board and staff, the institutions, and the legislature. A review of Master Plan III reveals that many of its goals have been realized or are being implemented. One goal, increasing students' financial access to the state's colleges, has been implemented by increases in state funding for student aid. Upon the recommendation of the plan, the General Assembly established the Missouri Guaranteed Student Loan agency. (Most student aid, however, still comes from the federal government.) In addition, all of the institutions with the help of generous individuals have established extensive scholarship programs.

Other goals that have been achieved include the adoption of a uniform fee policy and the regulation of "diploma mills" and proprietary career schools. The legislature also has adopted other recommendations of the plan, including increases in state aid for the community colleges and legislation enabling community colleges to offer off-campus classes outside their districts.

The goal of equal opportunity for people of all races is still being pursued. The institutions actively recruit minority students, make special funds available for financial assistance, and provide remedial aid to help students succeed academically. All of the institutions have increased their efforts to recruit minority faculty and staff.

During the 1980s the coordinating board shifted its attention to institutional planning, requiring each institution to prepare and annually update a strategic plan. The purpose of these first plans was to help the institutions to identify areas of strength and weakness, compare their competitive position with the other institutions, and identify unique areas in which they were particularly strong. The institutions also were asked to review and revise their mission statements. The statements, which can be found near the front of most college catalogs, are an expression of the philosophy and purposes of the institution.

Program Review

After several unsuccessful attempts to curb the rampant growth of new degree programs on the college campuses during the 1960s and early 1970s, the General Assembly in the 1974 reorganization of state government granted power to the Coordinating Board for Higher Education to review new and existing degree proposals as well as the power to approve, subject to legislative enactment, the establishment of new campuses.

Review of New and Existing Degree Programs

In reviewing new degree proposals, the staff does not attempt to evaluate the academic requirements for the new degree. The focus of the review is on the demand for the program and whether the institution has sufficient resources to support a quality program. A most important consideration is whether the proposed degree duplicates a similar degree being offered by another campus, public or private. The concern is not so much with the basic liberal arts degrees as with the more expensive specialized degrees and graduate programs. Since 1982, the board has required the institutions to reallocate internal resources to finance the new degree programs.

Duplication also can be avoided through institutional planning. All of the institutions are required to have a board-approved plan, including an annual update, which includes a mission statement defining the institution's fundamental purposes and educational philosophy. In submitting a new degree proposal, the institution must show how the degree is related to its mission. The coordinating agency has pressured the institutions to refine their missions and to sharply differentiate them from other campuses. Each institution is encouraged to focus on programs that are unique to that campus or that are particularly strong, and to phase out programs that are inconsistent with its mission.

The board initiated a policy of campus-based program review in 1983. The institutions were asked to draw up a five-year plan under which 20 percent of their programs would be reviewed each year. The purpose of this internal review was to identify areas of strength and weakness, programs with low enrollments, and programs in which faculty and support facilities needed improvement. As a result of the first review cycle, 260 academic programs were eliminated and more than $40 million was reallocated to higher-priority programs and services.[8]

Establishment of New Campuses

Supporters of coordination had hoped that the most expensive form of duplication, the establishment of new colleges for political rather than educational purposes, could be prevented by granting authority to the Coordinating Board for Higher Education to approve new colleges and residence centers as well as new degree programs.

Although the board is authorized to approve the establishment of new colleges and residence centers, the General Assembly appropriates the funds and enacts the enabling statutes. The pork barrel nature of a new institution, bringing new jobs and prestige to a community, encourages log rolling among legislative coalitions. Without the support of the governor, the

8. CBHE News Brief 9:3 (December 1989).

board recommendations will be ignored by the powerful outside forces and legislative coalitions. This is not to say that its recommendations have no influence. The study and analysis of a new campus proposal can be very helpful to the governor and the legislators if they choose to use it.

The importance of politics in founding new colleges is demonstrated by the establishment of Missouri Western and Missouri Southern state colleges as well as the School of Optometry at the University of Missouri–St. Louis (UMSL).

A coalition of legislators from St. Joseph and Joplin, led by Senator Richard Webster (Republican—Carthage) and Senator John Downs (Democrat—St. Joseph) launched a campaign in the early 1960s to turn their community colleges into state-supported senior colleges. They met with little success, however, due to the opposition of the other institutions and to the fact that each community college was located less than fifty miles from a regional university. In 1964 when Warren Hearnes was running for governor, he promised the people of St. Joseph and Joplin that he would support the proposal for their colleges if he was elected. Hearnes did become governor, but the opposition to the colleges continued and the General Assembly agreed only to fund the last two years for each college, leaving the financing for the first two years similar to arrangements for community colleges. The Joplin–St. Joseph coalition continued to push for full state funding, and finally in 1975 the General Assembly agreed to the funding, beginning in 1978 on the recommendation of the new coordinating board. Reportedly, the board had recognized that the legislation was imminent. To limit duplication, it recommended that the two colleges specialize in vocational technical training and retain their com-

muter status rather than becoming residential campuses.[9]

The board's need for the governor's support is illustrated by the establishment of a School of Optometry on the UMSL campus in 1980. In 1968 UMSL administrators formed a coalition of state optometrists, St. Louis business leaders, and the large St. Louis delegation to lobby for the new school. Although it had not been approved by the University Board of Curators or the coordinating board, because of other more pressing priorities, the St. Louis group succeeded in pushing through the legislation, establishing the school in 1980. It was signed by Governor Joseph Teasdale, who was seeking reelection. Five years earlier, Governor Christopher Bond had vetoed a $5 million appropriation for the school because the coordinating board had not been consulted.[10]

Budget Review

Prior to the 1974 reorganization each institution prepared its budget request according to a simple formula that had been recommended by the advisory Commission on Higher Education. Although the formula was based on enrollments, there was no uniform method for calculating or verifying enrollments. During the appropriation process, each president lobbied his own budget, making deals and picking up support where he could. Competition was keen, and those with the most political clout wound up with the most money. The legislators were forced to appropriate money without really knowing what the higher education needs of the state were. Consequently, some parts of the state were

9. For a more detailed account, see Welch, 140–55.
10. Ibid. This is a greatly condensed version of a complex undertaking that extended over a period of twelve years with many other actors involved.

well served while others suffered from the uneven distribution of resources.

Operating Budgets. As one of its first priorities, the coordinating board appointed a task force to develop a uniform financial data reporting system. The task force employed outside consultants and spent several years in developing an expenditures reporting system. Other groups were appointed to meet with the state auditor's staff to develop uniform methods for reporting enrollments. This latter task also was essential because state funding for many functions is based on credit hours generated.

With improved data, the agency staff could then begin to develop a formula that would be acceptable to the institutions and the elected officials as a framework for budgetary decision making. Briefly, formula budgeting uses the average cost per activity to compute the money needed to carry on this work through the year. In contrast to traditional budgeting practices, it multiplies averages instead of adding up individual requests that have been collected in great detail from the bottom. To estimate an institution's expenditures for the fiscal year, for example, the amount generated by each component of the formula is summed.

The formula varies according to the mission of the institution, program offerings, institutional pricing, and expenditure trends. In addition, "add-ons" to the formula are made, to allow for individual differences between campuses. Estimated income from fees and other local revenues is subtracted from the total. Auxiliary enterprises such as dormitories are self-supporting and are not included.

The preparation of the consolidated budget request by the staff has won the acceptance of both the elected officials and educational administrators. The availability of detailed budgetary data and a coordinating agency staff to answer questions opens up the financial operation of the institutions to official scrutiny and enables elected officials to hold the institutions accountable. At the same time, the consolidated budget request enables the board and the institutions to identify and request additional funds for the most urgent statewide needs. Finally, preparing the budget jointly reduces the instability inherent in the budget process and ensures more equitable outcomes.

Capital Improvement Budget. Although the staff has succeeded in winning acceptance of the formula as the decisional framework for the operating budget request, it has been less successful with the capital budget recommendation, which is considered in a separate bill. The board and the institutions have employed outside assistance from time to time to help prepare a statewide facilities plan that ranks the needs for maintenance and repair, renovations, and new buildings on all the campuses.

There has rarely been enough money in the state budget to provide for new buildings. During the late 1980s the capital improvement budget was so limited that the coordinating board allocated the entire amount to maintenance and repair to protect the state's investment of more than $2 billion in physical facilities.

In addition to the rare appropriation for a new building, the state's colleges and universities have several other ways to finance new buildings. During the 1970s the General Assembly set aside a large part of the state's revenue sharing funds for new buildings and maintenance and repair on the college campuses.[11] In 1982 and 1994 the General Assembly referred to the voters capital improvement bond issues that included money for other new state construction as well. The General

11. Ibid., 188–93.

Assembly also authorized institutions to issue revenue bonds, which can be used to construct dormitories or other buildings that generate income. With the growing scarcity of state funds, many institutions have launched fund-raising campaigns for new buildings, as well as for other purposes. Using this variety of procedures, Missouri's public colleges and universities have doubled the number of buildings on campuses in the last thirty-five years.

IV. Decision Making at the Periphery

The Governor Proposes Reforms

After winning reelection in 1988, Governor Ashcroft undertook to reform the state's system of higher education. He announced his proposed reforms at the Fourth Annual Governor's Conference on Higher Education, held in Kansas City on November 30, 1989. Among the proposed changes were: raising admissions standards, greater specialization and refinement of missions to reduce duplication, increases in graduation rates, improvements in assessment, and increased performance evaluations with a portion of the state's appropriation to higher education being tied to performance. Ashcroft stated that increased funding alone would not solve these problems. However, if the institutions made progress, he would be "able to support the case for higher education even more strongly."[12]

The presidents and chancellors did not agree that there was unnecessary duplication in the system. All of the institutions had just undergone the first five-year cycle of internal program review, in which more than 260 academic programs had

been eliminated and more than $40 million reallocated.[13] And since 1982, all new degree programs had been financed by the reallocation of resources.

In response to a question by the *Kansas City Star*, Shaila Aery, former Commissioner of Higher Education (1982–1988), agreed with the administrators, stating that most of the fat had been wrung from the system except that which could not be eliminated for political reasons. In fact, higher education's share of the state budget had declined by five percentage points between 1977 and 1988, and Missouri had declined to 10 percent below the national average in appropriations per student. From 1984 to 1988, tuition and fees had increased an average of 62 percent.[14]

Ashcroft turned his attention next to the regional universities, where he said duplication could be reduced by a refinement of missions to allow each college to specialize in a few areas. As an example, he cited Northeast Missouri State University, which had become a four-year liberal arts college, and the University of Missouri–Rolla, which had always had a mission limited to science and engineering. When the presidents responded that very little would be saved by closing baccalaureate programs and that specialization would be more costly and would limit access for many students, Ashcroft agreed, but stated that the proposed changes would strengthen the system.[15]

Receiving little encouragement from the governor for increased state support or a tax increase, the presidents formed a lobbying association to inform the public and legislators about the needs of higher education.

12. Fourth Annual Governor's Conference on Higher Education, Kansas City, Mo., November 30, 1989 (on file Jefferson City: CBHE).

13. CBHE News Brief, December 1989.

14. "Colleges Told to Set Emphasis," *Kansas City Times*, December 1, 1989; CBHE Information File, September 1987.

15. "Colleges Told to Set Emphasis."

Known as "Missourians for Higher Education," it enlisted the support of prominent citizens and businessmen as well as key legislators. Later, after the General Assembly had approved Proposition B, this group conducted a statewide campaign on behalf of the tax increase.

Missouri Business and Education Partnership Commission

In response to the continued pressure for a tax increase, Ashcroft proposed that the General Assembly establish a commission to make a study of the state's needs in higher education. The commission was composed of state administrators, legislators, and businessmen, appointed by the governor, the speaker of the house, and the senate president pro tem. The commissioner of higher education was also a member of the commission. The Missouri Business and Education Partnership Commission was authorized to function for two years and to employ a staff and consultants.[16]

Reportedly, conflict between the legislators and businessmen was continuous, but despite the difficulty of reaching consensus, the commission issued a report (and a minority report as well) on January 15, 1991. The commission declined to recommend a form of governance, but it did recommend that the Coordinating Board for Higher Education should have authority to:

• Establish an overall framework plan for higher education
• Approve missions and mission implementation plans, including admissions standards, for state higher education institutions in accordance with that plan

• Develop and seek legislative endorsement of five-year educational goals
• Transfer, or if necessary eliminate, programs inconsistent with the plan
• Measure and report on institutional performance toward mission achievement and goal realization.[17]

Significantly, the report did not recommend closing any institution. All were economically viable, and the gains to be made in economic efficiency would not be sufficient to warrant closing an institution and reallocating resources to other institutions. Instead, it recommended that unique missions be developed for each of the thirteen state institutions, noting that potentially significant differences already existed in roles and missions.

Not surprisingly, the commission did find that increased funding was needed. It proposed a $300 million annual increase plus a one-time capital investment of $340 million. However, by this time the state had entered an economic slump, and other state agencies were also in need of funding. Ashcroft lent his support to a smaller tax increase to be shared with the public schools. As the price for his support, all of the recommendations of the commission would be included in the statute authorizing the tax increase.

Proposition B

Section A of senate bill 353, entitled "The Economic Security Act of 1991," was referred to the voters as Proposition B in November 1991. It proposed an annual tax increase of approximately $385 million, with the money to be divided between

16. The General Assembly appropriated $250,000 to provide support services for the commission (CBHE Annual Report 1990). The staff was provided by the National Center for Higher Education Management Systems.

17. Missouri Business and Education Partnership Commission, Report of the Missouri Business and Education Partnership Commission (Jefferson City, January 14, 1991), 23.

higher education and public education, except for 1.4 percent that would be allocated to the Department of Economic Development for job training by private industry.

The bill authorized the coordinating board to establish an overall framework for higher education, including any necessary changes in institutional mission and admissions standards, subject to the approval of the governor and the General Assembly. The legislation authorized the coordinating board to measure and report on institutional performance in student academic achievement, retention rates, graduation rates, and other areas.[18]

Funds for mission enhancement, reform, and change (more than 55 percent of the total new revenues) would be appropriated to the coordinating board, but none of the funds could be disbursed until all of the mission implementation plans had been approved by the board and the General Assembly. In addition, up to 2 percent of the state's general revenue appropriations to higher education could be appropriated to the board to use as incentive funds to reward performance on the general accountability measures.

Proposition B failed in the November 1991 election by a margin of more than two to one despite the $1.5 million campaign that had been waged on its behalf; opponents had spent less than $60,000. It had been endorsed by prominent business leaders, newspapers, and organizations such as the Chamber of Commerce and the Farm Bureau. Educators, college students, and legislators had worked hard for its passage.

Several explanations were offered for its defeat: the economic downturn and loss of consumer confidence; the traditional antipathy of Missourians to tax increases; and the complexity of the proposition (to print the entire bill required four pages of small newspaper print). Many of its provisions were unintelligible even to the informed voter. Resentment of massive state funding for desegregation of the St. Louis and Kansas City school districts and the distrust of voters who had thought that proceeds of the Missouri Lottery were earmarked for education were also cited.[19]

Critical Choices Task Force

With the defeat of Proposition B, the Coordinating Board for Higher Education lacked both the authority and the funds to implement the proposed reforms. However, it decided to press ahead through the creation of a special task force. The establishment of the Task Force on Critical Choices in Higher Education, consisting of the chairs of the governing boards from public and independent colleges and universities throughout the state, was authorized at its December 1991 meeting. When the presidents and chancellors of the public institutions complained that they were being shut out, they were invited to attend the meetings as guests.

The task force met four times, beginning on March 26, and its report was adopted by the coordinating board at its June 1992 meeting. Seeking to reduce duplication among the institutions, the cost of remedial

18. These included: student retention and graduation rates; percentage of students meeting admission standards; success of remediation programs; measurable communication skills including writing, speaking, and critical thinking; percentage of students attending graduate or professional schools; demonstrated student achievement through use of standardized testing; employer satisfaction; student access and student body composition; support from service area community of interests; implementation of state goals expressed by the coordinating board in operational terms, and measurements of success at meeting the community college's or the state institution's functional emphases.

19. "Officials Blame Education Defeat on Voter Distrust," *Warrensburg Daily Star Journal*, November 6, 1991.

classes, and high freshman dropout rates, the task force proposed an admissions schema that called for the institutions to differentiate their missions on the basis of entering student populations.[20] Each institution was asked to select an admissions category, ranging from open to highly selective, with the selection automatically affecting a change in the institution's mission. Any degree programs that did not fall within an institution's newly defined mission could be terminated or transferred by the board.

Other aspects presented practical problems. First, all institutions, except the community colleges, were requested to adopt a board-recommended high school core curriculum as a part of their admissions requirements. Some small rural schools, however, could not afford to establish new classes to meet these core requirements.

The problem of adequate financing was another major concern. The various changes of mission and of admissions requirements could result in a smaller student body for some institutions. Financing for those institutions could be reduced because state appropriations are based on credit hours generated. Also, the greater the enrollment, the greater the income from student fees.

Most of the institutions did choose one of the more selective admissions categories. Whether they would actually become more selective in their admissions was uncertain. Few institutions would willingly adopt policies that would cause them to lose students and income, especially since no new funds were appropriated for this purpose.

20. Task Force on Critical Choices for Higher Education, Suggested Statewide Public Policy Initiatives and Goals. Report to the CBHE, adopted June 5, 1992, Jefferson City, 5.

What Happened to Reform

Governor Ashcroft sought to reform the state's system of higher education to make it more efficient and to improve the quality of education. First he proposed to require most institutions to specialize more, by reducing or eliminating programs that were available elsewhere or for which there was limited demand. Second, he sought improvement in the quality of education through increased controls (the accountability measures and incentive funding), and third, he wanted to enhance the powers of the coordinating board to enable it to implement these reforms.

The governor was successful in one of his major reform endeavors—the development by all institutions of a comprehensive plan for assessing student academic achievement. In this he was assisted by nationwide trends, including the adoption of similar requirements by some of the national accreditation associations. In addition, the governor allocated sizable sums for the implementation of this program, looking upon it as a means of holding the institutions accountable, making them prove, as he said, that their students were actually learning something.

The governor was less successful in getting his other proposals for reform through the legislature due to (1) domination of the legislature by the opposition party; (2) the close relationship between the institutions and powerful legislators; (3) the state's lack of resources; and (4) his leadership style, which was seen as partisan and strident by his opponents. Nevertheless, the legislature and the institutions had accepted the governor's reform proposals as the price for his support of Proposition B. The defeat of Proposition B left the governor without funding or leverage to impose further reform proposals.

V. Conclusions

Coordination and State Policy Making.
Perhaps the greatest influence of coordination is on the policy process itself, on how decisions are made. Coordination forces the individual institutions to come together to address and resolve statewide academic problems that might otherwise be ignored or addressed in a hit-or-miss fashion. The bureaucratic agency provides an environment in which extensive discussion and debate are possible, and in which professional criteria can help to shape decisions.

Another contribution of coordination is that it provides a means for resolving conflicts between the competitive institutions. When conflicts are resolved within the bureaucratic environment, this leaves control in the hands of the institutions and prevents improper legislative interference. Institutional administrators and departmental staff spend many hours working out agreements and balancing interests. Once the agreement has been reached, it is formalized by the staff and translated into officially binding policy by the board.

The coordinating board's policy-making powers are embedded in its authority to plan—to gather data, make analyses, and set goals. Short-range planning is continuous, informing decision making in budget and program review and other areas. Master planning is comprehensive, identifying state problems and setting statewide goals. It is necessarily incremental because of resistance to change and the lack of resources needed to make significant changes.

The board has had mixed success in fulfilling its second major responsibility, the review of new and existing degree programs and the approval of new campuses. The requirement that the institutions establish an internal program review process by which every degree program is reviewed every five

years has resulted in the phasing out of hundreds of weak degree programs and the shifting of resources to more viable programs. The board's power to review new degree proposals has halted the proliferation of weak degree programs and costly duplication among the institutions. The board has been less successful in curbing duplication in expensive graduate programs within the University of Missouri system.

The board's authority to prepare the operating budget request has brought stability and fairness to the budget process, which in the past was fraught with uncertainty and danger for the institutions and was unsatisfactory to the elected officials. On the other hand, the Coordinating Board for Higher Education has met with mixed success in its capital budget recommendations, again because of the pork barrel nature of the issue.

Who Gains and Who Loses? Coordination tends to maintain the status quo. Any decision that adversely affects an institution, or group of institutions, would immediately be thrown into the legislative arena where the outcome would be determined by the legislators. The patron–client relationship between the institutions and powerful legislators discourages significant changes.

Coordination has favored two groups of institutions—the community colleges and the independent colleges. Both lobbied extensively in 1974 for a strong board, and they also lobbied to be brought under its jurisdiction. Coordination has given these two groups a place at the bargaining table and has forced the state to take into account their needs and contributions.

Should the Powers of the Coordinating Board Be Enhanced? Even though there has been no statutory change since the 1974 reorganization, the powers of the board have increased significantly. This is partly due to the nationwide demand for accountability, which requires more bureaucratic controls. Declining enrollments and state support also created a demand by the elected officials for more oversight to improve economy and efficiency.

If Proposition B had passed, the powers of the board would have been enhanced considerably. It did not pass, and it is unlikely that the legislators will again grant significant new powers to the board, absent a sharp decline in enrollments, a depression, or some other major force. Legislators fear that the board will be captured by either the governor or the institutions. They are vitally interested in the institutions in their districts. Although legislative intervention on behalf of an individual institution is at times unfair, and detrimental to the system as a whole, the institutions find it beneficial.

Without increased statutory powers, the enhancement of the board's strength will depend, as it has since 1974, upon the political skills of the governor and to a lesser extent the commissioner.

CHAPTER 17

Funding for Education in the 1990s: A Case Study
by Gregory Casey and James W. Endersby

If you think education is expensive, try ignorance.—Bumper sticker

Political struggles over education funding and reform from 1990 to 1993 show the continuing involvement of many interest groups in the policy process. This process includes the stages of initiation, decision, and implementation. Interest groups are constantly active in their own sector or sphere of interest, and occasionally become active in other policy sectors when threatened or when concerned with crusading for collective goals. Interest groups look for timely opportunities when political institutions and office holders are suddenly more receptive than expected to their basic philosophies and policy preferences. They stake out positions, bring forth proposals, and react to political leaders' agendas.

I. Background

Education in Missouri is considered chronically underfunded. It usually ranks low among the fifty states in expenditures per capita (forty-second through forty-seventh from 1988 to 1992). This average measure covers a wide range of variation, with the lowest spending per student coming in poorer rural districts (especially in southern Missouri) and the highest found in the suburbs of the two larger cities, which are rich in tax base (and often lacking in large numbers of students). Teachers'

salaries lag behind those in other states, again with wide variation across the state. Popular rhetoric, even among teachers, accepts that the low funding levels are not all bad; the cost of living in most locations within the state is considered low to moderate. Of course, virtually no groups in the education sector would refuse more financial support.[1]

The Revenue Basis for Education. Elementary and secondary education is supported by a blend of local and state revenues. Property tax is the prime local component of school revenue, and is a function of two factors: the assessed value of local real property and the levy rate for the school district. As is common throughout the country, the value of real property is highest in the suburbs and lowest in poorer, rural districts. Levy rates for operating costs of a school district also vary substantially across the state, and tend to be highest in

1. Lobbyists in other sectors view education as "greedy"; one business lobbyist told us that education often seemed as if it would gladly accept 110 percent of the state budget. The expenditure per capita rankings were computed by the authors from data from the U.S. Bureau of the Census, 1989–1993. The rankings of educational expenditures per elementary and secondary pupil are from *States in Profile: The State Policy Reference Handbook 1990* (McConnellsburg, Pa.: Brizius and Foster and State Policy Research, Inc.), Table G–12 and Table G–10.

the suburban and urban areas and lowest in the rural areas, particularly in the southern part of the state. Thus, poorer districts usually have lower levy rates on less valuable real estate, while wealthier districts feature higher levy rates on more highly valued real estate—a situation making for considerable disparity in the property tax revenue basis for school support.

State revenues for education are raised through the school foundation formula and from earmarked taxes, especially from a one cent sales tax adopted in 1982 (Proposition C) to benefit schools. The foundation formula was originally designed to benefit poorer school districts, but part of the formula also rewards local tax effort—so that school districts with higher levy rates (generally, wealthier areas) also receive substantial aid. Proposition C monies provide some redistribution of wealth in that they are collected disproportionately in wealthier areas of the state but distributed equally on a per student basis to the school districts as a supplement to the other revenue streams contributing to the school district's funding.[2]

For the education lobby, increasing funding for elementary and secondary education thus involves a double focus. One eye must be kept on local support for the levy rate. But the other eye must watch state government, particularly the foundation formula, whereby funds are distributed to the local districts and the level of funding is determined. The level of funding is an annual decision, while the foundation formula is only rarely altered; before the 1993

revision, the last previous change had been in 1977, and before that in 1969.

Funding in the 1980s. The adoption of the state's revenue and tax ceiling in 1980 (the Hancock Amendment) indicated public skepticism about substantial increases in funding for education. The proportion of total state revenues (including federal funds and earmarked funds) spent on education hovered around 24 and 25 percent in the late 1970s and early 1980s. The comparatively low level of state support for education was a fundamental motivation underlying the education lobby's work on Proposition C in 1982. The Missouri State Teachers Association (MSTA) took the lead in sponsoring the initiative drive for Proposition C; the two other teachers' groups, the Missouri National Education Association (MNEA) and Missouri Federation of Teachers (MFT), both based in the urban centers, lent support, and signatures were gathered inexpensively at PTA meetings throughout the state. Proposition C was passed by voters in 1982. Even so, appropriations for elementary and secondary education increased only slightly, from 24 percent of all state revenues to 25 or 26 percent in later years.[3]

Funding prospects for all programs, and certainly for education at all levels (including higher education), looked glum throughout the 1980s. The state's revenue ceiling made tax increases so difficult to

---

2. Some county level revenues other than property taxes (such as railroad and utilities taxes) go to support local schools. Other earmarked state revenue taxes include a four cent cigarette tax distributed on a per pupil basis, a tax on out-of-state insurance companies designated for textbooks, and earmarked appropriations distributed separately for vocational education and food service.

3. The state constitution requires that at least 25 percent of the state revenue, exclusive of interest and sinking fund, shall be "applied annually to the support of the free public schools." "State revenue" has been interpreted to mean "general revenue," excluding federal funds and earmarked funds. Using this definition, general revenue expenditures for elementary and secondary education constituted 31 percent of all general revenue in fiscal year 1988 and 29 percent in fiscal year 1992. In fiscal year 1993 the legislature included desegregation in the education appropriation, raising the total appropriated for elementary and secondary education to 37 percent of general revenue minus interest and sinking fund.

attain that the idea of a tax increase became almost a taboo topic.[4] Political candidates became unwilling to commit to increased taxes, and in many cases they were skittish about even discussing the subject.

Lobbying for Funding in an Antitax Climate. In this environment, an interest group seeking greater funding for particular programs cannot demand increased appropriations outright, since it is necessarily asking for cuts in other programs, which would activate opposition from groups in other sectors, neutralizing its own influence and setting itself up for defeat. Therefore, the reasonable sequence of tactics for any group seeking greater funding is first to identify a specific tax source that could be designated for its use, and then to have the actual tax enacted by a public vote. The revenue thus gained would not count against the revenue ceiling, leaving the previous fiscal equilibrium balanced and not threatening other groups. A third rule of thumb for operating in this fiscally conservative environment, when going for a public vote, is to show the specific benefits to the public of more funding.

Following these precepts, lobbies could win earmarked taxes in public votes; thus, the voters approved a one-tenth cent sales tax in 1984 for state parks and soil and water conservation (like Proposition C, this was put on the ballot by initiative petition). Another public vote in 1987 resulted in a higher gasoline tax; spurred by poor repair of roads and bridges, and the looming necessity of appropriating monies from general revenues to avoid losing federal matching funds, the legislative leadership and Governor John Ashcroft worked out a proposal for a four cents per gallon tax increase to be put on the ballot in April 1987. The General Assembly rubber-stamped the deal. Since several previous efforts to increase the gasoline tax had failed (a three cents per gallon tax increase for better roads in 1978 had gone down to crushing defeat, with 87.7 percent disapproval), the Highway Department identified the local projects that would receive first priority from the tax. With state leaders in agreement, an ad hoc committee was formed to campaign for the measure, potential benefits were specified for the voters, and the measure passed. Many supporters of roads wanted more than a four cent gas tax increase, and even Ashcroft favored a six cent increase—but in the antitax popular climate of opinion, four cents looked like the safest number.

II. Policy Initiation and Development, Round I: Daring to Talk of Taxes

In 1984 Ashcroft was elected to the first of his two terms of office as governor, and his stands on education thus began to affect the education lobby's strategic environment. Deeply interested in education and a former educator himself, Ashcroft styled himself the "education governor"; his policy on additional funding was to emphasize reform as a prior condition for more funding. An Excellence in Education Act in 1985 aimed at improving teaching and assessing student progress was the first result of his leadership. A fiscally conservative Republi-

---

4. Raising taxes more than 1 percent above the revenue ceiling could have precipitated a tax refund on a pro rata basis to income taxpayers, both personal and corporate. Substantial concern about triggering a refund haunted Missouri state politics during most of the 1980s; many argued that if the refund were triggered and tax refunds begun, a lawsuit would prevent them from continuing because taxes paid in the form of excise and sales taxes would be paid out only to income taxpayers, and that once a lawsuit found the refund provision unconstitutional the revenue limitation would be dead. But the refund provision has not yet been triggered, leaving the revenue limitation in place.

can, Ashcroft generally was opposed to new taxes.

Even in the antitax environment, the MSTA success with Proposition C in 1982 was influential. Hopeful ideas were being discussed. In 1985 several college presidents organized a new education lobby, Missourians for Higher Education, to join with elementary and secondary educators in pushing for a tax increase for all levels of education. In 1986 the Commissioner of Higher Education proposed a one-year elimination of all sales tax exemptions (for example, farm machinery and prescription drugs) to develop a fund for increasing salaries at the public universities and colleges.

The MSTA held joint tax hike parlays in 1987 with the college group, focusing on a tax hike to raise a kitty of money for both higher and K–12 education. But negotiations broke down; many in the college group wanted an income tax increase rather than a sales tax increase, and when the college heads wanted additional time to consult their boards before committing, MSTA's executive director broke off discussions and developed an initiative drive to support only elementary and secondary education, casting higher education adrift. But lack of consensus in the K–12 sector wounded the MSTA's initiative drive, enough so that it failed.

Meanwhile, higher education groups took the initiative, and business groups gradually came aboard in support of additional funding; a blue-ribbon committee, the Missouri Business and Education Partnership, was formed and eventually recommended (in January 1991) an additional $300 million for college and vocational education, premised on reform.

A Tax Program Emerges: Proposition B. The two key legislative leaders (House Speaker Bob Griffin and Senate President Pro Tem James Mathewson) had each previously dared to propose increased taxes for education. With the business and education sectors now both in favor after one and one-half years of discussions, the house and senate passed different packages in the 1991 session; at this point, pressures for a public vote for additional educational funding increased to the point where Ashcroft became willing to lend his support. Governor Ashcroft and legislative leaders then whittled down the amounts in the two chambers' packages and together developed a complex proposal for a referendum on increased taxation for both higher and K–12 education. The legislature readily voted to put this package on the ballot for November 1991; known as Proposition B, this measure was a mixture of taxes, reforms, and benefits.

If approved by the voters, Proposition B would raise $385 million in revenue, $190 million to benefit K–12, the same amount to benefit higher education (including community colleges), plus $5 million for job training and development to benefit business. The additional revenue would come from another sin tax on cigarettes, a three-eighths cent sales tax, a limitation on use of the federal income tax deduction in calculating state income tax payments, and additional taxes for large corporations (actually this would only make permanent a temporary business tax increase put into effect two years previously to pay off tax refunds ordered by the United States Supreme Court to federal retirees). Among specified uses of the K–12 monies were reducing class sizes in the early grades to fifteen students and establishing new programs to involve parents in learning. All newly raised monies were to be put in trust funds to prevent shifts to other programs. Accountability measures promised were annual report cards for school districts and standards for high school graduates. The main umbrella organization working for passage of Proposition B, Missourians for Quality Education, spent about $1.5 million, while two smaller organizations in opposition spent only about $60,000.[5]

III. Policy Decision, Round I: Defeat

Despite the far larger amount spent to persuade the voters to adopt this measure, and despite support from Ashcroft, the legislature, most of the education lobby, and business groups such as the Farm Bureau and the Chamber of Commerce, Proposition B was soundly defeated in November 1991, with slightly less than one-third of voters favoring the package.[6] Postmortems were agonizing, because if the voters were now going to balk at approving tax increases, the revenue ceiling could stifle funding needs for all programs. Moreover, this result called into question the strategy worked out (after 1980) of going to the voters for earmarked taxes to circumvent the revenue ceiling and avoid the unpopularity of general tax increases.

Aftermath of Defeat. Several liberal organizations had opposed Proposition B on the grounds that it perpetuated the inequity in taxation (with its inclusion of the regressive sales tax), and that it ignored the

low level of other human services; among these opponents were the League of Women Voters, the Missouri Association of Social Welfare, Missouri Protection and Advocacy Services, a regional council of the UAW, and ACORN. The last two groups formed one of the small organizations that raised funds to fight Proposition B.

Yet the opposition of these groups struck observers as less significant than voters' questions about previous tax hikes and expenditures. The voters questioned why Proposition C wasn't sufficient, how much of the tax money raised might be given over to court-ordered desegregation programs in St. Louis and Kansas City, and why the monies from the lottery weren't sufficient for education.[7] Criticisms also suggested that the package was too diverse, with elements thrown together in too far-flung a coalition—a grab bag of reforms, tax increases, tax breaks, and earmarked funds.

Failure to reform the foundation formula played a role also; an attempt to rework this had come to naught when the house and senate passed different versions, neither supported by Ashcroft. Some school superintendents had complained earlier in the campaign that Proposition B monies would be unfairly distributed because the foundation formula remained inequitable; to allay their fears, the Commissioner of Education maintained that a new formula would be put in place soon, by the courts if the General Assembly did not act. But

5. These figures are from "1991 Statewide Ballot Measures of Committee Financial Activity," November 5, 1991, Special Election, *1991 Missouri Annual Campaign Finance Report,* Roy D. Blunt, Secretary of State (Jefferson City, April 1992).

6. The governor's chief of staff took leave from his position to work as campaign director of Missourians for Quality Education. The Missouri Federation of Teachers, the smallest of the teachers' groups, opposed the measure because of its provisions for a longer school year and for allowing college graduates to obtain teacher certification with a minimum of education training. Virginia Hick and Susan C. Thomson, "Tax Plan Is Hot Topic among Teachers," *St. Louis Post-Dispatch,* November 1, 1991.

7. Negative voters were asked why other voters might have voted against the proposition. About 20 percent indicated distrust in general of officeholders or specifically of the governor and legislature, or distrust founded in disappointment in how the lottery turned out. Twenty-five percent mentioned simple opposition to a tax increase, and another 10 percent felt that education would not spend the money suitably. (David Leuthold, "Proposition B—What Happened?" *Governmental Affairs Newsletter* 26 [January 1992], 5–8.)

promising to rewrite the foundation formula only after adoption of the tax in effect violated the tactical rule of thumb of obtaining popular approval by identifying specifically where the benefits will flow.

Gubernatorial Candidates React. Underfunding was still chronic enough that all gubernatorial hopefuls for the 1992 election voiced either an intention to raise more money or gave an alternate plan for doing so. However, discussion now involved only K–12 education; higher education disappeared from the agenda in most campaign statements.

Of the Republican gubernatorial candidates, the most far-reaching proposal came from Roy Blunt, then secretary of state. Blunt advocated a constitutional amendment earmarking one-third of the state's general revenue for elementary and secondary education (up from one-fourth in the current Constitutional provision), foreseeing an increase of roughly $400 million per year. Blunt did not neglect higher education, proposing as an alternative constitutional amendment the earmarking of half of all general revenue for all education, including higher education. Wendell Bailey, then state treasurer, supported a Republican plan that had been developed to increase funding by $150 million without a public vote, and also suggested closing loopholes in the state's sales tax laws. William Webster, then attorney general, wanted to earmark proceeds from the state lottery, then running about $70 million per year, for education (this measure was adopted in a public vote in August 1992).

Democratic gubernatorial hopeful Mel Carnahan, then lieutenant governor, supported a tax increase, and the other Democratic candidate, Vince Schoemehl, mayor of St. Louis, proposed an infusion of $200 million to $225 million more into the foundation funding formula, with revenues to come from the lottery, closing off sales tax exemptions, and other budget savings.[8]

Certainly, no candidate could reasonably suggest that the schools had enough money. One common view was the grim diagnosis that the voters could not be counted on to support a tax increase in the wake of Proposition B's defeat: the antitax climate of opinion had hardened.

IV. Policy Initiation and Development, Round II

The next cycle of policy development featured a lawsuit, the gubernatorial general election campaign of 1992, and eventual reaction to the court ruling in the legislative session of 1993.

Litigation. By the time Proposition B was being considered in the fall of 1991, two lawsuits already had been filed in trial court in the state capital over the school funding formula. One plaintiff was a group of suburban Kansas City school districts, and the other was a large grouping of rural school districts, mostly in southern Missouri. The cases were consolidated into one suit involving 124 school districts, and trial was set in the court of activist Circuit Judge Byron Kinder. The plaintiffs contended that the state's foundation formula was so unfair and inequitable that it violated the state constitution's guarantee of free public schools.

Litigation had been a tactic used productively by the education lobby in other states, such as New Jersey, Kentucky, and Texas, but in Missouri it was more of a response to severe financial difficulties. Commissioner Bartman stated in December 1991 that

8. Virginia Hick and Jo Mannies, "Politicians Share Ideas on Schools," *St. Louis Post-Dispatch*, November 7, 1991; John A. Dvorak, "Education Platforms Long on Ideas, Short on Details," *Kansas City Star*, December 7, 1992.

the schools needed at least another $190 million, which meant a tax increase—but he conceded the improbability of this in light of the fate of Proposition B.[9] About one-third of the state's school districts had begun engaging in deficit spending in the 1990-1991 school year, and trends were worsening, particularly in rural areas. Testimony in the trial (in the fall of 1992) showed that total spending per pupil in the state then ranged from $9,750 to $2,653. Some school districts defended the formula because they were losing enrollments and were favored by a "prior-year constraint" facet in the formula, while school districts undergoing rapid growth were among those suing. The MSTA submitted a brief in amicus curiae on behalf of the plaintiff school districts.

Gubernatorial General Election Campaign. In the general election, Carnahan promised higher taxes (a hike of about $200 million) for schools, with higher corporate and cigarette taxes and higher personal income taxes for the wealthier. He proposed to put this package to a popular vote. Carnahan persisted in the face of substantial concern from his campaign staff that candidates who advocated tax increases often lost at the polls. The Republican candidate, Webster, became involved in a scandal, and Carnahan handily won the November election.

Shortly after his inauguration, Carnahan held a joint press conference with legislative leaders Griffin and Mathewson, at which he promised a new foundation formula in 1993. But then the governor's budget offered very little new revenue at all and his budget speech contained only one reference to his promise of more money for education. After his speech, Carnahan told reporters that he still wanted to come up with the additional $200 million promised in his campaign, but that first the state's foundation formula had to be changed.[10]

The Court Ruling. Soon afterwards, the foundation formula case decision was announced: Judge Kinder declared education a fundamental right, found the current foundation formula irrational and unconstitutionally inequitable, and ordered the General Assembly to find a new way to pay for it to provide equal opportunity for all children. The commissioner of education lauded this ruling, and Carnahan commented that he expected the decision and was in general agreement. The judicial order was timed to become effective ninety days after the close of the regular legislative session (May 15) to give the political branches a chance to work out a reform.

The New Strategic Environment. In setting expectations that the legislature would act, the judicial decision altered the strategic situation. A joint committee was already at work on a new funding formula, and its work was the more serious because Carnahan demanded a new formula before figuring out how to raise the revenue. But how to devise a new formula? The political risks of a new formula seemed even higher than those for new taxation measures; and now policy leaders had to reckon with the risk that the cost of continued indecision would be highest of all. If the General Assembly adopted no new taxes because it could not afford to work out a new funding formula, the court might take over the school system, impose a new formula, and even impose new taxation.

In late January the Missouri School Board Association brought 230 members to Jefferson City for its annual meeting with

---

9. Barbara Barrett, "The Budget Crunch," *Columbia Missourian*, December 4, 1991.

10. Terry Ganey, "Carnahan Offers $11 Billion Budget," *St. Louis Post-Dispatch*, January 14, 1993.

legislators, and most members thought that the only way to an acceptable formula would be to create a bigger budgetary pie that would raise funding for the poorer districts rather than reduce state aid to wealthier districts; a formula in which many school districts would lose money was considered politically infeasible. Martha Karlovetz, leader of MNEA, agreed that no district should lose funding. Committing to new taxation, so difficult in recent state history, would nonetheless be easier than changing the formula to redistribute the funds.[11]

But soon teachers' organizations found the altered strategic environment to be hazardous to their professional independence: policy leaders intended to seize the opportunity of the court ruling to require new educator accountability provisions. Annette Morgan, chair of the Elementary and Secondary Education Committee in the house, wanted more rigorous state standards, assessment of student progress toward standards, and reporting of results. She also advocated rewarding teachers whose students succeeded, penalizing teachers whose students failed, suspending teachers in academically deficient districts, and dissolving failing school districts.[12]

The joint committee used consultants and computers to determine, with short turnaround time, how shifts in the formula affected school districts, and eventually came out with a proposal that required an estimated $558 million additional revenue for funding. Only 12 out of 538 districts would lose money, and property tax school

levies would have to be at least three dollars per one hundred dollars assessed valuation in every district, a provision that would require raises in many districts. The teachers' lobby was still resistant: Karlovetz found the assessment and accountability measures unacceptable, and eventually Kent King of MSTA stated that these provisions would make "teachers the focal point of blame," and foster a "teach the test mentality." Yet some in the education lobby testified favorably: the State Board of Education, the St. Louis and Kansas City school districts, and the school administrator's association.[13]

The Senate Education Committee voted out a school funding formula carrying a cost of $502 million for the state plus a local contribution of $185 million (to be made up by raising the levy rate). But opposition arose on many fronts. A poll of senators revealed that the majority were opposed or leaning against the package; most thought the cost too high. Teachers' groups still opposed penalties for teachers and school districts where students failed to perform up to standards. Rural school superintendents fretted that the legislature might not adopt a new formula, and that Judge Kinder might then adopt an alternative simplified formula more favorable to the St. Louis area school districts; meanwhile, St. Louis area superintendents and school boards became worried about losing state aid under the new formula because of their high assessed property valuations and high local property tax. Senator Wayne Goode of St. Louis County indicated that the senate would have to revise the plan to make it more

11. Virginia Hick, "School Funding Ruling Prompts Worries," *St. Louis Post-Dispatch*, January 24, 1993; Helen Gray, "School Finance Is Hot Topic," *Kansas City Star*, February 7, 1993.

12. Terri Gleich, "Lawmakers Want to Overhaul Education First," *Springfield News-Leader*, February 15, 1993.

13. Will Sentell, "Legislative Panel Outlines a Direction for School Finance," *Kansas City Star*, February 27, 1993; Fred Lindecke, "Panel Proposes School Aid Plan," *St. Louis Post-Dispatch*, March 11, 1993; Sally Wells, "School Money Plan in Peril," *Columbia Missourian*, March 11, 1993.

palatable to his county's school districts, with a hold-harmless clause for school districts already drawing substantial aid under the old formula (a hold-harmless clause would provide that no school district would receive less money per pupil than it had been receiving).[14]

It therefore remained obvious that the new formula was going to require new revenue; it could not just redistribute the same level of funding. Carnahan continued work on a tax package, but insisted at a breakfast (hosted by the Missouri Association of Secondary School Principals) that funding increases be tied to school reforms: only a new "compact between schools and taxpayers" could justify the higher taxes.[15] He was reportedly still undecided on the amounts needed to fund the formula, the types of taxes to raise, and whether to submit the proposal to a statewide vote or just run it through the legislature.

The teachers' lobby (all three groups) advanced its own plan (dubbed "shared visions" as opposed to the senate's "new visions" plan) showcasing the key reform of significantly smaller class sizes for grades K–4.[16] Shared visions would suspend performance penalties for teachers if the state funded the formula at less than 90 percent, and would postpone all deadlines for one year each year the legislature funded the

formula at less than 90 percent. School administrators expressed fear that putting any tax to a public vote would ensure defeat; Bob Howe, Executive Director of the Association of School Principals, stated that any effort to ask Missouri voters to approve a major tax increase for the schools would be wasted. Some principals agreed wholeheartedly, but a few disagreed and felt that the proposal should go to the voters.

V. The Policy Decision, Round II

Finally, on April 8, with little more than a month to go in the legislative session, Carnahan asked the General Assembly for a tax hike of $365 million, to be added to $50 million in state government cuts to make up a pool of $415 million for the funding formula. The governor asked the legislature not to refer the tax to a public vote, but rather to pass it outright. The tax increase would raise the corporate income tax rate increase 5 percent to 7 percent and would limit, for high-income filers, the deductibility from state income of federal income tax paid. Carnahan endorsed the senate's pending funding formula, asking only that the minimum levy rate be changed from the senate's $3 to $2.75 to cut the cost of funding the formula to the governor's overall estimate of $415 million.[17]

Complaints and Hesitations. As legislators left town for Easter break after Carnahan's speech, commentators expressed a general gloom at the difficulty of the work awaiting them. Speaker of the House Griffin called the tax plan the hardest task before the General Assembly in twenty years.[18] Time was short, and selling the plan to

14. By mid–1996 the state Board of Education would have to develop criteria of academic deficiency, and teachers could eventually lose tenure if their schools were found deficient. One suburban school district, Affton, had managed its first successful levy increase in twenty-two years in February 1992, and now the new formula would reduce its take from the formula by 52 percent!

15. "Governor: Education Funding Hike Must Be Tied to Reforms," *Jefferson City Post-Tribune,* March 30, 1993; Scott Charton, "Carnahan Tried to Tailor Funding Plan," *Springfield News-Leader,* March 31, 1993.

16. Small classes were the primary factor shown in the education literature to salvage K–4 kids who otherwise might fall between the slats and become irrecuperable for learning at later ages. (Interview with Kent King, Executive Director, MSTA, October 8, 1993.)

17. By lowering the minimum levy rate, school districts that only went to the minimum would have lower local tax effort and therefore less take from the formula, making funding less expensive.

18. Will Sentell, "School Plan Aims at Rich, Businesses," *Kansas City Star,* April 9, 1993.

the teachers' lobby was a formidable challenge. The business sector also resisted: the Chamber of Commerce president called the plan "a narrow attack on business." Although the Missouri Association of School Boards hopped aboard, teachers' organizations withheld endorsement until viewing the details. Republicans in the legislature announced opposition.

Getting Carnahan's plan through both houses would be very tricky since neither chamber had yet passed even the funding formula. To fend off the teachers' groups, Marc Farinella, the governor's chief of staff, announced that the school reforms were nonnegotiable; Carnahan would veto any legislation lacking accountability provisions. Carnahan met with leaders of the Chamber of Commerce and Associated Industries of Missouri (AIM), but could not win their support. Carnahan began devoting his entire schedule to lobbying the legislature for the tax and funding formula package. Mrs. Carnahan began hanging around the legislature to talk it up as well.

Movement toward Decision. The senate now started making headway on the funding formula. The problem of resistance from the affluent school districts around St. Louis was solved with an amendment to reduce loss of state aid if the formula were not fully funded. An amendment that would have stripped the reform provisions was defeated 18–13. By this time the teachers' groups were coming aboard: Karlovetz of MNEA now praised the retention of the reform provisions, obviously impressed by Carnahan's resolve to veto legislation without educator accountability.

Two senate amendments brought the package closer to the preferences of the teachers' lobby by clipping the state board of education's curriculum powers. Instead of establishing a curriculum framework, the state board would be prohibited from requiring any school board to adopt its curriculum suggestions, and instead of determining how student learning was to be demonstrated, it could now only suggest criteria to the local boards. During these votes, Carnahan was in a hallway outside the chamber. Under the senate version, the foundation formula would need about $100 million more than the governor's plan had foreseen, but Carnahan still supported the bill and planned now on getting the extra costs removed in the house. The package even managed to attract some Republican support; for instance, Senator Johnson of Lee's Summit voted for it because it cleared up underfunding problems plaguing constituencies in several school districts (including Lee's Summit, a key district in the lawsuit).[19]

Senate victories raised the hopes of formula supporters. Action now shifted to the Elementary and Secondary Education Committee in the house, where education lobbyists spoke for the tax hike and new funding formula, but cautioned against putting the tax increase on the ballot. Business lobbyists spoke in opposition; AIM proposed an alternate plan that would use sales taxes and surtaxes on personal and corporate incomes to make up the amount necessary, and the Taxpayers Research Institute (TRIM) urged maintaining deductibility of federal income taxes for corporations calculating their Missouri income tax.[20] Despite business sector protests, the committee voted out the tax increase.

An Alternative Tax Plan. But the senate had not yet considered a tax package to fund the formula. Senator Mathewson now announced a tax plan more amenable

19. Rudi Keller, "Blunder Imperils Education Plan," *Columbia Tribune,* April 14, 1993.

20. Rudi Keller, "Hearing Sets the Stage for Vote on Education Package," *Columbia Tribune,* April 28, 1993.

to the business lobby: a one-eighth cent sales tax gradually to be replaced over four years by increasing the corporate rate to 6 percent, with the sales tax revenue tiding the formula over until the higher business tax payments began flowing.[21]

Defeat in the House. On the house floor, a Republican attempt to strip the reform component from the package seemed to pass, but Griffin allowed voting to continue for a longer time than usual while Annette Morgan and other reform supporters lobbied their fellow legislators for vote changes to defeat it. The Republicans were opposed to giving too much power to education bureaucrats in the state capital; one member branded the reform "the latest fad in socialistic education." Morgan did accept a change in wording to ensure that standards used for measurement of learning would be academic standards rather than attitudes or values. To rally spirits, Carnahan met with the house Democratic caucus and indicated his disagreement with the Mathewson sales tax proposal.

But the next day, in a severe setback, the house voted 79–75 against the education package, with the Republicans voting as a bloc against it. The Republicans professed to want the new formula and the tax increase, but wanted the tax package put on the ballot. With legislators going home for the weekend, Carnahan planned on lobbying to change votes so that a positive vote to reconsider could be taken up the next Monday. Griffin offered a compromise amendment that would put the tax increase on the ballot only if the state supreme court held that the present tax system was unconstitutional.

Shortly after the house voted against the

package, the senate took up the Mathewson tax proposal: an AIM proposal using a higher sales tax (0.275 cents), no alteration in the federal tax deduction, and a system of income tax surtaxes was voted down, as was a proposal to impose higher taxes on corporations. The senate then voted to approve Mathewson's proposal, and also voted against sending the tax plan to the voters. This positive development brought decision closer, but the Mathewson plan was substantially different from what might come back from the house, and the house still had to be turned around.

Again, Carnahan showed great energy, working with teachers' organizations to list names of state representatives whose votes could possibly be changed. MSTA activated its grassroots technique of lobbying; teachers acquainted with the targeted legislators started working to persuade them to turn around. Carnahan spent much of the weekend on the telephone with reluctant legislators, and even sent his plane to pick up a house member who anticipated difficulty getting back to the capital for the vote to reconsider on Monday. MNEA and MSTA members mustered at the legislature on Monday, wearing green ribbons on their lapels to signify their support for the bill. The vote to reconsider was 100–56, then the vote to pass the measure was 88–71; teachers cheered from the gallery at the final vote. Lobbyists viewed Carnahan's support as having made the difference: "The governor put his bacon on the line," said King of the MSTA, and other lobbyists acknowledged Carnahan's leadership as having turned the issue around.[22]

---

21. "Senate Leader Says Hancock 'Trust Zone' Allows Tax Increase," *Jefferson City Post-Tribune*, April 30, 1993.

22. Interview with Kent King, October 8, 1993; Rudi Keller, "Taxes Remain Sticky Issue for Education Bill," *Columbia Tribune*, May 11, 1993; Ronald Paul Keeven, "Dirty Politics Pushed Education Bill Through," *St. Louis Post-Dispatch*, July 28, 1993; Fred Lindecke,

Conference and Victory for Senate Bill 380. Some modifications took place in conference: Mathewson's sales tax plan was dropped, the corporate tax rate was raised to 6.25 percent, and the deductibility of federal income taxes was limited rather than removed altogether. The minimum levy rate was kept at $2.75 per $100 of assessed value, the house compromise to put the issue on the ballot only if the state supreme court overturned the trial court's decision on funding was retained, and further language was added to provide that the tax increases would be voided if the supreme court threw out the tax increase language of the trial court ruling. The conference report drew a six-hour filibuster in the senate in protest against not taking the tax measure to the voters, but this was overcome and the combined tax and funding formula reform sailed through to victory early on the last day of the session.

Aftermath of Decision. The intensive legislative battle now yielded to analyses of how it happened, as well as of precisely what did happen (the legislation was more than one hundred pages long and contained many provisions not carefully scrutinized during the debate). Supporters uniformly praised Carnahan, with many asserting that "gridlock" had been broken. Considering the lack of movement on the funding problem over the years, the governor's commitment certainly seems the *sine qua non* of the policy decision. Carnahan's leadership lowered legislators' political risk by providing "cover" for them: with both political branches clearly for the tax, responsibility was diffused and risks associated with the increased tax were lessened. In addition, legislators could point to the additional funding to be received by their local schools. In discussing his strategy afterwards, Carnahan specifically mentioned how the timing of the decision would help reduce legislators' risks; the benefits should begin to be apparent by the election of 1994, and in the intervening year and a half the voters would be more likely to forget about the tax increase.[23]

The court decision certainly contributed to lowering risks by throwing into the equation the (potentially catastrophic) costs of doing nothing compared to increasing taxes. So the actions first of the judge and then of the governor were the most instrumental in facilitating the policy decision. Support for taxes already existed among the legislative leadership and even among the membership in earlier years, but lacking then was any outside intervention comparable to the court decision to force the issue and a governor willing to take the risk of leading a campaign for a tax increase. Yet the role of the education lobby is also key: these groups kept the tax increase on the agenda during the policy initiation stage (even using litigation), and kept up the pressure. They supported the formula alteration, which was essential to the tax increase, worked with the reform (accountability) provisions so as to make them more palatable, and campaigned with the governor for reconsideration in the house at the crucial moment when the measure was temporarily defeated.

"House Approves School Aid Bill," *St. Louis Post-Dispatch*, May 11, 1993.

23. Fred Lindecke, "Carnahan's Tax Strategy," *St. Louis Post-Dispatch*, May 16, 1993. One of those praising Carnahan for breaking the gridlock was Chris Straub, Jefferson City School Superintendent and a lobbyist for the school administrators association, who stated: "Finally, the logjam [of the last four sessions] has been broken." ("Senate Approves Education Plan after Day Long Filibuster," *Jefferson City Daily Capital News*, May 14, 1993.)

VI. Policy Implementation

Kent King of MSTA called the victory "the decision of the decade for education," and predicted major impacts on school financing, curriculum, and testing of students. Martha Karlovetz of MNEA commented: "It is a reform backed up with money."[24] The legislation's tax provisions were discussed the most in the last month of the legislative session, but various other provisions would work consequences on curriculum and local taxation in ways yet unforeseen.

New testing, assessment, and punitive measures for school districts were of highest interest to the education lobby. To assess student progress, a standard knowledge test worked out over the course of the 1980s (the MMAT) is to be replaced by a new test of students' ability to use knowledge. Working this out will involve the education lobby in continual interaction with the Department of Elementary and Secondary Education (DESE). School districts and individual schools found academically deficient in terms of their students' assessed knowledge through test scores and other measures will have a state management team sent in to determine why; if still below par two years later, the school board would have to put the superintendent and principal on one-year contracts and eventually revoke tenure of teachers in the affected school(s). School board members in affected districts would also face recall. Developing standards and procedures for undertaking these actions will be a long process, and the education lobby will be working closely with DESE in framing the rules and regulations.

Carnahan signed senate bill 380 at the end of May. By this time, the Republican party was "sharpening campaign trail daggers" because, as education lobbyist Buddy Beetsma of the Missouri School Boards Association said, legislators voting for the tax "stuck their necks out."[25] Carnahan's idea had been that the association would be forgotten by the time of the 1994 elections. To keep the issue alive, one Republican senator filed a constitutional objection to the bill, specifically finding unacceptable the requirement of a $2.75 minimum levy rate without taxpayer approval (as a violation of the Hancock Amendment requiring local votes on all local tax increases).

By this time, school districts with low levy rates had begun to realize that their levy rates had to be set at the minimum, $2.75, by September 1, 1994. More than 100 of the state's 548 school districts were below the $2.75 levy rate required by senate bill 380; most of these were in southern Missouri. Districts began putting the levy increase on the ballot in August 1993 to give themselves several more chances to get voter approval in case of disapproval the first time. However, levy increases to the $2.75 minimum were passed in many districts in August.[26] Many of the remaining districts voted for $2.75 levies the following April.

These concerns and worries, significant as they were, were overshadowed by Hancock II, a tax limitation proposal on the November 1994 ballot. Congressman Mel Hancock and his supporters, explaining that they were angry about the tax increase and particularly the failure to provide for a public vote on the tax increase, circulated initiative petitions for a proposal to reduce state revenues and require popular votes on all state tax increases. Governor Carnahan and education supporters spent

24. Joan Little, "School Aid Bill Will Install Accountability," *St. Louis Post-Dispatch*, May 16, 1993.

25. John Dvorak, "Sponsors of Bill on School Aid Become Targets," *Kansas City Star*, May 23, 1993.

26. Lisa Yortgitis, "Educators to Consider Levy Issue," *Jefferson City Daily Capital News*, August 20, 1993.

untold hours and more than $1.5 million in their ultimately successful effort to kill the proposal.

VII. Senate Bill 380's Overall Significance

One of the ironic twists of all the work that went into senate bill 380 is that the disparities in per student spending between wealthy and poor school districts were not reduced greatly. The court decision in January 1993 found a range of $2,653 to $9,750 per student inequitable, but new formula estimates ranged from $3,000 to $9,000! The change is small, and the reform is thus marginal. Yet the tax increase binds state government's hands by using up a high proportion of the slack under the state revenue ceiling, and also puts the squeeze on other state services (set to suffer a $50 million reduction to contribute money needed for the formula rewrite).

With senate bill 380, education interests won out (somewhat), and business interests lost and will largely foot the bill for the new formula. But even though it was an epochal legislative breakthrough, senate bill 380 is only one noteworthy event in a continuing struggle over influencing state government. The education lobby had to wait a long time for its breakthrough, and the price of the breakthrough was a long period of patience and vigilance while waiting for the right circumstances to come together, for the right time to strike. The two factors that made opportunity available were (1) the court decision, which changed the strategic environment by increasing the costs of standing pat on educational spending for legislators and the governor, and (2) Carnahan's active role in leading the fight for a tax increase. Legislators (mostly Democrat) were thus freed from having to worry about the risk of fa-

voring a tax increase in the antitax climate of opinion because (1) not straightening out the formula would potentially cost far more in the long run due to the court decision[27] and (2) with the formula agreed on, supporting the tax measure was easier because Carnahan was working for it and would sign it.

VIII. Conclusion

This case study demonstrates how a variety of competing interests intervene in the political process to pressure for preferred public policy decisions. Coalitions may form (as in the coalition among business groups, the higher education lobby, and the elementary and secondary education groups), then fall apart; interest groups (business/elementary and secondary education) allied on one campaign, such as Proposition B, may be adversaries on another (senate bill 380), and groups previously allied (education at the college and elementary/secondary levels for Proposition B) may separate without locking horns in later campaigns. Interest groups represent diverse constituencies of individuals and organizations.

A variety of strategies are available to groups over time, but at any one time the structure of policy opportunity may make one strategy particularly advantageous. The teachers' lobby thus found a way of increasing state funding for education in 1993, but at the cost of accepting accountability measures for teachers and school districts. A supportive governor

27. Governor Ashcroft had continually emphasized the high costs of court-imposed desegregation programs for the St. Louis area and for Kansas City school districts; by the time of Judge Kinder's decision, these costs were running more than 6 percent of state general revenues. Avoiding court-ordered foundation formula rewriting and possible court-imposed taxation that would further damage the state budget was considered an important goal.

and a windfall judicial decision made 1993 the time to strike. At another time, major benefits like senate bill 380 might be simply unattainable—no strategy could help. Successful adoption of favorable policies may also require groups to use many different tactics. The Missouri political environment has evolved over time into a moderately strong interest group system. A healthy, pluralist society allows competing interests to lobby openly and encourages public officials to choose policy options favorable to the membership of the organizations that are represented.

CHAPTER 18

Health and Welfare in Missouri

by Jerena E. Giffen and Richard L. Koon

For every talent that poverty has stimulated it has blighted a hundred.—John Gardner

One measure of a state's social development is its historical pattern of concern and care for its dependent citizens. Missouri's pattern reflects an increase in concern for the development and care of the disadvantaged, and increased resources that have allowed governments to act on their concerns. Local responsibility at the community or township level, rather than state control, characterized treatment of the disadvantaged in the original thirteen colonies; Missouri adopted this pattern upon becoming a state.[1] Later, Missouri met its responsibilities by establishing state institutions for those with special needs. In more recent years, many of these institutions have been closed, and care has been provided at home or in community-based institutions.

I. Historical Patterns

The Poor. Before statehood, Missouri was a territory of the United States for nearly twenty years. One welfare program of this era dealt with homeless persons, more commonly referred to as vagrants. Adult vagrants were placed with the highest bidder—a system likened to a "form of personal slavery."[2] The law had one provision that was fairly modern: money obtained from the "employment" was used to pay debtors or provide support for a wife and children. The latter part of that law is similar in intent to the Child Support Enforcement Program, which is administered in the 1990s by the Department of Social Services to secure support payments from parents who are absent from the home as a result of divorce or desertion.

After Missouri became a state, the poor were cared for in almshouses—homes for the poor—and in county poor farms. In 1827 St. Louis County accepted a donation of land for an almshouse. A law passed in the early twentieth century authorized county courts to buy 160 acres for use as poor farms—a designation reflecting the idea that residents would use the land for raising crops to offset operational costs.[3] During their early years, these facilities were used for the custody of a variety of needy—poor of all ages, orphans, and the mentally and physically handicapped including the blind, deaf, and epileptics. In 1918 the number of such county facilities reached

1. Thomas J. Anton, *American Federalism and Public Policy: How the System Works* (New York: Random House, 1989), 43.

2. George B. Mangold, "Social Reform in Missouri: 1820–1920," *Missouri Historical Review* 15 (October 1920), 192.

3. Ibid., 199–200.

its peak of some one hundred institutions. In 1944 legislators found that eighty-seven counties and the city of St. Louis still operated county homes or almshouses. Most of the remaining counties cared for poor or elderly people in private homes or sent them to institutions in neighboring counties.[4] Widespread reports of abuses combined with improved treatment programs eventually resulted in the closing of all such facilities throughout the state.

Children. Territorial laws established a system for dealing with orphans that was to remain in place for nearly a century. Girls were apprenticed until they were eighteen and boys until they were twenty-one. They were to be taught some art, trade, or business, as well as a minimal amount of reading and writing. Apprentices usually received little or no pay for whatever help they provided the master craftsmen to whom they were assigned. Older children who were homeless were also put out as apprentices.

After Missouri became a state, orphanages were established. Mary Whitney Phelps, the wife of Civil War general and later Missouri Governor John Smith Phelps, started a home for orphans in Springfield in the 1860s. Mary Whitney Phelps used a twenty thousand dollar appropriation from Congress to finance the project. The appropriation was one of the few ever approved by the national legislature for an individual.[5]

Other institutions were established for children with special needs. A state school for deaf children, one of the first west of the Mississippi River, was established in Fulton in 1851, and a school for blind children was founded in St. Louis that same year. Each of these schools is still operating; the Missouri School for the Deaf provides elementary and secondary education and special training in a residential school environment, while the Missouri School for the Blind provides elementary and secondary education in a residential day school for those who are legally blind, or deaf and blind.

In more recent times, efforts by decision makers have deemphasized reliance on institutions to focus instead on providing for the needy and neglected in home settings. Abandoned children under the care of the Missouri Department of Social Services are now placed in one-family homes for temporary or even permanent care.

Assistance for most needy children is combined with assistance for their parents under the program of Aid to Families with Dependent Children (AFDC). Funded through combined appropriations from the federal and state governments, the program frequently is the main—sometimes the sole—source of income for ninety thousand families in Missouri. During the 1993–1994 fiscal year, a total of $283 million was available for AFDC payments— $112 million of that from state funds.[6]

The Aged. For many years, needy aged people were cared for by relatives. Those without relatives or resources were housed at poor farms and almshouses operated by local governments or charitable organizations. In 1935 the first old-age assistance law was passed in Missouri, and the first payments were issued in 1936 to some fifty thousand persons age seventy or older. This public assistance program awarded money to needy elderly persons to help pay for food, clothing, and rent. The first appropri-

4. Mark Hale and Jennette Gruener, "Social Services," *Missouri: Its Resources, People, and Institutions,* edited by Noel P. Gist et al. (Columbia: Curators of the University of Missouri, 1950), 478–79.

5. Jerena East Giffen, *First Ladies of Missouri: Their Homes and Their Families* (Jefferson City: Von Hoffmann Press, 1970), 114.

6. Information from the Missouri Division of Family Services.

ation was for $2.5 million, to be matched by the same amount in federal funds.[7] The federal funds were provided under the Federal Social Security Act of 1935, which also established the Old Age and Survivor's Insurance (OASI) program, popularly known as Social Security. Increasingly high percentages of workers have qualified for retirement payments under this program.

Not all of the needy elderly, however, have been covered by such programs. In an effort to provide assistance to some of the people who were not covered, Congress in 1974 established Supplemental Security Income (SSI), an extended program combining assistance to the aged, the permanently disabled, and the blind. SSI payments are supplemented in Missouri by state funds to meet special needs as determined by the Division of Family Services, which is a major part of the Department of Social Services.

II. Health Programs

Public medicine historically has been concerned more with prevention than with treatment of diseases. Government involvement in health care started in this nation with preventive safeguards such as quarantine, vaccination, and sanitation measures.[8]

Epidemic Diseases. Programs aimed at preventing epidemics were the primary concern of public health efforts in the early years of the United States. These programs reflected the types of illnesses prevalent in the late 1700s and the 1800s, such as cholera, a disease nearly extinct in this nation in the twentieth century. Cholera, with symptoms such as stomach cramps and high fever, often threatened the entire population of small communities. Cholera epidemics killed thousands of people in the

state and caused mass evacuations in 1832–1833, 1848–1849, and 1853. Ironically, one of the victims in 1849 was Dr. William Carr Lane, seven-term mayor of St. Louis and the pioneer in establishing public health services in the city.

One of Missouri's earliest and most prominent physicians, Dr. John Sappington of Arrow Rock, rang a bell twice a day to remind residents to take doses of quinine to prevent malaria, another disease that was widespread at the time.[9] Many of these early illnesses were spread by poor sanitation and, therefore, public health efforts were directed toward cleaner facilities, food, and water, as well as increased vaccination.

Today cholera has been controlled by better sanitation, especially by the development of sewage systems throughout the state. Many of these systems have been financed by the sale of bonds authorized by public vote, to be repaid by user charges. Improved sanitation in food handling, cleaner water, and vaccinations have also reduced the impact of cholera. Malaria has been controlled by the elimination of mosquito breeding places. Many of the childhood illnesses—measles, mumps, whooping cough, diphtheria, polio, and typhoid, for example—have been controlled by immunization. Promotion of immunization programs is the responsibility of the Bureau of Immunization in the Department of Health. Prevention of such potentially epidemic diseases as viral hepatitis, bacterial meningitis, and food-borne illnesses is the responsibility of the Bureau of Communicable Disease Control in the Health Department. Efforts to control another serious health threat, the recent epidemic of sexually transmitted diseases, particularly AIDS, are coordinated by the

---

7. *Official Manual, State of Missouri, 1937–1938,* 763.
8. George Rosen, *A History of Public Health* (New York: MD Publications, 1958), 2.

9. Giffen, 57.

Bureau of Sexually Transmitted Diseases and the Bureau of AIDS Prevention.

Premature Births. A program to prevent the birth of premature babies is an example of a modern health care program combining preventive and alleviative approaches. Started in the early 1970s and supported at first entirely by state funds, the program was meant to reduce the infant death rate resulting from premature births. Women diagnosed with high-risk pregnancies were provided funds to pay for close medical supervision prior to delivery and for deliveries at major medical centers that are best equipped for high-risk births. The program also paid for the care of newborns in neonatal intensive care units—one of the most expensive areas of modern hospitals. The program is alleviative since it treats an existing condition, and preventive since it helps to forestall possible health problems. After some twenty years of success as a state effort, the program in July 1990 became funded as part of the federal Medicaid program, which provides health care for eligible needy nationwide.

Health Care Services. For the 1995 fiscal year, Governor Mel Carnahan recommended state expenditures of $242 million for the Department of Health. In essence the department would be providing, on average, fifty dollars' worth of health care for every Missourian. The department was charged with expanding access to preventive and primary care services and reducing health disparities in special populations, especially minority populations.

Medicare and Medicaid. The health care of many elderly and needy Missourians is provided today through two federal programs, Medicare and Medicaid. Medicare, authorized in 1965, provides hospital insurance and medical insurance for people who are age sixty-five and older and who are covered by Old Age and Survivors Insur-

ance (social security). This program is also available to disabled people under sixty-five who are entitled to social security disability benefits.

In contrast, Medicaid is a federally aided, state operated, and state administered program providing medical benefits to low-income people, including the aged, blind, disabled, and members of families with dependent children where one parent is absent, incapacitated, or unemployed. The cost of Medicaid has been significant for Missouri's state government, given increases in health care costs, federal mandates to cover additional groups, and judicial mandates to provide higher rates for health care providers. For the 1996 fiscal year, Carnahan recommended that the state spend almost $2.8 billion for the Medicaid program—$460 million from state funds and $2.3 billion from federal funds. One of every eight Missourians, more than six hundred thousand people, are eligible for Medicaid. The governor also recommended a health care reform program using much of the Medicaid program, but his proposal was not passed by the legislature.

III. Mental Health Programs

In 1847 the state of Missouri began its first mental health program, establishing a state hospital in Fulton, then called Lunatic Asylum #1. Subsequent hospitals in St. Joseph, Nevada, Farmington, and St. Louis were all called lunatic asylums until the early 1900s, when the names were changed to hospitals for the insane, and then merely to state hospitals. Today the Fulton State Hospital includes a 159-bed adult psychiatric center that offers rehabilitation services for long-term-care patients, and a 235-bed maximum-security hospital for persons committed by the criminal courts for psychiatric treatment. The

133-bed St. Joseph State Hospital serves as a psychiatric center for northwest Missouri and provides long-term care for residents of greater Kansas City. The 220-bed St. Louis State Hospital provides care for mentally ill adults in the St. Louis metropolitan region.

Although hospitalization remains necessary for certain treatment programs, administrators are working to shorten the stay of mental patients. Regional centers also have been developed to provide hospital-type care closer to the patients' places of residence. The state hospitals at Nevada and Farmington have been closed and converted into mental health centers serving their regions. Other mental health centers have been established in St. Louis, St. Louis County, Kansas City, and Columbia. Resident treatment for children and adolescents is provided in centers in St. Louis and Cape Girardeau.

A facility at Marshall was first called the Colony for the Feeble-Minded and Epileptic. Its name was changed in the mid-1920s when it was designated a state school to recognize the teaching and training programs available for the young patients. Today the school is one of six centers providing residential care for severely disabled persons. The Division of Mental Retardation and Developmental Disabilities serves a population with mental retardation, cerebral palsy, head injuries, autism, epilepsy, and certain learning disabilities. The division also has eleven regional centers, which provide assessment and case management services including oversight for community placement facilities.

Establishment of a separate cabinet-level agency concerned with mental health did not occur until the Omnibus Reorganization Act of 1974. The act separated care for mental diseases from the administration of health and welfare programs by creating the new Department of Mental Health. Three major missions are identified by mental health administrators in the 1990s: preventing mental disorders, developmental disabilities, and substance abuse; treating and rehabilitating Missourians who suffer from those conditions; and improving public understanding and attitudes.[10]

IV. Public Welfare Programs

Assisting the unfortunate has long been recognized as an important, though often controversial, government responsibility. Just as the early colonists continued to observe numerous other English traditions, they carried on the tradition of the English poor law, which consisted of a system of local parish relief funded by local taxes. This system provided cash and in-kind assistance to those not expected to work and assisted the able-bodied with the raw materials to make goods for sale. By the eighteenth century, this system had evolved into a system of workhouses where the unemployed lived and worked at various tasks.[11]

By 1789 public assistance was one of the largest items of expenditure in many American cities. In the nineteenth century, however, responsibility for providing aid to certain groups of poor gradually began shifting to state governments. By midcentury the federal government began to provide some assistance to disabled veterans and their widows and orphans, and some aid to former slaves.[12]

In the early twentieth century, the trend toward state responsibility of caring for the poor accelerated. Wisconsin enacted the first workmen's compensation law in 1908. By 1930 most states had workmen's

---

10. *Official Manual, State of Missouri 1993–1994*, 458.

11. Irwin Garfinkel and Robert Haveman, "Income Transfer Policy in the United States," in *The Handbook of Social Intervention*, edited by Edward Seidman (Beverly Hills, Calif.: Sage Publications Inc., 1983), 481–82.

12. Ibid.

Table 18-1. Characteristics of a "Typical" AFDC Family

Family composition:	Mother with two children
Age of mother at birth of first child:	22 years
Length of time on welfare:	19 months
Educational attainment:	11.2 years
Average family monthly grant:	$265
Geographic location:	52% in St. Louis City, St. Louis County, or Jackson County;
	48% in rest of the state.

Source: *Missouri on the Move, Fiscal Year 1995* (Jefferson City: Governor's Office, 1994), p. 54.

compensation programs, more than half had widows' pension programs, and several had programs of aid for the aged. In 1932 Wisconsin and New York enacted the first unemployment compensation programs. Missouri had the distinction of enacting the first mother's aid law in the United States in 1911. In fact, the Missouri law was enacted prior to the 1913 establishment of a state agency responsible for dependent and neglected children.[13]

The Great Depression in the 1930s precipitated a dramatic shift in responsibility for financing and administering public assistance programs. The federal government's involvement in providing welfare income began with the goal of providing a means of subsistence for a large segment of the population that otherwise had none. When the Aid to Dependent Children program (ADC) was enacted in the 1930s, 88 percent of the families that received benefits were needy because the father had died. The proportion of ADC (or AFDC) children whose fathers were deceased fell to 42 percent by 1949 and 3 percent by 1977. In the latter year, more than 80 percent of the families on AFDC consisted of divorced, separated, deserted, or unmarried parents.

Most of the remainder were families with incapacitated and unemployed fathers.[14]

Since the Great Depression, the nature and emphasis of welfare in this country has gradually shifted from a substitute for work that does not exist to a supplement for low earnings and an alternative to work.[15] Prior to the 1960s, women with children generally were regarded as unemployable since a woman's place was considered to be in the home caring for children. In recent years, however, women have entered the labor force in unprecedented numbers. The rationale for excluding able-bodied welfare mothers from labor force participation is now questioned, especially when the majority of nonwelfare mothers with children are in the labor force.

This changing perception of the role of women in the labor market has led to changes in the administration of the AFDC program. Between 1935 and 1962, the federal government did not stress work requirements in return for welfare benefits. In fact, work requirements in return for

13. Garfinkel, 481–82. Missouri State Social Security Commission, *Index of Public Assistance in Missouri* (1939), 319.

14. Nancy Dickinson, "Which Welfare Strategies Work?" *Social Work* 31 (July/August 1986): 266. In 1962 the ADC program was expanded and renamed Aid to Families with Dependent Children (AFDC). By 1992, 206,000 individuals, about 4 percent of Missouri's population, were receiving aid under this program.

15. Lawrence M. Mead, *Beyond Entitlement* (New York: The Free Press, 1986), 69.

AFDC benefits were prohibited prior to 1962.

What makes this situation important is that one-half of all children born in America will spend part of their childhood in a family headed by a mother who is divorced, separated, unwed, or widowed. About one-half of these families are headed by single women who are poor and dependent to some extent on welfare. Studies have shown that the mothers and children in such families tend to have poorer than average mental health and to use a disproportionate share of community mental health services. Also, single mothers heading families dependent on welfare tend to have lower educational levels and lower self-esteem than women in two-parent families.[16]

Even more distressing is that in comparison with children who grow up in two-parent (husband-wife) families, children from welfare families headed by a single mother are on average less successful as adults. These children are more likely to drop out of school, give birth out of wedlock, divorce or separate, experience substance abuse problems, be involved with the criminal justice system, and become dependent on welfare.[17]

The number of children living in families at or below the poverty line is increasing. In 1966, 18 percent of all children under eighteen years of age lived in poverty; the current figure is more than 21 percent. There is little optimism that this trend will be reversed soon since both the number of individuals living in poverty and the number of AFDC caseloads continue to grow. In the 1993 fiscal year an average of 14.1 million individuals, 5.4 percent of the population, received AFDC each month, the largest number in the history of the program. This included approximately 4.6 million adults, mainly single women, and an estimated 9.5 million children.[18]

During the 1991 fiscal year, the most recent year for which data are available, AFDC benefits and administrative expenditures alone cost American taxpayers more than $30 billion. It is obvious that it is very expensive to allow large segments of the population to live on welfare. There are enormous costs associated with AFDC and other benefits such as Medicaid, public housing, mental health services, food stamps, and child care, in addition to collateral costs associated with substance abuse, child abuse, crime, and illiteracy. The American Public Welfare Association estimates that total spending by all levels of government is more than $225 billion per year on seventy-five separate public welfare programs, and that approximately 4 percent of the total U.S. economy is devoted to public welfare. These figures do not include expenditures for assistance programs available to both the middle class and the poor, such as Social Security and Medicare.[19]

In all fifty states, the income threshold for receiving AFDC is below the officially established poverty level. Each state sets its own standard of need for food, clothing, and shelter, and AFDC payments are then calculated on this formula. In Missouri, the 1993 standard of need for a family of

16. Larry Bumpass, "Children and Marital Disruption: A Replication and Update," *Demography* 21 (February 1984): 71–82. Irwin Garfinkel and Sara S. McLanahan, *Single Mothers and Their Children: A New American Dilemma?* (Washington, D.C.: Urban Institute Press, 1986), chapter 2.

17. Irwin Garfinkel, "Welfare Policy in America," Institute for Research on Poverty, University of Wisconsin–Madison, Discussion Paper No. 847–87 (October 1987), 1–2.

18. U.S. Department of Health and Human Services, Information Memorandum No. ACF-IM–94–3 (June 14, 1994), 6.

19. Telephone interview, American Public Welfare Association, June 15, 1992.

three was $312, but the state had not allocated sufficient funds to meet that level; as a result, the maximum AFDC grant for a family of three per month was $292. If the maximum food stamp grant were also counted, this family received a total of $596 per month. This same family would have needed $1,027 to rise above the poverty line.

V. The Permanent Poverty Group

Census data indicate that although 1993 was a year of economic recovery, the number of Americans living in poverty reached the highest level in three decades. The number of children growing up in poverty increased to 15.7 million in 1993, almost 23 percent of all children in the United States. A little more than half of these children lived in families receiving public assistance. The large number of people on welfare has helped fuel the calls for welfare reform, particularly because many analysts and political leaders now believe that a hard-core poverty "underclass" exists, sustained by a public welfare system that contributes to dependency and family breakup, and that undermines the incentive to enter the labor market.[20]

The concern about a hard-core poverty underclass is based on a disturbing percentage of welfare recipients who continue on welfare for interminable periods of time,[21] and the disturbing number who grew up in welfare families. This concern does not extend to many welfare recipients—the elderly and disabled, for example—who are not expected to be able to get off the welfare rolls. The focus is largely on welfare recipients who have the health and energy to allow them to participate in the labor force, mainly the young mothers who receive funds under the AFDC program. In earlier years, the view was widely accepted that society would be stronger if these children were being raised by a mother who was home to care for them. Now that view is being called into question, given the disturbing percentage of those children who themselves end up on welfare as well as the example of the large number of children being raised by single mothers who are not on welfare.

Why is there a permanent poverty group? Three explanations have been offered for its development:[22]

1. An explanation based on expectancy theory assumes that people who fail repeatedly will lose their motivation to try. Those who succeed gain confidence, while those who fail lose confidence. For some individuals, welfare becomes a trap that increases the individual's passivity and isolation. People become overwhelmed by circumstances and lose the capacity to use available opportunities to change their condition. The increased isolation and feelings of lack of control decrease feelings of self-worth, which in turn play a critical role in family structure patterns.

2. Cultural models focus on the cultural patterns that develop in poverty neighborhoods, embracing a population that "feels excluded from society, rejects commonly accepted values, and suffers from behavioral as well as income deficiencies." For

20. Center on Budget and Policy Priorities, "Despite Economic Recovery, Poverty and Income Trends Are Disappointing," *Newsletter*, October 1994. Kenneth Auletta, *The Underclass* (New York: Random House, 1982).

21. In his budget message, Carnahan reported that 6 percent of Missourians on welfare remained there more than five years, and 18 percent remained on welfare for two to five years. *Missouri on the Move* (Jefferson City: Governor's Office, 1994), 56.

22. David T. Ellwood, "The Origins of 'Dependency': Choices, Confidence, or Culture?" *Focus* 12 (Spring/Summer 1989): 6.

such adverse values to develop and persist, groups of people must be isolated geographically and socially from the rest of society. These groups live together and have little contact with the rest of society. Groups of disadvantaged and relatively unsuccessful people who share the same values often pass their values to succeeding generations. "Families with distorted values, or children raised in homes where welfare was the primary source of income, find welfare, out-of-wedlock births, and lack of work a normal and acceptable fact of life." As a result, the pathologies of one generation are passed on to the next.[23]

3. Rational choice models view long-term welfare dependency as a series of reasoned choices in light of available options. The rational choice for a typical single welfare mother with two children may be to remain on welfare rather than take a minimum wage job with no health benefits. For a large number of Missouri women receiving welfare, working will not immediately improve their economic situation and allow them to earn their way out of poverty. In Missouri, a woman with two children who earns ten thousand dollars a year (or roughly five dollars an hour) is only slightly better off than a woman who remains on welfare. The working woman will have her earnings, plus be eligible for an earned income tax credit. On the other hand, she will have to pay social security taxes and she probably will have substantial work expenses, including day care for her children and transportation to and from work. Most important, she will lose her Medicaid protection, her food stamps allotment will be reduced, and she may lose what eligibility she has for housing assistance, energy assistance, child care assistance, or educa-

tion assistance. Her five-dollar-an-hour job may not include health benefits to replace Medicaid.[24]

These considerations point out some of the problems with our present AFDC system, problems caused by competing policy goals—trying to provide a basic level of support for the poor, while trying not to provide support so generous that it encourages people to avoid work and become dependent on government public assistance payments. The problem is complicated further by the fact that many of the recipients of AFDC aid are children. Many would argue that children should be guaranteed an adequate level of support without being expected to work or assume responsibility for the actions of their parents.

VI. Welfare Reform

Fighting poverty and fixing the "welfare problem" have proved to be persistently difficult tasks. Since the advent of the Great Society programs of the 1960s, there have been many programs targeted at helping people escape poverty, thereby reducing the welfare rolls. Some of the major programs included:

Work Incentive program (WIN), 1967–1989
Comprehensive Employment and Training Act (CETA), 1973–1981
Job Training Partnership Act (JTPA), 1981–Present
Job Opportunities and Basic Skills Training program (JOBS), 1989–present.

In addition, numerous smaller programs such as Job Corps, Concentrated Employment Program, National Supported Work

---

23. Ellwood, 10–11. See also Kenneth Auletta, *The Underclass* (New York: Random House, 1982).

24. Detailed calculations for various income levels, based on Pennsylvania's welfare payments in 1989, are provided in Institute for Research on Poverty, *Focus* 12 (Spring 1989), 8.

Demonstration, Negative Income Tax Experiments, and the Manpower Development and Training Act were created to provide education, job training, job search assistance, and work opportunities for people living in poverty and on welfare. In many respects, these programs were probably successful at providing education and job skills training to numerous individuals. In aggregate, however, they probably did not move a lot of people out of poverty and off welfare.

Federal Government Proposals. During the 1992 presidential election, candidate Bill Clinton again raised the issue of the "welfare problem." He frequently criticized the present welfare system as trapping people in poverty and encouraging dependency, and promised to end welfare as we know it.

Clinton's recommendations for welfare reform included:

1. Expansion of the Earned Income Tax Credit (EITC) for the poor, so that the EITC will pay a poor person forty dollars for every one hundred dollars that person earns in wages, thus providing additional incentive to work.

2. Provision of health insurance for everyone, so that welfare recipients should not have to worry about losing their health coverage—Medicaid—if they choose to leave welfare and go to work. This proposal was part of the extensive national debate on health care.

3. Provisions for child care for welfare mothers who go to work.

4. Strengthening the child support enforcement system, so that more children will be supported by now delinquent fathers rather than public welfare.

5. Providing more education and training programs to make welfare recipients more employable. The most likely change is to modify the Job Opportunities and Basic Skills Training program (JOBS) to place a greater emphasis on work. While education is very important, some of the more successful JOBS projects from around the nation are finding that education in combination with work, or work experience prior to education, produces better long-term results. Additional sanctions are likely to be imposed.

6. Increasing flexibility of JOBS to address the problems of people who reenter the welfare system. Single mothers in typical entry-level jobs often do not stay in those jobs for long. If they have a sick child, or if they get sick, and they don't have sick leave or vacation days to use, they often lose their employment.

7. Imposing limits on the length of time that healthy people can receive cash assistance.[25]

Clinton's recommendations were not adopted, having been postponed by Congress until after the 1994 health care debate.

Welfare Reform in Missouri. Missouri has several welfare reform initiatives currently in the planning or initial implementation stages. First is the Twenty-First Century project in the Kansas City area. This project will place AFDC recipients on a job and divert the recipients' cash grant to the employer in order to supplement workers' wages for up to forty-eight months. The recipient will be working and will continue to receive other benefits such as food stamps and Medicaid as long as they are eligible. The employer will be responsible for training the recipient through a defined series of job progressions, and will be expected to pay the worker above the minimum wage level.

Missouri has two projects in operation—in Kansas City and St. Louis—that are

25. "Ellwood on Welfare Reform," *W-Memo*, American Public Welfare Association 5:8 (September 1993): 23–26.

providing education, employment, and training services to parents who are not paying child support. Missouri also has received a federal waiver that will allow for a "Learnfare" type of experiment in several selected school districts. Missouri's program will provide education, skill training, and support services to children from AFDC families who are having school attendance problems. Each school district selected to participate in this project will hire its own school-based counselor/case worker and will receive funding from the state Department of Social Services for its administrative and services costs. If a child's attendance problem continues, the family risks losing a portion of its AFDC cash grant.

Governor Carnahan recommended to the 1994 General Assembly a welfare reform initiative, focused on expanded education for welfare recipients, encouragement of employment, and increased use of technology. The technology included an electronic benefits transfer system that would give welfare recipients a single debit card, much like a credit card, which would reduce fraud and lower state costs for printing and mailing checks and food stamp coupons. The General Assembly did pass a welfare reform measure, including the electronic benefits transfer system and a program designed to help teenage mothers avoid additional pregnancies. The assumption of that program is that mothers with only one child may well return to high school, complete their degree, and become employable, but that arrival of the second child creates enough additional obstacles to discourage a return to school.

VII. Conclusion

Human services—health and welfare programs—involve a substantial part of the Missouri budget. In the 1994 fiscal year, the departments of mental health, health, and social services had budgets totaling more than $3.4 billion, about one-third of all state government expenditures. More than half of these social service funds are provided by the federal government, but that still leaves a staggering sum of $1.5 billion or so provided each year from Missouri funds, a figure equal to the amount of state money spent on higher education and highways and transportation combined.

States began to assume many of these responsibilities in the nineteenth century, only to feel a great sense of relief when the federal government assumed a greater share of responsibility, starting during the Great Depression. One underlying thrust of the state human services program has been to increase the number of social service recipients who contribute economically to society. This is represented, for example, by programs to help disabled people develop sufficiently to work at a job.

The high costs of social services today, and in some cases their limited impact, have led to revisions in policies and sharp debates about future policy making. In the case of mental health, various state institutions have been closed or converted into community treatment centers, moving from expensive institutional care to less expensive residential care, and also emphasizing individualized development. In the case of assistance to poor people, attention has focused on programs that will help healthy young people get the training and circumstances that will enable them to work enough to be able to support their families.

CHAPTER 19

Economic Development, Energy, and the Environment in Missouri

by Robert Dewhirst

The era of low cost energy is almost dead. Popeye is running out of spinach.—Peter G. Petersen, Secretary of Commerce in the Nixon administration, testifying before the Senate at his confirmation hearings in 1972

The task of meeting the demands for economic development, energy, and environmental protection has sparked much rhetoric from public officials and interested citizens alike. The increase in talk, however, has been coupled with decreasing expenditures to meet the challenges posed within each of these areas. Grappling with challenges posed in these three areas has strained the American federal system. The national government, increasingly strapped with its own fiscal problems, has told the states that they will have to rely on their own resources even more than in the past to develop answers to these serious and complex issues.

State governments feel a tension between having a clean environment on the one hand, and a desire to grow economically and have an abundance of energy on the other. One side of the debate argues for economic growth and abundant energy, while the other side works for a clean and safe environment. During each of the two energy crises in the 1970s, the federal government responded to public pressures to set aside environmental regulation deadlines in favor of attaining energy and economic growth goals.

This tension is at the heart of a second controversy confronting state governments. The conflict has become a zero-sum game. First, the universal inclination for every state is to work for maximum economic growth and abundant energy within one's own state while exporting the state's environmental problems (such as chemical, biological, or nuclear waste) into other regions of the nation. Citizens have become increasingly hostile not only to having hazardous waste dumped nearby but even to having waste transported through their area to distant disposal sites. Second, states want to attract economic development, even at the expense of neighboring states. Hence, state politicians work to make their state as attractive as possible for outside developers.

For the past half century the federal government has assumed primary responsibility for maintaining and promoting the economic health of the national economy. The federal government has attempted to meet this responsibility by manipulating such prominent macroeconomic tools as monetary and fiscal policies. Monetary policies involve manipulating the flow of money in the economy by changing the interest rates charged for borrowing. Fiscal policies deal with governmental taxing and spending.

State governments traditionally have focused their economic development efforts on the level of microeconomic policies—those dealing with individual businesses. During the past three decades states have become increasingly aggressive in promoting themselves as places for businesses to locate or expand. Governors and their entourages visit the headquarters of businesses in other states or even overseas. "Winning" a new business for a state can help ensure jobs and economic expansion for state residents, and political rewards, such as winning reelection, for public officials.

The nation needs substantial energy to fuel economic growth. At the national level, significant efforts were made in the 1970s to establish a federal energy policy. In the 1980s a new administration reversed course, believing that decisions about the supply of energy should be made in the private sector, governed by market forces. That free market pattern will probably prevail for the foreseeable future. Pressures from industrial interest groups plus growing budgetary limitations have combined to reduce the work of active regulatory agencies.

Other energy issues are likely to remain equally formidable. The publicly stated goal of attaining national energy independence from overseas suppliers is still far from being achieved. One possible solution, nuclear power, continues to be extremely controversial and expensive. Only two factors appear to remain certain. One, energy needs are going to continue to exceed domestic supplies, and two, financing energy

needs will strain both the public and private sectors.

The need for energy has raised significant environmental issues. For example, energy production and consumption of all types (but primarily motor fuels, electricity production, and natural gas consumption) have accounted for about 75 percent of all air pollution nationally.[1] At the federal government level, most emphasis has been placed on attaining energy and economic development goals, even at the expense of possible long-term environmental damage. However, such highly publicized events as the Exxon Valdez oil spill or the Three Mile Island accident have swayed public concerns away from energy and economic development goals and toward environmental goals, for at least a short time.

I. Economic Development Issues

Economic Development Efforts in Missouri. State public officials have become more aggressive in their efforts to establish programs and policies promoting the economic development of Missouri. The governor and other statewide-elected officials increasingly have traveled throughout the United States and abroad trying to attract new businesses to the state. In 1984 Missouri voters approved an amendment to the state constitution changing the name of an existing department to the Department of Economic Development, thereby also mandating a shift in primary emphasis. The department was made the state's main agency for attracting capital investment to Missouri and helping firms create jobs. Efforts have been made to attract tourists, develop existing businesses, train and retrain

---

1. Environmental Improvement and Energy Resources Authority, Missouri Department of Natural Resources, *Missouri Statewide Energy Study*, vol. 1 (May 1992), 45.

workers, create targeted tax abatements and enterprise zones, and help finance businesses.

The Department of Economic Development houses six business regulation divisions and the divisions of tourism and job development and training. The department's economic development programs are divided into the following areas:

- The National Business Development program markets the state to businesses nationwide, responds to inquiries, and tries to match company needs with sites in the state. Its employees accompany business leaders during tours of possible sites throughout the state.
- The Research and Planning group provides prospective companies with an array of information about the state, including statistics on such factors as available skilled labor, transportation facilities, taxes, and utility rates.
- The International Business Development program attempts to attract foreign investment to the state and to develop international markets for goods produced in Missouri. The program maintains offices in Düsseldorf, Germany; Tokyo, Japan; and Seoul, South Korea.
- The Existing Business Development Program works to retain businesses in the state and helps them to expand their efforts.
- The Small Business Office helps small businesses get started and helps existing small firms to expand. The office also seeks new markets for the products of small businesses.
- The Office of Minority Business provides technical, financial, and managerial assistance to minority and women business owners.
- The High Technology Program provides information and research grants to help technologically based businesses.
- The Missouri Economic Development Information System (MEDIS) is a computer system providing businesses with information about economic opportunities in the state.
- The Information Services staff produces printed and electronic materials promoting the benefits to businesses of locating in or expanding in Missouri.
- The Tax Benefit Program produces tax studies for firms interested in moving to or expanding in the state. The staff also administers the state's enterprise zone program. Created in 1982, this program provides reduced taxes for businesses agreeing to locate in economically depressed areas targeted for redevelopment. Missouri is one of twenty-two states having such a program.[2]

The department, together with elected officials throughout the state government, has produced an overall economic development program similar to, and competitive with, those efforts found in most states. For example, Missouri governors and other state officials frequently have led official trade delegations overseas. In addition, the state is the site of two foreign trade zones, one in Kansas City and the other in St. Louis County. Foreign trade zones can stimulate the economic development of surrounding areas by providing participating businesses with a special status of not being legally within United States Customs territory. Merchandise, whether produced abroad or domestically, may be brought into a zone under favorable conditions, such as being exempted from customs duties or excise taxes and not being governed by quota limitations.

2. *Official Manual, State of Missouri, 1993–1994* (Jefferson City: Secretary of State, 1994), 333–36.

How have the state's efforts been viewed by others? One evaluation that assessed states on their desirability as sites for factory relocation ranked Missouri twenty-second among the states. Another study that rated states on their treatment of small businesses (using criteria such as capital availability, labor resources, and level of business activity) listed Missouri thirty-second. Two other analyses have rated the state's economic climate as "just above average," with employment being the primary area of concern. While such ranking schemes have been criticized and debated at length, they do provide at least an attempt to assess how well states have been performing. In the all-important measure of employment, Missouri has grown by 38 percent since 1969, compared with 52 percent nationwide.[3]

Economic Growth Patterns in Missouri. How well has the state's economy developed? In terms of per capita income, Missouri has grown at much the same rate as the rest of the nation—per capita personal income in Missouri was 95 percent of the national average in both 1960 and 1992. This means that in the 1990s Missouri tends to rank near the middle of the fifty states in most personal economic indicators: twenty-fourth in per capita personal income, thirtieth in median household income, twenty-third in average annual pay, and twenty-eighth in average hourly earnings of production workers on manufacturing payrolls. Finally, the statewide ranking of disposable personal income per capita of Missouri's residents increased from twenty-eighth in 1980 to twenty-sixth in 1993.

In terms of the gross state product (GSP), the total production of all economic goods and services in the state, Missouri grew from $41.1 billion in 1977 to $103.7 billion in 1990. This represents an average annual growth rate of 7.4 percent per year, compared with an annual national growth rate averaging 8.3 percent during that period. The GSP is a state's counterpart of the better-known gross domestic product, which represents the total value of goods and services produced within a nation during a selected time. Missouri's lower than average growth rate is reflected in the state's lower than average population growth. While the state's population has increased steadily, the rate of growth has been less than that for the nation as a whole, so that Missouri's portion of the national population fell from 2.4 percent in 1958 to 2.03 percent in 1993.

The state's ability to attract foreign investment has been of particular economic and political importance. One study found that 180 foreign-owned companies had 277 plant sites employing more than 40,000 workers in the state. Many of the employees were in firms with owners from the United Kingdom and Canada (21 percent each), with Germany third (13 percent), and Japan fourth (11 percent). These businesses manufactured such things as auto parts, electronics, and food products. Why were these firms interested in Missouri? The state's central location near many of the nation's markets and manufacturing plants was found to be the main reason. The state's moderate business and political climates, plus a strong work ethic among employees, also appeared to be important factors.[4]

3. Anne M. Bowman and Richard C. Kearney, *The Resurgence of the States* (Englewood Cliffs, N.J.: Prentice Hall, 1986), 196–97; *Missouri Statewide Energy Study*, 25; "Just Average: Missouri, Illinois Rated Mediocre in Economic Climate," *St. Louis Post-Dispatch*, April 24, 1991; *Federal Reserve Bank of St. Louis Review*, Federal Reserve Bank: St. Louis, May/June 1990, 27, and Bureau of Economic Analysis (Regional Economic Measurement Division), U.S. Department of Commerce, Washington, D.C., 1991.

4. "Foreign Firms Increase Investment in Missouri," *St. Louis Post-Dispatch*, November 24, 1993, and "Mod-

In this search for new business, Missouri has been in intense competition with other states. For example, Missouri for many years ranked second nationally in passenger car assemblies. In recent years, however, only one new automotive plant has been constructed (in Wentzville), and even it has had production stoppages and slowdowns at times. On the other hand, some existing plants have reduced their work force at times. In addition, Missouri was unsuccessful in competing for new plants, such as a Saturn plant, which went to Tennessee, and a Toyota plant, which went to Kentucky. As a result, the state's automotive production fell from 12 percent in 1978 to 7.4 percent of the national total in 1992, and Missouri's ranking among the states declined from second to fourth, falling behind Ohio and then Illinois.[5]

Missouri also has long been a major site for the defense industry. For example, the state has been ranked seventh nationally in terms of Department of Defense expenditures, fifth in per capita Department of Defense expenditures, and second in per capita Department of Defense contracts awarded. The state's major primary contractor has been McDonnell-Douglas, headquartered in St. Louis County. But the state also has Allied Signal Aerospace Company in Kansas City, plus numerous firms producing subcontracting work for these and other major firms around the nation.

One of the major growth industries in the state has been tourism, which added more than $11.2 billion to the state's economy in 1991 through the efforts of about 250,000 workers. While the state has many popular tourist attractions in the St. Louis and Kansas City metropolitan areas plus the Lake of the Ozarks district in central Missouri, much of the state's more recent tourist development has taken place in Branson in the Ozark region. More than five million people visited Branson in 1992, with many attending one of the live country music shows for which the area is best known.

Job growth in Missouri has varied markedly among sectors of the state's economy. The largest employment gains have come from service industries—hotels and lodging, amusement industries, and health services, for example—which grew by 113 percent from 1969 through 1990. This statewide development was typical of, but smaller than, trends recorded for the nation as a whole. Likewise, during this same time the finance (banks), insurance, and real estate sector grew by 78 percent, while construction and retail trade grew by 49 percent each. However, statewide manufacturing employment declined by 6 percent, with the most significant decline in the manufacture of durable goods such as automobiles, airplanes, electronics, and furniture. Hence, statewide employment shifted from manufacturing to other segments of the economy, a pattern similar to nationwide trends.[6]

In sum, Missouri has been growing economically, but at a slightly slower rate than the nation as a whole, a rate roughly comparable with neighboring states in the Midwest. Missouri's economic development efforts are similar to those of most

eration, Location Two of State's Strengths," *St. Louis Post-Dispatch*, November 24, 1993.

5. *Statistical Abstract for Missouri: 1993*, 137; Research and Planning Program, Department of Economic Development, *Missouri's Economic Development Status 1993*, December 9, 1993, 2. In 1994 automobile manufacturers announced expansion of production in their Missouri plants, raising the possibility that Missouri might again achieve a higher ranking.

6. *Missouri Statewide Energy Study*, 26–28; *Federal Reserve Bank of St. Louis Review*, 27; Bureau of Economic Analysis (Regional Economic Measurement Division), United States Department of Commerce, Washington, D.C., 1991.

states, in that each year more effort and resources have been devoted just to keeping pace with accelerated competition.

II. Energy Production, Consumption, and Controversy

Energy has been a continuing source of concern in Missouri. On the one hand, Missouri power plants have generated ample supplies of electricity, even enabling producers to export large quantities to other states. Overall statewide production of electricity has increased steadily during the past decade. On the other hand, the state overall has lacked the capacity to produce fuels to meet the needs of consumers, and it consistently has been a major importer of natural gas, coal, and petroleum.

The state government's energy policies have been made by the governor working in conjunction with the General Assembly and in part implemented by the Division of Energy, a component of the Department of Natural Resources. The Division of Energy has been assigned three tasks: to help reduce energy costs in the state by designing conservation and development programs; to encourage the efficient use of energy resources; and to administer federal court-ordered oil overcharge funds.

Statewide energy production has been limited to coal electrical (83 percent), nuclear power (15 percent), and hydroelectric generation (2 percent). Coal mined in Missouri has accounted for about 17 percent of that consumed statewide. More widespread use of Missouri coal has been limited by its comparatively high sulfur content, which requires special control devices to prevent air pollution when the coal is burned. This high sulfur content led to the 1993 closing of Missouri's largest coal-mining facility, the Thomas Hill Mine in the north central part of the state. Leaders of Associated

Electric, a cooperative headquartered in Springfield, said they would instead import low-sulfur coal from western states.[7]

The demand for energy in Missouri increased steadily through the 1960s and part of the 1970s, but then remained flat for much of the 1980s. The reduction in demand reflected conservation efforts by motorists concerned about the price of gasoline, and by electric utilities that found it less expensive to urge consumers to conserve than to build and operate new power plants. By 1990 state residents were spending about $9.7 billion each year (or about $26 million each day) on energy. Missouri residents spend about 10.6 percent of their annual income on energy, compared with the national average of 10.2 percent. Explained another way, converting all energy use into terms of petroleum consumption, the average Missourian uses about thirty-six barrels, or fifteen hundred gallons of petroleum, each year.[8] A breakdown of annual energy consumption in Missouri is listed in Table 19–1.

Missouri uses less power per person than the average state, ranking thirty-fifth in per capita energy consumption. Missourians have lower heating costs than residents of northern states and lower cooling costs than residents of southern states. Missouri is above the national per capita average in consumption for residential, commercial, and transportation uses, but well below average in the industrial sector. In sum, Missouri's energy production and consumption patterns have tended to mirror those of the nation as a whole, with demand often exceeding local production, hence requiring the state to import fuel.

7. "State's Main Coal Mine to Close Next Month," *St. Louis Post-Dispatch,* January 12, 1993.
8. *Missouri Statewide Energy Study,* 9.

Table 19-1. Fuel Sources for Energy Consumed in Missouri, 1987

Fuel Source	Percentage of Statewide Consumption
Petroleum products (motor gasoline and distillate fuels) (imported)	42.4
Coal (from Missouri, Illinois, and Wyoming)	36.6
Domestic natural gas (imported from Southwest)	16.3
Nuclear generation of electricity (Callaway)	4.7
Hydroelectric plants (Lake of the Ozarks etc.)	1.0
Total	101.0

Note: Total exceeds 100 percent due to rounding

III. A Missouri Energy Case Study: The Callaway Nuclear Facility

The development of the Callaway nuclear facility is a classic example of the inherent tensions that develop between society's desires to have ample supplies of energy while also having a clean, safe environment. The Callaway facility is a massive nuclear reactor constructed in rural Callaway County, one hundred miles west of St. Louis and ten miles southeast of Fulton, near the small town of Reform. The plant was constructed for and is operated by Union Electric, a large utility headquartered in St. Louis. Union Electric began construction in 1976, the first nuclear fuel was delivered in late 1982, and operations began in 1984. The eleven-hundred-megawatt plant cost $2.85 billion and was the eighty-eighth plant to be licensed in the United States—the first and still only plant in Missouri. During its first year of operation the plant set a national record by producing 8.47 billion kilowatt-hours of electricity. The plant employs about nine hundred workers and generates about 25 percent of the electricity in the Union Electric system, serving the eastern half of Missouri and about one million customers in Illinois.

Throughout its history, the Callaway nuclear plant has attracted opposition from not only environmentalists but also those opposed to paying the larger utility bills (originally electric utilities had thought that nuclear power would be cheaper than conventional power, but ultimately it proved to be more expensive). Union Electric officials have fought off opponents who have challenged the company in the state's courts, General Assembly, and Public Service Commission, with election referenda, and before the federal Nuclear Regulatory Commission. Statewide voters frequently were brought into the fray. In 1976 an initiative proposal to prevent the utility from charging customers for construction work in progress won electoral approval. Construction costs could only be passed on to customers after the plant was producing electricity. In 1980 Union Electric successfully defeated an initiative proposal that would have prohibited the operation of a nuclear plant in the state until the federal government approved a method to dispose of radioactive waste. In 1984 a $4.8 million campaign, financed largely by Union Electric, buried another initiative proposal that sought to limit electrical rate increases and prohibit utilities from charging customers for their errors. In addition, five religious orders sought unsuccessfully to have Union Electric stockholders require management to update the company's study of the cost of decommissioning the Callaway plant.

In another arena, Union Electric officials asked for increases in electricity rates to recover costs of constructing the plant. Union Electric sought rate increases worth $639 million in Missouri and $78 million in Illinois, phased in over a five-year period. The proposed increases were sufficiently high that the General Assembly passed a modified "rate shock" bill designed to ease the rate of increase in utility costs. In addition, the company lost in state court in an effort to recover $106 million in funds spent on the never finished Callaway II, a planned matching nuclear facility on the same site.

By the end of the 1980s, operation of the Callaway plant continued with only occasional public controversy. In 1988 the facility ranked fourth among all nuclear plants in the nation in producing electricity. By the end of the decade the federal Nuclear Regulatory Commission was citing the plant for maintaining a consistently good safety record.

In sum, the breadth and intensity of feelings on both sides of the nuclear power issue nationwide have been illustrated in the protracted struggle among Missourians over the construction of the Callaway plant. Part of the objection was concern about environmental problems, particularly the disposal of nuclear waste, illustrating again the extent to which the energy and environmental debates are intertwined.

IV. Environmental Issues in Missouri

Statewide environmental policies have been made by the governor and the General Assembly, and most often have been implemented by the state's Department of Natural Resources. The department's divisions of Environmental Quality and of Geology and Land Survey have been especially important. The Division of Environmental Quality has six commissions acting as administrative policy-making bodies:

Air Conservation, Clean Water, Hazardous Waste Management, Land Reclamation, Safe Drinking Water, and Soil and Water Districts.

The state has been confronted with an array of potential pollution problems. Missouri has extensive urban areas whose industrial development and dense populations contribute to pollution. In addition, the state has a well-developed agricultural sector with pollution problems, such as those stemming from use of herbicides and pesticides. Missouri residents have felt strongly that polluters should pay for cleaning up their messes. A poll reported that 86 percent of state residents wanted industries that polluted the environment to finance their cleanup, even if the action later caused consumer prices to rise. Respondents said they were most concerned about having clean drinking water, with 94 percent of the respondents saying they would support a tax increase if the funds would be used to protect drinking water.[9]

Another prominent area of concern has been clean air. A survey conducted by the Department of Natural Resources of 1,863 manufacturers and processors of toxic chemicals estimated that more than 18,000 tons of toxic air pollutants have been emitted annually in the state. Part of the threat to the state's air quality comes from energy production. Because a higher than average percentage of Missouri's electricity is produced from coal, the air above Missouri has had greater amounts of carbon dioxide and sulfur dioxide than that found over most neighboring states.

Another concern was the finding by a

9. "Pollution Accountability Backed," *St. Louis Post-Dispatch*, July 29, 1992. The survey was conducted by the Public Policy Research Center at the University of Missouri–St. Louis for the state Department of Natural Resources. The questions were asked by telephone of 702 state residents in mid-May.

federal Environmental Protection Agency (EPA) study that more than five hundred companies in the state reported releasing some toxic chemicals into the environment, for a total of 163 tons given off in the year of the report. On a per capita basis, Missouri ranked twenty-second in industrial releases of toxic chemicals in 1991.

Missouri shares another environmental problem with most states: a number of hazardous waste disposal sites. Fifty-six hazardous waste sites are on record with the state's Division of Environmental Quality. Any or all of the sites, in virtually all areas of Missouri, could be placed on the EPA's national priorities list of the most serious environmental hazards. Missouri currently has 23 sites on this list of 1,236 scattered throughout the nation.

These hazardous waste sites can be cleaned up either by the state or federal governments, or privately by any or all of those responsible for creating the site. The state government's share of the cost for such activities was more than $116 million in the fiscal years 1985 through 1988. In addition, Missouri officials have signed an agreement with the EPA to clean up five sites in the state.

The state's Department of Natural Resources has responded to environmental emergencies. For example, during the year following July 1, 1987, the department received reports of 804 emergency response incidents, of which 8 percent were considered major. After receiving a report, department officials examine sites to determine if an emergency exists, and to calculate what action should be taken to solve the problem.

V. A Missouri Environmental Case Study: Times Beach

Just two days before Christmas in 1982, the 2,037 residents of Times Beach were stunned to learn from federal officials that dangerous levels of a chemical had been found in soil samples taken earlier from the town. The residents, just moving back following a flood from the nearby Meramec River, were urged to flee for their safety once again. The substance threatening the lives of the seven hundred families of the small town twenty-three miles southwest of St. Louis was dioxin, at that time widely regarded as one of the most toxic chemicals ever manufactured.

Dioxin, an undesired by-product of the production of some cleansers, pesticides, and food preservatives, was found to be present in some Times Beach soil samples at levels as high as one hundred parts of dioxin per billion parts of soil. The federal Center for Disease Control (CDC) in Atlanta, Georgia, the facility conducting the tests, warned that levels above one part per billion could cause health hazards. Most of the dioxin in Times Beach was found along twenty-three miles of road, shoulders, and ditches in the community. An investigation suggested that dioxin was present in waste oil that had been sprayed on unpaved roads to settle dust from the late 1960s through the mid–1970s. Most of the roads were subsequently paved. Testing revealed that most of the contamination was limited to the roads and not the structures of the town.

Times Beach was evacuated at the end of 1982 by order of the EPA. At that time it was speculated that the move was the largest evacuation of a toxic waste site in American history. Later the town's residents were bought out by federal and state governments at a price of more than $30 million. The federal government paid 90 percent of the cost, with the state financing the remaining 10 percent.

Several residents sued two firms involved in the production or distribution of dioxin to the community. The seven-month trial ended in June 1988 with the jury ruling that the town residents had failed to prove that their health problems were conclusively linked to the dioxin sprayed in the community. However, before the verdict was announced, one of the firms settled out of court for $14 million, a sum to be divided among 1,230 claims made in the state. Later the Justice Department filed suit seeking reimbursement for cleaning up the dioxin contaminating Times Beach and more than twenty other sites throughout the state.

To clean up the site, EPA officials decided to locate a temporary mobile incinerator in Times Beach to burn off, and thereby decontaminate, dioxin-contaminated soil from the town and nearby sites. Ashes from the incinerator would be deposited in a landfill to be located near the site. Residents from nearby towns expressed concern that fumes from the incinerator might contaminate surrounding areas and that the facility might be made permanent. The Gateway Green Alliance of St. Louis maintained that the incinerator could not totally destroy all of the dioxin, thereby allowing dangerous levels of the chemical to remain in the area.

After a legal battle, a federal court mandated that the dioxin be incinerated on the Times Beach site. The governing body of St. Louis County responded by approving an ordinance halting operation of the incinerator. Council members admitted they lacked legal authority to enforce their regulation against the federal government, but hoped their gesture would provide a legal mechanism that environmental groups could use to fight the project.

Also debated was the extent of the danger dioxin presented to the public. In the early 1990s, the EPA retested dioxin. The EPA reported that the chemical was a "weak carcinogen," as industry had long maintained, but expressed concern that the chemical could impair "immune and reproductive systems, as well as the endocrine system."[10]

The dioxin debate expanded further in response to the 1993 and 1994 flooding of rivers near Times Beach. The massive flood in the summer of 1993 left plastic bags containing fifteen hundred tons of dioxin-contaminated soil floating in a building in which they were being stored. State and federal officials concluded that the soil remained safe within the bags in the building. That flood, plus another the following April, rekindled fears of environmentalists and nearby residents that floodwater would wash into the incinerator, constructed on the Meramec River floodplain, and then escape out into the nearby region. An earthen levee surrounds the 8.3-acre site for the incinerator, which has not yet been built. Missouri Department of Natural Resources officials responded that the levee had held.[11]

In sum, environmental concerns surrounding the incident at Times Beach have not been resolved. Times Beach continues to provide Missourians and observers elsewhere with a graphic reminder of just how fragile the environment is and how easily and quickly it can be damaged. Moreover, the speed with which news of the event spread throughout the nation indicated just how deeply citizens have grown to fear environmental mishaps. Finally, the extensive cost of cleaning up the chemical further documents the expense in failing to keep the environment clean. Remaining uncalculated have been costs in human terms ranging from the immediate evacuation from homes to possible long-term

10. *The 1994 Information Please Environmental Almanac* (Boston: Houghton Mifflin Company, 1994), 179.

11. "Flood Swamps Dioxin," *St. Louis Post-Dispatch*, August 4, 1993; "Incinerator Site Dry despite Flood," *St. Louis Post-Dispatch*, April 16, 1994.

medical problems that could strike former Times Beach residents in the years to come.

VI. Conclusions

Economic development, energy, and the environment present as challenging a group of issues to Missouri governmental leaders as they do to state leaders throughout the nation. Unfortunately, the possible solutions often appear to be complex, expensive, or controversial. Moreover, such a matrix of issues seems to be as much a preface for the twenty-first century as it is a pending epilogue for the twentieth.

CHAPTER 20

State Agricultural Policy
by Rickert Althaus

> Farming looks mighty easy when your plow is a pencil, and you're a thousand miles from the corn field.—Dwight D. Eisenhower

From a position atop the dome of the capitol in Jefferson City, a bronze statue of Ceres, the Roman goddess of agriculture, watches over the seat of Missouri government. The statue's prominent placement is entirely appropriate, as it clearly symbolizes the prominence of agriculture in Missouri.

Agriculture and agriculture-related industries are of great importance to the state. Though Missouri has significant manufacturing and service industries, agriculture continues to be a major component of the state's economy. Cash receipts from the sale of crops and livestock brought Missouri farmers $4.4 billion in 1992.[1] Production of that magnitude is not possible without support from other industries, including those that provide seed, agricultural chemicals, machinery, and farm credit. Likewise, these commodities support extensive marketing and processing activities throughout the food industry. Obviously, agriculture means more than the planting, harvesting, and animal husbandry that occurs on the individual farm. Farming is the basis of an extensive industry that underlies the entire state economy.

Missouri's agriculture is incredibly diverse. Missouri ranks among the top ten states in the nation in the production of dozens of different agricultural commodities. To give a few examples, the state ranks second in beef production, fourth in grain sorghum production, fifth in turkeys raised, sixth in rice production, and seventh in the production of American cheese.[2] This diversification can be an obvious strength, because it decreases the likelihood that any one factor could affect state agriculture disastrously in any one year. However, this same diversity complicates policy making by state officials because so many variables and potential effects must be considered.

If diversity characterizes Missouri agriculture, federalism characterizes its agricultural policies. Farming and related activities occur in a policy environment consisting of federal institutions and programs, state institutions and programs, and other programs and activities that are jointly administered by both levels of government. In fact, even local governments are involved in actions that affect agriculture, such as zoning and other land-use regulations.

1. *Statistical Abstract for Missouri 1993* (Columbia: Business and Public Administration Research Center, University of Missouri, 1994), 181.

2. *1992 Missouri Farm Facts* (Missouri Department of Agriculture, October 1992), 2.

The federal role in agriculture is very extensive, partially because of the success of rural members of Congress in establishing years ago a large, well-funded, and powerful United States Department of Agriculture (USDA) and in maintaining that agency today. The prominence of USDA has meant that most state agricultural policies have been crafted to fit existing federal programs. The supplemental role of the state will become evident as we examine Missouri's agricultural programs.

I. Governmental Institutions

The major state governmental body dealing with agriculture is the Missouri Department of Agriculture (MDA). For years it has been the smallest of the executive departments in both number of employees and annual budget. (Recently, the department was edged out in these two areas by the newly created Department of Insurance.) In 1994, for example, the MDA employed only about 450 people and spent only $30 million, less than 0.3 percent of the total spent by the state. The department consists of seven divisions: administrative services, animal health, grain inspection and warehousing, market development, plant industries, state fair, and weights and measures.

The department is structured to perform two main types of activities: commercial regulation and agricultural promotion. The MDA regulates farm animal health standards, quality of grain in the marketplace, control of crop diseases and weeds, and accuracy of commercial scales and measuring devices. For many Missourians, the department's regulatory activity is at its most visible at gas stations. In most parts of the state, the MDA regularly verifies the calibration of gas pumps at retail outlets. When motorists fill their gas tanks, they may notice the MDA sticker on the pump attesting to its accuracy.

The MDA's role in agricultural promotion has been described by one student, Kevin Sexton, as that of an "agricultural chamber of commerce." The annual state fair held by MDA in Sedalia is an example of this type of promotional activity. Visitors to the fair learn about Missouri agriculture as they tour the various booths and displays or view a livestock judging or auction. In addition, MDA's AgriMissouri program publicizes agricultural products produced in the state. In this way, Missouri consumers are made aware of the home-grown products in their stores. The MDA is also active in many other ways in trying to create additional markets for the agricultural goods produced in the state.

Though the MDA's major responsibilities are evident from looking at its organization chart, the dovetailing of the state and federal governments in administering these programs is less easily seen. The following examples illustrate this "agricultural federalism": (1) the MDA and USDA jointly support the Missouri Agricultural Statistics Service in Columbia, an information bureau that gathers and distributes statistical information on Missouri agriculture; (2) the MDA Livestock Grading Program applies USDA grading standards to the state's livestock; (3) the MDA Animal Health Division enforces federal regulations dealing with the livestock trade and cooperates with USDA's Agriculture Research Service in disease control programs; and (4) the MDA International Marketing Program works with USDA's Foreign Agricultural Service in export promotion. Many other examples of federal-state cooperation could be cited.

The Department of Agriculture is one of

only two departments not covered by the state's merit system. One might think that the department would have many changes in personnel following a change of governors, since that is a characteristic commonly found in patronage agencies, but apparently that has not been the case. Recent court decisions have made it much more difficult to terminate even nonmerit employees, so partisan turnover is greatly limited. In addition, recent administrations have tended not to use party loyalty as the chief criterion for employment in the department, but instead have stated an emphasis on the qualifications and abilities of potential employees.

The Department of Higher Education also plays a role in state agriculture because of the department's responsibilities for the universities of the state, two of which are a part of the land-grant college system. The land-grant system, first created to support agricultural and mechanical colleges, was established by Congress through a series of laws enacted in the nineteenth century. The Morrill Act of 1862 gave federal lands to the states to be used in establishing land-grant institutions. In 1887 the Hatch Act provided yearly funding to the states for agricultural research, which led to the university-affiliated state agricultural experiment stations. The Smith-Lever Act of 1914 established the joint federal-state Agricultural Extension Service, which was to be involved in research, teaching, and outreach so that the fruits of this educational activity could be made available to farmers and rural Americans.

The University of Missouri and Lincoln University are both land-grant institutions involved in Cooperative Extension. They are both supported with state funds, but their extension programs are funded by a combination of state, county, and federal money, student fees, and grants and contracts. These programs are carried out at the county level.[3]

Each county in the state has a local extension council, made up of elected and appointed citizens. The council directs the local extension effort and approves the appointment of county-based faculty who are called extension specialists (formerly county agents). Although extension involves primarily agriculture and home economics (now known as Human and Environmental Sciences), its scope has expanded over the years to include programs in business, industry, labor, community development, and services for youths. The direction of extension programs is, of course, affected by funding decisions made in the USDA's Extension Service division. The provision of information and education is truly a cooperative effort.

Still other state executive departments are involved, whether directly or indirectly, in agriculture. The Department of Natural Resources (DNR) is responsible for soil and water conservation. The eight-person commission in charge of DNR soil and water conservation programs consists of five farmers, along with the directors of DNR and MDA and the dean of the University of Missouri College of Agriculture,

---

3. A second Morrill Act in 1890 provided for direct annual appropriations to each state and territory to support land-grant colleges. It also prohibited racial discrimination in admissions to colleges receiving such funds. However, seventeen states, including Missouri, initially evaded this provision by establishing separate institutions for White and Black students if such funds were equitably but not necessarily equally divided between the institutions. Lincoln University is one of the 1890 land-grant institutions resulting from the second Morrill Act. Lincoln does not receive state funding for its Cooperative Extension programs, which generally are delivered through county-based Cooperative Extension faculty employed by the University of Missouri or through Lincoln's campus-based Cooperative Extension faculty.

Food, and Natural Resources, who serve as ex-officio members. This commission assists the counties in establishing special soil and water conservation districts to promote farming practices consistent with resource maintenance. A large part of the DNR's soil conservation effort is funded by a portion of an earmarked state sales tax of one-tenth of a cent. The DNR is also involved in matters of water quality, feedlot runoff and animal wastes, and wetlands regulation, all of which are issues of interest to farmers.

The Department of Conservation is also funded to a great extent by another earmarked sales tax, of one-eighth of a cent, which is used to support wildlife conservation. The department's wildlife conservation effort involves agriculture because farmers are encouraged to use the land in a manner compatible with the state's wildlife population.

Because a transportation system that efficiently moves products from farms to processors is crucial to keeping agribusinesses in Missouri competitive with other states, the activity of the Department of Highways and Transportation also pertains directly to agriculture. The Department of Economic Development likewise has the potential to affect agriculture. One division of the department promotes economic and community development, which is especially important to depressed rural areas. Other divisions are responsible for regulating utilities and thrift institutions, which provide the energy and financial credit essential to the agricultural sector. The Department has been involved recently in a joint effort with the MDA to establish a trade office in Mexico, to try to stimulate exports of Missouri agricultural products to that nation. Obviously, the diversity of agriculture and its interrelatedness with many other activities means that agricul-

ture will be affected at least indirectly by much of what state agencies do.

Obviously, the General Assembly enacts legislation that governs the state's agriculture. With each of the latest reapportionments of legislative districts, rural areas have lost representation in the legislature to urban areas. Although the legislature is becoming less rural, that does not mean it is ignoring agricultural policy. After all, about one of every six senators and one of every seven representatives list farming or related fields as their occupation.[4] In addition, many legislators come from rural areas and are naturally attuned to some of the basic concerns of Missouri farmers. Even urban legislators, knowing the significance of agriculture to the state, are fairly sensitive to this policy area. Their constituents are all consumers of food and are therefore concerned with its availability, quality, and price. Likewise, urban representatives have an interest in the overall economic health of the state, in which agriculture plays such a great part.

As might be expected, committees have been established in the senate and the house to deal with agriculture. In the senate, the Agriculture and Local Government Committee deals with agricultural legislation. There have been two house committees related to agriculture since 1981: the Agriculture and the Agri-Business committees. Prior to that time, the single Agriculture Committee had been one of the largest in the house. In 1981 the newly selected speaker of the house, Bob Griffin, who was from a rural area (Cameron), decided to split that committee into two. Almost all of the members on each of the current house committees are from rural areas.

4. House of Representatives, "Missouri House of Representatives Occupation List," January 4, 1991; and Senate, "Interesting Facts about the Missouri State Senate," April 1993.

Creating the second house agricultural committee has had at least two important consequences. First, the speaker can now reward an additional supporter with a committee to chair. Second, twice as many agriculture-related bills may now reach the floor during the first part of the session, since individual committee chairpersons are limited in the number of bills they can recommend for floor action.

How effective is the General Assembly in making agricultural policy? It is fairly effective at passing agricultural bills, although that is not necessarily the same thing as making comprehensive policy. Of the bills that do pass, most originate in one of the two house committees, rather than in their senate counterpart. This may substantiate the impressions of some observers of state government who see the house committees as the more effective. If this is so, two possible explanations are that the senate committee has to deal with the entirety of agriculture while the subject is divided between two committees in the house, or that the typical senator serves on more committees than the typical representative, and is therefore less able to focus on any one specific subject.

Other committees, such as those in taxation and transportation, also handle bills that affect Missouri agriculture. The proposals of those committees often come under close scrutiny by rural-area legislators for potential impact on agriculture. Even legislators from urban areas who serve on other committees have the potential to affect agricultural policy and administration. Legislation was introduced and ultimately passed that required the MDA to begin regulating so-called puppy mills. The MDA didn't necessarily want this responsibility, nor did the agriculture committees actively seek to give it this responsibility, but legislative and public opinion pressures from largely metropolitan areas led to the legislation being enacted.

II. Political Party and Interest Group Activity

There are few noticeable differences between Democrats and Republicans in Missouri concerning farm policies. Both parties draw up state platforms regularly, but those documents rarely differ significantly on agricultural matters. The positions on agriculture are usually rather general, acknowledging the importance of that industry to the state's economy and calling for increased market development, especially in exports. Such issues are hardly controversial. The debate on free markets versus government intervention that often colors agricultural policy making at the national level is not often raised at the state level, perhaps because agricultural production policies involving acreage reduction, diversion payments, commodity loans, and other price support mechanisms are set at the national level.

While the Democrat/Republican factor does not significantly affect state agricultural programs, one factor that certainly does affect those programs is the farm lobby. Groups most directly concerned with agricultural policy usually fall into one of three main categories: general farm organizations, commodity groups, and agribusiness.

The general farm organization that has been most active before the General Assembly is the Missouri affiliate of the American Farm Bureau Federation. In recent sessions, the senate report forms showed five registered lobbyists from this group, while the house forms listed four.[5] Those

5. House of Representatives, "Missouri House of Representatives Lobbyist Registration System, All Lobbyists," September 28, 1992; and Senate, "Missouri Senate Registered Lobbyist Report," February 22, 1993.

numbers are significantly higher than those of any other agriculture-related group. Indeed, the general farm organizations that are prominent in other parts of the country seem not to be active at all before the Missouri legislature.

The Missouri Farmers Association (MFA), the large Missouri-based cooperative association of farmers, is in some respects a hybrid group. It is most similar to the general farm organizations, but it owns grain elevators and conducts purchasing and sales services on behalf of its members, so it has certain characteristics of an agribusiness organization. The legislature's report forms show only a very limited formal lobbying presence by MFA, but the organization's headquarters is in Columbia, so it is possible that MFA communicates its concerns in less formal ways.

The most active commodity groups traditionally have been the pork producers and the cattle, corn, and soybean associations, although dairy, poultry, and tobacco interests maintain a lobbying presence. More recently, the wine producer groups have been active, corresponding to the growth in Missouri's significant wine industry.

As might be expected, agribusiness also takes an active role in lobbying activities. The Missouri Agricultural Industries Council (MO-AG) is the main agribusiness trade association active in the state capital. It often coordinates a coalition of agricultural interests. MO-AG has a reputation for being very effective at influencing the policy decisions of the legislature. In addition to this umbrella group, individual farm equipment manufacturers and dealers have a registered lobbying presence, as do the large agricultural chemical producers such as Monsanto, Union Carbide, Du Pont, and Pfizer. Anheuser-Busch, one of the state's largest consumers of agricultural commodities, is very well represented before the legislature, both in terms of numbers and effectiveness of lobbyists.

This list of agriculture-related groups provides only a brief sketch of the different kinds of groups making demands on the state's legislators. Obviously, other groups communicate their interests to Jefferson City. However, the listing of these largest, most active groups should provide a sense of the major kinds of interests and priorities to which the General Assembly is likely to respond.

III. Current Policy Issues

At the present time, Missouri policy makers face few major agricultural issues that are purely at the state level. This is consistent with the concept of agricultural federalism. State agricultural policies supplement and fill in around the broader policies of the federal government.

To be sure, federal policy makers are currently dealing with issues that will affect agriculture across the nation, Missouri included. International trade policy, biotechnology, food safety, sustainability of farming operations, and government regulation of private property are all current topics of national agricultural policy debate. As decisions are made in these areas, Missouri agriculture will respond.

For several years, a regional dispute with agricultural implications has concerned state policy makers. The water level of the Missouri River has become the subject of a disagreement between the upstream states of Montana, North Dakota, and South Dakota, who want to retain water in their reservoirs for recreation purposes, and the downstream states of Nebraska, Iowa, and Missouri, who want water released to sustain commercial barge traffic. The agricultural interest in this issue comes from the fact that barges transport large amounts of grain and fertilizer throughout the region. A resolution of this issue will no doubt involve both the national and state governments.[6]

After the 1992 gubernatorial election, a transition advisory group was created to make recommendations to the new governor regarding the Missouri Department of Agriculture. The group's report suggested that MDA should (1) increase opportunities to market Missouri agricultural products; (2) improve its own internal administration; (3) increase ways to enter farming for those who want to; (4) address environmental and consumer issues; and (5) improve its function as an information channel.[7]

Early in 1993 the president of the Missouri Farm Bureau (himself a former director of MDA) traveled the state publicizing the state issues that his group felt were important. Among them were: (1) education funding that treats rural schools fairly (an issue largely resolved by the passage of the revised foundation formula later in 1993); (2) maintenance of the sales tax exemption on the purchase of farm machinery; and (3)

strengthening of property rights, assuring that proper procedures and compensation be used in any instance where government takes or restricts the use of privately owned land. The group also has concerns about environmental and other tax issues that will be addressed at the national level.[8] In late 1994 the Farm Bureau president announced that the group would work for passage of a constitutional amendment requiring that all major state tax increases be submitted to public vote.

IV. Conclusion

It can be said that Missouri agriculture is very diverse, and so, too, are the forces working on it. Government action regarding state agriculture can be characterized as "agricultural federalism." Any policies that are exclusively state policies treat areas that have not been addressed by the federal government. Although many pressing concerns of agriculture have yet to be resolved, agriculture's importance to Missouri ensures that most of these topics will eventually be addressed by policy makers.

6. For more detailed information on the Missouri River controversy, see "Missouri River Causing New War between the States," *St. Louis Post-Dispatch,* September 15, 1991; "Bond Calls Agency All Wet in Study on Missouri River," *St. Louis Post-Dispatch,* February 8, 1992; and "Lawmakers Attack River Plan," *St. Louis Post-Dispatch,* February 19, 1993.

7. Missouri Transition Government, "Report of the Agricultural and Economic Development Transition Advisory Group," Jefferson City, December 1992.

8. See "Issues Facing State Farm Bureau Varied," *Southeast Missourian,* February 12, 1993.

PART IV

Local Government and Politics in Missouri

CHAPTER 21

County Government in Missouri
by John Ballard

County governmental organization is characterized by diversity, not only from state to state but even within states. . . . As has been aptly observed, if any "principle" could be distinguished in American county government, it's the principle of confusion.—Russell W. Maddox and Robert F. Fuquay

Counties are an oddity. Theorists, reformers, and urbanites for years have used such terms as *obsolete, archaic,* and *horse-and-buggy* to describe county government, suggesting that these relics would soon disappear, to be replaced by more modern and more efficient structures. However, that has not happened. While counties may not have gained much governmental power, neither have they lost much. Counties remain the only form of local government serving almost the entire population, and they seem to enjoy considerable public support. Every state except Connecticut has counties, although they are called *boroughs* in Alaska and *parishes* in Louisiana, and in some New England states "towns" serve as the equivalent.

I. Origin of Counties

The recorded history of counties is long, dating back as far as A.D. 603 in England. Kings found that administering large kingdoms was simplified if representatives of the crown were assigned to deal with people in different locations. The first division was into shires, with the king appointing a reeve (shire-reeve, or sheriff) to govern each shire. The ancestry of these sheriffs can be traced to at least 787. The Norman Conquest of England changed the shire to the conte, or county, after 1066. The signing of the Magna Carta in 1215 brought the king's representatives, who by this time included counterparts of auditor, treasurer, recorder, and coroner, as well as sheriff, under the law. By about 1300 a start had been made toward locally electing rather than centrally appointing county officials.[1]

When Missouri was designated a territory by the United States Congress in 1812, the governor was required to "lay off the parts of said territory . . . into convenient counties."[2] Five counties were "laid off": St. Louis, St. Charles, Ste. Genevieve, Cape Girardeau, and New Madrid. In 1813, upon petition by residents, western Ste. Genevieve County became Washington County. Western New Madrid County became Lawrence County in 1815 but was later dissolved; its southern portion

1. Governmental Research Institute, *Governmental Facts* (Cleveland, Ohio, March 1980), 71-E.
2. The quote is from the 1787 Northwest Ordinance, which established governmental provisions for U.S. Territories.

became a part of Arkansas Territory, while the northern portion became Wayne and Madison counties. By 1820, when proceedings toward statehood began, there were fifteen counties in Missouri Territory. When statehood was granted in 1821, Missouri had twenty-five counties. The first state constitution called for appointed justices of the peace and elected sheriffs and coroners in every county.[3]

II. Organization

Today, Missouri has 115 counties, each of which is unique in at least some respects. They range from the independent city of St. Louis to Worth, an agricultural county in northwest Missouri that is the least populated (2,440 inhabitants) and smallest (266.5 square miles) county in the state. Only three states—Texas, Georgia, and Kentucky—have more counties.

Article VI, Section 8, of the state constitution designates four general classes of county, based on assessed valuation (the total value, for taxation purposes, of all property in the county, as determined by the county assessor). A change in classification is automatic when a county has maintained the requisite valuation for five years. Table 21–1 shows the counties by classification.[4] The primary differences between classes are in the number and compensation of elected and appointed officials and, in first-class counties, the maximum tax levy allowable.

Though the constitution specifies that "all counties within the same class shall possess the same powers and be subject to the same restrictions," the legislature has passed numerous laws applicable only to one county. In 1994 the Missouri Supreme Court called into question these special laws when it declared unconstitutional a statute which applied only to St. Louis County rather than all first-class counties.[5] The legislature responded by referring to voters a proposed constitutional amendment retroactively approving all laws applicable to only one or a few counties.

Structural Options. Two organizational options are available, at least to certain counties. All first-class counties may, if they choose, design their own governmental structure under a home-rule charter. The city of St. Louis has such a charter dating back to 1876. St. Louis County has operated under a charter since 1950. Jackson County adopted a charter in 1970 after several tries, and in its second effort St. Charles County followed suit in 1992. Several other eligible counties have considered and voted against charter proposals at least once: Buchanan County did so in 1949 and 1974, Clay County in 1969, Jefferson County in 1972, Greene County in 1980, and Boone County in 1982.

Third-class counties may divide certain governmental responsibilities among townships, which number from seven to twenty-four among counties that have taken this option. In township counties (Table 21–1), collecting taxes and maintaining roads are township responsibilities, and planning and zoning are permissible if voters so choose. Until recently, tax assessment was also a township function. Township counties appear to be largely

3. M. Ohman, "Missouri County Organization 1812–1876," *Missouri Historical Review* 76 (1982): 253–81.

4. Complications arose when the valuation requirements for all classes were changed in 1988; five counties that had qualified for Class 2 status would have had to return to Class 3 with the change. They were arbitrarily put into the newly vacant Class 4 by the General Assembly, but they operate under Class 2 statutes. (Earlier, Class 4 counties were the smallest in assessed valuation, but only one remained in 1988, and it was about to become third class.)

5. *State ex rel. Ellisville v. St. Louis County,* 877 S.W.2d 620 (Mo banc 1994).

Table 21-1. Counties by Class, 1994

Class 1 ($450 million & above)[3]	Class 2[1] ($300–$450 million)	Class 3 (under $300 million)			Class 4[2]
Boone	Callaway	Adair	Hickory	Phelps	Johnson
Buchanan	Camden	Andrew	Holt	Pike	Lafayette
Clay	Cape Girardeau	Atchison	Howard	Polk	Pettis
Franklin	Cass	Audrain	Howell	Pulaski	St. Francois
Greene	Cole	Barry	Iron	Putnam[5]	Saline
Jackson[4]		Barton[5]	Knox	Ralls	
Jasper		Bates[5]	Laclede	Randolph	
Jefferson		Benton	Lawrence	Ray	
Platte		Bollinger	Lewis	Reynolds	
St. Charles[4]		Butler	Lincoln	Ripley	
St. Louis[4]		Caldwell[5]	Linn[5]	Schuyler	
St. Louis City[4]		Carroll[5]	Livingston[5]	Scotland	
		Carter	Macon	Scott	
		Cedar	Madison	Shannon	
		Chariton[5]	Maries	Shelby	
		Christian	Marion	St. Clair	
		Clark	McDonald	Ste. Genevieve	
		Clinton	Mercer[5]	Stoddard[5]	
		Cooper	Miller	Stone	
		Crawford	Mississippi	Sullivan[5]	
		Dade[5]	Moniteau	Taney	
		Dallas	Monroe	Texas[5]	
		Daviess[5]	Montgomery	Vernon[5]	
		DeKalb[5]	Morgan	Warren	
		Dent	New Madrid	Washington	
		Douglas	Newton	Wayne	
		Dunklin[5]	Nodaway[5]	Webster	
		Gasconade	Oregon	Worth	
		Gentry[5]	Osage	Wright[5]	
		Grundy[5]	Ozark		
		Harrison[5]	Pemiscot		
		Henry[5]	Perry		

[1] Counties entering this classification after September 28, 1987, were relieved of five obligations required under Class 2: juvenile detention center, deputy sheriff for every 5,000 population, separate circuit clerk and recorder of deeds, elected county auditor, and reduction in the percentage allowed for cost of assessment from 1 percent to 0.5 percent. Presently, this affects only Camden county.

[2] These counties operate under Classification 2 statutes but lack the required assessed valuation. See text.

[3] An option is now given to counties to begin the five-year waiting period when they reach $400 million in assessed valuation, rather than waiting to reach $450 million.

[4] Home rule charter

[5] Township organized

those originally settled by immigrants from northern and eastern states, who use the township as the local government unit. The more southern states, from which many of Missouri's settlers came, commonly use the county as the basic unit of local government.

III. County Officials

Organizationally, the county is an aggregation of semi-independent powers, with officials for the most part elected separately. This can often make the officials accountable only to the voters, creating at least the appearance that no one is in charge. Such appearances sometimes are not far from reality. Table 21–2 itemizes elected and appointed officials in the various counties.

Elected officials generally serve four-year terms, although associate commissioners serve two-year terms. Appointed officials usually do not serve for a specified term, and there are considerable variations as to how, and by whom, these officials are appointed.

In the past, the prerequisites for holding most offices in Missouri were, as one county official was fond of saying, "Twenty-five dollars filing fee and a lot of friends." This appears to be changing in typically slow Missouri fashion. To receive full salary, assessors must now attend a state-approved training course. For a brief period the requirement was to "successfully complete" the course, but the weaker "attend" proved more acceptable. Newly elected sheriffs must complete some training between being elected and assuming the office, although those in office when the requirement was adopted are permitted unlimited reelection without regard to training. All other officers have a portion of their annual salary linked to completing a twenty-hour training course yearly. Since government in every county is in some respects unique,

a portion of any official's training must be received on the job.

County Commission. Before January 1985, the county commission was known as the county court. A three-member administrative body, the commission handles the county's budget, its business, and its road system. A presiding commissioner (previously, judge) is elected countywide for four years. Judges of the county court became commissioners in 1985. The statutory change required shrewd political maneuvering. The original proposal called for lengthening the term of associate judges to four years. The change in title was also included. Many counties endorsed the proposal because of the change in term length, which was then struck from the bill in committee, leaving only the title change. Associate commissioners each represent a half-county district for two years. Through its budgetary authority, this board approaches having supervisory powers, although lines of authority are thin and easily breached.

County Council. In St. Louis County, this seven-member body represents county districts and is somewhat like a large city's aldermanic board. Unlike the presiding commissioner of other counties, the county executive is not the presiding officer. The council may enact ordinances on matters of local concern, but on statewide matters, county ordinances must comply with state law.

St. Charles County, the latest home-rule county, also has a county council with a mix in representation. Seven members are elected by district and at large.

County Legislature. Jackson County's lawmaking body consists of nine members, six elected from districts and three at large. This legislature possesses considerably more budgetary authority than its St. Louis counterpart and consequently seems

Table 21-2. County Officials in Missouri

E=Elected; A=Appointed (Parenthetical = optional)

Office	Classes					County Charters		
	1	2 & 4	3	3 with Township	St. Louis City[1]	S.L. County	Jackson	St.Charles
Presiding Commissioner	E	E	E	E	—	—	—	—
2 Associate Commissioners	E	E	E	E	—	—	—	—
County Executive	—	—	—	—	—	E	E	E
7 Council Members	—	—	—	—	—	E	—	E
9 Legislators	—	—	—	—	—	—	E	—
Prosecuting Attorney	E	E	E	E	E	E	E	E
Sheriff	E	E	E	E	E	A	E	E
County Clerk	E	E	E	E	—	A	A	E
Assessor	E	E	E	E	E	A	A	E
Collector	E	E	E	—	E	A	A	E
Treasurer	E	E	E	E[2]	E	A	A	—
Circuit Clerk	E	E[5]	E[3]	E[3]	E	A	—	E
Recorder of Deeds	E	E[5]	E[3]	E[3]	E	A	A	E
Public Administrator	E	E	E	E	E	A	A	A
Auditor	E	E	—	—	—	A	A	A
Coroner	—	E	E	E	—	—	—	—
Medical Examiner	A	(A)[4]	(A)[4]	(A)[4]	A	A	A	A
Surveyor	—	E(A)	E(A)	E(A)	—	—	—	—
Highway Engineer	—	(A)	(A)	(A)	—	—	—	—
License Collector	—	—	—	—	E	—	—	—
Highway Administrator	A	—	—	—	—	A	—	—
City Counselor	A	—	—	—	—	A	A	A

[1] County offices retained when city became independent in 1876
[2] Also ex-officio collector for township collectors
[3] Circuit clerk may serve ex-officio as Recorder of Deeds
[4] Mandatory in 1st class and some 2nd class; optional in all others
[5] Camden county has combined circuit clerk and recorder; does not have auditor

better able to support or oppose the actions of its executive.

Since the charter governments are so different from the governments of the other counties, the operation of most offices is also different. The following descriptions, therefore, generally refer to counties other than Jackson, St. Louis, and St. Charles.

County Clerk. This office is the administrative center of county government. While commissions, councils, or legislatures meet at intervals and frequently convene at places other than the courthouse, the clerk's office is open any time the courthouse is, and all other offices must make at least periodic contact with this office. Reports, notices, purchases, and details of all kinds pass through the clerk's office. In most counties in the state, the clerk is also the chief election officer for all public bodies, and in third-class counties the clerk is also the budget officer. Extension of taxes (calculation of the various levies against property valuation) is another common function of the clerk. Typically, the clerk in this instance is intermediary among the assessor, the tax levying entity, and the collector.

Assessor. The assessor determines the taxable value of nearly all real property (real estate) and all tangible personal property (motor vehicles, livestock, boats, and airplanes) in the county. (State officials establish the total value of most railroad and utility property, and distribute that value among appropriate counties.) Recent court rulings and legislative actions have required that assessors work more closely with the State Tax Commission. Because the state is now providing part of the funding for the assessor, the State Tax Commission has some authority over the budgets of county assessors.

Collector. Except in cities that choose independent tax collection, the collector is in charge of collecting all property taxes levied. Township counties have no county collector, as this function is performed separately in each township. Some collections in the city of St. Louis are made by the license collector. At one time, collectors in third-class counties received as their pay a percentage of collections rather than a salary. Later this was converted to salaries, which still vary from county to county. All collectors assume personal liability for the total taxes due, which is relieved through periodic settlement. Collectors also conduct sales of property forfeited for delinquent taxes.

Treasurer. All collections, plus fees, fines, grants, and income from other sources, are placed in the custody of the treasurer. Disbursements of funds are made by the treasurer upon order of the county commission. This office has little contact with the general public, serving primarily as an internal control.

The loss of some officials can paralyze county government. Resignation, removal, or death of a collector or treasurer freezes in place all of a county's revenues. Before a new collector can begin collecting unpaid amounts, an audit must be made of all funds in hand but not yet turned over for settlement by the old collector. Until a settlement has confirmed the balances on hand of the old treasurer, a new treasurer cannot take office and no county funds can be paid out. Furthermore, selection of each new official is by the governor, who usually waits for local political committee concurrence.

Auditor. Voters in first-, fourth-, and second-class counties except for Camden elect an auditor whose task is to maintain a continuous audit of county operations. St. Louis and Jackson counties have appointed auditors. Third-class counties and Camden County are served by the state auditor, who is currently on a two-year audit cycle. Some federal programs require counties with an elected auditor to have an additional audit by an outside auditor to ensure independence. The elected county auditor is usually the budget officer.

Recorder of Deeds. In Camden County and most third-class counties, the circuit court clerk also serves as the recorder of deeds. Large counties and those who have chosen by election to do so have a separate recorder.

Sheriff. The chief law enforcement officer in all counties except St. Louis is the sheriff. Since most counties possess scant lawmaking power, sheriffs deal primarily with state law. Keeping the county jail, transporting prisoners to state custody, and serving various legal papers and processes are all common duties. Many sheriffs patrol roads, although this is required only in first-class and some second-class counties. It has become commonplace for sheriffs to dispatch by radio for other political subdivisions, such as cities or ambulance districts. New laws aim at further facilitating cooperation between sheriffs and city or state officers.

Circuit Clerk. The clerk of the circuit court serves as a scheduler and record keeper for the judiciary. As the unified court system has been phased in (see chapter 12), circuit clerks have come under the direct supervision of the state courts administrator. The clerk and at least one deputy clerk are now paid by the state. In most third-class counties, the circuit clerk also serves as ex-officio recorder of deeds. Passports and naturalization for citizenship also begin with the circuit clerk. This is the largest patronage office in the city of St. Louis and consequently is thought to carry considerable political weight. Attempts to make this post appointive rather than elective statewide have so far met with little success.

Prosecuting Attorney. In all of the state's counties, the job of prosecuting attorney is an elective one. The job of course includes prosecuting violations of state law, but duties have been expanding in recent years. For example, the prosecutor's duties might include locating parents of children receiving public assistance in order to collect support from them. Prosecutors often serve as legal advisers to county officials and the county itself. In first-class and some second-class counties, prosecutors must serve full-time. The prosecutors in the other counties are allowed to maintain nonconflicting private practices.

County Counselor. First-class counties and all charter counties have, by appoint-

ment, a legal adviser who serves as the county's attorney. The counselor does not prosecute or defend, except as the county itself is a party to the action. The county counselor also provides legal advice for other county officials.

Coroner/Medical Examiner. In all of the counties that have not chosen to appoint medical examiners, a coroner is elected. First-class and charter counties must have examiners. The duties of the coroners fall somewhere between law enforcement and medicine: checking violent or unattended deaths, ordering investigations or autopsies when necessary, and on occasion impaneling a six-member coroner's jury. In the absence, incapacity, or disqualification of the sheriff, the coroner becomes acting sheriff (in those counties with medical examiners, these duties fall to the prosecutor). Unlike coroners, it is permissible for a medical examiner to be shared by two or more counties.

Public Administrator. The public administrator settles estates of unknown or unclaimed dead and manages the estates of some children and incompetents. Many counties have little such business to do, and the post commonly goes unfilled. Compensation is entirely from the value of estates handled, on a percentage basis.

Surveyor. The surveyor conducts official surveys of property upon request, and is paid by the requester. Holders of this office must be registered land surveyors. Because few such surveyors are available, they are eligible to be elected in more than one county. First-class counties do not have this office.

Highway Engineer (Administrator). This post is optional, except in first-class counties. Where the post is mandated, the highway engineer usually must have some engineering credentials. Where the job is optional, such credentials may or may not be required. The highway engineer's task, of course, is to oversee the county's road system. In Class 1 counties the engineer or a staff member does official land surveys.

Judiciary Offices. Under the unified court system adopted in 1976, all courts, some of which were county offices, became direct state agencies. The transition was phased in over several years. Even so, all associate circuit judges are elected from a single county, and all circuit court judges are elected from a circuit, which may include more than one county. The courts are explained in chapter 12.

Boards and Commissions. In some counties, certain operational or advisory duties are formally or informally assigned, permanently or on an ad hoc basis, to groups resembling committees. The following list briefly explains some, but certainly not all, of these.

1. Board of Election Commissioners. In the city of St. Louis as well as St. Louis, Jackson, Clay, and Platte counties (and in Kansas City), the conducting of elections is assigned to a four-member board. Commissioners are appointed by the governor and confirmed by the senate, two from each major political party. The staff of these boards must also represent the two major parties in equal numbers.

2. Board of Equalization. The county commission, assessor, and surveyor, with the county clerk as secretary, annually hear complaints and equalize assessments of taxable property. Some cities can have representation during consideration of assessments within their limits. In certain counties, the board of equalization is composed of taxpaying, property-owning residents instead of officials. This board reviews assessments and makes adjustments, which may be appealed.

3. Planning Commission. Counties may, with voter approval, have planning commissions that ensure coordinated physical development within the counties. Such

commissions include a separate board of zoning adjustment and possibly a building commission. Numerous alternatives are provided, some by county class. About one in five counties, primarily the larger ones, regulate land use in some fashion.

4. Highway Commission. Some third-class counties can, with voter approval, turn over all road operations to a highway commission made up of elected district representatives plus the members of the county commission. Under this arrangement, a qualified engineer is appointed and tax revenues for roads are spent within incorporated cities as well as on the county road system. Newton and Stone counties have such a system; Cooper County did, but abandoned it.

5. Board of Jail Visitors. This six-member board has three women members and no more than three members of the same political party. Appointed by the circuit court, it visits, examines, and reports on the jails. Not all circuits have such a board.

6. Port Authority. Counties along a navigable waterway may create a port authority to promote and develop the use of waterways. Several have done so. Seven commissioners, no more than four from one political party, administer a port district.

7. Development Authority. Numerous development authorities have been formed in recent years. These are county-sanctioned groups empowered to issue revenue bonds for industrial development, broadly defined. Such bonds provide a tax-exempt status for investors, enabling debt to be incurred at minimal cost.

8. Political Committees. At each primary election voters in every township and large city ward elect a committeeman and committeewoman for their party. These compose the county committee. The committee in turn nominates judges of election to administer polling places. Each commit-

tee submits to the election authority twice as many names as there are positions to be filled. The election authority then selects equivalent numbers of workers from each party for two-year terms.

9. Semi-Connected Boards. A number of special-purpose boards, such as library, road district, or hospital boards, may or may not be under limited county jurisdiction. This usually depends upon how the district was organized. Centralized administration of elections has brought many of these semiautonomous boards into a closer relationship with the counties.

10. Ad Hoc Boards. Issues or problems often can be defused by appointing study commissions or advisory boards. At the same time, these bodies can provide a visible reward to a politician's supporters, whether or not their findings are to receive consideration.

IV. County Finance

Unlike many other governments, counties generally operate on a calendar year basis rather than on a fiscal year basis. This is because the basic county revenue is the property tax, based on ownership as of January 1. Counties must budget before spending, and budgets must be balanced. Debt may be incurred only with the approval of two-thirds of the voters, and even then for no more than twenty years. Borrowings during any budget year must be repaid before the end of that year and thus are not debt as usually defined. For the average third-class county, the percent of general revenue from each major source has been:

42 percent from sales taxes
19 percent from service charges
18 percent from property taxes
14 percent from intergovernmental transfers

1 percent from interest earnings
6 percent from other sources

Intergovernmental revenues (motor fuel tax) constitute a much greater percentage of road and bridge funds.

Borrowing against Anticipated Revenues. Statutes governing finance can be interpreted two ways: counties should collect taxes at year's end with which to fund operations the following year, or counties should collect taxes at year's end to repay the year's borrowings against anticipated revenue. (Counties are allowed to borrow up to 90 percent of anticipated revenue.) Some counties have rarely or never borrowed against anticipated revenues. It is not unusual for adjoining counties to adhere to diametrically opposing views on the question of borrowing. Politically there seems to be considerable advantage to the cash-in-hand position, as the public is seldom favorably inclined toward governmental borrowing. On the other hand, the use of short-term credit has long been a valuable tool of good management. The argument will not be easily resolved. Credit counties cannot become cash counties without finding a massive windfall. Cash counties could become credit counties but, after a single year of riches, would find it difficult ever to return to a cash operation.

Financial Hardship. Worth, the tiniest county both in area and population, chronically faces financial hardship. To reduce expenses (and to convince voters of the necessity of a levy increase), the courthouse was closed one winter. Officials did business from their homes or from donated space. Nevertheless, voters defeated the proposed levy increase. Subsequently, some officials resigned and their replacements lived on the restricted budgets. In Oregon County, a proposal by county commissioners to close the courthouse was thwarted by the opposition of the state tax commission, the circuit court, and others having authority. The county borrowed money to pay bills instead of closing.

Optional Sales Taxes. Historically, revenue sources for counties other than property taxes have been few. Legislative authorization in 1979 for an optional county sales tax gained acceptance more quickly and widely than is usual for new ideas—especially taxes. (Since the original authorization, several other options for additional sales taxes, with voter approval, have been adopted.) In less than four years, seventy-two counties had gained voter approval for the tax, at least half of which must be committed to property tax reduction. (See Table 21–3.) This represents the beginning of a shift away from the use of property taxes to finance county government. The disparities of the property tax are well known. The disparities of the sales tax, with uneven retail outlet distribution, are beginning to be noticed.

Fees. For many counties, fees represent a major source of revenue. External changes have modified the fee system over the years. The unified court system mentioned earlier shifted most court fees from counties to the state when the state began to pay court-related salaries. Land-transfer fees represent significant revenue only when considerable property is changing hands. Fees from sales of national forest products or payments in lieu of tax on federal or state holdings are rather erratic, both in amount and timeliness of payment, rendering them difficult to budget. Some counties have few of these fees, while others depend heavily upon them. Decisions as to the level of fees charged, amount of payment in lieu of tax-exempt property, and similar matters are made beyond the county level and usually without county consultation.

Intergovernmental Transfers. Intergovernmental fund transfers have dropped in recent years. However, they are still important in county finance, more so in other states than in Missouri. The major one available in Missouri distributes a portion of state gasoline tax revenues and fees. This is a permanent program mandated by the state constitution, but proceeds fluctuate.

State sharing of gasoline tax proceeds (plus half the sales tax on motor vehicles) is constitutionally set at 10 to 15 percent for the counties and 15 percent for the cities, and is earmarked for roads. County allocations are determined by a formula measuring state-approved county road mileage and rural unincorporated assessed valuation, and comparing each county against the total for all the counties.

Other intergovernmental transfers vacillate between lucrative and nonexistent. Larger counties generally are more likely to receive these grant funds, although the number of these programs and funds has been declining. A wide array of grants and programs fall under this heading: community-development grants, employment programs, economic development grants, historic preservation funds, and numerous others.

V. Operations

The day-to-day operations of counties fall under four general headings: finance, law, roads, and administration. The assessor, collector, treasurer, and auditor (where one is available) all deal with various aspects of county finances. The circuit courts, circuit clerk, prosecutor, sheriff, coroner, and public administrator all handle a portion of the enforcement and application of state laws within the county's boundaries. The highway engineer, surveyor, and county commission are responsible for building and maintaining all county roads

Table 21-3. Types of Sales Taxes in Missouri Counties, 1994

County	*Regular*	*General*	*Capital Improvements*[1]	*Law Enforcement*[1]
Adair	1981			
Andrew	1987		1987–96	1990
Atchison		1989	1994–04	
Audrain	1986		1989–99	
Barry	1993		1986–96	
Barton	1983			1990
Bates				1988
Benton	1980		1991–95	
Bollinger	1980	1989		
Boone	1980	1993–98	1986–91	
Buchanan	1981	1993	1984–88	1990–96
			1987–96	
Butler	1981		1994	1994
Caldwell	1983		1986–97	1993–98
Callaway		1994		1988–93
Camden	1980			
Cape Girardeau	1980		1986–89	
Carroll	1983			
Carter	1983	1988		
Cass	1982			
Cedar	1981			
Chariton	1986		1984–93	1993
Christian	1986		1986–97	1990
Clark	1987		1985–96	
Clay	1980	1988	1994–94	
Clinton	1980		1984–97	
Cole			1987–96	
Cooper	1988	1993	1985–96	
Crawford	1986		1986–98	
Dade	1982			1988
Dallas	1986		1985–94	1989
Daviess		1988		1988
DeKalb	1981	1990–94	1985–94	
Dent	1986			
Douglas	1984	1991		
Dunklin	—	—	—	—
Franklin	1983		1984–00	
Gasconade	1981	1991	1984–90	
Gentry		1988		
Greene	1985			
Grundy	1980	1989		
Harrison		1988–93	1985–96	
		1993		
Henry	1983			
Hickory	1981	1988	1984–87	1992

(Continued)

Table 21-3. *Types of Sales Taxes in Missouri Counties, 1994 (continued)*

County	Regular	General	Capital Improvements[1]	Law Enforcement[1]
Holt	1981	1990–95	1987–94	
			1993–98	
Howard	1987		1985	1991
Howell	1985			
Iron	1987			
Jackson	1980	1990–97		
Jasper	1981		1987–98	
			1994	
Jefferson	1980		1986–01	1988
Johnson	1980		1985–94	1993
Knox	1981	1990–97	1985–96	
Laclede	1985			
Lafayette	1994		1984–98	
Lawrence	1980		1985–99	
			1994–95	
Lewis	1981	1989–99	1985–96	
Lincoln	1980		1987–97	1988
Linn	1985		1985–94	
Livingston	1983			
McDonald	1981		1992–96	
			1994	
Macon	1981	1993–95	1986–96	
Madison	1988		1988–92	
Maries	1981	1990		
Marion	1980		1987–03	
Mercer	1982	1988		
Miller	1981			
Mississippi	1984		1987–97	
Moniteau	1981		1985–87	
Monroe	1981	1988–98		
Montgomery	1981	1994	1994–14	
Morgan	1981		1985–85	
New Madrid	1981			
Newton	1982	1992	1988–88	
Nodaway	1981	1994		
Oregon	1986	1990		
Osage	1981			
Ozark	1986	1989	1986–88	
Pemiscot	1980			
Perry	1980		1987–90	
Pettis	1980			
Phelps	1982		1991–97	
Pike	1981			1990
Platte	1981			
Polk			1994	1989–92
				1993

(Continued)

Table 21-3. Types of Sales Taxes in Missouri Counties, 1994 (continued)

County	Regular	General	Capital Improvements[1]	Law Enforcement[1]
Pulaski	1984		1984–86 1988–97	
Putnam		1988		1991
Ralls	1984	1991–96		
Randolph	1981			
Ray	1980	1988–95	1984–98	
Reynolds	—	—	—	—
Ripley				1988
St. Charles	1980	1992	1983–87 1986–96 1992–06	
St. Clair	1985			
St. Francois	1982		1986–86 1986–94 1994–00	1994
St. Genevieve*	1980		1986–97	
St. Louis Co.**	1978			
Saline	1981		1984–84	
Schuyler	1988		1984–87 1988–96	1989
Scotland		1988–89 1991	1986–97	1988–89 1991
Scott	1980		1986–89 1987–89	
Shannon	1988			
Shelby	1981	1990		
Stoddard	1988			
Stone	1983		1993–01	1990
Sullivan	1981	1988		
Taney	1980	1993–03	1984–98	
Texas	1982			
Vernon	1981			
Warren	1980		1994	1993
Washington	1985	1993–99	1988–98	1988
Wayne	1985		1993	
Webster	1983		1987–96	
Worth	1982		1985–96	1990
Wright	1981			
St. Louis City	—	—	—	—

[1] The second year listed (i.e. 1987–96) indicates the expiration date.

*Ste. Genevieve also had a storm water sales tax from 1986 to 1987.

**St. Louis County also has a public mass transit sales tax; the first passage was in 1973, the second in 1994 will expire in 1999.

and receive the complaints regarding this function. The many other necessary duties fall under the general category of administration. These duties include such specifics as recording of deeds and such generalities as representing the county. The county clerk and county commission are the hub of administrative operations.

Financial Operations. Financial operations generally have been relatively independent and self-sustaining. Treasurers in township counties face some difficulty in handling from seven to twenty-four separate collectors, but seldom are there major problems. Assessment costs are now partially shared by all taxing units rather than absorbed by the counties alone. One recent trend in the financial sector has been increased sophistication in the counties' management of money. A proposal for statewide pooling of idle funds for investment was defeated in 1978, but individual counties have been sharpening investment skills, and a few have instituted local pooling.

Legal Operation. Law operation is the most frequent source of administrative conflict within county government. Much of the money spent in this sector can, through court order, go off-budget or be ordered spent without regard to the budgetary processes. An appellate board for conflicts between state courts and counties deals with disagreements; in places, even federal courts have entered the arena, ordering replacement or closure of jails. Such items as pay for juvenile court personnel, uniform allowances for deputy sheriffs, or air conditioning of courtrooms have on occasion come into dispute. Whether through legislative mandate, as in mandatory sentencing for certain offenses, or indirectly, as in requiring all law officers to receive standardized training, law enforcement

seems to be changing from a county to a state operation.

Road Operations. Historically, the construction, maintenance, and repair of roads and bridges has been viewed as the primary, or perhaps the sole, responsibility of the county commission. In parts of the state, members of the commission are still called *road judges.* Except in township counties, the county is responsible for all roads and bridges that have been accepted as county roads and that are not within an incorporated place or a special road district. Because the counties have histories stretching back well past one hundred years, and because their records range from recent and complete to long since missing, determining which road is the responsibility of whom is far less simple than it would appear. Added to this is the confusion accompanying the fact that acceptance of roads into county systems until recently was often informal. It is not difficult to understand the volume of complaints that roads generate, given such an environment of uncertainty. Counties in recent years have been attempting to bring some order to this chaos, with agonizingly slow progress.

A new road problem has arisen in recent years. The increase in the rural, nonfarm population has brought a disproportionate increase in road management problems. Counties equipped and experienced with gravel and dirt roads, or even some asphalt roads, have found themselves with streets to maintain and citizens accustomed to city-level street services. Counties may and do refuse to accept subdivision streets as county roads. However, this is never politically easy and may be politically impossible. To add to the difficulty, as automobiles have become smaller, bumps and holes have become more threatening. Many questions regarding streets and roads remain to be answered.

Administrative Operations. The other duties and problems falling upon county government come under the broad category of administration. These range from seeing that a flag is displayed at every polling place (which the board of election commissioners does in a few counties and the county clerk does in others) to certifying the enumeration of school-age residents or annually inventorying county property (a county clerk duty). Most administrative chores are performed by the clerk, usually under the direction of the county commission. The clerk and commission often serve as intermediaries between county officials, between citizens and officials, between the county and the state or federal governments, and between the county and bureaucracies. All duties not specifically assigned elsewhere seem to become the responsibility of the commission and the clerk, either by stipulation or by habit.

Operational Conflict. Much of the confusion surrounding counties, and much of the difficulty surrounding new ideas, can be directly tied to the way counties are perceived. It is logical to view county officials as unified in their actions. It is also incorrect. Although the media often delight in referring to "the courthouse gang," it seldom exists as such. Within broad parameters, officials cooperate with each other as far as possible. On occasion, partisanship, politics, or personalities might interfere with the operations of the county government, but each official generally tries to consider the entire county and its population in performing the assigned tasks. However, occasions can arise in which two officeholders become adversaries. The assessor's determination of taxable value, for instance, can cause the collector to receive many complaints from taxpayers if the taxes are high. At the same time, if the assessed valuation does not increase sufficiently to move the county to a higher bracket, some county officials will forfeit a pay raise. This ongoing movement between ally and adversary may be what has maintained public support for the so-called obsolete county governmental structures.

VI. Change

Article VI, Section 2, of the state constitution says, "The existing organization of counties shall continue." It goes on to say that further provisions may be made. Several have been, but no Missouri county has used these provisions. Consolidation is permitted (Section 3), with each county retaining its outstanding liabilities. Dissolution is permitted (Section 5) through annexation to adjoining counties. Joint operations are permitted (Section 14) to a maximum of ten counties. Five methods for rejoining St. Louis County with the city of St. Louis are set forth: (1) merge county into city; (2) merge city into county as separate city; (3) allow city annexation into county; (4) jointly govern all or part; or (5) some other arrangement. For the most part, these have received scant notice and little serious consideration. A metropolitan sewer district, a zoo/museum district, and a mass transit operation are about the only implementations of these options. Why Section 2 remains so solidly in place is worth examining.

One presumption underlying all these provisions is that the public would in some fashion gain from a different form of governmental organization. On occasions when schemes have been presented, the contention has been either that existing services could be provided more economically, or that more and better services could be provided. Missouri voters, ever skeptical, find this difficult to believe. In most of the township counties, impassioned campaigns have stressed the increased efficiency possible through the abolition of township governments. Only one county has abolished townships, not to gain efficiency but because the county entered second-class status, and township organization is an option only open to third-class counties.

A study made in 1969 simulated the consolidation of two counties and calculated benefits and costs.[6] The two were ideal representatives, one prosperous and one poverty-stricken, adjoining and accessible. Savings from the elimination of the poor county, its elected officials, and its operation were itemized and tallied. On the cost side only one item was included: the additional mileage for an average of two trips per family per year from the eliminated county to the new county seat. At four cents per mile, costs outweighed savings. Informal replications suggest an identical outcome would be achieved for most counties today, adjusting mileage allowances to the times. Consolidation, in other words, does not appear to offer the savings that

6. T. Klindt and C. Braschler, "Costs, Revenues and Simulated Consolidation of Selected Missouri Counties," *Research Bulletin 949* (Agricultural Experiment Station, University of Missouri–Columbia, 1969).

are often presumed. The other reason for consolidation—better services—generates little support when it is emphasized. For those either satisfied with or resigned to the level of services presently received, improved services hold slight attraction. Article VI, Section 2, does not appear to be at risk.

This does not suggest, however, that counties do not change. As needs have arisen, counties have responded. An effective statewide association and individual associations of county officers (treasurers, sheriffs, and so on) have met with considerable success in convincing the General Assembly of county needs. County officials, particularly the county clerks and county commissions, have expanded their scope. Information sharing has become much more commonplace, both among counties and statewide. The statewide association, associations of officials by office, and a few Cooperative Extension agents have all been factors in improving communications. More aggressive county officials have also had marked impact. Fortuitous or unfortunate circumstances, as with court-ordered jail closure or state-mandated property revaluation, have focused public attention on counties. Intercounty cooperation seems to be flourishing. The long-predicted demise of county government does not appear to be close at hand.

CHAPTER 22

Special Districts in Missouri and the Nation
by Richard R. Dohm

> Special districts are the least known and least understood units of government in the United States.—W. G. Thrombley

Special districts are governments that serve a limited purpose. In contrast to municipalities and counties, which perform many functions and are called "general-purpose governments," special districts usually are confined to one service. For example, fire protection is needed by rural as well as urban residents. Yet county governments, which traditionally serve rural populations, are not authorized to provide fire protection. Voluntary efforts may be made to help fight fires, but the need for expensive equipment requires stable financing of some sort. The solution in many areas is to organize a fire protection district. This district represents a new government with taxing authority sufficient to provide the service.

Special districts are probably the least-known form of local government. Citizens generally are familiar with municipalities (cities, villages, incorporated towns), counties, and school districts, but are probably only vaguely aware of the special districts in their area. Yet St. Louis County has eighty-three special districts, which may surprise many of its residents. All states but Alaska have at least some special districts, and the number of special districts is growing as population increases and disperses.

Because of their low visibility, special districts have been termed "phantom governments" by John C. Bollens, who has written one of the classics on the subject.[1] As Bollens points out, many people are unaware of the existence of these governments, even though half of all governing board members are elected by the voters. In fact some observers question the effectiveness of special districts because so few voters participate in special-district elections. Accountability to the electorate is not present, say critics, if only 2 percent of the voters mark ballots for board members at an election.

In their defense, special districts are often the only way to provide a needed service. If a community in a fringe area needs water because individual wells are inadequate, a special district may be necessary to make drinkable water available. If the situation is desperate, affected citizens will not be very receptive to arguments about the undesirability of creating another new government.

1. John C. Bollens, *Special District Governments in the United States* (Berkeley: University of California Press, 1957). See also William H. Cape, Leon B. Graves, and Burton M. Michaels, *Government by Special Districts* (Lawrence: University of Kansas, Governmental Research Center, Research Series Number 37, 1969).

Table 22-1. Number of U.S. Local Governments, by Type, 1952–1992

	1952	1972	1992
General Purpose Governments			
County	3,052	3,044	3,043
Municipal	16,807	18,517	19,296
Township	17,202	16,991	16,666
Special Purpose Governments			
School District	67,355	15,781	14,556
Special District	12,340	23,885	33,131
Total Local Governments	116,756	78,218	86,692

Source: *1992 Census of Governments, Preliminary Report*

In a sense, creating special districts is akin to earmarking revenues by type of government, something public administrators and legislators abhor. Earmarking means dedicating revenues, a tax, or a portion of a tax for a specific function or service. For example, proceeds from the Missouri cigarette tax have been earmarked for primary and secondary education. In the case of a special district, a new government is created to perform a special function, and is given authority to tax. Because the new government is limited to one function (usually), all of the taxes or revenues it collects are earmarked for that function.

In this chapter, we will examine national trends in special districts and discuss in more detail the reasons for their creation. The chapter's final section focuses on special districts in Missouri, including types, selected organizational features, and geographic concentration. A note of caution: Special districts include a wide variety of types and are rapidly growing in number. There is some difficulty in attempting to classify them and even greater difficulty in arriving at an accurate count. U.S. Bureau of the Census figures are used in this chapter, but these figures are open to question given the survey method used to obtain

data, as well as the rapidity with which new districts are being formed.

I. National Background and Trends

Although special districts were used in England as early as the thirteenth century, their early use in the United States was primarily for education. The commitment to public education and the agrarian nature of early America led to a huge number of small districts, in which children could walk to school. As Table 22–1 indicates, in 1952 there were 67,355 school districts in the United States.[2] By 1972 the number had dropped to 15,781, a 77 percent loss over twenty years. School district decline tapered off after 1972, falling by only about 8 percent, to 14,556 districts, by 1992.

Overall, local governments increased in number from 1972 to 1992. The number of county governments remained relatively stable, as did the number of township governments. However, both municipalities and special districts increased, with the dramatic gain being in special districts—up 39 percent from 1972 to 1992. There were

2. U.S. Bureau of the Census, 1992 Census of Governments, Preliminary Report, "Governmental Units in 1992."

33,131 special districts in the United States as of 1992.

By 1972 special districts had become the largest category of local government, and they are increasing their lead. Today, special-district governments are found everywhere. Bollens has categorized them geographically into (1) metropolitan; (2) urban fringe, or the developing areas around cities; (3) conterminous with the boundaries of a related government; and (4) rural. Functions vary from one area to another; for example, highly urban services such as transportation and air pollution control are confined primarily to metropolitan areas.

Table 22–2 indicates which states have the greatest number of special districts. A glance will indicate that Midwestern states are well represented.

There is great variety among the special districts in the United States. The largest category by far (found in all geographic areas) is fire protection; there were more than five thousand such districts in the United States as of 1992. Rural areas have had an increasing need for fire protection as the population disperses. New residents in rural areas are concerned about protecting their property, and as rural areas become more populated, more fire protection districts are likely in the future.

The second largest category of special districts is housing and community development, which reflects urban needs. Water supply is third, reflecting the many districts created during the last decades to furnish drinkable water to rural residents. With increasing population dispersion, individual wells are no longer adequate for water supply. Drainage and flood control is the fourth largest category, with soil and water conservation next. Both of these categories relate to rural needs, with farmers wanting to put more land into production and prevent flooding. Soil and water conservation districts are formed to prevent wind and water erosion.

There are many other varieties of special districts: the list includes cemeteries, libraries, hospitals, highways, airports, and health. Still other special districts are organized in some areas for exotic functions such as mosquito abatement. The Minneapolis–St. Paul metropolitan area, for example, has many lakes and wetlands where mosquitoes breed. Because the wind can blow mosquitoes for many miles, the district's boundaries include a large geographic area. Spraying is conducted regularly to keep the pests in check, and a special property tax is levied throughout the jurisdiction to provide funds for the service.

Another unusual type of special district is the noxious-weed district. A special tax is levied within the district's boundaries to provide funds for the eradication of harmful weeds such as johnsongrass, which is a hay crop in some areas but a weed in cultivated lands. Missouri has several of these jurisdictions, although there is some question about whether they are actually districts. One neighboring state, Nebraska, used to have more than eighty such districts.

Revenues are a crucial consideration for all governments, including special districts. Indeed, districts are often created to avoid tax limitations imposed on general-purpose governments—a point that will be returned to later. Special districts differ from municipalities and counties most dramatically in that they rely far less on the property tax and more on user/service charges. Only 11 percent of special-district revenues come from the property tax, and indeed only 53 percent of all special districts can levy a property tax (all general-

Table 22-2. Top States in Number of Special District Governments and in Number of Special Districts per 100,000 Population, 1992

State	Number of Special Districts	State	Number of Special Districts per 100,000 Population
Illinois	2,995	North Dakota	117
California	2,897	Wyoming	86
Texas	2,392	Idaho	70
Pennsylvania	2,244	Montana	70
Kansas	1,506	Nebraska	67
Missouri	1,443	Kansas	60
Colorado	1,317	South Dakota	39
Washington	1,192	Colorado	38
Nebraska	1,075	Oregon	29
Indiana	1,000	Delaware	29
		Missouri	28

purpose governments can do this).[3] According to Bureau of the Census reports, more than one-half of all special-district revenue comes from direct charges for services.

II. Factors Stimulating Creation and Growth

There are many factors that can encourage the creation of special districts. In general, though, these factors can be classified as either ideological, political/legal, or economic.

Ideological Factors. The ideology behind special districts relates to conservatism in general but more specifically to the values associated with Thomas Jefferson. Jefferson believed in maximum political freedom and a minimum of governmental activity, declaring, "I am for a government rigorously frugal and simple." Furthermore, he considered public power potentially dangerous to liberty and was in favor of dispersing it: "It is not by the consolidation or

concentration of powers, but by their distribution, that good government is effected." Such an ideology opposes concentration of power in any given government (or branch of government), supporting instead a preference for governments small enough to be considered "close to the people."

This support of small governments is evident in the rather conservative Midwest. As noted earlier, many Midwestern states are among those states with the largest number of local governments. Illinois is highest with 6,810; Missouri ranks ninth with 3,368.[4]

Another result of Jeffersonianism is that state legislatures have placed many restrictions on existing governments. Local governments are subservient to state governments, and most state legislatures exert considerable control over them. The preference for small, personal governments (if one has to have government) is structured by state statute (the legal "playing field"). In the past, rural interests dominated state legislatures, and anti-city legislation was

3. U.S. Bureau of the Census, *Finances of Special Districts,* 1987.

4. "Governmental Units in 1992."

common. Although this has changed with reapportionment and an increased urban population, many state laws still reflect rural biases. For example, early annexation laws and court decisions in St. Louis County hindered cities from expanding their boundaries. The requirement of two majorities in annexation elections (nonresidents and residents) stifled most efforts. It was easier to create new municipal and special district governments (only one majority was needed). As a report by the Advisory Commission on Intergovernmental Relations explains, "Faced with alternatives of leaving these decisions (regarding services and taxes) to county officials or of being annexed by other, adjacent municipalities, citizens of much of St. Louis County chose local self-government."[5] Such restrictions were extended to the rest of the state in the 1970s, and large annexations outstate have been stopped. Populations outside cities usually fight being absorbed.

In rural areas, county governments are not able to perform many urban services because of state law, despite the desire of expanding populations outside of cities and villages for such services. These laws are not changed because of financial pressures, and because of the disinclination of county officials to take on additional responsibilities. Again, it is easier to create new special-district governments with additional taxing authority.

Political and Legal Factors. Institutions and public policies are never neutral, favoring some groups or populations while disfavoring others. Federal government activism since the Great Depression has resulted in many new policies, and several have directly or indirectly stimulated creation of special-district governments.

5. Advisory Commission on Intergovernmental Relations, *Metropolitan Organization: The St. Louis Case,* September 1988, M–158, 17.

For example, in 1936, in response to dust bowl conditions caused by drought, Congress passed the Soil Conservation and Domestic Allotment Act, which is the basis for a Missouri state conservation law. Both the federal and the state laws are designed to stimulate the formation of soil conservation districts to protect against erosion, a concern of increasing interest today. Missouri voters in August 1984 approved an increase of one-tenth of a cent in the state sales tax for five years; half of the revenues are to be used for soil conservation, and half for state parks. Voters renewed the tax for another ten years on November 8, 1988, by a wide margin—1,263,644 to 576,790. As a direct result of such policies, almost every county in Missouri now includes a soil conservation district.

Indirectly, federal policy stimulated creation of many special districts in metropolitan areas following World War II. The federal government made home loans with low down payments and low interest rates available to returning veterans and others. Together, the G.I. loans and the Federal Housing Administration (FHA) loans stimulated much home building outside of the central cities. (Most central cities— at least in the eastern half of the United States—were already developed and did not have sufficient space to accommodate the huge demand for single-family housing.) As a result of this policy, thousands of new subdivisions were created, many of which were incorporated as cities and villages. This phenomenon became known as "proliferation," or the development of a great many new (but generally small) suburban governments.

A major problem resulting from proliferation is the mismatch between the area needing services (which may be the entire metropolitan area) and the governmental structure, which may consist of hundreds of suburban governments. How can a service be performed for all when suburban governments are independent entities jealously guarding their autonomy? An existing city cannot perform a service for another unless there is a legal contract between the two. However, when as many as ninety cities are involved (as in St. Louis County), contracts are almost impossible to negotiate. Also, there are often geographic gaps between cities consisting of unincorporated (county) land. *Only special districts can coexist with or extend into another government's territory to provide a service.* Thus, for such metropolitanwide functions as transportation, most metropolitan areas develop a special district that can cross city, county, and even state lines (the latter only by interstate compact).

The politics of establishing such a district can be very interesting. Problems usually have to reach crisis proportions before political action is taken, and the political battles may have to be resolved in the state legislature. Usually, "muddling-through" approaches will be tried until the problem (perhaps polluted drinking water) becomes a crisis. Then, out of desperation, some groups and officials will propose a "metropolitan" solution. Jealousies among local governments and officials will arise, scare tactics will be used, and fears of loss of local identity will surface. These and other factors (sometimes pure self-interest) will extend the political battle over many months, even years. Solutions will sometimes be comprehensive, but more often piecemeal or partial adjustments will result.

Another political reason for creating special districts relates to the desire of professionals or interested citizens to separate a given function from city hall. City halls often are considered "too political," and many

perceive city hall politics to be "too dirty." Therefore, they push for independence for their favored functions and help create independent school districts (meaning independent from city or county government), library districts, or special districts for technical functions such as water supply or sewage disposal. Engineers generally distrust politicians and prefer to see technical functions under special-district control, where engineers can be more influential. The rationale for this splitting-off process is that some functions are so important that "they must be taken out of politics."

Rural or outstate areas also use special districts, such as road, hospital, and fire protection districts. Rural residents often need or want the same services as their urban counterparts, although perhaps not to the same extent. For example, the Federal Highway Safety Act had the effect of forcing private ambulance operations out of business. Mortuaries often provided such services in rural areas, but when confronted with the necessity of paying minimum wages to personnel on duty and providing constantly ready ambulances and trained personnel, they simply dropped the services. (Before the act, ambulance personnel could be paid by the run rather than by the hour and could sleep in the mortuaries between calls.) If existing hospitals did not pick up the service dropped by the mortuaries, special-purpose ambulance districts were required. Again, federal policy had an effect at the local level of stimulating the creation of new governments, when existing city-based hospitals were reluctant or unable to service rural areas.

Of extreme importance is the legal framework of local government. This is the structure that establishes "rules of the game." Originally, political factors such as Jeffersonianism affected the legal framework, but once such a framework is set, it is very difficult to change. The most basic and enduring rule in terms of local government was that given by Judge John F. Dillon in 1868; in a crucial court opinion, he ruled that cities are mere "creatures of the state." In other words, all local governments are political subdivisions of the state and cannot act without state authorization. As a result of Dillon's rule, state governments have "protected" local units by imposing tax and indebtedness restrictions on them, the most severe of which apply to counties. Consequently, county governments are faced with budgetary problems and often cannot respond to requests for new services. As a result, new governments in the form of special districts are established.

Economic Factors. Economic factors related to the creation of special districts have been touched on already in this chapter. Many governments are too small, in terms of both geographic area served and tax base, to provide a needed service. The services usually involve a large capital outlay and/or large budgets for operation, and small governments are unable to finance them through their own resources. Cooperation between governments to share resources is extremely difficult, and an approach designed to tap the resources of a large area becomes necessary. The special district is often the answer and has the additional advantage of preserving the status quo; that is, it does not threaten the independent status of existing governments.

In summary, special-district governments are created for a wide variety of reasons. Federal policies have been a factor, professional groups (such as engineers) are interested in having technical functions "taken out of politics" by separating them from general-purpose government, and some governmental units lack the legal and taxing authority to perform certain services. In addition, existing governments may prefer to create special districts to avoid pressures for consolidation. Sometimes even unadorned self-interest is involved. As Bollens points out,

> One illustration relates to the actions of private concerns anxious to sell equipment and supplies. Judging that their business opportunities will be enhanced, they sometimes provide the principal stimulus for the establishment of special districts. . . . The result in one instance was the creation of a sanitary district which laid sewer pipes far in excess of needs of both the present and the foreseeable future population. . . . Another example of self-interest is the desire of local residents to realize a return on tax money collected in their area. This self-centered attitude explains the establishment of a number of road districts in Missouri.[6]

There are almost as many reasons for establishing special districts as there are types of districts, but the prevailing culture may well be the most important.

III. Special Districts in Missouri

"Government for every purpose" aptly describes local government in Missouri, particularly special-district governments (see Table 22–4). As of 1992, Missouri ranked eighth among the states in total number of local governments and sixth in special districts, according to the Census of Governments. In road districts, Missouri ranked first, having almost half of the nation's total at that time.

There are so many special-district governments, with such a variety of purposes, that it is difficult to get an exact count. Furthermore, new ones are added frequently, and in some cases consolidation or abolition changes the total. Deciding when a unit is governmental is sometimes difficult.

---

6. *Special District Governments,* 14–15.

Table 22-3. Top Missouri Counties in
Number of Special Districts per
1,000 Population, 1992

County	Number of Special Districts per 1,000 Population
Holt	3.81
Atchison	3.08
Carroll	2.61
Worth	2.46
Ripley	2.19
Putnam	2.17
Howard	1.97
Dade	1.88
Cedar	1.82
Lewis	1.76
Scotland	1.66
St. Clair	1.54
Shelby	1.44
Sullivan	1.42
Schuyler	1.42
Ray	1.27
Osage	1.25
Clark	1.19
Gentry	1.17
Daviess	1.14
Barry	1.13
Knox	1.12
Carter	1.09
Saline	1.06
Henry	1.00

For example, housing authorities are sometimes independent of city government. In Missouri these are often counted as special districts, but they really do not qualify. They are created without an election, have appointed directors, and do not have taxing authority. However, they do issue revenue bonds, pay off their debts with revenues from housing facilities, and have some degree of autonomy.

In another example, the state auditor classifies soil and water conservation districts as independent governments, even though they do not have taxation authority. Indeed, they are expressly forbidden to levy taxes, but otherwise have many characteristics of independent governments. To make things even more complicated, soil and water conservation *subdistricts* do have taxing authority. Should the subdistrict but not the district be classified as a local government because of its taxing authority? This is part of the difficulty in determining exactly how many special-district governments there are in Missouri or, for that matter, in the nation.

The state auditor probably has the most accurate count of special districts, because the auditor's office relies on more than questionnaire returns. In its February 1992 report, the office classified 1,437 units as special-district governments (see Table 22–4). In 1981 only 1,205 special-district governments were counted.

Types of Districts in Missouri. Although the state auditor has identified twelve categories of special districts, there are at least twenty-nine enabling acts or state laws for the creation of districts. Obviously, if there is a strong need for a service not being performed by private enterprise, the General Assembly is willing to pass authorizing legislation. This receptivity would appear to contradict Missouri's antigovernment posture, but when examined more closely, it reflects the state's anti-BIG government bias. Politicians often inveigh against the federal government because of its size, remoteness, and insensitivity to state and local needs. Yet there appears to be no particular bias against small, personal governments.

Table 22–4 lists the types and numbers of special districts in each county in Missouri. Missouri still has a disproportionate number of road districts. In all, seven of the twelve categories include more than one hundred districts, with three—road, fire

Table 22-4. Missouri Special Districts by County, 1992

County	Road Districts	Fire Protection	Water	Libraries	Drainage Levies	Soil/ Water	Ambulance	Sewers	Health	Nursing Home	Miscel- laneous	Total
Adair	1		1	1	1	1	1			1		7
Andrew		4	4	1	2	1	1			1		14
Atchison	5	4	1	1	10	1	1					23
Audrain	9	1	2	1		1	1		1	1		17
Barry	26			1		1	2		1			31
Barton		1	1	1		1	1		1			6
Bates	2	1	4	1		1	1					10
Benton	3	1		1		1	2			1		9
Bollinger		1		1		1	1					4
Boone	1	2	7	4	1	2	1	1				19
Buchanan		3	2	2	3	1		2			1	14
Butler		2	3	1	2	1	1				1	11
Caldwell			2	2		1	1			1		7
Callaway	2	4	2	1	1	1	1					12
Camden	2	3	2	1		1	1					10
Cape Girardeau	1	4	3	4	1	1			1		1	16
Carroll		2	1	2	19	2	1			1		28
Carter			2	1		1	2					6
Cass	1	9	11	1			2	1	1			26
Cedar	17		1	1		1	1		1			22
Chariton		4	2	1		1	1					9
Christian	11	4	2	1		1	1					20
Clark	1	1	1	2	1	1	1			1		9
Clay	5	2	8	1	2	2			1			21
Clinton	2		4			1	3			1		11
Cole			5	3	1	1		1				11
Cooper		1	1	1		1	1		1	1		7
Crawford		2		1			2					5
Dade	7			2		1	1		1	2		14
Dallas	1	1		1		1						4
Daviess	3	1	1	1		2	1					9
DeKalb			1			2						3
Dent		1	1	1		1			1			5
Douglas				1		1	1					3
Dunklin			2	1	8	1	1					13
Franklin	4	7	3	4	1	1	6	7		1	1	35
Gasconade	1			1	1	1	2		1	1		8
Gentry		3	1	2		1	1					8
Greene		9	3	1		1			1		1	16
Grundy			1	1		1				1	1	5
Harrison			1			4	2		1			8
Henry	13	1	1	2		1	1		1			20
Hickory	1		1	1		1						4
Holt	4	3		2	13	1						23
Howard	2	1	2	3	7	2	1		1			19
Howell		2	2	3		1	3					11
Iron	3	1		2		1	1					8
Jackson		7	7	2	1	1			1		1	20
Jasper	8	3	2	3	1	1						18

(Continued)

Table 22-4. Missouri Special Districts (continued)

County	Road Districts	Fire Protection	Water	Libraries	Drainage Levies	Soil/ Water	Ambulance	Sewers	Health	Nursing Home	Miscel- laneous	Total
Jefferson	2	12	10	5		1	5	6			1	42
Johnson		2	2	2		2			1			9
Knox			1	1		1	1			1		5
Laclede	4	2	3	2		1						12
Lafayette	10	5	2	1		4						22
Lawrence	12			1		1	1			1		16
Lewis	3	3	1	2	2	5	1			1		18
Lincoln	1	1	2			2	1		1			8
Linn	2	2	1	1		2	1					10
Livingston		1	4	2		1	1			1		9
McDonald	4		1	1		1						7
Macon	3		1	2		1	1			1	2	11
Madison			1	1		1				1		4
Maries	3			1		1	2					7
Marion			1	1	4	1	1			1		9
Mercer				1		1	1					3
Miller	3	3	1	2		1	1			1		12
Mississippi		1		1	5	1	1				1	10
Moniteau			2		1	1	1					5
Monroe	2		1	1		1	2			1		8
Montgomery	2		1	2	1	1	1					8
Morgan	4	3		1		1				2		11
New Madrid		3	2		9	1	1					16
Newton	7	5	1	2		2	1				1	19
Nodaway	1	9	1	1		6	1				2	21
Oregon	1		1	1		1	1					5
Osage	7		4	1	1	1	1					15
Ozark						1	1					2
Pemiscot			1	3	4	1			1			10
Perry	1		2	1	1	1			1			7
Pettis	1	1		3		1				2	1	9
Phelps			2	2		1	1		1			7
Pike	2	1	1	1		2			1		1	9
Platte	5	8	8		3	1		9				34
Polk	16			2		1			1			20
Pulaski		2	3	2		1	2		2			12
Putnam	2	2	1	1		2	1		1	1		11
Ralls			2			2	1					5
Randolph	1	1		2		1	1				1	7
Ray	7	2	3	1	10	2	1		1	1		28
Reynolds			1	1		1	1		1			5
Ripley	19		2	1		3	1		1			27
St. Charles		8	1	1	5	1	1	2			1	20
St. Clair	7	1		2		1			2			13
St. Francois	1		3	3		1	1				1	10
Ste. Genevieve	1		1	1	2	1			1			7
St. Louis		24	1	10	3	1		32			12	83
Saline	7	1	3	2	8	1	3					25

(Continued)

Table 22-4. *Missouri Special Districts (continued)*

County	Road Districts	Fire Protection	Water	Libraries	Drainage Levies	Soil/ Water	Ambulance	Sewers	Health	Nursing Home	Miscel- laneous	Total
Schuyler	1		1	1		1	1			1		6
Scotland			1	1		3	1		1	1		8
Scott	2	3		3		1	2					11
Shannon	1					1	1					3
Shelby	2		1	2	1	1	1			2		10
Stoddard	6		6	2	3	1	1					19
Stone		2	1	2		1	1					7
Sullivan	4		1	1		1	1		1			9
Taney	1	2	3			1	1					8
Texas			3	1		1			1			6
Vernon			5	1		1	1					8
Warren		3	2	1		1	2					9
Washington		1		1			1		1			4
Wayne		1	1	1		1	1					5
Webster	1	1		1		1						4
Worth			1			3	1			1		6
Wright				1		1						2
St. Louis City												0
TOTALS	295	209	207	169	139	146	110	64	35	34	29	1437

1. Soil and water conservation districts include soil and water conservation subdistricts.

Source: Missouri State Auditor Report, February 1992

protection, and water—being the most numerous at more than two hundred districts each. These three categories include almost half of all special districts in the state.

Selected Organizational Features. There are several organizational variations among the twenty-nine different types of special districts authorized for Missouri, according to an earlier study by Jack Timmons of the University of Missouri–Columbia.[7] More than half of the authorizing state statutes provide for creation by election and also call for election rather than appointment of those serving on governing boards. Most of the statutes provide for annexation and dissolution, although less than half allow merging or consolidation of more than one district (again, tilting the playing field toward proliferation).

Taxing authority is provided in all but two types of districts—port authorities and common sewer districts. Slightly more than half (fifteen) can issue general obligation bonds for capital improvements, backed by the full faith and credit of the special-district government. Public water supply, common sewer, and johnsongrass districts can only issue revenue bonds, however, whereas four types can issue both, and six types have no bonding authority at all. Revenue bonds are retired by fees or charges levied on the service being offered, and generally have become more popular as anti–property tax sentiment has increased.

Distribution and Geographic Concentration. The state auditor's report includes county totals as well. Table 22–4 shows the distribution of special districts through-

7. Paper prepared by Jack Timmons, University of Missouri–Columbia, Department of Community Development, January 21, 1976.

out the state. Twenty-one counties have twenty or more special districts each; ten of these counties are located in the two major metropolitan areas. Every county has at least two special districts.

The metropolitan counties include a number of different types of single-function districts, with the largest number (eighty-three) located in St. Louis County. There are thirty-two sewer districts and twenty-four fire protection districts in St. Louis County. Metropolitanwide (multicounty) entities such as the Bi-State Development and Transportation districts have been created to perform functions on behalf of the entire metropolitan area (including territory in Missouri and Illinois). Kansas City also has an areawide transportation authority. Support of the St. Louis Zoo is shared between the city of St. Louis and St. Louis County through the Metropolitan Park and Museum District.

Rural counties with high numbers of special districts have many road districts or drainage/levee districts, or sometimes both. In contrast, metropolitan St. Louis County has many more districts associated with urbanization, such as sewer districts. Jefferson County reflects more of a mixture of rural and urban special districts because of its more recent urbanization, confined primarily to the northern part of the county.

Sixty-six counties have 295 road districts, according to the state auditor. Most of these are found in southwest Missouri, whereas township governments act as road districts in the northwest. Interestingly, northwest citizens support road taxes at a higher rate than southwest citizens do, which may relate to early immigration patterns, and to the different soil structures, since it is less expensive to build roads on the rocky soil in southern Missouri. Drainage/levy districts, in contrast, are found in areas with flood-

plains and thus are associated with counties on or near major rivers.

The fastest-growing rural districts are those providing urban-type services. There have been dramatic increases in hospital, water, library, nursing home, and ambulance districts since 1977. Water districts are most numerous in growth areas, including the counties of Boone and Jefferson. However, they are also widespread in that eighty-nine counties have at least one. This also gives testimony to the effectiveness of the Farmers Home Administration, which has actively pushed for creating water districts and safe, drinkable water. Hospital and nursing home districts of course reflect the need for health care for the aged. Fire protection also has been a priority for sparsely settled areas and has been authorized for several decades.

IV. Summary and Conclusions

Every state in the nation uses special districts to some extent, but there is an abundance of such districts in the Midwest. Heavy reliance on districts is related to agricultural needs, population dispersion, and commitment to Jeffersonian values supporting small, numerous local governments.

State laws favor the creation of new governments rather than an increase in the power and scope of old ones. It is rather easy to establish a new municipality or special district, but much more difficult to increase the size of cities or to add functions to county government. New special-district governments avoid tax limitations imposed on old governments, but have the effect of earmarking taxes by type of government. Special districts generally are established to perform only one function, and their taxing authority is therefore limited to the specified service.

Once an area is built up with many local units of government, only a few approaches can be used to perform a service for the entire area. Cooperative agreements or contracts are sometimes effective, but not for areawide functions such as transportation or air pollution control. Expanding a county government's authority in a metropolitan area is helpful, but it is not necessarily the answer in metropolitan areas that include more than one county. In this situation, only a special district can overlay the many jurisdictions found in a multicounty area.

Although special districts have been termed phantom governments because of their low visibility in the public eye, they are often the only way to provide certain services. When a problem is severe enough, a special district may have to be created to cope with it. If the problems of special districts in turn become a major concern, it is perhaps then that comprehensive reorganization of all local governments will become an item on the public agenda.

CHAPTER 23

The Politics of Planning and Zoning in Missouri
by Richard R. Dohm

> The ability of zoning battles to turn ordinarily reasonable people into wide-eyed fanatics is a never-ending source of amazement.—Clan Crawford

Of the many powers of local government in Missouri, none are more controversial than those relating to planning and zoning. Controls over land use have always generated opposition, but some regulations have a fairly long history. However, zoning ordinances, which create zones for particular types of development, have had legal sanction only since 1926.[1]

Many Missourians dislike even the concept of land use planning, associating it with socialism and too much government. To them, planning suggests conspiracies and control. Zoning is considered even worse in that it can prevent an individual property owner from maximizing profit; for example, by not allowing an owner to change property from residential to commercial status, which would usually increase the value of the land.

Planning may be defined as a process that involves goal setting, fact gathering, and study and analysis. Zoning is part of the planning implementation process (together with other regulations), and involves establishing land use districts; that is, agricultural, industrial, commercial, and residential areas. Zoning powers are outlined in an ordinance or local law and are based on a city's police powers, which include authority to protect the health and welfare of citizens.

The passions generated by planning and zoning became meaningful to one university-based land use planner following a night seminar on planning and zoning in a rural county. He had been invited to make the presentation by supporters interested in some sort of regulation to cope with existing and future problems. After the meeting, however, opponents told him not to return for any more presentations relating to planning and zoning, and he definitely felt he would have suffered bodily harm should he have done so. This is a more extreme example of opposition to P and Z (as participants call it), but attempts to adopt county zoning do bring about spirited—sometimes even fanatical—opposition.

Many Missourians are highly individualistic, and they resent and distrust government. This dislike is most apparent in opposition to taxes, but it applies to some regulation as well. These people believe government's role in decision making should be minimized, and they see little need for planning and zoning. However,

1. *Village of Euclid, Ohio, v. Ambler Realty Co.,* 272 U.S. 365, 1926.

the ideological dimensions become blurred because liberals and conservatives can be found on either side of the issue. Liberals usually support planning and zoning because they are willing, if necessary, to use governmental powers to bolster community improvement. Moderate conservatives are often supportive as well because they want to maintain property values, which they feel can only be safeguarded through regulation. On the other hand, archconservatives oppose planning and zoning on principle because it involves using governmental powers. Switches in traditional positions do occur, though, if enough personal gain is involved.

Opponents can be vociferous in their opposition. They view zoning, for example, as a violation of property rights. No one should be able to restrict such rights, they feel. For example, the governmental power of eminent domain, which refers to the power of government to take a person's property after due process and with just, or fair, compensation, is thought to be "unconstitutional" by many opponents. At least one recent U.S. Supreme Court decision, it should be noted, appears to be questioning zoning authority more intently, thus giving more support to this point of view.

Support for planning and zoning is strongest in urban areas. Almost every county in or near a large city has planning and zoning save for the counties by Joplin. In contrast, few rural counties have adopted planning and zoning, the main exceptions including three tourism-impacted counties in southwest Missouri and a half-dozen counties in northwest Missouri. In total, twenty-nine counties have adopted zoning, and eighty-five counties have not (see Table 23–1). Some of the latter counties have adopted planning authority alone; Missouri is one of the few states that allows county voters to adopt either planning or zoning, or both.

Threats to health and the environment, however, are strong motivators for embracing planning and zoning. Recently, several very rural counties experienced environmental threats such as large-scale landfills that might cause future problems. One of these counties voted in county zoning to try and cope with the situation. Others pushed for legislation that would allow an area smaller than a county to approve zoning authority. The result was state legislation authorizing township zoning.

Townships are much smaller governments than counties. They have been established in only twenty-three Missouri counties, most of which are in northwest Missouri. With authority provided to townships, zoning can then be limited to the immediate area affected by, for example, a landfill, while sparing the rest of the county from zoning controls. At least six townships have adopted zoning to date (of which five are in northern Missouri and suffering economic decline). This trend, it should be noted, is diametrically opposed to what professional planners would recommend—namely, that entire regions be under common policies.

I. What Is Planning?

Although planning connotes governmental control to many, it is actually a process of applying forethought to solve or avoid problems. Planning is an allegedly neutral process that involves taking an inventory of present land use and development, mapping it, and then projecting future trends. Historical analysis is part of the process, as is the application of computer mapping.

Planning is used to reach some preconceived goal for the community's use

Table 23-1. Counties and Townships with Zoning Authority*

County	Township	Year Adopted or Implemented
Boone		1971
Buchanan		1962
Caldwell		1991 (implemented in 1993)
Cape Girardeau		1972
Carroll		1960s (implemented in 1992)
Cass		1959
Chariton		1966
Christian		1990
Clay		1952
Clinton		1966
Franklin		1966
Greene		1964
Jackson		1943
Jefferson		1986
Lafayette		1984
Livingston		1964
Marion		1964
Monroe		1964
Pemiscot		1964
Platte		1952
Ralls		1964
Ray		1966
St. Charles		1959
St. Louis		1946
Schuyler		1989
Stone		1993
Taney		1966
Warren		1983 (implemented)
Worth		1994
Barton	Union	1994
Mercer	Madison	1991/92
	Medicine	1991/92
	Washington	1991/92
Putnam	Lincoln	1994
	York	1991

*Information for this table is based upon a 1985 survey with additions. In the 1960s, some additional counties adopted planning only or both planning and zoning to qualify for loans for public water supply districts, but never implemented the new procedure.

of land, rather than leaving development to the mercy of whatever external forces are operating. Goals are crucial here. The problem becomes goal-setting: what does a community want to do? It is also considered crucial to follow the democratic process in setting the goals. There should be broad participation in goal-setting, although city councils and county commissions will have the final say. Some argue that there should be public votes on comprehensive land use plans, but this is not required by state law in Missouri.

How the plan will be implemented is of equal importance. How is a community to meet its goals? Implementation involves both governmental restrictions and, in the case of land use planning, incentive programs for some desired goals such as building and clearance projects. (Planning is equally important for other health and welfare concerns, but the focus here is land use and development.) Implementing tools include zoning, subdivision regulations, and code enforcement (building, plumbing, electrical, housing codes, and others). Also, special financing and incentives including loans might be a part of a program to bring about desired change, such as housing rehabilitation.

As noted, planning can be separated from plan implementation at the county level in Missouri. The reasons for this go back to the 1960s, when the Farmers Home Administration required planning authority before loans could be made for water districts. Planning and zoning had been tied together, but a change in the law allowed counties to vote for the much less onerous planning without zoning. (Voter approval is needed for either or both.) Adoption of planning, though, did include the ability to regulate subdivisions. Conversely, counties can vote for zoning without planning, which boggles the minds of planners and other sympathizers. They cannot comprehend zoning without going through the planning process first.

II. Pros and Cons of Planning and Zoning

Obviously, planning and zoning can be controversial. Ideology is often part of the debate over the desirability of adopting planning and zoning, and excellent arguments pro and con can be advanced. Several years ago an attitude survey regarding planning and zoning was administered in one rural county. Although not totally scientific (the sample was drawn in random order from voter registration lists), the responses provide some excellent insights into the views of supporters and opponents.

From the responses, it appears that there are certain fundamental assumptions made by supporters. Supporters assume that governmental powers should be used to enhance the community, or the wider "public interest." The emphasis should be on "community" or "commonwealth." Furthermore, they believe that all growth is not necessarily progress. The purpose of the community is to maximize the "good life." Growth should not threaten the amenities that make the community attractive.

Some survey responses of supporters (paraphrased) included:

Planning and zoning maintain property values by preventing mixed land uses. Auto salvage yards are not allowed in residential areas. Maintaining single-use districts (sometimes with buffer zones) will protect the property owner.

Planning and zoning can help maintain and expand the tax base of a community. Without such controls or regulation, shoddy development can take place, perhaps causing outflow of people and investment.

Planning and zoning saves dollars by coordinating additions to the infrastructure. Roads are planned to match up and sewers and water mains are added on a rational basis. Rebuilding water and sewer mains because of initial undersizing is very expensive.

Planning and zoning can be used to preserve amenities that otherwise would be lost. Open space for parks or buffer zones can be very enhancing. Certain physical features such as scenic places should be and can be preserved. Planning and zoning can prevent congestion and overcrowding, two problems which detract from urban life and can lead to individuals, institutions, and commercial/industrial interests leaving the community.

Planning and zoning powers and code enforcement can be used to regulate nuisances such as noise, smells, and dangerous conditions such as garbage, vermin, cesspools, and fire hazards.

Planning and zoning and subdivision regulations can help prevent urban sprawl and suburbs which become immediate slums. Subdivision regulations are particularly useful for this purpose.

Opponents also hold certain assumptions regarding planning and zoning. They believe that free enterprise and the marketplace should determine property decisions in the community. The emphasis should be on individualism. Furthermore, they believe growth *is* progress. Growth is necessary to maintain the economy. Development helps create jobs and fuels the local economy. Communities without growth, they argue, are dying.

Specific disadvantages taken from survey responses included:

Planning and zoning adds controls and restrictions which increase development costs, and may discourage new investment. Some may be absorbed by developers, but not if they reach certain levels.

Planning and zoning restricts individual decision making, leaving more authority with the local government and its bureaucracy. This works against imaginative development.

Planning and zoning requirements merely add complexity to a natural economic process, with the result of adding further costs without equivalent gain. Increased costs can easily stifle development.

Planning and zoning favors those who can manipulate the system—the rich or influential. Developers, commercial/industrial interests, and individuals who stand to gain can usually get zoning changes that advantage them.

Planning and zoning is an urban power which impedes agriculture and rural development; it puts the minority farmer under urban control. It is not needed in rural areas.

Planning and zoning may result in increased taxes by artificially creating higher-use zones with accompanying tax increases, allegedly for additional services.

Planning and zoning tends to concentrate both the rich and the poor, leading to increased costs and problems.

III. Planning/Zoning, the Environment, and Economic Development

Although controversial, planning and zoning are invoked when problems cannot be solved privately. Cities have a long history of using planning and zoning, basing its use on the government's police powers to maintain the "health and welfare" of the community. In the nineteenth century, some developers constructed housing next to heavy-industry factories, assuming that workers could save transportation costs if they lived close to where they worked. In the twentieth century, local governments began to prohibit such housing because the air and water pollution from the factories affected the health of the families of the workers. Mixed land use was considered damaging not only to health but also to property values. Although mixed development is becoming fashionable today (especially development combinations such as commercial convenience stores in residential areas), most city and county zoning ordinances continue the pattern of separating development, usually starting with zoning districts for commercial, industrial, and residential land use, as well as agricultural districts where applicable.

Zoning authority is a state government power, although traditionally it has been delegated to cities and counties, except in the case of coastal zoning in some states bordering on oceans (and Hawaii). The federal government does not use zoning, although it has programs that call on the states and localities to zone.

Environmental problems are more evident today because of more intensive use of the land and greater efforts by those interested in preserving habitats (the Greens and Sierra Club members among others). Conflicts occur between advocates of environmental and developmental causes, often over issues such as finding locations for trash incinerators and sewage disposal plants, which stimulate NIMBY (Not In My Back Yard) reactions.

In 1990 concern over Missouri's rivers, which were thought to be degenerating, led to a petition drive for a Natural Streams Act. The act called for zoning Missouri's fifty-two rivers and adjoining land in an attempt to maintain stream quality. Pesticide runoff, trash and litter, off-road vehicle use in stream beds, and overuse were thought to be causing the degeneration. Supporters claimed that owners with property along rivers were not doing a good job of managing the streams and adjoining land. Opponents called the act a variety of unprintable names, and they certainly resented the proposed use of governmental regulation on "their" rivers. Voters had a chance to express their opinions in the

1990 general election, and there was a clear indication of sentiment. Not one county approved the act: indeed, except for the city of St. Louis, where 45 percent of the voters supported the act, no county gave the act more than 25 percent of its votes. Twenty-three counties voted at least 95 percent against the proposal.

With respect to economic development, zoning usually is used as a tool for controlling growth. That is, it restricts industrial and commercial development to those areas or zones that have been allocated for such land use under the plan. Existing development, of course, strongly affects what is built in adjoining areas. Also, whatever is built first will often dictate similar development for the immediate area. This is why land use planners are so concerned that communities get an early start in the planning/zoning process. After ten years, existing growth is a given and tends to cause similar development. Commercial strip building on highways, once underway, is very difficult to stop or ameliorate.

Zoning controls in some rural areas have been stimulated by economic development, especially by corporate farming, large-scale landfills, and tourism. Corporate farming includes hog and cattle operations with highly concentrated activities. Some of these operations are very large and lead to obnoxious odors and sewage disposal problems. Large-scale landfills have been a threat to some counties. Prime locations for such landfills have been in sparsely populated counties in northern Missouri. Schuyler County in northeast Missouri voted for countywide planning and zoning in response to a proposal to bury trash from other states in abandoned mines in the county. Tourism, especially the phenomenal development of Branson as a center for country and western entertainment, has led to adoption of land use controls in southwest Missouri.

IV. Growth Management

Limiting or controlling growth has been a goal in some communities faced with overwhelming urban pressures. Several states, including Hawaii, California, New Jersey, Vermont, Florida, and Oregon, have developed approaches for controlling growth statewide or for targeted areas such as the fragile and sought after coastal properties. However, pioneering work has been done at the local level as well. Ramapo, New York, and Petaluma, California, were the first localities to use planning and zoning powers to control or limit growth. Ramapo adopted a phased growth plan where permits are required and issued only after services have reached the location to be developed. Builders and developers can proceed before the required municipal services are available, but only if they pay for them (another variation of this is impact fees). As one observer notes, "The Ramapo plan implied an annual quota on residential development."[2]

In contrast, Petaluma uses a fixed quota for development. A system was originated that gives points to builders and developers for: (1) access to existing services with spare capacity; (2) design characteristics; (3) including open space in the development; and (4) providing for low-income housing. Builders/developers compete annually, and those with the most points get to proceed with developmental projects.

Several studies have examined the effects of local growth management policies. The studies found that results are mixed. One researcher concludes, after review and analysis, that such policies are not particularly

effective at the local level—if pressures are severe enough, development will occur just outside the area of control. For this reason he argues that growth policies must be applied regionally or statewide, an idea that planners have long supported for any planning process.[3]

Rural Areas and Small Communities. In many rural communities, poor economic conditions often lead to a concern for generating growth rather than controlling it. Where planning and zoning is in place, there is often a tendency to designate larger-than-necessary industrial zones, in the hope that new business will be enticed to the community. This is referred to as "overzoning" for industry, and the practice often reflects unrealistic estimates of what may be achieved. In these same communities, and in many suburbs as well, the desire for economic development also leads to a wish to accommodate requests to change residential zones to commercial or industrial. Businesses or industries that wish to locate in an existing residential zone often have little trouble gaining a zoning change because of the community's desire to add to the economic base. The community fears loss of business or industry should they refuse such a change, and this may be a correct assessment in some instances.

V. Metropolitan/Urban Problems and New Approaches in Zoning

Zoning has been part of the urban landscape for decades. Although accepted more readily in cities than in rural areas, there have been controversial points that have led to attacks on both the concept and its implementation. In major metropolitan areas that include many municipalities, planners and policy makers have strongly criticized

2. J. Barry Cullingworth, *The Political Culture of Planning* (New York: Routledge, Inc., 1993), 125.

3. Ibid., 132.

the inability to create areawide zoning; zoning is instead on a city-by-city basis, which leads to great inconsistencies. For example, a residential neighborhood on the border of one municipality may be next to an industrial zone in an adjoining city. It is very difficult to get all city governments to act together in their development plans.

Suburbs also have been criticized for "exclusionary zoning." The flight of the wealthy from the problems of the central city has been well documented. Under the guise of protecting property values, but often to maintain "purity" and prevent "undesirables" (usually, minorities) from moving in, suburbs often resort to large-lot zoning. That is, lots of perhaps one acre or more are prescribed by the zoning ordinance. This means the cost of the land alone is substantial, plus the owner may have to meet a large minimum footage in building a residence to conform with the subdivision regulation ordinance. Obviously, costs are escalated through legal requirements requiring large residential lots and homes.

A third area of criticism relates to zoning procedures and involves favoritism. Planning commissions appointed by city councils develop comprehensive land use plans. From these are written zoning ordinances, which are approved by city councils and become local law. Obviously, changes are sometimes needed and the planning commission then often acts as a zoning commission, to grant zoning changes when necessary. If changes are disallowed, appeals may be made to the city council and ultimately to the courts. For specific relief from a zoning ordinance, a variance is requested from a separate Board of Zoning Adjustment; if denied, a property owner can appeal only to the courts, not to the city council. For example, changes in zoning from residential to commercial are made by the Planning/Zoning Commission, whereas a request for a nonconforming use, to continue until the property is sold, is handled by the Zoning Board of Adjustment.

Many individuals claim the system is biased in favor of the wealthy or influential, who appear to be able to get changes approved with relative ease. In some communities the planning commission consists only of people involved in real estate businesses, who certainly have a stake in the system but may tend to grant most requests for change. They readily approve change from a more restrictive to a less restrictive economic use. (More money can usually be made from property after rezoning from a restrictive residential use to a less restrictive commercial use, because of more intensive development.) However, too much change undercuts the comprehensive plan, and can lead to undesirable growth and development, such as strip commercial development on highways, or junkyards next to residential areas.

Manipulation, then, is a down side of the zoning system, according to many observers; the system is a "special interest heaven," say some. However, other critics complain that the system is so rigid that it creates requests for zoning changes or variances that would not be necessary with a better system. They point out that under the city's police powers, it was earlier thought necessary to be very specific about requirements, and zoning ordinances traditionally spelled out permitted uses in great detail. This led to undue restriction and forced many requests for legitimate change from affected property owners. In response to the narrow legalistic approach of earlier ordinances, there have been several new developments leading to greater flexibility.

VI. New Zoning Approaches

New zoning developments generally lead to greater flexibility for planning and zoning commissions. Since their inception, zoning approaches have been fairly standard. The general idea for residential areas was to specify the size of lots and the yard space required for each lot. Even curved streets did not change the ratios of lots to buildings. Such an approach, according to Herbert H. Smith, is what stimulated new approaches such as "density zoning and cluster development." Such approaches keep density the same but create more open space. Cluster development, for example, reduces lot size and concentrates development in compact areas, but leaves more common open space than would be the case in traditional same-size lot development. The same is true of planned unit developments (PUDs), which allow for mixed lands and more intensive development. PUDs are often associated with the creation of "mini-communities" or "new towns" within a community.

Another approach is called "impact or performance zoning," which reverses the traditional approach of detailed ordinances spelling out permitted uses. Instead, performance standards are used together with a rating or point system, which creates more flexibility. A lower score on the rating system indicates that impact is lower and the project is likely to fall within existing standards.

Other innovations include: (1) growth management plans and development codes, which centralize requirements for controlling growth; (2) cluster zoning and planned unit development (PUDs), where development is concentrated on part of the site but leaves open space on the rest, for recreation or other purposes (overall density remains the same); (3) inclusive zoning that requires developers and builders to build some low-cost housing in higher-cost subdivisions; (4) special-district zoning, which refers to such areas as the New York Theater District, the Special Garment Center District, or special downtown business or community districts (San Francisco has sixteen), which are generally "fixes" in response to local political pressures; (5) site plan and design review, which require developers to gain approval for street alignment and landscaping, among other things; and (6) floodplain zoning, which has been pushed by the federal government to prevent or control development in floodplains; such restrictions are necessary for property owners to acquire flood insurance.

"Down-zoning" is an approach that reverses the usual pattern of zoning. The usual pattern, as noted, is to rezone to less restrictive uses. In the case of down-zoning, the change is made to a more restrictive use. For example, if a downtown area has been zoned commercial, apartment housing on the fringe is in danger of being turned into commercial use. Pressures may very well develop to down-zone the fringe from commercial to multifamily residential to preserve the apartments. The same is true for some single-family housing neighborhoods next to urban campuses. There are tremendous pressures to turn large, old homes into rooming houses or student apartments. This leads to some overcrowding and often to considerable congestion on the streets because of little off-street parking. One solution is to resist change from single-family to multifamily dwellings, but another is to rezone back from multifamily to single-family residences. This is very difficult to achieve because of the economic loss that can be incurred by owners. One approach is for the city or a neighborhood trust to purchase the dwellings and subsequently restore them to single-family status. Still another is to allow individuals to down-zone their lots. If a substantial number of property owners do so, then large-scale commercial or apartment projects are thwarted.

Zoning in rural areas has been mentioned already in connection with township planning and zoning, which was adopted in 1989 in response to environmental concerns. At least six townships in Missouri have adopted township zoning (see Table 23–1).

Preserving Agricultural Land. There has been considerable interest in some states for preserving agricultural land, not only for farming purposes, but to provide open space and buffer zones. Federal legislation was passed in 1981, but it only required that federal agencies consider the impact their activities had on converting farmland to other uses. State governments have relied mostly on tax breaks to sustain farmers threatened by urbanization. Local governments have played the most prominent role and have basically used three approaches: (1) agricultural zoning; (2) the purchase of development rights; and (3) the transfer of development rights.[4] The most effective way to preserve agricultural land is outright purchase by a land bank or private association, of course, but this is much too expensive. Even the purchase of development rights, which involves less cost than outright purchase, strains resources.

The *transfer* of development rights is a relatively new approach that "separates the development value of land from its existing use, and 'transfers' that development value to another site."[5] Owners of land in an agricultural area to be preserved can transfer their development rights (TDR) to developers in designated "receiving" areas. Although simple in concept, transfer of development rights is very complex in detail and implementation. A program in Montgomery County, Maryland, is one of the best known.

Houston and the Case for Nonzoning. Houston is often cited as a city that works without zoning. Indeed, many argue that it looks remarkably similar to other cities that use zoning. Instead of zoning, a system of deed restrictions or restrictive covenants is used to control land use. Some have argued that the Houston approach is superior to using zoning ordinances. However, others point out that the city has always relied on more than just deed restrictions; that is, it uses a building code that specifies minimum distances between buildings and designates setback requirements: "It has a capital investment program, a comprehensive planning process, and subdivision regulations which apply to newly developing areas. It also has a major thoroughfare plan, which requires developers to dedicate right-of-way if the major streets adjacent to their property are not wide enough to meet city standards."[6]

Recently, concern over poorer neighborhoods has led to increased calls for protection. Buildings in these areas were often shoddy, and areas of the city that did have zoning had higher prices for the same type of housing. Reaction led to a unanimous decision by the city council in 1991 to create a comprehensive zoning ordinance. It would appear that Houston may be moving toward zoning for control purposes, and thus is in danger of losing its uniqueness as the only major nonzoned city in the nation.

VII. Summary and Conclusions

Planning and zoning can be highly ideological and controversial. Controversy is

4. Ibid., 129.
5. Ibid.

6. Ibid., 229.

more likely to occur in small communities and rural areas, but it can and does happen in metropolitan areas as well. Although many criticisms about fairness are raised and conflicts can arise over goals, the planning/zoning process is neutral. Some communities want economic growth at all costs, whereas others include populations that prefer to cap or control growth. There are advantages and disadvantages to planning and zoning, and the types of individuals and groups that either support or oppose planning and zoning can be surprising.

Planning and zoning generally has been an urban approach to control development. However, the process is also cited as a method to encourage growth, by showing the community's commitment to maintain property values and protect existing amenities. It also is used in connection with redevelopment and further developing amenities such as civic centers, parks, and open space. Supporters argue that preserving or increasing the attractiveness of communities helps attract new investment. Opponents argue that the additional governmental controls help repel or stifle new investment.

Planning and zoning, although being modified in some urban areas, are still considered crucial policy tools in carrying out certain community goals, be they oriented toward development or conservation. Their use will increase with increased urbanization, and more rural counties will consider their adoption if threatened with "unsatisfactory" economic development.

Conflicts over land use policies will certainly remain prevalent while Missouri is experiencing further urbanization. The politics of planning and zoning will consequently become even more interesting in the next century.

CHAPTER 24

Municipal Government in Missouri

by Richard R. Dohm

A strong America depends on its cities—America's glory and sometimes America's shame.—
John F. Kennedy, State of the Union Address, January 11, 1962

Almost three-fourths of the people in the United States, and two of every three Missourians, live in municipalities or incorporated cities and villages.[1] Incorporation means that the community has followed procedures established by its state to become a legally recognized local government with established boundaries, a specified form of government, and the ability to tax. This chapter examines municipalities in Missouri, especially incorporated municipalities. It begins with a brief discussion of the evolution of municipalities in America, with emphasis on major political reforms and the effects of federalism. Next, the analysis turns to Missouri's municipalities, discussing recent demographic trends, describing the system used by the state government to classify cities, and explaining the various forms of city government used throughout the state. The chapter concludes with a discussion of municipal tax revenues in Missouri.

I. Background

Since 1920, when almost half of the population was rural, there has been an enormous shift in population to cities and metropolitan areas. Indeed, following World War II there was considerable city building, with many new suburbs established. However, a countertrend has been discerned since 1970. Some older Eastern metropolitan areas have declined in population, as have many older central cities, some suburbs, and some outstate cities. The population has become more dispersed, with people moving to rural areas and outer suburbs (often called exurbs). However, urban populations have increased in the South and the West, and some newer cities have also gained population.[2]

In terms of sheer numbers, both municipalities and metropolitan areas have been growing, making the United States one of the more urbanized nations in the world. Economic benefits and opportunities for work have accompanied urbanization, but there have been problems as well. In an earlier time, industrial cities were confronted with sometimes violent labor movements. Because the larger central cities traditionally have housed minority populations and

---

1. In some states boroughs (smaller than a city) are also incorporated units of local government. New York City also has boroughs, but these are administrative subunits of city government.

2. Some redevelopment efforts have enticed individuals back to central cities. Older townhouses and flats have been rehabilitated and restored for middle- and upper-income housing. This process is often called gentrification.

the poor, problems in those areas have surfaced periodically. The urban riots of the 1960s and 1970s are an example, as well as the more recent disturbances in Los Angeles in 1992, in which Blacks protested law enforcement practices. Furthermore, the infrastructure of older cities is wearing out, and the necessity of rebuilding sewage, water, and transportation systems is coming to public attention.

Political Machines and Reform Reaction. Cities have been important in industrializing the nation and have also influenced political developments. In earlier eras they acted as assimilators of European and some Asian immigrants; today the immigrants are mostly Hispanic or Asian. The immigrants in the nineteenth and early twentieth centuries were generally poor, but they did have voting power. In some cities, one of the major political parties (usually but not always the Democrats) would seek their votes in exchange for jobs and handouts. A political machine would develop, powered primarily by immigrant voters, that would perpetuate itself through many elections.

Political machines existed in several eastern cities such as New York and Boston, but they also developed in midwestern cities such as Kansas City, St. Louis, and Memphis, which did not have large numbers of immigrants. Where a political boss was in control, however, there was an undermining of democracy; if elections could not be won legally, the political machine often would use illegal tactics to maintain office. Political machine rule inevitably led to fraud, abuse, and corruption, which in turn created a reaction called the *reform movement*. Municipal politics can still be explained in large part by the desire of reformers to "take politics out of government," that is, to eliminate strong political partisanship.

Reformers perceived the political parties as the villains. To reduce the influence of the parties, reformers supported nonpartisan elections (in which a candidate's political party is not identified on the ballot), the Australian secret ballot, campaign reform, direct primaries at all levels, merit or civil service systems, and many other changes. The weakened political parties of today testify to the successes of reformers, and efforts for reform continue.[3]

Another series of reforms involved the organization of city government. The traditional structure was the *weak mayor* form, which appeared to foster machines. This structure was very decentralized because many of the administrative officials were independently elected. This left few appointments for the mayor, who was thus weakened. Such cities also were likely to have large councils, with aldermen or councilmen elected from districts or wards. Political parties become dominant by capturing wards and certain city departments, whose jobs were used for patronage. Political bosses often were not part of city government but did control the party, which chose candidates and dispensed patronage and favors. Richard Daley Sr. of Chicago, although mayor in a weak mayor system, was powerful by virtue of being chairman of the Cook County Democratic Committee (Chicago is in Cook County, and the Democratic party prevails there). In contrast, Tom Pendergast, political boss of Kansas City, was never mayor.

The reformer's response to political ma-

3. Efforts today include some support for a national initiative and public funding of political campaigns at the state level. H. Ross Perot, independent presidential office seeker in 1992, suggested an electronic referendum where voters could respond to policy initiatives. Concerns about the weakened political parties have also developed, however, with some, including columnist David S. Broder, arguing for strengthened political parties.

chines and weak mayor structures was to deemphasize politics and centralize city government. This was accomplished by developing three new city government structures—the commission, council/manager, and strong mayor forms. The first two forms emphasize nonpartisanship and are unitary in the sense of having the administrative and legislative branches combined. The council/manager and strong mayor/council forms emphasize centralized administration, although the latter generally maintains partisan and ward elections as well. These forms of government are discussed at greater length later in this chapter.

Cities in the Federal System. Cities are not mentioned in the U.S. Constitution, and this neglect affects their legal status. Furthermore, a crucial decision by Judge John F. Dillon in 1868 laid down the principle that municipal governments can only exercise those powers specifically granted to them by state legislatures, or those powers that are indispensable in carrying out their responsibilities.[4] If there is any reasonable doubt about the municipality having the power, it is denied.

The effect of the Dillon decision has been momentous, and although the ruling has been challenged, most of the challenges have been unsuccessful. Cities have become mere "creatures of the state," relying on state authorization for any new authority. This means that the states and local governments do not share power in the same manner as in the federal-state model. States still have some exclusive functions in the state-federal relationship; municipalities have virtually none in the city-state relationship. Local governments, including cities, must look to state law for permission to perform all activities and must also be aware of state prohibitions.

Home Rule. The home rule movement, a reform effort to provide autonomy for cities and counties, has been widespread but not entirely successful. Most state governments continue to exert considerable influence over all cities and counties, including those with home rule charters. Only a few states have unleashed home rule governments so that they enjoy real autonomy in local functions.

In 1875 Missouri became the first state to provide for home rule through its constitution rather than through state statute. However, successive state supreme court decisions, legislative acts, and even efforts of city leaders weakened the provision, and Missouri home rule cities have little more autonomy than others. A 1971 constitutional amendment changed the home rule approach from specific grants of authority to one of residual powers. This new approach allows cities to act if the action is not prohibited by the constitution, statute, or the city's own charter. However, the new approach has had a mixed record. There has been a crosscurrent of state supreme court cases regarding the new approach, although James Westbrook, law professor at the University of Missouri–Columbia (and "father" of the 1971 amendment), considers the state to be definitely one of residual powers. In taxation, though, St. Louis and Kansas City have preferred to gain new legislation (following the old system) rather than risk possible legal challenge by assuming they have the power to mandate taxes.

II. Number of Municipalities

Missouri ranked sixth among the states in number of municipalities (933) in 1992, a much higher ranking than its rank in

---

4. *City of Clinton v. Cedar Rapids and Missouri Railroad Co.,* 24 Iowa 455 (1868).

overall population.[5] The explanation for this phenomenon relates to the state's political culture, with its preference for small, personal governments rather than large, impersonal ones. This culture has affected the legal structure, which reinforces such values through state laws.

The process of urbanization involves city residents and others moving to areas outside cities for any of a variety of reasons, both positive and negative. It may be the desire for more space or "better" school systems, or an aversion to city problems and taxes, to name only a few. However, although there is some anti-city sentiment on the part of such populations, there is also a desire for urban-type services such as fire protection, especially by those previously having such services. These services can be met by expanding existing municipal boundaries through annexation, or creation of new local units. State laws make annexation difficult, while new incorporations are relatively easy to create.

Missouri's two major metropolitan areas of St. Louis (St. Louis city and St. Louis, Franklin, Jefferson, St. Charles, Lincoln, and Warren counties) and Kansas City (Jackson, Clay, Ray, Platte, Cass, and Lafayette counties) contain more than half of the state's population and more than a fifth of the state's municipalities. St. Louis County has by far the largest number of municipalities of any county in the state, with 88 as of 1992. Consequently, with 143 cities, the St. Louis region ranks first among the state's six metropolitan areas in number of municipalities.

The reasons for St. Louis County's high number of municipalities include the following: (1) St. Louis leaders successfully sought from the 1875 constitutional convention a home rule provision that allowed

the city to separate itself from the county and triple its area, but that also prohibited the city from any further annexations; (2) a 1963 law that required the cities in St. Louis County wishing to annex new territory to secure the approval of a majority of voters in their city and a majority in the area to be annexed; (3) an early 1960s court decision that allowed the St. Louis County government to intervene and block annexations (*City of Olivette v. Graeler*, 338 SW2d 827 [Mo. 1960]); and (4) a state law that provided few barriers to incorporations of new communities. The law requiring dual majorities was particularly important because of the difficulty of securing a majority among the fringe area residents, many of whom had moved to the country to avoid city regulations and taxes.

In contrast, Kansas City (Jackson County) had fewer barriers to annexations, and extended its boundaries into the adjoining counties of Clay, Platte, and Cass. In response, several Kansas City suburbs conducted annexations of their own. As a result there are fewer incorporations of suburbs in the Kansas City metropolitan area (ninety-eight in 1992).

In 1976 the scope of the law requiring dual majorities was expanded from St. Louis County to the entire state, sharply reducing the number of annexations in the Kansas City area as well as in other Missouri counties. The stimulus for this change occurred when Columbia annexed a large tract of Boone County east of the city. The annexation was opposed by residents outside the city, who challenged the election as unconstitutional because fringe area residents were not permitted to vote. The state supreme court upheld the validity of the election, but then Senator Roger Wilson introduced legislation to enfranchise noncity voters in subsequent annexation elections. The legislation was passed and now two majorities are required; if fringe

---

5. U.S. Department of Commerce, Bureau of the Census, *1992 Census of Governments* and *1990 Census of Population*.

area residents oppose, another election is held for the entire affected population, and two-thirds must vote "yes" for approval.

Outstate metropolitan areas contain many municipalities as well. They include Joplin (Jasper and Newton counties), with forty-two municipalities in the two counties (ranking it third among the state's metropolitan areas). Springfield (Greene and Christian counties) has the fourth most municipalities with fifteen, followed by St. Joseph (Buchanan and Andrew counties) with fourteen. Columbia is the only designated metropolitan area entirely within a single county (Boone), and consequently has the fewest municipalities with eight.

In summary, the present legal "playing field" favors creation of new local units over the expansion of existing city boundaries. Annexations were relatively easy when only city residents voted on the issue. When the law was changed to require two majorities, annexations became much more difficult and city-initiated proposals dropped dramatically. Although the new law allows a single majority in a second election if fringe areas vote against a proposal, approvals are still rare because of the two-thirds supermajority required. Most of the action today involves property owners outside cities requesting to be annexed.

III. Classification of Missouri Cities

Classification of municipalities is required by the 1945 Missouri Constitution. Article VI, Section 15, states that no more than four classes of municipalities shall be created, and the powers of each class shall be defined by general laws so that all municipal corporations within the same class will hold the same powers and be subject to the same restrictions. State legislatures have traditionally classified cities to minimize special legislation affecting individual cities. Prior to the introduction of classes, individual laws passed by state legislatures (often called special-act charters) established the organization and powers of municipalities. Obviously, with great numbers of new cities being established after the Civil War, legislatures soon became glutted with special legislation affecting cities, both in new acts and in amendments to old statutes. Seeking a device to limit the number of such bills, municipal reformers and concerned legislators developed classification schemes, usually based on population.

Following this development, new cities did not need a special law to begin operation, but followed incorporation procedures and began functioning under the general act or law appropriate for their population. The results of this approach were twofold: the number of special acts was reduced, due both to classification and prohibitions of special acts in some cases; and an unintended abuse of classification occurred with the arbitrary introduction of new classifications (special acts affecting only one city or municipality but disguised as a general law). This latter result has been prominent in Missouri. One study reports as many as 167 classifications of cities, not merely the 4 called for in the state constitution.[6]

A classic example of a special act disguised as a general law is the following:

> 72.300. Any two or more municipalities which are adjoining or contiguous to each other on two or more sides and which are located in a county of the third class having a population of not less than twenty-five thousand nor more than thirty thousand

6. *Missouri Local Government at the Crossroads*, Report of the Governor's Advisory Council on Local Government Law, 1969, 12. The council was chaired by P. Wayne Goode, state representative from the 32d District and Peter W. Salsich Jr. of St. Louis University. The number of statutory cities was based on a study by George F. Nickolaus of the University of Missouri–Columbia Governmental Affairs Program, and then mayor of Columbia.

Table 24-1. Classification of Missouri Municipalities and Optional Forms of Government

Class of City	Population Requirement	Optional Forms of Government Authorized by Statute
III*	3,000–29,999	Mayor–Council Commission Council–Manager Mayor–Council (Administrator)
IV	500–2,999	Mayor–Council (Board of Aldermen) Mayor–Council (Administrator)
Village	Less than 500 (for incorporation)	Elected Board of Trustees. If population is less than 2,500, there are five trustees. If population is more than 2,500, there are nine trustees.
Constitutional Charter City (Home Rule)	More than 5,000	Any republican form of government. As set forth in the individual legislative charter.
Special Legislative Charters (special charters are prohibited by the Missouri Constitution, although six approved before 1875 are still in effect in Carrolton, Chillicothe, LaGrange, Liberty, Miami, and Pleasant Hill).		

*Classes I and II statutes were repealed in 1975.

may provide for the absorption of the corporate existence and the territorial limits of one or more of the municipalities by another such municipality in the manner provided in Sections 72.300 to 72.350.

Although this statute may possibly apply to more than one situation, it was enacted specifically to allow the city of Mexico in Audrain County to absorb the village of Vandiver. It can readily be seen how there can be as many as 167 classes of cities!

Missouri currently has two general classes of cities (Classes III and IV), which are based on population, and general laws for towns or villages. In addition, there are six special-act charter cities and pro-

visions for home rule charter cities (see Table 24–2). Class I and II city statutes were repealed in 1975 because no cities had operated under them for decades. Cities with a population entitling them to Class I and II status chose instead to become home rule cities and develop their own charters (or mini-constitutions).

Constitutional home rule is available to cities having a population of at least 5,001. Thirty-two cities have gone through the process of charter drafting and have established their own governmental structures. Home rule is the ultimate in local self-government, but it has not been used in Missouri as much as one might expect.

Table 24-2. Cities Operating under Constitutional Charters, 1994

Cities	Year of Charter	Form of Government	Population 1990
Berkeley	1957	Council Manager	12,450
Blue Springs	1994	Mayor Council–Admin.	40,153
Bridgeton	1966	Mayor Council–Admin.	17,779
Cape Girardeau	1981	Council Manager	34,438
Carthage	1993	Mayor Council–Admin	10,747
Clayton	1957	Council Manager	13,874
Columbia	1949	Council Manager	69,101
Creve Coeur	1974	Mayor Council–Admin.	12,304
Ellisville	1993	Council Manager	7,545
Ferguson	1954	Council Manager	22,286
Florissant	1963	Mayor Council	51,206
Fulton	1986	Mayor Council–Admin	10,033
Hannibal	1957	Mayor Council	18,004
Hazelwood	1969	Council Manager	15,324
Independence	1961	Council Manager	112,301
Jefferson City	1986	Mayor Council–Admin.	35,481
Joplin	1954	Council Manager	40,961
Kansas City	1925	Council Manager	435,146
Kirkwood	1983	Mayor Council–Admin.	27,291
Maplewood	1978	Council Manager	9,962
Neosho	1973	Council Manager	9,254
Nevada	1979	Council Manager	8,597
Olivette	1976	Council Manager	7,573
Palmyra*	1982	Mayor Council	3,371
Richmond Heights	1988	Council Manager	10,448
St. Charles	1981	Mayor Council–Admin.	54,555
St. John	1974	Council Manager	7,466
St. Joseph	1961	Council Manager	71,852
St. Louis	1914	Mayor Council	396,685
Springfield	1953	Council Manager	140,494
University City	1947	Council Manager	40,087
Webster Groves	1954	Council Manager	22,987

*Palmyra had been a special charter city. Legislation was passed (sponsored by Senator Norman Merrell of Northeast Missouri) allowing special charter cities to adopt home rule charters, even though their population was below the constitutional requirement of 5,001.

Source: *Missouri Municipal Directory, 1994–95.*

More than seventy cities (in addition to the thirty-two above) are eligible for home rule but have not adopted charters. One explanation might be the close association of home rule to reform structures. Many home rule cities have chosen the council/manager form of government, so potential home rule communities may fear that reform structures will be adopted if they engage in charter drafting. Population size may also be a factor—almost all of the larger eligible cities have adopted charters, probably because of the increased complexity associated with larger populations.

Confusion over classification is rather common, and some cities are unsure of their status. Slightly more than one-third of all municipalities are misclassified. The major reasons for the confusion are that (1) a municipality is not required to change classification when its population warrants; (2) little incentive exists for change; and (3) a change must be approved in an election.

One may quickly ask, however, whether such misclassification adversely affects municipal government. Although it is very difficult to identify all statutes affecting cities and villages, most municipalities are operating rather well, and relatively few suits have been filed challenging the right of municipal governments to perform or regulate some service.

Some lawyers and elected officials are interested in simplifying the mess, though. A committee was appointed at one time to study the matter, and a bill for codifying municipal statutes was introduced in the 1982 session, although it did not make much progress. Similar bills have been introduced since 1982, but none have cleared committee. Such codification means repealing out-of-date laws, combining similar laws, and eliminating conflicts between laws. The task is extremely complex and involves both technical and political efforts. Guiding any codification bill through the General Assembly will be a challenge. Many cities are comfortable with existing statutes, and codification might bring unpleasant surprises.

IV. Optional Forms of Municipal Government in Missouri

Figure 24–1 shows the forms of government available to Missouri's municipalities.

Municipalities generally can be classified as weak mayor/council, council/manager, city administrator, commission, or village structures.

Weak Mayor/Council. This form has been adopted by more than 80 percent of Missouri's cities. It is a traditional form of government, usually involving the complete separation of powers between the executive branch (the mayor) and the legislative branch (the city council). However, in Missouri the separation is blurred by having the mayor preside over council meetings and vote in case of ties. The mayor is the chief executive officer of the city but does not make any major appointments; several administrative officials are directly elected. This is in contrast to the strong mayor form, in which the administration is centralized under the office of the mayor. The mayor appoints the major department heads or has a chief executive officer make the appointments. There are no good examples of the strong mayor form in Missouri, although the mayor of St. Louis does have considerable legal authority (financial powers, however, are shared with the Board of Estimate and Apportionment). Another characteristic of the weak mayor form in Missouri is ward elections rather than elections at large.

Council/Manager. The council/manager structure is a very "pure" type under Missouri's law; that is, it is the epitome of a reformed or centralized municipal organization. The city council is charged with policy making and appoints a city manager to carry out its policy. The manager is not part of the council but has sole authority to appoint and remove department heads. The statutes also require nonpartisan and at-large election of five council members with staggered terms of office. Once adopted, the structure must be retained for six years before abandonment can be considered.

Figure 24-1. Most Common Forms of Municipal Government in Missouri

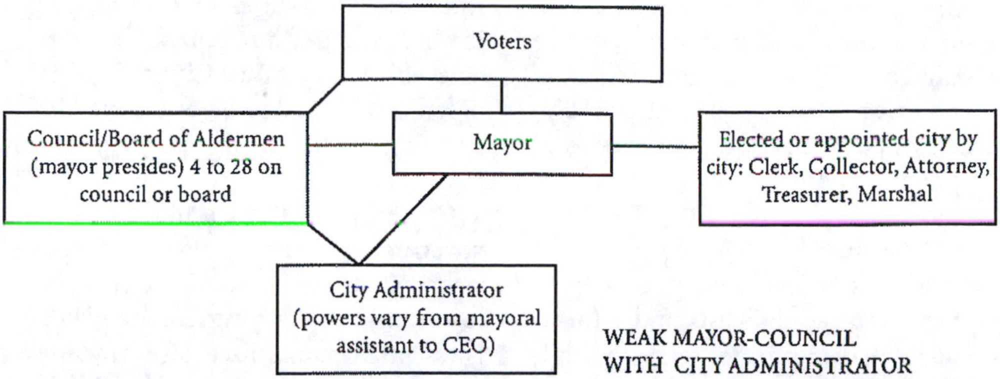

```
                        ┌─────────────────────┐
                        │       Voters        │
                        └─────────────────────┘
┌──────────────────────┐  ┌─────────────────┐  ┌──────────────────────────┐
│ Council/Board of      │  │     Mayor       │  │ Elected or appointed city│
│ Aldermen              │  │                 │  │ by city: Clerk, Collector,│
│ (mayor presides) 4 to │  │                 │  │ Attorney, Treasurer,      │
│ 28 on council or board│  │                 │  │ Marshal                   │
└──────────────────────┘  └─────────────────┘  └──────────────────────────┘
                   ┌──────────────────────────┐
                   │    City Administrator     │
                   │ (powers vary from mayoral │
                   │   assistant to CEO)       │
                   └──────────────────────────┘
```

WEAK MAYOR-COUNCIL WITH CITY ADMINISTRATOR

Mayor-council organizations are "weak" in Missouri because the mayor has limited legal authority to appoint officials. The mayor presides over the council but is not a member and cannot vote except to break ties. City administrators can be authorized by ordinance and are appointed by the mayor and council.

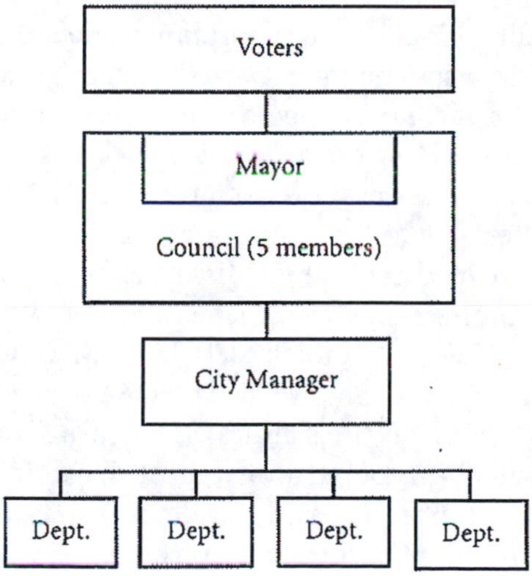

```
         ┌─────────────────────┐
         │       Voters        │
         └─────────────────────┘
         ┌─────────────────────┐
         │       Mayor         │
         │ Council (5 members) │
         └─────────────────────┘
         ┌─────────────────────┐
         │    City Manager     │
         └─────────────────────┘
  ┌──────┐ ┌──────┐ ┌──────┐ ┌──────┐
  │ Dept.│ │ Dept.│ │ Dept.│ │ Dept.│
  └──────┘ └──────┘ └──────┘ └──────┘
```

COUNCIL-MANAGER

The voters elect the council, which determines policy. Administration is the responsibility of a city manager, chosen by the council. In Class III manager cities, the council chooses one of their number to act as mayor. In Missouri home-rule manager cities, extensive variation is possible; often the mayor is elected directly by voters.

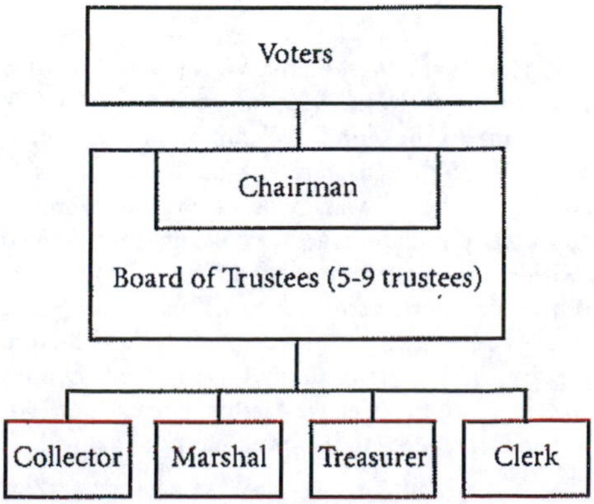

```
         ┌─────────────────────────────┐
         │           Voters            │
         └─────────────────────────────┘
         ┌─────────────────────────────┐
         │          Chairman           │
         │ Board of Trustees (5-9       │
         │ trustees)                    │
         └─────────────────────────────┘
  ┌─────────┐ ┌────────┐ ┌──────────┐ ┌───────┐
  │Collector│ │Marshal │ │Treasurer │ │ Clerk │
  └─────────┘ └────────┘ └──────────┘ └───────┘
```

VILLAGE

Villages have the least complicated form of government. There are approximately 260 villages in Missouri with populations ranging from two to more than three thousand. The trustees select one of their members as chairman and also appoint the four officials.

The council/manager form has been increasing in number nationally, but has been used by about the same number of communities (now thirty-six) for many years in Missouri. Traditional communities dislike and fear council/manager government—managers are commonly referred to as "dictators" by opponents of this system—and a campaign for adoption often meets fierce resistance.

City-Administrator. A more recent structure in Missouri represents a compromise between traditionalists and reformers. The city-administrator form, which is basically a variation of the mayor/council organization, was established in several Missouri cities even before there was state-enabling legislation. Several communities faced problems fostered by rapid growth, and the elected officials perceived the need for a full-time administrator similar to a city manager. However, they also realized their populations would not adopt the council/manager plan, so they created the office of city administrator by ordinance.[7] The mayor's executive authority (or part of it) is delegated to a city administrator, appointed by mayor and council, who assumes full-time administrative duties. However, the office can be eliminated at any time by repeal of the ordinance, unlike other abandonments that require a vote of the people.

The city-administrator form is an effective compromise between traditional and reformed structures and has had dramatic acceptance, having now been adopted by 114 Missouri cities. Many are recognized by the International City Management Association, which is the national association created to support manager cities,

and many administrators are active in the Missouri City Management Association. The push-and-pull of traditional and reform forces has led to a tilt toward reform in this instance, but only after considerable effort and time. City-administrator organizations had to be bootlegged before enabling legislation was passed legitimizing the structure.

Commission. The commission form of government is an early reform structure. It was created in Galveston, Texas, in 1900 following a devastating hurricane and flood. It is essentially committee government, with each member of the council directly administering a major department. Thus there is no separation of powers between branches; indeed, there is no chief executive officer at all. This unitary organization worked effectively in rebuilding Galveston, though, and was therefore adopted by hundreds of cities throughout the nation. The lack of a chief executive has proved to be the major weakness, and commission governments have declined in number. Missouri has only two commission governments at present.[8]

Village. Approximately 260 of Missouri's municipalities are villages (also called "towns" in the statutes). They usually are small in population—most have fewer than five hundred residents—and have the simplest form of government. Several, however, have more than one thousand residents, and at least one has a population

---

7. See Richard R. Dohm, *Reform from Within: The Development of the City Administrator Form of Government in Small Missouri Cities* (Columbia: University of Missouri–Columbia Extension Division, UED 1, 1970).

8. Monett and West Plains. West Plains discarded the commission form in 1985, but regained it in 1987. It has increased the number of commissioners from three to five through state statute. Monett did not want the change, so the bill was made applicable to only those cities with populations greater than five thousand except "within a third class county which adjoins three other third class counties and one second class county and the state of Arkansas. . . ." (78.080 of Revised Statutes of Missouri 1991). Interestingly, this involved definition of class legislation, which was designed to exclude Monett, was in error. Monett, however, has not changed.

of more than three thousand. Most of the largest villages are in St. Louis County. In the village form, voters elect a board of trustees of five to nine members. A chairman, elected from the board by other trustees, presides over meetings and votes on any issue. The board may pass ordinances on about forty topics specifically itemized in state statute, and it also appoints the collector, marshal, treasurer, and clerk.

In summary, some political forces across the nation favor centralization of municipal government, while others favor decentralization and dispersion of governmental power. Of the optional forms of government in Missouri, the council/manager structure requires considerable centralization, and the number of communities using it has remained virtually frozen for many years.

V. Municipal Functions

Most individuals are familiar to some degree with cities and their services, but how do city governments differ from county governments, the other main type of general-purpose government? The term *general purpose* refers to the many services or functions performed by cities and counties. In contrast, most special-district governments (including school districts) perform only a single function and are therefore termed single- or limited-purpose governments.

Counties are really administrative subunits of state government. When states were first organized, some cities existed, but the state was unable to rule vast areas of wilderness because of problems in transportation and communication. The solution was to establish county jurisdictions to implement state law. In Missouri, the plan was to create a jurisdiction small enough to put the county seat within a day's journey by horse and buggy of the most remote citizen (about a thirty-mile round trip).

Counties were assigned the responsibility of implementing state laws important to all citizens. Such responsibilities included law enforcement, which was to be administered by the county sheriff, and maintaining records on property transactions. Also, some governing body for rural residents was needed other than state government, so elected county courts or commissions were established in addition to the other elected offices.

Counties, then, perform functions considered by the General Assembly to be absolutely necessary for the health, safety, and welfare of all citizens. Cities perform some of these same statewide functions, but they have another array of functions as well: urban functions or services considered to be necessary for the "convenience" of local populations. These include fire protection and additional services usually associated with utilities, such as water and gas supply, electrical generation and/or distribution, refuse collection and disposal, and transportation. What is quickly evident about these services is that they are often provided by private companies or corporations. In earlier times they were often private, but if they became unprofitable, cities often took over ownership and operation. Some cities even call these services "enterprise" or "corporate" functions, and they all generate revenues from user charges.

Governmental and Proprietary Functions. The two sets of functions explained above are described legally as governmental and proprietary. Governmental functions are those imposed by state government, whereas proprietary functions are adopted for local convenience. This division has important implications for governmental liability in negligence lawsuits. In the past, cities generally have been liable for damages in negligence suits that involved proprietary functions, but immune from damage suits associated with governmental functions. In the latter, the cloak of state sovereignty was extended to cities. However, governmental immunity has been abolished or weakened in many states since World War II, including being voided by the courts in Missouri. However, it was reestablished by the General Assembly with certain exceptions.[9]

The range of services or functions that cities perform varies considerably from city to city, depending on population and other factors. In general, of course, the larger the city, the greater the number of services and the increased per capita costs. Cities have been squeezed financially since the Great Depression. World War II delayed many public improvements, and cities were then hit by the population explosion following the war. Because of the common unresponsiveness of state governments to urban problems, due mainly to rural domination of state legislatures until 1962, cities lobbied the federal government for financial aid. They were often successful because many of the election districts of Congress included substantial urban populations. The high point of federal aid came with general revenue sharing, which provided quarterly checks from the U.S. Treasury with few restrictions, based on a city's population and other criteria. A variety of categorical grant programs also provided monies to cities, and aid reached 21 percent of local general funds in 1981. Since then, federal aid has been decreasing and cities have been forced to support programs previously funded by the federal government.

9. See the discussion of sovereign immunity in chapter 7.

VI. Municipal Tax Revenues in Missouri

One might say that in today's context, the name of the game is finance. Taxation and finance have always been important for municipalities, but they are crucial today given the state of the economy, reduced federal aid, tax and spending limitations, and additional mandates by the state and federal governments.

Furthermore, Missouri's municipalities receive less help from state government than do cities in most states. Traditionally, Missouri state government has not supported sharing its revenues with cities, except for portions from road-user and intangible taxes.

Local Option Sales Tax. An example of Missouri's response to local fiscal needs occurred during the second term of Governor Warren Hearnes, from 1969 to 1973. At that time, cities relied heavily on the property tax, but the tax was (and still is) unpopular. In addition, many cities were at the maximum levy limit allowed without a two-thirds vote and could not find alternative revenues sufficient to offset increasing costs. The largest Missouri cities developed a campaign, led by the Missouri Municipal League, to persuade Hearnes and the General Assembly to pass tax-sharing legislation. The campaign urged an increase in either the state income or sales tax, with the extra revenue to be shared with municipalities.

The campaign was only partially successful; no tax sharing was forthcoming, but legislation was passed allowing cities to impose a local sales tax, if approved by a majority of voters. Hearnes included the local option sales tax as part of his Creative Localism policy, and the tax has been adopted by more than 60 percent of the municipalities as of 1994.[10] Up to 1 percent can be levied by a municipality on all items covered by the state sales tax. Merchants collect the tax and forward receipts to the state, which then returns the local share to originating cities after deducting a percentage for administration. The tax can be considered regressive in that it is imposed on food and clothing, but it has enabled user cities to reduce their reliance on the unpopular and equally regressive property tax. (In addition, a half-cent sales tax is authorized for transportation in cities with a population of more than five hundred, and a half-cent tax for capital improvements may be levied by any city.)

The local sales tax is inequitable in other ways as well. It is a bonanza for cities with regional trade centers that generate millions in sales, but not for a neighboring community that loses trade and sales tax receipts to the trade center. Also, the General Assembly has excluded many products from the tax, reducing revenues and leading to cries of "special preference." Nevertheless, the city sales tax has broadened the tax base and allowed cities to rely less on the very unpopular property tax. In 1980 the city sales tax became the major source of revenue for Missouri's cities. According to the Missouri Municipal League, the city sales tax produces more than 43 percent of municipal revenue, while the property tax produces about 16 percent of total revenues.[11]

Indeed, counties and schools took note of the success of the city sales tax. Counties now have a variety of sales tax options, in addition to the initial tax of up to 0.5 percent, with half of the revenues pledged to

property tax reduction. Schools sought and gained a one cent increase in the state sales tax with the increased revenues returned to school districts, again with half of the funds required to be used for property tax reduction.

The second largest revenue producer for Missouri cities (after sales tax) is the "nonproperty tax" category, as identified by the Missouri Municipal League. This includes such items as the cigarette tax (Columbia and some other cities charge a dime a pack), automobile and utility taxes, court fines and charges, and occupation and liquor license fees. Of this group, by far the largest revenue producer is the gross receipts tax, which is applied to utilities.

Some cities, however, own their own electrical distribution systems and buy power wholesale to sell to their residents. Others own their own generating plants as well. Obviously, these municipalities cannot use a gross receipts tax per se, but they do make use of a PILOT or "payment in lieu of taxes," which they charge their resident users.

The property tax is now the third largest revenue producer for Missouri cities, providing about 16 percent of municipal revenues, a far cry from the 1960s when it was the only major tax available. (It remains first in local revenue for schools, though, and is all that is available for many special districts. Counties also rely heavily on the property tax.)

Obviously, there has been a conscious policy of reducing reliance on the property tax for cities, and this has been successful. It is still very important for the smaller municipalities, however, and also for long-term borrowing. Indeed, the property tax may become more important in the future if there is a drop in sales tax revenues. A weakening economy or further exclusions

10. Missouri Department of Revenue, "Sales Tax Audit/Update Rate Table," October 1, 1994.

11. Missouri Municipal League, *Taxation and Revenue in Missouri Municipalities,* 1995.

of products subject to sales tax could reverse property tax trends.

Federal Aid. Another source of revenue is federal funds. Earlier, Missouri did quite well in maximizing categorical aid grant dollars from the federal government, which are available for specific areas of need. Municipalities and state governments would apply for such funds, documenting their need through long and involved applications. Federal aid gained considerable importance in the late 1960s with President Johnson's Great Society programs, and Missouri made efforts to make certain of its share. A later program that local officials particularly liked was general revenue sharing (supposedly funded by the peace dividend due to the end of U.S. involvement in the war in Vietnam) passed during the first Nixon administration and implemented in 1973. This program had few strings attached, and checks were automatically mailed by the U.S. Treasury to general-purpose local governments (municipalities and counties) and to state governments as well during the initial phase. The program was discontinued under President Reagan, who sought to reduce the federal role in national-state relations. Concern for annual budget deficits also led to cuts in financial assistance to cities, but another motivation was the desire to eliminate many of Johnson's social welfare programs, which often focused on central-city populations. The final year for distribution was 1986.

As of 1990, the estimated federal aid to state and local governments in Missouri was $109,202,355. Federal aid to cities and towns declined during the 1980s, with the most precipitous drop occurring from 1986 to 1987 when federal general revenue sharing ended. In 1986 Missouri's cities and towns received $181,930,132, whereas in 1987 the total fell to $72,305,376. The total amount increased in the late 1980s, but it

may never again reach the high point of the decade—$194,977,961 in 1984. When compared with the other states, Missouri ranked fourteenth in amount of aid received from the federal government for its cities and towns. This is slightly better than its ranking in population (fifteenth).[12]

Although Missouri politicians often inveigh against big government, they are pragmatic when money is involved. Federal funds can substitute for local and state revenues, thus allowing Missouri to continue to pursue its long-standing goal of low taxes. There are few instances of local officials turning down federal aid, although it is impossible to document how many have not applied for grants or loans because of ideological antipathy or hostility to the federal government.

State Aid. Unlike cities in some states, Missouri's municipalities cannot rely on state government for substantial financial help. Traditionally, state government has not supported sharing its revenues with cities (as noted, it only shares portions from road-user fees and a financial institution tax—formerly known as the intangibles tax). According to 1990 Census information, per capita state aid was $71.39 to local units in Missouri, ranking it forty-seventh among the fifty states. (Counties and special districts do no better than municipalities in state aid. Indeed, counties fared worse until the gasoline tax percentage allocated to counties was increased.)

Future Fiscal Trends. Historically, the property tax was the major revenue producer for municipalities. This has changed over the last three decades, with efforts being made to reform, reduce, and limit the property tax, both in Missouri and across the nation.

12. Kenneth N. Bickers and Robert M. Stein, *Federal Domestic Outlays 1983–1990—A Data Book* (New York: M. E. Sharpe, Inc., 1991), 26–121.

Table 24-3. State Aid to Local Governments Per Capita, 1990

(Excluding Education and Welfare Expenditures)

1.	Alaska	$497.65
2.	Wyoming	474.89
3.	Wisconsin	424.04
4.	Massachusetts	395.76
5.	Minnesota	350.65
6.	Nevada	329.70
7.	Michigan	298.18
8.	New Mexico	293.93
9.	Arizona	275.22
10.	Nebraska	258.62
11.	California	234.09
12.	Maryland	217.75
13.	Iowa	209.98
14.	New York	207.78
15.	Oregon	205.23
16.	Ohio	195.07
17.	New Jersey	193.01
18.	Mississippi	190.91
19.	Indiana	186.47
20.	North Dakota	185.92
U.S. Average		**177.64**
21.	Illinois	172.13
22.	Pennsylvania	154.16
23.	Idaho	149.70
24.	North Carolina	146.98
25.	Florida	142.36
26.	Tennessee	137.00
27.	Connecticut	133.29
28.	Alabama	131.99
29.	Washington	127.61
30.	Virginia	125.17
31.	Oklahoma	115.51
32.	South Carolina	112.14
33.	Arkansas	110.97
34.	Kansas	107.71
35.	Colorado	97.99
36.	Kentucky	93.30
37.	Louisiana	88.49
38.	Maine	85.77
39.	Vermont	84.90
40.	Montana	83.85
41.	Hawaii	82.25
42.	South Dakota	82.18
43.	Delaware	81.32
44.	Georgia	77.71
45.	Utah	74.06
46.	Rhode Island	71.60
47.	Missouri	71.39
48.	New Hampshire	59.96
49.	Texas	44.24
50.	West Virginia	33.02

Source: U.S. Census Bureau data, reported in *Governing*, January 1992, 42

The tax has been challenged for over-burdening real estate owners because many local units tax the same property. It is also cited as unfair because of "value being in the eye of the beholder." It is very difficult for several assessors or appraisers to come up with the same value for the same property. It is difficult to administer because of the valuing process, which involves field work and requires extensive computer capability. Furthermore, in the past there were many differing practices between jurisdictions, contributing further to inequities.

Many of the challenges to the property tax have been by school districts because of financial inequities; districts with larger and wealthier tax bases could use lower tax rates but still generate more revenues than the poor districts. The most significant court challenge to the property tax came, however, not from the school districts but from St. Louis developers who challenged the policy of taxing new construction more than old. In most counties, only real estate that changed hands was reassessed or revalued for tax purposes. This meant that in a period of inflation property held for a long time by one owner was taxed much less than new construction.

The courts upheld the developer's challenge and forced the State Tax Commission to order statewide reassessment, which meant equalizing values of similar property. This has now been accomplished, and biannual updates are now required as well.

Pressures to further limit property taxes generally were stimulated by the adoption of Proposition 13 in California in 1978. Thirty-one states had some form of limitation prior to 1970, but there have been many additions since then.[13]

Missouri, it should be noted, has had a tradition of tax limitations, and there have been property tax limits on cities and villages for generations (one dollar per one hundred dollars assessed valuation in third- and fourth-class cities, and seventy-five cents per one hundred dollars for villages), as well as election approval required for adoptions or increases up to the limit. (In some instances over-the-limit increases can be added with a supermajority vote in an election.)

With respect to cities caught by some form of tax or spending limitation, several escape hatches are available, including the use of local sales and income taxes, special assessments, user charges, special districts, and privatization (turning services over to private companies). Missouri, as noted, allows local option sales taxes for cities and counties, but only Kansas City and St. Louis are presently authorized to use local income/payroll taxes. Special assessments have long been used by Missouri cities, but no increase in use has been noted in recent years. User charges are certainly in the arsenal of city taxes and have become more prominent despite the Hancock Amendment's voter-approval requirement. This latter requirement has been modified by a Missouri Supreme Court decision that establishes a distinction between constitutional fees, which require voter approval, and ordinary fees, which can be increased

when needed without voter approval.[14] A five-part test was established for determining the difference.

With respect to special districts, which rely primarily on user fees, Missouri has had a policy of favoring their creation and thus ranks high among the states in total number of user fees. Such special-purpose governments add to the taxing and bonding authority of an area, sometimes negating the necessity of incorporating a new municipality to provide wanted local services. Such support can be expected to continue, and more special-purpose governments will undoubtedly be created.

Privatization of services has also occurred in some Missouri cities. Many have private refuse collection, and others are served by private water companies. More contracting out for services to private companies is likely in the future as budgets continue to be squeezed.

A final comment should be made regarding the Hancock Amendment. Congressman Mel Hancock was elected to the U.S. House of Representatives from Republican territory in southwest Missouri (the Seventh District) following his sponsorship of the Missouri constitutional amendment eight years earlier, and after unsuccessful campaigns for the U.S. Senate and lieutenant governor. He gained invaluable statewide visibility through these efforts. Although he may not have been aware of the national trend for cities to shift to user charges at that time, his section requiring a local vote on "tax, license, and fees" for local units certainly focused on one escape hatch. The Advisory Commission reports that "the public now clearly favors greater use of service charges if additional revenue

13. ACIR, "For the States, a Time of Testing," *Intergovernmental Perspective* 8:3 (Summer 1982), 22.

14. *George Keller, et al. v. Marion County Ambulance District, et al.,* Missouri Supreme Court 72979, December 17, 1991.

is needed to finance local governments."[15] Indeed, the commission suggests the following poem as comment:

> Don't tax me and don't tax thee.
> But charge that user a darn good fee.

The November election in 1982 saw the first votes on fee increases as required by the Hancock Amendment, and there was a high approval rate. Subsequent votes on fees generally have been supported as well, and voters appear to like the idea of voting on taxes.

VII. Conclusion

Missouri state and local governments will continue to be squeezed financially for the foreseeable future. Decreased federal aid and citizen disgruntlement over any new taxes have added to their problems. Cities will continue to be innovative in finance where possible, but "revenue enhancement" (a euphemism for additional taxes or revenues) will continue to be difficult.

In the past, change has been gradual, due primarily to the state's political culture and the impact of Dillon's Rule. However, a major crisis or continual problems of great severity may at some point stimulate an overhauling of the entire tax system. Realistically, with so many vested interests benefiting from the present system, it is difficult to predict that comprehensive reform is just around the corner. Such difficulties are pointed out very well in an article in *Alabama Heritage*:

> Among the most daunting problems facing reform-minded legislators are the special exemptions, deductions, and exclusions which currently overburden Alabama's tax code. These exemptions constitute subsidies for specified activities, often for some special interest group with strong ties to the legislature . . .
>
> Each group, of course, is prepared to fight any attempt to reduce its special advantage. Therefore, if tax reform is to succeed, the legislature must make major changes which affect all special interest groups simultaneously so that everyone's ox is gored at the same time and all share the pain of change. And all groups must share responsibility for serving the greater good of the state rather than their own special interests.[16]

Missouri is no different.

---

15. "For the States," 22.

16. Wayne Flint and Keith Ward, "Taxes, Taxes, Taxes: The History of a Problem," *Alabama Heritage* 24 (Spring 1992), 15.

CHAPTER 25

Politics in St. Louis
by E. Terrence Jones

A century ago, St. Louis seemed to be at the center of America: . . . the site . . . of the World's Fair of 1904 that produced the hot dog, the ice cream cone and, eventually, the musical "Meet Me in St. Louis." . . . In [those] days, St. Louis's old street grids . . . were filled with densely packed brick houses, with people living within walking distance of streetcar lines; but when autos came in, the people moved to the suburbs.—Michael Barone and Grant Ujifusa, *The Almanac of American Politics 1992*

About three of every ten Missourians live in the city of St. Louis or in St. Louis County. Although state government affects their daily lives, St. Louisans have learned that more often than not, politicians in Jefferson City have been less than enthusiastic about their fate. Rural interests have long dominated most of the state's policy making. Even though outstate Missouri no longer has as much strength in numbers, a mix of Show-Me State inertia and political cohesion has enabled rural forces to retain the edge.

As a result, the state's urban residents must look more to their local governments than to the state to address their needs. This chapter describes St. Louis's demographic and economic setting in the second half of the twentieth century, identifies the key policy issues confronting the St. Louis area, and analyzes how the local political and governmental process deals with these issues.[1]

1. Although the official U.S. Bureau of the Census definition of the St. Louis metropolitan area includes the

I. The Setting

Urban areas occupy relatively small portions of land, but they are filled with people, homes, wealth, and jobs. St. Louis has only 61 square miles and St. Louis County has only 510; together they constitute less than 1 percent of Missouri's territory. But the St. Louis/St. Louis County area is important because of the immense amount of human activity occurring there. The nature of this activity greatly influences the issues confronting St. Louis and the ways that governments can choose to handle these issues. To understand the politics of St. Louis, it is important to know something about its trends in population, socioeconomics, housing, and employment.

independent city of St. Louis, five Missouri counties (St. Louis, Franklin, Jefferson, Lincoln, and St. Charles) and five Illinois counties (Clinton, Jersey, Madison, Monroe, and St. Clair), this chapter concentrates on the two central units: the city of St. Louis and St. Louis County. Together, they contain about 60 percent of the metropolitan area's population and a much greater share of the economic and cultural activity. Unless otherwise qualified, the phrase *St. Louis* refers to the combined central units.

Figure 25-1. Cities in St. Louis County, 1994

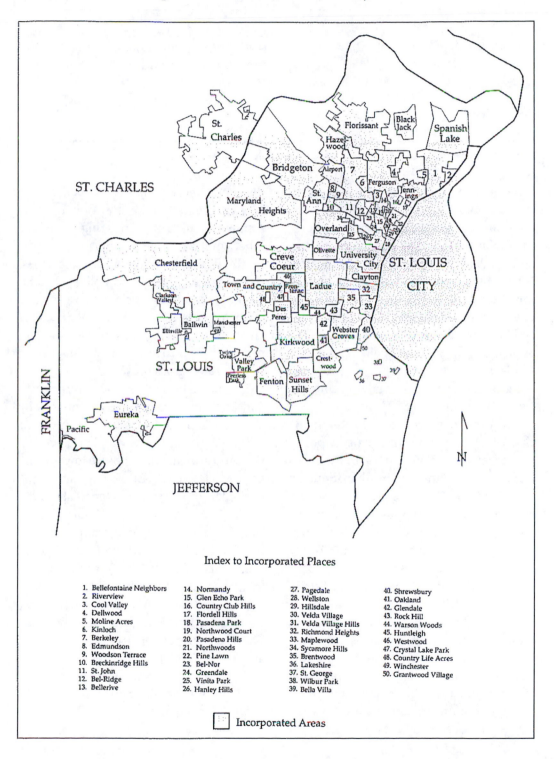

Index to Incorporated Places

1. Bellefontaine Neighbors
2. Riverview
3. Cool Valley
4. Dellwood
5. Moline Acres
6. Kinloch
7. Berkeley
8. Edmundson
9. Woodson Terrace
10. Breckinridge Hills
11. St. John
12. Bel-Ridge
13. Bellerive

14. Normandy
15. Glen Echo Park
16. Country Club Hills
17. Flordell Hills
18. Pasadena Park
19. Northwood Court
20. Pasadena Hills
21. Northwoods
22. Pine Lawn
23. Bel-Nor
24. Greendale
25. Vinita Park
26. Hanley Hills

27. Pagedale
28. Wellston
29. Hillsdale
30. Velda Village
31. Velda Village Hills
32. Richmond Heights
33. Maplewood
34. Sycamore Hills
35. Brentwood
36. Lakeshire
37. St. George
38. Wilbur Park
39. Bella Villa

40. Shrewsbury
41. Oakland
42. Glendale
43. Rock Hill
44. Warson Woods
45. Huntleigh
46. Westwood
47. Crystal Lake Park
48. Country Life Acres
49. Winchester
50. Grantwood Village

☐ Incorporated Areas

Table 25-1. St. Louis Population Trends, 1950–1990

	1950	*1960*	*1970*	*1980*	*1990*
Population:					
St. Louis City	856,796 (68%)	750,026 (52%)	622,236 (40%)	453,085 (32%)	396,685 (29%)
St. Louis County	406,349 (32%)	703,532 (48%)	951,671 (60%)	973,896 (68%)	993,259 (71%)
Total	1,263,145 (100%)	1,453,558 (100%)	1,573,907 (100%)	1,426,981 (100%)	1,389,944 (100%)
Percent Black:					
St. Louis City	18%	29%	41%	46%	47%
St. Louis County	4%	3%	5%	11%	14%
Total	14%	16%	19%	22%	24%

Source: U.S. Bureau of the Census, Census of Population and Housing, 1950–1990.

Between 1950 and 1990, the population of St. Louis and St. Louis County became smaller, more elderly, and more predominantly Black. The population peaked at 1,573,907 in 1970; it had declined to 1,389,944 by 1990 (see Table 25-1). Most of this drop occurred in the 1970s when the entire metropolitan area, not just St. Louis and St. Louis County, lost population. The population of the metropolitan area as a whole rebounded during the 1980s, but the growth occurred in outlying counties such as Jefferson and St. Charles.

The drop has been precipitous in the city, which lost more than half its population between 1950 and 1990. St. Louis County's population more than doubled from 1950 to 1970, an era of rapid suburban growth, but its population has subsequently plateaued at slightly less than one million. The combined city and county population is projected to either stay about the same or continue to decline slightly in the foreseeable future.

That St. Louis's population is likely to remain fairly steady overstates the area's vitality. Since the birth rate exceeds the death rate in the United States, population of any area should grow naturally. When St. Louis's numbers either stay the same or decline, it actually means that tens of thousands more people are departing the area each decade than are moving to it. Although a minority of this migration is to other counties in the St. Louis region, primarily Jefferson and St. Charles counties, most are leaving the metropolitan area. St. Louis is not holding its own as an attractive place for people to live and work. Since an area's economic prosperity is based on people wanting to locate there, a stagnating growth rate signals problems.

The percentage of Blacks in St. Louis and St. Louis County has grown steadily since 1945. In 1950 about one in seven city or county residents was Black; by 1990 the ratio was moving closely toward one in four. The city's Black population increased from 18 percent of the total in 1950 to 47 percent in 1990. St. Louis County stayed overwhelmingly White until 1970, but from 1970 to 1990 the Black population increased from 5 to 14 percent of the total. Although this increase was generated initially by migration from the rural South, recent and future increases will be the product of natural growth; Blacks in the St. Louis area are on average younger than Whites, and they also have a higher birth rate. As a result, St. Louis's Black population should continue to expand more rapidly than its White population.

Race is a salient feature in American politics, and it is an especially important underlying dimension in St. Louis. Historic discrimination and institutionalized segregation have deprived Blacks of an equal opportunity to achieve the American dream. As Blacks become a larger portion of the St. Louis population, there is an impact on many areas of life: education, housing, and employment, to name a few. The share of these valued resources received by Blacks and Whites becomes a recurring item on the area's agenda. Procedurally, the need to include everyone in community decision making is causing St. Louis–area governments to reexamine formal rules and informal practices.

The average age of an area's population can rise or fall, depending on the mix of birth, death, and migration rates. In St. Louis, however, the average age continues to creep upward. In 1950 about one in twelve persons was sixty-five or older; in 1990 almost one in seven was in this age category. How does this affect governmental policy? Senior citizens typically need and demand immediate public services such as health care and welfare payments; on the other hand, since their life expectancies are relatively shorter, they are less likely to support long-term public investments in education, revitalizing the infrastructure, or other areas.

Since World War II, St. Louis has reflected the national trends toward better education and higher incomes, but the economic gap has widened tremendously between the city and the county (see Table 25–2). The percentage of city and county residents age twenty-five and older with high school degrees has increased from 31 percent in 1950 to 77 percent in 1990. The median annual income of St. Louis families, measured in constant 1990 dollars to adjust for inflation, has risen 140 percent, from $16,650 in 1949

to $39,920 in 1989. This increase has almost kept pace with the national rise. The typical St. Louis family earned 12 percent more than the average American family in 1949; the advantage was 11 percent in 1989.

City and county residents have shared very unequally in this economic progress. While county incomes were increasing 135 percent between 1949 and 1989, city incomes were rising by only 57 percent. As a result, there is a steadily growing gap between city and county residents' economic well-being. In 1949 the average city family earned eighty cents for every dollar received by its county counterpart. By 1989 the ratio was fifty-four cents for every county dollar. Since 1969, city incomes have actually declined slightly and the poor are becoming more concentrated, with one of every four city residents now earning an income that is below the poverty line.

As the income difference between city and county broadens, the likelihood becomes greater that they will take divergent views on issues and that it will become more difficult to cooperate on joint ventures. The city will guard ever more jealously its remaining assets, and the county will grow more suspicious that any city overture is a thinly disguised raid on its treasury. In addition, as the city's population becomes poorer, it has greater demand for governmental services but fewer resources to pay for them.

Although the St. Louis city/county population has risen only modestly since World War II (and has even dropped since 1970), the number of housing units continues to increase, going from 381,934 in 1950 to 596,758 in 1990 (see Table 25–3). This jump has been fueled not by families moving to St. Louis, but by the baby-boom generation moving out of parents' homes and establishing new households. Combined with lower birth rates, this has dropped the aver-

Table 25-2. St. Louis Socioeconomic Trends, 1950–1990

	1950	1960	1970	1980	1990
Persons 25 and Older, Percent High School Graduates:					
St. Louis City	26%	26%	33%	40%	63%
St. Louis County	42%	48%	60%	62%	82%
City and County Combined	31%	34%	34%	55%	77%

	1949	1959	1969	1979	1989
Median Family Income, 1990 Dollars:					
St. Louis City	$15,420	$21,060	$25,600	$24,190	$24,270
St. Louis County	$19,240	$29,610	$38,770	$40,030	$45,210
City and County Combined	$16,650	$25,170	$33,570	$35,000	$39,920
City/County Ratio	.80	.71	.66	.60	.54
Total/Nation Ratio	1.12	1.14	1.12	1.12	1.11

Source: U.S. Bureau of the Census, Census of Population and Housing, 1950–1990.

Table 25-3. St. Louis Housing Trends, 1950–1990

	1950	1960	1970	1980	1990
Housing Units:					
St. Louis City	263,037 (69%)	262,984 (56%)	238,441 (45%)	201,951 (36%)	194,919 (33%)
St. Louis County	118,897 (31%)	207,408 (44%)	291,593 (55%)	357,827 (64%)	401,839 (67%)
Total	381,934 (100%)	470,392 (100%)	530,034 (100%)	559,778 (100%)	596,758 (100%)
Median Value, Single Family House, 1990 Dollars:					
St. Louis City	$44,325	$47,200	$41,300	$41,820	$49,700
St. Louis County	$55,080	$59,000	$58,820	$76,990	$82,600
City and County Combined	$47,670	$52,400	$50,940	$64,300	$71,850
City/County Ratio	.80	.80	.70	.54	.60

Source: U.S. Bureau of the Census, Census of Population and Housing, 1950–1990.

age number of persons per household from 3.31 in 1950 to 2.50 in 1990.

Again, there are stark differences between the city's and the county's trends. The city's housing stock dropped by one-fourth from 1950 to 1990, while the county's was almost quadrupling. In 1945 the county had less than half as many housing units as the city, but forty years later it had twice as many.

The county's greater attractiveness as a place to live is reflected in the housing prices. The median value of single-family houses, in constant 1990 dollars, rose from $55,080 in 1950 to $82,600 in 1990. In

Table 25-4. St. Louis Job Trends, 1959–1989

	1959	*1969*	*1979*	*1989*
Manufacturing Jobs:				
St. Louis City	141,102 (72%)	137,785 (59%)	99,166 (47%)	50,514 (29%)
St. Louis County	54,570 (28%)	95,321 (41%)	110,450 (53%)	122,903 (71%)
Total	195,672 (100%)	233,106 (100%)	209,616 (100%)	173,417 (100%)
Non-Manufacturing/ Private Sector Jobs:				
St. Louis City	215,084 (76%)	244,908 (63%)	201,382 (41%)	207,017 (32%)
St. Louis County	67,461 (24%)	145,428 (37%)	293,771 (59%)	436,554 (68%)
Total	282,545 (100%)	390,336 (100%)	495,153 (100%)	643,571 (100%)

Source: U.S. Bureau of the Census, County Business Patterns, 1959–1989.

the city, the median value declined from $44,235 in 1950 to $41,820 in 1980 before rebounding modestly to $49,700 in 1990. A typical city house had 80 percent of the value of a county house in 1950, but by 1980 the relative value was only 54 percent. With the city tearing down some of its worst housing stock and with selected neighborhoods experiencing a renaissance, the city's average house value improved to 60 percent of the average county house value in 1990. Since a local government's ability to provide adequate public services depends partially on the value of its residential property, the present divergence between city and county housing values creates very unequal governmental capacities.

The number of nongovernmental jobs rose significantly in St. Louis between 1959 and 1989, but the patterns vary noticeably. Manufacturing jobs, which typically pay the best incomes and add the most wealth to a region, have declined in number from 195,672 in 1959 to 173,417 in 1989 (see Table 25–4). The drop in the city has been precipitous: more than ninety thousand manufacturing jobs were lost between 1959 and 1990.

As in the nation as a whole, job growth has occurred in the service and information sectors in St. Louis. More than 360,000 such jobs have been added to the St. Louis economy during the past thirty years, including almost 150,000 during the past decade alone. These increases, however, are almost entirely in the county. While the city has struggled to keep its private-sector nonmanufacturing jobs above 200,000, the county's total has moved from less than 70,000 in 1959 to more than 400,000 in 1990.

II. The Issues

Although the issues described in this chapter are rooted primarily in local politics, the U.S. political system is complex enough that each level of government is involved to some degree in every issue. For example, defense is primarily a national issue, but St. Louis governments are very concerned about how many fighter planes are built by McDonnell Douglas, the area's largest employer. All levels of government must work together to help the St. Louis economy adapt to a post-cold-war world in which less money is spent on the military.

A brief review of demographic and employment trends in St. Louis reveals that possible population and economic stagnation (especially the latter) threaten to lower the area's quality of life. Like most older midwestern and northeastern metropolitan areas, St. Louis is highly vulnerable to the population movement from the Frost Belt to the Sun Belt and to the employment shift from manufacturing industries to the service and information sectors.

In the 1960s and 1970s, the federal government offered substantial assistance to areas such as St. Louis that were not faring well in the regional competition for jobs. In the 1980s under the Reagan administration, however, metropolitan areas were told they had to compete with their own resources. Paradoxically, the Reagan defense buildup provided a public stimulus to the St. Louis economy, but defense cutbacks in more recent years are removing that impetus. There is a growing consensus that St. Louis needs to do more about its economic development, but much disagreement about who is to direct such an effort, who would benefit from development, and who should pay for investments needed to attract it.

Different governments (city, county, municipalities in the county, and existing and proposed special districts) and a range of interest groups including major corporations and labor unions struggle for control. Each part of the area wants to make certain that its residents receive more from economic development efforts than they pay to support them. And almost everyone hopes that the tax dollars used to attract new jobs to the area will be paid primarily by someone else.

The 1980s debate about whether the St. Louis area needed a new stadium, in large part for a National Football League team, is an excellent example of this phenomenon. Years were spent working out where the stadium would be located and who would pay for it. While the negotiations wound on, the football team moved to Phoenix. Even after agreements were reached on location and financing, disputes arose over who would receive the construction contracts and jobs.

Maintaining the physical quality and economic value of housing is another significant issue in St. Louis. A home represents the major asset owned by most American families, and they are understandably concerned about protecting their investment. In the city, the loss of population has led to a depressed market in many neighborhoods. This has generated a strong effort by city government, neighborhood organizations, and others with an economic or psychological stake in city residential property to increase demand for housing in the city. Controversial aspects of this attempt include which city neighborhoods are to receive the most emphasis, which private developers shall obtain the most governmental assistance, and what happens to low-income residents displaced by middle-class persons reentering the city. To further complicate matters, the city's elected officials must balance these neighborhood concerns against developmental interests in downtown St. Louis.

In the county, the housing issue takes a somewhat different form. Most county residences are now middle-aged: the average house is about thirty years old. As the county matures and the homes continue to age, the percentage of deteriorating structures is likely to rise. Differences occur over how aggressively county and municipal governments should adopt and enforce tough residential codes, and over how much money and whose tax dollars should be spent on home rehabilitation.

A third major issue in the St. Louis area concerns public elementary and secondary education. The problem has two dominating dimensions: dollars and race. As enrollments in the public schools have declined, expenses have not dropped comparably.

More money per pupil is needed, and it must be raised through state or local tax increases. Those most directly connected with the schools, such as parents and teachers, press for these tax hikes, while those most economically vulnerable to property taxes, such as senior citizens on fixed incomes, oppose them.

Race underlies almost all local issues in St. Louis, but it is especially visible in education. When the U.S. Supreme Court declared in 1954 that educational segregation was unconstitutional, St. Louis's schools were racially segregated because the Missouri Constitution required it. Since 1954, political conflict on school desegregation has been an ongoing issue, with much of the discussion taking the form of litigation in the federal courts. In the early 1980s, at a time when almost two-thirds of the area's Blacks attended city schools, a voluntary plan was negotiated in which county districts having few or no Blacks would accept significant numbers of these students. This program and other aspects of racially integrated education continue to be controversial.

In addition to these three major issues, the standard services provided by local governments are perennial sources of conflict. Examples include public facilities such as roads and bridges, public safety, mass transit, and public health. There are both persistent and transient differences of opinion over how much should be done, where it should occur, how it should be distributed, and who should pay for it.

In the county, for example, the most recently developed areas have not improved their road systems sufficiently to serve their increased populations. There are too many cars on roads that are too narrow. If the roads are improved, which ones should be widened first, and who should pay for the bonds needed to finance the construction—the area immediately affected or the entire county? As another example, in the city, the need to eliminate some of the police stations and firehouses as the population declines is a recurring issue. Which neighborhoods should have their public safety facilities closed?

III. The Political and Governmental Process

How does the St. Louis area reach decisions about what actions should be taken on which issues? It is difficult to find a straightforward answer to this question because the formal decision making structure—the numerous governments and their hundreds of elected officials—is highly decentralized. The best one-word answer to the question, "Who is in charge in St. Louis?" is "Nobody."

All power, however, does not reside in government. In a capitalist society, those who control the major economic enterprises have the potential to be highly influential. In St. Louis, the private sources of power are more concentrated than are the public ones. Certain organizations, most notably Civic Progress, a small body dominated by the chief executive officers of the major locally headquartered corporations, contain substantial wealth. Moreover, because their key participants head large organizations, they have access to a wide range of resources.

This private power is limited, however, by the need to work through the fragmented local governments in achieving any public action. Even if the corporations, working together through Civic Progress, agree on what ought to be done, they often cannot effectively implement their wishes because the many governments involved are uncoordinated and respond to very different constituencies.

Types of Public Authority in St. Louis

General Governments. General governments possess the broadest authority to conduct the public's business at the local level. Although state law can and does limit their powers to raise revenues, regulate activities, and provide services, the twentieth century has seen a movement toward home rule in which local units can assume much more discretion and responsibility. In St. Louis, the general governments are the city of St. Louis, St. Louis County, and the approximately ninety separate municipalities within St. Louis County.

General government within the city of St. Louis is highly dispersed. First, like most American governments, power is divided between an elected executive (the mayor) and an elected legislative body (the Board of Aldermen, with twenty-eight ward-based members and a citywide-elected board president). Both entities have the legal ability to stalemate the other. Second, the mayor does not possess all of the executive power. One key function, the power to propose the annual budget, is held by the Board of Estimate and Apportionment. The mayor has only one of the three votes in this body, with the others held by the separately elected comptroller and the president of the Board of Aldermen. Third, for reasons that reach back to Civil War antagonisms, the elected city officials do not control one major city service: the police force. Instead, four of the five members of the Board of Police Commissioners are appointed by the governor, with the fifth position occupied ex-officio by the mayor. Fourth, because the city also has county functions, it has separately elected county offices such as license collector and recorder of deeds. These elected officials and their operations are responsible directly to the people. The mayor and the Board of Aldermen have little control over them.

Two factors partially offset this dispersion and occasionally bring some cohesion to city policy making. The first unifying factor is the prestige and attention commanded by the mayor. Far more than any other single city official, the mayor can publicize and dramatize a particular issue. This ability, when employed creatively, can mobilize public support for an initiative. The second force is the Democratic party. Almost all of the city's elected officials are Democrats. Although party influence has declined during the past four decades in the city, the party still serves as a common forum.

Because formal power is so dispersed within the city, policy proposals rarely move decisively in a clear-cut direction. Instead the two most frequent outcomes are division of the spoils and stalemate. On issues where it is possible to distribute the goods or services (for example, allocating $20 million in federal aid for community development), an extended bargaining process typically ends with every interest obtaining a piece of the pie. On issues where the goods or services are not so divisible (for example, deciding whether or not to end the city's involvement in running hospitals), usually no participant has sufficient power to determine the result quickly, and the norm becomes prolonged or indefinite stalemate punctuated occasionally by the mayor's attempts at unilateral action.

The principal general government in the county is the St. Louis County government. It performs certain functions for the entire county such as providing public health services and maintaining arterial roads, and it acts as the sole general government for the county's unincorporated areas, where approximately two-fifths of the county population lives.

Under the St. Louis County Charter adopted in 1968, formal power is concentrated in a strong county executive. Elected countywide, this office has much more authority than the relatively weak seven-member county council. The first four county executives have expanded this formal supremacy by establishing tight control over the county bureaucracy.

Things are not so simple within the county's municipalities, where the remaining three-fifths of county residents live. These fall into one of four governmental types: (1) strong mayor cities in which full-time elected executives play the dominant role because they have strong formal authority or because their personalities and energies are potent; examples include Florissant and Jennings; (2) council-manager cities in which an elected council sets overall policy but the daily executive function is handled by an appointed city manager; examples include Clayton, Ferguson, University City, and Webster Groves; (3) administrator-council cities in which the elected council sets the policy but the executive function is handled by an elected mayor who is then assisted by an appointed administrator; examples include Ballwin, Des Peres, Fenton, and Glendale; and (4) cities with an elected council and mayor or an elected board of trustees but no full-time appointed professional manager (typically a city clerk is the highest-ranking paid staff member); this form is found most often in smaller, low-service municipalities.

Decision-making styles and the role of government also vary considerably among the county's municipalities. In some cities, a single individual, most often the mayor or a longtime city manager, is very influential. In other municipalities, there is little disagreement about public issues, and hence policies proceed in the same manner year after year. In still other cities, most of the conflict is due to personality differences among the elected officials rather than deep-seated controversy within the larger community. On the whole, suburban cities have very homogeneous populations, and consequently the residents and their elected representatives agree on most municipal issues. The role of government in county suburbs ranges from high-tax, high-service cities such as University City to low-tax, low-service municipalities such as Riverview.

On countywide matters, the political process depends on whether the issue is an exclusive function of county government, such as health and hospitals, or whether it is a function shared by the county and municipal governments, such as police protection. In exclusively county issues, the county executive is the key actor. In issues shared between the county and municipal governments, the county executive must negotiate with the municipal officials. This bargaining most often occurs under the auspices of one or both of two organizations: the St. Louis County Municipal League and the Mayors of Large Cities.

School Districts. School districts also represent a type of public authority in St. Louis. Public elementary and secondary education in St. Louis is governed by twenty-four separate school districts, one in the city and twenty-three in the county. The school boards are elected at large from the entire district rather than from separate subareas within each district. As a result, minority interests are typically underrepresented.

Each district's elected school board appoints a superintendent, who is responsible for administering the school system. Teacher groups and parent associations are often quite active in educational policy making, and their views are usually given serious attention. Debate on school issues typically is conducted in a we-all-agree-that-the-goal-is-better-education rhetoric, but this apparent consensus frequently masks serious disagreements about curricula, discipline, and allocation of the district's resources among different neighborhoods.

Special Districts. A third type of public authority in St. Louis is special districts. Many local public goods and services are handled outside the general government. St. Louis values the autonomy of its local general governments, but has seen the need to have larger units handle specific functions. When this happens, the governing apparatus established to administer the good or service is called a special district. Examples include mass transit (the Bi-State Development Agency), fire protection and emergency medical assistance (more than twenty areas in the county have separate districts for these services), sanitary and storm water sewers (Metropolitan Sewer District), special education (Special School District), and cultural institutions (Zoo–Museum District).

Some special districts are governed by boards elected directly by the public: examples include the fire protection districts, the Special School District, and the St. Louis Community College District. Others are directed by boards appointed by elected executives. The Metropolitan Sewer District and the Zoo–Museum District boards, for example, are appointed by the mayor of St. Louis and the St. Louis county executive.

Whatever the selection procedures, unless some scandal occurs or the district needs a tax increase, most of the public is unaware of what is happening inside the operation. Typically, only those closely connected to the particular service, such as major suppliers, become actively involved in the special districts' political and governance process.

Major Informal Sources of Power

Groups with a major stake in what happens within local governments usually organize to promote their interests. Sometimes these organizations are tightly structured, with clear programs and single leaders. More often, they are less compact and more than one voice claims to speak for a particular segment.

Large corporations in St. Louis typically reach agreement about public policy positions through Civic Progress. With few exceptions, only the chief executive officer of the largest locally headquartered corporations (such as Anheuser Busch, Emerson Electric, and Monsanto) belong. Civic Progress shuns publicity and usually communicates its views behind the scenes to public officials. It has begun, however, to take a slightly more visible role in the past few years. Understandably, its principal concern is economic development.

A second and much larger business organization is the Regional Commerce and Growth Association (RCGA). Although RCGA also includes labor unions and not-for-profit organizations among its membership, its boards and its activities are dominated by business interests. Indeed, some observers argue that it is essentially controlled by Civic Progress, pointing to the fact that there is seldom any discrepancy between the two organizations' agendas.

Firms that benefit from additional development, such as home builders and road contractors, are also active in local politics. New land development drives their enterprises, and they wish to have some say over where and how development occurs.

For the most part, the labor unions in St. Louis work politically through the St. Louis AFL-CIO Labor Council, although historically, two large unions—the Teamsters and the United Auto Workers—have had a shaky relationship with this umbrella group. In the past, labor unions have focused more on national and state policies than on local politics, but this is changing as local units take on more responsibility for economic development. The construction trades are the most involved, since both development and building code regulations directly affect their members.

As the Black portion of the population has increased in St. Louis, Black organizations have become more prominent in local decision making. Once almost exclusively on the outside looking in, Blacks in the 1990s occupy top city positions including mayor, comptroller, and police chief. Among groups representing Black interests are the local chapters of the Urban League and the National Association for the Advancement of Colored People (NAACP).

In addition to these groups representing private interests, there are public interest groups that attempt to influence policies in St. Louis. Examples include the local chapter of the League of Women Voters and Confluence St. Louis. The latter is a membership group of about one thousand citizens who form task forces to study key problems, make recommendations, and then work to have those recommendations implemented.

Advantages and Disadvantages of Decentralized Government

Because government in St. Louis is so decentralized, there have been several consolidation attempts during the past century. The most recent, a 1988 proposal that included dividing the entire county into about forty municipalities and four fire protection districts, never came to a public vote because the U.S. Supreme Court ruled that the process that produced the recommendations was constitutionally flawed.

When these centralizing efforts recommending sweeping changes have been put before the voters, as they were in the late 1950s and early 1960s, they have been decisively defeated. When attempts at centralization have been more limited and have only dealt with a single good or service such as sewers or community colleges, they often have succeeded.

Some argue that there should be even more metropolitanwide governance and point to the existing fragmentation as a major obstacle to the region's development. Certainly many of the major issues challenging the area—economic vitality, housing quality, education—are beyond the resources of any single government. Other reasons to support more centralization are that coordination among existing governmental units is inadequate, that there are so many governments and procedures that almost no one can understand what is happening, that having a large number of small governments— especially the miniature municipalities in the county—is economically inefficient, and, finally, that the whole apparatus is just too messy. Corporate leaders in particular seem to long for a governmental structure that would be easier to work with and through.

Despite all these arguments, St. Louis persists in having very decentralized governmental arrangements. Why? First, having many governments accommodates the region's social and economic diversity and promotes the notion that government should remain close to the people, especially to "my kind" of people. Second, few present governments wish to go out of existence and therefore fight attempts to change. Third, the county resists centralization efforts that would unite the city and county, because one of the consequences might be that county residents would have to pick up more of the tab for services in the city. Fourth, many Blacks in the city oppose consolidation because it would rob them of the political influence there that they have fought so hard to gain. Fifth, having many distinct municipalities gives people more choices about the kind of city in which to live. They can select from a wide range of tax and service combinations. If there were a single general government, there would be no options about the tax-service levels. Sixth, in the grand American tradition, dispersing power among many governments lessens the probability that any single point of view or set of interests can tyrannize the rest.

IV. Conclusion

During the past few decades, St. Louis's population has stopped growing and the portion of elderly citizens has increased, its facilities have aged, it has become more racially diverse, and its economy has moved from manufacturing industries toward the service and information sectors. These trends, along with other factors, indicate that St. Louis must work even harder to maintain and enhance its quality of life. St. Louisans, however, have great pride in their region, and hard work is part of their ethic. The challenge for St. Louis is to maintain the advantages of decentralized governments while responding to the need to act decisively as a region.

CHAPTER 26

Politics in Kansas City
by G. Ross Stephens

Evrythin's up to date in Kansas City, they've gone about as far as they c'n go.—Oscar Hammerstein II

Greater Kansas City is a political maze covering a ten-county metropolitan area in two states—one-third of its 447 local governments and more than 35 percent of its residents are on the Kansas side of the state line. In 1992 the metropolitan area had an estimated population of more than 1.6 million within a complex of both discrete and overlying governmental jurisdictions—a political labyrinth for both the citizen and the public official. Moreover, the Kansas City area abuts smaller metropolitan areas to the north (St. Joseph, with about 83,000 inhabitants) and to the west (Lawrence, Kansas, with about 82,000 residents). If Topeka, Kansas, and its population of about 161,000 west of Lawrence is included, the region might be called a mini-megalopolis.

This chapter describes Kansas City's governmental maze and the problems it creates, and presents some idea of how government operates in the Kansas City area. The chapter begins with a review of growth patterns in the metropolitan area. The area's social and economic characteristics are examined next, followed by a description of the forms of local government, a look at the most influential economic factors, and, finally, an analysis of some of the political attributes that make the Kansas City area unique.

I. History and Growth

Kansas City, Missouri, was incorporated as a municipality in 1850, and by the turn of the century it had reached a population of 164,000. Except during the Great Depression–era 1930s, the city grew until 1970, when it reached a high of about 507,000 inhabitants. Thus from the end of World War II until 1970, Kansas City did not experience the decline in population so common to older, larger central cities in the Northern and Eastern United States. While St. Louis lost nearly 400,000 people, almost half its population, between 1950 and 1980, Kansas City avoided a similar decline by annexing land in Jackson, Platte, and Clay counties. Kansas City increased in size from less than eighty-five square miles to more than three hundred square miles in the 1950s and early 1960s. Partly in reaction to this "land grab," some suburban cities in the region embarked on their own annexation programs, including Independence, Lee's Summit, Grandview, Grain Valley, Oak Grove, Buckner, Platte City, Parkville, and several others.

Table 26-1. **Population of Counties in Kansas City Metropolitan Area, 1970–1990**

State & County	Area in Square Miles	Population (in Thousands)			Percentage Increase in Population by Decade	
		1970	1980	1990	1970–1980	1980–1990
Missouri						
Cass	699	39.3	51.0	63.8	+29	+25
Clay	397	123.7	136.5	153.4	+10	+12
Jackson	605	654.2	629.3	633.2	− 4	+ 1
Lafayette	629	26.6	29.6	31.1	+12	+ 4
Platte	420	32.1	46.3	57.9	+44	+25
Ray	570	17.6	21.4	22.0	+22	+ 3
Subtotal	3,320	893.6	914.4	961.4	+ 2	+ 5
Kansas						
Johnson	477	220.1	270.3	355.1	+23	+31
Leavenworth	463	53.3	54.8	64.4	+ 3	+17
Miami	577	19.3	21.6	23.5	+12	+ 9
Wyandotte	151	186.8	172.3	162.0	− 8	− 6
Subtotal	1,668	479.5	519.0	605.0	+ 8	+17
10 County						
Total	4,988	1,373.1	1,433.5	1,566.3	+ 4	+ 9

Sources: Bureau of the Census, *1990 Census of Population* and the *State and Metropolitan Area Data Book 1991.*

Although Kansas City, Missouri, was able to delay population decline, it could not fend it off entirely. The city lost 59,000 residents during the 1970s and another 13,000 during the 1980s. The city's population was listed at about 435,000 in the 1990 Census. Kansas City, Kansas, has shown a similar pattern: after annexing territory and avoiding population loss up until 1970, its population declined, from about 168,000 in 1970 to about 150,000 in 1990.

The population of the ten-county Kansas City metropolitan area has grown substantially since 1940, from less than 800,000 in 1940 to about 1,566,000 by 1990. However, the growth rate has slowed from almost 28 percent in the 1950s to 4 percent in the 1970s and then 9.3 percent in the 1980s.

Still, the suburbs have grown significantly in comparison with the central city. In 1940 nearly three of every five residents of the metropolitan area lived in Kansas City, Missouri; in 1990 the ratio was less than three in ten.

As in many other metropolitan areas, growth has taken place in the outlying cities and counties. Of the Kansas City area's population increase of 193,000 from 1970 to 1990, nearly 70 percent—135,000—was accounted for by Johnson County, Kansas. Most of the rest of the increase came about equally in three Missouri counties—Clay, Platte, and Cass—each of which added 25,000 to 30,000 residents over the 1970s and 1980s. In contrast, the central counties of Jackson in Missouri and Wyandotte in

**Figure 26-1. Population Growth and Decline, by County,
Kansas City Metropolitan Area, 1970–1990**

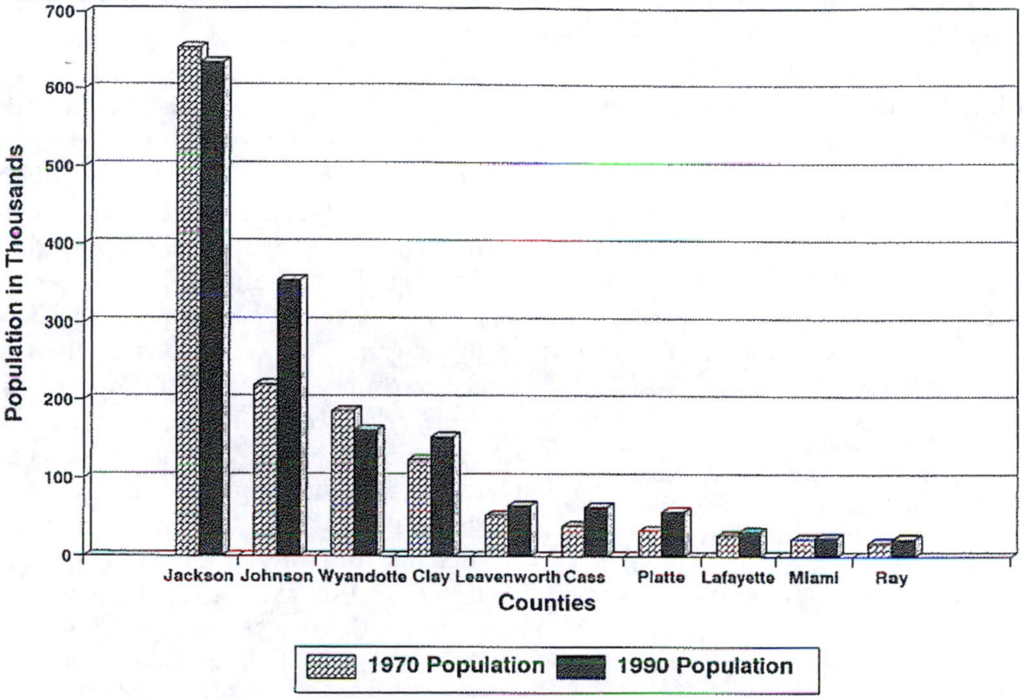

Source: *Statistical Abstract of the United States, 1993*, Bureau of the Census.

Kansas lost about 35,000 residents over the two decades. The cities that grew the most were Olathe, Kansas, which grew by 45,000 and Overland Park, Kansas; Blue Springs, Missouri; and Lee's Summit, Missouri; each of which increased by about 30,000 to 35,000.

Much of the area's population change is related to the changing character of the local economy. In a reflection of a nationwide trend, employment in manufacturing dropped from 25 percent of the Kansas City–area labor force in 1970 to 18 percent in 1989, while employment in service industries more than doubled. Since services are less tied to a central portion of the metropolitan area and are able to locate on the fringe of the urbanized area, this helps to account for the population shift from the central cities to the suburbs. But other changes have also taken place. Due to continued construction of circumferential highways, less dependence on rail transport, and an increase in the manufacture of smaller, higher-value goods, some manufacturing and warehousing operations have moved away from the congested core. Retailing has always followed the population to the suburbs. Other factors also have been involved, including the quality of state and local governmental services, which will be discussed later in this chapter.

In spite of this trend toward suburban growth, not all of the suburban municipalities grew in the 1970s and 1980s. Fifty-two of the 132 area municipalities lost population during these years (some of the population decline was accounted for by a 16 percent drop in the size of households since 1970, a reflection of another nationwide trend). The largest declines outside the central cities were in Prairie Village, Kansas, which lost five thousand residents, and Raytown, Missouri, which lost three thousand. Independence, the largest Missouri suburb, remained stable throughout this twenty-year period, despite (or perhaps because of) large-scale annexations in the 1970s.

The population patterns were described succinctly and pessimistically by the Mid-America Regional Council (MARC):

> Metropolitan Kansas City faces a daunting yet inescapable challenge: its urban core has declined steadily in recent decades and continues to suffer population loss, disinvestment and deterioration. It is spreading. And it affects the entire region.[1]

II. Social and Economic Characteristics

Blacks composed 13 percent of the area's population, or about two hundred thousand people, in 1990. Whites constituted 85.5 percent of the population, but this category included many different ethnic groups; those claiming English or German descent made up the largest segments. (However, half the population either did not report its ancestry or claimed descent from two or more ethnic groups.) There are more than thirty thousand residents of Latin American descent, plus fifteen thousand to twenty thousand residents of Asian descent. Nearly nine of every ten Blacks and most Latinos live in the two central counties, but quite a large number of Asian Americans live in Johnson County.

In the metropolitan area, per capita personal income (PCI) for 1992 averaged $20,948, which was 4.2 percent above the national average. Per capita personal income in the area ranged from about 35 percent above the metropolitan average in Johnson County, Kansas, to about 30 percent below the average in Wyandotte County, Kansas. In fact, Johnson County ranked in the top 5 percent in PCI among the nation's 740 metropolitan counties and city-counties.[2] Within the Kansas City area, the proportion of the population below the poverty line was highest in the two central counties and Lafayette County, Missouri, and lowest in Johnson County. The metropolitan area's PCI is higher than that for Omaha, Wichita, and Springfield, about the same as that for Des Moines, and lower than that for Denver, Dallas, and St. Louis. If one were to take the cost of living into account, Kansas City metropolitan area residents were better off than residents of most large metropolitan areas.

Like the national population, the population of the Kansas City area is becoming more elderly. The proportion of the population under 25 years of age is marginally lower than nationally and for other metropolitan areas; the productive age group from 25 through 64 is proportionally higher; while the age group of 65 and older is below the average for the nation and for metropolitan areas.

The number of employed in the area increased by 22 percent in the 1970s and by 25 percent in the 1980s, and stood at about 860,000 in 1993. The unemployment rate was usually about one or two percentage points below the national average. Compared to other metropolitan areas, Kansas City was a bit below average in percentage

1. Mid-America Regional Council (MARC), *Metropolitan Kansas City's Urban Core* (1993), 1.

2. United States Bureau of the Census, *State and Metropolitan Area Data Book 1991.*

Figure 26-2. Private Non-Farm Employment,
Kansas City Metropolitan Area, 1989

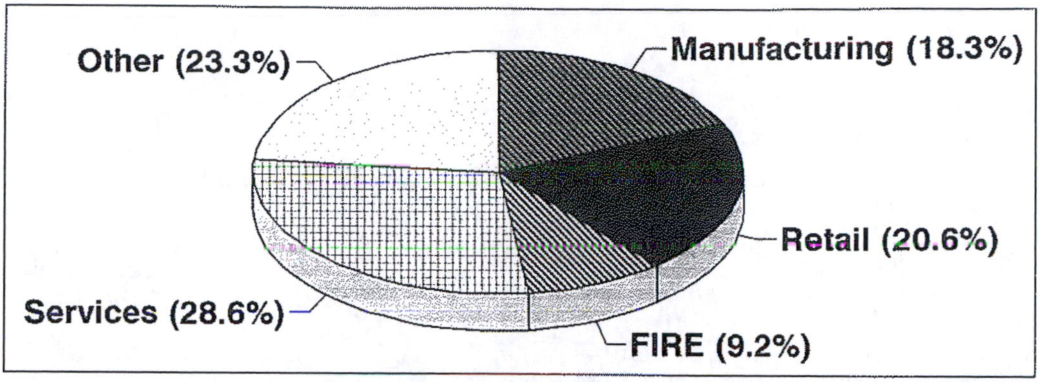

Sources: *State and Metropolitan Area Data, Data Book 1991;* and *Statistical Abstract of the United States, 1993;* Bureau of the Census

of the work force employed in manufacturing, retail trade, and service employment, but above average in finance, insurance, and real estate (FIRE) and in other miscellaneous types of economic activity.

In the past two decades, employment has increased in such occupations as law, data processing, health, and restaurants. At the same time, declines in employment were recorded in garment manufacturing, barber shops, drug stores, and dry-cleaning establishments.[3] There were very significant increases in the 1980s in office space and in business activities in Johnson County, with some increases also in southern Jackson and northern Cass counties as well as in the central business district of Kansas City.

Another area of increased employment in the 1970s was government of all levels— federal, state, and local. During that period, there was a 50 percent increase in government employment in the area. The number of employees with federal and local governments increased by about 40 percent, while

that for the states more than doubled. In the 1990s government employment accounted for 15 to 16 percent of the labor force, but it was no longer a high-growth sector relative to area employment. Since 1980, area federal government employment has remained stable, while that for state and local governments had increased an estimated 4 percent by 1991. Most of the 1980s increase in local government employment took place in the suburban areas.

Part of the reason for the more rapid growth of the suburbs and especially of Johnson County was the perceived quality of local schools. During much of this period, school expenditures in Johnson County were about one-third higher than those for the Kansas City, Missouri, and Jackson County school districts. This led to considerable migration of Missouri middle-class parents with school-age children across the state line to Johnson County. During the late 1980s and early 1990s, federal court–ordered integration tax increases and expenditures by both the state of Missouri and the Kansas City school district led to large increases in district

3. Ibid.; U.S. Department of Labor, Bureau of Labor Statistics. *Missouri Area Labor Trends,* 1990.

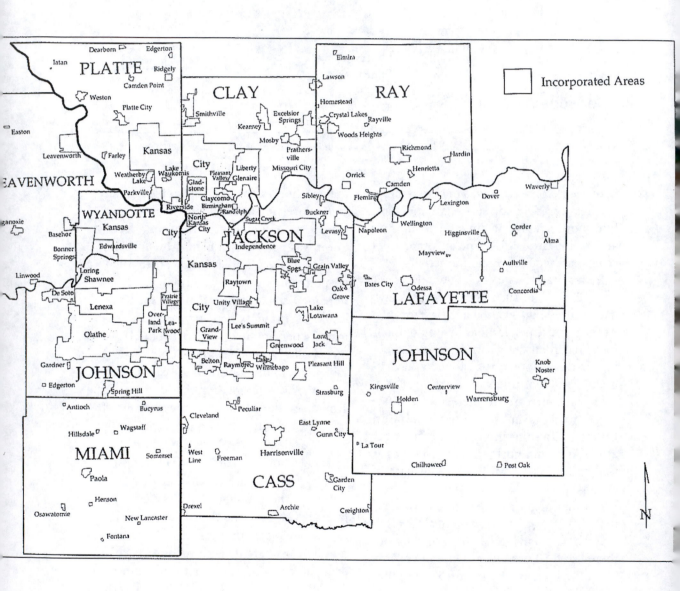

spending, raising substantially the expenditures per pupil. The increased expenditures, however, proved an insufficient lure; few middle-class children transferred or moved into the Kansas City school district.

Though not always recognized as such, Kansas City is the home of a number of institutions of higher education. The University of Missouri–Kansas City with its several professional schools is the largest in the metropolitan area, but there is also the University of Kansas Medical Center and the Kansas University Regents Center, which is being expanded. There are a number of smaller colleges, including the Kansas City Art Institute, William Jewell, Park, Avila, and Rockhurst. In addition, community colleges and college systems exist in Kansas City, Missouri; Kansas City, Kansas; and Johnson County, Kansas. Also the University of Kansas at Lawrence is only thirty-five miles from downtown Kansas City. This listing does not include extension programs by both in-state and out-of-state colleges and universities such as Webster and Central Michigan, technical training institutes, and Bible colleges.

III. Local Government

As mentioned earlier, the ten-county Kansas City metropolitan area contains numerous political subdivisions and boundaries, many of which overlie one another. Of the 447 local governments in the ten-county metropolitan area in 1992, 131 were municipalities (cities, villages, and towns); 207 were special districts; 66 were school districts; and 33 were townships (all of the townships were in Kansas). Sixty-five percent of these governmental entities and 60 percent of the area's population were located in Missouri, as were three-fourths of the municipalities. The smallest was the town of Iaton in Platte County with a population of 47. According to the 1990 Census, some sixty-seven municipalities had populations of less than one thousand; fifty-one had less than five hundred inhabitants.

General-Purpose Governments. Most of these 131 municipalities are organized as villages, towns, or fourth-class cities. Three operate with legislative charters passed before 1875. The overwhelming majority have weak mayor systems. Virtually all of the 26 municipalities with more than five thousand residents, as well as Johnson County, have council-manager or administrator forms of local government.

Kansas City, Missouri, operates under a constitutional home rule charter passed in 1925 and amended numerous times since then. Kansas City has a council-manager system that has been considerably modified and now contains the characteristics of both the manager and mayor-council organizational structures. The mayor is elected for a four-year term and presides over the city council. These elections are nominally nonpartisan, but the party affiliation of the candidates is almost always known. The mayor is a full-time functionary and appoints, with council approval, the members of numerous boards and commissions—some of whom run departments and regulatory activities. (One exception, however, is the police department, which is funded by the city but governed by a commission made up of the mayor and four members appointed by the governor.) Emanuel Cleaver was elected as the city's first Black mayor in 1991.

The twelve members of the city council also are elected for four-year terms, half at large and half by wards. In 1990 an amendment to the city charter limited the mayor and council to two terms in office. The result was a turnover of nearly half

Table 26-2. Local Governments in the Ten-County Kansas City Metropolitan Area, 1990

State & County	Municipalities	Civil Townships	School Districts	Special Districts	Totals*
Missouri					
Cass	18	—	11	22	52
Clay	20	—	6	22	49
Jackson	17	—	13	22	53
Lafayette	13	—	6	25	45
Platte	17	—	4	36	58
Ray	13	—	5	25	44
Missouri Subtotal	98	—	45	152	301
Kansas					
Johnson	20	9	7	16	53
Leavenworth	6	10	6	15	38
Miami	4	13	3	15	36
Wyandotte	3	1	5	9	19
Kansas Subtotal	33	33	21	55	146
Ten-County Total	131	33	66	207	447

* Totals include county governments.

Sources: Bureau of the Census, 1990 *Census of Population*; 1992 *Census of Governments* GC92(1)–1; *State and Metropolitan Area Data Book 1991*.

the council in the 1991 election. Voters in Kansas City also elect municipal judges under the Nonpartisan Missouri Plan for judicial selection.

The manager is appointed by the city council for an indefinite tenure. The fact that the mayor is more important in Kansas City than in most manager cities has at times led to conflict between the mayor and the manager.

Other area cities with council-manager plans include Gladstone, Independence, and Excelsior Springs. Those with the mayor–council–city administrator forms of government include Grandview, Lee's Summit, Belton, Liberty, and Harrisonville. In the 1980s Kansas City, Kansas, switched from a city commission to a mayor–council–city administrator system.

Jackson County, operating under a county charter, has an elected executive, a nine-member county legislature, and an elected prosecuting attorney and sheriff. All other Missouri counties in the Kansas City metropolitan area have a three-member county commission along with numerous other elected county officials. Kansas counties use a similar system, except that Johnson County uses a five-member commission with an appointed county administrator.

School Districts. School districts in Missouri are seldom coterminous with other political boundaries. The Kansas City, Missouri, school district covers only a small part of the city. The city's residents are served by a dozen school districts and the Metropolitan Community College District. The Kansas City School District has experienced great turmoil over integration, financing, and issues related to meeting the directives of the federal district court. In 1987 the court ordered a major increase in the local property tax and a 25 percent surcharge on the state income tax to fund the schools. The surcharge was thrown out on appeal to higher federal courts. The tax increase and mandated state funds are being used to fund magnet schools.

The results of these imposed changes are at best mixed. Not only are the standardized reading and mathematics test scores for the upper grades below the national averages, they are significantly below those at other large-city public schools. The district also has been unable to attract nonminority students, so the district remains rather highly segregated.[4]

Special Districts. Nearly all of the 207 special districts and authorities in the area are minor entities, with two or three exceptions. The Kansas City Area Transportation Authority (KCATA) was created by an interstate compact between Missouri and Kansas with its governing board appointed by the two states' governors. Originally, the KCATA was to serve a six-county area, but some of the local units have been opting out. Much of their activity is concentrated in Missouri because Kansas City, Missouri, has supported it with a half-cent sales tax. Another large district is the Kansas City, Kansas, Board of Public Utilities, which provides water and electricity. Most other special districts provide fire protection, minor highway maintenance, drainage, water and sewerage services, or housing, although there are also several cemetery districts on the Kansas side.

IV. Economic Leadership

Political and economic leadership in

4. Lynn Horsley, "The Color of the Class," *Kansas City Star*, May 9, 1993.

Kansas City is divided in orientation by the state line and other political boundaries. Economic leaders are continually criticized for their inability to carry out concerted action to revitalize the inner cities and downtown areas. Very little has been done to make use of the riverfront. The one real attempt to do so, the River Quay development, ended in failure when organized crime groups took over some of the establishments and started fighting among themselves. In the early 1990s there were moves or proposals to rehabilitate the River Quay area and the old Union Station, but not much was being accomplished. Bartle Hall was expanded, and there were proposals for new downtown hotels to attract more conventions. There was an abortive attempt in 1993 to recall the mayor by one of the midcity "wine and cheese" groups over the issue of what to do with Union Station.

Kansas City has the usual business associations, such as chambers of commerce and downtown development organizations, but their success has been limited. Business continues to move to the periphery. A number of brokerage firms and other businesses have moved to the Country Club Plaza, a midtown integrated shopping area; or to suburban areas, particularly Johnson County. One organization, the Civic Council, composed of chief executives of business firms, has worked quietly to promote economic development and other projects in the area, but so far its accomplishments have not been very visible. Local bankers are often criticized for failing to provide risk capital for development. As a result of the suburbanization of business activity, some of the old-line, formerly all-male clubs such as the Kansas City Club, the University Club, and the Athletic Club have had difficulty in maintaining membership.

To some degree they are being replaced by outlying country clubs.

Not all is failure. Some convention facilities have been developed in suburban Johnson County. Hallmark Cards and the Hall family helped to successfully redevelop the midtown area just east of Union Station, an area that became known as Crown Center. In the 1980s new construction provided more office space in the central business district as well. There also has been a vast increase in office space in Johnson County along College Boulevard and in Missouri along Interstate 435. Unfortunately, Kansas City, like many other cities, has a surplus of office space both downtown and in outlying areas. In comparison to cities such as Portland and Minneapolis there has been little concerted action in Kansas City to upgrade the central business district. Federal and state offices are still located principally in the central business district, but government is no longer a growth factor in the local economy except for suburban municipalities and school districts.

V. Political Leadership

It is not easy to understand Kansas City politics without some knowledge of the city's history and the rise and fall of the Pendergast Machine. The Citizen's Association, which grew out of the fight to undermine the Pendergast machine in the 1930s, still sanctions candidates for city offices, though its influence is not as pervasive as it once was. City elections are nonpartisan, and the Association could be called a political action group pointing the way to the "good, the true, and the beautiful." However, it tends to be a self-appointed group of second- and third-level business and community leaders who try to influence city elections. Their main thrust is to prevent any alteration of the manager form of government or of the nonpartisan elections.

In the 1950s and early 1960s, city politics tended to be factional, with the influential politicians including some who had been members of the Pendergast machine as well as many who had opposed the machine. Among those who had supported Tom Pendergast were Jim Pendergast, Alex Presta in the Italian community, and Henry McKessick in the Black community. With few exceptions, these factions were unable to work together.[5]

Since that time, factionalism has eroded and Kansas City politics has become more atomistic, with each person going off in his or her own direction. Nonpartisan elections have their costs. State government in Missouri is partisan, and through its nonpartisan elections, the city is at least partly cut off from state political officials—even though both city and state tend to be more Democratic than Republican. There are those who think nonpartisan elections are continued so that Republicans can be elected in a city that would otherwise elect a solid slate of Democrats.

In Kansas City, instead of asking, "Who governs?" perhaps we should ask, "Does anyone govern?" and, "In whose interest is this lack of governance?" Economic leaders, even those with substantial holdings in Missouri, live mostly in Kansas in Johnson County. This limits their ability to influence political leaders in Missouri. Concerted action is frustrated by the existence of the state line, multitudes of political jurisdictions, and toy governments, some of which are designed to frustrate economic development or to build fences to keep out "undesirables."

5. Edward C. Banfield and James Q. Wilson, *City Politics* (Cambridge: Harvard University Press, 1965), 134–35.

Many of the problems of Kansas City, Missouri, cannot be solved by the city itself. They are either caused or exacerbated by governments with overlying jurisdiction, in particular, the school districts and the state government. Missouri has never been out in front in experimenting with either new methods of taxation or the provision of public services. It is the Show-Me State.[6]

Missouri might more aptly be called the Do-Nothing State if it is judged by its low levels of spending (both per capita and as a percentage of total personal income) for state direct services plus aid to local governments. In both cases Missouri ranks forty-ninth out of the fifty states. Until the mid–1980s Missouri ranked dead last, but small increases in state taxes moved the state ahead of New Hampshire. In the Kansas City metropolitan area, property taxes are significantly higher on the Kansas side than on the Missouri side of the state line. On the other hand, Missouri municipalities levy higher gross receipts taxes on utilities of all kinds, and Kansas City, Missouri, also levies an earnings tax.

Over the past few decades, school districts in Johnson County have spent more for public education than have Jackson County districts; state aid to local governments and to education has been higher in Kansas than on the Missouri side of the state line. This is important because Kansas City, Missouri, and other Missouri communities are in competition with Kansas, particularly with Johnson County, for taxpaying residents and businesses. This is crucial when it comes to the quality of public education, which is an important factor when residents determine where to locate their homes and businesses. There are no physical barriers to free movement across the state line. Missouri is in competition with Kansas for economic development, and Missouri is losing the battle, as is evidenced by the major gains in population, income, and employment in Johnson County over the past few decades. Given the heavy competition for development in a high-tech, information-based, service-oriented economy, this can be a handicap for communities located on the Missouri side. It seems unlikely that these conditions will change in the near future given limitations on federal expenditures in the 1990s and the failure of Missouri state government to adequately fund state and local public services.[7]

Many Missouri legislators and politicians have long maintained that low taxes will attract business and commercial activity. But if the example of Kansas City is relevant, residents and businesses do not always opt for lower taxes if lower taxes also mean that they must accept inferior services. Low-quality public education is another location-shifter for middle-class residents.

VI. Conclusion

The Kansas City metropolitan area has great diversity in its cultural and social activities and, taken as a whole, a reasonably stable economy. However, there are problems, particularly with respect to the state line and the diversion of population and resources to Johnson County, Kansas. Competition flourishes between the numerous political subdivisions on both sides of the

6. When the author served on a governor's council a few years back, he suggested that the state create a commission to regulate annexation and incorporation of municipalities and the creation of special district governments. At this point a long-term state legislator noted that "if the other forty-nine states do it, *then* we might consider it."

7. G. Ross Stephens, "Federal Spending and State Economic Development in Missouri, 1968–1988," in Kimberly J. Kempf, J. Fred Springer, G. Ross Stephens, and David J. Webber, eds., *Missouri Policy Choices*, University of Missouri–Columbia, UED 86 (1991), 152–69.

state line and between the states as well. In the battle for economic development, the central cities (Kansas City, Missouri, and Kansas City, Kansas) and the state of Missouri are losing, but the average citizen is probably not aware of these losses.

On a more positive note, although the central cities have lost population and business to the suburbs, these losses are minimal compared to the situations of the cities of St. Louis, Missouri, and East St. Louis, Illinois. Kansas City has displaced St. Louis as Missouri's largest city. The Kansas City metropolitan area as a whole is economically healthy and is gaining in population.

About the Authors

Rickert (Rick) Althaus is Associate Professor of Political Science at Southeast Missouri State University, Cape Girardeau, where he teaches American government and politics. He has published (with Dean Yarwood of the University of Missouri–Columbia) in *Public Administration Review* and has written extensively on U.S. agricultural policy and public administration pedagogy. He has just completed a term as president of the Missouri Political Science Association, and is active in university governance and community political organizations. He received his Ph.D. from the University of Missouri–Columbia in 1987.

John Ballard is President of Governmental Services, Inc., in Ashland, Missouri. He publishes the monthly *Governmental Affairs Newsletter* and provides a variety of services to Missouri's local governments. He is a former Extension Specialist of the University of Missouri–Columbia's Governmental Affairs Program and has written many publications. He also has been a frequent contributor to both the print and electronic media in Missouri. As an Extension Specialist, he participated in programs for local and state officials, and he continues to do so as a private consultant. He has a master's degree in Community Development from the University of Missouri–Columbia.

Roy Blunt served two terms as Missouri Secretary of State (1985–1993), and in 1993 became President of Southwest Baptist University at Bolivar, Missouri. Prior to being Secretary of State, he served twelve years as County Clerk and Election Authority for Greene County and Springfield. He has taught American government and history in both secondary and higher education. Additionally, he has written many publications relating to voting rights, elections, and election procedures, both for state government and the University of Missouri's Governmental Affairs Program. He received his M.A. from Southwest Missouri State University at Springfield, and has participated in many programs involving local and state government officials.

R. E. Burnett is currently the Associate Director of the Patterson School of Diplomacy and International Commerce at the University of Kentucky; he is also an Assistant Professor of International Affairs. He has worked in Washington, D.C., as a political and economic consultant to the United States Information Agency and the State Department, and as a business and political consultant to MCI Telecommunications, Inc., and to General Dynamics Corporation. He received his master's degree in international affairs from George Washington University after completing work on his bachelor's degree at UMC. His doctorate work was also completed at UMC. He has studied at Sophia University in Japan and has taught at Stephens College in Columbia. He also acted as manager in Richard (Rick) Hardy's 1992 congressional campaign.

Joseph J. Carrier is a doctoral student in political science at the University of Missouri–Columbia, where he teaches courses in American politics. He received his B.A. in criminal justice from Southeastern Louisiana University, and earned his M.A. in political science from the University of Missouri–Columbia. Additionally, he has ten years of law enforcement experience, including five years with the Air Force Office of Special Investigation, conducting criminal and counterintelligence investigations. His current research interests include constitutional law and judicial behavior.

Gregory Casey is Associate Professor of Political Science with the University of Missouri–Columbia. He gained his Ph.D. from Georgetown University in 1968 and has been with the University of Missouri's Department of Political Science since 1967. His many publications include "Public Perceptions of Judicial Scandal: The Missouri Supreme Court 1982–88," published in *Justice System Journal*, and "Political Controversy on Missouri's Supreme Court: The Case of Merit vs. Politics", which appeared in *State and Local Government Review* (both coauthored with Kenyon Bunch). He has won many teaching awards for his classes on the U.S. Constitution, the judiciary, and American and state government and has a variety of present research interests.

Robert Dewhirst is Associate Professor in the Department of Government and Economics at Northwest Missouri State University in Maryville. His teaching and research interests are in American government and politics, legislative politics, and presidential/executive politics. He has recently become interested in environmental and energy issues, particularly as they affect economic development. He gained his Ph.D. from the University of Nebraska in 1983.

Richard R. Dohm is Professor Emeritus of Political Science at the University of Missouri–Columbia, and former Director of the department's Governmental Affairs Program (GAP), its University Extension and outreach effort. As Director, he supervised and coordinated applied research and training efforts for Missouri public officials. He also edited the monthly *Governmental Affairs Newsletter* and wrote many publications on policy matters of interest to state and local officials. His current interests include developing relations with the newly created Academy of Public Administration in

Moldova (previously Moldavia of the former Soviet Union), as well as training proposals. He received his Ph.D. from the University of Minnesota in 1965.

James Endersby is Assistant Professor of Political Science at the University of Missouri–Columbia, with interests in research methods and statistics; American politics; voting, public opinion, and elections; formal theory; and interest groups and legislative behavior. He has many publications, including "Nonpolicy Issues and the Spatial Theory of Voting," in *Quality and Quantity*; and "Spotlight on Vermont: Third Party Success in the 1990 Congressional Election," in *Social Science Journal* (coauthored with David Thomason). He gained his Ph.D. in 1990 and his M.A. in 1982, both from the University of Texas at Austin.

Bryan Forbis is presently Deputy Director for Administration with the Division of Child Support Enforcement, Missouri Department of Social Services. He supports a staff of more than eleven hundred in twenty different facilities for the Division, which has grown considerably since 1985. Prior to this, he was Director of the Department of Social Services' Division of Aging, which has programs serving 945,000 older Missourians, and legislative director for the Department of Natural Resources. He completed his undergraduate and graduate work at the University of Missouri–Columbia, gaining B.A. degrees in interdisciplinary honors and political science and an M.A. in political science (public policy) in 1981.

Jerena E. Giffen gained her Bachelor of Journalism degree from the University of Missouri–Columbia, and was a staff writer and bureau director for United Press International's Jefferson City office before holding several positions as public information officer in Missouri state government. She returned to graduate school at the University of Missouri–Columbia, where she gained her Masters of Public Administration degree in

1980 and her Ph.D. in 1989. She has taught at Lincoln University, Columbia College, the University of Missouri–Columbia, and the University of Missouri–Rolla. She has a variety of publications, including *First Ladies of Missouri: Their Homes and Families* and several others on women in Missouri, and has scripted two television shows concerning political participation for national educational networks.

Richard J. Hardy is Associate Professor of Political Science at the University of Missouri–Columbia and former Director of the department's Masters of Public Policy Program. He received his Ph.D. from the University of Iowa in 1978. His areas of interest include American government, state and local politics, and constitutional law. He has published in such journals as the *American Journal of Political Science, Policy Studies Journal, Law and Policy Quarterly,* and *Teaching Political Science.* He is also the author of the widely adopted *Government in America,* published by Houghton-Mifflin; has won many awards for teaching; and has been a candidate for Missouri's 9th District congressional seat.

Earl W. Hawkey is currently Registrar for the University of Nebraska at Lincoln. Previously, he worked for the Registrar's Office at the University of Washington, and as Manager of Facilities Analysis, Programming, and Energy Planning in the Office of Facilities Management at the University of Missouri–Columbia. Still earlier, he worked as a Planner and Budget Analyst in the Division of Budget and Planning for the State of Missouri, Office of Administration. He received his A.B. in government and international studies from the University of Notre Dame and his M.A. and Ph.D. from the University of Missouri–Columbia.

E. Terrence Jones is Dean of the College of Arts and Science at the University of Missouri–St. Louis. He has a B.S. in Economics from St. Louis University and re-

ceived his Ph.D. in Political Science from Georgetown University in 1967. He is the author of *Conducting Political Research* (1972 and 1984), and his articles on urban politics, public policy, and public opinion have appeared in many journals, including *Policy Studies Journal, Public Opinion Quarterly,* and *Urban Affairs Quarterly.* He often appears on television as a political analyst and conducts frequent public opinion polls. He is also active as a political consultant.

James D. King is Associate Professor of Political Science at the University of Wyoming at Laramie. Previously, he was at Memphis State University, where he taught courses in American Politics and State Government, and served as department chair. His research on various aspects of legislative politics and electoral behavior has appeared in *Presidential Studies Quarterly, Journal of Politics, Social Science Quarterly, Political Methodology, Western Political Quarterly,* and other publications. He received his Ph.D. from the University of Missouri–Columbia in 1983.

Richard L. Koon has worked with employment and training programs at the state and federal levels since 1971, and is currently administrator of the Missouri FUTURES program for the State of Missouri (Jefferson City). He received his B.S. in Public Administration from Southwest Missouri State University at Springfield in 1971. Additionally, he acquired a Masters of Public Administration degree in 1983 and a Ph.D. in Political Science in 1993, both from the University of Missouri–Columbia.

David A. Leuthold is Professor Emeritus of Political Science at the University of Missouri–Columbia, having taken early retirement in 1992 to work on special projects of interest. His research interests include public opinion and election campaigns, state government, and public policy. Since his retirement, he has planned and directed a conference on economic/political relations between Missouri and South Korea and spent a semester at the University of Sibiu in Romania as a visiting scholar and lecturer. Following the general election of 1992, he also organized and directed a conference on campaign politics, which involved the campaign managers of both successful and defeated political candidates for office. The proceedings of the conference were included in *Campaign Missouri 1992*, published by the University of Missouri Press in 1994. He received his Ph.D. from the University of California–Berkeley in 1965.

Michael P. McConachie has taught political science at Stephens College, the University of Tennessee at Martin, Texas A&M University at Galveston, Cumberland College in Kentucky, Texas Christian University, and the University of Missouri–Columbia. He gained his bachelor's degree from the University of Texas at Austin, and his master's and doctorate degrees from the University of Missouri–Columbia. Presently, he is pastor of First Christian Church (Disciples of Christ) in Paris, Missouri, and teaches part-time at Moberly Area Community College.

Donald Phares is Professor of Economics and Public Policy at the University of Missouri–St. Louis. In addition, he has served as director of an urban research center, chairperson of the Department of Economics, and Vice Chancellor for Budgeting and Planning at the University of Missouri–St. Louis. He has written several books, including *Who Pays State and Local Taxes?* and *State-Local Tax Equity: An Empirical Analysis of the Fifty States*. He also has written or coauthored more than one hundred professional articles and technical and governmental reports. He served as coeditor of the *Urban Affairs Quarterly* and was on the editorial board of the *Journal of Urban Affairs*. He received his B.A. from Northeastern University, and his M.A. and Ph.D. from Syracuse University.

Denny E. Pilant is Professor of Political Science and Associate Dean, College of Humanities and Public Affairs, Southwest Missouri State University in Springfield. His present and long-term research interests focus on the unanticipated consequences of political reform in American politics and political theory. His research has been published in the *Journal of Black Studies, American Politics Quarterly,* the *Journal of Political Science,* and in chapters in several books. His fields of interest include political theory, American government and politics, and methodology. He received his Ph.D. from Duke University in 1964.

Cordell Smith was educated at the University of Missouri–Rolla (B.A. history, 1988) and at the University of Missouri–Columbia (M.A. political science, 1993). He has served as Saline County Coordinator, Missourians for Roy Blunt (1992); Director of Research, Hardy for Congress (1992); Delegate and Alternate, respectively, for the 1988 and 1992 state Republican conventions; Salt Fork Township Committeeman, Saline County Republican Committee; officer of the University of Missouri–Rolla and the University of Missouri–Columbia College Republicans; and as Republican nominee for state representative, district 116 (1988). In addition, he has been a contributing author to the University of Missouri–Columbia's *Governmental Affairs Newsletter.*

G. Ross Stephens is Professor Emeritus from the University of Missouri–Kansas City, from which he still pursues his research interests. He received his Ph.D. and two Masters degrees—one in urban planning—from the University of Wisconsin–Madison. He is the author or coauthor of more than fifty articles, monographs, research reports, and books. He has worked as a consultant to federal, state, and local governments, universities, and private businesses, and is past president of the Missouri Political Science Association.

David Valentine is Director of Senate Research (Missouri General Assembly). As Director, he supervises twenty employees who prepare bills for legislators, including conducting background research and analysis on matters of public policy. He has taught at St. Louis University and the University of Arkansas at Monticello, and has published in *American Politics Quarterly* and *State Legislatures.* He received his Ph.D. from the University of Missouri–Columbia in 1977.

Jeanette B. Welch earned her Ph.D. in Political Science from the University of Missouri–Columbia in 1982. She has taught at Central Missouri State University and Northwest Missouri State, as well as in Central Missouri State University's graduate program at Whiteman Air Force Base, and the State Fair Community College at Whiteman. She edited Central Missouri State University's 1986 strategic plan and both the 1984 and 1994 institutional self-study reports required for reaccreditation by the North Central Association of Colleges and Schools. Her interests include public administration, public policy (education), and American government and politics.

Larry Whatley is Associate Professor of History and Political Science at Southwest Baptist University in Bolivar, Missouri. He received his B.A and his M.A. in History from Mississippi State University at Starkville. Among his publications is an article entitled, "The Works Progress Administration in Mississippi," *The Journal of Mississippi History,* February 1968.

C. Cartwright Young is Professor of Political Science at Northeast Missouri State University in Kirksville, where she teaches courses in American government, public administration, and public policy. She has published articles on organizational leadership, Missouri politics, interest group and agency influence on public policy, Olympic politics, and educational assessment. As a consultant to numerous universities, she has been a pioneer in developing comprehensive assessment programs. She has also received many honors for her teaching, including a 1993 Governor's award for excellence. She received her M.A. in 1975 and her Ph.D. in political science in 1982, both from the University of Missouri–Columbia.

James V. Young is Professor of Political Science at Central Missouri State University in Warrensburg. He earned his B.A., J.D., and Ph.D. degrees at the University of Iowa, where he also won a Big Ten Medal for Scholarship and Athletics. His teaching career includes service at St. Olaf College in Minnesota from 1964 to 1968, and at Central Missouri State University from 1968 to the present. He is the author of three books, including *Landmark Constitutional Law Decisions* (1993). His teaching and research interests include American government and politics, federalism (state politics and intergovernmental relations), and public law/judicial process.

Glossary

Abortion. The process of terminating a pregnancy before term. Before 1973, few abortions were allowed in the United States, but the United States Supreme Court decision in *Roe v. Wade* established that states must allow abortions. Missouri legislators passed laws attempting to restrict the use of abortions, but most of these laws were declared unconstitutional. In 1987 the U.S. Supreme Court, in *Webster v. Reproductive Health Services*, upheld Missouri legislation imposing several restrictions.

Absentee voting. An electoral process that enables qualified citizens to vote by mail if they are away from home or incapacitated on election day. Absentee ballots in Missouri are secured from the county clerk or board of election commissioners (in St. Louis, St. Louis County, Kansas City, Clay County, or Jackson County) no sooner than thirty days prior to the election and must be received by election authorities no later than 7 P.M. on the day of the election.

Ad valorem. A tax imposed "according to the value" of property, usually calculated per $100 or per $1,000 of the assessed valuation.

AFDC. Aid to Families with Dependent Children. This is a public assistance program that provides payment to low-income families with dependent children. AFDC is jointly sponsored by the state and federal governments, with the states setting benefit levels and eligibility requirements and the federal government providing matching funds.

Affirmative Action. In the 1960s this term meant the elimination of rules or procedures that kept women and minorities from certain jobs. Later it came to mean taking compensatory action to ensure that appropriate numbers of disadvantaged groups were hired or received other opportunities.

Amicus curiae. Written arguments filed in a court of law by individuals or groups who are not directly involved in a case but have an interest in the outcome. The term literally means *friends of the court.*

Appellate court. A court having jurisdiction to review or hear appeals of decisions rendered by a trial court. In Missouri the appellate courts are the three courts of appeals (eastern, western, and southern) and the Supreme Court of Missouri.

At-large election. The selection of one or more legislators by all the voters of a jurisdiction, rather than by ward or district designation. In 1932, the Missouri legislature did not agree on new congressional district boundaries, and the state's congressmen were all elected in one at-large (statewide) election, with each voter getting to select up to thirteen candidates.

Bail bond. Money posted or left with the courts as security in exchange for a defendant's freedom until his or her case comes to trial.

Block grant. Money given by the federal government to state and local governments for general use in a broad area, such as law enforcement or community development. Few strings are attached to such grants.

Board of equalization. The county board that hears appeals from citizens dissatisfied with property valuations. The board of equalization usually consists of the county commissioners, assessor, surveyor, and clerk.

Brown v. Topeka Board of Education. The 1954 case in which the U.S. Supreme Court declared that racial segregation in the public schools was unconstitutional. Some Missouri school districts integrated quickly after the Supreme Court decision, while others delayed. Missouri had a clause in its constitution requiring separate schools for white and colored children. Although Missouri voters finally repealed this segregation provision in 1976, federal judges used its long existence as justification for requiring the state government to pay much of the cost of the desegregation programs in St. Louis and Kansas City.

Building code. A body or collection of regulations governing the construction of commercial or residential buildings within a community or county.

Calendar. In the legislative process, the listing of the order in which bills are to be considered by either house of the legislature. In the Missouri General Assembly, controversial bills are placed on the "perfection" calendar; noncontroversial bills are placed on the "consent" calendar.

Categorical grant. Money given by the federal government to state and local governments for specific purposes with uniform rules. Usually many strings are attached to such grants.

Charter. A local government "constitution" or basic law for a city or first-class county. Charters are developed by a committee of citizens, then sent to local voters for approval or disapproval. Many Missouri cities have adopted charters. State law allows several large counties to adopt charters if they wish, and three have done so.

Circuit breaker. A provision in Missouri to limit property taxes for certain individuals such as the elderly or poor.

Civil liberties. Fundamental rights of a free society that are protected by the Bill of Rights against the power of the government. These rights include the freedoms of speech, press, religion, and assembly.

Civil rights. Fundamental rights of all citizens, especially minorities, to enjoy full equality and equal protection under the law.

Civil service. Also known as the merit system, this is a system of hiring and promoting government personnel on the basis of merit and competence rather than on the basis of partisanship.

Comity. The practice among the states of recognizing each other's citizens as they do their own. Article IV, Section 2, of the U.S. Constitution is known as the "comity clause."

Commutation. The power possessed by the governor to lessen punishment, such as to release a prisoner early or change a death penalty to life imprisonment.

Concurrent powers. Powers exercised independently by both national and state governments, such as the powers to tax, establish court systems, pass criminal laws, and maintain road systems.

Conference committee. A legislative committee whose members are drawn from both houses of the legislature to reconcile differences between each house's version of the same bill.

County seat. The capital of a county, usually located near the center of the county, so that all county residents could go to the county seat and return in one day on horseback.

De facto segregation. Literally, "by fact" separation of the races resulting from housing patterns.

De jure segregation. Literally, "by law" separation of the races resulting from legal sanctions.

Debt limitations. Laws prohibiting state or local governments from incurring specific kinds of debts beyond a certain amount. The Missouri Constitution of 1945, for example, stipulates that a debt exceeding $1 million in any one year must be approved by a majority of the voters and that all bonds of indebtedness must be repaid within twenty-five years. Since 1945, Missouri voters have approved several proposals to incur debt to construct state buildings and water and sewage systems.

Desegregation. The process of ending racial separation or imbalances in schools, employment, housing, or public accommodations.

Double jeopardy. The provision in the Fifth Amendment of the U.S. Constitution and in Article I, Section 19, of the 1945 Missouri constitution guaranteeing that a person may not be tried twice for the same crime at the same level of government. If the person did something that violated a federal law and also violated a state law, that person could be tried at each level. The courts have ruled that two such trials are not double jeopardy.

Due process. The requirement established in the Fifth and Fourteenth amendments of the U.S. Constitution and in Article 1, Section 10, of the 1945 Missouri constitution that any person involved in a legal dispute must have a fair, unbiased hearing or trial. The courts have interpreted this to include the right to a speedy trial, the right to have an attorney, the right to be tried by an impartial jury, and so on.

Earmarking. The process of reserving tax revenue for specific purposes. Proposition C, passed by voters in 1982, established an additional one cent sales tax, half of which was earmarked for elementary and secondary education and half for reduction of property taxes.

Eminent domain. The power of the national government (under the Fifth Amendment of the U.S. Constitution) or the state government (under Article I, Section 26, of the 1945 Missouri constitution) to take private property for public use, provided the owners are given just compensation. Such authority is also available to local governments, which use it to acquire land for a variety of public projects, such as airports, water wells, and land clearance.

En banc. All of the judges of a court sitting together to hear a case. The term *banc* refers to the bench.

Enterprise zone. An area or region designated for increased industrial development. Usually businesses will receive some tax or other incentive to establish an industrial site in such a zone. The state of Missouri has authorized enterprise zones in various rural and urban areas.

Entitlements. Government programs that pay benefits to individuals or groups that meet eligibility requirements set by law. Cost to the government depends on the number of people who qualify. Examples are social security, unemployment compensation, and Medicaid.

Equal protection. A phrase in the Fourteenth Amendment of the U.S. Constitution interpreted by the U.S. Supreme Court to require states to provide equal treatment to U.S. citizens in a variety of substantive areas. Also found in Article I, Section 2, of the 1945 Missouri constitution.

Ex post facto law. Any law that "after the fact" makes an act criminal. Such laws are prohibited by the U.S. Constitution (Article I, Section 9) and by the 1945 Missouri constitution (Article 1, Section 13).

Excise tax. A tax levied on specific goods produced, manufactured, sold, transported, or used within the nation or state. The most common state excise taxes are on gasoline, tobacco, and liquor.

Felony. A crime punishable by death or imprisonment in a penitentiary for more than one year. In Missouri, there are four classes of felonies: class A (a term of not less than ten years or more than thirty years, or life imprisonment), class B (not less than five years or more than fifteen), class C (not less than seven years), and class D (not more than five years).

Fiscal year. An annual accounting period that for the government of Missouri begins on July 1 and ends on June 30 of the following year. The number of the fiscal year (for example, FY95) is the calendar year in which the fiscal year ends; the 1995 fiscal year ends on June 30, 1995.

Foundation formula. A method of education funding in Missouri designed to combine state and local revenues to reach a predetermined amount of aid per pupil.

Full faith and credit. A provision in Article IV, Section I, of the U.S. Constitution requiring states to honor each other's legal documents, such as wills, deeds, licenses, contracts, and vital papers.

General-obligation bond. An instrument of indebtedness issued by a state or local government to long-term creditors guaranteeing the "full worth and credit" or use of the government's taxing power to pay off the bonds. In Missouri, a state general obligation bond requires a majority vote for approval, while local general obligation bonds require approval by more than a majority, either four-sevenths or two-thirds of the voters.

Gerrymandering. Drawing of legislative district boundaries in such a way as to magnify or reduce the power of a particular group of voters.

Grand jury. In Missouri, a body of twelve persons who hear evidence presented by the prosecuting attorney against persons accused of a crime. The grand jury decides by majority vote whether there is sufficient evidence to warrant bringing the accused to trial.

Grant-in-aid. Funds made available by Congress to state and local governments in accordance with prescribed standards or conditions. See also *Block grant* and *Categorical grant.*

Greens. A term often used to refer to people with a strong sense of concern about the environment. The Green party qualified as an established party in the Ninth Congressional District when the 1992 Green congressional candidate received more than 2 percent of the vote.

Hancock Amendment. The 1980 amendment to the Missouri Constitution initiated by Springfield businessman Mel Hancock and the Taxpayers Survival Association. This complex, voter-approved amendment limits state taxes, except for yearly adjustments based on the total income of persons in Missouri or in the case of emergencies; prohibits local tax or fee increases without a popular vote; prohibits state expansion of local responsibility without state funding; adds a *rollback* provision for local governments to prevent "windfall" revenues because of increased property tax assessments; and authorizes lawsuits by citizens to ensure compliance and to recover costs.

Impeachment. The formal accusation of misconduct in office by a public official, made by the Missouri house of representatives. A trial is then held by the Missouri Supreme Court.

Incrementalism. Making changes of policy a little at a time, rather than making a major reform. Proponents of incrementalism argue that it is easier to get sufficient political support to make a smaller rather than a larger change, and that the possibility of error is minimized.

Indictment. An accusation by a grand jury charging a person with a crime.

Infrastructure. The physical facilities needed to develop and sustain economic activities. The example given most frequently is roads and bridges, but other facilities would include electrical and natural gas utilities, water and sewage facilities, and other transportation facilities, such as railroads, airlines, and barge lines.

Initiative. An electoral procedure allowing citizens to propose constitutional amendments or legislation and to refer the decision to a popular vote by obtaining a required number of signatures on a petition.

Injunction. A court order commanding a person to do a specific act or to refrain from committing an act that would injure another's personal or property rights.

Institutionalization. Requiring people to enter and remain in a state institution, such as a mental hospital, training school, or prison, until they have developed appropriate behaviors or skills or have served their sentence.

Interstate compact. An agreement between states on concerns such as water projects, flood control, or transportation, as authorized by Article 1, Section 10, of the U.S. Constitution.

Item veto. A procedure by which the governor of Missouri may strike out or veto part of an appropriations bill (except educational funding) while signing or approving the remainder of it. Item vetoes may be overridden by a two-thirds vote of the total membership in both houses of the General Assembly.

Jurisdiction. Authority vested in a court to hear and decide certain types of cases. Literally, jurisdiction means "to say the law."

Libertarian party. A political party emphasizing individual liberty and very little government organization or regulation. Libertarians prefer that the postal service be managed by a private company, and that laws against drug usage be repealed. In 1992, Libertarian supporters secured enough signatures on petitions to put several Libertarian candidates on the ballot. Those candidates received enough votes so that the party was able to put its nominees on the ballot in subsequent elections without circulating petitions.

Litigation. The act of contesting the law: a lawsuit brought by the plaintiff(s) against the defendant(s).

Lobbyist. A person, often representing an interest group, who seeks to influence the content of pending legislation, the outcome of legislative votes, or decisions of executive agencies.

Lottery. A form of gambling now used in many states to raise revenue and finance internal improvements. The use of the lottery in Missouri was approved by voters in November 1984. Missourians bet about $225 million per year on the lottery, and about $75 million of that amount is turned over to the state, for use in education. The $75 million, while it sounds large, is a very small portion of the amount spent by Missourians on education.

Mail ballot election. Missouri law allows election authorities to mail ballots to all voters

and to have the voters vote at home and return the ballot in person or by mail, in special elections with only one issue on the ballot. Mail ballot elections have been conducted in Kirksville, Boone County, and some small jurisdictions. One result has been much higher turnouts than are usually achieved with polling place elections.

Mass transit. A transportation system that transports large numbers of people in a short time, usually in urban areas. Local bus systems can be considered mass transit systems, but sometimes the term is used to mean exclusively a system running on fixed routes, such as a rail route. An example would be the Metrolink system in St. Louis.

Means test. A determination of the "means" or income that a person has. Usually a means test requires that a person prove that he or she has no income or sufficiently low income to qualify for public welfare or other government services designed for low-income people.

Medicaid. A public assistance program established in 1965 to help low-income persons pay hospital, doctor, and medical bills. The program is financed through general federal, state, and local taxes.

Medicare. A federal social insurance program established in 1965 that provides hospital and doctor services to elderly persons through the social security system.

Merit system. See *Civil service.*

Misdemeanor. A crime punishable by a fine or imprisonment of less than one year, or both. In Missouri, misdemeanors fall into one of three categories: class A (a term not to exceed one year); class B (not to exceed six months); and class C (not to exceed fifteen days).

Missouri plan. A hybrid court plan adopted by Missouri in 1940 that serves as a national model for selection of judges. It combines appointive and elective systems of judicial selection.

Municipal court. A division of Missouri's

circuit courts that has jurisdiction over traffic offenses and misdemeanors committed within the geographical boundaries of the circuit.

NIMBY. The acronym for *Not In My Back Yard,* referring to the opposition from local residents when government leaders propose to establish a landfill or some other undesirable facility in a particular location. During the 1970s citizens protested against prisons in their communities, but by the 1980s communities began to compete for these facilities, which increase local employment.

Nonpartisan election. An election in which the ballot does not reveal the party affiliation of the candidates.

Outstate. In Missouri, the areas outside the major metropolitan regions of Kansas City and St. Louis. Springfield, St. Joseph, Columbia, and Joplin are all considered outstate, although each is large enough to be the center of a smaller metropolitan area.

PAC. A political action committee formed by an interest group to support political candidates. Many PACs are formed by managers of corporations or leaders of labor unions, but some are formed by associations of people in the same occupation, such as realtors or doctors. Others are formed by people who share similar attitudes, such as political conservatives or conservationists.

Pardon. An action by the governor that relieves one from punishment for a crime and restores the rights and privileges lost as a result of that crime.

Party platform. The policies, principles, and promises proposed or adopted by a political party.

Patronage. The power to make partisan or political appointments or to distribute jobs, franchises, licenses, contracts, and so on, on the basis of partisanship.

Petit jury. In Missouri, a trial jury consisting of twelve persons whose function is to evaluate the evidence and determine guilt or innocence in criminal cases, or to make

a judgment for the plaintiff or defendant in civil cases.

Pluralism. The assumption that the major decisions in a community or state are made by different groups of people, depending on the issue involved. Few people are influential in most or all areas. For example, some people make decisions on education policy, while others make decisions on urban renewal. See *power elite* for an alternative viewpoint.

Police power. The power of state governments to restrain personal freedoms and property rights to protect the public health, safety, welfare, morals, or convenience. Police power is a reserved power of the states subject to national and state constitutional limitations. Such powers are also delegated to local governments.

Power elite. The assumption that all or most of the important decisions in a particular community or state are made by a small group of people, often business leaders. See *pluralism* for a competing assumption.

President pro tem. The officer in the Missouri senate elected by the members to preside over that body in the absence of the lieutenant governor, who is the president of the senate. The president pro tem makes all chair and committee assignments for his or her party.

Primary election. An election prior to the fall general election in which voters select the candidates who will run on each party's ticket. Missouri has an open primary election in which the voter is not registered by party, but rather asks for the ballot of one of the parties at the polls on primary election day. Missouri primary elections are held in August of even-numbered years.

Progressive tax. A tax that requires the wealthy to pay a greater portion of their income than the poor. See also *Regressive tax.*

Property tax. A state or local tax, based on the value of real or personal property. In Missouri, the tax is applied mostly to real property—land and buildings.

Public assistance. A welfare program or policy that distributes public funds to people who are needy. Usually no prior contribution is necessary.

Public Service Commission. In Missouri, the Public Service Commission is a five-person body charged with ensuring that public utilities (investor-owned electricity, natural gas, telephone, and sewer and water services) provide adequate amounts of utility services and that they receive a reasonable return on their investment.

Reapportionment. The redrawing of legislative district lines following each decennial census to keep districts within each house of the legislature equal in population.

Reassessment. In Missouri, the process by which county assessors take inventory of all property in the state and determine the current value of that property for taxation.

Recall. A method of removing a public official by popular vote after submission of a petition signed by a requisite number of registered voters.

Referendum. An electoral device whereby voters can approve or disapprove a state legislative act. In other words, in a referendum the proposals of the state legislature are "referred" to the voters. Referendums may be called either by the legislature or by citizens submitting sufficient signatures through the initiative process.

Regressive tax. A tax that requires the poor to pay a greater portion of their income than the rich. See also *Progressive tax.*

Revenue bonds. An instrument of indebtedness issued by a state or local government pledging revenues from a project to retire the bonds. Examples of such revenues would be tolls for a bridge or rent paid by a manufacturer using a city-owned factory building. Special district governments such as water districts often use such financing for their facilities, paying off the bonds from part of the monthly fees paid by their customers.

School choice. Allowing students to choose to attend a school other than their neighborhood school, among those schools in their school district that have room for additional students. Some school districts in Missouri allow such choice already. The term is also used for proposals for a voucher system, in which parents would receive vouchers for the cost of their children's education, which could be used either in a public school or as part or full payment in a private school.

Small-claims court. A special court created in Missouri in 1976 under the jurisdiction of the Associate Circuit Division to hear civil cases involving sums of less than one thousand dollars. Small-claims courts do not use juries or formal rules of evidence, and attorneys are optional.

Speaker of the House. The leader of the Missouri House of Representatives, nominated by the majority party caucus and elected formally by the entire House membership in January to preside over sessions and to appoint committees and chairpersons.

Special session. An extraordinary meeting of the General Assembly, to last not more than thirty days, called by the governor or by petition of legislators, to consider particular issues. The number of special sessions was reduced substantially when the constitution was amended to allow five-month sessions each year.

Spoils system. The practice of providing numerous government jobs to workers who had supported the winning candidate. "To the victor belongs the spoils," spoils now meaning jobs that can go to the winners. Years ago, many state jobs changed hands every four years when a new governor would appoint his supporters. Today most state employees are under a merit system of some type, and governors have few "spoils" to pass to their party workers.

Stare decisis. The judicial practice of basing decisions on similar cases decided in the past, establishing precedent. This is an important principle of common law, meaning literally "let the decision stand."

Suffrage. The right to vote.

Sunset laws. Legislation requiring that a program or an agency be given a definite life span beyond which it cannot exist without further legislative approval.

Sunshine laws. Missouri statutes requiring that public meetings, public records, and public votes be open and accessible to the public and the media. Sunshine laws are also known as *open meeting* or *open records* laws.

Supplemental security income. A federal cash assistance program developed in 1974 to supplement social security benefits and to help replace inadequate state and local programs for the aged, blind, and disabled. SSI helps provide a nationwide, uniform minimum standard.

Tort. A civil breach, violation, or injury of another person's personal or property rights, independent of any contractual obligation. Torts include negligence, strict liability, assault, or trespass.

Township. The geographical subdivision of a county for the administration of elections and the selection of jurors. All Missouri counties have townships, but only 23 of the state's 114 counties permit their townships to operate a separate township form of government.

Urban renewal. A term used during the 1950s and 1960s to designate the rebuilding or rejuvenation of blighted urban areas, often through large building projects. Federal government funds for urban renewal were switched in 1974 to the Community Development Block Grant Program, and these funds are distributed annually in many Missouri cities.

Veto. The power of the governor to prevent a bill passed by the state legislature from becoming law (veto literally means "I forbid"). Bills rejected by the governor are returned to their house of origin with reasons for rejection. A two-thirds majority in both houses of the General Assembly is necessary to override a governor's veto.

Voir dire. The preliminary questioning of prospective jurors by the court and/or attorneys to assess their qualifications to sit on a jury. Literally, *voir dire* means "to speak the truth."

Ward. A municipal territorial subdivision for the purpose of electing members to the city council.

Suggested Readings

State Government and Politics—Missouri

Barone, Michael, and Grant Ujifusa. "Missouri." In *The Almanac of American Politics 1994*, 726–53. Washington, D.C.: National Journal, 1993.

Botner, Stanley B. "The Office of Governor of the State of Missouri." Ph.D. diss., University of Missouri, 1963.

Brekke, Jerald D. *Understanding the Missouri State Constitution*. Dubuque, Iowa: Kendall-Hunt, 1991.

Bunch, Kenyon D., and Gregory Casey. "Political Controversy on Missouri's Supreme Court: The Case of Merit vs. Politics." *State and Local Government Review* 22 (1990): 5–16.

Carter, John J., and David A. Leuthold. "Missouri." In *Reapportionment Politics: The History of Redistricting in the 50 States*, edited by Leroy Hardy, Alan Heslop, and Stuart Anderson, 181–85. Beverly Hills: Sage Publications, 1981.

———. "Missouri." In *Redistricting in the 1980s: A 50-State Survey*, edited by Leroy Hardy, Alan Heslop, and George S. Blair, 151–55. Claremont, Calif.: Rose Institute of State and Local Government, Claremont McKenna College, 1993.

———. "1991 Redistricting in Missouri." *Governmental Affairs Newsletter* 26 (July 1992): 17–22.

Casey, Gregory, and James D. King. "Missouri: From Establishment Elite to Classical Pluralism." In *Interest Group Politics in the Midwestern States*, edited by Ronald J. Hrebenar and Clive S. Thomas, 165–91. Ames: Iowa State University Press, 1993.

Chen, Stephen C. S. *Missouri in the Federal System*. 3d ed. Lanham, Md.: University Press of America, 1986.

Connelly, Michael D. "Budgetary and Policy Analysis in Missouri." Ph.D. diss, University of Missouri–Columbia, 1981.

Constitution, State of Missouri. Secretary of State, Jefferson City, 1995.

Derge, David R. "The Lawyer as Decision-Maker in the American State Legislature." *Journal of Politics* 21 (1959): 408–33.

———. "Metropolitan and Out-State Alignments in Illinois and Missouri Legislative Delegations." *American Political Science Review* 52 (1958): 1051–65.

Dorsett, Lyle W. *The Pendergast Machine*. New York: Oxford University Press, 1968.

Dunne, Gerald T. *The Missouri Supreme Court: From Dred Scott to Nancy Cruzan*. Columbia: University of Missouri Press, 1993.

Dvorak, Tom. "State Campaign Finance Law: An Overview and Call for Reform." *Missouri Law Review* 55 (1990): 937–74.

Faust, Martin L. *Constitution Making in Missouri: The Convention of 1943–1944*. New York: National Municipal League, 1971.

Fenton, John H. *Politics in the Border States*. New Orleans: Hauser Press, 1957.

Flader, Susan, ed. *Exploring Missouri's Legacy: State Parks and Historic Sites*. Columbia: University of Missouri Press, 1992.

Giffen, Jerena East. *First Ladies of Missouri: Their Homes and Their Families*. Jefferson City: Von Hoffmann Press, 1970.

Karsch, Robert F. *The Government of Missouri*. 14th ed. Columbia: Lucas Brothers Publishers, 1978.

Kempf, Kimberly L., J. Fred Springer, G. Ross Stephens, and David J. Webber, eds.

Missouri Policy Choices. Columbia: University of Missouri Extension, 1991.

Kirkendall, Richard S. *A History of Missouri, Volume V, 1919 to 1953.* Columbia: University of Missouri Press, 1986.

League of Women Voters of Missouri. *Missouri Voters' Handbook.* St. Louis: League of Women Voters, 1992.

Leuthold, David A. *Campaign Missouri 1992.* Columbia: University of Missouri Press, 1994.

———. "The Legislature in Missouri's Political System." In *Midwest Legislative Politics,* edited by Samuel C. Patterson, 67–88. Iowa City: Institute of Public Affairs, University of Iowa, 1968.

———. *The Missouri Legislature: A Preliminary Profile.* Columbia: Research Center of the School of Business and Public Administration, University of Missouri, 1967.

McCullough, David. *Truman.* New York: Simon & Schuster, 1992.

Masters, Nicholas A., Robert H. Salisbury, and Thomas H. Eliot. *State Politics and the Public Schools: An Exploratory Analysis.* New York: Alfred A. Knopf, 1964.

Meyer, Duane G. *The Heritage of Missouri.* St. Louis: River City Publishers, 1982.

Midwest Research Institute and Capper Press. *The Missouri Quick-Fact Book.* Topeka, Kans.: Capper Press, 1991.

"Missouri." In *Politics in America: 1994, the 103rd Congress,* edited by Phil Duncan, 859–94. Washington, D.C.: CQ Press, 1993.

The Missouri Budget, Fiscal Year 1996, State of Missouri. Jefferson City: Governor's Office, 1995. Published each year.

Missouri ex. rel. Gaines v. Canada. 305 U.S. 337 (1938). The Supreme Court said that the University of Missouri School of Law must admit Lloyd Gaines, a black student denied admission because of his race.

Missouri v. Holland. 252 U.S. 416 (1920). This ruling, concerned with migratory fowls, established supremacy of a national treaty over Missouri law.

Missouri v. Jenkins, 110 S.Ct. 1651 (1990). This is the Kansas City school desegregation case.

Mitchell, Franklin D. *Embattled Democracy: Missouri Democratic Politics, 1919–1932.* Columbia: University of Missouri Press, 1968.

Murphy, Thomas P. *Metropolitics and the Urban County.* Washington, D.C.: Washington National Press Inc., 1970. This book focuses on Jackson County.

Official Manual, State of Missouri, 1993–1994. Jefferson City: Secretary of State, 1994. Published every two years.

Papastathopoulos, Catherine, David A. Leuthold, and Robert S. Friedman. *State/Provincial Administrators in Michigan, Missouri, and Ontario: A Report to Respondents.* Ann Arbor: University of Michigan Institute of Public Policy Studies, 1969.

Parrish, William E., Charles T. Jones Jr., and Lawrence O. Christensen. *Missouri: The Heart of the Nation.* 2d ed. Arlington Heights, Ill.: Harlan Davidson, 1992.

Peirce, Neal R. "Missouri: Microcosm U.S.A." In *The Great Plains States of America: People, Politics, and Power in the Nine Great Plains States,* 29–78. New York: W. W. Norton & Co., 1972.

Peltason, Jack. *The Missouri Plan for the Selection of Judges.* University of Missouri Studies, vol. 20, no. 2. Columbia: University of Missouri, 1945.

Perry, Robert T. *Black Legislators.* San Francisco: R and E Research Associates, 1976.

Pilant, Denny E., ed. *Reinventing Missouri Government: A Case Study in State Experiments at Work.* Fort Worth, Tex.: Harcourt Brace College Publishing, 1994.

Planned Parenthood of Central Missouri, Inc., v. John Danforth et al., 428 U.S. 52 (1976).

Rafferty, Milton D. *Historical Atlas of Mis-*

souri. Norman: University of Oklahoma Press, 1981.

Robertson, Edward D. Jr., and Duncan E. Kincheloe III. "Missouri's Tax Limitation Amendment: Ad Astra per Aspera." *UMKC Law Review* 52 (1983): 1–21.

Schmandt, Henry J., Paul G. Steinbicker, and George D. Wendel. *Metropolitan Reform in St. Louis: A Case Study*. New York: Holt, Rinehart and Winston, 1961.

Schmandt, Henry J., George D. Wendel, and E. Allan Tomey. *Federal Aid to St. Louis*. Washington, D.C.: Brookings Institution, 1983.

Statistical Abstract for Missouri, 1993. Columbia: B&PA Research Center, College of Business & Public Administration, University of Missouri, 1994.

Thelen, David P. *Paths of Resistance: Tradition and Democracy in Industrializing Missouri*. Columbia: University of Missouri Press, 1991.

U.S. Advisory Commission on Intergovernmental Relations. *Significant Features of Fiscal Federalism, 1994*. Vol. 2. Washington, D.C.: Advisory Commission on Intergovernmental Relations, 1994.

Watson, Richard A., and Rondal G. Downing. *The Politics of the Bench and the Bar: Judicial Selection under the Missouri Nonpartisan Court Plan*. New York: John Wiley and Sons, 1969.

Webster v. Reproductive Health Services, 109 S.Ct. 3040 (1989).

Westbrook, James E. "Municipal Home Rule: An Evaluation of the Missouri Experience." *Missouri Law Review* 33 (1968): 45–79.

Yarwood, Dean L. "Lieutenant Governors: Gubernatorial Transitions in Missouri." In *Gubernatorial Transitions: The 1983 and 1984 Elections*, edited by Thad L. Beyle, 297–303. Durham: Duke University Press, 1989.

Yarwood, Dean L., and Richard J. Hardy. "The Norm of Standing Aside: Gubernatorial Transition in Missouri in 1984." In *Gubernatorial Transitions*, 70–102.

State Government and Politics—General

Abney, Glenn, and Thomas P. Lauth. *The Politics of State and City Administration*. Albany: State University of New York Press, 1986.

Berman, David R., ed. *County Governments in an Era of Change*. Westport, Conn.: Greenwood Press, 1993.

Beyle, Thad L., ed. *Governors and Hard Times*. Washington, D.C.: Congressional Quarterly Press, 1992.

———. *State Government: CQ's Guide to Current Issues and Activities 1991–1992*. Washington, D.C.: Congressional Quarterly Inc., 1991.

Byrnes, Timothy A., and Mary C. Segers, eds. *The Catholic Church and the Politics of Abortion: A View from the States*. Boulder, Colo.: Westview Press, 1992.

Council of State Governments. *The Book of the States*. Lexington, Ky. This is a compendium of statistics, facts, laws, and structural changes in the fifty states, published biennially since 1933.

Duncombe, Herbert Sydney. *Modern County Government*. Washington, D.C.: National Association of Counties, 1977.

Dye, Thomas R. *Politics in States and Communities*. 8th ed. Englewood Cliffs, N.J.: Prentice-Hall, 1994.

Elazar, Daniel J. *American Federalism: A View from the States*. 3d ed. New York: Harper & Row, 1984.

Francis, Wayne L. *Legislative Issues in the Fifty States: A Comparative Analysis*. Chicago: Rand McNally & Co. 1967.

Glick, Henry Robert, and Kenneth N. Vines. *State Court Systems*. Englewood Cliffs, N.J.: Prentice-Hall, 1973.

Gray, Virginia, Herbert Jacob, and Robert B. Albritton, eds. *Politics in the American States: A Comparative Analysis*. 5th ed. Glenview, Ill.: Scott, Foresman, 1990.

Harrigan, John J. *Politics and Policy in States and Communities*. 3d ed. Glenview, Ill.: Scott, Foresman, 1988.

International City Management Association. *The Municipal Year Book*. Washington, D.C.: ICMA. Published annually.

Jewell, Malcolm E. *Parties and Primaries: Nominating State Governors*. New York: Praeger Publishers, 1984.

Jewell, Malcolm E., and David M. Olson. *Political Parties and Elections in American States*. 3d ed. Chicago: Dorsey Press, 1988.

Jones, Ruth S. "Campaign and Party Finance in the American States." In *Campaign and Party Finance in North America and Western Europe*, edited by Arthur B. Gunlicks, 41–67. Boulder, Colo.: Westview Press, 1993.

Magelby, David B. *Direct Legislation: Voting on Ballot Propositions in the United States*. Baltimore: Johns Hopkins Press, 1984.

Moakley, Maureen, ed. *Party Realignment in the American States*. Columbus: Ohio State University Press, 1992.

Osborne, David, and Ted Gaebler. *Reinventing Government: How the Entrepreneurial Spirit Is Transforming the Public Sector*. Reading, Mass.: Addison-Wesley, 1992.

Phares, Donald. *Who Pays State and Local Taxes?* Cambridge, Mass.: Oelgeschlager, Gunn and Hain, 1980.

Rosenthal, Alan. *Governors and Legislatures: Contending Powers*. Washington, D.C.: CQ Press, 1990.

———. *Legislative Life: People, Process, and Performance in the States*. New York: Harper & Row, 1981.

———. *The Third House: Lobbyists and Lobbying in the States*. Washington, D.C.: CQ Press, 1993.

Sabato, Larry. *Goodbye to Good-Time Charlie: The American Governor Transformed*.

Washington, D.C.: Congressional Quarterly Press, 1983.

Stumpf, Harry P., and John H. Culver. *The Politics of State Courts*. New York: Longman, 1992.

Tarr, G. Alan, and Mary Cornelia Porter. *State Supreme Courts in State and Nation*. New Haven: Yale University Press, 1988.

Thomas, John Clayton, and Dan H. Hoxworth. "The Limits of Judicial Desegregation Remedies after *Missouri v. Jenkins*." *Publius* 21 (Summer 1991): 93–108.

Wahlke, John C., Heinz Eulau, William Buchanan, and Leroy C. Ferguson. *The Legislative System*. New York: John Wiley, 1962. This is a comparative study of legislators in California, New Jersey, Ohio, and Tennessee.

Walker, Jack L. "The Diffusion of Innovations among the American States." *American Political Science Review* 63 (September 1969): 880–89.

Journals on State Government

American Politics Quarterly. Published since 1973 by Sage Publications.

Comparative State Politics. Published bimonthly since 1979 by the Legislative Studies Center, Sangamon State University, Springfield, Ill.

ecos: The Environmental Communique of the States. Published bimonthly by the Council of State Governments.

Governing. Published monthly beginning October 1987 by Congressional Quarterly.

Intergovernmental Perspective. Published quarterly since 1975 by the Advisory Commission on Intergovernmental Relations.

Judicature. Published by the American Judicature Society.

Legislative Studies Quarterly. Published since 1976 by the Comparative Legislative Research Center, University of Iowa.

National Civic Review. Published bimonthly by the National Civic League.

Public Administration Review. Published by the American Society for Public Administration.

Publius. Published since 1971 by the Center for the Study of Federalism, Temple University.

Spectrum: The Journal of State Government. Formerly known as *The Journal of State Government.* Published quarterly since 1990 by the Council of State Governments. Published bimonthly from 1986 to 1989.

State Court Journal. Published quarterly since 1977 by the National Center for State Courts.

State Government News. Published monthly since 1956 by the Council of State Governments.

State Government Research Checklist. Published bimonthly since 1968 by the Council of State Governments.

State Legislatures. Published monthly since 1987 by the National Conference of State Legislatures.

State and Local Government Review. Published since 1976 by the Institute of Government, University of Georgia.

State Policy Reports. Published bimonthly since 1983 by State Policy Reports.

Stateline Midwest. Formerly known as *Midwesterner.* Published monthly by the Council of State Governments.

Suggested State Legislation. Published annually since 1941 by the Council of State Governments.

Urban Affairs Quarterly. Published since 1965 by Sage Publications.

Western Political Quarterly. Published by the University of Utah. Official journal of Western Political Science Association.

Index